ROYAL NAVAL AIR SERVICE

OPERATIONS REPORTS

26th November 1915
to 30th June 1917

Parts 1 to 36

The Naval & Military Press Ltd

Published by

The Naval & Military Press Ltd
Unit 5 Riverside, Brambleside
Bellbrook Industrial Estate
Uckfield, East Sussex
TN22 1QQ England

Tel: +44 (0)1825 749494

www.naval-military-press.com
www.nmarchive.com

In reprinting in facsimile from the original, any imperfections are inevitably reproduced and the quality may fall short of modern type and cartographic standards.

ROYAL NAVAL AIR SERVICE.

OPERATIONS REPORTS,
Nos. 1—29
(with Royal Flying Corps Reports attached).

26th NOVEMBER 1915—16th MARCH 1917.

The Naval & Military Press Ltd

NAVAL STAFF,
  OPERATIONS DIVISION.
    October 1917.

ROYAL NAVAL AIR SERVICE.

REPORTS OF OPERATIONS
Nos. 1–29.

INDEX.

Report No.	Page.
1	1
2	4
3	6
4	9
5	11
6	14
7	18
8	22
9	26
10	31
11	33
12	37
13	41
14	44
15	51
16	57
17	70
18	81
19	88
20	96
21	105
22	114
23	125
24	137
25	152
26	158
27	178
28	196
29	225

ROYAL NAVAL AIR SERVICE.

REPORT OF OPERATIONS No. 1.

November 26th.

(1) Colonel Maitland (airship section), for the purpose of a test, carried out a parachute descent from a spherical balloon at a height of 10,500 feet. He descended safely.

No. 1 WING.

November 27th.

(2) Flight Sub-Lieut. Lea, with A. M. Norris, on submarine patrol, descended to a height of 50 feet in order to observe bell buoy, Ostend. Heavy anti-aircraft fire was directed against the machine, the majority of shots falling well over. One shell hit the water 200 yards behind the machine.

November 28th.

(3)—(a) Flight Sub-Lieut. Brackley, No. 1 Wing, with Petty Officer Franklin, in Caudron No. 329, engaged on hostile aircraft patrol, observed at 8.55 a.m. a hostile machine approaching Dunkerque from the direction of Bergues, which, on being approached, immediately made off for the lines, crossing them at Dixmude, where it was heavily fired at by our anti-aircraft guns. Owing to the speed of the hostile machine being greater, it was impossible to get within range to open fire.

(b) Flight Sub-Lieut. Talbot, No. 1 Wing, with Sub-Lieut. Collinson, in Nieuport No. 318, were engaged on coastal reconnaissance, and observed one hostile machine coming in the direction from Ypres for Dunkerque, which, on being approached, turned and headed for the lines. The pilot was unable to get within firing range.

(c) Flight Sub-Lieut. Beard, No. 1 Wing, in Nieuport No. 3178, observed one hostile machine at about 10,000 feet between La Panne and Dixmude. The pilot was then only 6,500 feet high, and by the time the enemy's altitude had been reached, the hostile machine had turned back, returning over the lines in the direction of Westende.

(d) Flight Sub-Lieut. Ferrand, No. 1 Wing, and Air Mechanic Oldfield, in a seaplane, engaged upon submarine patrol, observed when about $2\frac{1}{4}$ miles N.E. of Nieuport a German T.B.D. and four German seaplanes, two of which were on the water about 3 miles N. of Westende. Dropped one bomb on T.B.D., but missed. Height of seaplanes about 1,500 feet. Seaplanes were apparently patrolling above the T.B.D., which on sighting them returned towards Ostend. Flight Sub-Lieut. Ferrand then proceeded to attack the seaplanes, three of which turned and went back to Ostend; the fourth came towards our machine. The air mechanic fired 47 rounds at 100 yards, and the German machine, an "Albatross" seaplane with long floats, nose-dived into the water until only her tail was visible. Her tail disappeared shortly afterwards.

(e) Flight Sub-Lieut. Perham, No. 1 Wing, with Air Mechanic Crispin, in a seaplane, engaged upon submarine patrol, observed when off Nieuport a German seaplane in the water, about 2 miles N.N.E., elevator and rudder being just visible. A German destroyer was making towards it, but on being approached, turned in the direction of Ostend.

(f) Sub-Lieut. Viney and Lieut. Le Comte de Sincay proceeded at 11.30 a.m. in Henri Farman No. 3620, with two 65-lb. bombs, to look for submarine previously reported off Zeebrugge. When off Middelkerke, about 6 miles seaward, observed submarine proceeding west. Pilot immediately steered towards it. Submarine was on the surface, and two men were observed on the conning tower. Immediately after the first submarine had been seen, a second submarine was observed, apparently stationary. Height at this time 5,000 feet.

The first submarine was lost sight of whilst the pilot was spiralling down to 1,500 feet. When next observed the first submarine had turned round northwards and was diving. The second submarine was still stationary on the surface. The pilot then proceeded directly over it and at a height of 1,200 feet released both bombs, which dropped nearly together, one of them being seen to hit the deck fairly amidships. The burst of the other bomb was not observed. The submarine was for a moment hidden by the smoke of the 65-lb. bomb, and when that cleared away seemed to be sinking, apparently broken amidships, as its ends were stuck up in the air. Flight Sub-Lieut. Viney, circling round for some minutes, observed a large quantity of oil coming up on the spot where the submarine had sunk.

(g) Flight Sub-Lieut. Potts, in Nieuport No. 3971, whilst on hostile aircraft patrol over Dunkerque and La Panne, observed at 11.45 a.m. a hostile machine 3 to 4 miles seaward, approaching Dunkerque. On being approached the hostile machine turned seawards, disappearing into the clouds.

(h) Flight Sub-Lieut. Mulock with Sub-Lieut. Casey, in Nieuport No. 3970, whilst on hostile aircraft patrol, between Nieuport and Dixmude, observed one large hostile machine off La Panne, at 12,000 feet, which disappeared into the clouds when approached.

The following reports from Over-seas Squadrons have been received during the week :—

November 13th.

Flight-Commander Smyth-Piggott, No. 2 Wing (Dardanelles), volunteered to attack a railway bridge at Kuleli Burgaz. He carried out a night flight of over four hours' duration, being frequently under heavy anti-aircraft fire, and descended to within 300 feet of the bridge before releasing bombs. The result was difficult to see, but both bombs apparently hit the western extremity of the bridge. The pilot plainly felt the heat of the explosion, and the machine was badly bumped about. Just before the bridge was reached the engine started running badly, and it gave trouble all the way back. This flight is probably the longest night flight undertaken during the war.

November 19th.

Squadron Commander Davis and Flight Sub-Lieut. Smylie carried out an attack on Ferrejik Junction. On the return journey Smylie's machine was struck by machine-gun fire and brought down, landing in marsh near Maritza River. Smylie lighted and burnt his machine, and before the enemy, who were approaching over the marsh, could arrive, Squadron Commander Davis descended, took up Smylie, and got away in safety.

Air Department, Admiralty,
  1st December 1915.

REPORT OF OPERATIONS No. 2.

The following report from Overseas Units have been received since the issue of the last communiqué :—

I.—(a) Flight Commander Edmonds (H.M.S. "Ben-my-Chree"), in a Short seaplane, left the water at 11.34 a.m. to attack Kuleli Burgaz Bridges. He crossed the coastline to the west of Enos and followed the Maritza Valley to the north-east. Kuleli Burgaz was reached after $1\frac{1}{4}$ hours' flight. He kept on the east bank of the river whilst approaching the railway, descending 1,500 feet, and as soon as he reached the railway followed it across the river, and dropped bombs when he got into a favourable position.

The first bomb hit the north side of the embankment at the east end of the East Bridge, but it did not appear to have damaged the railway line. The second bomb fell in the middle of the island about 50 yards north of the railway.

There was considerable rifle and gun fire, and the seaplane has two or three hits in it.

(b) Flight Lieut. Dacre (H.M.S. "Ben-my-Chree"), in a Short seaplane, left the water at 12.33 p.m., about four miles east of Enos, to attack Kuleli Burgaz Bridges, and climbing to 2,000 feet flew inland up the Maritza River, climbing 4,200 feet. He reached the objective after 1 hour 12 minutes, and proceeded to fly above the railway eastward of the bridges, descending to about 3,000 feet. He aimed at the western bridge with both bombs. The first struck the middle of the Dedeagach lines about 100 yards from the bridge. The second hit the river bank south of the bridge and about 12 yards from it. Heavy machine-gun fire was opened upon him. One bullet struck the tail-float and passed through the empennage.

(c) Wing Commander C. R. Samson. D.S.O. (Pilot), Captain Edwards (Observer), attacked the railway bridge on the River Maritza at Kuleli Burgaz, dropping two 100-lb. bombs simultaneously at the centre of the bridge from a height of 800 feet. Both fell together, making a perfect detonation, about five yards to the south of the bridge. It was impossible to see the extent of the damage done to the bridge, as the aeroplane was being fired at by machine guns and rifle fire and could not, therefore, fly a second time over the bridge at such low altitude.

II.—The following from No. 6 Kite Balloon Section operating with the military on the Western Front, is inserted as a matter of interest and gives a summary of the work done between August 17th and November 13th :—

(1) On first inflation, 139 tubes used; on re-inflation, 139 tubes used. Total number of tubes used, 662.
(2) Number of days balloon ascended, 53.
(3) Number of ascents, 88.

(4) Total time in air, 232 hours 35 minutes.
(5) Longest time in air by one observer, 10 hours 20 minutes. Longest time in air by two observers, 9 hours 9 minutes.
(6) Highest altitude, one observer, 3,200 feet. Highest altitude, two observers, 3,000 feet.
(7) Greatest wind pressure, 49 miles an hour.
(8) Different positions worked from, 7.
(9) Greatest distance moved inflated, $3\frac{1}{2}$ miles.
(10) Batteries worked with, 23   Armoured train, 1.
(11) Targets registered, 86.
(12) Batteries located by flashes, 42.
(13) Types of guns worked with :—6-in., 4·7-in., 4·5-in., 60-prs., and 18-pr.
(14) A large number of trains and signal lights observed and reported in the enemy's lines.
(15) Average distance from enemy's line, 7,500 yards.
(16) Greatest distance target registered at, 12,000 yards.
(17) Greatest number of targets registered in one day, 12.
(18) On one or two occasions balloon was connected by telephone with a 6-in. gun and an 18-pr. battery at the same time, and registered targets for both satisfactorily.

III.—The following is an extract from the report of No. 2 Kite Balloon Section operating on the Western Front :—

November 24th.

To-day, in a small way, was a record for this Balloon Section, as there were eight successful shoots, besides one unsuccessful one, which accounted for 18 rounds and 40 minutes of fine weather.

November 30th.

IV.—Flight Sub-Lieut. Hardstaff, No. 4 Wing, attached to No. 1 Wing, while carrying out coastal reconnaissance in a Nieuport, observed one hostile machine at 11.30 a.m., which made off towards Ostend. At 11.45 a.m. he sighted two hostile machines at Pervyse proceeding in a north-easterly direction towards Dixmude. On being pursued, both machines disappeared through the clouds south of Ostend.

December 14th.

Sub-Lieut. Grahame, No. 1 Wing, in a Nieuport, with Sub-Lieut. Ince as Observer, when carrying out patrol from Dunkerque, attacked a large German seaplane near La Panne. The German seaplane caught on fire, nose-dived, and exploded as it struck the water. No trace could be found of the machine, pilot, or observer.

The Nieuport was struck in the petrol tank by machine-gun fire and was forced to descend. The officers were picked up safely, but the machine sank.

REPORT OF OPERATIONS No. 3.

December 14*th.*

(1)—(*a*) Flight Sub-Lieut. Simms, No. 1 Wing, with Flight Sub-Lieut. Collison, in a Nieuport, whilst returning from a coastal reconnaissance observed two seaplanes off La Panne at a very low altitude quite close to the shore. When approached they fired red and white Very's lights respectively. This was evidently a signal to the anti-aircraft guns, and in view of the heavy fire Sub-Lieut. Simms broke off the engagement.

(*b*) Flight Sub-Lieut. Dallas with Air Mechanic Watt, in a Caudron, while carrying out hostile aircraft patrol over the "stranded" vessel off La Panne, observed a hostile machine coming in from a north-easterly direction, as if coming towards the "stranded" vessel. He proceeded towards the enemy "Aviatik" and opened fire at a range of 300 yards. After firing about 30 rounds the hostile machine turned and circled out to sea. It came back for a second attack, which was made in a similar manner. After firing another 20 rounds the hostile machine was finally driven off and disappeared in the direction of Ostend. The pilot did not pursue machine further, as it would have left the "stranded" vessel unguarded.

(*c*) Flight Sub-Lieut. Price with Air Mechanic Bell, in a Caudron, carried out patrol over "stranded" vessel. When in the vicinity of Dixmude observed a hostile machine engaged by two French machines, but before pilot was able to get within firing range hostile machine had turned back over lines.

(2) The following further particulars have been received as regards the bringing down of an Albatross seaplane by Flight Sub-Lieut. Graham (pilot) and Flight Sub-Lieut. Ince (observer) in a Nieuport on December 14th. The Nieuport easily had the speed of the enemy and overhauled him rapidly, getting within a range of 100 yards. The pilot manœuvred his machine so as to be behind and below the enemy's tail at a range about 50 yards. The observer fired 15 rounds, and on ceasing firing clearly observed bullet holes and an appearance of smouldering beneath the enemy observer's seat. The enemy carried a pilot and passenger, and beyond one slight alteration in course did not appear to manœuvre. Flight Sub-Lieut. Graham succeeded twice in getting his machine into position, the passenger each time firing into the enemy. Finally the German machine turned sharply round and dived vertically nose first into the water. Flaming wreckage was seen on the water below and the pilot volplaned. Only the enemy's empennage was visible above water. The engine of the Nieuport

then failed, presumably owing to the petrol tank having been holed by a bullet, and a forced descent was made in the sea. Machine turned over in the water, but both pilot and observer succeeded in releasing themselves from their belts and supporting themselves until rescued by H.M.S. "Balmoral."

(3) **The following is a synopsis of the work carried out by No. 3 Squadron during operations in the Dardanelles from March 28th to November 9th :—**

Maximum number of pilots, 11.
Average number flying daily, 6 to 7.
Number of miles flown, 137,934.
Number of flights to control either fire of ships or shore batteries, 394.

(The majority of these flights were of $2\frac{1}{2}$ hours' duration, the shortest one never less than $1\frac{3}{4}$ hours.)

Bombs dropped.—One hundred and seventy-nine 100-lb. bombs and five hundred and seven 20-lb. bombs.

Engagements with Hostile Aircraft.—These have occurred almost daily, and none of them have ended in our defeat.

Hostile Aircraft brought down.—Two. (*Note.*—On many occasions the hostile aircraft escaped by descending to a low altitude over its own territory. Every combat in the air has taken place over the enemy's country.)

Reconnaissances.—Long-distance reconnaissance and bombing flights have taken place very frequently, penetrating as far as 100 miles in the enemy's lines.

Night Flights.—A large number of night flights have been carried out for the purpose of bombing camps and landing-places.

Attacks on Enemy's Battleships, Destroyers, and Transports.—One transport was sunk by bombs. One battleship was badly damaged. ("She arrived at Constantinople with her centre turret damaged, and 10 men killed as the result of an aeroplane bomb.")

Damage to the Enemy's Communications.—The main landing pier at Ak Bashi Lima was severely damaged on May 17th by 100-lb. bomb. Four attacks have been made on the Kuleli Burgas Railway from low altitudes. Eleven attacks have been made upon Ferrijik Railway Junction from low altitudes. Two flights have been made at an altitude of 1,000 feet above the enemy's first line of trenches at the request of general headquarters to determine how thickly they were held by troops.

Conditions.—All the flights carried out necessitated long flights over the open sea on aeroplanes unprovided with floats. Three aeroplanes have been lost by falling into the sea. On one occasion the occupants were $1\frac{1}{2}$ hours in the water before being picked up. Flights have been frequently carried out in winds of gale force. It has frequently taken machines capable of 75 m.p.h. 40 minutes to cover 16 miles.

Cape Helles Aerodrome has daily been used under heavy shell fire. Four aeroplanes have been wrecked there by shell fire. In case of engine failure the machine is almost bound to be lost either by falling into the sea or in the hands of the enemy. The only landing places are Suvla and Cape Helles. Both these are in view and within range of the enemy. Aeroplanes landing at either are immediately fired upon. Of aeroplanes which landed at Suvla up to date, only one has been saved.

Submarines.—Hostile submarines have been sighted on two occasions and attacked with bombs.

Photography.—Photographs have been taken of the whole sphere of operations.

Flying Records.—On April 25th (landing day) 37 hours were spent in the air. June 4th, 33 hours.

22nd December 1915.

REPORT OF OPERATIONS No. 4.

December 25th.

(1) Flight Sub-Lieut. Mulock with Sub-Lieut. Furnival (No. 1 Wing), in a Nieuport, whilst returning from a reconnaissance carried out over Wenduyne, Meetkerke, St. Andre, Bruges, Sysserre, Middleburgh, Oostekerke, Dudzerle and Ostende—this reconnaissance being carried out at an average of 5,500 feet and a great deal of useful information being obtained—when over the Zeebrugge Canal was approached by a large German tractor biplane coming from the westward. It followed him at the same height and was evidently giving a range to the anti-aircraft battery by means of different coloured lights; the shooting of the battery was in consequence excellent. The German machine was appreciably faster in climb and speed than the Nieuport but did not close for attack. A second German machine well above the Nieuport also did not attack, but was probably correcting for Middelkerke Batteries in the same manner.

December 30th.

(2) A practice bombing expedition was carried out by No. 1 Wing on the sheds at Ostende situated to the north of T. 4. The following machines took part:—

         13 Nieuports,
         4 Caudrons,
         3 Henri Farmans.

Three of these machines were detailed for fighting patrol only. Bombs were dropped as follows:—

On sheds.—Thirteen 16-lb. bombs and seven 65-lb. bombs.
On batteries at T. 4.—Five 16-lb. bombs.
On Westende.—Four 65-lb. bombs.
On Ostende docks.—Three 65-lb. bombs.
On anti-aircraft batteries north-east of Bassin à Flots.—Five 16-lb. bombs.

Results were very difficult to observe owing to very heavy high-explosive anti-aircraft fire. Several machines were hit.

The following incidents during the course of this expedition are interesting:—

    (a) Flight Sub-Lieut. Mulock attacked a German biplane, and after firing about half a tray of ammunition the hostile machine was last seen in a steep nose-dive near Dixmude.

    (b) Flight Sub-Lieut. Allen when near Ostende and about to drop his bombs observed a white German tractor biplane. He fired half a tray at the hostile machine, which turned away and thus enabled pilot to drop his bombs. The same machine again approached, and after Flight Sub-Lieut. Allen had fired the remainder of the tray the enemy was driven off.

(c) Flight Sub-Lieut. Petre when about to release bombs was attacked from behind by a Fokker monoplane with a deflector propeller. Pilot immediately turned his Nieuport round to enable him to face his opponent and opened fire at about 80 yards' range. Pilot fired two trays of ammunition at the hostile machine, and while endeavouring to reload the third tray, machine got into a spiral nose-dive and the Lewis gun fell overboard. Pilot was forced to abandon the fight and steered straight for Nieuport with the enemy machine still firing behind him. The Nieuport machine was hit in many places. However, when passing over Westende hostile machine broke off the engagement.

December 30th.

(3) Flight Commander Bone, No. 1 Wing, in a Nieuport, whilst carrying out hostile aircraft patrol between La Panne-Nieuport-Dixmude, observed two German machines at 8,000 to 10,000 feet flying in company crossing back over the lines. He attempted to pursue them, but owing to engine trouble was forced to land on the sands near Bray Duns.

(4) The following report has been received during the week from Eastern Mediterranean :—

December 2nd.

Flight Commander Busk, with Captain Joppe, Royal Australian Field Artillery (observer), whilst engaged in spotting for one of H.M. Ships, observed the ship being attacked by a hostile aeroplane. He dived down and closed within 50 yards, opening fire with his machine gun. The German machine attempted to escape, but was followed down to an altitude of 1,000 feet. Flight Commander Busk eventually discontinued the action owing to the Taube getting down to 200 feet and to his own machine gun jamming. The whole fight took place well within the enemy's lines, and our machine was subjected to heavy machine-gun fire from the ground.

5th January 1916.

REPORT OF OPERATIONS No. 5.

January 9th.

1.—(*a*) Flight Sub-Lieut. Goble, No. 1 Wing, with Sub-Lieut. Bellamy, in a Nieuport, whilst on a coastal reconnaissance to Ostend, observed, when opposite Raverside, a big German land machine (a tractor) coming down the coast from the direction of Ostend. While manœuvring to open fire on the enemy a second hostile machine appeared coming in from the sea, which opened fire from above at a practically vertical range of 60 yards. Sub-Lieut. Bellamy opened fire on the second machine, firing half a tray at a range of 60 yards. The gun jumped its socket and was used as an ordinary rifle against the first machine at a range of 300 yards, firing the remainder of the tray. The second machine only fired one tray and proceeded towards Ostend. Three other hostile machines were observed at a higher altitude over Ostend.

(*b*) Flight Sub-Lieut. Dallas, No. 1 Wing, with Air Mechanic Watt, in a Nieuport, observed two hostile machines at a high altitude over Nieuport being heavily shelled by our anti-aircraft guns. The hostile machines, on being pursued, made off in the direction of Ostend.

(*c*) Flight Lieut. Huskisson, No. 1 Wing Depôt, Dover, in a Bristol Scout, proceeded with three other machines in chase of a large white German seaplane, which had approached Dover Harbour at a height of 6,000 to 7,000 feet, and which turned tail as soon as anti-aircraft fire was opened on it. Flight Lieut. Huskisson chased the seaplane for a considerable distance, and finally lost it in a bank of clouds.

January 12th.

2. Flight Lieut. Petre, No. 1 Wing, in a Nieuport, ascended on a report being received of hostile aircraft over Calais, and proceeded towards Gravelines. He encountered heavy clouds at 4,500 feet and turned towards Nieuport. When off Zuydcoote he observed anti-aircraft fire and shortly afterwards observed a hostile machine and proceeded to give chase. The hostile machine, on being pursued, immediately turned in the direction of Nieuport. Flight Lieut. Petre gave up the chase on the enemy disappearing into the clouds.

January 14th.

3. Flight Sub-Lieut. Peberdy, No. 1 Wing, with Air Mechanic Hamlin, in a Nieuport, whilst carrying out hostile aircraft patrol between Nieuport and Dixmude, sighted a hostile machine over Nieuport. On making towards it the machine turned back over the German lines and was lost in the clouds.

January 17th.

(a) Flight Sub-Lieut. Sims, No. 1 Wing, in a Nieuport, ascended on receiving a report of hostile aircraft over Nieuport, and proceeded up the coast five miles out to sea. When off Nieuport, at 11,000 feet, he observed an enemy machine coming from the direction of Westende, at about 13,000 feet. The pilot manœuvred to head him off, gradually climbing to enable him to engage. This was successfully accomplished, and when 40 yards below, and behind the enemy, he opened fire, emptying half a tray. The German machine, which was observed to be of the large Aviatik type, with pilot in front and passenger behind, made half a turn to the left, bringing his gun into position, and at the same time opening fire. Flight Sub-Lieut. Sims again manœuvred for position, and when at close range emptied the remainder of his tray into the German machine. The bullets were clearly observed to strike the fuselage beside the pilot and passenger, who were apparently hit. Flight Sub-Lieut. Sims was then forced to turn away to change his ammunition tray, but at the same time observed the German machine dive towards Ostend, and immediately dived after him, but was forced to abandon the chase owing to heavy anti-aircraft fire.

(b) Flight Sub-Lieut. Minifie, No. 1 Wing, in a Nieuport, while carrying out hostile aircraft patrol, observed when off Dixmude, at 10,000 feet, heavy anti-aircraft fire off Dunkerque, and proceeded in that direction. When over Oost-Dunkerque he observed an enemy machine well out to sea. He immediately gave chase, but was unable to overtake the machine before it was lost to view in the clouds.

5. The following are extracts from reports received during the course of the last week as regards Naval Kite Balloon Sections operating with the military :—

October 3rd.

"Captain Macneece, No. 2 Kite Balloon Section, remained up in a very heavy wind and sent most valuable information to Third Group, H.A.R., with reference to the German artillery."

October 4th.

(a) "Arrangements were made to observe for the 52nd French Battery, Armoured Train, and 22nd Brigade, R.G.A. Owing to heavy rain the balloon began to come down rapidly, and the cable got in contact with some electric high-power wires, which fused the cable, and the balloon broke away with about 1,200 feet of cable. Flight Lieut. Ogilvie-Davis and Sergeant Barard were in the basket, and the former made a perfect landing with the help of some gunners near Houchin."

6. The following is an extract from a report received from the Naval Air Service Unit operating with Force "D" (Mesopotamia).

October 4th.

"Squadron Commander Gordon proceeded on reconnaissance with a Short Seaplane to discover enemy's position at Tesiphon. At Azizeah the propeller sheathing stripped and vibration broke the petrol pipe. The pilot landed and repaired pipe and later repaired propeller with solder. He then continued the flight and found enemy's position astride the river at Tesiphon. He could see no troops in trenches, but was fired at from the enemy's right flank by one gun. Height, 4,500 feet. He returned to Azizeah and reported to D.H.Q. He returned to Kut after flying a total distance of over 240 miles.".

19th January 1916.

REPORT OF OPERATIONS No. 6.

January 19th.

1.—(a) Flight Sub-Lieut Norton, No. 1 Wing, in a Nieuport, while on hostile aircraft patrol between Nieuport and Dixmude, observed a hostile machine between Ypres and Dixmude. He immediately gave chase and followed the machine well over the other side of the lines. When drawing near, the pilot overhauled the enemy machine, which on being approached dived and was lost sight of.

(b) Flight Sub-Lieut. Sims, No. 1 Wing, in a Nieuport, while on hostile aircraft patrol, Nieuport–Dixmude–Ypres, when at an altitude of 12,000 feet observed a hostile biplane tractor patrolling at about 10,000 feet. Pilot immediately dived towards it and the enemy machine turned back over its own lines, leading the way over the Foret d'Houthaulst, where very heavy anti-aircraft fire was encountered, and the enemy machine descended.

January 23rd.

II.—(a) Flight Sub-Lieut. Leather, No. 1 Wing, in a Nieuport, while on hostile aircraft patrol, Nieuport–Dixmude, observed a German biplane making towards its own lines. The pilot followed and was able to get underneath. The iron crosses were distinctly visible. When within 70 yards he opened fire, expending one tray of ammunition. Immediately the pilot opened fire the hostile machine put his nose down and dived straight for the German lines, so that the pilot was forced to abandon the chase. So far as could be observed the hostile machine did not open fire.

(b) Flight Sub-Lieut. Sims, No. 1 Wing, in a Nieuport, proceeded with four 16-lb. bombs to locate a submarine previously reported and observed a submarine half blown 10 to 12 miles west of Ostende, steering south-west. While coming down from 3,000 to 500 feet the submarine was seen to fire two green lights. The submarine immediately began to dive, and at the moment of releasing the bombs from a height of 500 feet the periscope only was visible. The pilot was unable to observe the effect; nothing was visible but black marks in the water close to where the periscope was last seen.

(c) Flight Sub-Lieut. Norton, No. 1 Wing, in a Nieuport, proceeded with four 16-lb. bombs to locate the same submarine. He located the submarine and observed the four bombs of Flight Sub-Lieut. Sims, and immediately came down to 500 feet and dropped one 16-lb. bomb. The top of the periscope was only just visible and he was unable to observe the result.

January 24th.

III.—(*a*) Flight Sub-Lieut. Mulock, No. 1 Wing, in a Nieuport, while carrying out photographic reconnaissances to Ghistelles and Ostende, encountered a hostile tractor biplane at 7,000 to 8,000 feet when off Nieuport. The hostile machine was at a much lower altitude. The pilot therefore manœuvred over the enemy machine and at a steep angle opened fire. After a few rounds the hostile machine was observed to dive steeply in the direction of Westende. The pilot pursued the enemy machine until reaching an altitude of 5,000 feet, when heavy anti-aircraft fire was encountered from the Westende batteries. Low-lying clouds prevented the pilot keeping in touch with the hostile machine, but when last observed it was on the ground near Westende. The hostile machine was observed to be a large brown biplane with a large overhang on the upper wing and a black cross on the upper part of each upper wing on a white background.

(*b*) Flight Sub-Lieut. Sims, No. 1 Wing, in a Nieuport, whilst carrying out hostile aircraft patrol to Ostende and the vicinity, when at a height of 11,000 feet off Nieuport machine on the return journey, observed a Nieuport machine and a hostile seaplane below. He dived and manœuvred for position, and when at about 7,000 feet he attempted to engage the enemy. The Lewis gun would not fire owing to the spring being too weak to overcome the resistance due to the oil thickening on account of the cold. The hostile machine fired 60 to 80 rounds. The pilot dived and eventually was able to bring the gun into action. Returning to the attack, he fired two trays of ammunition at 100 yards' range. The hostile machine returned a continuous fire up to this point, when he turned away and was lost sight of, going in the direction of Ostende.

(*c*) Flight Sub-Lieut. Leather, No. 1 Wing, with Flight Sub-Lieut. Furness, while on coastal reconnaissance, observed in the vicinity of Nieuport a hostile seaplane at about 4,000 to 5,000 feet and one mile inland. The pilot manœuvred to engage the seaplane and at the same time observed a Nieuport Scout, also manœvring to attack. The seaplane immediately nose-dived to a low altitude, thereby getting shelter from its own anti-aircraft guns, and was almost immediately lost sight of in the low-lying mists. The pilot therefore abandoned the chase and returned.

(*d*) Flight Sub-Lieut. Peberdy, No. 1 Wing, in a Nieuport, proceeded to investigate the report of a German seaplane having been seen off Dunkerque. When about three miles off Nieuport, at a height of 5,000 feet, he engaged the seaplane. The seaplane was being shelled by our anti-aircraft fire, which stopped to allow the pilot to engage it. The pilot opened fire at 200 yards' range, emptying one tray of ammunition. When changing trays the enemy machine was observed to withdraw, and was lost sight of in the mist.

January 25th.

IV.—(a) Flight Sub-Lieut. Keeble, No. 1 Wing, in a Nieuport, while on a hostile aircraft patrol north of Ostende and seawards, when at an altitude of 10,000 feet off Nieuport observed a seaplane 7 miles out to sea, at about 2,000 feet, which was climbing, and when at a height of 4,000 feet the pilot observed it to be a hostile seaplane. The pilot therefore manœuvred to engage by nose-diving to a position about 60 yards below and behind his tail. When in this position the pilot expended one tray of ammunition. The enemy was observed to turn to the left as if manœuvring to open fire, but at this moment he descended at a very steep angle and landed on the sea. The pilot turned round and when vertically over released one 16-lb. bomb but was unable to observe the result. Immediately after releasing the bomb the pilot observed a hostile machine at a high altitude coming straight towards him, but owing to his own low altitude he proceeded in the direction of Nieuport.

January 26th.

V.—Flight Sub-Lieut. Mulock, No. 1 Wing, in a Nieuport, while patrolling in the vicinity of Nieuport, acting as escort to a machine registering the calibration of gun-fire on Westende, observed a large white German biplane making for the Fleet. The pilot manœuvred to get well under his tail and opened fire, expending half a tray of ammunition. The hostile machine dived steeply down through a thick bank of clouds. The pilot pursued him, keeping up an incessant fire. On coming up through the clouds the hostile machine was seen to be in a vertical spinning nose-dive.

The German machine was a large biplane carrying a passenger and two guns, one fitted on the side mounting and the other on the upper plane. It was also fitted with bombs. The German machine fired only a few rounds from the rear gun.

(*Note.*—Flight Sub-Lieut. Mulock reports that after the first shells from the Monitors had been fired large fires were observed on the sands which produced a big volume of smoke, and which were observed to be lighted from windward. These were apparently " smoke-screens " across the line of fire to prevent observation of the fall of shot from the land observation stations.)

October 24th.

VI.—The following is an extract from the report received from the Naval Air Service Unit operating with Force D in Mesopotamia :—

(a) . . . Flight Lieut. Rober in a Short Seaplane proceeded to attempt to blow up a Turkish pontoon bridge. He descended to 1,000 feet above 4,000 Turks and dropped one 100-lb. bomb among them. He then proceeded to the bridge but did not hit it. He returned for more 100-lb. bombs and dropped them, but the target was too small.

October 25th, 1915.

(a) . . . Flight Lieut. Blackburn bombed a large body of Turkish Cavalry which were moving round our right flank . .

VII.—The following is an extract from the report of No. 2 Kite Balloon Section operating with the military at the Western front :—

(a) . . . The following has been received from the O.C., 2nd Wing, R.F.C.: "You and your section did fine work " yesterday. It may interest you to know that you were seen " at daybreak by the whole of the Army Staff, who realised " that your balloon had been up while it was still dark."
. . .

2nd February 1916.

REPORT OF OPERATIONS No. 7.

February 1st.

(1) Information having been received by No. 1 Wing on the evening of January 31st that Zeppelins were over England, arrangements were made to attack them if they returned *via* Belgium.

The following pilots took part in anti-Zeppelin patrol:—

    Flight Commander Breese.
    Flight Lieut. Petre.
    Flight Lieut. Graham.
    Flight Lieut. Mulock.
    Flight Sub-Lieut. Leather.
    Flight Sub-Lieut. Sims.
    Flight Lieut. Dallas.
    Flight Sub-Lieut. Jackson.
    Flight Sub-Lieut. Penley.
    Flight Sub-Lieut. Clayton.

All these machines (Nieuports) were fitted with 16-lb. bombs, except one machine, which carried Ranken darts.

These 10 machines proceeded at three-minute intervals, $1\frac{1}{2}$ hours before sunrise, to take up position at about 10,000 feet between Nieuport and Zeebrugge about 5 miles out to sea.

All machines were in their allotted positions more than half an hour before the sun rose.

The visibility high up was very good, and a Zeppelin could have been seen for a long distance against the dawn.

Machines patrolled from 10 miles seaward to about 5 miles inland, and were apparently not observed from the ground, due to rising of thick mist.

All were completely lost on coming down to a low altitude, but all managed to strike the coast at various points between Gravelines and Cape Grisnez, with the exception of Flight Sub-Lieut. Clayton, who missed Cape Grisnez and ran out of petrol, and was finally picked up in the water about 30 miles N.W. of Dieppe.

He succeeded in landing his machine without it capsizing, and the machine floated owing to the empty petrol tank.

Two pilots, Flight Lieutenants Mulock and Petre, were able to identify their position on striking the coast, and found their way back to the aerodrome, aided by the large petrol flares, which showed up through the haze for a distance of 2 or 3 miles.

Flight Sub-Lieut. Penley ran out of petrol and planed down to the water. He fortunately sighted the high-water mark on the way down, and was just able to reach the sands. It was, however, such a near thing that he had to make a cross-wind landing on a soft patch, and capsized the machine.

During the forenoon, Flight Lieut. Mulock went out in a two-seater machine with mechanic, tools, &c., and found five machines and pilots who were down on the sands, gave them the necessary directions, and started them home.

February 12th.

(2) Although the weather conditions were most unfavourable, two pilots with their observers attempted a reconnaissance over Ostende Harbour to observe the whereabouts of two monitors that had been previously reported. Flight Sub-Lieut. Keeble and Midshipman Rogers obtained a clear view of the harbour through a pocket in the clouds, but no monitors or submarines were observed.

(3)—(a) Flight Commander Breese, No. 1 Wing, with Sub-Lieut. Furness, in a Nieuport, while carrying out fighter patrol, intercepted a hostile machine flying over Leke in a westerly direction at about 10,000 feet. On being approached, enemy machine turned and disappeared in the direction of Thourout.

(b) Flight Commander Dallas, No. 1 Wing, in a Nieuport, while carrying out fighter patrol, when near Dixmude, at 10,000 feet, sighted a hostile biplane. Enemy observer was in the rear seat, and as far as could be observed had only one gun. When at a range of 200 yards pilot opened fire, enemy machine returning the fire. The enemy observer suddenly stopped firing, the hostile machine took a sharp left-hand turn, and was lost sight of in the thick clouds. It is thought that the hostile observer must have been hit, as at the time when he stopped firing he was still in a good position to have continued the combat.

(c) Flight Sub-Lieut. Hervey, No. 1 Wing, in a Nieuport, while on fighter patrol Nieuport-Dixmude, observed hostile machine north of Dixmude well behind its own lines and proceeding south-east, but owing to its rapid descent to a low altitude it was impossible to engage it.

February 18th.

(4) Flight Sub-Lieut. Clayton and Sub-Lieut. Haines, No. 1 Wing, while on coastal reconnaissance, when 2 miles seaward of Ostende, encountered enemy machine, which fired 20 rounds and then dived for Ostende.

February 22nd.

(5) A night bomb attack was arranged on 11 craft, previously reported by reconnaissance as being in Bassin-de-Leopold, Ostende. It was intended to attack with six Twin Caudrons and five Nieuports (No. 1 Wing) and six Voisin (French), but owing to the high wind the attack had to be carried out by the British five Nieuport machines only. The

machines left at 5.15 a.m., 1 hour 50 minutes before sunrise. Each machine carried five 20-lb. bombs. The machines flew at from 3,000 to 5,000 feet during the journey. The first machine to arrive (Flight Commander Breese) glided down from seaward and attacked at 500 feet. The second machine (Flight Sub-Lieut. Goble) attacked from 3,000 feet. The third machine (Flight Sub-Lieut. Clayton) ran into a thick cloud on the way. The machine became unmanageable, drifted back, and did not reach Ostende until after daylight. He attacked from a height of 4,000 feet. Throughout the attack heavy anti-aircraft fire from rockets and guns was encountered, including much high explosive.

In the fourth machine (Flight Sub-Lieut. Hervey) the instrument light circuit failed shortly after leaving ground, and the pilot was unable to judge altitude and direction, and finally came down in daylight at St. Omar, after two hours' flying. It was impossible to observe the results of the bomb explosions, owing mainly to the searchlights on the north side of the new basin.

February 29th.

(6) At 9.25 a.m. Flight Sub-Lieut. Sims, in a Nieuport Scout (single-seater) 3981, fitted with two machine guns, left to attack German machines, reported by telephone to be crossing the lines. He chased one German machine 5 miles beyond the German lines and lost sight of him.

At 10.30 a.m. he observed a hostile machine being shelled behind the Allies' lines, and got between the German machine and the lines. The two machines approached each other end on. He fired while approaching, the two machines passing each other starboard to starboard, while the German machine opened fire with a machine gun worked from behind by the passenger. The British machine turned sharply to starboard, came round under the tail of the German machine, opened fire with the left gun, which jammed. At the same time the German continued to fire his machine gun. Flight Sub-Lieut. Sims continued to fire with the right gun, and the German machine dived, bringing the British machine on top and behind. He continued to dive, and the German machine fired his right gun.

During the fight many tracer bullets were clearly seen to hit the fuselage of the German machine. Later there was an indication that the German machine was on fire, and it was last seen diving steeply with steam and smoke trailing behind.

The encounter took place off Dixmude, and was witnessed by Belgian soldiers in the trenches, who saw the German machine fall in flames in the flooded area just in front of their trenches near Dixmude.

(7) The following report has been received during the week from Squadron Commander Cull's squadron in East Africa:—

On January 27th Flight Sub-Lieut. Dawson, in a Voisin (?), and Flight Sub-Lieut. Brown, also in a Voisin, carried out a bomb raid over Salaita and Taveta. Flight Sub-Lieut. Dawson succeeded in dropping his bombs in Taveta, and from intelligence reports succeeded in killing two whites and several Askaris, while a good many natives were severely injured. Flight Sub-Lieut. Brown's engine failed over Salaita, and he dropped his bombs at an altitude of about 2,000 feet. At 800 feet he observed a company of Germans on the road, who opened fire on him, cutting his rudder controls and several stay wires. He was consequently obliged to make a landing in the bush. The machine struck a tree and nose-dived to earth. Flight Sub-Lieut. Brown, realising that the machine was beyond repair, and that the Germans were closing in on him, retreated rapidly. After travelling two miles he fell in with a party of Baluchis, who returned with him to destroy the machine.

8th March 1916.

REPORT OF OPERATIONS No. 8.

EXTRACT FROM REPORT OF No. 1 WING.

March 13th.

Four German machines dropped bombs on Dunkirk. Two of our machines which were coming back from a reconnaissance observed one of the hostile machines and pursued it over the German lines, but had to give up through lack of petrol, and only just got back to the aerodrome.

March 19th.

(a) Flight Sub-Lieut. Leslie, Dover Air Station, in a Bristol Scout, proceeded at 1.52 p.m. in chase of a hostile seaplane. At about 2.12, when at a height of 5,000 feet, he passed a hostile machine which was approximately 5,000 feet above him. At 2.32, having drawn well ahead, he returned to the attack at a height of 7,000 feet, but enemy seaplane being at least 2,000 feet higher, Lewis gun could not be brought into action, owing to fixed mounting. He continued to fly directly under the hostile machine and eventually succeeded in discharging six rounds at it, apparently with no effect. Position being then 15 miles north-east of Westende, he landed at Dunkirk.

(b) Flight Commander Bone, No. 4 Wing, in a Nieuport Scout, proceeded from Westgate in chase of a hostile seaplane. After pursuing it for about 30 miles out to sea, his superior climb and speed enabled him to get in position almost directly over the hostile machine. He did an almost vertical nose-dive, firing his Lewis gun. Later he continued the action from under the tail of the hostile machine, which ceased to fire, and the observer, from his attitude, was seen to be either dead or seriously injured. The pilot of the hostile machine eventually dived, his engine (tractor) being brought up all standing, evidently as a result of one of the shots from the Lewis gun.

The hostile pilot succeeded in making a landing and fired a Very's light, upon which a second hostile machine, which until then had not been observed, came down on the water close to the first. Flight Commander Bone, being unable to do anything further, returned to Westgate.

(c) Flight Sub-Lieut. Clayton, No. 1 Wing, when at a height of 6,500 feet, in a Nieuport, 8 miles out to sea, observed a hostile machine 3 miles to the north-west. He gave chase for 25 minutes, but without gaining on it.

March 20th.

(a) A bombing raid upon the aerodrome at Houttave was carried out by a combined force of British, French, and

Belgian machines. The following British machines took part:—

    Flight Sub-Lieut. Goble,
    Flight Sub-Lieut. Hervey,
    Flight Sub-Lieut. Bryant, } in Caudrons, No. 1 Wing.
    Flight Sub-Lieut. Potts,
    Flight Sub-Lieut. Keeble,

    Flight Sub-Lieut. Woolley,
    Flight Sub-Lieut. Blagrove, } in H. Farmans, No. 5 Wing.
    Flight Sub-Lieut. Hughes,

    Flight Lieut. Wood,
    Flight Sub-Lieut. Dallas,
    Flight Sub-Lieut. Neville with Sub-Lieut. Gow, } in Nieuports, fighter patrol, No. 1 Wing.
    Flight Lieut. Mulock with Sub-Lieut. Nelson,

The British machines dropped twenty-five 65-lb. bombs with excellent results, as far as could be observed.

(b) On the same morning a bombing raid was carried out on the seaplane base situated on the Mole at Zeebrugge by British seaplanes:—

FROM SEAPLANE BASE, DUNKIRK.

    Flight Sub-Lieut. Perham with Sub-Lieut. Inge,
    Flight Sub-Lieut. Coley with Sub-Lieut. Slater, } in two Short seaplanes with four 65-lb. bombs each.

FROM SEAPLANE CARRIER "A."

    Flight Lieut. Stewart,
    Flight Lieut. Arnold, } in Short seaplanes with four 65-lb. bombs each.
    Flight Lieut. Price,

Flight Lieut. Price was unable to drop his bombs, due to a broken compression cock, which forced him to land at Nieuport and taxi back.

FROM SEAPLANE CARRIER "B."

    Flight Lieut. Towler with Sub-Lieut. Hopcraft,
    Flight Lieut. Reid with Chief Petty Officer Mullins, } in Short seaplanes with three 65-lb. bombs each.
    Flight Lieut. Openshaw with Midshipman Hoblyn,
    Flight Sub-Lieut. Knight with Midshipman Isaacs,

As far as could be observed, very satisfactory results were obtained. A large fire was still burning on the Mole during the afternoon of the 20th.

(*Note.*—In the raid on Houttave 10 French bombing machines and nine fighting machines took part. The Belgians supplied 11 bombing machines and five fighting machines.)

March 26th.

A Seaplane Carrier carried out bombing operations against airship sheds in the island of Sylt.

The following took part :—

Flight Lieut. Towler with
  Sub-Lieut. Hopcraft,
Flight Sub-Lieut. Knight
  with Midshipman Hoblyn, } in Short seaplanes.
Flight Lieut. Reid with Chief
  Petty Officer Mullins,

Flight Lieut. Openshaw, } in Sopwith Baby sea-
Flight Sub-Lieut. Hay, } planes.

Frequent snow squalls were met and there was bad weather throughout the flight.

Flight Lieut. Towler, failing to find any signs of an airship station at Hoyer, continued his search for some considerable time, and eventually dropped his bombs on a factory, which was apparently set on fire. He reports that it appears absolutely certain that there are no sheds at Hoyer.

Flight Lieut. Openshaw, having failed to discover any sheds at Hoyer, proceeded inland to Tondern. He sighted three large sheds when at a height of 3,000 feet and dived steeply, passing over the sheds at 1,000 feet. His bombs failed to release, even after repeated efforts, owing probably to the frozen condition of their oil. He was under considerable anti-aircraft fire, but the shooting was bad.

The remaining pilots have failed to return.

Damage to the railway line, to a military grain store, to the railway junction at Niebull, and to the military steam ferry between the island of Sylt and Hoyer, is reported (Daily Aeronautical Report No. 17 A.W.S.).

It is also reported that two of the missing machines were shot down and that the third landed with engine trouble.

The following additional reports have been received from overseas units since the date of the last communiqué:—

(*a*) Extract from report of V.A., Eastern Mediterranean Squadron:—

On the 17th March, at the Dardanelles, a reconnoitring aeroplane, which had become separated from her escorting fast machine through the presence of clouds, was attacked by an enemy aeroplane. The latter was driven off, but not before the British pilot and observer had been wounded. British machine managed to reach aerodrome at Imbros.

No. 4. KITE BALLOON SECTION.

Monday, 6th March.

(b) 3 p.m. German aeroplane circled over balloon and dropped a light. Within a few minutes, three shells burst close to winch siding.

3.30 p.m. Locomotive arrived and winch drawn out on to main line, where balloon ascended with Captain Blake, R.F.C., and Sub-Lieut. Bell as observers to altitude of 1,900 feet.

4.35 p.m. German started shelling. Large shells burst on level near balloon. Hauled down 800 feet. Shells followed descent and continued to burst on level with balloon.

4.50 p.m. Hauled down altogether. Put out no ballast, so as not to disclose bagging down position, and man hauled winch on truck towards Paperinghe.

Shelling continued with shrapnel very close to balloon, and ground was searched with H.E. shells.

Balloon hauled down in dark with difficulty, owing to wind having changed and cable fouling the trees. Balloon was also leaking and had lost her lift.

No. 8 KITE BALLOON SECTION.

Observation ascent. Flight Sub-Lieuts. Sadd and Smith successfully ranged on battery H. 3 D. 84. Thirteen rounds of H.E. were fired at target, which was registered with the fifth round. Both hostile batteries ceased fire.

1st April 1916.

REPORT OF OPERATIONS No. 9.

March 16*th.*

Flight Sub-Lieut. Nicholson and Sub-Lieut. Portal (No. 2 Wing), in a Henri Farman, carried out a reconnaissance of shipping in the Dardanelles, escorted by Flight Sub-Lieut. Thorold in a Nieuport Scout. Owing to the cloudy weather the escorting machine was lost sight of. The Henri Farman completed the reconnaissance, and when over Anzac, on its return journey, was attacked from behind by a hostile monoplane of the Fokker type. The Farman endeavoured to turn in order to bring its gun to bear, but the superior speed of the Fokker enabled it to keep close behind, (50 to 100 yards). It broke off action, probably having exhausted its ammunition. The Farman did not succeed in getting off a single round.

(*Note.*—The Farman withstood a speed of 95 knots by the air speed indicator after both the front and rear spars of the lower plane had been pierced through their centres on the same fore and aft line, a considerable amount of metal being shot away.)

March 17*th.*

Flight Sub-Lieut. Thorold and Sub-Lieut. Portal (No. 2 Wing), in a Nieuport, carried out a reconnaissance of shipping in the Dardanelles, escorted by Flight Sub-Lieut. Hooper, in a Nieuport Scout. When abreast of Chanak, on their return journey, Flight Sub-Lieut. Hooper sighted a Fokker type monoplane. He turned towards it, opening fire as the Fokker passed over him. When directly overhead the Fokker turned very steeply and dived, opening fire at the same time and scoring several direct hits, the most serious of which carried away the induction pipe of the Nieuport engine. The pilot was hit in the boot. The Fokker then made off towards the Asiatic coast. Flight Sub-Lieut. Thorold, in the two-seater Nieuport, turned and crossed his bows, opening a heavy fire with 20 $\%$ tracers, most of which were seen to pass into the hostile machine. The Fokker, drawing aft, also opened fire, hitting the Nieuport several times, inflicting a severe wound in the pilot's back, and wounding the observer in the thigh and lodging a bullet in his arm. The pilot lost control of the machine and nose-dived. He soon regained control, and found the Fokker still following. The observer succeeded in firing two magazines, when the Fokker sheered off and disappeared towards Galata. The escorting Nieuport witnessed the last part of this action, but was unable to keep up, having lost much H.P. through its broken induction pipe.

Altogether 250 rounds were fired at the hostile machine. Both of our machines returned safely, the wounded pilot making a perfect landing before fainting.

(*Note.*—The apparent ineffectiveness of the large number of hits poured into the fore part of the Fokker seems to indicate that the machine and pilot are protected by armour against fire from ahead.)

March 29th.

Flight Sub-Lieut. Hervey, with Sub-Lieut. Mullens, No. 1 Wing, in a Nieuport machine, made a reconnaissance over Ostend and vicinity, and obtained 18 satisfactory photographs of the country from Dixmude to Ostend, showing position of "T. 4" gun emplacements, &c. They were attacked by a Fokker monoplane, which was driven off after a short fight at 400 yards' range.

March 30th.

(*a*) Flight Sub-Lieut. Eyre, with Sub-Lieut. Mullens,
Flight Sub-Lieut. Leather - - -
Flight Commander Haskins - - -
} No. 1 Wing, in Nieuport machines,

while on fighter patrol to Nieuport and Ypres, sighted enemy machine and chased it over the lines without fighting.

(*b*) Flight Sub-Lieut. Tooks and Sub-Lieut. Slatter, R.N.V.R. (Dunkirk Seaplane Base), in a Short seaplane, after patrolling for $2\frac{1}{2}$ hours in enemy water, attacked a submarine 7 miles off Ostend.

A 65-lb. bomb with delay action fuse was dropped from 1,000 feet, followed by another with impact fuse. The explosion caused a great commotion in the water, and three streaks of oil were observed..

Destruction of this submarine is claimed by the officers concerned.

March 31st.

(*a*) Flight Sub-Lieut. Bailey and Sub-Lieut. Slatter, R.N.V.R. (Dunkirk Seaplane Base), in a Short seaplane, attacked a submarine 4 miles off Zeebrugge. Three 65-lb. bombs with delay fuses were dropped. No traces of oil observed.

(*b*) From G.O.C., Aden :—

Reconnaissance this morning by seaplanes from Seaplane Carrier showed main enemy camp about $1\frac{1}{4}$ miles east of Waht. Fifteen bombs were dropped into this camp, six in and near Waht, and two in Darb. Observation near Fiyush difficult. All seaplanes returned safely. (Arabs report 20 Turks, 6 Arabs, 29 mules, 7 gun bullocks, 1 camel, and many military huts destroyed, and all Arabs fled to Wadikabir.)

The attack was also continued next day.

April 10th.

Sub-Lieut. A. G. McEwan, Polegate Airship Station, in "S.S. 6" (airship), carried out a patrol over the Channel from 4.40 a.m. to 5.20 p.m., making a total of 12 hours 36 minutes in the air, and covering a distance of 325 miles.

April 15th.

Squadron Commander Smyth-Pigott
Flight Sub-Lieut. Dickinson
Flight Lieut. Savory
Flight Sub-Lieut. Barnato
} No. 2 Wing,

carried out a bombing raid on Constantinople and Adrianople.

Flight Lieut. Savory arrived at Constantinople and dropped proclamations. He descended to 500 feet in an unsuccessful endeavour to find Zeitunlik Powder Factory, and was heavily fired on, his machine being hit twice. He dropped eight incendiary bombs on aeroplane hangars, producing a fire.

Flight Sub-Lieut. Dickinson reached Constantinople and dropped proclamations. He dropped eight bombs on Zeitunlik, but ran into heavy wind and thunderstorms over Marmara, and, being exhausted and behind time, came down near Trawler 348 off Cape Xeros. Most important parts of machine salved.

Flight Sub-Lieut. Barnato sighted Marmara, but the land was obscured, and owing to threatening weather he had to return.

Squadron Commander Smyth-Pigott dropped pamphlets on Adrianople and bombs on Adrianople Station.

Length of flights to Constantinople and Adrianople, 360 and 230 miles respectively. Fine weather at start, which developed into rain and thunderstorms.

April 16th.

(a) Flight Sub-Lieut. Souray, No. 5 Wing, whilst bringing a Caudron from Paris to Dunkirk, lost his way and crossed the lines. He was attacked by a Fokker and wounded in the right side.

He succeeded in landing at Furness and is now in hospital at La Panne.

(b) Flight Lieut. Gerrard and Sub-Lieut. Mullens, in a Nieuport, whilst on a photographic reconnaissance, engaged the hostile machine mentioned in the preceding paragraph. When within range of 50 yards, fire was opened, and after 20 rounds the enemy was observed to nose-dive over Westende. It appears probable that the machine was seriously damaged.

April 21st.

(a) Sub-Lieut. Bailey with Air Mechanic Fryer, No. 1 Wing, in a Short seaplane fitted with a Lewis gun and carrying one 65-lb. bomb, while patrolling off Blankenburgh Pier, sighted two German destroyers. The seaplane attacked one destroyer with its bomb, from a height of 2,000 feet, and succeeded in damaging the deck and stanchions. The pilot then dived to 1,000 feet and attacked the destroyer with the Lewis gun, firing one tray at a distance of 300 yards, the tracer bullets showing several hits on the deck and fore part. During the attack the machine was under heavy fire from both destroyers, who were armed with four pom-poms and two or three machine guns each.

(b) Sub-Lieut. Tooke with Sub-Lieut. Inge, R.N.V.R. (No. 1 Wing), in a Short seaplane, left Dunkirk with the object of repeating the attack on the destroyers, but did not discover them. They therefore carried out a surprise attack on Zeebrugge, dropping two 100-lb. bombs on the lock gates. Both bombs fell within about 20 yards of the objective in the vicinity of the operating mechanism. Heavy fire was opened from the anti-aircraft guns, and the machine was hit several times.

April 23rd.

An attack was carried out by No. 5 Wing on the enemy aerodrome at Mariakerke. Owing to the inclement weather only nine machines could get away, but the majority of these reached their objective with apparently good results. All were heavily fired on and hit, but all machines landed safely.

Flight Sub-Lieut. Dallas, in a Nieuport Scout, attacked an enemy aeroplane which was chasing a British machine. After a short fight the enemy dived, and Flight Sub-Lieut. Dallas followed down to a height of 2,000 feet, firing all the time. When last seen the enemy was close to the ground and out of control. The Nieuport was heavily fired at, but got back safely. The pilot had a piece of shrapnel in his cap.

April 24th.

(a) The attack on Mariakerke was continued by 12 machines from Nos. 4 and 5 Wings, in co-operation with the Belgians. Thirty-four 65-lb. and twenty-four 16-lb. bombs were dropped. Heavy anti-aircraft fire was met with, but all machines returned safely.

(b) Flight Sub-Lieut. Sims with Flight Lieut. Furness, No. 1 Wing, in a Nieuport, attacked an enemy seaplane, about 5 miles off Zeebrugge. The enemy pilot was killed, and the machine dropped, the observer falling out while the machine was still at a height of 3,000 feet. The seaplane crashed into the sea and sank.

(c) Flight Lieut. Gerrard, No. 1 Wing, in a Nieuport, while on fighter patrol along the coast, observed two German seaplanes. He attacked one, firing 20 rounds, but the result was not observed, as the enemy made off. The second seaplane was then chased, and the Nieuport obtained a position 10 feet behind and below, but the pilot was unable to open fire owing to gun having jammed. Enemy disappeared in the direction of Zeebrugge.

April 24th/25th.

During the operations against the German battle cruiser squadron, which appeared off the east coast on the morning of the 25th instant, two Zeppelins were pursued by Flight Lieut. Hards and Flight Lieut. Nicholl in B.E. 2 C. R.A.F. machines over 60 miles out to sea. Bombs and darts were dropped apparently without serious effect.

Flight Lieut. Smith, in a Bristol Scout, attacked two enemy submarines with 12 grenades. The enemy at once submerged and made off.

Flight Sub-Lieut. Hall and Sub-Lieut. Evans, R.N.V.R., in a seaplane, attacked the enemy squadron approximately 10 miles east of Yarmouth. Heavy fire was opened by all the ships upon the seaplane, and the pilot was seriously wounded in the shoulder. Although very weak from loss of blood, he succeeded in bringing his machine back to Yarmouth and landing safely.

Flight Sub-Lieut. Wemp, in a B.E. 2 C. R.A.F., armed with eight 16-lb. bombs, pursued the German squadron. He attacked the rear ships of the line and dropped his bombs, but was unable to observe the result. He was subjected to heavy anti-aircraft fire.

Squadron Commander Oliver, in a seaplane, armed with five 65-lb. bombs, flew along the whole line of the enemy fleet, dropping his bombs. He was subjected to considerable anti-aircraft fire, but was not hit.

Flight Lieut. Smith again proceeded to attack an enemy submarine some 15 miles eastward of Southwold, which immediately started to submerge. Pilot dived to 500 feet and dropped three 16-lb. bombs. Although he could not ascertain the result, he is of opinion that he either sank or seriously damaged the submarine.

April 25th.

A Caudron bombing machine patrolled the coast between Nieuport and Westende in search of hostile submarines and destroyers. He attacked two large T.B.D.'s and a number of small T.B.'s. The first two bombs fell one in front and the other behind the last T.B.D., and the next two fell on the beam of the first T.B.D., about half a length off their mark.

April 26th.

Flight Sub-Lieut. Bailey with Sub-Lieut. Slatter, R.N.V.R., No. 1 Wing, in a seaplane, bombed Zeebrugge lock gate with two 100-lb. bombs.

Air Department, Admiralty,
  1st May 1916.

REPORT OF OPERATIONS No. 10.

April 30*th*.

Flight Sub-Lieut. Leather, No. 1 Wing, in a Nieuport, while on fighter patrol, observed a hostile aeroplane off Ostend. He chased it back over Westende, firing half a tray of ammunition at a range of 500 yards. The enemy then disappeared.

May 3*rd*.

(*a*) Sub-Lieut. Sims, No. 1 Wing, in a Nieuport, patrolled seawards with a view to cutting off enemy machines which were dropping bombs on Ramsgate and Dover. He observed a hostile seaplane coming towards Zeebrugge, and, altering his course, chased it for 20 minutes, slowly gaining on it. When nearing Zeebrugge he opened fire at a range of 800 yards, but after firing half a tray of ammunition his gun jammed. The enemy descended and replied with a machine gun. Sub-Lieut. Sims fired another tray from the second gun, but by this time the German seaplane had descended into Zeebrugge, and the chase had to be abandoned.

(*b*) One of our machines proceeded on a reconnaissance flight north of Zeebrugge. The pilot observed a hostile submarine and dropped five 65-lb. bombs. The submarine immediately submerged, and the result could not be seen.

(*c*) A raid was made against the Bulgarian coast by all available machines in the Eastern Mediterranean Squadron. Seaplanes from Stavros and seaplane carriers attacked points of military importance. All machines returned.

May 4*th*.

(*a*) The pilot of a patrolling machine observed a hostile submarine, and made three separate attacks from a height of 600 feet, dropping one 65-lb. bomb each time, all of which fell 30 to 60 feet from the objective. The submarine was observed to turn back towards Zeebrugge. The seaplane was seriously damaged by gun-fire from the submarine, and was only just able to reach port.

(*b*) Nineteen machines carried out a raid on Mariakerke Aerodrome and fifty 65-lb. bombs were dropped. A great many anti-aircraft incendiary shells or rockets were fired, which gave a green-coloured light, and were composed chiefly of magnesium. They were probably fired with the idea of setting fire to the wing material. One pilot flew through one of these bursts, and although the magnesium appeared to touch the planes, it did no apparent damage. All the machines returned safely, except two, Flight Sub-Lieut. Van Allan in a Caudron, and Flight Sub-Lieut. Greensmith in a B.E. 2. C. being lost.

May 5th.

(a) Flight Lieut. Petre,
Flight Sub-Lieut. Leather,
Flight Sub-Lieut. Dallas,
} No. 1 Wing, in Nieuport machines,

were despatched to Dixmude upon a report that a heavy artillery action was taking place, and that German machines were spotting for their artillery. Lieutenant Petre engaged an Aviatik and from a range of 500 to 1,000 feet fired two trays. The tracer bullets were observed to pass very near the hostile machine, which opened fire whilst diving steeply into the enemy lines.

(b) Flight Lieut. Sims, with Sub-Lieut. Mullens as observer, left on fighter patrol and did not return. Two patrols were sent out to search for the missing machine, but no trace could be found. The body of Lieut. Sims was picked up during the day by one of the mine-sweepers.

May 6th.

(a) Flight Lieut. Openshaw, H.M. Seaplane Carrier "A," in a Baby Sopwith, attacked Tondern Airship Base and dropped two 65-lb. bombs, but, owing to the mist over the land, the result could not be determined. Pilot and machine were hoisted on board without injury.

(b) Flight Lieut. Walmesley, H.M. Seaplane Carrier "A," in a Baby Sopwith, struck the mast and wireless apparatus of H.M. T.B.D. The pilot was not seen again and the machine was lost.

(c) Flight Lieut. Price, H.M. Seaplane Carrier "B," in a Short seaplane, attacked two enemy destroyers off Ostend with five 65-lb. bombs. He was subjected to anti-aircraft fire and the machine was hit, but he returned safely.

(d) Flight Lieut. Stewart and Flight Lieut. Gregory, H.M. Seaplane Carrier "B," in Short seaplanes, attacked hostile submarines off Zeebrugge. The submarines immediately submerged.

Air Department, Admiralty, S.W.,
16th May 1916.

REPORT OF OPERATIONS No. 11.

May 6th.

Flight Sub-Lieut. Cowley and Sub-Lieut. Inge (Dunkirk Seaplane Station), in a Short seaplane, proceeded on a patrol flight and did not return. Two seaplanes reconnoitred for the machine during the day, but could find no trace.

According to the official communiqué issued on May 7th by the Berlin Admiralty they were taken prisoners by a German torpedo boat, together with their machine.

May 16th.

Flight Lieut. Petre and Flight Lieut. Gerrard (No. 1 Wing), in Nieuport Scouts, proceeded on a reconnaissance patrol with the object of carrying out a sweep of the lines and cutting off enemy machines engaged in spotting in the neighbourhood of Nieuport. They observed a hostile "L.V.G." biplane south-west of Dixmude, and Flight Lieut. Petre dived vertically down to 5,000 feet, firing one tray of ammunition at a range of 250 feet. The tracer bullets were seen to hit the enemy's fuselage, whereupon the enemy turned and dived down into its own lines. The attack was then continued by Flight Lieut. Gerrard, who fired a tray of ammunition at 300 to 400 feet. By the time the tray had been changed and the gun recharged the enemy had disappeared in a south-easterly direction, after being chased 5 miles over his own lines. This engagement was carried on by our machines under very intense and accurate anti-aircraft fire by the enemy batteries in the neighbourhood of Dixmude.

May 18th.

During the morning hostile machines appeared over Dunkirk, and fighter machines were immediately despatched from all three wings.

One seaplane was seen and chased, but lost in the mist. A second hostile machine fired unexpectedly from above on to one of our machines at a height of 12,500 feet over Dixmude, but was also lost sight of.

A third enemy machine (either an Aviatik or Albatross) attacked one of our aeroplanes, using tracer bullets. The enemy made off after receiving a tray and a half of ammunition.

During the afternoon a constant patrol was kept up, but no other hostile machines were observed.

May 19th.

(a) A bombing raid was carried out on the Ghistelles Aerodrome by nine machines. Twenty-four 65-lb. and twenty 16-lb. bombs were dropped from very low altitudes. The majority of the bombs were observed to fall on and among the hangars and on the railway siding at the south end of the aerodrome.

(b) An attack was made on the Mole at Zeebrugge by a seaplane carrying nine 65-lb. bombs, seven of which were released from a height of 2,600 feet. As far as the pilot could ascertain all seven fell on the Mole. Several explosions were heard, but the damage could not be observed.

(c) Flight Lieut. Gerrard, in a Nieuport (No. 1 Wing), while on fighter patrol, observed a hostile seaplane off Middelkerke. He dived from 14,000 to 7,000 feet and fired two trays at a range of approximately 400 yards. During the recharging the enemy was observed with nose well down, and was lost to sight. A search was made out to sea and inland, but without success. Every tracer bullet was observed to hit the machine somewhere, mostly in the centre.

May 20th.

(a) Flight Sub-Lieut. Dallas (No. 1 Wing), in a Nieuport Scout, when 4 miles off Blankenburghe, observed a German seaplane. Diving down to 4,500 feet the pilot succeeded in getting above and behind the enemy, and fired half a tray at close range. Enemy machine was observed to swerve and dive into the water. It sank, and reappeared in a sinking condition. Shortly afterwards the seaplane sank. A grey-coloured motor boat (apparently a motor patrol boat) was observed about a quarter of a mile away, and Flight Sub-Lieut. Dallas descended to about 900 feet and emptied the remainder of his ammunition (half a tray) into it.

(b) A fighter patrol was carried out to Nieuport and Dixmude and along the lines. One pilot, from a height of 17,000 feet, observed Ghistelles Aerodrome and one machine on the ground. Two German seaplanes were sighted in the vicinity of Dixmude. Fire was opened at long range, but both enemy machines retreated.

May 21st.

(a) During the early hours an allied raid by the English (R.N.A.S. and Second Army), French, and Belgians was carried out on the enemy's aerodromes and places of military importance. Sixteen R.N.A.S. machines dropped thirty-eight 65-lb. bombs and seventeen 16-lb. bombs on Mariakerke Aerodrome. One seaplane dropped one 100-lb. and two 65-lb. bombs on the Solway Works, Zeebrugge.

All these machines returned safely with the exception of one.

(b) An attack was made upon Dunkirk by hostile aircraft. Several machines went up with the object of cutting off the enemy on their return journey, in the vicinity of Nieuport Flight Sub-Lieut. Dallas, No. 1 Wing, in a Nieuport Scout, attacked three machines at a range of 400 yards. He opened fire on one machine with half a tray of ammunition, and observing another about 900 feet above him making seawards, gave chase, and fired the rest of the tray. He then changed trays, and reclimbing to 10,000 feet, encountered a large two-seater, which opened fire at long range. Flight Sub-Lieut. Dallas fired a tray of ammunition and observed tracer bullets entering the machine, which started to smoke violently, and nose-dived towards the sea, not towards the land, as might have been expected had it been under proper control. The Commanding Officer of the French Escadrille No. 26 was in the air at the same time, and states that he observed, in the same locality, what appeared to be a machine on fire, enveloped in a volume of black smoke. A fourth hostile machine was encountered, and after manœuvring, a full tray was fired into it in volleys. Flight Sub-Lieut. Dallas was unable to continue the chase as all his ammunition had been expended.

(c) Flight Sub-Lieut. Eyre, No. 1 Wing, in a Nieuport Scout, when six miles out to sea, over Zuydcoote, observed five hostile machines together, and another one a little way behind. Climbing rapidly, the pilot attacked the last one at close range of 100 yards, and expended quarter of a tray of ammunition. The hostile machine suddenly dived steeply, but pilot was unable to ascertain the result, as he was attacked from behind by three scouts, probably Fokker biplanes, at a range of 100 feet. Flight Sub-Lieut. Eyre turned round to meet them, and reloading, continued to fire. These machines, however, made good their retreat over the lines.

(d) Flight Commander Mulock, No. 1 Wing, in a Nieuport Scout, followed the raiders out to sea, opening fire when off Mariakerke. He closed with three machines, one of which was seen to topple over suddenly and nose-dive out of sight. Reloading, the pilot attacked another machine, which, after a few rounds, was observed to dive steeply. The third machine did not attempt to engage, but flew back over the lines. The same pilot, when returning, encountered another machine near Furness. Six single shots were fired at him, but the chase had to be abandoned owing to the heavy shelling over St. Pierre Capelle. It is probable that one, and possibly two, of these machines were destroyed.

(e) Flight Lieut. Huskisson and Lieutenant St. John, No. 5 Wing, in a Sopwith, engaged and drove off three machines. One of these appeared to be of a new type, and, if anything, much faster. The upper surface of the wings was chocolate colour. It was a large two-seater biplane, with swept-back wings and gun firing through propeller.

(f) Flight Sub-Lieut. Allen (No. 4 Wing) engaged several machines, and having expended five trays of ammunition, was forced to abandon the chase.

May 22nd.

Flight Sub-Lieut. Goodenham, in a Nieuport Scout, observed five hostile machines in close formation, and one further in the rear, which he attacked. At very close range and from underneath, he emptied a tray into the machine, the tracer bullets entering the fuselage. The observer of the enemy machine fired a few rounds and then broke off, as though killed or wounded, our machine still being an easy target. The other hostile machines drew away, while Sub-Lieut. Goodenham was changing trays, and were seen to be joined off Ostend by three other machines coming in from the sea.

Later in the day hostile machines (undoubtedly those encountered by Flight Sub-Lieut. Goodenham) were observed dropping bombs on Dunkirk. There were no casualties and no damage to the aerodrome.

A report was received of hostile machines proceeding towards Dunkirk from Bergues, and patrols were made in that vicinity, but no hostile machines were observed. Information was subsequently received that the machine stated to have been seen over Bergues was encountered in the neighbourhood of Cassel by a French pilot, who succeeded in bringing it down in a damaged condition.

May 26th.

An armed German trawler was attacked three miles N.E. of Ostend by one of our seaplanes. Two 65-lb. bombs were dropped without success, and the observer of the seaplane opened fire with a Lewis gun. The trawler replied with a machine gun, and although the seaplane was hit three times, no serious damage was caused. The tracer bullets were observed to pass very near, and probably hit the trawler. Owing to the proximity of the shore and the low altitude at which the seaplane was flying, the attack had to be abandoned.

Note.—Flight Sub-Lieut. Greensmith, who was reported lost on May 4th, is now interned in Holland. He was obliged to land (owing to engine trouble) at Gadzand (about 50 yards from the Dutch frontier), and endeavoured to pull his machine into Holland, but it was stuck too far in the sand, and, as German soldiers were approaching, he crossed the border and gave himself up to the Dutch military authorities.

Air Department, Admiralty, S.W.,
30th May 1916.

REPORT OF OPERATIONS No. 12.

FORCE D.—MESOPOTAMIA.

March 3rd.

Flight Sub-Lieut. Hume, while on a reconnaissance patrol, was obliged to make a forced landing, owing to a broken petrol pipe. He landed near one of our cavalry patrols, and borrowing a horse, rode eight miles to the aerodrome to obtain a new pipe. He then repaired the machine, and flew back.

This officer had never been on horseback before.

March 26th.

Sub-Lieut. Dunn, Second Lieut. Peck, and Sub-Lieut. Hume proceeded on a bombing raid over the Turkish aerodrome. Sub-Lieut. Hume succeeded in damaging the hangars.

During the month of April the R.N.A.S. machines and pilots took part, together with the R.F.C., in dropping food into Kut, 150 to 200 lbs. being carried at a time by the seaplanes. A total of 19,500 lbs. of food and a quantity of medical stores were dropped between April 15th and 29th. The pilots were Flight Lieut. Elliott and Flight Sub-Lieuts. Dunn, Hume, Hodges, Leigh, Gasson, and Murray.

On April 26th a Short machine was shot down while carrying food, the pilot, Flight Sub-Lieut. Gasson, being wounded and made prisoner, and the observer, Second Lieut. Thornless, killed.

EASTERN MEDITERRANEAN.

April 24th.

A Short seaplane reconnoitred for a submarine base round Port Lagos, and dropped bombs on the seaplane station on the west side of Lake Boru. Her escort, a Schneider Cup seaplane, meanwhile engaged an enemy seaplane over the lake.

May 1st.

Two Nieuport Scouts proceeded in pursuit of an enemy aeroplane, which was dropping bombs on Imbros, but, as the hostile machine flew directly into the sun, it was lost sight of and escaped.

Attacks were made from Long Island, Mitylene, upon an aeroplane shed on Smyrna racecourse, and upon landing stages in the Gulf.

May 2nd.

A hostile seaplane appeared over Mudros, and was driven off by anti-aircraft guns. Within six minutes of its appearance over Mudros scouts from Imbros were in the air, with the object of intercepting the enemy.

Spotting for a monitor by a seaplane from H.M. Seaplane Carrier "D" resulted in three direct hits being obtained on a three-arch railway bridge south of Aya Suluk.

MUDROS.

Reconnaissances showed little activity on the part of the enemy, either in the Dardanelles or Gallipoli.

May 3rd.

One Short seaplane from Stavros attacked a large bridge-building depôt on the Nestos river. Another attacked barges at a reported submarine base on Feror Burna.

A Short seaplane from H.M. Seaplane Carrier "E" left to attack a reported Zeppelin shed and alleged concentration of troops at Ferejik, but finding no trace of these, dropped 65-lb. bombs on the barracks.

May 10th.

One Short and two Schneider seaplanes from H.M. Seaplane Carrier "E" dropped bombs on Budrum Fort, and on a house reported to be occupied by German officers.

The same machines destroyed sheds at Dalian and Kuluk, and unsuccessfully attacked Kuteli Bridge, all in the Gulf of Mendalia.

May 11th.

An aeroplane from Mitylene attacked a tug with its Lewis gun and drove her ashore. Tug was reported with decks awash. Another tug was attacked with bombs and damaged.

May 13th.

Short and Schneider seaplanes bombed the barracks at Milas and again attacked Kuteli Bridge.

Two aeroplanes from Imbros dropped bombs on Krithnia, Maidos, and on the seaplane shed at Kusa Burna.

May 17th.

H.M. Seaplane Carrier "E" proceeded to El Arish, where Lieutenant Wright and Lieutenant Baxter, in a Short seaplane, spotted for monitors for 50 minutes in difficult circumstances and under heavy anti-aircraft fire. The carrier then proceeded to Rafa, where the camp at Khan Yunis was reconnoitred and bombed.

May 31st.

H.M. Seaplane Carrier "E" was ordered to send a seaplane (Flight Lieut. Rutland pilot, and Assist. Paymaster Trewin observer) to scout for the enemy fleet. A number of cruisers and destroyers were sighted. Owing to the presence of low clouds a descent to 1,000 feet was necessary, when the machine came under heavy fire from anti-aircraft and anti-torpedo armament. Shortly after the enemy altered course 16 points to the south, which, with their numbers and disposition, was signalled by W/T to the Battle Cruiser Squadron. The seaplane was later on obliged to descend owing to a broken petrol pipe. The defect was made good, and the machine ordered to return to the carrier.

DUNKIRK.

May 29th.

Flight Lieutenant Bell, No. 1 Wing, in a Nieuport, when patrolling between Nieuport and Dixmude, encountered a hostile machine over Dixmude. When within 70 yards the British pilot opened fire with his front gun, firing 1½ trays of ammunition. Tracer bullets were observed to hit enemy machine, which dived towards its own lines, obviously in difficulties. Flight Lieutenant Bell was obliged to abandon the chase, owing to the low altitude and heavy anti-aircraft fire. The observer was unable to assist in this combat, owing to the rear gun jamming.

June 1st.

Flight Sub-Lieut. Daly, No. 4 Wing, in a Nieuport, upon information that a German machine was spotting for Westende guns, proceeded on a reconnaissance in search of the enemy. At Nieuport he sighted two hostile machines, and on his approach one landed and the other retired in the direction of Ypres. The latter machine, however, suddenly returned and opened fire at long range. Flight Sub-Lieut. Daly, who was at 9,000 feet, was about to return the fire, when he was hit twice in the right arm, and, looking up, saw an Albatross about 100 feet above him. He dived and turned, and attempted to return the enemy's fire, but his gun jammed after firing a few shots, owing to a bullet striking the tube. His starboard gun miss-fired at the first pull, and he was unable to re-cock with his left hand; he therefore dived and made good his escape with a missing engine. Finding that he was losing much blood, he had to hold the artery with his left hand, flying the machine with a stick between his knees. He made a safe landing at the aerodrome and is now in hospital. His machine was covered with shot holes and had a large piece chipped off the propeller.

June 3rd.

A seaplane, while on a reconnaissance patrol, was attacked by two hostile seaplanes. Two trays of ammunition were fired on the enemy, which enabled the British machine to return safely.

No. 8 KITE BALLOON SECTION.

June 2nd.

The section, whilst engaged in spotting, was heavily shelled by a 10-cm. gun. The first round burst just over the balloon, and over 30 shells were fired, making more than 400 shrapnel holes in the fabric. The balloon descended so rapidly as to make it difficult to haul in the slack, and it drifted towards the German lines, but was eventually safely landed. The observer, Flight Lieutenant Sadd, continued to give corrections as long as the target was visible.

No. 11 KITE BALLOON SECTION.

June 3rd.

A German battery opened fire on the balloon just as it was about to ascend, the first shell bursting within 15 yards of the basket containing the observers. The cable was immediately cut, and the balloon dragged by the crew at the double for three-quarters of a mile, shells following them all the way. The balloon ultimately had to be ripped, and the crew were ordered to scatter until fire had ceased.

The kite balloon was hit but not seriously damaged.

The report of the Heavy Artillery Corps states : "Throughout " the operations No. 18 Squadron Royal Flying Corps, and " Nos. 6, 8, and 10 Kite Balloon Sections gave most useful " information as to the activity of the enemy batteries."

REPORT OF OPERATIONS No. 13.

DUNKIRK.

June 8th.

(a) Flight Sub-Lieut. Dallas, No. 1 Wing, in a Nieuport Scout, while on fighter escort to a coastal reconnaissance machine, sighted and attacked, off Ostend, a large hostile machine of great speed, which was about to attack the reconnaissance machine. He fired quarter of a tray at the enemy, who made off to Ostend immediately he observed the Nieuport, and Flight Sub-Lieut. Dallas was unable to get within close range. The enemy machine was of a light brown, almost red colour, with black nose-piece, and was extremely fast.

(b) Flight Sub-Lieut. Graham, in a seaplane, sighted three German Torpedo Boat Destroyers N.W. of Zeebrugge, which opened fire on the seaplane, firing 18 shells and making very accurate shooting. Flight Sub-Lieut. Graham turned back, pursued by the enemy, to inform the Fleet of the position of the enemy. Unfortunately the W/T installation broke down, but the observer (Petty Officer Boyd) made temporary connections with a piece of wire and succeeded in informing the Fleet, in spite of injuries to his hand caused by the spark.

June 10th.

Flight Sub-Lieut. Woolner and Chief Petty Officer Ellen, H.M. Seaplane Carrier "L," proceeded in search of a minelayer reported by W/T. They attacked with three 65-lb. bombs, but missed the objective.

June 10th.

Carrier pigeons were used, with very satisfactory results, to report result of patrol, being released from two seaplanes at 4,000 feet between Zeebrugge and Ostend. Carrier pigeons would be most useful to report cases of engine trouble or casualties.

June 18th.

Flight Lieut. Price and Chief Petty Officer Ellen, H.M. Seaplane Carrier "L," while flying at 3,000 feet, were obliged to descend in an enemy minefield, as their engine had caught fire. Three enemy machines, one aeroplane and two seaplanes, attacked them with machine guns, but were driven off by fire from the Lewis gun without injuring the British seaplane. The tide bore them towards Nieuport and they were safely rescued.

EASTERN MEDITERRANEAN.

May 19th.

An attack was made by 10 machines from No. 2 Wing on the shipping, piers, and seaplane shed in the Dardanelles. Ninety bombs were dropped on Charak, Maidos, Kilie Line, Kusa Burna, and Seddul Bahr.

May 20th.

Bombs were dropped on military works at Gumuljina by one French and eight British aeroplanes.

May 22nd.

A further attack was made on shed and shipping in Chanak Bay.

May 25th.

One Short and two Schneiders proceeded from S.E. of Samos up the valley of the Bijuk Mendere river to Sokia, where the railway line and station were bombed. On the following days, in the course of a series of attacks, considerable damage was done to Fouges and Merdivan Scala, and to the station at Smyrna.

June 1st.

Camps between Xanthi and the Nestos river were bombed by British and French machines from Thasos.

June 7th.

(a) A reconnaissance of El Arish was made in a Short seaplane from Seaplane Carrier "K" and bombs were dropped, the seaplane remaining over the town for 55 minutes, at a height of 1,500 feet.

(b) Spotting flights were carried out by Flight Sub-Lieut. Arnold and Lieutenant Torrington, in a Short seaplane from H.M. Seaplane Carrier "L"—(1) For monitors firing at the railway bridge N.W. of Scala Nuova. Range 17,600 yards. Two direct hits were scored. Two shells burst under the bridge and the remainder all fell close. (2) For cruiser and monitor at battery south of Scala Nuova. Several hits were obtained by cruiser.

(c) A spotting flight was carried out by Flight Commander Sitwell in a Short seaplane for a cruiser firing at gun emplacements north of Scala Nuova, and five hits were obtained.

Thasos.

During the week ending June 9th constant attacks were made by British and French flights on hostile camps.

The seaplane station at Gereviz, on Lake Boru, was bombed and petrol store destroyed.

On June 8th attacks were made with incendiary bombs upon the crops, with fair success.

Imbros.

Two aeroplanes engaged hostile mine-sweepers with Lewis guns, and shipping generally was attacked.

On June 8th a Fokker started to attack our bombing machines, but sheered off on the approach of a Nieùport Scout.

Mitylene.

On June 7th a reconnoitring aeroplane and escort attacked a hostile launch with a Lewis gun.

June 9th.

One of the seaplanes supplied to the Belgian Government by the Admiralty was flown by Belgian officers from Toa Albertville to Kigoma, on Lake Tanyanika (100 km.), and successfully bombed the "Graf von Gotzen."

Air Department, Admiralty, S.W.,
    28th June 1916.

REPORT OF OPERATIONS No. 14.

DUNKIRK.

June 17th.

(a) A Nieuport Scout escorted a French machine east of Ostend, and came under very heavy anti-aircraft fire. The machine was hit several times, and the pilot suffered from deafness on his return.

(b) Flight Sub-Lieut. Minifie, in a Nieuport Scout, encountered a large white enemy biplane at 12,000 feet off Westende, and fired two trays of ammunition at from 300 to 25 yards, while being subjected to heavy anti-aircraft fire. The enemy then retreated.

June 18th.

Flight Sub-Lieut. Bailey and Sub-Lieut. Slatter patrolled to locate and protect British Seaplane 7' N. of Middelkerke. The position of the machine when found was given to a British minelayer, which towed the machine into harbour.

June 22nd.

Flight Sub-Lieut. Hinshelwood encountered an enemy machine one mile seaward from Wendwyne at 12,500 feet. The enemy opened fire, the bullets passing through main bay. Flight Sub-Lieut. Hinshelwood closed to 100 yards and fired, and the enemy immediately dived dead vertical from 2,000 feet and then made towards Blankenberghe. On being engaged the German pilot dropped smoke bombs and flares.

June 23rd.

Flight Sub-Lieut. Graham and Sub-Lieut. Mardock sighted and engaged three enemy seaplanes from Zeebrugge and Blankenberghe, reporting position of enemy by W/T. One seaplane attacked our machine under tail and the other two from the rear and above. Two were within 100 yards, the third 250 yards away and 200 feet above. Our machine was hit five times in the tail, but not seriously damaged. Two of the enemy seaplanes were hit, and they all retreated towards Ostend.

July 1st.

Flight Sub-Lieut. Dallas, in a Sopwith triplane, encountered two large enemy biplanes north of La Panne, at 12,000 feet. One machine was easily overtaken and 40 rounds fired at it. Tracer bullets were seen entering the machine, which was observed, nose down, diving towards the sea. Flight Sub-Lieut. Dallas was forced to retire when attacked by a second machine, owing to his gun jamming.

July 8th.

Flight Lieut. Gerrard, in a Nieuport machine, acting as escort to French spotters, encountered a new type Fokker at 13,000 feet 2′ seaward of Ostend. The pilot dived down and fired 1¾ trays of ammunition at from 20 feet to 200 yards into the enemy machine, which rolled right over and nose-dived towards the sea. After reloading no sign of the enemy was visible. All tracer bullets appeared to enter the cockpit of the Fokker. Later in the day the same pilot encountered another Fokker off Westende. He succeeded in getting behind it and dived 3,000 feet, firing 1½ trays of ammunition at from 200 to 30 yards. The enemy was last seen diving towards Westende. Flight Lieut. Gerrard also engaged an Aviatik off Nieuport, firing two trays of ammunition. The enemy dived towards Mariakerke. Both the two latter machines were hit, but not seriously damaged.

July 9th.

Over 100 fighter patrols were carried out, and numerous engagements took place, three of which were apparently decisive in our favour. Fourteen escorts to French spotters were carried out. Twenty-four hostile machines were encountered, and at least two Fokkers destroyed.

(*a*) Flight Sub-Lieut. Little, in a Bristol Scout, encountered a Fokker, and opened fire at from 1,000 to 50 yards. Tracer bullets were seen to hit cowl and fuselage of the hostile machine, which nose-dived and landed in the German lines S. of Ypres.

(*b*) Flight Sub-Lieut. Dallas, in a Nieuport machine, encountered a Fokker above Mariakerke aerodrome. A full tray was emptied into the hostile machine at a few yards range. The pilot was seen to fall back dead, and the Fokker dropped vertically. On the return journey the Nieuport assisted a French machine to drive off a large enemy biplane.

(*c*) Flight Sub-Lieut. Irving encountered a Fokker at 10,000 feet off Middelkerke. He fired 20 rounds from one gun and a few rounds from the other, both guns jamming. The Fokker fell over and went down spinning vertically. While clearing the jams the pilot was attacked by an enemy biplane at close range, his top plane being holed. The engine failed, and a forced landing had to be made on the beach at Nieuport. Being under heavy anti-aircraft, machine, and rifle fire, the machine was soon entirely destroyed. The pilot escaped safely.

(*d*) Flight Sub-Lieut. De Quincey-Quincey, when at 13,000 feet off Middelkerke, encountered five hostile machines flying in V formation. The pilot attacked them single-handed, and four retreated. About 20 rounds were fired into the fifth, a Fokker, which was last seen diving steeply towards the sea at Ostend.

The pilot then found himself close to a large Aviatik, into which he fired the rest of his tray, the Aviatik diving steeply towards the coast. The same pilot encountered another Aviatik near Mariakerke, and dived at it from 13,000 feet, forcing it to descend.

July 9th.

(e) Flight Sub-Lieut. Hervey (pilot) and A. M. Pearce (observer), in a $1\frac{1}{2}$ Strutter, encountered three large hostile machines about 2 miles out to sea from Westende. The pilot spiralled down from 14,000 to 10,000 feet, and was attacked by two of the enemy. One of his guns jammed, but a tray was fired from the other, and tracer bullets were seen in line of the hostile machine fired at, which nose-dived, and was last seen close to the sea still in the nose-dive.

(f) Flight Sub-Lieut. Booker (pilot) and Gunlayer George (observer), in a Sopwith, while patrolling, observed five hostile machines between Westende and Ostende. The pilot spiralled down in order to enable the observer to attack with the after gun, as the front gun had jammed. The observer fired eight trays at ranges varying from 1,000 to 300 yards. All the machines were fired at, and some of our tracers were observed to go very near, if not through, the fuselage of one machine. When last seen four machines were making eastward, and one was spiralling down with the intention, apparently, of landing at Mariakerke aerodrome.

July 10th.

A party from No. 1 Wing, consisting of W. H. Golden, Chief Petty Officer; A. N. Grice, Petty Officer; G. Workman, First Air Mechanic; H. Hamlin, First Air Mechanic; and R. Worgan, First Air Mechanic, volunteered to salve parts of a Nieuport machine abandoned west of Nieuport, in range of the enemy's guns, and, working from midnight to 3 a.m., succeeded in salving the engine, Lewis gun, and other valuable parts.

EASTERN MEDITERRANEAN.

Thasos.

During the week ending June 16th French and English flights effected enormous damage with incendiary bombs to large tracts of crops.

During the week ending June 30th continued operations with French aeroplanes were carried out. Xanthi was twice bombed, first at night, when 52 bombs were dropped, besides 16 on Yeniji Karasa, an important military centre, and second, by day, when 47 bombs were distributed over the town and railway. The destruction of crops was continued, large tracts being set on fire. The time of day most suitable for this work being the hottest is also the most difficult for flying, on account of the violent remous experienced.

On June 29th Flight Commander Rainey and Sub-Lieut. Luck were injured by the overturning of their machine, due to this cause.

The Zeppelin shed at Gumuljina is stated to have been damaged during the raid on June 20th.

Imbros.

Dardanelles kept under observation. Seaplane sheds at Nagara Point and stores at "V" beach bombed. On June 15th launches at Helles attacked by bombs and machine guns. Long-distance reconnaissances carried out of the Ferejik Malgara and Keshan districts. Grenades dropped on lighters and on the ferry in Morto Bay. Pamphlets dropped at various places describing the results of the battle of Jutland. Regular reconnaissances of the Dardanelles by "C" flight.

Thermi.

Reconnaissances and spotting in the Gulf of Smyrna carried out by "B" flight. On June 11th Smyrna Railway Station was attacked by three bombing machines and two escorts. On returning two tugs were attacked with Lewis guns. One machine was hit by return fire and damaged beyond repair in landing near Long Island. The pilot and observer were picked up by another machine.

On June 14th aeroplanes attacked tugs and lighters south of Long Island, which replied with machine and rifle fire.

Stavros.

Photographic reconnaissance of the country in advance of the British front carried out. A seaplane flying from Stavros to Mudros was fired at by a submarine from a gun forward of conning tower when almost vertically overhead. Armed boarding steamer informed of whereabouts.

Airship Station.

Long daily flights made for submarine scouting, and the entrance to Mudros Harbour searched for mines. On one occasion an object taken for a mine turned out to be a turtle asleep beneath the surface.

Mudros.

During the week ending June 23rd incendiary bombs have been dropped whenever circumstances were favourable upon enemy crops between Boru Lake and the Nestos river. Great damage was effected, the crops being completely destroyed round many villages and the inhabitants panic-stricken and fleeing to the interior.

On June 20th allied aeroplanes dropped 64 bombs on the barracks, camps, and buildings at Gumuljina. The principal camps in the area E. of Lake Boru have also been bombed.

June 21st/22nd.

Fifty-eight bombs dropped on camp and seaplane base at Gereviz. During a reconnaissance on Port Lagos two enemy seaplanes were attacked by Flight Lieut. E. H. Dunning, D.S.O., and Sub-Lieut. C. B. Oxley, R.N., in a Nieuport. The enemy machines put to flight, one being damaged. Flight Lieut. Dunning was wounded in the leg, and the observer took the controls while a tourniquet was being applied.

RED SEA.

H.M. Seaplane Carrier "C." Ben-my-Chree

June 7th.

A reconnaissance of hostile camps in the Lahej Delta was carried out.

June 8th.

Two Sopwith and one Short seaplane proceeded to bomb the camps. Commander Samson, with Lieutenant Wedgwood Benn, dropped a 16-lb. bomb on a camel camp at Mahalla, and one 112-lb. and two 16-lb. bombs on the camp north of Lahej. The machine was under heavy fire, being hit twice, and owing to atmospheric conditions could with difficulty attain 800 feet.

Flight Lieutenant England dropped a 65-lb. bomb and 500 flechettes, and Flight Lieutenant Bankes Price, four incendiary and four 16-lb. bombs, upon Waht while under fire.

June 9th.

A reconnaissance flight was carried out by Commander Samson and Lieutenant Benn, and an incendiary bomb dropped upon Darb while under heavy rifle fire.

Flight Lieutenant M. Wright carried out a reconnaissance flight over Darb, Waht, Subar, Bir Abdulla, and Assela. An incendiary bomb was dropped on an encampment at Mokaija, and an explosive bomb on Bir Abdulla. Heavy shell fire was experienced.

Flight Lieutenant Bankes Price, while flying at 1,000 feet, was obliged to release all his bombs in order to lighten his machine, owing to engine trouble. He succeeded in getting back to the sea safely.

Flight Lieutenant Wright and Lieutenant Wedderspoon dropped one 112-lb. bomb and two 16-lb. bombs on Darb, while under gunfire.

Flight Lieutenant Paine dropped one 112-lb. bomb in the middle of Waht.

June 11th.

Flight Lieutenant England and Lieutenant Wedderspoon dropped four 20-lb. bombs and two incendiary bombs on the town of Lahej, while under shrapnel fire from Fiyush, Subar, Waht, and Lahej.

Commander Samson carried out a reconnaissance flight and dropped a 65-lb. bomb on tents at Darb.

June 12th.

Flight Lieutenant Bankes Price dropped six incendiary and two 20-lb. bombs on the camp at Subar, causing an extensive fire.

June 13th.

A series of attacks were made on positions in the vicinity of Sheikh Seyyid.

Flight Lieutenant Bankes Price gave line of fire for ship by dropping incendiary bombs in line of camp at Jebel Akrabi, and dropped five explosive bombs into the camp.

Flight Sub-Lieut. England carried out a spotting flight, and also bombed the camp.

Flight Sub-Lieut. Wright and Lieutenant Wedderspoon bombed the camp near Jebel Barika and Khor Gherera under heavy fire, their machine being hit twice.

Flight Sub-Lieut. Paine and Lieutenant Clarke bombed camp south of Jebel Akrabi.

June 15th.

Flight Lieutenant England dropped 65-lb. bombs among soldiers at Jeddah, and fired at trenches north of the town.

Flight Lieutenant Bankes Price dropped 65-lb. bomb on trenches south of the town and opened fire on soldiers.

Commander Samson and Lieutenant Benn carried out reconnaissance flight over the town under very heavy fire. The machine was hit several times, the propeller blade being pierced and elevating wire nearly severed.

June 16th.

Jeddah surrendered. The moral effect of the seaplane attacks appears to have been very considerable.

DUNKIRK.

July 15th.

Flight Sub-Lieut. Galbraith, No. 1 Wing, in a Nieuport, patrolled 10 miles out to sea, and when approaching Ostende, at about 12,000 feet, encountered a German seaplane — single engine, Tractor type — 500 feet below him. The enemy manœuvred for a position behind and below the Nieuport, both machines meanwhile executing a steep glide. Flight Sub-Lieut. Galbraith thereupon looped over and above, and the enemy passed underneath. The British pilot thus gained the desired position behind, and emptied one tray into the seaplane at a range of 100 yards. Tracer bullets were observed to pass in behind the pilot's seat. The German pilot, who was palpably hit, made a vertical nose-dive. The machine was last seen in flames falling headlong downwards.

Air Department, Admiralty,
  19th July 1916.

REPORT OF OPERATIONS No. 15.

FRANCE AND HOME STATIONS.

(1) On July 15th, Flight Sub-Lieut. Hodge, Dover Seaplane Station, while on a patrol, observed that the switch wire of his seaplane was broken, thereby rendering it impossible to switch off the engine. He pointed the defect out to his observer, First Air Mechanic McCredie, who climbed out of his seat, across the pilot's seat, and kneeling on the front main spar behind the pilot's seat, mended the switch wire whilst in flight, with the engine running at full speed.

(2)—(a) On July 21st, Flight Sub-Lieut. Mack with Sub-Lieut. Sims (No. 1 Wing), in a Nieuport, obtained three photographs of Tirpitz Battery at a height of 14,000 feet. The machine was subjected to very heavy anti-aircraft fire, the fuselage being hit. The same pilot and observer also obtained photographs on the 9th and 19th instant, and on both occasions were subjected to heavy anti-aircraft fire, which hit the machine.

(b) Flight Sub-Lieut. Graham, Dunkirk Seaplane Station, in a Sopwith Fighter seaplane, when at 11,000 feet, encountered a hostile aeroplane (two-seater biplane). The British pilot dived on the hostile machine, which, in the meantime, was manœuvring for position under his tail, opening fire at the same time. The machines met nose on, both firing. The Sopwith pilot fired one tray at close range, the machines passing within 20 feet of each other. The hostile machine then turned and made for the coast. The British pilot followed, but owing to lack of petrol was forced to descend.

(c) Flight Sub-Lieut. Goble (No. 1 Wing), in a Nieuport machine, encountered a hostile two-seater biplane, three miles east of Dixmude, at 9,000 feet. Whilst the pilot was manœuvring for position the hostile machine opened fire, but the British pilot was eventually able to get behind, and opened fire at 100 yards, which was reduced to 30 yards before the tray was fired. Tracer bullets entered the enemy's fuselage, and the machine was seen to nose-dive and spin with full engine on and black smoke issuing from the machine. It was eventually seen to fall at 6,000 feet, obviously out of control.

(3) On July 24th, Flight Sub-Lieut. S. J. Bailey, Dunkirk Seaplane Station, while carrying out a patrol in search of a missing machine, was attacked by an enemy seaplane, and a running fight was kept up at ranges varying from 100 to 150 yards. The hostile machine turned back when opposite West-ende as the anti-aircraft guns commenced a heavy fire. The British seaplane was hit in four places.

The hostile machine had the appearance of a French F.B.A., having similar floats, but with new wings of slightly different shape.

(4)—(a) On July 28th, Flight Lieut. Gerrard (No. 1 Wing), in a Sopwith triplane, sighted a hostile machine returning towards Nieuport. Diving from 14,000 feet to 10,000 feet and manœuvring to get behind the enemy, he opened fire at close range. Unfortunately, whilst the attack was being carried out the machine experienced a strong concussion and got out of control, diving steeply, spinning to the left, and dropping some 2,000 feet. Flight Lieut. Gerrard, with the greatest difficulty, was eventually able to get his machine under control, and made a safe landing. The triplane was found to have the whole upper surface of the left-hand plane and two-thirds of the right-hand top plane stripped of fabric.

(b) Flight Commander Petre, D.S.C., No. 1 Wing, in a Nieuport, encountered the same German machine, having witnessed the Sopwith's fall and recovery. Pilot was at 10,000 feet one mile to seaward of Coxyde, and met the enemy, apparently a Roland biplane, end on. Turning sharply, pilot emptied both trays from behind at 300 to 100 yards, and tracer bullets were seen to hit fuselage and pass between the planes of the enemy machine, which kept up a hot fire from a rear turret mounting, and hit the propeller of the Nieuport. The enemy machine, however, was not seriously damaged, and being very much faster soon drew right away from the Nieuport.

(c) Flight Sub-Lieut. Hervey (pilot) and Lieutenant St. John, R.N.V.R. (observer), in a Sopwith, sighted an enemy machine about six miles eastward of Calais at about 10,000 feet, with shrapnel bursting all round her. The British observer fired a recognition light to warn our anti-aircraft gunners that they were about to attack, and the firing ceased. The enemy then bore away inland and a running fight ensued, the hostile machine firing with the after gun, and the Sopwith replying with its Vickers gun, the pilot having to stall machine in order to bring the gun into action. The British observer also fired over the top plane, and many tracer bullets were seen to enter the fuselage of the enemy machine, which ceased firing, and when last observed was diving into the clouds. The chase had to be abandoned owing to lack of ammunition.

It is probable that the enemy observer was hit, as the hostile machine did not fire in the latter part of the engagement.

July 31st.

(5)—(a) Flight Sub-Lieut. J. L. Northrop, in a B.E. 2 C., R.A.F., pursued and attacked a Zeppelin, 30 miles off Southwold. He sighted the enemy about 1,500 feet above him, and fired two trays of ammunition. After reloading, his third tray came away from the gun and hit him on the head. He was temporarily dazed, and by the time he had gained control of his machine the Zeppelin had disappeared in the clouds.

(b) Flight Lieutenant Fowler with Lieutenant Gow, in a Sopwith, accompanied by two fighting machines, proceeded on a photographic reconnaissance. Five hostile machines were seen, and one attacked the Nieuport, but was driven off by the fighters. These two machines kept close to the reconnaissance machine throughout, under heavy anti-aircraft fire, and by this undoubtedly prevented the other hostile aircraft attacking, and enabled successful photographs and observations to be obtained.

NOTE.—On July 23rd, at 18,000 feet, vertically over Nieuport Ville, the Schuddebeurze Wood anti-aircraft battery burst several salvos of high explosive exactly level with, and slightly in front of, the Sopwith triplane. As an experiment, pilot then climbed to slightly over 20,000 feet and circled round and over Nieuport at that height for some time without being shelled.

EASTERN MEDITERRANEAN STATION.

July 1st–7th.

(6) Our machines have maintained a steady offensive in Southern Bulgaria, which has had a most demoralising effect on the enemy. Places where the heaviest anti-aircraft fire was encountered have been singled out for special attention, with the result that our machines now fly over these places with little or no opposition. Much damage has been done to transport vehicles and huts.

(7) Crops in the Nestos districts which have not been burnt by our incendiary bombs have been cut, regiments of soldiers having been detailed for the duty. Large fires have been caused among the remaining crops all over this part of the country.

(8) Our machines have maintained a regular patrol of the Dardanelles, attacking all shipping seen with bombs and machine-gun fire.

On June 27th Flight Sub-Lieut. Blandy with Midshipman Snow (observer) attacked a fast launch with bombs, and failing to hit came down 400 feet and attacked with a Lewis gun. The machine was brought under shrapnel fire from the shore and forced to abandon the attack.

July 7th–14th

(9) On July 8th–9th Flight Commander Rainey, with Sub-Lieut. Jameson, R.N.V.R. as observer, carried out attacks on Geréviz seaplane station with 100-lb. bombs. These attacks were most successful, one hangar being seen to collapse.

(10) Flight Lieut. Bush with Sub-Lieut. Wright, R.N.V.R., carried out an attack with three 100-lb. bombs on Zinelli

Village, where troops were quartered, and later dropped a 65-lb. bomb among some road wagons, six of which were destroyed.

(11) Operations against the enemy's crops have continued with very good results, a certain amount of corn already in "stooks" being destroyed, as well as standing crops. One fire alone cleared an area of $1\frac{1}{2}$ miles by $\frac{1}{4}$ to $\frac{1}{2}$ mile broad.

(12) On July 10th, Flight Lieut. Jacob, in a Nieuport, carried out a reconnaissance over the Dardanelles and attacked a hostile seaplane which was examining British minefields. The enemy seaplane was apparently seriously damaged and came down across wind off Kum Kale.

EAST INDIES STATION.

(13) On July 6th, Flight-Lieut. Bankes Price, H.M. Seaplane Carrier "C," in a Sopwith, carried out an inland reconnaissance in the vicinity of El Arish, and bombed trenches in the Wadi. The machine was under very heavy shrapnel fire, and flying inland towards the enemy's aerodrome, was headed off by two hostile aeroplanes and forced to return.

(14)—(a) On July 7th, Commander Samson, R.N., and Second Lieut. Wedgewood Benn, from H.M. Seaplane Carrier "C," in a Short machine, carried out a reconnaissance of Bierut and nearby fortifications. Bombs were dropped on sailing ships in the harbour.

(b) On July 7th, Flight Lieut. T. England, H.M. Seaplane Carrier "C," proceeded to reconnoitre Turkish garrison and railway. Two hundred horses were seen and fired on with the Lewis gun. Ten casualties were caused and the remainder stampeded.

(15) On July 10th, Commander Samson and Flight Lieut. Bankes Price, from H.M. Seaplane Carrier "C," each in a seaplane, proceeded to attack tugs in the Nahr el Kebir. Eight bombs were dropped, but the vessels were not sunk. On the return journey Turkish troops opened fire from a small post near the mouth of the river. The fire was returned by both machines.

The same seaplanes carried out two more attacks on the same objective, on each occasion coming to low altitudes and engaging the Turkish troops.

(16) On July 1st, Flight Lieut. Brook, from H.M. Seaplane Carrier "K," carried out a reconnaissance of El Arish and environs. Heavy and accurate gunfire, both H.E. and shrapnel, was met with. Two bombs were dropped from 3,000 feet, one of which hit the outhouse of the ammunition store.

(17) On July 2nd a reconnaissance of Haifa was carried out by Flight Lieut. Dacre, D.S.O. (pilot) and Lieut. Ravenscroft, R.F.A. (observer) in a Short, and Flight Sub-Lieut. Man, in a

Sopwith, from H.M. Seaplane Carrier "K." Bombs were dropped on the bridge and on the Customs wharf.

The Sopwith failed to return and was observed half a mile from Acre drifting to the shore in a sinking condition. The Short landed a few yards from the Sopwith and took aboard the pilot. As it was impossible to salve the machine, it was fired at and sunk. The Short then returned to the ship, carrying three persons. The observer had to sit on the top of the petrol tank, as this was the only position in which the balance of the machine could be maintained.

(18) On July 6th, Flight Lieut. Brooks (pilot) and Second Lieut. King, K.O.S.B. (observer), from H.M. Seaplane Carrier "K," flew from Castelprizo eastwards as far as Cape Pyrgo and set fire to the scrub. The fire spread rapidly and burned for some two hours.

(19) On July 7th bombs were dropped by a Short and a Sopwith from H.M. Seaplane Carrier "K" in the Levisi district.

The Governor of Castelprizo considers the moral effect of the seaplane work to be great and that the fires caused by the bombs were most effective.

July 15th–22nd.

(20) Owing to the renewed activities of enemy submarines, a continual patrol was necessary. This was carried out by means of a succession of flights by Sopwith and Short machines. Since the patrol was instituted no submarines have been detected in the neighbourhood of Port Said, and no further casualties have been suffered by shipping.

The total gross tonnage entered and cleared July 15th–21st is stated to be about 323,730 tons.

CAPE STATION.

(21) Information has been just received that Flight Sub-Lieut. Terraneau (pilot) and Captain Bruno (observer), who left on April 29th in a Voisin machine to reconnoitre in German territory, were unfortunately killed, their machine having been found badly smashed to the south-east of Lake Gipe.

FRANCE AND HOME STATIONS.

(22)—(a) On July 30th, in conjunction with the French, an attack was made by machines of No. 3 Wing on the benzine stores and barracks at Mulheim. The machines met with very heavy anti-aircraft fire, but carried out a successful bombardment.

(23) On August 2nd, 14 machines from the various wings took part in a bombing raid upon the aerodrome at St. Denis Westrem and the ammunition depôt at Ghent.

A number of the sheds and billeting buildings of the aerodrome were badly damaged, and bombs were dropped on eight hostile machines in the aerodrome.

Bombs were clearly seen to fall on the ammunition depôt and arsenal, and also on the railway trucks in the siding.

Heavy anti-aircraft fire was experienced in places, but all the pilots returned safely except Flight Lieut. R. G. A. Baudry, in a Sopwith. A shell was observed to burst near his machine, which immediately nose-dived out of sight.

(b) Flight Lieut. Freeman, from H.M. Seaplane Carrier "M," in a Bristol Scout aeroplane, ascended from the deck at 7.30 p.m. and proceeded to attack a Zeppelin sighted about 10 miles away.

He dropped two containers of Ranken darts, one of which apparently took effect, as the Zeppelin almost immediately dropped from 8,500 feet to 5,000 feet.

The pilot followed her down in a nose-dive, but having no further armament, was unable to again attack. On switching on his engine he discovered that his pressure had failed, and he was obliged to come down in the sea near the North Hinder Lightship. He was supported by the air bags in the tail of his machine for about two hours before being picked up by a Belgian steamer, which landed him in Holland.

August 2nd–3rd.

(24) Flight Sub-Lieut. Pulling, in a B.E. 2 C., attacked a Zeppelin over Burgh Castle, and hit it repeatedly with his machine gun. While reloading he lost sight of the enemy, and owing to the darkness was unable to get in touch with it again.

Air Department, Admiralty, S.W.,
    10th August 1916.

REPORT OF OPERATIONS No. 16.

DUNKIRK.

August 1st–30th.

The usual large number of reconnaissances and patrols were carried out, and, in addition, a large amount of W/T spotting in connection with the bombardment of Battery Tirpitz.

Photographic reconnaissances of the Hindenberg Battery and all places of interest in the enemy's country were regularly undertaken.

Shipping along the coast to Ostende and beyond was kept regularly under observation.

Fighter patrols and anti-submarine and Zeppelin patrols were constantly carried out, as necessary.

The following are a few of the more interesting events during the period:—

August 1st.

A photographic reconnaissance (pilot Flight Lieut. Fowler, observer Lieutenant Gow) resulted in two good photographs of Hindenberg battery from an altitude of 12,000 feet. The machine was under constant and heavy anti-aircraft fire, and was twice hit. The accompanying four fighting machines were also under heavy fire from Ostende.

August 2nd.

Fourteen machines carried out an attack on St. Denis Westrem Aerodrome and the Ammunition Depôt at Ghent, as reported in last communiqué.

Ten fighters accompanied the bombing machines, and eleven fighters met them on their return journey and patrolled the lines between Nieuport, Dixmude, Ypres, Roulers, and Thourout.

One of the fighters (Flight Sub-Lieut. Baudry) was brought down by anti-aircraft fire.

August 3rd.

(1) Two machines spotting for the firing on Battery Tirpitz were under very heavy fire from the Westende, Middelkerke, Mariakerke, and Ostende batteries, shrapnel bursting several hundred feet above machine at a height of 16,000 feet. A fighter attached to the spotting machines observed a hostile seaplane endeavouring to get under the tail of our machine. He dived and opened fire, and while executing this manœuvre was in turn attacked by a Fokker monoplane. One tray was emptied into him at long range. Whilst changing trays our machine lost sight of the enemy, which did not return to re-engage.

(2) A fighter patrol sighted three enemy aeroplanes behind their own lines. One large L.V.G. was apparently spotting for the others higher up. The Nieuport climbed to the level of the L.V.G. at 12,000 feet, and got within 300 yards of it before being discovered. The L.V.G. at once dived towards Mariakerke Aerodrome in a steep spiral and the Nieuport followed, firing whenever his guns bore on the enemy, whose passenger appeared to be firing. The Nieuport gave up the chase when all ammunition was spent. The other two machines made no attempt to support the third machine.

August 6th.

A fighter patrol, when over Ypres, at 7,000 feet, sighted two hostile machines. When within 100 yards three trays were emptied into one of the enemy planes and tracers were observed to pass on all sides. The enemy then both retreated in the direction of Ostende.

August 9th.

(1) A fighter (Flight Lieut. Legh) was despatched to report on two German machines over Nieuport. When about one mile S.E. of Lombartzyde the pilot sighted two L.V.G.'s above him. He climbed to 11,000 feet and attacked one of the machines from above. There ensued a running fight lasting for about 15 minutes, in the course of which the L.V.G. was hit. The Nieuport machine chased it down to a height of 3,000 feet above Mariakerke, during which time two trays of ammunition were expended. The hostile machine was last seen diving steeply towards Mariakerke. This machine used tracer bullets and hit the Nieuport once. It was much faster than our machine and manœuvred very quickly.

The Nieuport passed below the kite balloon at Wilskerke, which was at 4,000 feet, and was immediately hauled down. The pilot encountered very heavy anti-aircraft fire, and left the enemy's coast at a height of only 2,300 feet.

(2) On the same day a successful raid was carried out by Flight Sub-Lieut. Collet and Flight Sub-Lieut. Harkness in Sopwith machines, on the Zeppelin sheds at Berchem St. Agathe and Evere, near Brussels. Flight Sub-Lieut. Collet, when coming down to attack the Berchem St. Agathe shed, observed the eastern door wide open and nothing inside the shed. He therefore continued coming down and dropped 12 bombs on the Evere shed, from a height of 200 feet. At least eight bombs were observed to hit, and immediately a dense volume of black smoke began to come from the shed. No anti-aircraft fire was opened until the first bomb had been released, when very heavy fire of all descriptions followed.

Flight Sub-Lieut. Harkness observed the bombs dropped by the first pilot to strike the shed, but owing to the intense anti-aircraft fire he was forced to drop his bombs from a height of 8,000 feet. He dropped eight bombs, most of which hit their mark. A few seconds later still more smoke was observed to pour out of the shed. He released the remainder of his bombs on the Berchem St. Agathe shed, but was unable to observe the result.

August 15th.

At 7.30 a.m. Flight Sub-Lieut. Goble, in a Nieuport, was patrolling the Nieuport-Dixmude lines when the pilot observed two hostile seaplanes four or five miles out to sea over Nieuport. Immediately the hostile machines observed that they were being approached they turned eastwards. The pilot caught them up off Westende and opened fire on one of them from behind at a range of 100 yards. After firing $1\frac{1}{2}$ trays of ammunition the enemy was observed to sideslip inwards for about 500 feet. The left wing then collapsed and machine was observed to fall headlong through the clouds.

The machine was a large two-seater, rather slow, and built on the lines of an Avro.

The other seaplanes had meanwhile dived and disappeared.

August 18th.

At noon four machines left on a bombing raid on Lichtervelde ammunition dumps. Forty-eight bombs were dropped on the objective.

Very heavy anti-aircraft fire was experienced, but it was inaccurate. Two large fires were afterwards observed.

August 19th.

During a photographic reconnaissance by Flight Lieut. Keeble and Sub-Lieut. Betts, six plates were exposed off Beau Terrain. The machine was over the coast for 25 minutes under continual anti-aircraft fire, from 9,000 to 13,000 feet.

August 20th.

Night spotting was carried out for one of the monitors, and was found quite successful at a height of from 4,000 to 5,000 feet. The flash from the gun and the fall of shot were unmistakable, so that accurate spotting was quite practicable

August 21st.

A message was received by carrier pigeon that Flight Lieut. Tooke, Dunkirk Seaplane Station, is a prisoner, and his observer, Lieutenant Crowther, is dead; Sub-Lieut. Mardock, R.N.V.R., and Flight Sub-Lieut. Bailey were taken prisoner on the 4th August.

August 25th.

(1) A bombing raid was carried out on the Zeppelin sheds at Cogneloe, near Namur, by Flight Sub-Lieut. Collet, Flight

Sub-Lieut. Jamieson, and Flight Lieut. Wood, in Sopwith machines.

Flight Lieut. Wood lost touch with the other two pilots by getting into a very heavy bank of clouds, and was unable to pick up any landmarks. He searched for the other machines for an hour and twenty minutes, but without success, and therefore returned and patrolled the coast back to Dunkirk.

The other two pilots succeeded in reaching their objective (but Flight Sub-Lieut. Jamieson failed to return, and has since been reported interned in Holland) and dropped their bombs, straddling the two northern sheds. Heavy anti-aircraft fire was met with, and our machines took refuge in the clouds immediately after dropping their bombs, and were therefore unable to observe the results.

(2) Flight Sub-Lieut. Grange, while on fighter patrol, off Ostende, observed a L.V.G. proceeding towards Nieuport. On being approached the enemy turned towards Ostende. The pilot turned to head him off and opened fire at 100 yards. Two trays of ammunition were expended, and tracer bullets were observed to go through the enemy's fuselage. The hostile machine dived and disappeared in the clouds.

August 31st.

(1) A very comprehensive photographic reconnaissance was carried out along the coast as far as the Dutch frontier and about 7 miles inland over Heyst-Knocke road. No trace of the aerodrome reported south of the road could be found. Five plates were exposed to the landward end of the Zeebrugge mole. Prisoners' reports that seaplanes are kept on railway trucks are verified from these.

(2) A fighter accompanying a seaplane patrol observed a hostile seaplane making for the reconnaissance machine. The fighter manœuvred into position behind the hostile machine, and opened fire at a range of about 30 yards. Two and a half trays of ammunition were fired, many tracers entering the enemy's fuselage. Although the hostile machine appeared to be very fast, the pilot seemed disinclined to carry out any banking turns or quick manœuvres, and for this reason the Sopwith fighter was able to keep his gun trained on the enemy machine throughout the engagement. After five minutes' engagement the hostile machine stopped circling round and headed straight for Ostende.

(NOTE.—The enemy seaplane was very similar indeed to the Wight Scout seaplane and may easily be mistaken for this. The great difference is that the engine is stationary and not rotary.)

HOME STATIONS.

The usual large number of anti-submarine patrols and reconnaissances from all aeroplane, seaplane and airship stations have taken place, and the usual work has been done by seaplane carriers in the North Sea.

A considerable amount of night anti-Zeppelin patrols have taken place during recent raids. The following, however, are the only incidents of interest:—

August 9th.

Flight Lieutenant de Roeper, Redcar Air Station, in a B.E. 2 C. machine, proceeded in search of a Zeppelin reported to be in the vicinity of Hartlepool. Guided by the bursting bombs, he followed the airship, which eventually climbed to 12,000 feet. In order to gain altitude he dropped his four bombs into the sea, but was unable to reach the Zeppelin, which disappeared in the mist.

August 19th.

Flight Sub-Lieut. Fox, Killingholme Air Station, in a Sopwith Baby seaplane, proceeded in chase of a Zeppelin reported to be about 35 miles east of Spurn. He sighted the airship, and rising to 11,000 feet passed over it, dropping four 16-lb. bombs in succession and two boxes of Ranken darts.

The Zeppelin immediately turned a complete circle, her nose dropping very considerably. She was apparently hit.

Flight Sub-Lieut. Fox then discovered that his left float was punctured, probably due to a broken valve rocker.

The machine, after alighting, gradually sank by the left float, but the pilot was able to keep it up by sitting on the right wing tip.

EASTERN MEDITERRANEAN.

July 14th–August 11th.

Aeroplanes, seaplanes, and airships in the Eastern Mediterranean have throughout this period continued the usual duties of co-operating with the Fleet and harassing such of the enemy's country as is within reach of the coast.

A very large amount of patrol and reconnaissance work has been successfully carried out.

The following are the more interesting events:—

Thasos.

July 14th–21st.

Reconnaissance and offensive work has been continued in Southern Bulgaria. Crops within easy reach of Thasos have now either been burnt or harvested by the Bulgarian soldiery, and the crop-burning offensive is now being carried further north, on the higher land, where crops are still standing.

Raids have been made in the Xanthi area, and two escorted attacks were carried out on the two remaining seaplane hangars at Geroviz.

On the 16th July, at dawn, Flight Lieutenant R. Y. Bush (pilot), Sub-Lieut. G. E. Wright (observer), and Flight Commander T. A. Rainey (pilot), Lieutenant C. B. Oxley, R.N. (observer), with escorts, made an attack on Gumuljini. Four direct hits were scored on a large camp to the north-east of the town, and one 112-lb. bomb was dropped within 25 yards of the railway and probably caused damage. The machines were fired at by anti-aircraft guns, mounted on the rear wagon of a goods train travelling from Gumuljini to Dedeagatch.

On the 17th instant further raids were carried out on Xanthi itself and on the sheds at Naib-Obasi, where fires were observed.

July 21st–28th.

The enemy have concentrated machines of various types, including Fokkers, Albatross Scouts, and Aviatiks, in the Xanthi district, and various encounters have taken place. During one action an Albatross Scout was driven to earth, obviously damaged.

In spite of the unfavourable weather, a successful bombing raid was carried out on the 23rd on the important military centre of Yenije Karasu.

On the 27th July an enemy aeroplane appeared over Thasos aerodrome and dropped bombs on the camp, but no damage was sustained. The machine was chased but succeeded in escaping.

July 28th–August 4th.

The air station has several times been bombed by the enemy, but without effect. The attacks are usually delivered by Aviatik machines escorted by an Albatross Scout. On each occasion they have been pursued by our scouts, but the distance to their aerodrome is too short to give much chance of overtaking them.

An Aviatik which appeared over the aerodrome on August 1st was chased by a Nieuport machine.

He overtook the enemy and attacked at 250 yards, closing to 50 yards, but the hostile machine nose-dived and was lost sight of.

Offensive and reconnaissance work has been carried out continually in the Xanthi district and Gumulgina, and photographs have been obtained of the recent defensive works constructed at Kala Burun. Successful bomb attacks have been made on the hangars at Mizanli, sheds at Anakeui, and on the village of Kirajilar, where fires were started in the surrounding fields.

On July 31st and August 2nd incendiary bombs were dropped on Xanthi and Zinelli and also on Yenije Karasu, an important military centre, where large fires were started.

August 4th-11th.

Several reconnaissances were made by seaplanes with the object of locating enemy mines. On August 7th four mines were discovered.

On August 3rd, 4th, and 5th reconnaissances of the Nestos and Xanthi areas were carried out, and much useful information and successful photographs obtained.

Explosive bombs were dropped in Yenjije Karasu and Thermi, bombs in the maize fields at Gengerli and Karageuzli, where good results were obtained.

On 8th August the important military centre of Yenije Karasu was again subjected to bombardment. Twenty-five bombs were dropped and considerable damaged was observed.

Experiments have been made in burning woods which may form cover for the enemy. A deserter's report states that one of these fires raged for four days.

Thermi.

July 14th-21st.

On the 14th and 15th July machines were employed in spotting for the ships bombarding the batteries on the coast; the area was also photographed. On the 16th and 17th petrol bombs were dropped on the olive groves to the north and south of Aivalik, which caused fires. Further reconnaissances and spotting flights have been carried out during the week.

July 21st-28th.

Spotting for the ships was carried out on the 21st and 25th July.

On the 24th cattle raids were made to the north of Cape Baba. Three machines patrolled the area during the raids.

July 28th-August 4th.

Incendiary bombs have been dropped on the olive groves south-east of Aivalik and on villages near the coast. A large fire was started close to a group of threshing floors.

On the 29th July a H. Farman machine was flown from Imbros by Flight Sub-Lieut. H. G. Ford and was damaged on landing, the pilot being seriously injured.

August 4th-11th.

Anti-submarine patrols have been carried out in the Musellim Channel.

Imbros.

July 14th-21st.

A daily patrol of the Dardanelles has been maintained throughout the week. At dawn on the 16th instant a raid was made by three machines on the sheds to the north of Gallipoli town. One direct hit was obtained and several bombs fell close to the sheds.

On the 13th instant, during a reconnaissance flight, grenades and bombs were dropped on the store depôt and on the railway junction at Ferejik. The lines were ripped up and the station building wrecked. A small outpost camp south of Yazeuren was also bombed successfully.

At dawn on the 20th two machines attacked the barracks to the north of Gallipoli town. Explosive and incendiary bombs were dropped and direct hits were obtained. The buildings were on fire and were blazing fiercely when the machines left the district.

July 21st–28th.

The patrol of the Dardanelles has been maintained.

On the 21st July three machines attacked tents on the beach at Morto Bay. Visibility was bad, but one incendiary bomb hit some part of the objective, which burnt for a considerable time.

July 28th–August 4th.

A regular patrol of the Dardanelles has been maintained by " C " flight of No. 2 Wing.

August 4th–11th.

A daily patrol of the Dardanelles has been carried out whenever the weather permitted.

Anti-submarine patrols and mine-searching flights were also carried out.

Mudros.

H.M. Seaplane Carrier " A."

July 14th–21st.

The seaplanes at this station carried out usual anti-submarine patrols. S.S. 8 has commenced a daily submarine patrol in the vicinity of Mudros Harbour.

July 21st–28th.

Airship Station.

S.S. 8 has patrolled the entrance to Mudros Harbour every day during the week.

July 28th–August 4th.

H.M. Seaplane Carrier " A."

A Short seaplane acted as escort to the fleet, and patrolled he area from Lemnos to Strati in search of submarines.

August 4th–11th.

Airship Station.

On August 4th and 5th the usual patrol of the entrance to Mudros Harbour was carried out by S.S. 8. Mine searching patrols were also carried out.

Port Laki.

H.M. Seaplane Carrier " E."

July 14th–21st.

On the 12th July reconnaissance flights were made along the coast, which was photographed. Four 16-lb. bombs were dropped on the breakwater at the entrance to Derin Geuil.

July 28th–August 4th.

Seaplanes carried out successful bombing raids over the area surrounding the mouth of the Meander River; three 65-lb. bombs were dropped on a. bridge, the foundations of which were believed to be damaged.

On the 27th July the defences of "Lade Island," to the southward of the mouth of the Meander, were reconnoitred, and 65-lb. bombs dropped, one of which fell in a trench and caused a large explosion.

On the 28th July a direct hit was obtained upon a gun emplacement which contained a gun.

Kassandra.

August 4th–11th.

On 1st August Airship S.S. 17 sighted a submarine on the surface 8 miles off Kassandra. Immediately the airship approached, the submarine dived.

EAST AFRICAN AEROPLANE SQUADRON (KONDOA IRANGI).

June 6th–25th.

This squadron has continued to operate with General Van Deventer's column carrying out reconnaissances ahead of the army and bombing the German encampments. The results have been very satisfactory both in keeping the General fully informed of the enemy's movements and in causing much loss to the enemy by desertion of natives and by damage to transport and encampments. The country in which this squadron is now operating makes it impossible to land a machine without wrecking it, except in the aerodromes and sometimes in the river beds. Engine failure, therefore, nearly always entails wreckage. The climatic conditions entail a very arge percentage of sick.

The following are the more interesting events :—

June 6th.

Two Voisin aeroplanes, which had come down in the Massai Plain six days previously owing to the pilots having lost their way and run out of petrol, were found intact, and with the aid of 120 carriers a space was cleared sufficient for them to rise from. They were flown back to Kondoa.

June 9th.

During the course of reconnaissance over enemy's positions the engine of a machine was hit by machine-gun fire but she returned safely.

June 11th.

Bombs were dropped on South Hill. The machine was fired at as usual by a 4·1 gun. It has since been reported by deserters that 12 Askaris and two porters were killed and three Germans wounded. Many desertions took place in consequence, and the German porterage service is much disorganised.

June 12th.

Bombs were dropped on the enemy's positions; one caused a large fire in the camp—another fell in the enemy's trenches. Machine was shelled after leaving this area, but returned in order to draw fire and succeeded in locating the position of the gun. Machine was hit in five places. Throughout the day the aerodrome was shelled by the 4·1 gun from the " Konigsburg."

June 13th.

Aerodrome moved to a fresh position.

June 17th.

A machine dropped two 65-lb. bombs on Chambala camps. When the machine had landed after its return a swarm of bees settled on the engine and entered the induction pipes.

June 22nd.

Bombs were dropped on Gunneck and on South Hill. It was reported that ten natives were killed and many wounded as a result of these bombs.

June 24th.

While the enemy were retiring one of our machines dropped bombs upon them. One bomb caused a convoy of draft animals to stampede.

CAPE STATION.

June 27th–July 20th.

A careful watch has been kept on the enemy coast by seaplane and kite balloon reconnaissances from the kite balloon ship "I" and from an armed liner. The following are the only incidents of interest:—

June 28th.

An attack on the enemy camp at Gingwere Creek, which had previously been discovered by a seaplane reconnaissance, was carried out by indirect fire, a seaplane spotting. Several hits were obtained, a large building in the camp being totally destroyed. The site, when subsequently reconnoitred, was littered with debris.

July 4th.

A reconnaissance by seaplane and kite balloon of Dar-es-Salaam was carried out. The seaplane was under machine-gun fire, but no other signs of life were observed.

EAST INDIES (SUEZ).

July 25th-August 10th.

The seaplane carriers throughout this period have been employed mainly upon reconnaissance work over the enemy's country.

A very large number of photographs have been obtained of the defences and a considerable amount of machine-gun and rifle fire has been experienced by the machines.

Particular items of interest are as follows:—

H.M. Seaplane Carrier "C."

July 25th.

The ship, accompanied by a French Torpedo Boat Destroyer, left Port Saïd to carry out a series of reconnaissances between Nazareth and the El Arish–Auja road with a view to watching for the movements of troops and stores to reinforce the army in the Sinai Peninsula.

Seaplanes from the Carrier made several reconnaissances and photographic flights.

The Carrier and French Destroyer, in conjunction with a seaplane, made an attack upon three schooners which were bringing down ammunition and supplies to the enemy in Sinai. The crews abandoned the vessels, which were destroyed by gunfire. Rifle fire was opened from the shore but was soon silenced.

July 26th.

Commander Samson, R.N., and Captain Wedgewood Benn, in a Short Seaplane, proceeded along the railway line to El Afuleh. Heavy rifle fire was opened on the machine from a large camp north of Tubaum. Two bombs were dropped upon a train and set a coach on fire.

At Seminieh heavy anti-aircraft fire was experienced, a steel strut on the port side of the machine being destroyed by a shrapnel bullet and the planes and elevators hit.

Further reconnaissances were carried out during the day and bombs were dropped on trucks and wagons. Seaplanes were observed from the Carrier to be under fire from a Turkish post and several rounds fired, which silenced the Turks and destroyed their tents.

August 14th–15th.

The ship left Port Said escorted by a French Destroyer at 4.35 on August 14th.

A series of reconnaissances were carried out in order to examine the communication lines behind the forces in Sinai, with a view to seeing whether the camp has increased in size and to bomb suitable targets.

One hundred and sixty-five miles of coast were examined for a distance of 20 miles inland in the course of 24 hours with excellent results, both observation and photographic.

Bombs were dropped on the railways and trucks and camel convoys were attacked with machine-gun fire.

H.M. Seaplane Carrier "B."

August 5th.

A photographic reconnaissance was carried out by a Short Seaplane from H.M. Seaplane Carrier "B" over the El Maaden –El Arish road.

August 7th.

The ship proceeded to sea to carry out spotting flights for a French flagship. In preparation for this work, receiving apparatus has been fitted in the seaplane, and messages sent by this means were received more surely than by searchlight, the observer also being free to devote his whole attention to watching the fall of shots.

Successful experiments have also been made in connection with towing seaplanes by trawlers when no carrying ship is available.

August 10th.

Two flights were made with a Sopwith machine for the purpose of dropping bombs, and two with a Short machine for observation and direction of artillery fire. Two factories and a barracks were destroyed.

An attack was made on the ship by a large enemy biplane, which dropped four small bombs. She was driven off by anti-aircraft fire.

H.M. Seaplane Carrier "K."

July 26th–August 10th.

Seaplanes and landing parties from the ship were employed in carrying out a photographic survey in the Gulf of Akaba and the Red Sea.

According to instructions the defences in the various districts were thoroughly photographed and much useful information was obtained as a result of numerous reconnaissances.

On July 26th one large dhow and several small ones moored in the harbour were sunk by fire from the Carrier.

On August 10th two spotting flights were carried out for the bombardment of a camp N.E. of Bir-el-Mazar. One machine dropped four 16-lb. bombs to indicate direction to the Monitor and direct hits were obtained. The second machine, after giving the signal to the Monitor to open fire, was immediately attacked by a hostile aeroplane (L.V.G. or Fokker), which opened fire from underneath, hitting the petrol tank. The radiator was shot just afterwards and a running fight ensued, the seaplane landing beside the Monitor. It was then taken in tow and hoisted into the Carrier in a sinking condition.

Air Department, Admiralty, S.W.,
    11th September 1916.

REPORT OF OPERATIONS No. 17.

DUNKIRK.

September 1st to 15th.

A great deal of bad weather has been experienced during this period, but a considerable amount of offensive work has been undertaken, and the usual patrols and reconnaissances have been maintained.

The more interesting events are as follows :—

September 2nd.

At 3.10 p.m. four machines left to carry out a bombing raid on the shipbuilding yards at Hoboken, Antwerp. One machine was forced to return, but the other three succeeded in reaching the objectives by steering a compass course above the clouds and diving down when they thought they had reached their objective. After a considerable time they observed the yards and dropped 34 bombs from heights of respectively 1,000, 3,000, and 4,500 feet. No results could be observed, however, as a heavy hail storm was in progress.

One pilot, as soon as he was out of range of the shore batteries, was attacked by a hostile monoplane. The pilot fired nine rounds into the enemy, who then disappeared into the clouds.

Owing to the gaps in the clouds between Zeebrugge and Nieuport, all coast batteries kept the machines under continuous fire.

September 3rd.

Seventeen machines left at about 4.45 to bomb the Ghistelles aerodrome. Eighty-five bombs were dropped, but owing to the early hour and bad visibility the exact damage done was difficult to observe, but columns of smoke were seen arising from the aerodrome, and two hits were observed on the railway track.

Bombs were dropped from an average height of 5,000 feet.

One of the pilots had just crossed the lines when he was attacked by a Fokker, which completely out-manœuvred him. Unfortunately the pilot's gun jammed after firing the first few shots, and his machine got into an uncontrollable spinning nose-dive, falling about 2,000 feet. The pilot, after turning off his engine, succeeded in righting his machine. Fortunately a fighter which was close by succeeded in driving off the enemy.

Pilot then regained his height and dropped his bombs on the objective. He distinctly observed smoke rising from several of the sheds.

On the return journey this machine was again attacked by an L.V.G., which fired several drums from below and then turned back 5 or 6 miles east of the lines. Our pilot escaped injury, but the machine was hit several times by machine-gun bullets and splinters from anti-aircraft fire.

September 6th.

A fighter machine patrolling over Nieuport at 10,000 feet was hit by anti-aircraft fire, one compression strut in the fuselage being shot away.

September 7th.

(a) Eighteen machines left at noon to bomb St. Denis Westrem Aerodrome at Ghent. Six of these machines, when opposite Zeebrugge, were forced to return owing to the strong wind. Flight Sub-Lieut. Brackley, when returning, was shelled from Knocke and chased from Eccloos to Knocke by an L.V.G., which fired intermittently. The pilot was later attacked by a small seaplane which followed him from Zeebrugge to Ostende, firing continually. This seaplane was very much like a Schneider Cup. It gave up the chase when about 1 mile north-east of Nieuport piers at 800 feet. Flight Sub-Lieut. Brackley was able to make a successful landing, although his machine was severely damaged, the warp control being cut through, one elevator wire cut, the oil tank punctured, and altogether 40 holes made in the machine.

The remaining machines succeeded in finding their objective and dropped bombs from heights varying from 1,000 to 2,000 feet. It is estimated that considerable damage was done, but although the sheds were clearly visible at this low altitude it was impossible to observe the actual damage, as a heavy hailstorm was in progress.

One machine (Flight Commander Beard) is missing.

(b) At 2.10 p.m. a signal was received from No. 11 Kite Balloon stating that a hostile kite balloon was up at Wilskerke, and a Nieuport pilot (Flight Lieut. Mackenzie) was immediately despatched. Observing the balloon arriving at its position east of Steene the pilot flew out to sea until the balloon had reached a considerable altitude, and then proceeded over Ostende, throttling down at 16,000 feet. The pilot dived and attacked the balloon, and immediately afterwards saw it with at least three, if not more, flaming points in her. When last observed the balloon was falling, a mass of flames, with a large column of smoke above.

The pilot returned over Pervyse under exceptionally heavy anti-aircraft and machine-gun fire, at an altitude of about 2,000 feet.

(c) At 8.30 a.m. a Nieuport Scout encountered two enemy machines in company at a height of 11,000 feet. One of these machines was observed to be a large Aviatik, and the other a small, very fast Roland biplane. The pilot, who was alone, immediately dived into them from 13,000 feet, and opened fire on the Roland at a range of 60 yards. Unfortunately one Lewis gun jammed owing to a cartridge missfiring, and pilot continued with the second gun, closely following the enemy, who dived down in a steep spiral. A whole tray was emptied into the Roland, tracers going through the fuselage.

The Nieuport was fired at by both machines, but eventually they retreated, diving inland towards Ghistelles.

September 8th.

During the evening W/T spotting was carried out for a monitor firing on the Belgian coast. Excellent results were obtained, and although shots were over the target the line of fire was very good.

Spotting was carried out from inland over the canal, observer confirming that the best position for night spotting is between the target and the moon.

September 9th.

In the early hours of the morning two bombing raids were carried out on the aerodromes at Ghistelles and Handzaeme by four Caudron machines. Owing to the misty visibility the results could not be observed by the bombers.

A third raid was carried out on the Lichtervelde ammunition dumps in the afternoon by three Sopwith machines. Bombs were observed to fall on the railway siding.

The machines from all three raids returned safely, and none were attacked by hostile machines.

September 12th.

A fighter machine, accompanying a seaplane patrol, observed a hostile submarine 5 miles W. by N. of Westcappelle, heading S.W. The submarine immediately dived, and the pilot dropped two bombs on the spot and circled round in the vicinity for about 15 minutes without observing the submarine again. A reconnaissance machine later reported having observed the bombs dropped by the fighter. Immediately after the second bomb exploded the submarine appeared again on the quarter of seaplane, and remained with its periscope awash for about 5 seconds. The periscope only was visible, and this appeared to come up in almost the exact spot where the second bomb dropped. It is therefore considered that some damage may have been done to the submarine. The observer in the reconnaissance machine observed that the bombs dropped by the fighter were extremely well aimed.

September 15th.

In the early hours of the morning 10 Caudron machines carried out a bombing attack on the Hindenburg and Tirpitz batteries. In both cases bombs were observed to fall close to the objective, but accurate observations were impossible owing to the thick low-lying clouds and bad visibility.

Bombs were dropped from altitudes varying from 3,000 to 6,000 feet.

Several machines were occasionally picked up by searchlights and experienced anti-aircraft fire.

All machines returned safely.

Night landing lights were in use at Mariakerke Aerodrome, but were extinguished on the approach of bombing machines.

A searchlight south of Mariakerke Aerodrome appeared to pick up the machines very quickly.

EASTERN MEDITERRANEAN.

August 11th to September 1st.

A considerable amount of bad weather has occurred during the period under review. The usual regular patrols of the Dardanelles and anti-submarine patrols in other areas have, however, been carried out by aeroplanes, seaplanes, and airships.

Reconnaissances over the enemy's country have taken place almost daily.

The following are the more interesting episodes during this period :—

Thasos.

August 11th–18th.

Offensive and reconnaissance work has continued to show important results. Our persistent attacks on Xanthi have resulted in the military headquarters being removed to Yazi Euren in the mountains north of Xanthi, and the enemy machines which were formerly concentrated at Xanthi Aerodrome have been distributed to various other places where the hangars can be to some extent concealed by trees.

At Maswakli, two miles south of Xanthi, six hangars and a shed were observed, where two days previously there had only been two hangars. The growth of this aerodrome has been watched with interest, and being now considered ripe for destruction, it has been attacked twice during the week.

On the evening of the 11th August four machines dropped 30 explosive and carcase bombs on the aerodrome, three of which fell between the hangars, four on the wood, and the remainder on the landing ground about 70 yards from the hangars.

Whilst carrying out these operations one bombing machine was attacked by a perfectly new Fokker. Flight Sub-Lieut. Kinhead, in a Bristol Scout, engaged him from behind, firing three trays. The Fokker nose-dived about 2,000 feet and made off in the direction of Xanthi. The apparent immunity from damage, although attacked at close quarters, raises the presumption that the vital parts are armed. Beyond a hit in the cowling of the Bristol Scout, no damage was inflicted on our machines.

August 15th.

A further attack was carried out by seven machines. A full report of this operation has not yet come to hand, but it is known that some of the hangars were wrecked.

August 12th, 13th, and 17th.

Reconnaissance and bombing flights were carried out over the whole district round Kusilar on the frontier about 17 miles north-west of Xanthi, which is strongly fortified. Bombs were dropped at Yazi Euren, where military headquarters are reported, and also at Domirjik. Fires were started in both cases.

Submarine reconnaissances have been carried out as necessary.

August 11th.

Four bombs were dropped on Thasos Aerodrome by a hostile aeroplane but no damage was done.

A Bristol Scout proceeded straight to Xanthi, where he waited over the aerodrome for the return of the raiding machine, but failed to find it.

August 13th.

Another bombing attack on the aerodrome was frustrated by one of our machines, which engaged and drove off the enemy.

August 18th–25th.

On the morning of the 18th a reconnaissance reported a pontoon bridge had been built by the Bulgarians across the Nestos at a point east of Sarishaban. Movements of troops and lorries were observed and two Henri Farmans were despatched to bomb the bridge. A number of bombs fell close to the bridge without a direct hit, but damage was probably done to the lorries in the vicinity. During this attack twenty transport lorries were seen leaving Sarishaban and proceeding towards Kavalla. Thre Henri Farmans were sent to bomb the troops and transport on the road. Machines chose different sections of transport as a target and dropped heavy bombs close to them, one bomb causing a large explosion among the wagons.

The troops did not offer a good target, being seen to scatter as soon as an aeroplane was observed.

August 21st.

Sarishaban, having been abandoned by its inhabitants and being known to contain troops, was bombarded by three machines. Six bombs fell in the centre of the village and the remainder in the surrounding fields.

August 23rd.

A monitor was spotted on to troops encamped at Hanchiftlik on the Sarishaban-Kavalla road, and on the same day a hostile seaplane was chased and attacked by a Nieuport Scout. The seaplane made a bad landing, with his engine stopped, about a mile out to sea between the mouth of the Nestos and Kala Burum.

The Nieuport circled round and saw that the observer was hanging downwards over the side of the machine. The pilot could not be seen. It is probable that the machine was salved by the enemy, as lights were seen in that direction during the night.

August 25th, September 1st.

During the course of the Bulgarian advance continuous reconnaissance has been maintained and much useful information obtained.

Detailed information gained during the flights has been dropped for the use of the O.C. troops at Chai-Aghiji.

August 25th.

The railway station and bridge at Buk were attacked with bombs. On the same day the ships of the Fleet were spotted on to the fort north of Kavalla.

August 26th.

An attack was made by three machines on Drama railway station.

The first machine dropped two 100-lb. bombs, which fell close to the railway south-west of the station, and a large fire was seen to break out, which lasted for a considerable time. This was probably the petrol store.

Two of the machines attacked with small bombs the trucks, &c., in the sidings. Owing to the smoke and dust, it was impossible to see the extent of the damage.

Bombs were also dropped on buildings at Dokset, where troops are billeted.

August 27th.

A bomb attack was made on Okjilar railway station, where the headquarters of the 10th Division are now established. Twenty-three bombs were dropped on the line and trucks in the station and on the permanent way and station buildings, causing a fire to break out.

August 28th.

Drama station was again bombed. The station buildings were considerably damaged. On the same day bombs were dropped on Kavalla forts, with excellent results.

August 29th.

A raid was carried out at Porna. A reconnaissance on the previous day located a large body of infantry and transport concentrated in a village close to the railway station. These were attacked by three machines, and considerable havoc was caused in the village and among the troops, besides a large fire being started among the stores and transport.

The moral as well as the material effect of this bombardment seems to have been considerable, as a reconnaissance on the following day showed that all troops, camps, and transports had been removed from the district.

August 31st.

An attack was made on Angista railway station. Heavy bombs were dropped and direct hits were made, causing extensive damage.

Full details of this operation have not yet been received.

On the 28th, three hostile machines appeared over Thasos aerodrome. Three of our machines proceeded in pursuit, and Flight Sub-Lieut. Blandy, in a Nieuport, chased one machine to 8,500 feet, when the enemy commenced to dive. The Nieuport followed and opened fire at 75 yards, closing to 25 yards. Tracers were seen to enter the fuselage, and immediately the enemy landed in a field $\frac{3}{4}$ mile south-west of Ghengeli. The Nieuport descended to 400 feet and fired half a drum of ammunition at the machine. The pilot and observer were seen to climb out and leave their machine.

Flight Sub-Lieut. Kinhead, in a Bristol Scout, attacked a second machine at 7,000 feet above the mouth of the Nestor, closing up from a range of 150 yards. He was then attacked by a third machine from the starboard side, which he eventually got behind and attacked. The hostile machine then dived and was driven to land on rough ground two miles north-east of Zinelli.

Thermi.

August 11th–25th.

August 12th and 14th.

Reconnaissance and bombing flights were made over the Gulf of Smyrna. Bombs were dropped on a tug to the south of Long Island and on the hangar at Long Island Aerodrome.

15th and 16th August.

A Monitor was spotted on to two gun emplacements north of Deve Burnu, which had been previously located by a reconnaissance.

18th–25th August.

The machine spotting on the 16th (pilot Flight Sub-Lieut. Reid, observer Lieutenant D. Sassoon, 5th Dragoon Guards) was attacked by a Fokker, the first to be encountered in this district.

The Fokker attempted to attack four times, each time from the same direction, meeting the Nieuport and passing on the right side of the machine, firing at an angle of 45°. He only once fired his gun, firing 10 rounds, which grazed the under side of the left-hand lower plane of the Nieuport.

The Nieuport, armed with a fixed gun firing through the propeller, and worked by the pilot, as well as a gun behind, fired a tray from each gun. The Fokker was put into a spinning nose-dive for about 2,000 feet, after which it flattened out and disappeared across the Menimen Plain. The forward gun of the Nieuport was evidently a surprise for the Fokker and appeared to upset his predetermined method of attack.

Imbros.

11th–18th August.

August 13th.

A raid was made on Gallipoli by five machines. The primary object of attack was the flour mills on the water front, which formed a distinct target. The attack was carried out at night, and in spite of wind across the line of mills and warehouses, these were well sprinkled both with incendiary and explosive bombs. The pilots concerned were Squadron Commander R. Smyth-Pigott, D.S.O., Flight Lieutenants C. E. Brisley, A. F. F. Jacob, and L. P. Hardman, and Flight Sub-Lieut. A. M. Waistall.

Mudros Airship Station.

18th–25th August.

August 19th.

S.S. 8 sighted a mine 10 miles due east of Cape Thascoli, Strati Island. The pilot endeavoured to explode it by dropping two 16-lb. bombs. These failed to hit the target, and an indicating buoy was dropped. The mine was successfully located and sunk by H.M.S. "Grampus" later in the day.

EAST INDIES.

EGYPT SEAPLANE SQUADRON.

H.M. Seaplane Carriers "C," "K," and "B."

August 24th–29th.

Between these dates a rapid series of effective attacks on the enemy communications in Palestine were carried out, and the whole of the lines of approach from Adana were reconnoitred.

Although the railway line runs parallel to the coast, it is for the most part behind a range of mountains difficult for seaplanes to surmount, and has on this account been considered immune from attack.

The following are the more interesting events :—

August 25th.

H.M. Seaplane Carriers "C," "K," and "B" rendezvoused at Haifa. Ten seaplanes proceeded in starboard quarter line up the Haifa-Afuleh Valley. Very heavy rifle fire was encountered from Tubaum and from the camp north-west of it.

The defences of Afuleh proved to have been considerably strengthened and the camp greatly enlarged. A brisk rifle, machine-gun, and shrapnel fire was opened. A train proceeding south was bombed, the last coach being wrecked and the permanent way destroyed. The permanent way was also destroyed at various other places. A railway engine, 14 carriages, and a large amount of stores were burnt. The machines then proceeded to carry out their pre-arranged reconnaissances. All machines returned safely, but every one had been hit.

A further reconnaissance was carried out at between 1,200 and 2,000 feet, and machines were exposed the whole time to hostile fire from the valley, while from the Carmel Ridge they were under horizontal and plunging fire.

H.M. Seaplane Carrier "C."

August 26th.

H.M. Seaplane Carrier "C" arrived off Mahr El Kebir. At Askalan seven machines were hoisted out to attack the camp at Bureir and bomb the railway viaduct over Wadi El Hesy. The bombs failed to destroy the viaduct, but destroyed the line and embankment near by, and damage was done to the encampment, causing the camels to stampede, by Lewis gun fire. The operation was carried out under unusually heavy fire. One machine (pilot Flight Commander Dacre, D.S.O.) failed to return.

One machine failed to reach a greater height than 1,000 feet and was therefore unable to cross the mountains. A reconnaissance of the Coast Defences was therefore carried out.

Another machine flew to Homs and bombed the station (pilot Flight Commander England, observer Second Lieut. King). This flight, in a heavy seaplane, of 45 miles inland, with a strong wind causing very bad remous, and crossing hills 1,800 feet high, with clouds at 1,500 feet, was an exceptionally fine one. During this flight photographs were taken.

A Sopwith machine bombed a small camp at Tel Kale.

August 29th.

The Carrier arrived at Karatash Burnu. Two Shorts proceeded to reconnoitre and bomb Adana and the main railway line. One seaplane could not gain any height, and after a short reconnaissance of the coast returned to the ship. The other seaplane flew to Adana and bombed the railway station and bridge over the Jeiban Irmak.

A Sopwith was sent to Tarsus Chai and bombed lighters therein.

H.M. Seaplane Carrier " B."

H.M. Seaplane Carrier " B " arrived at Iskanderuneh, about 20 miles north of Jaffa.

A Short machine proceeded to bomb the station at Tulkeram and to reconnoitre the railway line.

Another Short machine proceeded to Ramleh and Ludd. Bombs were dropped on a large camp four miles north-west of Ramleh and on piles of stores near the station.

CAPE SEAPLANE SQUADRON.

A considerable number of reconnaissances have been made by seaplanes belonging to this squadron and valuable information and photographs obtained.

The following are specially interesting events:—

July 27th.

A Short seaplane (pilot Flight Lieut. Maclean, observer W.O. Lacey) made a reconnaissance over Sadani. Anti-aircraft fire was experienced, the fuselage being hit twice, but the firing ceased on the bombs being dropped.

July 29th.

A reconnaissance was carried out over Bagamoyo by a Short seaplane (pilot Flight Lieut. Maclean, observer Sub-Lieut. Fitzherbert). Bombs were dropped at Nuagwe, setting fire to one house and blowing the back out of another. Machine-gun and rifle fire was experienced.

Over easterly end of trenches a bullet passed through starboard plate into fuselage and hit the brass clip for air-bottles. The brass was splintered and a portion wounded pilot on leg and arm. The observer climbed out of his seat and bandaged the pilot's arm, and afterwards climbed down and inspected the floats for damage.

HOME STATIONS.

September 1st to 15th.

The usual large number of anti-submarine patrols and reconnaissances from all aeroplane, seaplane, and airship stations have taken place, and the usual work has been carried out by seaplane carriers in the North Sea.

A Zeppelin attack took place on September 2nd/3rd, and in this connection the following flight is of interest.

Grain.

Flight Commander Arnold, in a H. Farman machine, proceeded in search of a Zeppelin which he observed dropping bombs over Romford, but eventually lost sight of her. In attempting to land near Chelmsford he crashed and wrecked his machine, sustaining slight injuries.

September 9th.

Mullion.

C. 10, while patrolling in the vicinity of the Lizard, sighted a submarine between two burning vessels. The pilot attempted to bomb the submarine, but it submerged.

He warned ships and stations, and one of H.M. vessels was in consequence enabled to pick up the crews of burning vessels.

Air Department, Admiralty, S.W.,
  26th September 1916.

REPORT OF OPERATIONS No. 18.

DUNKIRK.

During this period the usual routine patrols and photographic reconnaissances have been maintained.

Spotting was carried out as requisite for H.M. ships.

The more interesting events are as follows :—

September 17th.

Flight-Lieut. Minifie, in a Nieuport Scout, encountered a small German seaplane with two long floats and no tail float at a height of 13,000 feet inland of Ostende. Pilot sighted the enemy 500 feet above and endeavoured for 10 minutes to climb and out-manœuvre him. The enemy was, however, vastly superior to the 80 Le Rhone Nieuport in speed and climb, and suddenly dived at the Nieuport, firing as it came. Flight Lieut. Minifie met this attack by stalling his machine and firing three-quarter tray of ammunition at close range. He then proceeded to change the tray of his single gun, while the German climbed rapidly and hid himself in the clouds at 15,000 feet.

September 22nd.

(*a*) Flight Sub-Lieut. Keeble with Sub-Lieut. Betts, in a Sopwith machine, carried out a photographic reconnaissance under very heavy anti-aircraft fire, the machine being twice hit at a height of 13,000 feet. Fourteen plates were successfully exposed from the coast west of the Villa Scolare up to the east end of Ostende and over Middlekerke. Two were also taken of Tirpitz battery.

(*b*) Three Sopwith machines carried out a bombing raid on St. Denis Westrem, accompanied by two Sopwith fighters. Twenty-four bombs were dropped, several of which were seen to burst by the observer of one of the fighters. It is certain that damage was done to the sheds and machines. Bombs were seen to burst all round one of the big sheds, and it is believed that two were actually hit.

While escorting the bombing machines a hostile single-seater biplane was engaged off Ostende by one of our fighters. The pilot fired $1\frac{1}{2}$ trays of ammunition from the after gun, upon which the enemy machine turned back and made for Ostende. The Sopwith followed, and pilot fired about 100 rounds from the front gun, which then jammed. When last observed the enemy was diving steeply towards Mariakerke.

(c) Flight Sub-Lieut. Cuckney and Sub-Lieut. Hodson, in a Short seaplane, carried out a reconnaissance, accompanied by Flight Sub-Lieut. Graham in a Sopwith fighter seaplane and Flight Sub-Lieut. Durston in a Short bombing seaplane. They encountered four hostile seaplanes off Zeebrugge. Flight Sub-Lieut. Graham attacked the first two and Flight Sub-Lieut. Durston the remaining two. After a short encounter Flight Sub-Lieut. Graham successfully drove off the first two and then turned his attention to the other pair. A fierce fight was kept up at a range of between 200 and 300 yards, and eventually both hostile machines were driven off by the Sopwith fighter.

The seaplane reconnaissance was successfully completed. It is thought that during the engagement one of the hostile observers was badly injured, as he was last observed leaning over his gun, which, although in range of the Sopwith, did not continue firing.

All three of our machines sustained slight damage.

September 23rd.

(a) A bombing raid was carried out on the enemy aerodromes at Ghistelles and Handzaeme by six Sopwith machines. Thirty-six 65-lb. bombs and forty 16-lb. bombs were dropped, but owing to the thick ground mist it was impossible to observe the damage. It is thought that a number of bombs fell very close to the sheds.

(b) Flight Sub-Lieut. Thom and Gunlayer Symonds in a Sopwith machine, while escorting a photographic reconnaissance, engaged a large seaplane at about 5,500 feet. Firing was opened by both Lewis and Vickers guns, tracers being observed to enter the machine. After firing about 30 rounds from the Vickers gun and about 60 rounds from the Lewis gun the hostile seaplane was seen to nose-dive steeply. When last seen it was still diving and was probably shot down.

Shortly after this a small, very fast, enemy seaplane attacked our machine, but after firing about 50 rounds it returned to Ostende.

(c) Flight Sub-Lieut. Travers, in a Nieuport, while accompanying a spotting machine, observed a large German seaplane going towards the fleet. The pilot escorted the spotting machine past Nieuport and then turned back and attacked the enemy, who opened fire at 150 yards. One tray was then fired into him and tracers could be observed going round his fuselage. After unloading for second tray the enemy was seen diving for Ostende, and our machine, being under heavy anti-aircraft fire, returned to the aerodrome.

On this day a number of hostile machines endeavoured to spot over the Nieuport and Dixmude area, but owing to the efficient patrol of our machines were rapidly driven back over their lines.

Five actual encounters took place.

September 24th.

Two hostile machines dropped bombs over Dunkirk. All available machines got away in remarkably short time. When in the vicinity of Ghistelles, Flight Sub-Lieut. Goble, in a Sopwith Scout, encountered two L.V.G.'s at a height of 12,500 feet. He got within 50 yards of one unobserved and opened fire with a burst of about 10 shots, whereupon the observer in the enemy machine jumped up, but before he could sight his gun Flight Sub-Lieut. Goble side-slipped under and across the enemy machine, thereby getting underneath and behind, from which position he fired 30 rounds. The L.V.G. fell over sideways and caught fire, falling in a spiral nose-dive, evidently quite out of control.

It would appear from the evidence that these two L.V.G.'s were the same machines which had just dropped bombs on Dunkirk.

September 25th.

(a) A number of successful photographs were taken of the area between Nieuport and Zeebrugge and the district south of the hospital at Middlekerke.

All three photographic machines and their accompanying escorts were under very heavy and accurate anti-aircraft fire.

(b) Flight Sub-Lieut. Grange, acting as escort to a photographic reconnaissance, observed, when off Ostende, a hostile seaplane about six miles out to sea at a height of 8,000 feet. He opened fire with a burst of 10 shots, and the enemy turned and got into a spin.

The tail of the hostile machine was observed to break and the machine collapsed, finally falling into the sea from a height of 6,000 feet.

Note.—On the following day a monitor, whilst on patrol, picked up parts of a German seaplane, which was probably the one shot down by Flight Sub-Lieut. Grange.

(c) Flight Sub-Lieut. Trapp, in a Sopwith, met and engaged a German machine, probably an L.V.G. His gun jammed, and while clearing it his machine was thrown into a nose-dive by anti-aircraft fire. The engine stopped, and when it picked up again was vibrating badly. The pilot therefore turned for home and had to make a forced landing at Malo. The Sopwith was twice hit by shell fire.

September 27th.

A bombing raid was carried out on the Zeppelin sheds at Evere, Etterbeek, and Berchem St. Agathe by four Sopwith machines. All three sheds were straddled with bombs from heights varying from 5,000 to 8,000 feet.

One of the pilots who attacked the shed at Evere observed that his bombs fell short and on some buildings adjoining the shed. A loud explosion followed and masses of smoke issued. It is probable that an ammunition shed was exploded.

All the machines returned safely.

September 28th.

Flight Sub-Lieut. Galbraith, in a Neuport scout, sighted an enemy seaplane at 11,000 feet, about six to eight miles off La Panne. Pilot, after manœuvring for position, opened fire at a range of 15 yards. The tail of the seaplane was seen to break off, and Flight Sub-Lieut. Galbraith followed the enemy down and emptied another tray, whereupon the machine blew up and was seen to fall headlong. The Nieuport was hit many times, the back sight of machine gun being carried away and a large hole being drilled in the wind screen.

This fight was witnessed by one of the French seaplane pilots, who was searching for the same machine, and he reports as follows :—

> Observed a fight going on between two machines. Proceeded at once towards the spot and recognised a German seaplane of big dimensions being attacked by an English Nieuport. After a few minutes the hostile seaplane went into a vertical dive towards the sea, followed by the English machine, and both disappeared in the clouds. The hostile machine appeared to be very badly hit.

September 30th.

(a) A German biplane which appeared to be directing artillery fire was observed by Flight Lieut. Dallas, D.S.C., in a Sopwith triplane, a short distance S.W. of St. Pierre Capelle. Pilot dived down about 1,500 feet and fired 60 rounds at the enemy, who dived and side-slipped, hopelessly out of control, and was lost to sight after falling several thousand feet.

Continuing his patrol, pilot observed a small German seaplane diving down, apparently on the point of attacking a Belgian machine. He engaged the enemy at rather long range, forcing him to retire and give up the attack.

EASTERN MEDITERRANEAN.

Reports Nos. 25 and 26.

September 1st to 15th.

Spotting has been carried out as requisite for H.M. ships.

The usual patrols of the Dardanelles and anti-submarine patrols of other areas have been carried out by aeroplanes, seaplanes, and airships.

A considerable number of reconnaissances over the enemy's country have taken place, in spite of a shortage of pilots owing to malaria.

The following are the more interesting events :—

Thasos.

Details have been received of the bombing attack on Angista railway station on August 21st, which has previously been briefly commented on.

The pilot of the bombing machine was Flight Lieut. Bush, with C.P.O. Marchant as observer. Bombs were dropped from a height of 11,000 feet. One 65-lb. bomb fell in the centre of the station building. Two 100-lb. bombs were dropped on the railway bridge.

The escorting machine was piloted by Flight Sub-Lieut. Mills.

September 4th.

(a) H.M.S. "Grafton" was spotted on to the earthworks with the object of drawing the enemy's fire, and reconnaissances were carried out over the same area, with the result that the position of some of the guns was located.

(b) A seaplane attack was carried out over the barracks and camps at Travishta. Four bombs were dropped on the barracks and 16 on the camp to the N.W. of the town by Flight Sub-Lieut. Barrington (pilot) and H. Howe, Air Mechanic 1 (observer).

September 8th.

Flight Sub-Lieut. Barrington with Sub-Lieut. Wright succeeded in locating and attacking with bombs gun emplacements and trenches on the spurs of the hills.

September 11th.

A reconnaissance was carried out over the railway in the vicinity of Xanthi.

September 13th.

A bombing raid was carried out on the hamlet of Bademli Chiftlik, the headquarters of the 10th Division, and considerable damage was done. A full report will follow.

H.M.S. "Empress."

September 12th and 14th.

Reconnaissances were carried out over the mouth of the Struma, and considerable artillery activity against the French and British lines was observed.

Thermi.

September 8th and 9th.

Two successful reconnaissances and anti-submarine patrols were carried out over Foujes Harbour.

September 11th and 12th.

Spotting was carried out for M. 22 and 33 at Cape Bianco. Two direct hits were made, one gun being apparently demolished. Spotting machine returned to Thermi the same day.

Imbros.

A sailing vessel was observed proceeding eastwards and was attacked with Lewis gun by a patrolling machine and driven back to Port Talbot.

Twelve bombs were dropped on Tenedos by a hostile seaplane, but no trace of it could be found by our fighting machines, which were sent up to cut it off from its base.

EAST INDIES STATION.

Egypt Seaplane Squadron.

31st August to 10th September.

Various reconnaissance operations have been carried out by this Squadron during the above period.

H.M.S. "Raven" was to have participated, but was unfortunately struck by a bomb from an aeroplane during an air raid on September 1st, casualties being one officer and eight ratings.

H.M.S. "Anne" therefore took her place and proceeded to carry out the operations ordered, from which she has not yet returned.

Aden.

A report received from the O.C. Perim gave the following results of the bombing flights and bombardments of Sheik Said :—

On June 13th—

(1) 25 powder barrels blown up at J. Reyu.
(2) 26 Turks and four Arabs killed.
(3) 15 Turks wounded.
(4) No Turkish guns hit.

No further reports have been received from this station during this period.

HOME STATIONS.

The usual number of routine anti-submarine patrols and reconnaissances from all aeroplane, seaplane, and airship stations have taken place, and the usual work has been carried out by seaplane carriers in the North Sea.

The more interesting events are as follows:—

September 22nd.

A hostile aeroplane visited Dover and dropped three bombs on the Duke of York's School, breaking a few windows. A bomb was also dropped on the Deal road, damaging a few telegraph wires, and another near the military aerodrome.

No casualties were caused.

September 23rd.

On this day a raid was made by 14 or 15 hostile airships and a number of machines went up from various stations.

Yarmouth.

(*a*) Flight Lieut. Kilner and C.P.O. Rose in a Short seaplane attacked a Zeppelin 45 miles east of Yarmouth. The airship was lost in the clouds and pilot was forced to land on the water on account of darkness.

(*b*) Flight Lieut. Galpin, in a Schneider Cup Seaplane, attacked a Zeppelin 30 miles east of Lowestoft. Pilot fired one tray into the Zeppelin but was compelled to return owing to darkness.

Calshot.

(*a*) Squadron Commander Bigsworth and Flight Lieut. Cooper in W. and T Flying Boats went up in pursuit of a hostile Zeppelin which was sighted, but were unable to overtake. Squadron Commander Bigsworth was forced to land owing to engine trouble, slightly damaging the machine.

September 24th.

(*b*) Flight Lieut. Cooper and Probationary Sub-Lieut. Spear, in a seaplane, observed a German submarine northeast of Casquets at a moment when it was preparing to sink a Norwegian steamer, the crew having already been ordered into their boats.

The pilot was unable to drop bombs on the submarine owing to the danger of hitting the steamer's boats, which had, under orders from the submarine, been pulled alongside her. Immediately after it had dived, however, and drawn ahead of the boats, the pilot released his bombs, but was unable to observe the result, and did not again sight the submarine, although he undoubtedly saved the Norwegian vessel from being sunk.

Air Department, Admiralty,
    13th October 1916.

REPORT OF OPERATIONS No. 19.

DUNKIRK.

During this period the usual routine patrols and reconnaissances have been maintained when weather permitted.

The following are the more interesting events:—

October 1st.

A seaplane patrol, accompanied by two Fighter machines, was attacked by an enemy seaplane. This machine was observed to be a two-seater with no wing extension, speed about 80 knots, no tail float, and only one gun firing on the beam aft, not forward.

Seven and a half trays of ammunition were fired by our seaplanes, and shots were observed to enter the fuselage of the enemy, who was eventually driven off towards Ostende.

Our machines were hit several times, one being forced to land owing to petrol trouble.

October 2nd.

A bombing raid was carried out on the airship sheds at Brussels by four machines. Two pilots were to attack the Evere shed and one pilot to attack the Etterbeck and Burchem St. Agathe respectively.

Very bad weather was experienced, and two out of the four machines were forced to return owing to engine trouble.

Flight Sub-Lieut. Chadwick failed to return.

The fourth pilot, Flight Lieut. Collet, although forced to travel nearly the whole journey by compass above the clouds, succeeded in reaching the objective, and dropped 12 Le Pecq bombs directly across the Evere shed.

LUXEUIL (No. 3 WING).

October 12th.

An attack was carried out by 15 Bombing machines and six Fighters, in conjunction with nine French Bombers and 25 Fighters on the Mauser factory at Oberndorf, the total distance flown being 223 miles.

The majority of the machines reached their objective, and it appears probable that considerable damage was done.

The machines were under heavy anti-aircraft fire and were, in a few instances, attacked by hostile machines.

One hostile machine was brought down by a Sopwith Fighter (pilot Flight Commander Jones, observer Sub-Lieut. Downs). A second was damaged and probably brought down by another Sopwith (pilot Flight Sub-Lieut. Smith, observer Gunlayer Clegg).

The French also claim to have brought down four machines.

Flight Sub-Lieut. Butterworth (in a Sopwith), and Flight Sub-Lieuts. Newman and Rocky, with Gunlayers Vitty and Sturdee (in Breguet machines), failed to return and are prisoners of war in Germany.

HOME STATIONS.

The usual number of routine anti-submarine patrols and reconnaissances from all aeroplane, seaplane, and airship stations have taken place when weather permitted, and the usual work has been carried out by seaplane carriers in the North Sea.

The following is the only interesting event :—

October 13th.

Sub-Lieut. Bittles, in a Short seaplane, sighted a floating mine between Cross Sands and Smith's Knoll and fired a Very's light to attract the attention of a trawler in the vicinity. On investigation by a mine sweeper six mines were swept up.

EAST INDIES STATION.

Egypt Seaplane Squadron.

1st to 17th September.

H.M.S " Ben-my-Chree."

September 16th.

H.M.S. " Ben-my-Chree " left Port Said at 9 p.m. for the purpose of carrying out spotting for the fire of H.M. Ships.

September 17th.

In the early hours of the morning six machines were hoisted out.

During the course of the operations a Short machine (pilot Flight Lieut. Maskell, observer Sub-Lieut. Kerry, R.N.V.R.) flew east of El Arish to a point where a complete observation of the aerodrome could be obtained. An enemy aeroplane was seen immediately to rise, climbing at a great speed. This machine easily overtook the Short and flew between it and its escort (two Sopwith machines). The enemy was first engaged by Flight Lieut. Bankes-Price, but after a few shots this pilot was killed and his machine fell to the water in a sheet of flame.

The enemy was then engaged by Flight Sub-Lieut. Nightingale, but owing to superior speed and armament he was able to hit our seaplane repeatedly through the tail, and finally pierced the petrol tank, compelling a descent. Flight Sub-Lieut. Nightingale was picked up by a Monitor and his seaplane by a trawler.

The hostile aeroplane then attacked the Short from below, but Flight Lieut. Maskell, by a skilful manœuvre, quickly dived, at a speed of 75 knots, and got under the enemy. While there the enemy could not fire and Sub-Lieut. Kerry was in a position to pour six hoppers from the Lewis gun into him. Many tracer bullets were seen to hit the enemy and he immediately made off.

H.M.S. "Ben-my-Chree" returned to Port Said.

H.M.S. "Anne."

Between September 1st and 16th operations were continued in the Red Sea with a view to supporting the Sheriff of Mecca and his allied tribes.

"Anne" moved from point to point as requested for carrying out wireless spotting for H.M. Ships, and a considerable number of bombs were dropped on forts, troops, and points of importance. Troops and camels were also continually harassed by Lewis gun fire.

A considerable number of reconnaissances were carried out.

Flights were also carried out with a view to impressing the Sherifian recruits.

CAPE STATION.

The following is an extract from the Report of C.-in-C., Cape, with reference to the capture of Bagamoyo by a naval force on 15th August 1916:—

"Meanwhile the 'Manica' had got up her Kite Balloon and was spotting, but her seaplane had engine trouble and was forced to come down in the breakers at the mouth of the Kingani River, returning undamaged. I accordingly called on 'Himalaya' (Captain Colin Mackenzie, D.S.O.), which was just leaving Zanzibar, and at 6 a.m. her seaplane flew across from Zanzibar and at once dropped bombs on the enemy in trenches, afterwards spotting. . . . . .

"At 6.30 it was reported from three sources (Kite Balloon, Portable W/T set ashore, and W/T from seaplane) that the enemy were retiring between the French Mission and the Sea, and were around the Mission. . . . . .

"Flight Lieut. D. Gill has brought his Kite Balloon Section to a high state of efficiency, and this officer, with Flight Sub-Lieut. J. W. Walton, was of the greatest use in pointing out the enemy's line of retreat. . . . . .

"On the 16th August the 'Manica' steamed back from Dar-es-Salaam to Zanzibar—34 miles, with the balloon up 2,000 feet, in a strong monsoon. . .

"Flight Lieut. Moon responded to my call for him with great promptitude and flew across from Zanzibar fully equipped with bombs, photographic apparatus, and W/T. Having dropped his bombs round the inner trenches he took most excellent photographs, and then remained spotting for the big ships until fire ceased about 9 a.m. He was ably assisted by Air Mechanic Wilmshurst.

"The scheme of landing was based on a most excellent photograph taken by Flight Lieut. Maclean and Sub-Lieut. Fitzherbert, R.N.V.R. (Observer) of the Royal Naval Air Service, which was of the greatest assistance and enabled me to frame a clear idea of the nature and possibilities of the defences."

EASTERN MEDITERRANEAN.

Reports Nos. 27, 28, and 29.

16th September to 6th October.

High winds, accompanied by low clouds and rain, have greatly interfered with flying during a part of this period.

The usual patrols of the Dardanelles and anti-submarine patrols of other areas have been carried out by aeroplanes, seaplanes, and airships, whenever possible.

Spotting has been carried out as requisite for H.M. ships.

The following are the more interesting events:—

Thasos.

September 16th.

The Bulgarian headquarters were located in a wood on the Drama–Kavalla road, and an attack was carried out on them. This was eminently successful, two 112-lb. bombs being dropped, which fell directly on the target, causing a large explosion to take place and a fire to break out among the buildings, which was seen to last for a considerable time.

A large amount of transport which had been previously observed proceeding along the road towards Drama was also attacked, the bombs exploding among the waggons and troops, causing considerable damage.

September 18th.

A large amount of railway stock and stores having been reported by reconnaissance to be at Drama Station, bombing machines were sent to attack. A further attack was also made on the following day, several 112-lb. bombs being dropped N.E. and S.W. of the station. The damage caused has not yet been ascertained, but it must have been considerable.

September 19th.

A quantity of small bombs were dropped on a column of troops and transport on the Kavalla–Drama road, which fell close to the transport waggons, causing damage and confusion.

September 21st.

A reconnaissance flight and bombing attack were carried out on points of military importance on the Serres–Drama Road, and a successful photographic reconnaissance of the new defences to the north of Kavalla was carried out on the same day.

Details have now been received of a bombing attack carried out on the Bulgarian headquarters on 13th September, briefly noted in previous report of operations.

Two machines participated in the attack, particularly good practice being made by Flight Sub-Lieut Whetnall, with C.P.O. Marchant. Eight 16-lb. bombs were released from 10,000 feet, all of which fell among the buildings.

September 25th.

A reconnaissance over Drama area having disclosed a large amount of transport, the village of Musralti, seven miles from Drama, was attacked by bombing machines, and five heavy bombs were dropped among the transport, causing considerable damage.

On the same day points of military importance at Kavalla were also attacked with bombs.

September 26th.

A bombing attack was made upon Chepelje, an important store depôt on the railway, immediately behind the Bulgarian lines. Direct hits were made and buildings were wrecked.

September 27th.

A further attack was made against Angista railway station, which was reconnoitred by "D" flight on the previous day. This is the chief transport centre for the Lower Struma sector. Two direct hits were made on the station buildings, and on a bivouac camp to the N.E. of the station.

September 28th.

A further attack was made on Angista Station. Large fires were started, one of which spread to a small camp north of the station.

September 30th.

A reconnaissance flight over the Upper Nestos area located two long goods trains proceeding towards Drama, and a considerable amount of transport in and around Buk. These were attacked with bombs and at the same time the important railway bridge at Buk was attacked.

October 3rd.

Troops and transport on the Kavalla–Pravista road were observed by a reconnaissance, and on 4th October, having arrived at Drama, they were bombed.

At the same time transport waggons on the road near Chatalja were attacked.

October 5th.

A bombing attack was carried out at the request of the 80th Brigade on Angista Station, the most important stores depôt for the Lower Struma sector of the Bulgarian line. Results of this raid are not yet known.

Imbros.

September 21st.

A hostile submarine having been reported off Helles two bombing machines started off from Imbros. One was totally wrecked, the pilot being slightly injured. The second machine observed the periscope of the submarine some distance away, but before he could reach the spot it had submerged, and was not seen again.

September 25th.

A Torpedo Boat sighted at Chanak was attacked with bombs.

October 5th.

A Torpedo Boat was observed and attacked with bombs off Chanak.

One of H.M. ships was successfully spotted on to Bodema junction, and the surrounding country was reconnoitred.

Mudros Airship Station.

Patrols were only possible on two days during the week ending September 30th.

October 5th.

A submarine was located by airship 4 miles S.W. of Cape Tigani and torpedo boats and trawlers proceeded to search the area.

Kassandra.

The usual patrols of the Gulf of Salonika have been carried out.

Struma.

Photographic reconnaissances over hostile batteries were carried out on the 25th, 27th, and 28th September, and spotting for Monitors on the 26th and 27th.

September 29th.

One of H.M. ships was spotted on to batteries at Dranli.

A spotting machine observed about 4,000 troops drawn up in squares outside the village. The ship was immediately directed to fire on these and one shell was seen to burst among a group of about 50 men. The troops then scattered up to the hills to the North, when they were again shelled with good effect.

Later in the day another of H.M. ships was spotted on to the village of Dranli, the northern end of which was demolished and set on fire.

The pilot was Squadron Commander Smyth Pigott, D.S.O., with Second Lieut. Barry, 1st Royal Irish, as observer.

These officers carried out the reconnaissances in this area on 24th, 25th, and 27th September, and 5th October, and obtained much useful information and photographs of enemy defence works.

October 2nd.

A reconnaissance and bomb dropping flight was carried out over the Lower Struma area. Bombs were dropped with good effect on batteries which were observed to be in action.

All machines operating over the Chai-Aghizi area have been subjected to very heavy anti-aircraft fire, which has, fortunately, up to date, been erratic.

H.M.S. "Empress."

September 21st.

H.M.S. "Grafton" spotted on to the two enemy observation posts reported by a previous reconnaissance flight, with the result that one observation post was demolished.

September 26th.

A reconnaissance flight by Flight Sub-Lieut. Arnold and Sub-Lieut. Hampton succeeded in definitely locating the position of seven anti-aircraft guns, and in obtaining much useful information about the Lower Struma defences.

September 28th.

A considerable number of reconnaissances were carried out by seaplanes from this ship over the Struma lines.

September 29th.

Bombs were dropped with good effect on the observation trenches on the coast line south of Orfano, which had previously been located by a reconnaissance.

Spotting flights were carried out on 29th and 30th September and 5th October. On the latter date an enemy gun was destroyed south-west of Dranli.

Thermi.

September 16th.

The shipping in Foujes Harbour was attacked, the bombs dropping on the quay.

September 18th.

A caique lying at anchor at Tuz Burnu was attacked with heavy bombs, and on the same day three 112-lb. bombs were dropped on emplacements on a hill to the N.E. of Tuz Burnu in the vicinity of a gun which was firing at one of H.M. ships.

During the greater part of the week ending 28th September flying was impossible on account of the weather. Reconnaissances were carried out, however, over the Gulf of Smyrna and a special reconnaissance over Aivalik on the 22nd and 28th respectively.

September 29th.

One of H.M. ships was spotted on to the small guns at Darlikli Burnu, Gulf of Smyrna previously located by a reconnaissance. Good results were obtained, also further information and photographs of these defences.

October 5th.

Bombs were dropped to the east of Tuz Burnu (Aivalik area), where a 6-inch gun is now reported.

Air Department, Admiralty,
    27th October 1916.

REPORT OF OPERATIONS No. 20.

DUNKIRK.

During this period the usual routine patrols and photographic reconnaissances have been maintained.

Spotting was carried out as requisite for H.M. Ships.

The weather had been exceedingly boisterous during part of this period.

The more interesting events are as follows :—

October 17th.

Flight Sub-Lieut. Galbraith, in a Sopwith Scout, No. 5181, while on fighter patrol in the Dixmude-Nieuport-Furnes sector, observed an enemy biplane of the Fokker type about 10 miles S.E. of Ghistelles, at 9,000 feet. A running fight ensued. The hostile machine was eventually out-manœuvred and dived, but although tracers were observed to enter the fuselage, it was apparently under control. The enemy also used tracer bullets.

October 20th.

(*a*) Flight Lieut. B. C. Clayton, in a Nieuport Scout, No. 3981, encountered an L.V.G. while flying near Dixmude, at 16,000 feet. The hostile machine being 1,000 feet below, Flight Lieut. Clayton manœuvred for position close behind him and got within 50 yards of the enemy before opening fire. The Lewis gun jammed, and by the time it was ready for action the hostile machine had turned away, diving towards Ghistelles.

(*b*) The same pilot sighted a new type of enemy machine, rather like a large Sopwith, with two bays, and pursued it towards Aire-Bethune, just being able to keep up with it, but out of range. At Aire, however, the enemy turned and pilot was able to close to about 100 yards, when he opened fire. The Lewis gun worked badly and finally jammed, and pilot was obliged to give up the chase.

(*c*) Flight Sub-Lieut. T. G. Culling, in a Nieuport Scout, No. 3987, while flying over Ghistelles, encountered an Aviatik at 14,000 feet. Pilot dived and attacked, opening fire at a range of less than 50 yards. Owing to the Lewis gun not working well pilot could not take advantage of his tracer bullets, and pilot escaped by diving out of reach.

(*d*) Flight Lieut. Leather, in a Nieuport Scout, No. 3956, while flying at 14,000 feet off Ostende, encountered a very large

German two-engined tractor seaplane 4,000 feet lower. Pilot dived, attacking on the port bow of the enemy and shooting the observer, who collapsed forward on his gun after firing a few rounds. The seaplane then made steeply for Ostende, followed by the Nieuport, which kept close up by swerving in astern.

Lieutenant Leather then shot the pilot, whereupon the hostile machine stalled, side-slipped, and fell vertically into the sea, about two miles off Ostende. It entirely disappeared under the water, but later a portion of the seaplane, apparently afloat, appeared on the surface.

The Nieuport Scout was, at this time, only 3,000 feet above the sea, and the complete destruction of the enemy machine was very clearly seen.

(e) Flight Lieut. E. W. Norton, in a Nieuport Scout, No. 3994, attacked the enemy kite balloon near Ostende. Pilot flew among the clouds searching for the balloon for about 20 minutes, eventually sighting it below him, at a height of 2,000 feet from the ground, about three miles inland S.W. of the Wellington racecourse. Pilot fired his rockets at close range, hitting the balloon, which immediately burst into flames and fell blazing to the ground. One parachute was observed to leave the balloon, but this caught fire and was destroyed.

Flight Lieut. Norton was subjected to very heavy fire from enemy batteries.

October 21st.

Flight Commander J. J. Petre, D.S.C., in a Nieuport Scout, when flying at 15,000 feet, encountered two enemy biplanes (Aviatik and L.V.G.) approaching Nieuport from the S.E. at a low altitude. Pilot dived to 6,000 feet and both the enemy machines turned towards Ghistelles. Pilot attacked the L.V.G. at less than 100 yards' range, firing 40 rounds. The German observer, who was standing up, fell backwards into the fuselage, evidently shot, and immediately after the L.V.G. went down vertically and then fell, side-slipping, and emitting a large cloud of smoke from the fuselage. The Aviatik, although close, made no attempt to fight. The anti-aircraft fire at this time being very intense, Flight Commander Petre was unable to see the end of the L.V.G., but from the report of a Belgian pilot who witnessed the whole of this fight it appears that the machine was entirely destroyed.

October 22nd.

(a) Flight Sub-Lieut. Culling, in Nieuport Scout, No. 3987, engaged a German machine which was spotting behind the enemy's lines near Nieuport. Pilot dived from 12,500 to 7,000 feet, getting into close quarters, and emptied a tray into the enemy. Tracer bullets were seen cutting into the fuselage of the enemy machine, but he dived out of reach under control, and apparently not seriously damaged. The Nieuport was then at 7,000 feet over Westende, under heavy fire, which forced him to fly out to sea.

(b) The same pilot, immediately after this engagement, encountered an enemy machine at 7,000 feet over the sea off Westende. After one tray had been fired at it, this machine retired, diving towards Ostende. Tracer bullets were used by the enemy machine.

(c) The same pilot, when over Dixmude, at 10,000 feet, sighted an enemy aeroplane about 500 feet above him. He could not get close up to him, so fired one tray at 150 yards. The enemy returned the fire, using bullets of which at least a dozen exploded round the Nieuport Scout, puffs of smoke being clearly seen and the sound of the bursts being audible. These bullets did not trace. The machine, which was a new type, rather like a Sopwith, had much higher speed than the Nieuport, and retreated towards Ostende.

(d) Flight Lieuts. Bell and Neville, in Sopwith Scouts, whilst on fighter patrol, observed two hostile machines at 12,000 feet between Handzaeme and Stadem. Both pilots dived towards the enemy machines, whereupon they immediately dived to the ground. Flight Lieut. Bell fired half a tray at long range.

(e) Flight Sub-Lieut. Galbraith, in a Sopwith Scout, while on fighter patrol off Blankenberghe, encountered an enemy seaplane. (Probably the one which dropped bombs on the Nore.) Pilot dived from 15,000 to 7,000 feet and emptied two trays into the enemy, whereupon the latter nose-dived straight into the sea. Pilot followed down to 3,000 feet and saw traces of the broken machine floating about. Distance was approximately $2\frac{1}{2}$ miles off Blankenberghe.

October 23rd.

(a) Flight Sub-Lieut. Casey, while on patrol in a Sopwith Scout, sighted a small German seaplane about five miles off Blankenberghe at about 5,000 feet. Pilot dived from 10,000 feet to attack, when enemy machine immediately dived. Tracers were noticed to go round the machine, but the enemy descended so low that the fight had to be abandoned.

(b) Flight Lieut. Keeble, in a Sopwith Scout, sighted four hostile machines below him, about 10 miles off Ostende. He dived to attack and found two white and two brown seaplanes. Pilot attacked a brown one which had separated a little from the others, and after a second dive succeeded in shooting it down. Machine crashed into the sea, and pieces of the wreckage were observed on the water. During the fight our machine was attacked by the three other machines. The Lewis gun jammed, and Flight Lieut. Keeble was obliged to abandon the attack. All these German machines used tracer bullets.

(c) Flight Lieut. Travers, in a Sopwith Scout, whilst on patrol, saw a German seaplane about 4,000 feet off Ostende. He dived from 12,000 feet, and when closing with the enemy fired about 90 rounds. Tracers were seen to enter the enemy's fuselage, but the Lewis gun jammed, and while Lieutenant Travers was clearing it the enemy escaped.

(d) Flight Sub-Lieut. Fisher, in a Sopwith seaplane, No. 8145, when at a height of 11,500 feet, about four miles off Ostende, sighted a two-seater L.V.G. biplane flying westwards at 11,000 feet and about a mile from the coast. Pilot dived and manœuvred for position under his tail; the L.V.G. seemed slightly slower than the Sopwith, but had better climb. The enemy opened fire at long range, but the Sopwith closed range and opened fire, shots appearing to enter the right side of enemy's fuselage. After eight rounds the Lewis gun jammed, due to faulty ammunition, and pilot was forced to abandon the fight.

NOTE.—Flight Sub-Lieut. Arnold J. Chadwick, who failed to return from the raid on the Zeppelin sheds near Brussels on October 2nd, succeeded in making good his escape from Belgium, and is now in England.

No. 3 WING.

October 23rd.

Two flights of Sopwith bombers and six Sopwith fighters carried out a raid on the ironworks and factories at Hagendingen, in conjunction with the French.

The operation was very successful, many bombs being seen to hit the objective.

Heavy anti-aircraft fire was experienced.

Flight Sub-Lieut. Smith with Air Mechanic Clegg attacked a captive balloon on the return journey.

HOME STATIONS.

Routine anti-submarine patrols and reconnaissances from all aeroplane, seaplane, and airship stations have taken place, and the usual work has been carried out by seaplane carriers in the North Sea when weather permitted.

The more interesting events are as follows :—

October 22nd.

A raid was made on Sheerness by a hostile aeroplane, four bombs being dropped on the dockyard without doing any damage, the machine making off in an easterly direction after dropping its bombs.

A second hostile machine (seaplane) was fired on by a torpedo boat and T.B.D. in the vicinity of the Tongue Lightship.

From reports received it would appear that this seaplane was the one brought down by Flight Lieut. Galbraith off Blankenberghe (see Dunkirk Reports).

Machines ascended from the following stations to attack these hostile machines:—Manston, Dover Seaplane Station, Dover Aerodrome, Eastchurch.

October 23rd.

A raid was made by a German aeroplane on Margate. Three bombs were dropped, but very little damage done. Machines ascended from Dover, Westgate, Manston, and Eastchurch, but did not encounter the enemy.

H.M.S. "Vindex."

October 22nd.

A special reconnaissance over the Heligoland Bight was carried out, in conjunction with a number of H.M. Ships, by Flight Commander H. F. Towler with Lieutenant Erskine Childers, R.N.V.R., and Flight Lieut. N. Halstead with Chief Petty Officer A. Blackwell, in Short seaplanes.

The operation was successful although somewhat hampered by fog, and valuable information was obtained.

Flight Commander Towler was chased by a Zeppelin and a Taube, but these quickly retired when fired on by the squadron.

EASTERN MEDITERRANEAN.
Report No. 30.

October 6th to 13th.

Spotting has been carried out as requisite for H.M. ships.

The usual patrols of the Dardanelles and anti-submarine patrols of other areas have been carried out by aeroplanes, seaplanes, and airships.

A considerable number of reconnaissances over the enemy's country have taken place.

Thasos.

Offensive and reconnaissance work has been carried out unremittingly by "A" flight throughout the week.

The following are the most interesting operations:—

October 10th.

A bombing attack was made on the railway stores at Musratli, which is an important supply depôt for the troops at Kavalla.

Two direct hits were obtained on the store buildings at Musratli, and three direct hits were made on the railway line at Burzanlar, about $\frac{1}{4}$ mile N.E. of Musratli Station.

No further details of this operation are yet to hand, but will be dealt with in the next issue.

October 11th.

It having been ascertained that the barracks at Pravi had been occupied by troops, a bombing attack was made, three direct hits being obtained.

The enemy air service in Southern Bulgaria has recently been reinforced, and is making serious endeavours to wrest from us the supremacy of the air, as the following operations show :—

October 8th.

An Aviatik and an Albatross Scout appeared on the aerodrome and dropped bombs from between 9,000 and 10,000 feet, immediately retiring, pursued by one of our scouts.

October 10th.

Two fast scouts again dropped bombs from a similar height over Thasos camp, causing slight material damage, and again retired, pursued by two scouts.

On neither occasion were the Thasos scouts able to overtake the enemy, owing to the fact that their machines have considerable speed, and the distance to their aerodrome is too short to allow our machines to overtake them while climbing.

October 11th.

A single-seater dropped bombs on the anti-aircraft guns to the east of the aerodrome and retired.

October 12th.

In order to ascertain the strength of the enemy a raid was carried out on Maswakli Aerodrome, the attacking flight being composed of one H. Farman, one Nieuport two-seater, and two escorting scouts. A seaplane was told off to patrol the Bulgarian coast to render assistance to any machine which might be compelled to come down in the sea.

Two big scouts and a large fast Aviatik were engaged over the aerodrome.

Only signalled reports of the action are available at present, but the pilots who returned report that Flight Sub-Lieut. B. A. Millard, who failed to return, was last seen attacking an Albatross Scout. A subsequent search located his machine, apparently undamaged, in a field to the north of Karageuzli.

It seems probable that either the pilot was wounded or his machine hit in the engine.

On the chance of Lieutenant Millard being able to make his way to the coast a monitor was detailed by the S.N.O. to watch the coast during the afternoon and succeeding night.

On the following day an enemy machine dropped a message at Thasos stating that the missing pilot is a prisoner of war and well.

All other machines returned safely from this operation, but no reports of the damage inflicted on the enemy have yet been received.

NOTE.—Details are now to hand of the raid carried out at the request of the 80th Brigade on Angista station and stores on October 5th. The attack was carried out by three machines, which, for the first time in this particular place, were fired on by anti-aircraft guns, the shooting being fairly accurate.

The first machine (pilot Flight Lieut. Bush, observer C.P.O. Marchant) dropped one 65-lb. bomb and two 100-lb. bombs from a height of 7,000 feet, all of which fell close to the waggons parked to the west of the station. The second machine (pilot Flight Sub-Lieut. Whetnall, observer Second Lieutenant H. E. Tansley, R.F.C.) dropped one 100-lb. and two 112-lb. bombs on the stores scattered around the station, all of which hit the target, and demolished a building at the western end of the station compound. The third machine (pilot Flight Lieut. Harden, observer Lieutenant Sassoon) dropped two 65-lb. bombs between the station and an isolated house to the south of the station, which appears to have been used as a store warehouse. Two photographs were taken of the station under bombardment by Lieutenant Sassoon. Mules were observed stampeding about the buildings during the attack. The escorting machine was piloted by Flight Commander H. Stanley Adams.

Stavros.

" D " flight continues to operate with the ships and the army on the Lower Struma sector, carrying out reconnaissance and spotting flights daily, and bombing attacks whenever suitable targets are located.

Much valuable information has been obtained.

October 6th.

A reconnaissance and bomb-dropping flight was made over the Proviata-Totolivo-Pravi-Orfano area. Two bombs were dropped on a train under way one mile east of Angista Station, both bombs being observed to burst alongside the train.

On the same day M. 18 was successfully spotted on to a battery 100 yards S. of Dranli.

October 9th.

Bombs were dropped on the Struma trenches and on Dedevalli village, which is used as a military depôt.

October 10th.

A number of spotting flights were made, and reconnaissances and bomb-dropping flights carried out over the Angista area, where direct hits were made on horse lines.

October 11th.

A bombing attack was made on the important military depôt at Razolivos.

October 12th.

A photographic reconnaissance was carried out over the Pravi and Angista regions, bombs being dropped on a party of troops near Proviata.

H.M.S. "Empress."

October 7th.

H.M.S. "Empress" returned from Mudros to Stavros, where she continues to operate with H.M. ships.

October 8th.

A reconnaissance and bomb-dropping flight was carried out over Orfano. New trenches were located and bombs dropped on them, direct hits being made.

October 11th.

Three bombing flights were carried out on Orfano, where a camp had been located from the air three days previously, and two direct hits were made.

Details of these operations and names of pilots will be given in the next issue.

OPERATIONS IN TURKEY.

Thermi Air Station.

October 6th.

A monitor was spotted by "B" flight on to the 6-in. gun emplacements on hill 440 to the E. of Tuz Burnu. Two direct hits were made and photographs of these defences obtained.

October 12th.

A hostile machine was sighted from the aerodrome and a Bristol Scout was sent in pursuit. The enemy was overtaken and attacked by Lewis gun-fire over the Gulf of Chandarli, being forced to make a landing on the Ali Agha plateau, which is probably being used now as an advance base for the machines operating from Chikli and Kasamir aerodromes.

Imbros.

The Dardanelles have been patrolled by "C" flight, scouts and bombing machines being sent on several occasions to bomb hostile shipping which had been reported, but without success.

October 5th.

A hostile machine was sighted and chased at Chanak. It avoided action by diving and was seen to land and apparently turn over in the aerodrome to the south of Chanak.

Details have now been received of the spotting flight carried out at Dedeagatch on this date, briefly reported in the last issue.

The first machine, Flight Lieut. Jacobs with Lieut. A. R. C. Douton, R.N.R., left Imbros at 8.0 a.m. for the 50-mile oversea journey. They reached Dedeagatch at 9.45 and proceeded to spot H.M.S. "Abercrombie" on to Bodoma junction. Several direct hits were made on the water towers and on the permanent way, which was ripped up. Severe engine troubles had been experienced on the outward journey, and after half-an-hour's spotting it was found necessary to return to Imbros.

The second machine, Flight Sub-Lieut. Marlowe with Paymaster A. Ewing, R.N., acted as "stand-by" for the spotting machine, and while over Dedeagatch dropped two bombs from 2,500 feet, both of which made direct hits on the barracks.

Mudros.

H.M.S. "Ark Royal" has, for the time, stopped other repair and erecting work in order to assist in the equipment of the Roumanian flight, and has landed special parties for the erection of machines at the repair base, and for the building of another Bessoneau to contain the machines.

Mudros Airship Station.

Daily patrols of the entrance to Mudros Harbour have been carried out by S.S. 8.

Kassandra Airship Station.

The usual patrol of the entrance to the Gulf of Salonika has been carried out daily by S.S. 7.

EAST INDIES STATION.

Egypt Seaplane Squadron.

No further reports have been received since the last issue.

CAPE STATION.

No further reports have been received since the last issue.

REPORT OF OPERATIONS No. 21.

DUNKIRK.

During this period the usual routine patrols and reconnaissances have been maintained when weather permitted.

The following are the more interesting events :—

November 6th.

Flight Lieut. R. S. Dallas, D.S.C., in a Sopwith triplane No. N500, when at 14,000 feet, encountered three enemy two-seater aeroplanes over Westende. All three were circling together, as though they were practising tactics. Flight Lieut. Dallas succeeded in approaching unnoticed by banking and rolling his machine in a similar manner, and when close behind one of the enemy machines he fired 40 rounds. His Vickers gun then gave trouble and pilot was forced to abandon the fight. He was then attacked by all three machines and was obliged to take cover in a patch of cloud. On emerging he found himself within a few yards of another enemy machine, narrowly avoiding a collision. A few minutes later pilot sighted all three of the enemy machines several thousand feet lower down retreating towards Ostende.

November 10th.

Twenty-four machines carried out two attacks upon the Atelier de la Marine Works, Ostende, and on the T.B.D.'s. in the harbour and also on the seaplane shed on Zeebrugge Mole.

A good deal of anti-aircraft fire was experienced, but none of the machines were hit.

Bombs were dropped from heights varying from 800 to 5,000 feet.

The following bombs were dropped during the raids: one 500-lb.; 75 Le Pecq bombs; 57—65-lb.; 38—16-lb.

Although it was difficult to observe the results of the operations, it is believed that very considerable damage was done by the two raids.

Flight Lieut. Hodge in a Short Bomber Seaplane No. 8016 failed to return and is reported as a prisoner of war.

November 12th.

Fifteen machines (Nieuport and Sopwith Scouts), escorted by a fighter squadron, carried out a raid on Ostende Docks.

Ten machines succeeded in reaching the objective and dropped their bombs, but the visibility was so bad that pilots could only with great difficulty make out the objectives, and practically no results could be observed, except in one case, when pilot dropped his bombs from a very low altitude and observed them fall at the corner of the Atelier de la Marine.

44-16-lb. and 36 Le Pecq bombs were dropped.

The pilots all returned safely eventually, but owing to the very thick mist had some difficulty in reaching the aerodrome, two being subjected to very heavy anti-aircraft fire, one over Westende and the other over the Nieuport trenches.

Another pilot landed on the water near Calais and was rescued by a French trawler, his machine being towed back in a practically undamaged condition.

One of the escorting machines observed a hostile machine and chased it through the fog to Calais. Owing to engine trouble pilot was obliged to land on the water but was rescued by a French patrol boat.

No. 3 WING.

October 23rd.

Referring to the raid carried out on this date on the works at Essingen and Hagendingen, the damage appears to have been considerable.

According to reports received, only two factory chimneys were left intact after the last bombs had been dropped. Therefore, although it is possible that part of the factories may be in working order, the majority of the works will be out of action for some considerable time.

November 11th.

A raid was carried out on Volklingen Iron Foundry works and blast furnaces by nine Sopwith bombers and eight fighting machines, 35-65-lb. bombs being dropped. Six hostile machines were engaged, three being brought down.

All machines returned safely, one observer being slightly injured.

Many bombs were seen to explode; full details of the operation will be furnished in the next issue.

November 12th.

A raid was carried out on the iron foundries and blast furnaces at St. Ingbert by nine Sopwith bombarding machines and seven fighting machines, 36-65-lb. bombs being dropped.

Sub-Lieut. Wilson failed to return, but he is believed to have landed in friendly territory.

Further details of this raid will be furnished in the next issue.

HOME STATIONS.

The usual number of routine anti-submarine patrols and reconnaissances from all aeroplane, seaplane, and airship stations have taken place when weather permitted, and the usual work has been carried out over the North Sea.

The following are the more interesting events :—

November 11th.

Calshot.

Flight Sub-Lieut. Pierce, in Seaplane 3639, while on patrol, sighted an enemy submarine steering westerly, 40 miles off Culvers, at 9 a.m. The submarine dived before the seaplane could get into a position to drop its bombs, but two were dropped in the position where the submarine submerged, but with no apparent effect.

Polegate.

S.S. 16 escorted the British passenger vessel "Osterley" for a distance of 130 miles, the flight lasting 4 hours 35 minutes.

November 13th.

Yarmouth.

A special wireless reconnaissance patrol was carried out to Smith's Knoll, Jim How, and Elbow Buoy to investigate gun fire heard N.E. A shipwrecked smack's crew was observed near Smith's Knoll, and three mine-sweepers in the vicinity were informed.

EASTERN MEDITERRANEAN.
Reports Nos. 31 and 32.

October 13th to 27th.

The usual patrols of the Dardanelles and anti-submarine patrols of other areas have been carried out by aeroplanes, seaplanes, and airships, whenever possible.

Spotting has been carried out as requisite for H.M. ships.

The following are the more interesting events :—

Thasos.

The following details have now been received of the operation carried out on the 10th/11th October, which was briefly reported on in the last issue :—

October 10th.

The attack on the transport at Parzalar was made by Flight Lieut. E. P. Hardman with 2nd Lieut. H. E. Tansley, R.F.C., as observer. Five 16-lb. bombs were dropped, all of which exploded among the store warehouses and transport waggons at the N. and N.W. side of the village.

A second machine; pilot Flight Sub-Lieut. Shoppee, with A. M. Howes as observer, attacked the railway line near Musratli with one 100-lb. and two 112-lb. bombs, two of which burst on the permanent way at a point $2\frac{1}{2}$ miles S.W. of Musratli.

The escorting machine was piloted by Flight Sub-Lieut. Magor.

October 11th.

An attack was made on Pravi barracks by Flight Sub-Lieut. Barrington with Lieut. E. Sassoon as observer.

Eight 16-lb. bombs were dropped, all of which fell in the barracks compound close to the buildings.

The escorting machine was piloted by Flight Sub-Lieut. Whetnall.

October 13th.

An enemy machine dropped a message bag containing a letter from Flight Sub-Lieut. Millard giving some further details of his action.

He attacked an Aviatik and succeeded in wounding the observer in the leg. The Nieuport Scout's engine, which had previously "cut out," then stopped entirely, and pilot was obliged to land in a field about four miles S.W. of Maswakli.

He started to effect the necessary repairs and had completed one half when he was captured. The engine trouble was not due to enemy fire, only one bullet having hit the cowl.

The letter stated that Flight Sub-Lieut. Millard was in good health and being well treated, and was to be sent inland on the succeeding day.

N.B.—Flight Sub-Lieut. Millard was reported missing on the 12th October, after the raid on Maswakli aerodrome.

October 15th.

An attack was made on the large and important railway bridge at Buk.

Three H. Farmans escorted by two Bristol Scouts took part in the attack, particularly good shooting being made by Flight Sub-Lieut. B. C. Shoppee with 2nd Lieut. Tansley, 4th K.R.R., who attacked the bridge from 1,200 feet under heavy rifle fire and dropped two 100-lb. bombs, two of which fell within 15 yards of the bridge, while the third fell directly on the permanent way of the second span of the bridge. Two photographs were taken of the bombs bursting.

October 16th.

A reconnaissance and bomb-dropping flight was carried out over the Kavalla-Drama area. Four bombs were dropped on Drama station, where a large transport park is established and where stores are assembled for distribution.

October 18th and 19th.

Anti-submarine patrols have been carried out over Thasos Strait and a further raid was also made on Maswakli aerodrome. The results of this attack are not yet known.

October 23rd.

A reconnaissance flight was carried out over the Buk area and it was discovered that the second span of the bridge was completely demolished and lying in the river, and the piers were badly damaged. Trains were observed on either side of the bridge and about 50 waggons were engaged in transporting stores from one train to another across the new foot bridge. Three 112-lb. bombs were dropped at these trains, which fell close enough to do considerable damage, although no direct hit was obtained.

During the afternoon of the same day Flight Sub-Lieut. G. K. Blandy with Lieut. R. G. Blakesley, R.N.V.R., as observer, in a Nieuport No. 8913, proceeded on a reconnaissance towards Buk with the object of harassing the railway traffic between Buk and Drama. The machine failed to return and a search was carried out by seaplane and aeroplanes during the evening and on the following day, but without success. Information was received later by means of an intercepted enemy Press message, that the machine had been shot down in the neighbourhood of Drama after an air battle lasting half-an-hour. On 25th October a message was dropped by a hostile machine stating that both pilot and observer had been made prisoners, the former being wounded in the leg, but doing well.

October 24th.

Bombs were dropped on the rolling stock at Drama railway station with considerable success.

October 24th and 25th.

Attacks were made upon an important objective on the Xanthi-Drama railway, viz., the small railway bridge at Yeni Keui (12 miles S.E. of Buk), which crosses a tributary of the Nestos about $\frac{1}{4}$ mile from the village. The damage caused is not known, but many casualties are reported, presumably amongst working parties.

Further details of these operations will be furnished in the next issue.

Stavros Air Station.

Offensive and reconnaissance work has been carried out by this flight throughout this period. Important photographs of enemy defence works have been obtained and successful spotting flights for H.M. ships and the Army have been carried out.

October 13th.

Two bombs were dropped on the transport at Angista.

October 15th.

An attack was made on Razolivos.

October 18th.

During a reconnaissance of the Pravi-Drama area bombs were dropped on transport proceeding along the road.

October 19th.

A bombing attack was delivered on Provista, two direct hits being made.

October 24th.

A bombing attack was delivered against a camp at Vitasta (S.E. of Angista Station), and bombs were also dropped on Tafel Kop, Hill 112, where trenches and observation post had been previously located from the air.

October 26th.

Spotting and photographic flights were carried out and bombs were dropped at Porna, Fotolovo, and Demirli, where a direct hit was made on a large store camp.

Details of operations and names of pilots will be furnished in the next issue.

H.M.S. " Empress."

" Empress " continues to co-operate with H.M. ships, supporting the British right flank and carrying out reconnaissance and spotting flights daily.

October 13th and 14th.

New guns were located by a reconnaissance and bombs were dropped on the fortified position, Tuzla Farm, at the mouth of the Struma.

October 15th.

Further new guns were located on to which one of H.M. ships was successfully spotted, direct hits being obtained, followed by large explosions.

October 18th.

During a reconnaissance over Orfano a detachment of cavalry was attacked with bombs and Lewis guns.

October 19th.

Three successful bombing flights were made in the Orfano region, bombs being dropped on Orfano itself and on the wood to the north-west of the village, in which stores and ammunition were thought to be concealed, and on the trenches and machine-gun positions outside the village, the latter being also attacked with Lewis gun fire.

Details and names of pilots in connection with this operation will be included in the next issue.

October 22nd/23rd.

A successful bombing attack was carried out on trenches and gun pits between Orfano and the seashore which had been previously located.

OPERATIONS IN TURKEY.

Thermi.

October 17th.

Bombs were dropped at the emplacements A.C. on Hill 440.

October 20th.

Submarine patrol was carried out, but was unable to find any trace of the enemy submarine reported in Mityleni Channel.

Imbros.

October 13th.

Bombs were dropped on the shipping at Chanak.

October 24th.

Pamphlets illustrative of the Allied advance on the Western front and of the Zeppelins brought down in recent raids, and other pamphlets indicating the German schemes for undermining the Mohammedan religion in Africa, were dropped in various villages on the Asiatic side of the Straits.

Mudros Airship Station.

While Airship S.S. 8 was carrying out a patrol of the swept channel to Mudros Harbour at 500 feet, an attack was made one mile south of Cape Irene by a hostile seaplane. Three bombs were dropped, the first two from 4,000 feet above the airship and the third from a lesser altitude. All the bombs hit the water astern of the airship, and the seaplane, on being fired at by trawlers, retired in an easterly direction. A Schneider Cup and Nieuport Fighter were sent in pursuit from Mudros, and machines from Imbros endeavoured to cut off the enemy from its base, but, owing to the thick haze, no trace was seen of it.

It is now advisable to escort the airship when doing her morning patrol, and for this a Schneider Cup machine is used when available. To avoid unnecessary wear to seaplanes the airship is not sent out unless the conditions for observing under water are good or there is some definite and important objective for her.

Kassandra Air Station.

The usual patrol of the entrance to the Gulf of Salonica has been carried out by S.S. 17, over 50 hours' flying being done between 13—20th October.

October 15th.

During the patrol six mines were located. These have been swept by trawlers, together with three others, all apparently having been laid recently.

The airship was deflated on 25th October owing to defects in the ballonet, and a new envelope is being sent from Mudros.

ROUMANIAN FLIGHT.

On 24th October preparations for the Roumanian Flight were completed, and a start was made from Imbros on 25th under the supervision of the Wing Captain. The following pilots were chosen for the expedition, under the command of Flight Commander H. Stanley Adams, in a Nieuport Scout, No. 3978 :—

Flight Lieut. L. A. Hervey, H. Farman, No. 3008.
   ,,   ,,   A. F. F. Jacob, Nieuport Fighter, No. 8525.
   ,,   ,,   G. A. Cox, Nieuport Fighter, No. 8524.
   ,,   ,,   R. Y. Bush, H. Farman, No. 3007.
   ,,   Sub-Lieut. H. V. Reid, Nieuport Fighter, No. 8514.

Flight Lieut. Bush failed to make a start owing to engine trouble, and Flight Lieut. Jacob landed in Russia.

The other pilots all completed the journey of 310 miles without mishap and arrived safely at Bucharest.

EAST INDIES STATION.

Egypt Seaplane Squadron.

No reports have been received during this period.

CAPE STATION.

Aeroplanes (East African Force)..

1st July to 9th September.

Over 13,000 miles have been flown in the enemy's country.

The height flown seldom exceeded 3,000 feet, and on occasions the aeroplanes descended to 300 feet to drop their bombs.

Flights of over three hours' duration have been carried out during adverse climatic conditions and over country which offers no possibility of making a safe landing, frequently through gorges enfiladed by machine-gun fire and flanked by high mountains.

Voisin aeroplanes have done excellent service. They have been without shelter since the beginning of June and since then have flown 6,500 miles.

Captured prisoners state that the presence of aeroplanes and dropping of bombs completely demoralises the German Askaris,

Seaplanes (Zanzibar).

21st August to 22nd September.

Flight Lieut. MacLean and Sub-Lieut. Fitzherbert in Short Seaplane No. 3096 carried out in the neighbourhood of Dar-es-salaam and the Rufiji Delta a series of photographic, reconnaissance, and bomb-dropping flights during this period.

Many successful exposures were made, and gun positions, trenches, and camps located, which were afterwards bombed.

REPORT OF OPERATIONS No. 22.

DUNKIRK.

During this period the usual patrols and reconnaissances have been maintained when weather permitted.

The following are the more interesting events :—

November 16th.

Ten indecisive encounters with German aeroplanes took place and three sharp seaplane engagements.

A report having been received that Flight Sub-Lieut. Graham had been wrecked, patrols were sent out, and his machine was observed upside down, the bottom of floats showing above water and the pilot sitting on the floats.

Flight Sub-Lieut. Woolner with Sub-Lieut. Hodson eventually succeeded in reaching the wreck, and although the sea was rough managed to pick up the pilot after he had been forced to swim for about 100 yards. Unfortunately the seaplane was unable to leave the water carrying the pilot and two passengers, but succeeded in taxying in a north-westerly direction, being eventually towed into Dunkirk by a French torpedo boat destroyer. A perpetual fighter patrol was kept up over the wrecked seaplane, an encounter taking place between an R.N.A.S. machine and two enemy seaplanes, both being successfully driven off towards Ostende. It is thought that one of these machines was badly hit.

November 18th.

(a) A bombing attack was carried out in the early hours of the morning on the Atelier de la Marine and Slyken's Electric Power Station, Ostende, and on the seaplane base on Zeebrugge Mole.

The following bombs were dropped :—

    81—" Le Pecq " bombs.
    24—100-lb. bombs.
    27—65-lb. ,,
    48—16-lb. ,,

All pilots returned safely, and only one machine was hit, which was obliged to make a forced landing on the west side of Nieuport owing to a punctured petrol tank.

On the approach of the bombing squadron to Ostende two torpedo boat destroyers were observed just outside the harbour, which opened fire with anti-aircraft guns. One of the pilots straddled these vessels with four bombs and firing immediately ceased. Pilot was unable to see whether the torpedo boat destroyers were actually hit or not.

Bombs were observed to fall in the middle of the Atelier de la Marine and one of the last pilots saw the explosions from his bombs, the flashes of which shone through the broken windows and holes in the roof. Although no direct hit was observed on the Power House, bombs were seen to fall in very close proximity and the lights were extinguished. Bombs were also observed to explode on the railway sidings and warehouses situated between the Bassin au Bois and the inner harbour.

Anti-aircraft fire was very heavy and more accurate than on previous raids. The searchlights also picked up some of the machines, but were unable to hold them very long.

The seaplane base at Zeebrugge Mole was straddled by nine bombs and pilot is of opinion that they hit their mark, but was unable to observe definite results.

(b) A large German seaplane was observed to come under very heavy fire from French anti-aircraft batteries over Nieuport. Seaplane glided down to the sea off Ostende and taxied very slowly into harbour. It is thought that this machine was shot down.

(c) A squadron of hostile machines bombed one of our aerodromes. There were no casualties and no damage of military importance was caused.

November 21st.

One enemy machine dropped bombs on Dunkirk, but no military damage was done.

November 25th.

Nieuport Scouts Nos. 3989 and 8748 engaged a hostile aeroplane over Mariakerke, diving on to it from 13,000 feet. One tray was fired, upon which the enemy retreated towards Ostende.

November 27th.

Two hostile machines were chased, one of which was brought to action, eight rounds being fired, when the gun jammed and fight had to be abandoned.

Another enemy machine was attacked near Middlekerke, but owing to superior speed of the hostile machine pilot was unable to approach nearer than 500 yards. Five trays of ammunition were fired, but chase had to be abandoned.

A bombing raid was attempted on Zeebrugge by four bombing machines escorted by four fighters. Machines encountered low clouds and thick fog. Two out of the four machines succeeded in reaching the objective, but the results could not be observed. All machines returned safely.

Flight Sub-Lieut. N. W. Frame of "A" squadron was accidentally killed during the day while landing in a fog.

HOME STATIONS.

The usual number of routine anti-submarine patrols and reconnaissances from all aeroplane, seaplane, and airship stations have taken place, and the usual work has been carried out over the North Sea.

The following are the more interesting events :—

Calshot.
November 28th.

Flight Sub-Lieut. Fox, with A. M. Redman as observer, in a 225-h.p. Short seaplane, while on patrol from Portland, sighted an enemy submarine and attacked it with two 65-lb. bombs.

November 27th/28th.

(a) A raid took place on the north-east coast, in which nine hostile airships were engaged.

R.N.A.S. machines went up from Burgh Castle, Yarmouth, Redcar, Scarborough, and Cranwell.

The following is an extract from a report from Commodore, Lowestoft, giving a detailed account of the Zeppelin destroyed on the 28th instant by R.N.A.S. pilots :—

At 5.7 a.m. a report was received that a Zeppelin was over Swaffham at 4.40 a.m. and at Dereham at 5.3 a.m.

On receipt of this information I ordered two aeroplanes (one from Bacton and one from Holt) to ascend in the hope of intercepting her before she got over the coast line.

At 6.5 a.m. Yarmouth reported : " Zeppelin overhead."

Aeroplanes were immediately despatched from Burgh Castle and Yarmouth, and as, by this time, dawn was breaking, they could clearly follow the course of the Zeppelin, which was then steering S.S.E. from Yarmouth.

Flight Lieut. Egbert Cadbury and Flight Sub-Lieut. Gerrard William Reginald Fane, from Burgh Castle, proceeded immediately after her, and Flight Sub-Lieut. Edward Laston Pulling (who had ascended at 5.0 a.m. from Bacton night landing ground), attracted by the sound of firing from the anti-aircraft guns at Great Yarmouth, proceeded south at full speed.

At 6.35 a.m., the Zeppelin then being about 9 miles E.S.E. from Lowestoft naval base, Flight Lieut. Cadbury and Flight Sub-Lieut. Fane had overtaken her. The former got under her at about 700 feet distance, and fired his Lewis gun into the after part of her, being at the time under heavy fire from the Zeppelin. The first tray not having the desired effect of setting fire to her, he changed trays and repeated the evolution, still with the same result. This evolution he performed altogether *four times,* until his ammunition was exhausted.

The Zeppelin at this time was proceeding at an estimated speed of 55 miles an hour, to which she had increased the moment Flight Lieut. Cadbury opened fire on her; previously she had been proceeding at about 30 knots.

On perceiving that Flight Lieut. Cadbury had exhausted his ammunition and that the Zeppelin was still apparently intact, Flight Sub-Lieut. Fane then approached to within *100 feet* of the starboard side of the Zeppelin and tried to open fire, but his Lewis gun jammed, probably owing to the intense cold and the oil having frozen.

Flight Sub-Lieut. Pulling, who had witnessed the two previous officers' attack, then approached. He advanced to within *60 feet* of the Zeppelin. The Zeppelin, by this time endeavouring to rise rapidly, had assumed an angle of about 45 degrees to the vertical. Flight Sub-Lieut. Pulling opened fire within 50 feet of her, being under a continuous fire from the Zeppelin's machine guns that would bear.

After about 10 rounds had been fired from his Lewis gun the Zeppelin caught fire, and within a few seconds was nothing but a fiery furnace. Flight Sub-Lieut. Pulling immediately dived to starboard to avoid the falling debris, and it is noteworthy that the crew of the Zeppelin continued to fire at him for some appreciable time after she was ablaze.

She then fell stern foremost into the sea, where she was engulfed and entirely sunk, leaving a large area of oil-covered water.

The height at which these officers attacked the Zeppelin was 8,200 feet, and, from my own personal observation from the pier, I estimate that it took about a minute from the time of her ignition to the time that she struck the water.

(*b*) On the same day a hostile aeroplane visited London about 11 a.m. and dropped six bombs, doing no military damage.

This machine landed near Boulogne owing to engine trouble, the occupants being made prisoners, a large-scale map of London, which was in the machine, being secured.

November 30th.

Flight Sub-Lieut. Ross, with Air Mechanic Redman as observer, in seaplane 8379, while on patrol, sighted an oil track, presumably a submarine, which he followed, and, after endeavouring to warn a Norwegian steamer, suddenly saw the submarine about three miles astern. He immediately turned and headed for the submarine, and when over it dropped a 65-lb. bomb, which fell about 100 feet short, the submarine at the time being almost completely submerged.

Unfortunately, on rising from the water after having landed to warn another ship, the machine stalled and side-slipped and was completely wrecked. Pilot and observer were picked up by one of H.M. ships.

No. 3 WING.

October 12th and 23rd.

With reference to the two raids on these dates on Oberndorf and Hagendingen, briefly reported in last issue, the following information has been received :—

The majority of bombs in the former raid appear to have fallen on new factories which were not in actual working order. Damage to buildings was considerable, but, owing to the machinery and personnel not being there, this objective got off very lightly.

With regard to the latter raid, the results are more satisfactory. Three out of the five blast furnaces were partly destroyed.

Referring to the raid carried out on Volkingen on November 10th, previously reported, it would appear that a further raid was carried out by the French on the same objective on the night of the 10th, and during the afternoon of the 11th a further attack was made by the R.N.A.S. on the same target with 14 bombing machines, accompanied by seven fighters. During this raid a number of enemy machines were engaged, two of which were driven down, but it is impossible to say whether they were damaged or dived to avoid further combat. Visibility was very bad indeed, so that it is impossible to say what damage was caused.

All machines returned safely. Flight Sub-Lieut. Harrower was obliged to land at Dijon, and was at first reported missing.

EASTERN MEDITERRANEAN.
Reports Nos. 33 and 34.

October 28th—November 9th.

The usual number of routine anti-submarine patrols and patrols of the Dardanelles have been carried out by aeroplanes, seaplanes, and airships whenever possible.

Spotting has been carried out as requisite for H.M. ships.

Roumanian Flight.

A few further particulars have been obtained from intercepted Press messages of the flight to Roumania on the 25th October.

Difficulties were experienced by apparently all the pilots owing to thunderstorms and thick mists.

Flight Lieut. Jacob experienced some slight engine defect and landed on Bulgarian territory to repair it. The ground which he selected to land on was found to be close to a Bulgarian camp, and pilot was only just able to effect repairs, restart his engine and get away without being captured.

After crossing the Danube he ran into rain and fog, completely losing his bearings, and ultimately coming down well into Russian territory, whence he returned to Bucharest by train.

Flight Lieut. Bush still remains at Imbros awaiting favourable weather to make the journey.

Thasos.

Bomb attacks for the purpose of rendering the Xanthi-Drama railway useless to the enemy for the supply of the Struma front have been continued by "A" flight.

After the destruction of the Buk bridge a reconnaissance disclosed the fact that the enemy was running trains from Xanthi and from Drama as far as the bridge head on either side of the river, and there transferring the stores from one train to another by means of the small trestled bridge and about 50 waggons. Accordingly, in order to make the railway useless as a means of transport it was necessary to block it or cut it again at two points on either side of Buk, between which road transport of heavy material could not easily be effected, and as far apart as possible, in order to segregate rolling stock which might be on the line.

The first point chosen for the attack was one between Buk and Xanthi, namely, the railway bridge at Yeni Keui, 12 miles S.E. of Buk, which crosses a tributary of the Nestos about ¼ mile N. of the village.

October 24th.

Flight Sub-Lieut. Shoppee with 2nd Lieut. Tansley, 4th K.R.R., proceeded to Yeni Keui in a H. Farman, and attacked from 1,000 feet with three 100-lb. bombs, one of which fell near a group of soldiers who were firing at the machine with rifles, killing all but one, while another fell on the right bank of the dry river bed in line with the northern end of the bridge and about 10 yards east of it.

The bridge is of stone resting on iron supports, and it is probable that this bomb has damaged the foundations of the stone work and strained the plate rivets sufficiently to prevent its being used for heavy traffic until repaired.

On the following day a further attack was made by two escorted machines. One 65-lb. bomb was dropped on the railway embankment about 10 miles south of the southern end of the bridge, damaging the permanent way.

Photographs of the bridge under bombardment were obtained on both days.

October 30th.

The railway was again attacked, the point selected being the bridge over a small river at Shimshirli, about half way between Buk and Drama. Two machines, with escorts, participated in the attack, particularly good shooting again being made by Flight Sub-Lieut. B. C. Shoppee with Second Lieut. R. E. Tansley, who approached the bridge at 1,000 feet under rifle fire and dropped three 112-lb. bombs. The first made a direct hit, falling on the third span from the Buk end and tearing a large hole in the permanent way. The second fell on or near the line about 16 yards west of the bridge, and the third near the line about 25 yards west of the second. After dropping the bombs machine-gun fire was directed on to the bridge guard, who were firing at the second machine, causing them to take cover while the second machine dropped her bombs. Photographs of the bridge were taken by the same observer.

According to later information it would appear that the two centre spans on the bridge have fallen into the river, and it seems probable that a train of nine carriages fell with it.

The attack on the rolling stock at Drama Station on 24th October, briefly reported in the previous issue, was made by Flight Sub-Lieut. Barrington with Lieutenant E. Sassoon as observer. There were about 50 trucks in the station at the time, and two 112- and one 65-lb. bombs were dropped, all of which fell close to the line just east of the station. Owing to a thin layer of transparent cloud the extent of the damage was not ascertained.

November 3rd.

Three H. Farman machines. with escorts, delivered an attack on Hill 122 or Tafel Kop, an advanced post on the Bulgarian line on the lower Struma front. The whole of this area is a network of trenches, emplacements, and dug-outs, and these were well plied with bombs, good shooting being made from all three machines, in spite of unfavourable atmospheric conditions.

November 4th.

A reconnaissance of the Nestos and Drama-Kavalla areas was carried out, and it was observed that the section of the line between Buk and Drama had been rendered useless since the bomb attack on the Shimshirli Bridge on the 30th October.

November 6th.

A bomb attack was carried out by two machines on Angista railway bridge, but owing to low clouds one of these lost her way and failed to find the objective, and, therefore, in accordance with previous orders, returned to Kavalla, making a reconnaissance of Fort B, where, that morning, monitor 18 had reported many new works and emplacements. Photographs were taken of these, and new works were bombed.

November 8th.

A bombing attack was delivered against Fort B, at Kavalla, about 2 miles from the town, where a considerable amount of defences had been previously seen.

Stavros (D. Flight).

Spotting flights were carried out by this flight for H.M. ships and for land batteries on most days.

October 29th–31st.

A reconnaissance of the Lower Struma lines was made, and pamphlets and proclamations were dropped on the villages and trenches.

November 1st and 2nd.

A further reconnaissance of the same area was made, and bombs were dropped on Lakovikia. A photographic reconnaissance was also carried out.

November 3rd.

A photographic flight was made over the Struma lines, and four bombs were dropped on enemy bivouacs.

November 4th.

Two reconnaissance flights were carried out in addition to spotting and photographic flights.

November 5th.

A reconnaissance was made of the Angista area. Bombs were dropped on the stores and defences previously located by aircraft from Stavros and Thasos.

November 6th.

A bomb attack was carried out on a camp near Serret.

November 8th.

Bombs were dropped on Porna, a supply depôt of some importance, and the last station to which trains are run by the enemy westwards of Drama.

Note.—The successful reconnaissance and bomb-dropping flight carried out over the Angista area on the 26th October, briefly reported in the previous issue, was made by Flight Lieut. Wood, with Lieutenant G. P. Morris as observer. Much useful information about enemy movements was obtained, and four bombs were dropped from 3,000 feet on a large store dump at Fotolivo.

H.M.S. "Empress."

A number of spotting and reconnaissance flights have been made by pilots from this ship. The following are of interest :—

October 29th.

Bombs were dropped on a new trench east of Tuzla Farm and also on Lakovikla.

November 2nd.

A reconnaissance flight was carried out over the area to the east of Orfano, bombs being dropped on Boblen.

November 3rd–5th.

Successful spotting flights were carried out for monitors.

November 6th

Bombs were dropped on trenches round Hill 154, north-west of Orfano, and a monitor was afterwards spotted on to the horse lines which had been located during the morning reconnaissance. The horses were also attacked with Lewis gunfire from the spotting machine.

Note.—A great deal of valuable information has been obtained recently by " Empress " seaplanes.

Referring to the reconnaissance flight made on October 18th by Flight Sub-Lieut. Malet with Sub-Lieut. Holcombe, R.N.V.R., as observer, 200 enemy cavalry were seen under the trees between Orfano wood and village. Incendiary bombs were dropped on the wood, and the cavalry took refuge in a ravine. This was immediately reported to H.M. ships and the ravine was shelled.

OPERATIONS IN TURKEY.

Thermi Air Station (" B " Flight).

October 28th.

A hostile machine flew over Poer Iero and dropped two bombs at the shipping. It was pursued by one of our machines as far as the Menemem plain, but could not be overtaken.

October 30th.

Spotting flight was carried out and also a reconnaissance of the shipping in Aivalik Harbour. Pamphlets in Turkish, illustrative of the German reverses on the western front and indicating their schemes for undermining the Mohammedan religion in Africa, were dropped on the town and surrounding villages.

November 4th.

A reconnaissance was carried out over the Gulf of Chandarli. Several new emplacements and trenches were located and bombs were dropped on occupied emplacements.

November 6th.

While carrying out a spotting flight over Cape Chemali, the spotting machine (H. Farman) was attacked by a Fokker and forced to land in the sea. Both pilot and observer were unhurt, but the machine was lost.

On the same day two other machines were damaged on landing, the pilots and observers being unhurt.

November 7th.

M. 22 was spotted on to four new gun emplacements which have been constructed at Cape Paramesa, Chesme. Two direct hits were made on the western emplacements.

Imbros ("C" Flight).

The usual patrols of the Dardanelles have been carried out by this flight. Nothing of importance has been observed except a steamer of about 1,000 tons at Chanak on 28th October and one of 1,500 tons on November 7th.

Flight Lieut. Bush, with H. Farman aeroplane, has been unable to start for Bucharest owing to bad weather.

Mudros Airship Station.

A Schneider seaplane has accompanied the airship during the patrol of the swept channel at the entrance to Mudros Harbour.

Kassandra.

During the patrol of 23rd October two submerged objects were seen and reported to S.N.O., Salonica, as probable mines. These proved to be enemy mines and have since been destroyed by trawlers.

The crew of the airship was the same as located the minefield on 15th October, viz., pilot Flight Lieut. T. P. Y. Moore, with Temporary Warrant Telegraphist J. R. Bamford.

EAST INDIES STATION.

H.M.S. "Ben-my-Chree."

"Ben-my-Chree" left Port Said on November 2nd to proceed to an agreed rendezvous at Adalia, arriving the next day.

Two flights were immediately carried out with a view to locating enemy guns which had recently fired on the French destroyer "Dard." Elaborate entrenchments and gun positions were discovered north of Lara and photographs taken.

Later in the day a Short machine spotted for the fire of one of H.M. ships and "Ben-my-Chree" on to these gun positions. W/T communication (receiving and sending) was effectively maintained during the whole flight, which lasted 1 hour 40 minutes.

The target at Lara was successfully destroyed, and the spotting machine reconnoitred the north end of the bay and photographed the trenches on the shore surrounding the mouth of the Arab Su.

Hostile machines having opened fire on "Ben-my-Chree," a seaplane was immediately hoisted out to locate the batteries. Five or six shots straddled the ship while stopped. As soon as the seaplane was hoisted out, "Ben-my-Chree" engaged the battery east of Adalia.

As the first seaplane could not locate the enemy a second seaplane was hoisted out, which located and bombed three guns, two of which were hit with 65-lb. bombs.

The shooting of the enemy was very good, and, although " Ben-my-Chree " was not hit, at least a dozen shells exploded extremely close and many passed over the ship on either side.

A battery which had been engaged at close quarters by the French guns was silenced.

At dusk, in accordance with orders received, the ship steamed to Castelorizo.

CAPE STATION.

No reports have been received during this period.

REPORT OF OPERATIONS No. 23.

DUNKIRK.

Owing to the extremely bad weather during this period it has, on many days, been impossible to carry out any flying.

The usual routine patrols and reconnaissances have been maintained when weather permitted.

The following are the more interesting events :—

December 5th.

A small balloon of peculiar shape was shot down by one of our fighting patrols. The balloon was cigar-shaped, red in colour, and about 8 feet in length. Attached to it was a small basket a foot in diameter. This latter appeared to be weighted on one side. Nothing was observed to fall out of it.

December 10th.

Engagements took place during the day with a single-seater Fokker biplane south of Ostende, and also with another German machine which was engaged in spotting, both machines being driven down. During a photographic reconnaissance off Blankenberghe two machines were constantly attacked by hostile machines, which were driven off by the fighter escort. Both photographic machines were under very heavy anti-aircraft fire for 45 minutes, one having two ribs smashed by shrapnel and the other being hit in ten places.

December 12th.

Three indecisive encounters took place with an enemy machine. In one case the pilot was able to get within close range, but after firing a few shots his Lewis gun jammed and he was too cold to clear it.

HOME STATIONS.

The usual routine anti-submarine patrols and reconnaissances have been carried out when weather permitted, but owing to the unfavourable conditions no special flights have been attempted.

On 11th December, Short seaplane 9054, while on patrol, nose-dived from a considerable height. The pilot, Flight Lieutenant Hume, and the observer, Chief Petty Officer Bradley, were both killed. Their bodies were recovered later and the engine salved.

DETACHED SQUADRON WORKING WITH ROYAL FLYING CORPS.

A report has now been received from the above squadron, of which the following are the most interesting events.

It is regretted that Flight Sub-Lieutenant W. H. Hope did not return from an offensive patrol on 23rd November and is still missing.

SUMMARY OF WORK.

November 1916.

No. of hours flown { Service flights, 246 03 / Test flights, 99 33 } Total, 345 36.

No. of days on which flying was possible, 12.

No. of combats { Decisive, 10 / Indecisive, 18 } Total, 28.

COMBATS.

Name.	Machine.	Decisive.	Indecisive.	Remarks.
F.S.L. Galbraith	Sopwith Scout	3	3	Two observers seen to be hit.
F.L. Goble	,,	3	1	
,, Mackenzie	Nieuport	1	1	
F.S.L. Corbett	,,	1	—	
,, Little	Sopwith	1	2	
,, Trapp	,,	1	2	
F.L. Hervey	,,	—	1	
F.Com. Huskisson	,,	—	1	
F.S.L. Lawson	Nieuport	—	1	
,, Simpson	,,	—	1	
,, Compston	,,	—	1	One observer seen to be hit.
Hope	Sopwith	—	1	
Grange	,,	—	3	One observer seen to be hit.

Following are details of some of the more interesting events:—

November 10th.

Flight Sub-Lieutenant Galbraith, while on an offensive patrol the other side of Bapaume, encountered a formation of Roland biplanes. He engaged the rear machine, getting between him and the sun, and fired about 50 rounds at close range under his tail. The hostile machine stalled and disappeared in a spinning nose-dive out of control.

November 16th.

Flight Lieutenant Goble while patrolling for hostile machines observed a Brown two-seater machine similar to L.V.G. proceeding in an easterly direction in the direction of Ablainzeville at 10,500 feet. He dived at hostile machine and fired about 25 rounds at close range. The machine fell over sideways and disappeared evidently quite out of control.

Flight Sub-Lieutenant Galbraith while on an offensive patrol saw a two-seater L.V.G. at 8,000 feet. He dived from 14,000 feet and came up under tail of machine and fired about 20 shots at from 15 to 20 yards range. The machine stalled, spun and then righted itself, finally disappearing in a bad side-slip apparently quite out of control.

November 17th.

Flight Sub-Lieutenant Trapp while at 15,500 feet on an offensive patrol saw three type L machines travelling south in formation. He got between rear machine and sun and dived to 12,000 feet, coming up under its tail, and opening fire at 15 yards range. Gun fired once and jammed with handle in the vertical position. While reaching to clear jam, he came so close that in order to avoid hitting hostile machine he did a right-hand vertical bank, clearing gun while so doing. On coming out of this position, pilot found himself directly behind the second type L. He then dived to position under tail and opened fire at about 15 yards. Pilot observed all tracery going about centre of fuselage, and machine at once went into a nose-dive. It then righted itself and proceeded to flutter down slowly, absolutely out of control. Pilot followed machine down to 6,000 feet when he observed three type J and three type L machines closing in from all directions. He headed straight for one type J and, after firing a few rounds, broke off the fight and climbed away.

November 17th.

Flight Lieutenant Goble while on an offensive patrol over Cambrai and Bapaume encountered a small hostile scout similar to a Spad at 7,000 feet. He dived at it and opened fire at about 75 yards range. The hostile machine dived and he dived after it, chasing it down to 1,500 feet and saw it land in a field five or six miles east of Bapaume, north of Cambrai road. It appeared to land all right, and then crashed into a fence and turned over.

November 23rd.

Flight Sub-Lieutenant Galbraith while on an offensive patrol encountered six hostile two-seater machines, similar to L.V.G.'s, over Estrum, east of Cambrai, at 16,000 feet. He attacked the last machine of the formation and getting under its tail fired about 60 rounds into it at close range. The hostile machine's left wing folded up and the machine went down out of control. Then the other five attacked him and he got under the tail of another one. He could not stay there long, however, as the other machines were closing in around him, so pilot put his machine up to a great speed and looped over the one who was coming up under his tail and came up under him, at whom he fired about 15 shots. The hostile machine went down in a slow glide and the other three went away.

Flight Lieutenant Mackenzie while escorting F.E. 2 B's on a fighting patrol suddenly saw one of the F.E.'s being attacked by two machines. He dived on one of the hostile aircraft and fired several shots at close range. Hostile machine turned vertically on his left wing, stalled and nose-dived, spinning all the time. The nose-dive was too steep to be natural.

Flight Sub-Lieutenant Corbett while escorting F.E. 2 B's on a fighting patrol saw three hostile machines come from westward and attack F.E.'s. He dived and attacked one of them and fired several shots at close range. The hostile machine turned and went over on his left-hand side to about 40° and went vertically downwards. Pilot saw the hostile machine lurch twice and finally disappear diving fast towards our lines apparently out of control.

Flight Sub-Lieutenant Little while on an offensive patrol encountered a two-seater type L. north-east of Bapaume steering south at 3,000 feet. He dived at it and opened fire about 150 yards away, keeping up a continuous fire until about 75 yards away, when the hostile machine caught fire. The machine went down at an angle of 85°, flames and white smoke coming out of it all the time. Pilot followed it down to about 6,500 feet and saw it still burning on the ground close to a small wood.

Flight Lieutenant Goble while on an offensive patrol saw a Brown two-seater L.V.G. about 1,000 feet below him. Suspecting it was a decoy, he looked behind him and saw four Roland scouts behind and about 1,000 feet above him. He pretended to dive at L.V.G. and after diving about 300 feet opened his engine up and "hoicked." The scouts passed him diving and then flattened out. He then got under the rear scout's tail and fired about 60 rounds at about 20 yards range. Machine stalled, caught fire, and went down out of control. The other scouts tried to get behind him, and in order to prevent this he tried to loop, which he did too quickly and spun. When he came out of the spin the hostile machines were nowhere to be seen.

EASTERN MEDITERRANEAN.

Reports Nos. 35, 36, and 37.

The usual patrols in the Dardanelles, and anti-submarine patrols of other areas, were carried out by aeroplanes, seaplanes, and airships whenever possible, but the weather has been exceptionally bad during this period.

Spotting has been carried out as requisite for H.M. ships.

Thasos.

November 10th.

A special reconnaissance was carried out in the Drama area by Flight Sub-Lieut. Magor, and an enemy aerodrome was located by him, the existence of which had been suspected in this district. On receipt of this intelligence, bombing machines and escorts were sent to Drama to attack the aerodrome, pilots being:—

Bombing Machines.

Flight Sub-Lieut. Shoppee. Observer, Second Lieut. Tansley, K.R.R.

Flight Commander Sitwell. Observer, Sub-Lieut. Corry, R.N.V.R.

Escorting Machine.

Flight Sub-Lieut. Magor. Observer, Mr. Constantino.

While one of the bombing machines was leaving the aerodrome, about 6,000 feet, he sighted a large hostile tractor biplane approaching the aerodrome about 4,000 feet above him. Observer fired two red Very's lights to attract the attention of the escorting machine, opening fire with Lewis gun at long range, causing the hostile machine to turn and disappear in the direction of Xanthi.

On arriving over Drama aerodrome, six 112-lb. bombs were dropped from 9,000 feet, one of which fell about 50 yards east of the north-east hangar and another 50 yards west of the north-west hangar. Both hangars were probably damaged during the attack. Two large hostile machines seemed to leave the ground but did not engage the bombing flight. A third machine remained in the aerodrome. Photographs of the aerodrome were taken, and useful information about the coast defences south-west of Kavala were also obtained on the outward and homeward journeys.

During the latter half of the week flying has been impossible owing to the heavy rainstorms accompanied by strong wind.

November 18th.

A bomb attack was arranged on Drama aerodrome, the bombing machines being escorted by two scouts and accompanied by another scout, whose orders were to act independently and engage any hostile aircraft seen, and afterwards, if possible, to reconnoitre the country as far as Buk. Owing to bad weather the bombing machine and her escorts returned to Thasos, but Flight Sub-Lieut. A. F. Whetnall in Nieuport scout, No. 3979, went on to Drama but failed to return, and according to information received from the military, a Bulgarian communiqué reports that "an English Nieuport No. 4979 was caused to land near Drama after combat, pilot being killed."

November 20th.

A further reconnaissance of the Buk area was made, which showed that the bridge had apparently been repaired, and that a considerable amount of transport was assembled in the vicinity. In the afternoon, therefore, machines were sent to bomb the bridge. Heavy bombs were dropped, and a signalled report states that the bridge was again probably damaged. No further details are yet to hand.

A number of anti-submarine patrols were carried out by this flight during this period.

November 24th.

A large transport park and stores, together with a number of trucks and covered wagons, having been reported in the vicinity of, and in the station at, Angista, by a machine from " D " Flight, two Henri Farmans from Thasos escorted by two scouts delivered an attack on the station. Unfortunately the transport park, stores, and most of the trucks were found to have been removed by this date. However, one machine dropped one 65-lb. bomb and two 100-lb. bombs, one of which exploded beside the line in the centre of the station. Other machines dropped eight 16-lb. bombs, all of which fell along the line in the station compound, causing considerable damage to the permanent way.

Pilot, Flight Sub-Lieutenant Shoppee. Observer, Second Lieutenant Tansley, K.R.R.

Pilot, Flight Sub-Lieutenant Aird. Observer, Midshipman R. J. Dashwood, R.N.R.

Escorting Machines.

Pilot, Flight Sub-Lieutenant G. A. Magor. Observer, Mr. Constantino.

November 26th and 29th.

Enemy seaplanes having been very active recently, their base at Gereviz was bombed by Thasos machines, considerable damage being done.

November 28th.

A further raid was made on the new aerodrome at Drama and on Drama Station by two Henri Farman machines with two other machines acting as escorts Only a signalled report has been received of this operation, but one direct hit was made on the station.

Stavros Air Station.

November 10th.

Two reconnaissance flights were made over the railway to the north-east of Lake Takhenos, bombs being dropped on store dumps at Porna and Angista. Considerable damage is believed to have been caused.

November 11th.

A further attack was made on Porna.

Stavros Air Station. "D" Flight.

A number of reconnaissance flights over the lower Struma have been carried out by this flight, and also spotting flights for land batteries.

November 18th.

Provista and Semultos were attacked with bombs.

November 19th.

Semultos was again attacked and a photographic flight over enemy lines was carried out.

November 22nd.

Proclamations in Turkish were dropped in the trenches and camps occupied by Turkish troops at the request of A.H.Q. at Salonica.

November 24th.

An attack was made by three machines on a camp of 2,000 men in a gully near Razolivos in the Prava-Angista area. After dropping bombs, machines flew low over the gully and attacked the camp with machine guns.

November 25th.

Three machines delivered an attack on Drama aerodrome. One shed which was damaged by the previous raid from Thasos had been removed and one of the three remaining was again damaged by a bomb.

November 26th.

Bombs were dropped near Provista, where large bivouac store sheds and stores had been observed.

November 27th.

Four bomb attacks were made on Porna, the store depôt on the railway between Drama and Serres, and on Doksambos on the eastern shore of Lake Tahinos, where machines from Stavros had previously located defence works and accumulations of stores. Photographic and spotting flights were also carried out during this week.

November 29th

Two machines again bombed Docambos. On the same day machines reconnoitring over the railway came down low and attacked a moving train with machine-gun fire. The engine-driver and stoker were seen to fall out of the engine, presumably hit, leaving the train to continue its journey.

H.M.S. "Empress."

November 5th.

A reconnaissance was carried out over the Ofano area. Pilot, Flight Sub-Lieut. Melly. Observer, Sub-Lieut. Holcombe, R.N.V.R. A large camp was observed on the northern slopes of Hill 154, and appeared to be occupied by over 1,000 men, and about 80 horses were tethered in front of the huts. On the following day the same pilot and observer dropped six bombs on the camp, and attacked the horses with Lewis gun fire from 2,000 feet. One of H.M. ships was then spotted on the camp, 60 per cent. of the shots being direct hits. Later in the day the same ship was again spotted on to the camp. Nine rounds of 6-inch high explosive were fired, three of which fell among the huts and horses. The other six were all within a few yards of the camp, and must have done considerable damage.

November 12th.

An L.V.C. or Aviatik attacked Port Iero and dropped two bombs in the anchorage and two on the French camp. No damage was caused. Flight Sub-Lieut. Mellings in a Bristol Scout was sent in pursuit, and first sighted the hostile machine at about 8,500 feet over Chikli (near Smyrna, and 55 miles from Therma aerodrome). The Bristol Scout opened fire at close range, the hostile machine being repeatedly hit. The pilot of the Bristol was obliged to discontinue the action after a time owing to difficulty in piloting his machine in the back-wash of the enemy, and on turning his attention to the hostile machine again he noticed it apparently out of control in a spinning nose-dive.

Details have now been received of engagements with a Fokker machine which took place over Cape Chemali on 16th November, reported in last issue. The pilot was Flight Lieut. Barnato, observer Sub-Lieut. A. E. H. Roberts, R.N.V.R. While searching for guns in a Henri Farman machine on which to spot for one of H.M. ships, they were attacked by a Fokker monoplane at a height of about 5,000 feet.

The Fokker attacked at close range from behind the Farman, and succeeded in injuring the radiator at the beginning of the action. On two occasions the R.N.A.S. pilot side-slipped his machine, causing the enemy to overshoot his mark, and enabling the Farman's Lewis gun to come into action. Owing to the above-mentioned damage, the Farman's engine failed through over-heating, and she was landed in the sea close to one of H.M. ships, both pilot and observer being uninjured. The Fokker was then engaged by the ship's anti-aeroplane guns when the Farman was sufficiently close to the water to render this possible.

November 17th.

Two machines spotted for one of H.M. ships.

November 18th.

A further spotting flight was carried out.

A Schneider seaplane was sent in pursuit of enemy machines which had attacked the ships anchored at Chai and Aghaizi.

November 19th.

An anti-submarine patrol was carried out in the Gulf of Orfano and a reconnaissance of the Karjani was made and bombs were dropped on the village.

November 20th, 21st, and 22nd.

Further reconnaissance, spotting, and anti-submarine flights were carried out.

November 23rd.

The area Orfano, Kahjani, Dranli was reconnoitred, bombs being dropped on Kahjani, and proclamations in Turkish were dropped in the trenches at Dranli.

Several photographs were taken by the spotting machine of Kahjani village (which, owing to frequent bombardments from sea and air, is now in ruins), and of the new defence works which have been constructed on the hills behind the village. Pamphlets sent from A.H.Q., Salonica, were, at their request, dropped in trenches near Dranli which were seen to be occupied.

On 26th November, during a reconnaissance of the Dranli-Orfano area, two 16-lb. bombs were dropped on Dedeballi village.

Later in the day a reconnaissance was made of Kahjani and two 16-lb. bombs were dropped on the ruins at Karacol in which trenches were concealed.

A number of spotting and photographic flights were carried out by machines from H.M.S. "Empress."

Thermi Air Station. "B" Flight.

November 21st.

A hostile machine approached Thermi aerodrome and was driven off by anti-aircraft fire. Two Bristol scouts went in pursuit, one of which, piloted by Flight Sub-Lieut. Hackman, overtook the hostile machine at 7,500 feet over the southern end of Mitylene island. The Bristol scout opened fire at 75 yards, whereupon the hostile machine dived steeply. The Bristol scout followed and continued to fire until its gun jammed. Pilot had to turn away in order to remedy it. On turning to re-engage, the hostile machine had disappeared.

November 17th, 20th, 21st, 22nd, and 23rd.

Usual reconnaissance of the Dardanelles was made on the 21st November. A Nieuport was sent in pursuit of two hostile machines which had been sighted over Tenedos. The same day two machines proceeded to Magara and attacked the seaplane base there, and in the afternoon the Nieuport was again sent to search for a hostile biplane which had dropped two bombs near one of H.M. ships and two on Mavro.

November 23rd.

Two hostile machines dropped 12 bombs on Imbros aerodrome. No damage was caused to the station. Two men of the King's Regiment were slightly injured. Two Nieuports pursued the hostile machines, one of which was engaged, and tracer bullets were seen to hit it.

November 21st.

A hostile aeroplane (L.V.G. type) and an F.F. seaplane approaching from the south-west and east respectively attacked the Mudros airship shed. The aeroplane made two attacks, dropping two bombs each time, one of which fell within 50 yards of the southern entrance of the shed. Small pieces of the bomb entered the shed and pierced the envelope of the airship. The seaplane was met by heavy A.A. fire and was only seen to drop one bomb on the hills a mile away. The enemy machine left in an easterly direction pursued by a Schneider seaplane (pilot Flight Sub-Lieut. Brandon), which engaged the F.F. seaplane at close range, firing three trays into it. The action commenced at 8,000 feet, and the enemy had dropped to 3,000 feet by the time the Schneider had finished her ammunition. Tracer bullets were seen to enter her fuselage.

It is probable that the enemy seaplane was hit in the radiator or engine, as she was discovered by one of H.M. ships in Yukyeri Bay (east of Tenedos) and destroyed by gun fire. Pilot and observer were seen to escape inland on foot.

Imbros Air Station. "C" Flight.

The usual reconnaissance of the Dardanelles was made on the 10th, 13th, 14th, and 16th November, but this was not possible during the remainder of the week. Owing to bad weather nothing of special importance was reported.

Mudros and Kassandra Airship Station.

Practically no patrols were undertaken during this week owing to bad weather.

Roumanian Flight.

November 21st.

Three machines left Mudros for Roumania, pilots being:—
    Flight Lieutenant C. E. Brisley, in Nieuport Fighter No. 8731;

Flight Sub-Lieutenant Mills, in Nieuport Fighter No. 8513;

Flight Sub-Lieutenant Barrington, in Henri Farman 3004; and a fourth machine left from Imbros, pilot being:—

Flight Lieutenant Bush in Henri Farman 3007.

All machines arrived safely in Roumania.

CAPE STATION.
Zanzibar.
H.M.S. "Manica."

A number of reconnaissances have been carried out by various pilots during this period, much valuable information having been obtained and numerous photographs secured.

September 8th.

A Short seaplane, No. 3096, pilot Flight Lieutenant MacLean, observer Sub-Lieutenant Fitzherbert, made a photographic reconnaissance, carrying bombs. Having examined coast near the Rufigi Delta, bombs were dropped over Msungu. Two further bombs were dropped near a camp a mile and a half inland near Kavinja, but fell short of the sheds. Other bombs were dropped on remains of the camp at Mjamamba. Photographs were taken.

On the 9th the same machine, pilot, and observer made another reconnaissance over the north arm of the delta. About 200 head of cattle were observed near Kirkale, and a bomb was dropped among them, scattering the natives and the cattle. Three more bombs were dropped in and around Kirkale. No huts were actually hit. Three photographs were also taken.

September 10th.

A reconnaissance was made over Gingwera River, bombs being dropped on a group of native huts.

September 27th, 28th, 29th, and 30th.

Reconnaissance raids were made over Rufigi Delta, bombs being dropped on suitable targets and photographs being obtained.

Flying in this part of the world is extremely difficult owing to the numerous heavy squalls and air being very bumpy.

EAST INDIES STATION.

No reports have been received from this station during the period under review.

MALTA SEAPLANE STATION.

The following report has been received from Malta Seaplane Base:—

It has been found very difficult to carry out patrols in consequence of the extremely heavy seas and strong winds, the seas taking considerable time to subside. In spite of this, however, firing has been carried out from the air on eight occasions, and live bombs dropped twice.

November 29th.

In spite of an appreciable swell, Flight Sub-Lieutenant Gorman, with Sub-Lieutenant Jenks as observer, succeeded in getting off the water and carried out a patrol of $3\frac{1}{4}$ hours in search of a reported submarine. Observer reported having seen a submarine 21 miles south-east of Malta, and this was at once communicated to the senior officer in charge.

The submarine submerged considerably before they arrived over the spot where she was sighted, but as they only had four 16-lb. bombs they fired Very's lights to attract the attention of two trawlers which were in the vicinity. They were then forced to return owing to shortage of petrol.

REPORT OF OPERATIONS No. 24.

HOME STATIONS.

The usual anti-submarine patrols and reconnaissances were carried out when possible. Weather during the whole period was unfavourable.

On 20th December, Short Seaplane 3227, pilot Flight Sub-Lieut. Ross, patrolling from Portland, sighted a hostile submarine on the surface proceeding to attack a transport. On sighting the seaplane the submarine commenced to dive. Pilot dropped one bomb, probably without direct effect. The seaplane remained over the ship until two patrol boats arrived 45 minutes later and prevented any further attack.

DUNKIRK.

The weather during the whole period has been unfavourable for flying. On six days no flying or balloon ascents were possible. Fighter patrols on other days did not encounter any hostile craft.

Photographic reconnaissances on Zeebrugge and Ostende were carried out on the 17th and 27th December under the usual heavy anti-aircraft fire. Coastal reconnaissances on the 20th, 24th, and 26th December.

R.N.A.S. Squadron, attached 22nd Wing R.F.C.

A report (A 03140) has been received from military sources of the work carried out during the period 3rd—16th December inclusive, as follows:—

During the period under report there have been only two days on which service flying has been possible.

On the 4th December the squadron had many combats in the air. They forced several hostile machines to land, and drove down three, apparently out of control. Four machines of the squadron acted as escort to a bombing raid.

Flight Sub-Lieut. the Hon. A. C. Corbett, while on patrol, was brought down near Delville Wood. He was killed, and is buried at Heilly.

On 10th December Flight Sub-Lieut. S. V. Trapp was killed whilst on a test flight.

On the 11th December four pilots escorted a bombing raid carried out by the 22nd Wing. One pilot engaged and drove down a hostile machine, the destruction of which was not definitely established.

No. 3 Wing.

No report has been received during the period under review.

Gibraltar and Malta.

No operational report has been received during the period under review.

ROUMANIAN FLIGHT.

The following further information has been received of the flight to Bucharest from Imbros, already mentioned in Report No. 23.

The flight took place on the 25th October, and owing to the very bad weather only one machine succeeded in making a non-stop flight to Bucharest. All machines, however, reached Bucharest later.

No. 1.—*Report of Flight Lieut. Hervey in Nieuport 8514.*

Imbros was left at 10.15, and a course due north steered for the coast. Drifting to eastward, the machine was carried east of Adrianople and was fired on by anti-aircraft guns. Turning west, the machine ran into a thunderstorm, which rendered its compass useless. The clouds were cleared at 9,400 feet, and course set W.N.W. for two hours In order to take bearings the machine was dropped to 1,800 feet over Razgrad railway station. The Danube was crossed 45 minutes later at 1,200 feet, under heavy machine-gun and rifle fire. Following the railway at 400 feet Bucharest was reached, and the machine landed on the aerodrome at 4.45 after $6\frac{1}{2}$ hours flight.

No. 2.—*Report of Flight Lieut. Cox, R.N., in Nieuport 8524.*

Steering due north after leaving Imbros at 10.23, the coast was crossed midway between Enos and Dedeagatch. On account of eastward drift a course was set 10° west for three hours, picking up the Danube at 7,000 feet. Although flying over heavy clouds sufficient landmarks were visible to enable the pilot to keep course, but north of the Danube it was necessary to descend and land in order to find out the exact position, which proved to be a village called Draganesti, about 65 kilos. S.W. of Bucharest. As the weather did not improve the machine was dismantled and brought to Bucharest by road.

No. 3.—*Report of Flight Commander Stanley Adams in Nieuport 3978.*

The machine left Imbros at 10.50, crossing the Bulgarian coast between Enos and Dedeagatch at 6,500 feet. The compass was corrected for drift, and course altered N. 15′ W., which gave almost the true map course. Much cloud was encountered during the flight, and partly owing to this and partly to engine and oil trouble, the machine eventually descended at Marsa, 16 miles S.S.W. of Bucharest, whence it was taken on a lorry to Bucharest.

No. 4.—*Report of Flight Lieut. A. J. Jacob in Nieuport 8525.*

After leaving Imbros at 10.30, good weather prevailed for the first two hours and good time was made to the Bulgarian coast, in spite of slight drift to eastward. The map was very accurate and useful. Passing westward of Adrianople much activity was observed, one large force of about 5,000, with transport but no guns, being seen going towards the town. The weather became rapidly worse on the Balkan mountains, and during a thunderstorm, enveloped in a large cloud, the pilot lost control. He fell from 9,000 to 1,000 feet, at which height he emerged from the cloud upside down, regaining control at 500 feet. He considers he must have been upside down several times, as not only did he feel his belt tighten, but various things fell out of the machine. His compass was now useless. The petrol in his front tank was almost finished, and pressure in the back tank faulty. The pilot consequently decided to land, which he did successfully, and repaired the defects with his engine running. A party of Bulgarians opened fire as he was taxy-ing off, and pilot charged them, firing a few rounds from his gun, whereupon all fell flat, and he was able to get away. While he was following down the course of a small river, in the hope of striking the Danube, a party of 30 Bulgarians on a barge fired at the machine with rifles. The pilot turned back and emptied a tray of ammunition at them, and then dived to within a few feet, causing them all to jump into the water.

Most of the last two hours' flying was done at about 50 feet owing to bad visibility.

The pilot, having flown for more than six hours, continually losing his way, decided to land. He found that he was about 20 miles north of Ismail, in Russia, and at length reached Bucharest on October 30th.

The pilot speaks highly of the engine, the excellent condition of which he attributes to C.P.O. J. E. Clarke.

EASTERN MEDITERRANEAN SQUADRON.

(*Extracted from Reports Nos.* 38 (*A* 03101) *for* 29*th November—* 6*th December, and* 39 (*A* 03208) *for* 7*th December—* 14*th December.*)

During the period the usual reconnaissances and spotting were carried out as requisite, in spite of unfavourable weather.

The more interesting events are mentioned below.

Thasos Air Station. " A " Flight, No. 2 Wing.

The following further particulars of the raid on Drama Station of 28th November have now been received :—

Of the two Henri Farmans employed, the first machine (Henri Farman 3905, pilot Flight Sub-Lieut. B. C. Shoppee and Second Lieut. H.E. Tansley, K.R.R.C., observer) dropped eight 16-lb. bombs and two 65-lb. bombs.

The second machine (Henri Farman 3916, pilot Flight Sub-Lieut. Grieg, with Sub-Lieut. R. Frazier, R.N.V.R., as observer) dropped two 100-lb. bombs on the Station Compound among the tents.

Though two hostile machines, one a small scout, left the aerodrome, neither attempted to attack.

The escorting machines (Nieuport Scout 3983 and Bristol Scout 3036) were piloted by Flight Sub-Lieut. G. A. Magor and Flight Sub-Lieut. Aird.

November 29th.

Gereviz Seaplane Base having been observed to have been considerably enlarged, two machines participated in an attack on this base. One of these (Henri Farman 3916, piloted by Flight Sub-Lieut. Grieg, with Sub-Lieut. Frazier, R.N.V.R., observer), descending to 300 feet, dropped eight 16-lb. bombs among outbuildings and tents to the north and west of the hangars and two 65-lb. bombs, one close to the large rectangular shed and the other 10 yards from a Bessoneau, causing the side to collapse. Some of the buildings hit by the 16-lb. bombs evidently contained petrol stores, as a large fire broke out and spread, owing to a strong east wind, towards the camp and Bessoneau. The flames rose to a height of 30 feet and immense volumes of black smoke were visible from Thasos, 35 miles distant.

The second Henri Farman (No. 3905, piloted by Flight Lieut. Cowper, with Lord Torrington as observer) attacked the large rectangular shed from 900 feet and dropped one 65-lb. bomb and two 100-lb. bombs, one of which fell within 25 yards of the target. After dropping the bombs this machine came under considerable rifle, machine-gun, and anti-aircraft fire.

Subsequent reconnaissance showed that one hangar and most of the camp and huts were completely destroyed. One hangar still remained.

December 1st.

The same pilots and observers, escorted by a Bristol Scout, proceeded to deliver another attack on this aerodrome. Ten minutes after starting, the engine of the Bristol Scout gave trouble and she had to return, and though another scout was despatched to search for the Henri Farman and circled round

Gereviz at 4,000 feet, observing that no further damage had been done, she failed to see anything of the bombers. No news has since been received of them. Probably these machines were brought down either by gunfire or by scouts from hostile stations in the vicinity.

December 2nd and 3rd.

Reconnaissances were made of the coast line, as works had recently been constructed for guns which would command Thasos.

December 10th.

In the afternoon a hostile seaplane was sighted about four miles distant from Thasos, evidently approaching the aerodrome with the intention of dropping bombs. A Nieuport Scout which was in the air at the time immediately went in pursuit, followed by a Schneider Cup Seaplane. A long chase ensued until the hostile machine finally put its nose down and rapidly disappeared, outdistancing both pursuing machines. A second Nieuport Scout, which was also unable to overtake the enemy, proceeded to Gereviz in order to intercept him, but sighted no hostile machine. The seaplane base was observed to have been considerably reduced since the raid of 29th November, only one small hangar surrounded by bivouacs remaining.

December 11th.

This was attacked on the following morning by one Henri Farman and a Schneider Seaplane, escorted by two Nieuport Scouts. On approaching the target accurate anti-aircraft fire was experienced by the Henri Farman. This fire was silenced by a 100-lb. bomb, which fell within 40 yards of the guns.

In the afternoon of the same day a hostile seaplane sighted off Thasos was pursued by two Nieuport Scouts to Gereviz, where a second seaplane was encountered. After an engagement lasting half an hour both machines were driven down to Lake Boru, apparently damaged.

Stavros Air Station. " D " Flight, No. 2 Wing.

November 30th.

Flight Sub-Lieut. Bradley, with Petty Officer Stanley as observer, proceeded to attack a train travelling from Porna towards Angista Station. The train was attacked first with bombs, one of which fell about five yards from the engine. The pilot then came down to within 50 feet and fired one tray of Lewis gun ammunition at the engine driver and fireman, both of whom were seen to jump from the footplate, leaving the train to proceed out of control.

Imbros Air Station. "C" Flight.

December 1st, 2nd, and 3rd.

Mavro and Phedo Island were visited by hostile aeroplanes and seaplanes, bombs being dropped, and though on each occasion a scout pursued the enemy machines, they were able to get away up the straits without being brought to action.

December 6th.

Five bombs were dropped on Imbros by a hostile machine.

December 13th.

On 13th December, the weather being favourable for a long-distance flight, a raid on Kuleli Burgas railway bridge was carried out by the three Henri Farmans (previously sent from Mudros fitted for carrying heavy bombs), one Henri Farman from Imbros, and two Bristol Scouts.

Soon after the departure one scout was compelled, by engine trouble, to return, and landed in the Salt Lake at Kephalo, the machine being wrecked, but the pilot unhurt.

The remaining five machines reached their objective at Kuleli Burgas, 90 miles distant from Imbros, and dropped three 100-lb. and nine 65-lb. bombs. Signalled reports of the operation state that several of these fell very close to the bridge and probably damaged it. Considerable anti-aircraft and rifle fire was experienced, but all machines returned safely, though Henri Farman 3915 was damaged on landing.

Thermi Air Station. "B" Flight.

The usual reconnaissances in the region of Smyrna were carried out.

H.M.S. "Ark Royal."

Usual routine has been carried out.

H.M.S. "Empress."

November 30th.

Flight Sub-Lient. Abbott, in Short 9758, was wounded in both legs by gunfire while on reconnaissance in the Karjani area, his machine having dropped 1,000 feet through engine trouble. Fortunately he was able to fly back to the "Empress."

December 1st and 2nd.

Bombs were dropped on trenches constructed recently in the Karjani area.

Kassandra Airship Station.

During the patrol on 14th December the airship was obliged, owing to engine trouble, to come down on the water 20 miles west of Kassandra. Assistance was rendered by one of

H.M. ships and the airship was towed back to Salonika by trawler. The envelope is now deflated, and extensive repairs will have to be made before the airship is ready for service again; she is accordingly being returned to Mudros for repairs, and Airship S.S. 8 from Mudros will be flown to Kassandra for duty there as soon as weather permits.

EAST INDIES STATION.

A report (A 03133) has been received of operations carried out on December 1st—3rd, 1916.

"Ben-My-Chree" proceeded on reconnaissance duties in company with a French Destroyer on December 1st, arriving off Haifa on December 2nd.

Flight Sub-Lieut. A. G. Nightingale, R.N., and Lieutenant P. M. Woodland, R.N.V.R., operating over the Jaffa district in Short No. 8372. The machine was seen to come suddenly under shell fire in the direction of Ramleh and dived to earth behind a ridge of hills. It has since been ascertained that both these officers are prisoners in the hands of the Turks.

Flight Commander England, D.S.C., and Captain Wedgewood Benn, in Short No. 8080 immediately undertook the reconnaissance ordered for No. 8372. The machine was vigorously attacked by A.A. fire and a float was pierced. The reconnaissance was, however, successfully carried out.

Two enemy aircraft made an unsuccessful bomb attack on the ship as one of her machines was being hoisted in.

CAPE STATION.

Zanzibar.

No. 8 Squadron.

A detailed report (A 03132) has now been received of the operations of this squadron for the month of August.

Various reconnaissances were carried out and much valuable information was obtained; spotting for H.M. ships was also successfully undertaken by seaplanes, and several hostile camps and buildings were bombed with good results.

The weather generally appears to have been unfavourable for flying and almost all pilots complained of high winds and generally bumpy conditions, which hampered operations to some extent.

BRITISH NAVAL ARMOURED CARS.

ROUMANIA.

A report (A 03190) received describes the preliminary orders and proceedings of the force and the subsequent active service operations of the Royal Naval Air Service armoured cars in conjunction with the Russian and Roumanian forces in the attack on the German and Bulgarian positions in the neighbourhood of the Cernavoda Bridge in the Dobrudja from 25th November to 3rd December.

Acting on the orders of the Chief of Staff of the Danube army at Braila, the force was successfully transported on barges from Reni to Hirsova, arriving there on 26th November. Commander Gregory left Reni on the 25th in order to make arrangements for their reception at Hirsova, finding great difficulty owing to the fact that the town had been sacked and burned by the Bulgarians less than two weeks before. He reported himself to the Chief of Staff, informed the latter as to the organisation of the force, and received instructions, necessary maps, and orders to take the field in 48 hours, a big battle being imminent. The force was completely disembarked by 1 p.m. on 27th November, and all three squadrons were immediately ready for action.

On 28th November the squadron leaders were ordered to reconnoitre the positions, roads, &c., in the area of operations, and during this reconnaissance two officers were wounded, Lieut. Commander Belt, R.N.V.R. (slightly and returned to duty), and Lieut. Smiles, R.N.V.R. (sent to base hospital). In the evening a conference was held and dispositions were arranged for the forthcoming battle.

At noon on the 29th the Chief of Staff at Braila cancelled all previous orders, and directed that the force should proceed to a destination in the vicinity of Bucharest. On examination of the roads, however, it was found impossible to move the force as directed, and after explaining this to the Chief of Staff of the Fourth Siberian army, permission was obtained from the headquarters of the Danube army for the force to remain where it was and participate in the forthcoming battle as arranged.

On the 29th orders were received to take up the positions assigned. Lieut.-Commander Wells Hood, R.N.V.R., proceeding with his squadron (No. 2) to the village of Panteleimon Ustin, and Commander Gregory with Squadrons 1 and 3 to the village of Topalul.

The main objective of the attack was to advance on Cernavoda.

Squadrons 1 and 3 were to operate on the right flank and Squadron 2 on the left; the latter being intended to cut off the enemy's retreat if the attack was a success, or to repulse a counter attack if the operation was a failure.

November 30th.

The attack opened at 9 a.m. on 30th November with an artillery bombardment in dull and misty weather most unfavourable for artillery observation, and was temporarily abandoned for this reason, but recommenced at 12.30, the weather conditions having improved.

Lieut.-Commander Belt's squadron (No. 1) went into action at 3.35.

A new and powerful type of Russian car with two Maxims and two turrets proceeded to act in concert with Sub-Lieut. Lefroy's car in enfilading the very strongly protected enemy trenches, but the Russian car, on reaching the enemy's wire entanglements and attempting to turn round for action, got bogged, and has never been extricated. Lieut. Lefroy's car had the whole superstructure shifted by a high explosive shell, and with great difficulty retired.

A second Russian car, accompanied by Acting Lieut. Walford's car, then proceeded into action, and though the former car got imbedded, Lieut. Walford succeeded in enfilading the enemy's trenches till his gun was shot through and put out of action.

Lieut.-Commander Belt took his car to the rescue of the Russian cars, but the soft ground and the oncoming darkness prevented him, and also Sub-Lieut. Gawlor, who followed him, from rendering assistance.

The motor cyclists accompanied the cars into action.

No infantry attack was made in support of these cars, but the concentration of troops and artillery by the enemy in consequence of the attack by these cars enabled the Russians to gain a success on the left flank.

The force was recalled, it being impossible to fight the cars in the dark, though the attack continued through the night.

Squadron No. 3 did not go into action on this day.

December 1st.

The action was continued, and though all these squadrons were ordered to take up positions for action, only No. 3 actually carried out operations, gallantly carrying out the duties assigned to them, running up to the enemy's trenches under very heavy shell, rifle, and machine-gun fire, firing into them, and retiring in full view of the enemy.

December 2nd.

A heavy counter attack by the enemy was expected, and Squadron No. 1 was sent to attack the enemy trenches unsupported by Russian infantry, while Squadron No. 3 was directed to be ready to move into any position required.

After two cars of Squadron No. 1 had attacked, this squadron stood by and eventually returned, operations being temporarily suspended on both sides.

In the meantime the enemy launched an attack on the left flank.

Lieut.-Commander Wells Hood (Squadron No. 2) gallantly led his cars into action and repulsed this counter offensive in its early stages before it was fully developed. It was eventually abandoned by the enemy.

All the cars of Squadron 2 were in action; two were bogged and their guns put out of action; afterwards the officers (Lieut. Ingle and Lieut. Mitchell) with the crews crept into a trench in the vicinity of the car and were all taken prisoners. The two cars were eventually brought in during the night of 2nd December by Lieut. Hunter after a counter attack by the Russians had driven the enemy away from the vicinity.

It was mainly due to the efforts of the British Armoured Car Division that the enemy did not capture the Russian trenches and break the line at this point, and Commander Gregory received an autograph letter from the General Commanding the 4th Siberian Army thanking officers and men for their brave and unselfish work, regretting the heavy losses, and giving permission for the cars to return to Hirsova, which they accordingly did during the night of 2nd December.

The medical arrangements under the command of Staff-Surgeon G. B. Scott were admirable.

The gallant conduct and devotion to duty displayed by the officers and men of all three squadrons are highly praised by their commanding officer.

ROYAL FLYING CORPS COMMUNIQUÉ No. 66.

December 10th.

Artillery Co-operation.—No work was possible on the fronts of the First, Second, and Third Brigades.

Captain Mackay, No. 4 Squadron, completed a successful artillery patrol in low clouds and frequent drizzle. He located and reported by zone call six active hostile batteries, one of which was silenced. A party of 30 infantry were located and dispersed by accurate gun fire opened within six minutes.

Bombing.—Three machines of No. 2 Squadron, during the night of the 9th/10th, carried out bombing raids. One returned owing to low clouds. One dropped two 112-lb. bombs on Salome and Billy respectively, wrecking houses. The third pilot, Second Lieut. Wadleigh, lost his way in the clouds, but eventually came within sight of the sea, where the sky was clear. He recognised that he was over Ostende, and dropped two 112-lb. bombs, observing the bursts on factories near the canal. He subsequently landed at Dunkirk.

Casualty.—Killed.—Flight Sub-Lieut. S. V. Trapp, R.N.A.S.

December 11th.

Artillery Co-operation.—Thirty-three targets were dealt with by aeroplane observers; many shots were interfered with owing to the mist; 17 hostile batteries were successfully engaged.

Hostile Aircraft.—The First Brigade had eight indecisive combats. An F.E. 8, attacked by two hostile machines, had its petrol tank shot through, and on the return journey to the lines ammunition drum flew out of the pocket and hit the propeller. The hostile machines were eventually driven off by a B.E. 2e.

A reconnaissance of No. 11 Squadron encountered a formation of German machines, variously estimated at from 15 to 20. Many combats ensued, and the enemy were eventually dispersed.

An offensive patrol of No. 60 Squadron, consisting of Lieutenants Caldwell, Daly, Whitehead, Weedon, and Meintjes, and led by Captain Grenfell, dived at an Albatross over Dainville. All our machines opened fire, and the German was at once forced to land. Captain Grenfell, who followed the German to the ground, was unfortunately injured on landing. The pilot of the German machine was injured in the foot. Before surrendering, his observer set fire to the machine, but was severely injured in the process, owing to an explosion occurring.

An Albatross, brought down by anti-aircraft fire, fell near our front line trenches, near Beaurains. The pilot was killed; the observer was captured.

A hostile machine, attacked by Captain Long and Lieutenant Pashley, No. 24 Squadron, and Captain Duffus and Second Lieut. G. O. McEntee, No. 22 Squadron, fell in Bapaume and burst into flames.

Flight Lieut. Goble, R.N.A.S., attacked and drove down a German machine east of Bacquoy. Its destruction is not verified.

Second Lieut. G. W. Dampier and Second Lieut. H. C. Barr, No. 10 Squadron, while on escort to a photographic patrol, were attacked and brought down in our lines. The pilot and observer were killed.

Bombing.—The dumps and railway sidings east and northeast of Mory were attacked by six machines of No. 23 Squadron. Nineteen bombs were actually seen to hit the dumps, from which large clouds of red and black smoke issued. Lieutenant B. P. G. Hunt, No. 32 Squadron, who was part of the escort, failed to return. His machine was seen to make a forced landing, apparently due to engine trouble, in the German lines.

Casualties.—Killed.—Second Lieut. G. W. Dampier and Second Lieut. H. C. Barr, No. 10 Squadron.

Wounded.—Second Lieut. R. B. Davies, No. 2 Squadron; Captain E. O. Grenfell and Second Lieut. E. J. L. W. Gilchrist, No. 60 Squadron.

Missing.—Lieutenant B. P. G. Hunt, No. 32 Squadron.

December 12th to 15th.

Very little flying was possible owing to unfavourable weather. There is nothing to record.

December 16th.

Artillery Co-operation.—Twelve targets were successfully dealt with by aeroplane observers. A thick ground mist considerably hindered observation.

The 153rd Siege Battery, with observation by Lieutenant Pemberton, No. 5 Squadron, caused two explosions in a battery on the south-west of Biez Wood.

The 16th Heavy Battery and the 113th Heavy Battery, with observation by Lieutenant Clarke, No. 5 Squadron, registered two hostile batteries. In the first case explosions were seen in two pits.

Hostile Aircraft.—The enemy aircraft were fairly active on his own side of the line. On the Second Army front six indecisive combats took place. In one of these the observer in the hostile machine appears to have been shot. A machine of No. 12 Squadron, engaged in photography, was attacked near Agny and brought down. The observer, Lieutenant Murray, was killed, and the pilot, Second Lieut. Thomson, slightly wounded. An officer of Y 12 Trench Mortar Battery reports having seen the combat, and states that the hostile machine appeared to be driven down damaged.

A hostile machine, attacked by Captain Knight, No. 29 Squadron, is reported by anti-aircraft observers as having been brought down, apparently out of control.

There were nine other indecisive combats on the Third Army front.

Bombing.—No. 6 Squadron dropped four 112-lb. bombs on hutments at Holle Bosch. One hut was completely demolished, and another bomb fell amongst the huts.

No. 20 Squadron dropped one 336-lb. bomb on hutments at Becelaere. The result was unobserved.

Casualties.—Killed.—Lieutenant H. G. Murray, No. 12 Squadron. Wounded. — Second Lieut. Thomson, No. 12 Squadron; Lieutenant J. P. Greenwood, No. 16 Squadron.

Head Quarters, Royal Flying Corps,
 17th December 1916.

ROYAL FLYING CORPS COMMUNIQUÉ No. 67.

December 17th, 18th, and 19th.

No flying. Nothing to report.

Casualties.—Killed.—No. 11378 1 A.M., A. Rogers, No. 3 Squadron. Wounded. — No. 7768 2 A.M., R. Oxley, No. 3 Squadron.

December 20th.

Successful reconnaissances were carried out by all brigades.

Artillery Co-operation.—Eighty-five targets were successfully engaged with aeroplane observation.

A hostile anti-aircraft battery was hit by heavy artillery of the First Army, and siege artillery obtained nine direct hits on three gun-pits, causing an explosion of ammunition. Nine direct hits were obtained on other targets.

With aeroplane observation by the Second Brigade, artillery obtained two direct hits on trench mortar emplacements.

Artillery of the Third Army, working with aeroplanes of the Third Brigade, secured three direct hits on hostile batteries.

Artillery, co-operating with aeroplanes of the Fourth Brigade, obtained thirteen direct hits on hostile batteries and trenches.

The 152nd Siege Battery, with observation by Captain Leigh-Mallory and Second Lieut. Parker, No. 5 Squadron, either destroyed or badly damaged three pits of a gun battery.

Second Lieut. Arnold and Second Lieut. Clarke, No. 5 Squadron, observed for the 47th Siege Battery. Seven explosions were caused in a hostile battery position.

Second Lieut. Mayo and Lieutenant Pemberton, No. 5 Squadron, observed for the 153rd Siege B. Battery, an explosion and the destruction of one pit in a hostile battery resulting.

The 153rd Siege Battery, with observation by Captain Johnson and Corporal Wilson, No. 5 Squadron, destroyed one pit and damaged two others in a hostile battery.

Hostile Aircraft.—Lieutenant E. L. Benbow, No. 40 Squadron, engaged an Albatross south of Lens. He dived at it and opened fire at a range of about 70 feet under its tail. The hostile machine was destroyed.

Twenty-six combats took place on the front of the Third Army.

A patrol of No. 11 Squadron was very heavily engaged by nine Albatross Scouts.

A patrol of No. 11 Squadron attacked four hostile machines near Monchy, one of which was driven down out of control by Captain Quested and Lieutenant Lutyens.

On the front of the Fourth Army one hostile machine was driven down damaged.

Second Lieut. Pateman and Second Lieut. Macaulay, No. 15 Squadron, engaged and drove down a Fokker biplane near Beaumont Hamel.

Flight Lieut. Hervey, Flight Sub-Lieut. Soar, Flight Sub-Lieut. Todd, and Flight Sub-Lieut. Little, all of the R.N.A.S. Squadron, had encounters with, and drove off, hostile machines.

Bombing.—The dump at the sugar factory N.W. of Vraucourt was successfully attacked by machines of No. 23 Squadron. Many direct hits were observed and several explosions caused. Large clouds of smoke were seen to issue from the factory. Our machines drove off repeated attacks by hostile aircraft and all returned safely.

Photography.—Seven hundred and forty-one photographs were taken during the day.

Contact Patrol.—Captain Leask and Second Lieut. Adkin, No. 16 Squadron, carried out a successful contact patrol in connection with an infantry attack made by the First Army.

Casualties.—Wounded.—Lieutenant W. O. Boger, No. 11 Squadron; Second Lieut. W. K. M. Britton, No. 29 Squadron.

Missing.—Second Lieut. L. G. D'Arcy and Second Lieut. R. C. Whiteside, No. 18 Squadron; Lieutenant C. H. Windrum and Lieutenant J. A. Hollis, No. 18 Squadron; Lieutenant R. Smith and Lieutenant N. Fiske, No. 18 Squadron; Captain A. G. Knight, No. 29 Squadron.

December 21st.

Six targets were engaged with aeroplane observation. The 72nd Siege Battery, with observation by Second Lieut. D. W. Davis and Second Lieut. W. M V. Cotton, No. 7 Squadron, damaged one gun-pit and obtained four direct hits on the position. This machine failed to return.

Casualties. — Killed. — Lieutenant H. Brereton, No. 15 Squadron.

Wounded.—Second Lieut. J. P. Morkham, No. 15 Squadron; Lieutenant H. M. Yeatman, No. 34 Squadron.

Missing.—Lieutenant D. W. Davis and Second Lieutenant W. M. V. Cotton, N. 7 Squadron.

December 22nd.

In spite of low clouds, strong wind and rain, thirteen targets were engaged with aeroplane observation, and an explosion of ammunition was caused by artillery of the Fifth Army.

23rd December.

Nothing to report.

Head Quarters, Royal Flying Corps.
23rd December 1916.

REPORT OF OPERATIONS No. 25.

HOME STATIONS.

The usual reconnaissances and patrols were carried out when possible. Flying was greatly interfered with throughout the whole period by unfavourable weather conditions.

DUNKIRK.

The weather has been unfavourable for flying during the whole period. On eight days a few fighter patrols were carried out, no hostile craft being encountered. On the remaining seven days neither flying nor kite balloon ascents were carried out.

Detached Squadron working with Royal Flying Corps.

A report has now been received from the above squadron of events during the month of December 1916. A report (A. 090) has also been received from military sources concerning the period 17th December to 30th December.

SUMMARY OF WORK.

No. of hours flown { Service flights, 151 hrs. 10 mins. / Test flights, 27 hrs. 35 mins. } 178 hrs. 45 mins.

No. of days on which flying was possible, 8.

No. of combats { Decisive, 14 / Indecisive, 16 } Total, 30

Date.	Name.	Machine.	Type of H.A.	Where brought down.
Dec. 4	Flight Sub-Lieut. Little.	Sop. Sct. 5182	Halberstadt	S.E. Bapaume.
4	Flight Lieut. Goble	,, ,, 5194		,,
4	Flight Lieut. Mackenzie.	Nieuport 8750	Type M.	N.E.
4	Flight Sub-Lieut. Simpson.	3956		
11	Flight Lieut. Goble	Sop. Sct. 5196	L.	E. Bucquoy.
20	Flight Sub-Lieut. Todd	,, ,, 5193	K.	N. Bapaume.
20	Flight Sub-Lieut. Little.	,, ,, 5182	K.	Fontaine.
20	Flight Sub-Lieut. Soar	5181	Halberstadt	Remy.
20	Flight Sub-Lieue. Soar	5181	2-seater Sct.	Fontaine.
20	Flight Lieut. Hervey	5184	White biplane	N.E. Bapaume.
26	Flight Commander Huskisson.	5186	Type K.	Ypres.
26	Flight Lieut. Croft	,, ,, A626	Single-seater Sct.	S. of Bapaume.
26	Flight Sub-Lieut. Compston.	Nieuport 8750	Albatross Sct.	2 miles W. Cambrai.
26	Flight Sub-Lieut. Woods.	Sop. Sct. 3691	Halberstadt	Uncertain, probably N.E. Bapaume.
26	Flight Lieut. Hervey	5197		
27	Flight Lieut. Mackenzie.	5198	Type L.	Achiet-le-Petit.

N.B.—When machine was certainly destroyed pilot's name is in *italics*.

Following are details of some of the more interesting events.

December 4th.

Flight Lieut. Goble, while escorting a bomb raid of F.E.'s, observed three Halberstadts at 12,500 feet trying to get behind the F.E.'s. The pilot dived at them. Two turned E., so he chased the other one, firing about 30 or 40 rounds. The F.E.'s then attacked it, and it appeared to go down out of control. Flight Lieut. Goble then climbed back to 13,300 feet and attacked three more Halberstadts. He got under the tail of one and fired about 100 rounds while circling round on a steep bank. The hostile machine dived towards Bertincourt in a very erratic manner, apparently out of control.

Flight Sub-Lieut. Little, while escorting a bomb raid of F.E.'s, observed a hostile scout coming towards them. He met him about half a mile from the formation and fired one round at close range, when his gun jammed in the second position. The pilot broke off the fight and the hostile machine attacked him while he was trying to clear the jam. His engine was running badly, so that he could not climb; he therefore dived west with the H.A. following, and firing continuously for about 30 seconds. He was forced to dive more steeply, crossed the lines at about 5,000 feet, and landed in a field just this side of the lines. He cleared the jam, got away again, and climbed to 10,000 feet. Seeing one of the F.E.'s being attacked by two H.A., he attacked the lower one, and fired about 20 shots at 50 yards range, when it side-slipped and nose-dived, going down out of control.

December 20th.

Flight Lieut. Hervey, while escorting a bomb raid, observed a white single-seater scout about 400 feet above him and to the eastward. He climbed about 200 feet above H.A. and dived at him with the sun behind him, opening fire at about 100 yards range. After about 20 rounds (several tracers were clearly seen to enter the enemy's fuselage) the hostile machine dived very steeply and apparently out of control, his engine being full on and emitting quantities of blue smoke.

Flight Sub-Lieut. Soar, while escorting a bomb raid, observed two H.A. at about 10,000 feet. He dived on both after getting between them and the sun, and opened fire at about 500 feet from them. One went down in a series of stalls with his engine on.

Flight Sub-Lieut Todd, while on an offensive patrol with F.E.'s, saw an F.E. being attacked by a type K over Bapaume. He dived and attacked at 9,500 feet. He opened fire at

50 yards range, closing up to 30 yards before H.A. stalled and went down in a spinning nose-dive out of control. He followed it down for some way, but did not see it recover.

Flight Commander Huskisson, while escorting a bomb raid, was attacked by a type K, who dived on him from behind. He put the machine down to gain more speed, then half stalled to allow the H.A. to pass underneath. He then dived on H.A. from above and opened fire at about 15 yards range. **The H.A. stalled, fell over on one wing, and then** nose-dived. Pilot saw this repeated down to 2,000 feet, but could not observe crash owing to mist.

Flight Sub-Lieut. Compston, while on an offensive patrol, was attacked by seven Albatross scouts N. of Cambrai. He dived at one, opening fire at about 30 yards range. The pilot saw his tracers entering the H.A., which then stalled and nose-dived, and went down out of control.

No. 3 Wing, France.

December 27th.

A report (A. 063) has been received of a raid on the blast furnaces of Dillingen. Nine bombers escorted by four fighters dropped 2,340 lbs. of bombs. Owing to the hazy weather it was impossible to observe the actual result. The machines were attacked on the return journey, but all got back safely.

GIBRALTAR.

No report from this station has been received during the period under review.

MALTA.

A report (A. 1231) has been received from this station.

The usual patrols and reconnaissances have been carried out.

This station is now complete.

EASTERN MEDITERRANEAN SQUADRON.

(Extracted from Report No. 40 (A. 034) from 15th–21st December.)

Note.—Strong winds and low clouds, prevalent throughout the Northern Ægean, have greatly interfered with all flying during the current week.

Thasos, "A" Flight of No. 2 Wing.

From the 15th to the 20th December anti-submarine patrols, reconnaissance, and bomb-dropping operations were carried out along the coast and in the Xanthi area.

December 20*th*.

Bomb attacks were made on Xanthi in the morning and on Gereviz seaplane base in the afternoon. Full reports are not yet available.

Stavros, "D" Flight of No. 2 Wing.

December 15*th and* 16*th*.

Spotting was carried out for H.M. ships.

December 17*th*.

Reconnaissance flights in the Orfano and Angista areas definitely confirmed the existence and location of a Turkish divisional headquarters.

December 18*th*.

One "D" flight machine, in conjunction with five R.F.C. machines, carried out a bombing attack on this objective. Five of the nine marquees housing the headquarters were observed to be damaged.

December 18*th,* 19*th, and* 20*th*.

Spotting flights and reconnaissances were carried out.

Thermi, "B" Flight.

Only practice flights have been carried out here.

Imbros, "C" Flight.

December 15*th,* 16*th, and* 17*th*.

Reconnaissance of the Dardanelles were carried out. Two enemy warships were attacked with bombs on the 16th, and two more on the 17th. No damage appears to have been done.

Further details have been received of the raid on 13th December on Kuleli Burgas Bridge mentioned in Report No. 39.

Flight Sub-Lieut. Williams with Midshipman Snow in H.F. 3002, Flight Sub-Lieut. M. Heriot with Sub-Lieut. R. F. Bentley in H.F. 3003, Flight Sub-Lieut. Devlin with Sub-Lieut. G. E. Wright in H. F. 3001, Flight Sub-Lieut. Waistell with Sub-Lieut. W. C. Jameson in H.F. 3915, with an escorting Bristol Scout (No. 8996) piloted by Flight Sub-Lieut. F. Marlowe, participated in the attack on the bridge.

One 65-lb. bomb, dropped by H.F. 3002, exploded on the island in the middle of the river which supports the centre portion of the bridge.

This was almost a direct hit, as smoke was seen to rise from both sides of the bridge, and it is probable that damage was caused by this bomb. Two 100-lb. bombs, dropped by the same machine, exploded 20 yards and 30 yards away from the bridge, and another 65-lb. bomb dropped by H.F. 3003 also fell 20 yards from the bridge.

Mudros, H.M.S. "Ark Royal."

Only test flights have been carried out on Shorts and Schneiders during the period from the 16th to the 20th December.

H.M.S. "Empress."

December 19th and 20th.

Reconnaissances were carried out and bombs dropped at Dranli and near Orfano.

Kassandra.

December 17th.

Airship S.S. 8 was transferred by air to Kassandra for patrol duty in the Gulf of Salonika in place of S.S. 43, which is being repaired.

EAST INDIES STATION.

Reports (A. 033 and A. 035) have been received of work done by H.M.S. "Ben-my-Chree" and H.M.S. "Raven II." during the period December 1st–23rd, 1916.

The following are the more interesting events:—

December 8th–19th.

H.M.S. "Raven II." carried out a series of reconnaissances and attacks on Turkish troops in the vicinity of Yenbo, on the Red Sea. A daily watch was kept on movements of troops, and bombs were dropped. Heavy anti-aircraft fire was experienced.

December 21st–23rd.

H.M.S. "Ben-my-Chree" carried out reconnaissances in the districts on Gaza, Jaffa, and Haifa. Bombs were dropped on the railway at Tubaun.

The ship was attacked by a Taube, which dropped six bombs, without effect.

CAPE STATION.

No. 8 Squadron, Zanzibar.

A report (A. 02) has been received for October 1916.

Reconnaissances have been carried out over various enemy camps and establishments. Bombs were dropped in some cases, and photographs obtained.

H.M.S. "Manica."

A report has been received (A. 039) dated November 3rd, which gives particulars of a seaplane flight over the Rufigi Delta.

Bombs were dropped, but no signs of activity were observed on the part of the enemy.

No. 7 Squadron with East African Field Force, Kilossa.

A report (A. 0122) has been received from Squadron Commander Nanson, with details of operations carried out between September 9th and October 16th, 1916.

Unsuitable weather has greatly hindered operations, the summit of the higher mountains being usually obscured by cloud, which has confined the sphere of activity to the less mountainous districts.

Reconnaissance and bombing expeditions have been carried out when possible from Dar es Salaam, where the new aerodrome has been completed.

R.N.A.S. ARMOURED CARS, EAST AFRICA.

A report (A. 097) has been received from this unit covering the period October 12th to December 3rd, 1916.

During this period no active operations took place.

REPORT OF OPERATIONS No. 26.

As the distribution list of this communiqué is now increased, it is opportune to state that the object of this publication is to keep officers in and out of the Air Service informed of the general work carried out. It is not in any way a complete record of work done.

HOME STATIONS.

The weather generally has been unfavourable for flying during the period under review.

A few flights in pursuit of reported hostile aircraft and the usual instructional and experimental flights have taken place whenever possible.

DUNKIRK.

Reports have been received covering the period 16th to 31st January 1917.

Owing to unfavourable weather, very little flying has been possible.

January 23rd.

A reconnaissance flight was made over Zeebrugge, Ostende, Bruges, and all harbours were reported as very quiet.

January 24th.

There were five engagements between fighting patrols on this day, and patrols between Zeebrugge and Ostende for the observation of shipping were carried out on the 25th, 26th, and 27th.

DETACHED SQUADRON WITH ROYAL FLYING CORPS.

A statement (A. 120657) has been received reporting Flight Lieut. Grange and Flight Sub-Lieut. Lawson wounded in combat on 7th January. Flight Sub-Lieut. Lawson, although badly wounded by a bullet which passed through the seat of his machine, brought back his machine, which was badly shot about, and made a perfect landing.

On the same date (7th January) Flight Sub-Lieut. Little accounted for his fourth hostile aircraft.

REPORT ON ROYAL NAVAL AIR SERVICE SQUADRON.
Attached 22nd Wing Royal Flying Corps.

A report (A. 0211) has been received from military sources of work carried out during the period 31st December 1916 to 13th January 1917 inclusive.

During the above period there have only been three days on which service flying has been possible.

On 4th January a pilot on patrol engaged and drove off three hostile machines in succession. Flight Lieut. Croft and Flight Sub-Lieut. Todd left on an offensive patrol at 2.30 p.m. on the 4th instant and have not since been heard of. Another pilot of the Naval Squadron reports seeing three hostile machines attacking a Sopwith Scout, and that the left planes of the Sopwith Scout came off during the combat. The three German machines followed the Sopwith down and he saw them land. He went down and saw what had occurred, but could see no trace of the Sopwith Scout. He saw a German machine on its back, and two others in the field near by.

On 5th January it was fine all day, and a good deal of flying was accomplished by the squadron. Only one indecisive combat took place.

On 7th January a pilot engaged and drove down a hostile machine. When last seen the German was turned over on its back and was falling out of control. Flight Lieut. Grange and Flight Sub-Lieut. Lawson were wounded during combats in the air.

There are now 16 flying officers serving with the squadron, which is composed of 16 Sopwith Scouts and one Nieuport Scout.

Headquarters, Royal Flying Corps,
    14th January 1917.

REPORT (A. 0408) ON ROYAL NAVAL AIR SERVICE SQUADRON.

Period 14th January to 27th January 1917, inclusive.

During the week ending 20th January no service flying was possible, and test flights only were carried out.

On the 21st and 22nd January the weather continued unfavourable for flying.

On the 23rd instant the weather was fine all day, and hostile aircraft were very active after 10 a.m. One pilot attacked the rear machine of a hostile formation of four machines N.E. of Bapaume. Several of his tracer bullets were seen to hit the German machine, which stalled, fell over on its wing tip, and nose-dived, with a great amount of smoke coming out of its engine. Something was also observed to drop from the hostile machine. When last seen it was completely out of control at a height of 2,000 feet. The combat took place at 12,000 feet. Another pilot, who was engaging a hostile machine, saw the observer drop his gun and fall inside the machine. It is presumed that the observer was either seriously wounded or killed. The squadron carried out many patrols on this day.

The 24th instant was again fine all day, but misty. The squadron had some indecisive fighting. Flight Commander Mackenzie set out on an offensive patrol at 11.15 a.m. He was last seen over Bapaume. No news has been received of this officer up to the time of writing this report, and he has been reported missing.

The 25th instant was again fine, and the squadron carried out several offensive patrols, damaging and driving down an Albatross.

The 26th instant was fine all day, but very misty. The squadron had some indecisive fighting. Flight Sub-Lieut. Soar was reported missing, but news has since come to hand that he is quite safe, and that he made a forced landing at Picquigny, N.W. of Amiens.

The 27th was fine all day, and patrols were carried out by the squadrons.

There are now 16 pilots serving with the squadrons, which is composed of 17 Sopwith Scouts.

Headquarters, Royal Flying Corps,
    29th January 1917.

No. 3 Wing, Luxeuil.

A report (No. A. 0213) has been received for the period 28th December 1916 to 16th January 1917.

During this period it has been impossible to carry out any operations owing to the very rough state of the weather.

No. 3 Wing, France.

A summary (A. 0176) has been received of all the operations carried out between 30th July and 31st December 1916.

EASTERN MEDITERRANEAN.

Report No. 41.

A report (A. 0153) has been received covering the period from 22nd to 28th December 1916, with an account of operations in South Bulgaria and on the Struma front.

Strong winds, low clouds, and rain-storms have greatly interfered with flying during the period under review.

Thasos "A" Flight.

December 22nd.

Bombing and reconnaissance flights were carried out at Xanthi, the railway station and Transport park being attacked with four 112-lb. bombs.

Photographs were taken of the railway lines and coast to the mouth of the Nestos, where new entrenchments were observed.

December 26th and 28th.

A further reconnaissance of the area to the south of Xanthi took place and the railway station was again bombed, considerable damage being done to the rolling stock according to reports, though no detailed accounts have been received as yet.

December 24th and 27th.

Anti-submarine patrols were carried out on these days.

Stavros Flight.

December 22nd and 27th, 1916.

Reconnaissance-photographic flights have been carried out, and also spotting for H.M. Ships and the Army.

Imbros Flight.

December 25th to 28th.

Reconnaissances of the Dardanelles were carried out; only small shipping was observed, with the exception of one T.B. at Chanak.

December 26th.

The aerodrome at Galata was attacked. Four machines and two escorts participated, and nine heavy and four 16-lb. bombs were dropped, direct hits being made on huts and living quarters, and considerable damage is believed to have been done to a hangar by a heavy bomb which dropped within 10 yards of it.

December 27th to 28th.

Tenedos was shelled by guns from the coast, and arrangements have been made to spot for one of H.M. ships to silence them.

Thermi "B" Flight.

December 23rd to 25th.

Reconnaissances were carried out over the coast line, and some trenches were attacked with bombs on the 24th, one direct hit being made.

December 26th.

A reconnaissance flight was made over the Chandarli Gulf. New gun emplacements and a new aerodrome were observed, and the Paradise racecourse has been reoccupied by the enemy.

H.M.S. "Ark Royal."

December 22nd to 27th.

Search was made for a sunk torpedo, and practice flights in Schneider Cup seaplanes were carried out.

H.M.S. "Empress."

December 22nd to 27th.

In a reconnaissance carried out in the Orphano district many new trenches were observed on the hills. A further reconnaissance of the same area was made the next day, and during this flight photographs were taken of the trenches, and a reconnaissance made of the Dranli area.

December 25th.

Two submarine patrols were carried out in the Orphano Gulf and two reconnaissances were also made of the Dranli area. A trench was attacked with four 16-lb. bombs, which put an end to some signalling which had been observed.

December 26th.

A further reconnaissance took place on the Dranli area, and four bombs were dropped on a redoubt. A spotting flight was also carried out for one of H.M. ships.

December 27th.

The ship proceeded to Mudros for exchange of old machines for new ones, and the transference having been completed she was ready for sea on the morning of the 29th.

Kassandra.

December 22nd to 27th.

Patrols of the entrance to the Gulf of Salonika by airship S.S. 8 were carried out.

Compiled from Report No. 42 (A. 0282) and Report No. 43 (A. 0203) of operations covering the period between 29th December 1916 and 10th January 1917.

Thasos.

December 29th to 31st.

Reconnaissance flights were made at Drama, and a bomb attack was made on the Buk Bridge, four bombs being dropped from a height of 10,200 feet. The 1½ Strutter in which the attack was made was heavily shelled. A Schneider seaplane acted as escort.

January 2nd and 3rd.

A successful bomb attack was carried out on Gereviz.

January 4th.

During the night an attack was made on Fort B to the east of Kavalla in a Short seaplane. Two 100-lb., one 112-lb., two 16-lb., and two incendiary bombs were dropped, and one tray of ammunition was fired at the fort.

January 5th.

A raid was carried out on the largest of the bridges on the railway between Xanthi and Gumultina. Two Henri Farman bombers, escorted by two Scouts, delivered the attack.

Flight Sub-Lieut. Haig and Sub-Lieut. T. E. Maxwell, R.N.V.R. (in H.F. 9140, Type 27, No. 4023) made particularly good practice, coming down to 3,000 feet and dropping two 100-lb. bombs, one of which exploded close to the bridge, and the other appeared to pass right through it, exploding underneath the water. Though the bridge was not wrecked, it is probable that the structure was severely shaken.

All machines came under heavy and accurate anti-aircraft fire. Two enemy anti-aircraft guns were definitely located.

After bombing the bridge Flight Sub-Lieut. Haig and Sub-Lieut. Maxwell, while proceeding on reconnaissance to Xanthi, attacked a train of 20 trucks about half a mile south-west of Xanthi station. Four 16-lb. bombs were dropped, and it was observed that the train did not proceed on its journey after the bombardment.

January 9th.

During a reconnaissance in a Sopwith bomber, accompanied by a 1½ Strutter, a camp of 400 bell tents and a bridge were bombed. Only signalled reports have been received of this operation.

Stavros.

December 29th, 1916, to January 11th, 1917.

Spotting flights were carried out for H.M. ships, photographs were taken of the Orphano district, and reconnaissances and two bombing expeditions, the first on a transport park at Angista, and the other in the Orphano-Pravi Valley, were carried out.

H.M.S. "Empress."

December 29th.

H.M.S. "Empress" returned to Stavros from Mudros. Reconnaissances took place on the following morning.

January 1st.

A large hostile machine of the Albatross type circled over Chai Aghizi at 7,000 feet apparently taking photographs. A Schneider seaplane was sent in pursuit from H.M.S. "Empress," and attempted to attack at 7,000 feet, but the hostile machine disappeared in the clouds.

January 5th.

Spotting and reconnaissance flights were carried out in the Karjani area and new gun emplacements were located, and a photographic reconnaissance was made of Dranli.

January 6th.

Spotting for one of H.M. ships resulted in part of a village in the region of Orphano being set on fire by bombardment.

Trenches to the south-west of Orphano were attacked with bombs from a height of 2,500 feet, and three bombs exploded in a redoubt and one in a trench.

January 8th.

A number of shelters and dug-outs in the Dedeballi and Orphano district, having been located during a morning flight, were attacked in the afternoon by Flight Sub-Lieut. Malet and Sub-Lieut. D. P. Rowland in Short 9758.

As a result the camp was set on fire, and was found burning by a second seaplane, which arrived on the scene half an hour later. Another bomb was dropped at a group of 50 men near the burning camp, and three more bombs at another camp in the vicinity of Orphano by the second seaplane.

January 9th to 11th.

Spotting flights were carried out for a monitor, and the Orphano-Lungo areas were again reconnoitred.

Thermi.

Nothing of importance took place. No Service flights were made during the period under review.

Imbros.

December 30th, 1916, and January 1st, 2nd, 3rd, and 4th, 1917.

The usual reconnaissances were carried out over the Dardanelles. A small torpedo boat was the only unusual shipping observed.

One machine has been sent to Tenedos, which is to be used as an advanced base to watch the Asiatic coast.

Several reconnaissance flights and bombing expeditions have been undertaken, one especially on the Kuleli Burgas bridge by moonlight. The following is an account of this operation :—

Three machines left Imbros at 1715, 4th January, and at 1720, and arrived over the target in the moonlight at about 1930.

The first machine (H.F. 3003) on approaching the bridge was fired at by an anti-aircraft gun on the Kuleli Burgas side of the river.

Two 16-lb. bombs were dropped at this gun, which was effectually silenced, no more flashes being observed from this gun till after the attack. Coming down to 2,000 feet, the bridge was attacked from the Uzun Keupri side with two 65-lb. and 100-lb. bombs, the following results being observed :—

The 100-lb. bomb exploded in the centre of the bridge, where it crossed the broad part of the river on the Kuleli Burgas side of the island, and one 65-lb. bomb exploded on the side of the bridge or on the abutments on the Kuleli Burgas bank of the river. These two bombs must have wrecked the section of the bridge on the western side of the island.

The second machine (H.F. 3001) attacked the Iron Road bridge to the south of the railway bridge with three 65-lb. bombs which were dropped from 1,000 feet. A direct hit was made with one of these, and the eastern half of the Bulgarian Span was seen to be enveloped in smoke and débris.

The third machine (H.F. 3002) descending to 1,000 feet attacked the railway bridge, straddling it from east to west. The first two bombs (65-lb.) fell alongside the viaduct on the island, and the third (100-lb.) made a direct hit on the western section of the bridge itself, exploding on the permanent way on the span nearest the island.

Considerable anti-aircraft rifle and machine-gun fire was experienced by all machines during the attack, and also from Kesham on the return journey.

The numbers of the machines and engines which carried out the former raid on Kuleli Burgas bridge on 13th December are as follows : -

H.F. No. 3002. Engine 155 h.p. Canton Unne, No. 4566.
H.F. ,, 3001. ,, ,, ,, ,, ,, 4687.
H.F. ,, 3003. ,, ,, ,, ,, ,, 4729.
H.F. ,, 3915. Engine 150 h.p. ,, ,, ,, 3508.
B.Sct. No. 8996. Engine 100 h.p. Mono Gnome. No. 5812.

With regard to the running of these engines, the only one which was entirely satisfactory was No. 4729 in H.F. 3003.

The Mono Gnome in the Bristol Scout failed when over the bridge (after a 90-mile flight), but picked up after the machine had glided 3,000 feet. It failed again on the return journey, and the pilot was only just able to make the aerodrome.

Details have now been received of the raid on Galata aerodrome, carried out on 26th December, and briefly reported in W.O.R. No. 41.

The attack was delivered by three Henri Farmans and a B.E. 2 C., escorted by two Nieuport two-seaters; the bombs were dropped from 6,500, 7,000, and 9,000 feet with the following results:—

One 65-lb. bomb exploded about 10 yards from the middle hangar on the north side of the aerodrome, which was seen to be considerably damaged, and another fell (65-lb. bomb) 25 yards from the same hangar.

Two 100-lb. bombs and two 65-lb. bombs fell on and among a group of huts and sheds to the N.W. of the aerodrome, presumably living quarters and storehouses.

One 100-lb. bomb exploded directly on a small shed to the S.W. of the above huts and sheds. Other bombs fell close to the remaining hangars, but these are protected by high earthworks, and it is doubtful whether any damage was done to them.

January 9th and 10th.

Owing to low clouds, the usual Dardanelles patrol was carried out on these days only.

January 9th.

The aerodrome was attacked about midnight by two hostile machines. Fifteen small bombs were dropped, but little damage was done. An hour later Galata was attacked, five 65-lb. bombs being dropped, but no details of this operation have been received, though it is believed that damage was caused.

Mudros.

(1) H.M.S. "Ark Royal."

Practice flights in Short and Schneider seaplanes were carried out on 30th and 31st December and 1st, 2nd, and 4th January.

January 10th.

Practice flights in a Short seaplane were carried out.

(2) Marsh Aerodrome.

Instructional and practice flights have been made in Sopwith Strutters, Nieuport Fighters, B.E. 2 C.'s. and Henri Farmans. Bomb-dropping practice has also been carried out.

(3) Airship Station.

Period between 29th December 1916 and 4th January 1917.

Airship S.S. 43 remains at Mudros undergoing repairs.

No patrols have been carried out during the current week, 4th to 10th January.

Kassandra Airship Station.

From 30th December to 9th January.

The patrol of the entrance to the Gulf of Salonica was carried out on 30th and 31st December and on 1st January by S.S. 8. During the remainder of the week bad weather prevented flying.

EAST INDIA STATION.

A report (A. 0346) has been received of operations 25th to 28th December.

December 27th.

Chikaldere bridge was attacked by seaplanes from H.M.S. " Ben-my-Chree " and H.M.S. " Raven II."

Short No. 8080 (Flight Sub-Lieut. Smith and Captain Wedgewood Benn) dropped bombs on bridge and track and scattered the bridge guard by Lewis gun-fire.

Sopwiths Nos. 3770 (Commander Samson, D.S.O.), 3778 (Flight Lieut. Clemson), and 8188 (Flight Lieut. Brooke) attacked at heights of 400 to 700 feet.

Further attacks were made by Short 8080 (Flight Lieut. Maskell and Lieutenant W. L. Samson, R.N.V.R.). Sopwith 3778 (Flight Lieut. Clemson), and Sopwith 3770 (Flight Sub-Lieut. Henderson). Flight-Lieut. Clemson on this occasion scored direct hits on the permanent way with both his bombs.

In all fifteen 65-lb. and twenty-four 16-lb. bombs were dropped, and at least four direct hits were observed.

Most of the machines were hit, but all returned safely and without casualties to personnel.

H.M.S. " Raven II."

A report (A. 0170) has been received of operations of 25th to 27th December.

December 27th.

Flight Sub-Lieut. E. King, R.N., with observer Lieutenant N. W. Stewart, Royal Flying Corps, left the ship in a Short seaplane 8004 and bombed the Chilkaldir Bridge, on the Constantinople Bagdad Railway. No direct hit was obtained.

Flight Lieut. Burling, R.N., with Observer Lieut. K. L. Williams, in 8075, dropped nine bombs on the bridge, one direct hit being obtained.

CAPE STATION.

Zanzibar.

A report (0335) has been received covering the month of November.

The usual reconnaissances and spotting flights were carried out over the Rufigi Delta.

No. 7 Squadron.

Kilossa.

A report has been received (A. 0321) of operations carried out between 16th October and 12th November 1916.

October 20th.

The following are the most interesting events :—

The selection of a site for a new aerodrome at Iringa and the transport of aviation stores, &c., was proceeded with, but the party with machine-gun detachment sent from Safari to carry out the operation, on reaching Iringa were obliged to retire northwards, as that place was threatened by the enemy in force. They were unable to return to Iringa until 4th November.

Great credit is due to Lieutenant Kearton (Royal Fusiliers, attached to the Royal Naval Air Service) for successfully completing this journey over mountainous and difficult country not yet clear of the enemy, the retirement to the north referred to being carried through without food, and the porters being in a state of mutiny.

November 2nd.

A reconnaissance flight was carried out on the Kilossa-Mabruge road, and it was ascertained that the enemy had partly repaired a bridge over the river, and a photograph was taken.

November 7th.

Various reconnaissances have been carried out from Iringa, aeroplanes Nos. 8489 and 8425 having arrived there, and much useful information has been obtained.

Finer weather has been experienced during the last month, and in spite of low clouds the work undertaken has been successful. Several flights have been made from Dar-es-Salaam, and bombing expeditions at the request of the General in command there.

ARMOURED CAR DIVISION.
East Africa.

A report (A. 0354) has been received from this unit for the period 3rd December 1916—8th January 1917. The division has left East Africa for Egypt.

ROYAL FLYING CORPS COMMUNIQUÉ No. 68.
Artillery Co-operation.

December 24th.

Forty targets were successfully engaged with aeroplane observation.

Four direct hits were obtained by heavy artillery co-operating with aeroplanes of the First Brigade, and Siege Artillery obtained 20 direct hits on five gun-pits, and two direct hits on trench targets. Three direct hits were also obtained on trench targets by field artillery.

With aeroplane observation by the Second Brigade, artillery successfully engaged eight hostile batteries; 28 direct hits were obtained on hostile batteries and trench targets. One explosion of ammunition was caused.

Artillery co-operating with aeroplanes of the Third Brigade secured two direct hits on enemy targets.

Artillery of the Fourth Army, co-operating with aeroplanes of the Fourth Brigade, successfully engaged two hostile batteries.

During the day some successful photographic work was accomplished, and bombs were dropped on places of military importance by machines of the First, Second, and Fifth Brigades.

Casualties.

Killed.—Corporal G. Dinnage, No. 1 Squadron.

Wounded.—Lieutenant W. B. Kellog and Second Lieut. T. B. Jones, No. 23 Squadron.

December 25th.

On the night of the 24th–25th bombs were dropped on Pont-à-Vendin, Douvrin, and Cité St. Theodore by machines of the First Brigade. Four bombs were seen to explode in Pont-à-Vendin.

Vaulx-Vraucourt was attacked by aeroplanes of the Fifth Brigade. One house was set on fire. Machine-gun fire was opened into the villages of Vaulx-Vraucourt and Grevillers.

On the day of the 25th no flying was possible.

Artillery Co-operation.

December 26th.

Co-operating with aeroplanes of the First Brigade, siege artillery obtained 12 direct hits on hostile batteries, and caused an explosion of ammunition. One direct hit was obtained on another target. Three direct hits were secured by field artillery on two targets.

Artillery of the Second Army successfully engaged two hostile batteries with aeroplane observation. One gun-pit was hit, and two explosions of ammunition caused.

Eight direct hits were obtained on enemy targets by artillery co-operating with aeroplanes of the Third Brigade.

Artillery of the Fourth Army co-operating with aeroplanes of the Fourth Brigade successfully engaged 11 hostile batteries, obtaining 21 direct hits. Five emplacements were damaged and two explosions caused. A working party was engaged and dispersed under zone call.

Some successful artillery work was accomplished with aeroplane observation by the Fifth Brigade.

Hostile Aircraft.

A hostile machine engaged by Captain Long and Lieutenant Sedgwick, both of No. 24 Squadron, was driven down in a damaged condition.

Second Lieutenant Zink and Second Lieutenant Mayhew, No. 18 Squadron, engaged a hostile machine near Velu. The German aeroplane broke off the combat and dived vertically.

Second Lieutenant Macdonald and Second Lieutenant Smith, No. 18 Squadron, engaged and drove down a hostile machine out of control.

A German aeroplane attacked by Second Lieutenant Lewis and Second Lieutenant Royffe, No. 18 Squadron, was driven out of control near Velu.

Flight Sub-Lieut. Compston, R.N.A.S. Squadron, engaged several Albatross Scouts, one of which he drove down out of control, and the rest broke off the combat.

A German machine engaged by Flight Commander Huskisson, R.N.A.S. Squadron, near Ypres, was hit and fell in a series of stalls, and appeared to be absolutely out of control.

Flight Lieut. Croft, R.N.A.S. Squadron, engaged two hostile machines near Bapaume, one of which fell apparently out of control.

Lieutenant R. W. P. Hall and Second Lieutenant E. F. W. Smith, No. 9 Squadron, on a B.E. 2 E., were attacked from behind by a Halberstadt. The B.E. 2 E. opened fire with the rear gun. When within about 90 feet range the German pilot was hit, and the machine dived to earth and crashed.

Bombing.

Places of military importance behind the German lines were attacked by aeroplanes of the First, Second, and Fifth Brigades.

A number of bombs were dropped by machines of the Fifth Brigade and were seen to burst in Vaulx-Vraucourt.

Casualties.

Killed.—Captain J. W. W. Nason and Lieutenant C. A. F. Brown, No. 46 Squadron.

Wounded.—Second Lieutenant G. A. Masters, No. 18 Squadron; Second Lieutenant W. H. Hubbard, No. 5 Squadron.

Missing.—Second Lieutenant Lewis, No. 24 Squadron; Second Lieutenant F. N. Insoll and Second Lieutenant H. E. Arnold, No. 5 Squadron.

Artillery Co-operation.

December 27th.

Eighty-six targets were successfully engaged with aeroplane observation.

Artillery of the First Army, with aeroplane observation, obtained 12 direct hits on battery and other positions.

Two direct hits on enemy targets were obtained by field artillery.

Co-operating with aeroplanes of the Second Brigade, artillery successfully engaged nine hostile batteries. Four gun-pits were hit, and two explosions of ammunition caused.

Artillery of the Third Army, with aeroplane observers, obtained 14 direct hits on hostile batteries. One explosion of ammunition was caused.

In co-operation with aeroplanes of the Fourth Brigade, artillery successfully engaged 20 targets and caused two explosions of ammunition.

With observation by aeroplanes of the Fifth Brigade, artillery obtained eight direct hits on gun positions; these gun-pits were damaged, and an explosion of ammunition was caused.

Hostile Aircraft.

During the day, Second Lieutenant R. B. Wainwright and Second Lieutenant H. R. Wilkinson, No. 20 Squadron, engaged and drove down two hostile machines, both of which are believed to have been badly damaged. The presence of other German aeroplanes prevented the fate of the two enemy machines being ascertained.

Second Lieutenant J. Blackwood and Second Lieutenant F. H. Bronskill, No. 20 Squadron, engaged two Halberstadt biplanes, one of which was destroyed near Zonnebeke, and the other driven off.

Twenty-one combats took place on the front of the Third Army.

Two German aeroplanes were brought down and seen to crash by No. 11 Squadron. One of these was destroyed by Captain Quested and Second Lieutenant Dicksee. A third hostile machine was forced to land in a field.

An offensive patrol of No. 29 Squadron encountered a formation of hostile machines over Adinfer Wood, and drove one down out of control.

A German machine engaged by Second Lieutenant J. V. Aspinall and Second Lieutenant J. M. R. Miller, No. 22 Squadron, was driven down and landed in a field west of Ruyaulcourt.

Captain S. H. Long, No. 24 Squadron, engaged and drove down a German machine out of control.

A German aeroplane which was attacked by Second Lieutenant Copeland and Sergeant Ware, No. 7 Squadron, was driven down out of control between Pys and Miraumont.

Photography.

Seven hundred and thirty-seven photographs were taken during the day.

Bombing.

Bombs were dropped by machines of the First and Fifth Brigades on places of military importance.

Casualties.

Killed.—Second Lieutenant E. F. W. Smith, No. 9 Squadron; Lieutenant C. W. H. Parker, No. 5 Squadron.

Wounded.—Second Lieutenant R. P. C. Fremantle, No. 9 Squadron; Captain J. R. Gould, No. 2 Squadron; Second Lieutenant E. F. Jones, No. 5 Squadron; Second Lieutenant H. J. H. Dicksee, No. 11 Squadron.

Artillery Co-operation.

December 28th.

Twenty-eight targets were dealt with by aeroplane observers. In co-operation with aeroplanes of the First Brigade heavy artillery obtained three direct hits on gun-pits.

Siege artillery obtained nine direct hits on gun-pits, four of which were destroyed and two badly damaged. A trench target was also hit.

Four hostile batteries were successively engaged by artillery co-operating with aeroplanes of the Second Brigade. Two gun-pits were hit, and two explosions of ammunition caused.

Artillery of the Fourth Army, co-operating with aeroplanes of the Fourth Brigade, obtained several direct hits on three trench points.

With observation by aeroplanes of the Fifth Brigade, artillery successfully engaged six hostile batteries and obtained direct hits on gun positions. Four gun-pits were damaged, and an explosion of ammunition caused.

Bombing.

Auchy and Lievin were attacked by machines of the First Brigade. In both places buildings were hit.

Bombs were dropped on Miraumont and a dump in Rossignol Wood by aeroplanes of the Fifth Brigade.

Casualties.

Wounded.—No. 22177, First Air Mechanic L. V. Bulmer; No. 24208, Acting Corporal J. Chappell, No. 46641, Second Air Mechanic L. Hadley; No. 40941, Second Air Mechanic J. Newman, all of No. 14 Balloon Company.

Missing.—Captain H. Spanner, No. 27 Squadron.

December 29th.

No flying; nothing to report.

December 30th.

Very little work was done owing to bad weather. Artillery of the Second Army, with aeroplane observation, engaged three hostile batteries. Two gun-pits were hit. Bombs were dropped on trenches and places of military importance by machines of the First Brigade. One bomb dropped in Cité de l'Abattoir was seen to burst on a house.

Headquarters, Royal Flying Corps,
 31st December 1916.

ROYAL FLYING CORPS COMMUNIQUÉ No. 70.

Artillery Co-operation.

January 7th.

Seventy-six targets were successfully engaged with aeroplane observation.

On the First Army front four direct hits were obtained on a gun-pit and six on an anti-aircraft battery. A successful shoot was carried out against Pont-à-Vendin. The railway line was damaged and an explosion of ammunition caused.

Artillery of the Second Army, with observation by the Second Brigade, successfully engaged five hostile batteries and caused four explosions of ammunition. The 160th Siege Battery obtained 18 direct hits on a hostile battery, and caused a large explosion of ammunition.

In co-operation with aeroplanes of the Fourth Brigade artillery successfully engaged 14 hostile batteries and obtained 11 direct hits, damaging three emplacements and causing one large explosion.

On the Fifth Army front 12 batteries were successfully engaged; 13 direct hits on gun positions and four explosions of ammunition were recorded. Four gun-pits were demolished.

Successful trench shoots with aeroplane observation were carried out on all army fronts.

Hostile Aircraft.

During the night of the 6th–7th six hostile aeroplanes appeared over Noeux-les-Mines at intervals of 15 minutes, flying at a height of under 1,000 feet. Each aeroplane dropped six bombs, causing some damage to the mines. They also fired their machine guns into the village.

Flight Lieut. Little, R.N.A.S., observed a hostile machine engaging a B.E. over Grevillers. He dived at the hostile machine and fired about 60 rounds. The German fell out of control, and was last seen turned on its back. Owing to the presence of other hostile machines its ultimate fate was not ascertained.

An offensive patrol of No. 32 Squadron engaged and dispersed a hostile formation north of the Bois des Vaux. One of the hostile machines was obviously hit. It side-slipped and nose-dived, but flattened out again when it had gone down about 3,000 feet.

Bombing.

During the day eighty 20-lb. bombs were dropped by the First Brigade on various objectives with satisfactory results.

Twenty one 20-lb. bombs were dropped on Miraumont by the Fifth Brigade.

Casualties.

Killed.—Second Lieut. E. G. W. Bisset, No. 6 Squadron.

Wounded.—No. 1396, Sergeant T. Mottershead and Lieutenant W. E. Gower, No. 20 Squadron; Second Lieut. J. W. Eckles, No. 22 Squadron; Flight Sub-Lieut. A. H. S. Lawson, R.N.A.S. Squadron; and Flight Lieut. E. R. Grange, R.N.A.S. Squadron.

Missing.—Second Lieut. E. G. S. Wagner, No. 32 Squadron, Major L. Parker and Second Lieut. F. A. Mann, No. 52 Squadron.

January 8th.

The weather was unfavourable and very little work was accomplished. Some successful artillery co-operation was accomplished on the fronts of the Fourth and Fifth Brigades.

During an artillery patrol, Second Lieut. Johnson and Lieutenant Bird, No. 4 Squadron, engaged three hostile machines, one of which was apparently damaged.

January 9th.

Nothing to report.

January 10th.

The weather continued unfavourable and little work was accomplished. On the Fourth Brigade front one hostile battery was successfully engaged, and on the Fifth Brigade front six hostile batteries were silenced.

Hostile Aircraft.

No. 2 Section's balloon was attacked and brought down in flames. Lieutenant S. Gavin and Second Lieut. Whitlock made successful parachute descents and landed unhurt. No. 10 Section's balloon was also attacked, but was hauled down safely.

Bombing.

On the night of the 9th-10th instant, bombs were dropped by No. 18 Squadron on hostile aerodromes. Six were dropped on Velu (or Lebucquiere), all of which were seen to burst, and a large explosion was caused. Six more were dropped on Villers le Cagnicourt. One fell among the hangars, and the remainder on or about the aerodrome. A hostile machine left the aerodrome and was attacked by the F.E. but was soon lost to sight. Six bombs were also dropped on Buissy from a height of 500 feet, all of which fell on the north-east edge of the aerodrome.

Contact Patrols.

Second Lieut. Sayer and Second Lieut. Davis, No. 15 Squadron, carried out a successful contact patrol at low altitudes, gaining valuable information as to the position of our troops and the condition of the enemy's positions.

On a pre-arranged plan Captain G. C. Bailey and Second Lieut. L. S. White, No. 2 Squadron, flew over the enemy's trenches just north of the double Crassier at a low altitude, and opened machine-gun fire. They fired Very's lights, and generally attracted the enemy in the trenches, who thus had their backs turned to the front line and were firing at the aeroplane with rifle and machine-gun fire. The Germans were so occupied with this work that our troops were enabled to leave their trenches and cross no man's land without being perceived, and without any previous artillery preparation. Two parties entered the German trenches, took eight prisoners, and bombed dug-outs which were full of Germans. Captain Bailey's machine was hit in a few places by anti-aircraft fire, but was untouched by rifle or machine-gun fire. During the flight he and his observer located 13 active hostile batteries.

January 11th.

Very little work was possible on account of clouds and snow.

Contact Patrol.

In connection with the operations of the Fifth Army a very successful contact patrol was accomplished by Second Lieut. Sayer and Second Lieut Davis, No. 15 Squadron, from a height of 300 feet. Flares were located in the captured objectives, and our men were seen waving their hands. This patrol was carried out in very inclement weather.

Bombing.

On the night of the 10th–11th instant two hostile aeroplanes dropped bombs on No. 16 Squadron's aerodrome at Bruay. One bomb hit a hangar, destroying five aeroplanes which were in it, and wounding one non-commissioned officer and two men. In retaliation aeroplanes of No. 2 Squadron left to attack the aerodrome at Provin. Owing to mist they were unable to find the objective, and dropped bombs with good results on Pont-à-Vendin, Carvin, and Salome.

Casualties.

Killed —Second Lieut. R. Hopper, No. 60 Squadron.

Wounded.—No. 24977, Sergeant J. Drew; No. 10726 First Air Mechanic A. Best; and No. 16398, Second Air Mechanic W. J. Callaghan, all of No 16 Squadron.

On 7th January Sergeant Mottershead and his observer, Lieutenant Gower, No. 20 Squadron, were attacked by a German aeroplane when about 9,000 feet over Ploegsteert Wood. The petrol tank of the F.E. 2. D. was pierced almost immediately and the machine burst into flames, compelling the pilot to break off the fight and make towards our lines. Two officers of the A/153rd Brigade, R.F.A., witnessed the descent, and could see the pilot enveloped in flames being sprayed with a fire extinguisher by Lieutenant Gower. Sergeant Mottershead selected a suitable landing ground in a difficult country, and made a successful landing in spite of the condition of his machine and the seriousness of his wounds. On touching the ground the machine collapsed, throwing the observer clear, but pinning Sergeant Mottershead under the burning wreckage. Again Lieutenant Gower checked the flames as much as possible by the use of his extinguisher. Sergeant Mottershead has since died of his wounds.

January 12th.

Unfavourable weather. Nothing to report.

January 13th.

Practically no flying. Low clouds, snow and rain all day.

Casualties.

Missing.—Second Lieut. G. W. Bentley and Second Lieut. D. R. Hinkley, 12th Yorks and Lancs Regiment (attached to No. 5 Squadron for signalling purposes).

Headquarters, Royal Flying Corps.
  14th January 1917.

ROYAL FLYING CORPS COMMUNIQUÉ No. 71.

January 14th to 20th, inclusive.

During this period there has been practically no flying owing to adverse weather conditions.

A few successful artillery flights have been carried out, and on the 15th instant bombs were dropped by the First and Third Brigades on various places in the hostile lines.

Casualties.

Wounded.—Captain J. McArthur, No. 12 Squadron; Lieutenant Balls, Sixth Corps Intelligence Officer, attached to No. 12 Squadron.

Headquarters, Royal Flying Corps,
  21st January 1917.

REPORT OF OPERATIONS No. 27.

As the distribution list of this communiqué has now increased, it is opportune to state that the object of this publication is to keep officers in and out of the Air Service informed of the general work carried out.

It is not in any way a complete record of work done.

HONOURS.

Commander Samson, D.S.O., R.N., has received a bar to his D.S.O. for conspicuous and continuous service.

The D.S.O. has been awarded to Flight Lieut. S. G. Goble, D.S.C., R.N.A.S-, for conspicuous bravery and skill in attacking hostile aircraft on numerous occasions.

The D.S.C. has been awarded to the following officers:—

Flight Commander W. G. Moore, R.N.A.S.
Flight Lieut. L. C. Shoppee, R.N.A.S.
Flight Lieut. E. R. Grange, R.N.A.S.
Sub-Lieut. R. A. Little.

Flight Commander Moore received recognition for his work in East Africa, and especially for his remarkable 300-mile flight to Mahenje.

Lieutenant Shoppee has shown great bravery and skill in bombing raids in the Eastern Mediterranean, and his particularly good shooting resulted in the collapse of an important bridge on the railway between Buk and Drama (*see* Report of Operations No. 22).

The other two officers mentioned have shown conspicuous gallantry in attacking hostile machines, and success in bringing enemy aircraft down.

Flight Lieut. D. M. B. Galbraith receives a bar to his D.S.C. for his exceptional gallantry in attacking enemy machines; on one occasion he attacked six hostile machines single-handed, and succeeded in driving down two of them and putting four to flight.

HOME STATIONS.

The reports received from home stations during the period from January 31st to February 16th all speak of the weather being unfavourable for flying. The usual patrols, experimental and instructional flights, have, however, been carried out whenever possible.

A report (A. 0382) has been received from Mullion Airship Station, giving details of the discovery of an enemy submarine in the vicinity of the Wolf Rock.

The captain of a coastal airship while on patrol noticed an oil track on the surface of the water, with bubbles rising at intervals of about one minute and moving at a speed of about 6 knots. After circling round for about 20 minutes, one 65-lb. delay-action bomb was dropped, which fell approximately 20 yards from the bubbles, which continued to rise to the surface, but were apparently hardly moving.

Two destroyers in the vicinity were then signalled to the spot, and the airship returned to its base, as the light was failing.

A further report has been received from Mullion Air Station with reference to the sighting of a submarine on February 12th.

In overcast and rainy weather a coastal airship sighted a submarine coming to the surface about one mile on the port bow, but she submerged again almost immediately. The airship dropped two 65-lb. bombs; about half a minute after the conning tower of the submarine disappeared. The first failed to explode, and the other, which was a delay bomb, exploded immediately over the swirl made by the conning tower. Large quantities of oil were observed to come to the surface, but there was no further sign of the submarine, although the airship remained in the vicinity or within 15 miles radius for four hours.

DUNKIRK.

No. 5 Wing.

January 3rd.

The torpedo boat destroyers in Bruges harbour were attacked, and a building was set on fire. Unfortunately several machines were wrecked owing to engine failure due to the oil freezing, though all pilots and machines have since been accounted for.

January 4th.

A further raid was carried out on the harbour at Bruges, eighteen 112-lb. bombs being observed to fall among the huts on the docks and West Basin. All three machines engaged in the operation safely returned.

January 7th.

Five machines, escorted by a fighter escort and a photographic machine, carried out a bombing raid on Bruges harbour, dropping sixty 22-lb. Le Pecq bombs on the shipping and docks. All the machines returned safely with the exception of one of the escort.

On the same evening and in the early hours of the following morning a further attack took place on the torpedo craft in this harbour. Twelve bombs of 112-lb. calibre were dropped, with good results, and a large fire was observed. All pilots and machines returned safely.

January 14th.

A bombing attack on the harbour and shipping at Bruges was carried out by seven machines in the early hours of the morning. Six machines found their objective, on which sixty 22-lb. Le Pecq bombs and eight 16-lb. bombs were dropped.

The shooting seems to have been particularly good. All bombs were dropped from 3,000 to 4,000 feet. Though visibility was rather hazy, the docks were clearly visible.

The railway junctions were destroyed, and the building at St. Michiels, occupied by Germans, was attacked. Three torpedo boats and a captured English vessel were also severely damaged.

An attack on some covered refuges for submarines also took place with unknown results.

Flight Sub-Lieut. Stewart, in Sopwith 5081, failed to return.

MONTHLY SUMMARY FOR JANUARY 1917.

NAVAL SQUADRON No. 8, ATTACHED 22nd WING, ROYAL FLYING CORPS.

Number of hours flown :—
Service flights, 159 hours 10 minutes   -) 205   hours
Test flights, 46 hours 40 minutes   -   -) 50 minutes.
Number of days on which flying was possible, 20
(including five days on which only practice flights were carried out).

Number of combats : Decisive, 3 ; Indecisive, 16 ; Total, 19.

Date.	Name.	Machine.	Type of H. A.	Locality.
Jan. 4	Flight Sub-Lieut. Grange (D.S.C.)	Sop. Sct. 5194	Type K.	South of Bapaume.
7	Flight Sub-Lieut. Little (D.S.C.)	5194	Type M.	Grevillers.
23	Flight Lieut. Booker.	5197	Albatross scout	N.E. of Bapaume.
*23	Flight-Commander Huskisson.	5186	Small two-seater	Arras.

* Hostile observer appeared to be hit.

Casualties.

January 7th.

Flight Lieut. Grange and Flight Sub-Lieut. Lawson wounded in action.

Missing.

January 4th.

Flight Lieut. Todd and Flight Lieut. Croft.

January 24th.

Flight Commander Mackenzie, D.S.O.

February 2nd.

Flight Sub-Lieut. Traynor. (Attached No. 8 Squadron from No. 3 Squadron.)

Honours.

Flight Lieut. Grange and Flight Sub-Lieut. Little. Awarded the D.S.C.

January 4th.

Flight Lieut. Grange, while on an offensive patrol, sighted two type K machines south of Bapaume at 12,000 feet, and attacked the nearest one. Pilot manœuvred about until he got his gun into position, and after about 50 rounds the hostile machine went down in a spin apparently out of control.

January 7th.

Flight Sub-Lieut. Little, while on an offensive patrol, saw a hostile scout, type K, diving on a B.E. Pilot dived on the H.A. and opened fire at a range of about 100 yards. After firing about 60 rounds, hostile machine nose-dived, apparently out of control. After diving for some distance it turned over on its back.

January 23rd.

Flight Lieut. Booker, while on an offensive patrol, attacked the rear machine of a formation of four hostile scouts. Pilot observed his tracers entering the fuselage of the H.A., whereupon it stalled, fell over on its wing tip, and nose-dived. A great amount of smoke appeared to be coming from the engine. Pilot also saw something fly off from the machine, which, when last seen, appeared to be completely out of control.

January 23rd.

Flight Commander Huskisson, while on an offensive patrol, attacked the rear machine of a hostile formation which attempted to cross our lines near Arras. Pilot opened fire at short range and saw the observer of the hostile machine, who was firing at him, drop his gun and fall back inside the machine.

General Remarks.

January has been a disappointing month generally. The weather was unsuitable for work over the lines until p.m. of the 4th, when two offensive patrols were carried out. The Germans were very active, and one of our patrols, consisting of Flight Lieuts. Grange, Todd, Croft, and Little, brought down a hostile machine near Bapaume, but Flight Lieuts. Todd and Croft failed to return. The weather remained unsuitable again until the 7th, when it was very fine all day. Hostile activity was above normal, and many combats took place.

Flight Sub-Lieut. Little brought down a machine near Grevillers, but we had the misfortune to have both Flight Lieut. Grange and Flight Sub-Lieut. Lawson wounded.

Flight Lieut. Grange was hit in the right shoulder, and although he lost the use of his arm and a great deal of blood, he landed his machine without damage. Flight Sub-Lieut. Lawson was hit in the right buttock, and also had his machine badly knocked about, and the rear flying wires on the left-hand side shot away. He, however, brought his machine back, and landed her without damage in the aerodrome.

From the 8th to the 23rd the weather was appalling; wet, cold, and foggy until the 17th inst., when a change took place, and we had snow and hard frost.

From the 23rd to the 31st we had intensely cold weather, but fine, with fair visibility, and flying was carried out every day over the lines.

On the 23rd, Flight Lieut. Booker brought a machine down near Bapaume, otherwise the luck was against us, and we had the misfortune to lose Flight Commander Mackenzie. He failed to return from an offensive patrol on the 24th inst., but we feel fairly confident that he is safe and a prisoner of war.

On February 1st and 2nd the weather was bad early, but became very fine later, and we carried out two escorts to the photographic reconnaissance machine of No. 23 Squadron, Royal Flying Corps. Naval Squadron No. 3 relieved us on February 3rd, and we returned to Dunkerque.

Hostile aircraft have been much more aggressive this month, and they have been flying at greater heights and in larger formations than during November and December. The Albatross Scouts and the two-seater (either a Roland or a Halberstadt) seem to be the most formidable. During the latter part of the month a number of H.A. crossed our lines, but showed no inclination to fight. They were extremely difficult to engage owing to the fact that they flew very high, and on sighting any of our machines immediately dived for their own lines.

No. 7 SQUADRON.—EXTRACT FROM REPORT OF OPERATIONS.
Raid on Ghistelles.

February 16th.

Flight Lieut. Brackley started at 4.55 a.m. on Short No. 9338, and flew along the coast to Nieuport, thence straight to Ghistelles. He reached his objective at 5.35 a.m.. which he could distinguish easily, as the aerodrome was well lit up; in fact, after passing Pervyse on the journey, he observed the lights showing very clearly. He steered straight for the lights and from S.W. to N.E. dropped two No. 112-lb. bombs and six No. 65-lb. bombs from 7,600 feet, which all exploded in the S. and S.E. corner of the aerodrome, two of them very near the railway siding. All the lights of the aerodrome were extinguished immediately after the explosion of the bombs. They were remarkably vivid. The big searchlight on the aerodrome lit up about two minutes after the bombs exploded. On the outward journey it was very difficult to see the ground owing to the haze. He has observed that whenever a night raid is carried out the searchlight at La Panne always comes into action when his machine passes, and suggests that this gives an indication to the enemy. He returned by Pervyse and along the coast, observing about a dozen searchlights in action along the coast from Ostende to Westende. H.E. was bursting very frequently, though no anti-aircraft guns fired at him. He saw no hostile aircraft.

Flight Sub-Lieut. Frame started at 5 a.m. on Short No. 9336, following the coast, and avoided Nieuport, passing to the southward. He was only able to see his objective fairly well through the ground mist, which he reached at 5.45 a.m., and he dropped six No. 65-lb. bombs and two No. 112-lb. bombs from 7,000 feet on the aerodrome, which he straddled from N.E. to S.W. over searchlights, which picked him up. He was also picked up by anti-aircraft guns from Ostende, but not at close quarters. He failed to make any observations on the aerodrome, which was in darkness. He saw no hostile aircraft. He returned over Pervyse.

Flight Lieut. Darley left at 5.11 a.m. He took the route along the coast and inland over Furnes and Pervyse. He reached his objective at 5.50 a.m., could see it, and dropped seven No. 65-lb. bombs from 5,700 feet (one bomb remaining hung up in the bomb rack owing to a broken Bowden wire). He observed them explode, one falling about the centre of the aerodrome and the remainder in a line straddling the headquarter buildings. He noticed searchlights and anti-aircraft firing at Ostende just before reaching the lines, but no searchlights or anti-aircraft guns picked him up, nor did he observe any hostile aircraft. He returned by the same route he took on the outward journey.

No. 3 Wing, Luxeuil.

A full report (A. 0384) has how been received of the bombing raid on the blast furnaces at Burbach on 23rd January.

Out of 24 machines which left the base, only 16 were able to reach the objective, owing to the intense cold. The atmosphere was clear, and considerable damage appears to have been done by the 2,600 lbs. of bombs which were dropped. All pilots, observers, and gunlayers behaved splendidly.

Flight Sub-Lieut. W. E. C. Wigglesworth, in Fighter No. 9667, met six German machines (Halberstadt type) at 12,000 feet, and fought five engagements with three, four, and five machines at one time, and succeeded in driving one of them down. W. Bunce, A.M. II., who was the gunlayer, behaved excellently, and although his gloves were blown away and his hands frostbitten, he fought to a finish. Lieut. Wigglesworth was also frostbitten.

MALTA.

A report has been received of operations carried on during the month of January.

The weather has seriously interfered with flying, only 14 days being suitable. When weather permitted a daily patrol has been carried out, in conjunction with minesweepers.

EASTERN MEDITERRANEAN SQUADRON.

Report No. 44 (A. 0440) has been received, covering the period 12th to 18th January.

Thasos Air Station ("A" Flight).

January 14th.

In the morning a reconnaissance with wireless was carried out by a Nieuport fighter over the Xanthi district. With the exception of a transport park at the east end of the town no concentration or movement was observed. When over the northern end of Boru Lake three hostile seaplanes were seen to leave Gereviez and start in pursuit of the Nieuport, which, however, kept well inland and soon lost sight of them. The presence of the enemy machines and the fact that the Nieuport was returning were reported to Thasos by W/T.

Immediately on receipt of this intelligence two scouts were sent up from Thasos with orders to meet the Nieuport and return with her.

The two scouts (a Bristol and a Nieuport) flying in company, passed the returning Nieuport without observing her, and continued their flight towards the north end of Boru Lake at 11,000 feet.

The Bristol Scout observed the Nieuport make a 16-point turn, and on turning also was unable to find the latter machine. Shortly afterwards he observed an enemy seaplane flying low along the coast from Kara Burnu towards Sarishaben, and dived to attack, but lost sight of the machine and failed to locate it again.

The Nieuport Scout No. 3983, with 80-h.p. Le Rhone engine No. 5152, piloted by Flight Lieut. Peberdy, failed to return, and it is thought probable that when he was observed to turn, his engine was giving trouble, and that his loss was due to engine trouble and not to attack by enemy seaplanes.

Search was made in the early afternoon by a seaplane of the area round Boru Lake, but no sign of the missing machine was observed, and no news of the pilot has since been received.

January 15th, 16th, and 17th.

Anti-submarine and coast patrol flights were carried out in the vicinity of Thasos Island.

Details of an attack on Tatar Bazarjik carried out on the 9th January have now been received.

The flight was carried out by Flight Sub-Lieut. Aird in Sopwith No. N. 5110, Clerget No. 1259, escorted by Flight Sub-Lieut. Mager with Mid. R. J. Dashwood, R.N.R., as observer in Sopwith N. 5086.

The machines left Thasos at 10.45 a.m. and arrived at Tatar Bazarjik—just over 100 miles distant—at noon. Four 65-lb. bombs were dropped, two of which fell between the railway station and the bridge over the Maritza River, one on some buildings close to the northern end of the bridge, and the fourth close to a large camp of 300 to 400 tents observed to the N.E. of the town. A reconnaissance of the roads, &c., in this area was made, and photographs of the town and railway station at Tatar Bazarjik were taken.

No anti-aircraft fire was experienced in this district, and both machines returned safely to Thasos, landing on the aerodrome at 1.15 p.m.

Stavros Air Station ("D" Flight).

January 13th.

A successful reconnaissance flight was carried out over the area of Hill 350, Dedeballi-Zdravik, and a considerable number of new defence works and camps were observed.

Early in the afternoon of the same day M. 20 was spotted on to the emplacements N. 4 to the S.E. of Hovil Hill, and a photographic reconnaissance was made over the Orfano valley. On returning from this latter flight the pilot, Flight Sub-Lieut. R. K. J. Vallings, and observer, Second Lieut. A. C. Panting,

6th Royal Munster Fusiliers, who had been lent to "D" Flight by the Army, were killed. Details not yet available.

January 14th, 16th, and 17th.

Further reconnaissance flights over the lower Struma lines and the Angista Valley were carried out, and a photographic reconnaissance of areas required by the Army was made on the 15th January, a spotting flight for H.M. ships being carried out on the same day.

Imbros Air Station.

January 14th, 15th, 16th, and 17th.

Reconnaissances of the Dardanelles were carried out on these days. With the exception of a steamer of about 1,500 tons at Chanak on 15th January, none but the usual shipping has been observed.

Details of the night attack on Galata aerodrome carried out on the 10th January, and already briefly reported in the last communiqué, have now been received, and are as follows:—

Flight Sub-Lieut. Devlin with Sub-Lieut. Jameson, R.N.V.R., in H.F. 3001, and Flight Sub-Lieut. Bisshe in B.E. 2 C. 8414, left Imbros at 2.40 a.m., and dropped five 65-lb. bombs on their objective from a height of 1,800 feet. Three of the bombs were observed to explode close to the hangars. The pilot of the second machine was unable to see the fall of his bombs owing to the flashes of anti-aircraft guns.

OPERATIONS IN TURKEY—THERMI AIR STATION,
"B" FLIGHT.

No service flights have been carried out during the period under review.

H.M.S. "Empress."

January 13th.

In the morning four 16-lb. bombs were dropped on Karjani with good effect. In the afternoon, a reconnaissance of the Orfano-Dranli area was made, and four 16-lb. bombs were dropped on trenches and redoubts in "Latrine Nullah."

January 14th.

One of H.M. ships was spotted on to the redoubts and emplacements in the region of Dranli and in "Latrine Nullah" (the spotting machine being escorted by a Schneider Cup Seaplane).

January 15th.

N. 32 was spotted on to the same redoubts and emplacements, the spotting machine being again escorted by a Schneider, which in addition to escorting dropped two 16-lb. bombs on

Mentesselli and two on Dedeballi. During the flight the pilot of the Schneider seaplane discovered an enemy machine of the Nieuport scout type above and behind him in a favourable position, but on flattening out could not locate the enemy machine, which, after having been discovered, made no attempt to engage either the Schneider or spotting machine.

The enemy machine was much faster than the Schneider, and flew off to the eastward.

Later in the day a large Albatross biplane approached Stavros anchorage at about 12,000 feet. A Schneider Cup seaplane was sent in pursuit, but the hostile machine had disappeared in the direction of Thasos, and was not sighted by the Schneider pilot.

January 16th.

One spotting flight was made for H.M. ships, and on the following day 25 bombs were dropped by four seaplanes on Boblem, where the headquarters of a regiment of Turkish irregulars is reported to have been established.

January 17th.

A reconnaissance of the Karjani-Dedeballi-Dranli area was also carried out.

Mudros.

(1) H.M.S. "Ark Royal."

Practice flights in Short seaplanes were carried out on 15th and 16th January, and a W/T test flight was made in a Short on the 14th January.

(2) Marsh Aerodrome.

Instructional and practice flights have been made whenever weather conditions have permitted.

(3) Airship Station.

No patrols have been carried out during this period.

Kassandra Air Station.

January 12th.

S.S. 8 was deflated. No patrols were carried out.

Note.—Strong winds from the southward, increasing to gale force at times, accompanied by low clouds and rain, have interfered with flying throughout the week.

Mudros.

A bomb attack was made on Buk Bridge on the night of 11th February, and later information reports damage to the Northern Pier, and interruption to the traffic appears to be certain.

EAST INDIES STATION.

A full report has now been received of the operations which concluded with the very successful attack on the Chilkaldere Bridge on December 27th.

This bridge carries the Bagdad Railway across the Irmak river, and is about 18 miles east of Adana. Its importance to operations by the Turks is obvious.

H.M.S. "Raven II." and "Ben-my-Chree" left Port Said on the 25th–26th and both proceeded to the Bay of Ayas, in the Gulf of Alexandretta. Unfortunately H.M.S. "Raven II." arrived late at the "rendezvous" owing to delay on account of mines in the channel, and the form of the attack was slightly altered in consequence.

Flight Sub-Lieut. Smith with Captain Wedgwood Benn as observer in Short 8080, and Commander Samson, Flight Lieut. Clemson and Flight Lieut. Brooke in three Sopwiths (Nos. 3770, 3778, and 3188) all got away about 11 o'clock in the morning, and made for the Chilkadere Bridge. Flight Sub-Lieut. Smith dropped one 65-lb. bomb at the bridge and two 16-lb. bombs at a train, but all failed to explode owing apparently to defective fuses. He then turned his attention to the defences at the south side of the bridge according to his instructions, and having dropped 16-lb. bombs, which exploded on the water and caused damage to the bridge, he put to flight with his machine-gun fire the bridge guard which had turned out.

The other pilots mentioned above then attacked at heights ranging from 400 to 700 feet, and were successful; Commander Samson scoring one hit, and Lieutenant Brooke and Lieutenant Clemson both causing damage.

"Raven II." sent out two Short machines about noon, each carrying one 65-lb. bomb and two 16-lb. bombs. One hit was scored by these machines. About 1.30 another Short was sent off from the "Ben-my-Chree," carrying two 65-lb. bombs, and two Sopwiths were also hoisted, carrying two 65-lb. bombs each.

Flight Sub-Lieut. Henderson secured one hit on the embankment, carrying away a large portion of it, and Flight Sub-Lieut. Clemson hit the bridge itself with two 65-lb. bombs.

There appears to be no doubt that the bridge was certainly rendered impossible for traffic, and that it will take some time to repair.

Most of the machines were hit.

Great credit is due to Engineer Lieut. Robinson, R.N.R., and his department for the splendid way in which, though shorthanded, he kept the ship steaming, and also credit is due to Flight Commander England, D.S.C., and to the ratings of the R.N.A.S., for their hard work in preparing the seaplanes for this special work at short notice. Thanks are due to the French escort, which, as usual, rendered extremely efficient and painstaking service.

The seaplane carriers returned to Port Said after the operations were concluded, as it was judged inadvisable to prolong the stay in these dangerous waters.

H.M.S. "Anne."

A report (A. 3648) has been received with particulars of the attack on Wej on the 23rd January.

On the night of the 19th the scheme of operations was received, and a practice landing and attack was carried out in conjunction with H.M. ships, one seaplane being sent up to spot for gunfire. The plan of attack on Wej had been prepared from reports of operations carried out by seaplanes in December last, and in order to obtain information as to the situation in Wej at the time of the attack the S.N.O. himself made a flight over the town to satisfy himself.

On the morning of the attack both the seaplanes spotted for H.M. ships.

During this operation Lieutenant Stewart, 7th R.S. and R.F.C., was fatally hit by rifle fire.

Wej was taken on the morning of the 24th January, and its fall marks the conclusion of the operations carried out with the assistance of the R.N.A.S. in the Red Sea.

Wej was one of the largest towns to the northward, was occupied for some time by the enemy, and was the object of many attempts at its reduction. The fall of this town renders it possible to raid the Hedjaz railway from the coast.

The difficulties of seaplane work in this climate are considerable, and the large results obtained by the small expenditure of aircraft is most noteworthy. The prestige of the Allies in Mohammedan countries is greatly increased by such successful operations against the Turks.

CAPE STATION.

No report of operations has been received during the period under review.

ARMOURED CAR DIVISION.

East African Field Force.

A report (No. 14) has now been received from the Naval Armoured Car Division operating in East Africa during the period December 6th, 1916, to January 4th, 1917.

Lieutenant Commander Howard Nalder, in command of these cars, seems to have had great anxiety over the health of the men under his command, and after negotiations with Headquarters the cars and personnel have been sent to Egypt, sailing from Kilindi for Port Sudan on January 4th, as briefly mentioned in the last communiqué.

ROYAL FLYING CORPS COMMUNIQUÉ No. 73.

Artillery Co-operation.

January 27th.

Forty-six targets were engaged with aeroplane observation.

Co-operating with aeroplanes of the First Brigade, artillery obtained 11 direct hits on three gun-pits and caused two explosions of ammunition. Twenty-three direct hits were obtained on a trench target, and a tramway terminus was wrecked.

In co-operation with aeroplanes of the Second Brigade, artillery successfully engaged five hostile batteries.

Artillery of the Third Army, with aeroplane observation, obtained two direct hits on gun emplacements and caused an explosion of ammunition.

In co-operation with aeroplanes of the Fourth Brigade, artillery successfully engaged six hostile batteries.

With observation by aeroplanes of the Fifth Brigade, artillery obtained 10 direct hits on gun positions.

Hostile Aircraft.

Captain Long, No. 24 Squadron, destroyed a German aeroplane, which fell in our lines near Norval.

A hostile machine engaged by Lieutenant Hudson, No. 54 Squadron, fell in "No Man's Land," near Courcelette.

A third German aeroplane, attacked by Lieutenant Woodhouse and Lieutenant Nickalls, No. 52 Squadron, fell on our side of the lines at Maurepas.

An offensive patrol of No. 32 Squadron met two hostile aeroplanes near Ervillers. The patrol dived on to one of the machines, which fell in flames, and was seen to crash near St. Leger.

Lieutenant Taylor, of the same squadron, engaged and drove down a second German aeroplane out of control.

Lieutenant A. Dennison, No. 41 Squadron, while on patrol on the 24th instant, engaged two hostile aeroplanes. He was severely wounded in the arm, but continued the engagement, and drove down one hostile machine. Infantry report that this machine fell out of control. Lieutenant Dennison continued fighting the second enemy aeroplane until his engine was hit, when he glided over the lines and landed safely.

Bombing.

Bombs were dropped by the First Brigade on places of military importance. In several cases the bombs were seen to explode on the objectives.

Miraumont and Biez Wood were attacked by aeroplanes of the Fifth Brigade.

Casualties.

Wounded.—Second-Lieut. L. G. Fauvel, No. 20 Squadron; Second Lieut. H. Butler, No. 70 Squadron.

Artillery Co-operation.

January 28th.

Fifty-six targets were engaged with aeroplane observation.

Siege artillery, with aeroplane observation of the First Brigade, obtained four direct hits on seven gun-pits.

Co-operating with aeroplanes of the Second Brigade, artillery successfully engaged six hostile batteries.

Artillery of the Third Army, with aeroplane observation, successfully engaged several hostile batteries. Two gun-pits were destroyed, and an explosion of ammunition was caused.

In co-operation with aeroplanes of the Fourth Brigade, artillery obtained two direct hits on hostile batteries and caused an explosion of ammunition.

Artillery of the Fifth Army, co-operating with aeroplanes of the Fifth Brigade, successfully engaged 16 hostile batteries. Eight direct hits were obtained on gun-pits. An explosion of ammunition was caused. Trenches were also damaged.

Hostile Aircraft.

Second Lieut. J. V. Aspinall and Second Lieut. J. M. R. Miller, No. 22 Squadron, engaged a hostile aeroplane over Villers-au-Flos. The hostile machine was driven down and crashed between Barastre and Bus.

Bombing.

Sixty-three 20-lb. bombs and four incendiary bombs were dropped by the First Brigade. A trench tramway, communication trenches and houses in Bailleul, Lens, and Salome were hit.

Bombs were dropped on Miraumont and Biez Wood by the Fifth Brigade.

Second Lieut. Davies, No. 32 Squadron, fired on ammunition lorries on the Bapaume–Arras road from 800 feet.

Casualties.

Killed.—Lieutenant F. G. Russell, No. 21 Squadron.

Wounded.—Second Lieut. A. F. Barker, No. 41 Squadron; Second Lieut. E. G. Herbert, No. 60 Squadron; Lieutenant B. S. Cole, No. 1 Squadron.

Missing.—Second Lieut. P. C. E. Johnson and Lieutenant C. B. Bird, M.C., No. 4 Squadron.

Artillery Co-operation.

January 29th.

Sixty-five targets were engaged with aeroplane observation.

Heavy artillery of the First Army, with aeroplane observation, obtained one direct hit on a gun-pit.

Siege artillery obtained eight direct hits on gun-pits and caused three explosions. Two of the explosions caused fires which burned for a considerable time.

Co-operating with aeroplanes of the Second Brigade, artillery successfully engaged five hostile batteries.

Seven gun-pits were badly damaged.

Artillery of the Third Army, co-operating with aeroplanes of the Third Brigade, scored several hits on hostile batteries, and caused three explosions of ammunition.

In co-operation with aeroplanes of the Fourth Brigade, artillery obtained four direct hits on hostile batteries.

Thirteen hostile batteries were successfully engaged by artillery co-operating with the Fifth Brigade. Thirteen direct hits on gun positions were obtained, and five explosions of ammunition caused.

Hostile Aircraft.

Five F.E. 2 B.'s, No. 25 Squadron, accompanied by three F.E.8 B.'s, No. 40 Squadron, encountered a formation of 12 hostile scouts, all Halberstadts, while on photographic reconnaissance. Second Lieut Blenkiron, No. 25 Squadron, was hit in the thigh at the beginning of the encounter, but managed to stand up and fire at a hostile aeroplane at point-blank range. This machine went down out of control with columns of smoke and then flames coming out of it.

This was confirmed by two other pilots. Second Lieut. Leith in another F.E. dived to the help of Second Lieut. Blenkiron, and fired a drum at 15 yards range into another hostile aeroplane. This German machine stalled and side-slipped, and was seen to fall out of control. Two more Halberstadts were forced to land, and the formation was entirely broken up.

Captain Meintjes, No. 60 Squadron, engaged a German aeroplane at a range of 35 yards. The hostile machine was seen to fall out of control and crash. Lieutenant Benge, No. 29 Squadron, also engaged and destroyed a German aeroplane.

Second Lieut. Caldwell, on a Nieuport Scout, attacked and drove down a machine. It was not seen to crash. He was forced to leave the formation owing to his petrol and oil tank being shot through, but landed safely.

Bombing.

On the night of the 28th–29th instant bombs were dropped by the First Brigade on Provin, Pont-à-Vendin, and Meurchin.

Aeroplanes of the Fifth Brigade attacked the sidings and dumps at Mory. Bombs were also dropped on Miraumont and Biez Wood.

Captain B. L. Dowling and Lieutenant C. F. Lodge, No. 11 Squadron, whilst leading an offensive patrol on the afternoon of the 29th instant, had an anti-aircraft high explosive shell burst just behind the right lower wing of the aeroplane.

The machine was completely riddled. Three tail booms were cut, one blade of the propeller was blown away, and all the controls except the elevator were put out of action.

The lower right-hand tail boom was completely severed by the destroyed propeller blade, and the aeroplane became uncontrollable. Realising this, Lieutenant Lodge climbed out three-quarters of the way to the right wing tip, in order to balance the machine. When about 900 feet from the ground the action of the observer balanced the machine, which glided evenly. At about 200 feet from the ground, owing to a slight movement on the part of the observer, the machine again began to spin, but the pilot was able to stall the aeroplane from a height of about 10 feet, and both the pilot and observer escaped unhurt.

This machine was hit just over the lines, but, owing to a strong east wind, was blown about 2,000 yards over our front line.

Casualties.

Wounded.—Lieutenant S. E. Goodwin, No. 53 Squadron; Second Lieut. A. W. Clarke, No. 5 Squadron; Lieutenant H. W. Golding, No. 20 Squadron; Second Lieut. A. V. Blenkiron, No. 25 Squadron; Second Lieut. H. A. Whistler, No. 3 Squadron; Corporal E. J. Hare, No. 3 Squadron.

January 30th.

The weather was unfavourable for Service flying.

Artillery Co-operation.

Siege artillery, with observation by aeroplanes of the First Brigade, caused an explosion of ammunition and silenced a hostile battery.

A gun-pit was also destroyed.

Artillery, with observation by Captain K. D. P. Murray, No. 52 Squadron, obtained 11 direct hits on a hostile battery and caused a fire.

Some successful work was accomplished by artillery co-operating with aeroplanes of the Fifth Brigade. The 144th Siege Battery demolished a bridge N.E. of Grandcourt.

Bombing.

20-lb. and incendiary bombs were dropped on Bailleul by aeroplanes of the First Brigade. Houses were hit, and the railway line destroyed in places.

Nine 20-lb. bombs were dropped on Miraumont by aeroplanes of the Fifth Brigade.

Casualty.

Wounded.—Second Lieut. H. G. White, No. 20 Squadron.

Artillery Co-operation.

February 1st.

Fifty-two targets were dealt with by aeroplane observers.

Artillery of the Third Army, with aeroplane observation, successfully engaged eight hostile batteries, and obtained two direct hits on a trench mortar. A number of direct hits were also obtained on a trench, and two explosions of ammunition were caused.

Two hostile batteries were successfully engaged by artillery of the Fourth Army, with aeroplane observation by the Fourth Brigade.

In co-operation with aeroplanes of the Fifth Brigade artillery obtained two direct hits on gun positions and damaged three gun-pits.

Bombing.

Forty-four 20-lb. bombs were dropped on Carvin by the First Brigade. Houses were hit and demolished. The railway and sidings were also hit. The sidings and a dump at Mory, and a dump at Fremicourt, were attacked on the night of the 31st January/1st February by the Fifth Brigade. Bombs were seen to burst on and round about the objectives.

Captain Jones and Second Lieut. Pickthorne, No. 22 Squadron, dived at a hostile A.A. battery on a lorry, and fired at it with their machine guns. The battery ceased to fire.

Casualties.

Wounded.—Lieutenant J. K. Stead, No. 20 Squadron; Lieutenant K. B. Brigham, No. 2 Squadron; Captain G. M. Moore, No. 15 Squadron.

Missing.—Second Lieut. W. A. Reeves and Second Lieut. F. H. Bronskill, No. 20 Squadron; Second Lieut. E. D. Spicer and Captain C. A. Carbert, M.C., No. 20 Squadron; Lieutenant P. W. Murray and Lieutenant D. J. McRae, No. 16 Squadron; Captain A. P. V. Daly, No. 29 Squadron.

Artillery Co-operation.

February 2nd.

Fifty-eight targets were dealt with by aeroplane observation.

In co-operation with aeroplanes of the First Brigade, siege artillery obtained 11 direct hits on gun-pits and five on trench targets.

Artillery of the Second Army, with aeroplane observation, successfully engaged four hostile batteries.

Three hostile batteries were successfully engaged by artillery of the Fourth Army, with aeroplane observation.

Co-operating with aeroplanes of the Fifth Brigade, artillery obtained eight direct hits on gun positions.

Hostile Aircraft.

Captain H. E. Hartney and Second Lieut. H. R. Wilkinson, No. 20 Squadron, engaged and destroyed a Halberstadt near Lille.

A German aeroplane was driven out of control by Major Gratton Bellew and Second Lieut. McCudden, both of No. 29 Squadron. In a general engagement between No. 32 Squadron and nine hostile aircraft, one enemy machine was driven down out of control and another forced to land.

Casualties.

Wounded.—Second Lieut. J. M. R. Miller, No. 22 Squadron.

Missing.—Second Lieut. H. Blythe, No. 32 Squadron; Flight Sub-Lieut. W. E. Traynor, R.N.A.S.; Second Lieut. R. F. W. Whitney and Lieutenant T. G. Holley, No. 23 Squadron.

Artillery Co-operation.

February 3rd.

In co-operation with aeroplanes of the First Brigade, heavy artillery obtained nine direct hits on gun-pits.

Siege artillery also obtained seven direct hits on gun-pits and caused a large explosion of ammunition.

Field Artillery obtained 13 direct hits on trench and other targets. Artillery of the Second Army, with aeroplane observation, obtained nine direct hits on gun-pits.

In co-operation with aeroplanes of the Third Brigade, artillery obtained five direct hits on hostile batteries and five on trench mortar emplacements. An explosion of ammunition was also caused.

With observation by aeroplanes of the Fourth Brigade, artillery successfully engaged seven hostile batteries.

Artillery of the Fifth Army, with aeroplane observation, obtained 17 direct hits on gun positions. Wire was also ranged on and considerably damaged.

A bridge over the railway near Grandcourt was destroyed. A large explosion of ammunition was also caused.

Hostile Aircraft.

Second Lieut. C. Gordon-Davis and Captain R. M. Knowles, No. 20 Squadron, engaged seven hostile aircraft during a patrol near Wervicq. One German machine was driven down out of control.

Casualty.

Wounded.—Captain J. C. McMillan, No. 4 Squadron.

Headquarters, Royal Flying Corps,
    4th February 1917.

REPORT OF OPERATIONS No. 28.

HOME STATIONS.

February 17th to 28th.

There is very little to report during the periods under review. The usual patrols have taken place whenever weather permitted, and a great deal of useful instructional and experimental work has been carried out.

A hostile aeroplane was signalled on the morning of the 17th February—by a Manstone patrol aeroplane—about 5 miles east of Ramsgate. The pilot went in pursuit, but was unable to overtake the enemy machine.

DUNKIRK.

R.N.A.S.

A summary of operations has now been received for the period 1st to 14th February. This report contains particulars and the names of pilots and observers who took part in the raids on Bruges, reported in R.N.A.S. Communiqué No. 27.

Weather Conditions.

The weather conditions during the period under review have only been fairly favourable for operations. Although there has been continuous sunshine, it has been accompanied by a certain amount of haze, and the temperature, especially at night, has been as low as 20° to 25° of frost.

Work has been carried out every day, except on the 11th and 12th.

Fighter Patrols.

Fighter patrols have been carried out from dawn till sunset, acting as escorts to photographic and coastal reconnaissances, French photographic reconnaissances, and bombing attacks, over the Nieuport-Dixmude-Ypres sector.

February 3rd.

On the morning of the 3rd three triplanes carried out a Zeppelin patrol at daybreak, as Zeppelins had been signalled in the early hours of the morning.

No hostile aircraft was sighted.

A few hostile machines have been observed. Two decisive combats took place; in both cases the hostile machine was successfully brought down. (*See* Combats.)

Photographic Reconnaissances.

Some very successful photographic reconnaissances were achieved during this period.

February 1st.

Photographs were obtained of the mole at Zeebrugge, Zeebrugge-Bruges Canal, and Bruges Harbour.

Photographs of Zeebrugge-Bruges Canal by Flight Lieut. Holden with Sub-Lieut. Betts, R.N.V.R. (Sopwith 9417), showed that the work of making ammunition stores along the east side of the canal is still in progress, and photographs of Bruges show that the harbour was congested with shipping; eight destroyers, 10 to 12 large torpedo-boat destroyers, and three submarines were clearly seen on the photographs. The whole harbour was covered with floating blocks of ice.

February 7th.

Successful photographs were taken by Sub-Lieut. Chase, R.N.V.R., pilot Flight Sub-Lieut. Tapscott (Sopwith 5172), of the harbour and Darse at Bruges at the same time as a bombing attack was being carried out there. The photographs show that for the first time the Darse at Bruges was being used to accommodate large destroyers—previous to this only cargo vessels had been moored alongside, whilst war vessels were berthed in the bassins.

The rest of the harbour was fairly empty, containing only four large destroyers and one large and three or four smaller submarines.

February 9th.

The same pilot and observer, on Sopwith 9419, succeeded in taking a very good photograph of Wenduyne, which showed very clearly two gun emplacements situated in the pleasure gardens on the sea front.

The photographic machines and fighter escorts on both occasions when photographing Zeebrugge and Bruges were subjected to very heavy and accurate anti-aircraft fire, but fortunately no machines were hit.

Bombing Attacks.

Eight successful bombing attacks have been carried out during this period, one during the day and the others by moonlight.

February 3rd.

During the early hours of the morning a bombing attack was carried out by Nos. 4 and 5 Wings on the torpedo boat destroyers in Bruges Harbour.

Twelve machines started at various times during the previous night, but owing to the extreme cold of $22\frac{1}{2}°$ of frost only six machines succeeded in reaching the objective; the others encountered severe engine trouble owing to the cold and were forced to land at various places.

This involved the wrecking of several machines, and in one case the pilot sustained slight injuries.

The following pilots succeeded in reaching the objective:—

    Flight Lieut. Darley. A.M. (G/L) Bager. (Short Bomber 9357.)
    Flight Sub-Lieut. Frame. A.M. (G/L) Young. (Short Bomber 9330.)
    Flight Sub-Lieut. Rouse. (Sopwith 9395.)
    Flight Sub-Lieut. Nelles. (Sopwith 9397.)
    Flight Sub-Lieut. Sieveking. (Caudron 9121.)

Twenty-three Le Pecq bombs and six 112-lb. bombs were dropped with good results.

The large shed on the east side of the West Bassin, upon being hit, flared up, giving off a large amount of smoke. The other bombs straddled the destroyers which were clearly observed in the west and east bassins. One bomb was observed to drop among the sheds on the dock.

Scarcely a shot was fired by the anti-aircraft batteries, and what there was, was very inaccurate.

The following pilots were forced to land owing to engine trouble, and did not reach the objective:—

    Flight Lieut. Brackley. A.M. (G/L) Woolley. (Short Bomber 9335.)
    Flight Sub-Lieut. Sproatt. (Sopwith 9382.)
    Flight Lieut. Blagrove. (Sopwith 9405.)
    Flight Sub-Lieut. Chadwick. (Sopwith 9394.)
    Flight Commander Wood. (Sopwith 9383.)
    Flight Lieut. Cerdner. (Sopwith 4423.)

Flight Sub-Lieut. Brackley started, but had to return owing to engine trouble, and again started a little later with no better result.

Flight Sub-Lieut. Frame lost his way on the return journey owing to a defective compass, and was forced to land at Le Crotoy.

Flight Sub-Lieut. Sieveking was forced on his way back to land on the beach at Malo, which was covered with lumps of ice. These lumps caused the machine to overturn, and the pilot sustained slight injuries and was taken to hospital.

At midnight on the 3rd a bombing attack on the same objective (Bruges Harbour) was carried out by No. 4 Wing, the following pilots taking part:—

Flight Sub-Lieut. Thorne (Short Bomber 9490), L.M. (G/L) Kent, dropped six 112-lb. bombs from 6,000 feet, which were observed to explode on the wooden huts and stores on the west side of the West Bassin.

Flight Sub-Lieut. Brackley (Short Bomber 9338), A.M. G/L Woolley, dropped six 112-lb. bombs, which fell near the railway on the south-west side of the West Bassin and on the buildings between the East and West Bassins.

Flight Lieut. Darley (Short Bomber 9776), A.M. (G/L) Bager, dropped six 112-lb. bombs, two of which were observed to fall on the south-west corner of the West Bassin.

A good deal of anti-aircraft fire was experienced, although very inaccurate.

Seven or eight searchlights were observed, which only succeeded in momentarily picking up the machines, all of which returned safely.

February 7th.

On the afternoon of the 7th, No. 5 Wing carried out a bombing attack on the shipping and docks of Bruges.

Sixty Le Pecq bombs were dropped on the harbour by the following pilots:—

Flight Sub-Lieut. Le Mesurier (Sopwith 9395),
Flight Sub-Lieut. Nelles (Sopwith 9397),
Flight Lieut. Gardner (Sopwith N. 5114),
Flight Sub-Lieut. Chadwick (Sopwith 9394),
Flight Sub-Lieut. Stewart (Sopwith N. 5081),

who were accompanied by two fighter escorts—

Flight Lieut. Blagrove. Air Mechanic (Gunlayer) Milne. (Sopwith N. 5102.)

Flight Sub-Lieut. Rouse. Air Mechanic (Gunlayer) Duggin. (Sopwith N. 5093.)

The bombs were dropped from varying heights between 9,800 and 13,000 feet.

Two fires, one at the south corner of the West Bassin and one in the north corner of the East Bassin, were observed, and another fire was observed to be started on the docks between the East and West Bassins.

For the most part the harbour was covered with floating blocks of ice, but a channel had been cut away to permit navigation.

Anti-aircraft fire was fairly severe over Bruges and particularly so over Dixmude, which the machines encountered on the return journey.

February 7th–8th.

During the evening of the 7th and early hours of the 8th another attack was carried out on Bruges Harbour by two pilots.

Flight Lieut. Brackley, Air Mechanic (Gunlayer) Woolley, on Short Bomber 9338, left at 9.56 p.m., and dropped six 112-lb. bombs on the objective from a height of 8,000 feet. Bombs were observed to fall on the sheds in the centre of the harbour works and one on the large ammunition store situated in the N.E. corner of the West Bassins. Immediately a dull red flame issued from the building for about five minutes.

Flight Sub-Lieut. Thorne, Air Mechanic (Gunlayer) Bager, on Short Bomber 9338, left at 12.33 a.m. and dropped six 112-lb. bombs. Bombs were observed to fall near the S.E. corner of the West Bassin, three of them near the Ammunition Stores and another close to the south end of the Torpedo Store, whilst the last bomb fell near the north end of the same shed. Pilot also saw a large fire, which broke out in the docks, and this was plainly visible as pilot landed again at 2.35 a.m.

February 9th.

A bombing attack was carried out during the afternoon on the enemy aerodrome at Ghistelles. Eight 16-lb. and 32 Le Pecq bombs were dropped, which were observed to fall close to the large shed on the east side of the aerodrome and on the wooden landing platform. Anti-aircraft fire was very severe and accurate, but no great damage was done. All pilots and machines returned safely. The following pilots took part :—

> Flight Sub-Lieut. Rouse. (Sopwith N. 5093.)
> Flight Sub-Lieut. Nelles. (Sopwith 9379.)
> Flight Lieut. Clarke. (Sopwith 9375.)
> Flight Sub-Lieut. Sproatt. (Sopwith N. 5114.)
> Sub-Lieut. Stewart, Sub-Lieut. Glazby, and Sub-Lieut. Chadwick were unable to reach the objective owing to engine trouble, and were forced to return.

Another bombing attack was carried out by a seaplane on Ostende. Machine left at 9.50 p.m. and dropped eight 65-lb. bombs from a height of 2,500 feet over the Ateliers de la Marine. Explosions were distinctly heard. Pilot, Sub-Lieut. Cuckney. (Short Seaplane Bomber 9406.)

February 10th.

Between midnight on the 9th and the early hours of the 10th a bombing attack was carried out by No. 4 Wing on the shipping in the Darse at Bruges. Sub-Lieut. Darley (Short Bomber 9338) and Flight Lieut. Brackley (Short Bomber 9338),

Air Mechanic (Gunlayer) Kirby, and Air Mechanic (Gunlayer) Woolley. Each pilot and gunlayer left on the same machine successively and dropped twelve 65-lb. and four 112-lb. bombs. The objective was harder to pick up than the remainder of the harbour, as the visibility was hazy. Bombs were observed to explode in the corner of the Darse and T.B.D.'s moored inside. One of the observers clearly saw that the south-west end of the Darse was packed with shipping. This was probably due to the constant bombing of the East and West Bassins, where hostile shipping had previously been observed.

Searchlights attempted to pick up the machines. The anti-aircraft fire was not accurate.

February 14th.

During the early hours of the morning a successful bombing attack was again carried out on the shipping in Bruges Harbour. Six machines from No. 3 Squadron and one from No. 4 Squadron (No. 5 Wing) took part. Seventy-two Le Pecq and eight 16-lb. bombs were dropped, but owing to the slight haze it was impossible to make any definite observations, but all bombs appeared to explode in a good line over the East and West Docks. All pilots and machines returned safely. The following pilots took part:—

    Flight Sub-Lieut. Nelles. (Sopwith 9379.)
    Flight Lieut. Clarke. (Sopwith 9394.)
    Flight Lieut. Gardner. (Sopwith 9395.)
    Flight Lieut. Mesurier. (Sopwith 9672.)
    Flight Sub-Lieut. Shadwick. (Sopwith 9376.)
    Sub-Lieut. Stewart. (Sopwith N. 5081.)
    Sub-Lieut. Bartlett. (Sopwith 9053.)

Bombing Patrols.

February 8th.

A bombing patrol was carried out on the 8th, accompanied by three fighter machines, on all hostile shipping between Nieuport and the Dutch frontier. The visibility was good, but no hostile shipping was observed. The following pilots took part:—

    Flight Lieut. Clarke. (Sopwith N. 5114.)
    Flight Lieut. Gardner. (Sopwith 9376.)
    Flight Sub-Lieut. Sproatt. (Sopwith 9395.)

The accompanying fighter machines were piloted by:—

    Flight Sub-Lieut. Glazby. Air Mechanic (Gunlayer) Simmons. (Sopwith N. 5096.)
    Flight Sub-Lieut. Rouse. Air Mechanic (Gunlayer) Powll. (Sopwith N. 5093.)
    Flight Sub-Lieut. Bartlett. Air Mechanic (Gunlayer) George. (Sopwith N. 5222.)

February 10th.

A similar patrol was carried out on the 10th by the following pilots:—

    Sub-Lieut. Nelles. (Sopwith 9379.)
    Sub-Lieut. Glazby. (Sopwith 9395.)
    Sub-Lieut. Chadwick. (Sopwith 9376.)

These machines were accompanied by three fighters:—

    Flight Lieut. Gardner. Observer, Lieut. St. John, R.N.V.R. (Sopwith N. 5096.)
    Flight Sub-Lieut. Griffin. Air Mechanic (Gunlayer) George. (Sopwith N. 5222.)
    Flight Sub-Lieut. Bartlett. Air Mechanic (Gunlayer) Smith. (Sopwith N. 5093.)

The visibility was poor, and no hostile shipping of any kind was observed.

Combats.

February 1st.

Flight Commander Dallas (Sopwith N. 5436) whilst returning from Ghistelles encountered a German two-seater Aviatik over Dixmude. Pilot manœuvred to get behind the enemy, and did so unobserved, opening on him at 50 yards range and firing 50 rounds. The enemy machine fell over sideways, and finished up in a spinning nose-dive; pilot followed the machine down, getting in occasional volleys, and at about 10,000 feet five white bursts of smoke were emitted from the German machine, which was later lost to view at 5,000 feet. Pilot afterwards observed what appeared to be a machine on the ground half a mile north-east of Dixmude.

Flight Lieut. Holden with Sub-Lieut. Betts, on Sopwith 9417, whilst returning from a reconnaissance, were attacked off Blankenberghe at 2.20 p.m. by a small single-seater stationary engine white biplane, which approached from the port quarter at a slightly greater altitude. No tracer bullets were observed from the enemy machine, though its gun was firing. Fire was opened on the hostile machine, and after half a tray had been fired it was seen to descend in a very steep spiral. The observer of the reconnaissance machine, by standing on the seat, was able to continue firing in an almost vertical position. Tracers were seen entering the hostile machine, and after changing tray it was observed diving very steeply in the direction of Wenduyne emitting thick clouds of smoke. The observer is confident that this machine was destroyed.

February 8th.

Flight Lieut. Norton, D.S.C., on Nieuport Scout N. 3184, whilst on an offensive patrol at 18,000 feet over the Forest of Houthulst, observed an Aviatik two-seater about 4,000 feet below. Pilot dived to within very close range and fired about a dozen rounds. He then made a complete right turn and came up under the enemy to within 50 yards, firing another burst of about 25 rounds. Tracers hit the enemy machine, which fell out of control, large clouds of black smoke coming from the fore part of the fuselage. Pilot followed it down to 10,000 feet, when anti-aircraft fire became intense.

When last seen the Aviatik was still falling erratically and emitting black smoke. Pilot of hostile machine made no attempt to manœuvre nor did the observer have time to open fire.

No. 11 Kite Balloon Section.

No ascents have been made during this period.

Seaplanes.

During this period the weather has been very unsuitable for reconnaissance and only two special patrols have been carried out, viz., on the 1st and 3rd.

February 1st.

Flight Sub-Lieut. Watson, observer Sub-Lieut. Hodson, R.N.V.R., on Seaplane 8013, accompanied by Sopwith Seaplane 8171, pilot Flight Lieut. Graham.

One of these machines being overdue, Flight Commander Welch left in search on Sopwith Seaplane N 1011, but was forced to land on the water. He was picked up and taken in tow by a drifter, and arrived back in harbour at 6.45 p.m.

February 3rd.

A second patrol was carried out on the 3rd by Flight Sub-Lieut. Potvin, observer Sub-Lieut. Hodson, on Short Seaplane No. 8013, accompanied by Fighter Seaplane 8145, pilot Sub-Lieut. Fisher.

There was nothing of importance to report on either of these patrols.

No. 3 WING, FRANCE.

A report (A. 0623) has now been received from the advanced base with particulars of the raid on Brebach of 25th January. Brebach is $2\frac{3}{4}$ miles S.E. of Saarbrucken, and the objective was a group of ironworks and blast furnaces.

Squadrons Nos. 1 and 2 each supplied Service bombers and three fighters.

Both detachments started within five minutes of one another and got off without a hitch, and kept a very good formation from the beginning and kept it throughout the operation.

Two pilots returned owing to trouble with their machines, and 13 bombers and 5 fighters reached the objective.

It appears that after dropping his bombs Flight Sub-Lieut. J. M. Sharman engaged a German machine of a monoplane type and claims to have shot it down out of control. Flight Sub-Lieuts. H. E. Edwards, Drummond, and Disette witnessed the fight, and agree that the machine was brought down out of control.

Flight Sub-Lieut. Pattison (Gunlayer P. O. Hinkler) was engaged with a Roland. Flight Sub-Lieut. Pattison's machine was hit in many places. The Roland was very much faster than the Sopwith, but the German machine eventually broke off the fight.

Flight Sub-Lieut. Redpath (Gunlayer A. M. Pinchon) was engaged by an enemy machine over the objective, and again later by three enemy machines on crossing the lines, with no decisive result.

Flight Lieut. Potter (Gunlayer A. M. Dell) was heavily engaged by four machines over Chateau Salines. He claims to have shot one down and was subsequently shot down by the other three, being, however, able to glide into our lines and landing safely. The machine is badly damaged by gunfire.

The number of enemy machines seem to have increased considerably and several minor fights of no importance occurred.

Several bombs were observed to hit the objective, though the target was small.

The machines were heavily shelled at the lines, and at Saarbrucken and in its vicinity. Enemy machines attacked at various points, but no decisive results took place.

The visibility was poor, the sky being clear above 3,000 feet but misty up to this height.

No. 8 SQUADRON. ROYAL NAVAL AIR SERVICE ATTACHED TO THE ROYAL FLYING CORPS.

This squadron has now been relieved by No. 3 Squadron, under Flight Commander Mulock, and it seems to be a fitting time to draw attention to the excellent work which has been carried out by No. 8 Squadron during its period of duty under Squadron Commander Bromet. The operations of the squadron have been ably carried out in conjunction with the R.F.C.

The personnel consisted of the following officers:—

Squadron Commander G. R. Bromet (in command).
Lieut. H. O'Hagen, R.N.V.R. (armament officer).
Lieut. D'Albiac, R.M.A. (records officer).
Mr. T. G. Brice, W.O. (stores).

"A" Flight.

Flight Lieut. S. J. Goble.
Flight Sub-Lieut. E. R. Grange (wounded).

Flight Sub-Lieut. R. A. Little.
Flight Sub-Lieut. W. H. Hope (missing).
Flight Sub-Lieut. S. V. Trapp (killed).
Flight Sub-Lieut. D. M. B. Galbraith (invalided on 7th December 1916).

"B" Flight.

Flight Lieut. C. R. Mackenzie (missing).
Flight Sub-Lieut. R. T. Compston.
Flight Sub-Lieut. H. L. Wood.
Flight Sub-Lieut. G. G. Simpson.
Flight Sub-Lieut. the Hon. A. C. Corbett (killed).
Flight Sub-Lieut. A. H. Lawson (wounded).
Flight Sub-Lieut. N. R. Cook.

"C" Flight.

Flight Lieut. J. C. P. Wood (withdrawn on 23rd November 1916).
Flight Sub-Lieut. C. E. Hervey.
Flight Sub-Lieut. C. Thom.
Flight Sub-Lieut. C. D. Booker.
Flight Sub-Lieut. C. H. B. Jenner-Parson (invalided 5th December 1916).
Flight Sub-Lieut. R. R. Soar.

In order to replace casualties the following officers have joined the squadron at various dates:—

Flight Lieut. A. S. Todd (missing).
Flight Lieut. J. C. Croft (missing).
Flight Sub-Lieut. W. R. Orchard.
Flight Sub-Lieut. W. N. R. Brown.
Flight Sub-Lieut. N. E. Woods (invalided 29th December 1916).
Flight Sub-Lieut. F. V. Branford.
Flight Sub-Lieut. J. A. Shaw.

During the period they were attached to the R.F.C. this squadron has carried out a large number of offensive patrols over the enemy's lines, and the following is a rough summary of the enemy machines destroyed or driven down, as computed after verification by the R.F.C.:—

Hostile aircraft certainly destroyed, 14.
Hostile aircraft brought or driven down, of which a large proportion must have been destroyed, 13.

In addition, there have been a very large number of indecisive engagements, which, in the majority of cases, were broken off by the hostile aircraft.

Although the percentage of casualties is higher than anticipated, it should be remembered that this squadron was employed entirely on operations over the enemy's lines during the whole of their period of service, and undoubtedly lessened the casualties of the R.F.C. by a very appreciable extent.

On 4th December the Field-Marshal, Commander-in-Chief, sent a personal message of appreciation to the squadron and mentioned them in the General Communiqué, and on two occasions Major-General H. Trenchard, C.B., commanding the R.F.C., has congratulated the squadron.

Field Marshal Sir Douglas Haig, in expressing his appreciation of the work of the squadron to the Army Council, writes as follows:—

"This squadron has had a good deal of fighting.

"The pilots have shown a great enterprise and dash and have always acquitted themselves admirably.

"The care of the machines has been beyond reproach, and the discipline of the unit very good.

"This unit is shortly leaving my command to rejoin the Royal Naval Air Service, and I request that the Lords Commissioners of the Admiralty may be acquainted with my appreciation of its fine work."

Squadron Commander Bromet has shown very high qualities both as an officer and a leader, and has maintained the moral of the squadron notwithstanding rather heavy casualties.

The petty officers and men have worked hard and cheerfully, and have maintained the engines and machines in first-class order.

The squadron as a whole, working in conjunction with the Army, has upheld the traditions of the Navy. While all officers and men carried out their duties very satisfactorily, the following officers and men should be noted for particularly good work:—

Squadron Commander G. R. Bromet.
Flight Commander B. L. Huskisson.
Flight Commander C. R. Mackenzie, D.S.O. (missing, 24th January 1917).
Flight Lieut. S. J. Goble, D.S.O.
Flight Lieut. R. J. O. Compston.
Flight Lieut. E. R. Grange (wounded, 7th January 1917).
Flight Sub-Lieut. R. A. Little.
Flight Sub-Lieut. S. V. Trapp (killed, 10th December 1916).
Flight Sub-Lieut. R. R. Soar.
Flight Lieut. D. M. B. Galbraith, D.S.C.
Flight Lieut. C. D. Booker.
Lieutenant H. O'Hagan, R.N.V.R.
   88   H. H. Scott, C.P.O.
12973   J. A. Rosling, C.P.O.
 4506   W. A. Hill, P.O.
 4685   H. Dawson, P.O.

935 F. T. McSorley, P.O.
2233 H. W. Newhill, L.M.
4494 S. Wylie, L.M.
4283 A. C. Drury, L.M.
4321 P. T. Clarke, A.M.
16401 L. M. Webb, A.C.M.
15156 H. Simson, A.C.M.

The Vice-Admiral at Dover has written expressing his appreciation of the good services rendered by this squadron, and expresses his regret at the loss of the officers killed and missing, especially Flight Lieut. Mackenzie, who was a brilliant officer.

EASTERN MEDITERRANEAN STATIONS.

The following reports have been compiled from information contained in Weekly Operation Reports, Nos. 45, 46, and 47 (A. 0490, A. 0496, and A. 0586).

A north-easterly gale, with rain and snow, has interrupted flying to a great extent, and low clouds and rainy weather have been prevalent throughout the locality. A certain amount of damage has been done to the Air Station buildings by the inclement weather.

Thasos "A" Squadron.

January 19th.

A hostile two-seated seaplane was engaged over Kavalla, and after being hit, was pursued in the direction of Gereviz

January 24th.

Flight Sub-Lieut. G. H. Major with Midshipman R. J. Dashwood, in Sopwith No. 5086, during a reconnaissance of the Xanthi area, observed two trains leaving the station, one in the direction of Okjilar and the other towards Gumuljina. The former was overtaken about three miles south of Xanthi, the pilot then flying at 900 feet. The train stopped on the approach of the aeroplane, and troops were seen to detrain and run into the fields. They were immediately attacked with machine-gun fire, and several were seen to drop before they had time to take cover.

January 28th.

A considerable amount of information was obtained regarding the aerodrome and anti-aircraft defences in a reconnaissance flight over the Xanthi area and the Nestos river.

Traffic was observed both by road and river, and a search was made in the Kavalla district for a Royal Flying Corps machine which was reported as having made a forced landing, the pilot being captured and the machine undamaged.

January 27th to 31st and February 1st.

Anti-submarine patrol flights were carried out.

On the 5th February attacks were made on the following targets in the Nestos area :—

(1) Yenikeui railway bridge—
    One direct hit was made on the bridge.
(2) Transport near Sarishaban—
    Two direct hits were made and many wagons were destroyed.
(3) One bomb was dropped on the fort to the west of Injenez.

Local patrol flights round Thasos Island, the coast of Athos Peninsula, the Gulf of Orfano, and Porto Lagos Bay were carried out by seaplanes on the 2nd, 3rd, 4th, and 6th February.

On 6th February Short Seaplane No. 9758 failing to return, search was made by seaplanes and ships, the missing seaplane eventually being found. The pilot and observer were uninjured, but the seaplane sank while being towed back to Thasos.

Stavros "D" Squadron.

January 19th, 22nd, 23rd, and 24th.

Reconnaissance, spotting, and photographic flights have been carried out on these days.

H.M.S. "Empress."

January 16th.

Flight Sub-Lieut. S. F. Abbott and Sub-Lieut. A. C. Holcombe, R.N.V.R., in Short No. 9758, spotted for one of His Majesty's ships on a camp about 1,200 yards south-east of Dranli.

This camp was set on fire by bombardment and entirely destroyed. Another result of successful spotting was the destruction of a gun emplacement near Dedeballi, on which a direct hit was scored.

In consequence of H.M.S. "Empress" having proceeded for refit on the 19th January, "D" Squadron has been operating both for the Navy and Army over the Stavros–Pelelinos, Drama, and Pravi areas, and the station has been strengthened both in personnel and machines.

A great deal of useful information has been obtained by reconnaissances, with reference to defence works, camps, enemy movements, roads, &c.

January 27th.

Bombs were dropped on the southern edge of Manterelli, and photographs taken of the area between Dranli and Orphano.

January 28th.

Four machines carried out a raid on Razobvos, 16 bombs being dropped on various enemy billets.

On 6th February a reconnaissance was made of the enemy's lines on the Neohori front and bombs were dropped on troops quartered in Lakovikia.

During the remainder of the week no flying was carried out owing to the swampy condition of the aerodrome, abnormally heavy rain having been experienced.

Thermi "B" Squadron.

January 25th.

With the exception of an anti-submarine patrol carried out on the Metylene Channel on this day, no Service flights were undertaken during the period under review till the 6th February, when reconnaissances were carried out over the Aivalik and the Muskonesi Islands, Chandarli Gulf, and the region around Smyrna.

A pontoon bridge connecting Mosko and Krommylo Islands was observed, and a seaplane station at Sanjak Kale, six miles due west of Smyrna, and the aerodrome at Kasamir were observed.

Imbros "C" Squadron.

January 19th, 23rd, 24th, 27th, and 28th.

Owing to low clouds and bad weather, the usual Dardanelles patrol was carried out on these days only. On 27th January a raid was carried out on the supposed aerodrome at Kephez, which had been located during the previous week.

Flight Sub-Lieut. J. R. S. Devlin, with Midshipman E. R. Snow as observer, in Henri Farman 3001 (155-h.p. Canton Unne), made particularly good practice, dropping three 65-lb. bombs from 5,000 feet, two of which fell among a group of bell tents, completely destroying them.

Flight Lieut. A. Maitland Heriot, flying a B.E. 2 C. during this raid, was attacked by a hostile monoplane (Fokker or Halberstadt) while his escort was occupied by a supposed enemy seaplane some distance off. The monoplane made three attacks, one at 700 and two at 4,000 feet. On each occasion Flight Lieut. Heriot dived and turned in the direction of the hostile machine, passing underneath him and thus preventing his adversary from getting his gun to bear. The enemy never approached nearer than 100 yards, and it was useless therefore for Lieutenant Heriot to use his automatic pistol, and he had no machine gun. After the third attempt the hostile machine broke off the attack and the B.E. returned to Imbros.

In view of the above account it is interesting to note a wireless press notice which appeared in Constantinople on 30th January, which runs as follows:—

> "In the Dardanelles on the 27th instant our aviator, Lieutenant Meinke, drove down an enemy two-decker in course of an air battle with six enemy machines. The aeroplane is in our possession."

(Reference Map, 1 : 20,000 squared, Dardanelles.)

Reconnaissance of the Dardanelles shipping was carried out on the 3rd, 4th, 5th, 6th, and 7th February.

During the morning of 4th February an explosion was reported from the direction of Anzac. A reconnaissance was accordingly made to investigate this. No indications or effects of the reported explosion were observed within a radius of three miles around W. Hill (105 T.U.), though subsequent reconnaissance carried out during the afternoon reported what was apparently another explosion on the shore at 91.0 (due west of Koja Dere).

Photographs of camps and gun emplacements on Chocolate Hill (105 L.) were taken.

At midday on the 6th February heavy firing was heard off Kum Kale. A reconnaissance was made and an object resembling a submarine was seen. As soon as this intelligence was received at Imbros, two bombing machines, with two escorts, were sent to attack, but before their arrival the target had disappeared. The bombs were accordingly dropped at a large tug and on the bridges at Boyaji and to the south of Kum Kale.

At midnight on the 6th and 7th February a raid was carried out by three machines on Nagara Base and the shipping in Nagara Bay—a steamer of 2,000 tons having been observed lying at anchor there during the whole of the previous day.

Five heavy and eight small bombs were dropped, two 100-lb. bombs exploding in the water within 30 yards of the 2,000-ton ship.

Small shipping in Kilia Liman and the wharfside at Chanak were also bombed.

Mudros.

H.M.S. "Ark Royal."

Only practice and W/T flights in seaplanes have been made during the period under review.

Marsh Aerodrome.

January 19th to 25th.

Practice flights have been carried out in Sopwith B.E. 2 C.'s and H.F.s, but no flying has taken place during the rest of the period under review owing to the bad weather and heavy rains.

Airship Station.

There is at present no airship available for this station, but in any case the weather conditions now prevailing would preclude flying. It is believed that by the beginning of March the weather will have settled sufficiently to start airship flights again.

Kassandra.

Owing to persistent gales the airship has not been inflated, and it is not intended to use the ship until more settled weather conditions prevail.

HOSTILE AIRCRAFT IN MACEDONDIA.

A report (A. 0484) has been received on hostile aircraft in Macedonia, which gives particulars of the principal enemy aerodromes in this fighting area, and information as to their personnel and numbers of machines.

The air service in Macedonia is commanded by Captain von Plomberg, who is directly responsible to General von Belon.

The six principal bases for the enemy air service are Uskub, Prilep, Hudova, Drama, Gereviez (seaplanes), and Xanthi; the last named being temporarily abandoned. At Uskub there are 18 machines, four of which are used for instructional purposes.

There are three squadrons at Prilep, consisting of 10 Fokkers and 14 Albatross machines. All these machines are of 1915 model. Six machines of the Albatross type are used exclusively for spotting for artillery.

Hudova is used in conjunction with Drama as an advanced base. There appear to be three squadrons at Hudova, the first two consisting of 12 Albatross machines (1915 and 1916 models), and the Bulgarian squadron, which has replaced a German squadron sent to the Dobrudja. The Bulgarians are said to fly very little, and have only four Albatross machines in their squadron (all 1915 models), and there is a considerable amount of bad feeling between them and the Germans.

At Drama there are three 1915 Albatross machines and one Fokker, and their duties are chiefly photographic reconnaissances on the Struma front, but only every two or three days with a definite object. Spotting is rarely undertaken, the principles of this kind of work being beyond the Bulgarian artillery. Whenever any hostile machines are signalled, no matter how many, the one Fokker is immediately ordered to attack.

There are probably at least three seaplanes at Gereviz, but no information could be obtained as to the exact number.

Plans of the various aerodromes and landing grounds are attached to the report.

February 17th.

Okjilar bridge is reported as having been destroyed by bomb attack, and the embankment was also considerably damaged. Okjilar is 6½ miles S.W. of Xanthi, on the Drama Railway to Constantinople.

NO DETAILED REPORT HAS AS YET BEEN RECEIVED.

ROYAL FLYING CORPS COMMUNIQUÉ No. 74.

Artillery Co-operation.

February 4th.

Forty-five targets were dealt with by aeroplane observation.

In co-operation with aeroplanes of the First Brigade, artillery obtained 15 direct hits on gun-pits, and one on an anti-aircraft battery.

With observation by aeroplanes of the Third Brigade, artillery obtained two direct hits on hostile batteries, and a direct hit on a trench mortar.

Co-operating with aeroplanes of the Fourth Brigade, artillery successfully engaged 12 hostile batteries.

Artillery of the Fifth Army, with aeroplane observation, obtained four direct hits on gun-pits, one pit being completely demolished.

On the night of the 3rd/4th instant, Major Henderson and Second Lieut. Nesbitt, No. 5 Squadron, located and reported by zone call 19 active hostile batteries. During this patrol a searchlight was attacked and extinguished by machine-gun fire from the aeroplane.

Hostile Aircraft.

As a result of an encounter with a German aeroplane, Second Lieut. Massey and Second Lieut. Vernham, No. 16 Squadron, had their machine brought down on fire. Second Lieut. Massey was wounded and Second Lieut. Vernham killed. Artillery officers state that the German machine was also shot down in this combat.

Lieutenant J. W. Boyd and Second Lieut. A. H. Steele, No. 16 Squadron, drove down a German machine, which went down under control, but crashed on landing.

Captain H. R. Hawkins and Sergeant Johnson, No. 22 Squadron, engaged three hostile aeroplanes near Haplincourt, one of which they destroyed.

Captain G. M. Clement and Lieutenant M. K. Parlee, No. 22 Squadron, while on offensive patrol, were attacked by three hostile machines, one of which was hit, and the propeller was seen to stop, but it glided away under control. Later, assisted by a De Havilland scout, the pilot and observer destroyed a German aeroplane near Rocquigny.

Two German aeroplanes were attacked by Captain Poellnitz, No. 24 Squadron, near St. Pierre Vaast Wood. The hostile machines were driven down, and one fell, apparently out of control.

Lieutenant E. C. Pashley and Lieutenant Saundby, both of No. 24 Squadron, observed eight German aeroplanes attacking 5 F.E.'s. They dived at the hostile machines and succeeded in destroying one of them. A second German aeroplane was driven down out of control by an offensive patrol of No. 14 Squadron.

An offensive patrol of No. 32 Squadron encountered a hostile formation near Achiet. A general encounter ensued. Captain Curphey drove down one of the hostile machines out of control. Several of our machines were badly hit. The patrol returned to their aerodrome, where Captain Curphey and Second Lieut. Randall changed their machines and went in search of the hostile aeroplanes. They had several combats, in one of which Captain Curphey, assisted by the other pilots, brought down a hostile machine, although he had been wounded in the head.

Second Lieut. Farquhar and Second Lieut. Blennerhasset, both of No. 24 Squadron, while on line patrol, were attacked by four German aeroplanes. One of these was driven down under control and a second out of control.

Bombing.

One hundred and five 20-lb. bombs were dropped on points of military importance behind the German lines by aeroplanes of the First and Fifth Brigades.

Casualties.

Killed.—Lieutenant J. W. Boyd, Second Lieut. A. H. Steele, Second Lieut. N. M. H. Vernham, all of No. 16 Squadron; Second Lieut. H. L. Villiers, No. 11 Squadron.

Wounded.—Second Lieut. H. M. Massey, No. 16 Squadron; Second Lieut. A. B. Coupal, No. 11 Squadron; Captain W. G. S. Curphey, No. 32 Squadron.

Missing.—No. 917 Sergt. J. F. Shaw, No. 15 Squadron; Second Lieut. G. W. B. Bradford, No. 15 Squadron.

Hostile Aircraft.

February 5th.

Captain G. Boumphrey and Captain L. Findlay, No. 46 Squadron, while on artillery observation, were attacked from behind by a Roland two-seater. An armour-piercing bullet struck a drum, with the result that six rounds exploded, and Captain Findlay was wounded, but continued fighting. Anti-aircraft gunners report that the German aeroplane fell out of control.

An offensive patrol of No. 32 Squadron met nine hostile aircraft from Grevillers. In the general combat which ensued

Captain Jones drove down a hostile machine, which fell completely out of control.

Bombing.

Douai aerodrome was attacked by aeroplanes of the First Brigade. The majority of the bombs, both 112-lb. and 20-lb., were seen to fall and burst on and around the aerodrome. Other places of military importance were attacked by machines of the First and Fifth Brigades.

Casualties.

Wounded. — Captain G. M. Boumphrey and Captain L. Findlay, No. 46 Squadron.

February 6th.

Thirty-five targets were dealt with by aeroplane observation.

In co-operation with aeroplanes of the First Brigade, artillery obtained six direct hits on gun positions.

Artillery of the Second Army, with aeroplane observation, obtained 12 direct hits on hostile batteries. One gun-pit, which was set on fire, burned for half an hour.

Co-operating with aeroplanes of the Fourth Brigade, artillery successfully engaged two hostile batteries. Four direct hits were obtained, and an explosion of ammunition was caused.

Artillery of the Fifth Army, with aeroplane observation, destroyed a gun-pit and damaged another.

Hostile Aircraft.

Captain R. J. Mounsey and Lieutenant L. M. Elworthy, No. 2 Squadron, while on artillery registration, were attacked by two hostile aeroplanes. The observer of one of the German machines was hit, and seen to fall into the machine.

Second Lieut. E. B. W. Bartlett, No. 41 Squadron, engaged a hostile machine, which he drove down in a vertical nose-dive, apparently out of control. A second hostile machine was driven down by a reconnaissance of No. 20 Squadron, and was last seen in a vertical nose-dive.

Second Lieut. McCudden, No. 29 Squadron, and Lieutenant Cockerell, No. 24 Squadron, each engaged and drove down a hostile aeroplane out of control.

Bombing.

A dump at La Chaudiere was bombed by aeroplanes of the First Brigade. Several of the bombs were seen to explode on the dump.

On the night of the 6th–7th bombs were dropped on Provin aerodrome by aeroplanes of the First Brigade. The bombs were seen to explode near the hangars. Bombs were also dropped on a train and on billets at Berclau. Bombs dropped on a dump at Provin Station were seen to burst on the objective.

Casualties.

Killed.—Second Lieut. H. L. Pateman and Second Lieut. H. J. Davis, both of No. 15 Squadron.

Wounded.—Second Lieut. F. W. A. Vickery, No. 23 Squadron; Lieutenant W. B. McDonald, No. 22 Squadron.

Missing.—Lieutenant E. B. Maule and Lieutenant T. C. H. Lucas, both of No. 20 Squadron; Second Lieut. M. E. Woods and Second Lieut. J. T. Gibbon, both of No. 20 Squadron.

Artillery Co-operation.

February 7th.

Sixty-nine targets were dealt with by aeroplane observation.

With observation by aeroplanes of the First Brigade, artillery obtained 13 direct hits on gun-pits, and one on an anti-aircraft battery.

Co-operating with aeroplanes of the Second Brigade, artillery obtained seven direct hits on gun-pits and caused two explosions of ammunition.

With observation by aeroplanes of the Third Brigade artillery obtained four direct hits on trench targets and one on a hostile battery.

Artillery of the Fourth Army, with aeroplane observation, successfully engaged seven hostile batteries, and caused two explosions of ammunition.

Co-operating with aeroplanes of the Fifth Brigade, artillery successfully engaged 12 hostile batteries. Two gun-pits were demolished and 10 damaged, and one explosion of ammunition caused. Seventeen direct hits on gun positions were recorded.

Hostile Aircraft.

A patrol of No. 40 Squadron engaged a German aeroplane, which was driven down under control, but in a badly damaged condition.

A photographic reconnaissance of No. 45 Squadron engaged six hostile aeroplanes near Menin. Two of the hostile machines were driven down out of control.

Sergeant Cunliffe and Second Air Mechanic Walker, No. 23 Squadron, whilst on line patrol, were attacked by five hostile aeroplanes near Combles. One of the German machines was driven down out of control and seen to crash.

A line patrol of No. 32 Squadron was attacked by nine hostile aircraft. One of the German machines, engaged by Captain Curphey, went down in a spinning nose-dive, with its engine full on. The fate of this machine could not be ascertained owing to the presence of other hostile aircraft. A second German aeroplane fell completely out of control, after being engaged by Second Lieut. Davies.

Photography.

Four hundred and ten photographs were taken during the day.

Casualties.

Missing.—Second Lieut. E. E. Erlebach and Second Air Mechanic F. Ridgway, of No. 25 Squadron.

Artillery Co-operation.

February 8th.

Seventy-one targets were dealt with by aeroplane observation.

In co-operation with aeroplanes of the First Brigade, artillery obtained three direct hits on eight gun-pits and two on trench mortars. An explosion of ammunition was caused. One of the shoots on a hostile battery was done at night by Second Lieut. E. J. Garland, No. 10 Squadron. He ranged the 150th Siege Battery on to a hostile battery between 10 p.m. and 1 a.m. on the night of the 7th/8th instant. Two direct hits were obtained in this shoot on a gun-pit. Incendiary shells were fired at the aeroplane, six being fired at a time. The flashes of the gun-firing were not observed.

With observation by aeroplanes of the Second Brigade, artillery successfully engaged 12 hostile batteries. Ten gun-pits were hit, and two explosions of ammunition were caused.

Co-operating with aeroplanes of the Fourth Brigade, artillery obtained five direct hits on batteries and 13 on trench points. A fire and four explosions of ammunition were caused.

Artillery of the Fifth Army, with aeroplane observation, successfully engaged 11 hostile batteries. Eleven direct hits on gun-pits were obtained. One gun-pit was demolished and seven damaged. A fire was caused, and three explosions of ammunition took place.

Hostile Aircraft.

Second Lieut. G. F. Haseler, No. 40 Squadron, drove down an Albatross two-seater. This machine landed in a field, and turned on its back after landing.

Bombing.

On the night of the 7th/8th instant Provin aerodrome was attacked by aeroplanes of the First Brigade. One bomb was seen to burst on a hangar and another on a shed. The remaining bombs fell on and around the aerodrome. La Pouillere aerodrome was also attacked, 13 bombs were observed to burst on the buildings and sheds of the aerodrome, and a considerable number fell on the aerodrome close to the hangars. A bomb dropped on Lattre Station was seen to burst on the sheds, and another near the railway line. Several other places were attacked during the night.

On the day of the 8th a dump and other places of military importance were bombed by aeroplanes of the First and Fifth Brigades.

Miscellaneous.

Captain Gould and Second Lieut. Taylor, No. 4 Squadron, whilst on artillery patrol, attacked and dispersed a party of hostile infantry with machine-gun fire.

Casualties.

Wounded.—Lieutenant W. H. Copeland, No. 4 Squadron.

Artillery Co-operation.

February 9th.

Sixty-eight targets were dealt with by aeroplane observation.

In co-operation with aeroplanes of the First Brigade, artillery obtained direct hits on nine gun-pits and one on a trench mortar.

Field artillery obtained four direct hits on trench and other targets.

With observation by aeroplanes of the Second Brigade, artillery successfully engaged three hostile batteries.

Co-operating with aeroplanes of the Third Brigade, artillery damaged a trench and hit two emplacements.

Artillery of the Fourth Army, with aeroplane observation, successfully engaged six hostile batteries. Three gun-pits were demolished and 13 damaged. Twenty-three direct hits were obtained on gun positions.

Hostile Aircraft.

A German aeroplane, which was engaged by Lieutenant Dunlop and Second Lieut. J. B. Weir, No. 25 Squadron, was driven down and fell in flames.

Sergeant Munro and Sergeant King, No. 25 Squadron, also drove down a German aeroplane in a damaged condition.

A hostile machine was brought down by anti-aircraft fire to the east of Neuville St. Vaast.

An offensive patrol of No. 32 Squadron engaged and drove down a hostile aeroplane, which is believed to have been badly damaged.

Photography.

Four hundred and fifty-three photographs were taken during the day.

Bombing.

Provin aerodrome was attacked by aeroplanes of the First Brigade. A number of bombs fell on the aerodrome, and one hangar was destroyed.

Other places of military importance were attacked by aeroplanes of the First and Fifth Brigades.

Casualties.

Wounded.—Second Lieut. H. V. Puckeridge and Lieutenant A. N. Nesbit, No. 5 Squadron.

Artillery Co-operation.

February 10th.

Sixty-eight targets were dealt with, with aeroplane observation.

Co-operating with aeroplanes of the First Brigade, heavy artillery obtained two direct hits on gun-pits. Siege artillery obtained four direct hits on hostile batteries, and caused a large explosion of ammunition. During a raid of the 11th Corps two active batteries were ranged on and silenced, 12 direct hits being obtained and an explosion of ammunition caused. Trench targets were also successfully registered. On the night of the 9th–10th Captain A. V. Robeson, No. 10 Squadron, attempted to range the 150th Siege Battery on to a hostile battery, but was only able to observe two bursts.

With observation by aeroplanes of the Third Brigade, artillery obtained a direct hit on a trench target. Captain McArthur, No. 12 Squadron, ranged the 35th Heavy Battery on to a hostile battery, and reported five direct hits, three emplacements damaged, and an explosion of ammunition.

With observation by aeroplanes of the Second Brigade, artillery successfully engaged nine hostile batteries; 12 gun-pits were hit, and six explosions of ammunition caused.

Artillery of the Fourth Army, with aeroplane observation, obtained 12 direct hits on hostile batteries and six on a brickfield.

With observation by aeroplanes of the Fifth Brigade, artillery successfully engaged nine hostile batteries; 13 direct hits were obtained, and two explosions of ammunition were caused.

Hostile Aircraft.

Captain Aizlewood, No. 32 Squadron, while on offensive patrol, engaged and drove down a German aeroplane, which was reported to have fallen out of control.

Bombing.

On the night of the 9th–10th aeroplanes of the First Brigade dropped twelve 20-lb. bombs on L'Adventure. All the bombs were observed to burst in the village. On the day of the 10th aeroplanes of the same brigade dropped bombs on infantry headquarters at Cantelaux. All the bombs were seen to burst on or near the objective. This attack was made in co-operation with a raid carried out by the 11th Corps.

Several other places of military importance were attacked during the day.

On the night of the 9th-10th aeroplanes of the Fifth Brigade attacked a dump and the sidings at Fremicourt, and an ammunition dump on the Mory–Sapignies road. All the bombs were seen to explode on the dump at Fremicourt, and a fire was caused. A bomb was seen to explode also on the railway line. The dump on the Mory–Sapignies road was hit with the bombs and with machine-gun fire. During the day of the 10th Biez Wood, Miraumont, and a group of hostile batteries near Miraumont were attacked with bombs.

Casualties.

Killed.—Lieutenant R. J. Docking, No. 43 Squadron; Lieutenant W. A. Porkess and Second Lieut. E. Roberts, No. 10 Squadron.

Wounded.—Lieutenant A. G. Stewart, No. 20 Squadron; Captain L. P. Aizlewood, No. 32 Squadron; Second Lieut. T. S. Edelston, No. 43 Squadron; Lieutenant J. M. J. C. L. Rock and Second Lieut. A. E. P. Smith, No. 43 Squadron.

Photography.

From the 4th to the 10th inclusive 2,643 photographs were taken.

Headquarters, Royal Flying Corps,
11th February 1917.

ROYAL FLYING CORPS COMMUNIQUÉ No. 75.

February 11th.

With observation by First Brigade, six O.K.'s were obtained on five hostile battery gun-pits, and three large explosions caused among ammunition.

In co-operation with Second Brigade, three hostile batteries were successfully engaged.

Thirteen targets were ranged on by Third Brigade, six of which were hostile batteries, on which two direct hits were obtained.

The Fourth Brigade ranged on 10 hostile batteries, obtaining five direct hits.

Four hostile batteries were engaged with observation by machines of Fifth Brigade, one gun-pit being destroyed.

Hostile Aircraft.

Four machines of No. 40 Squadron encountered four Halberstadts and one Albatross. One of the hostile machines was brought down in flames behind the German lines.

Photography.

Three hundred and sixty-six plates were exposed.

Bombing.

Sixty 20-lb. bombs were dropped during the day.

Miscellaneous.

Several trench and flash reconnaissances were carried out. Second Lieut. Sayer and Second Lieut. Morris, No. 15 Squadron, carried out a successful contact patrol. Several posts were located and communication obtained with Battalion Headquarters.

Casualties.

Wounded.—No. 3232 Corpl. H. Cottingham, No. 13 Squadron; Second Lieut. L. L. Brown, No. 15 Squadron; Second Lieut. F. J. Fleming, No. 34 Squadron.

Missing.—Captain J. Thornburn and Second Lieut. J. K. Howard, No. 13 Squadron.

Contact Patrol.

February 12th.

Second Lieut. Sayer and Second Lieut. Morris, No. 15 Squadron, carried out a successful contract patrol. No other work was possible owing to bad weather.

Artillery Co-operation.

February 13th.

Eight targets were dealt with by aeroplane observation.

Artillery of the Fourth Army successfully engaged three hostile batteries.

Hostile Aircraft.

Second Lieut. F. N. Hudson, No. 54 Squadron, engaged a hostile aeroplane near Le Transloy. The German machine was hit, and went down in a vertical nose-dive.

Lieutenant Burcher and Second Lieut Stroud, No. 9 Squadron, engaged two hostile machines near Sailly-Saillisel. One of the German aeroplanes was brought down in our lines.

Photography.

One hundred and ninety-seven photographs were taken during the day.

Casualties.

Killed.—Lieutenant T. S. Green and Second Lieut. W. K. Carse, No. 3 Squadron.

Artillery Co-operation.

February 14*th*.

Sixty-nine targets were dealt with by aeroplane observation. Artillery of the First Army obtained 12 direct hits on hostile batteries and trenches. Four hostile batteries were successfully engaged by artillery of the Second Army.

Artillery of the Third Army obtained three direct hits on hostile batteries and three on trenches. An explosion of ammunition was caused.

Eleven direct hits on hostile batteries and 14 on trench points were obtained by artillery of the Fourth Army.

Artillery of the Fifth Army obtained nine direct hits on gun positions, and caused an explosion of ammunition.

Hostile Aircraft.

Two German aeroplanes were driven down out of control during the day—one by a patrol of No. 60 Squadron near Monchy, and one by Flight Lieut. Mack, Naval Squadron No. 3, near Warlencourt.

Lieutenant Carbery and Lieutenant Vaile, No. 52 Squadron, destroyed a German aeroplane near Bouchavesnes.

Photography.

Seven hundred and fifty-four photographs were taken during the day.

Bombing.

Bombs were dropped by aeroplanes of the First Brigade on several places of importance behind the German lines. Two bombs were seen to burst on the railway line south of Avion.

On the night of the 13th–14th a machine of No. 6 Squadron dropped four phosphorus bombs over hostile batteries. After the first bomb was dropped the hostile battery attacked ceased fire for 20 minutes. The other batteries attacked were not seen to fire again during the period the machine was in the air. These bombs were dropped on batteries putting up barrage fire during an attack by the VIII. Corps.

On the 14th bombs were dropped on Biez Wood and Miraumont by the Fifth Brigade.

A successful contact patrol was carried out by Second Lieut. Sayer and Second Lieut. Morris, No. 15 Squadron, of our trenches north of the Ancre. Seven flares were observed.

Casualties.

Killed.—Second Lieut. F C. Young and Second Lieut. A. G. S. de Ross, No. 3 Squadron; Second Lieut. F. W. Nisbet and No. 45,071, Second Air Mechanic P. E. Knightly, No. 46 Squadron; Second Lieut. F. M. Myers, No. 20 Squadron.

Wounded.—Captain H. E. Hartney and Second Lieut. W. T. Jourdan, No. 20 Squadron; Second Lieut. F. J. Taylor, No. 20 Squadron; Second Lieut. C. F. Uwins, No. 1 A.D.; Captain G. C. Bailey, D.S.O., No. 2 Squadron; Second Lieut. W. J. Pearson, No. 8 Squadron.

Missing.—Second Lieut. C. D. Bennet and Second Lieut. H. A. Croft, No. 2 Squadron; Second Lieut. J. V. Fairbairn, No. 54 Squadron.

Hostile Aircraft.

February 15th.

One hundred targets were dealt with by aeroplane observation.

Artillery of the First Army obtained 15 direct hits on nine gun-pits. Three of the pits were set on fire. Eleven direct hits were obtained on trench mortars and trench targets.

Artillery of the Second Army obtained 11 direct hits on gun-pits, and caused an explosion of ammunition.

Artillery of the Third Army obtained six direct hits on hostile batteries, and three on trenches. Two explosions of ammunition were caused.

Artillery of the Fourth Army obtained 15 direct hits on hostile batteries, and caused four explosions of ammunition. Trenches were also hit.

Artillery of the Fifth Army destroyed one gun-pit and damaged ten others. Ten explosions of ammunition were caused.

Hostile Aircraft..

Hostile aircraft were driven down out of control by the following:—

> One by a patrol of No. 25 Squodron, near Avion.
> One by a patrol of No. 1 Squadron, near Hollebeke.
> One by Flight Sub-Lieut. Collison, Naval Squadron No. 3, near Bapaume.

Captain Jones, No. 32 Squadron, drove down a German aeroplane out of control near Grevillers. Although twice wounded, and with his machine badly shot about, he carried on with the patrol until the hostile formation was driven off.

Second Lieut. Pratt and Second Lieut. Bryers, No. 46 Squadron, brought down a German aeroplane, which fell in our lines near Vlamertinghe.

Second Lieut. McCudden, No. 29 Squadron, engaged two hostile aircraft over Adinfer Wood. One of the hostile machines was destroyed, and crashed east of Monchy.

While on patrol, Second Lieut. V. H. Collins, No. 1 Squadron, engaged and destroyed a German aeroplane.

A fourth hostile machine was destroyed west of Bapaume by Second Lieut. Huston and Second Lieut. Taylor, No. 18 Squadron.

Lieutenant E. L. Benbow, No. 40 Squadron, drove down a hostile aeroplane, which crashed near Douai.

Photography.

Four hundred and forty-one photographs were taken during the day.

Bombing.

Bombs were dropped on places of military importance by aeroplanes of the First and Fifth Brigades.

Casualties.

Killed.—Lieutenant H. E. Mulock and No. 0/75953, Private T. Booth, No. 52 Squadron; Second Lieut. A. E. Townsend, and No. 0/21732 Second Air Mechanic H. J. Honour, No. 34 Squadron.

Wounded.—Second Lieut. H. E. Rathkins and Lieutenant W. A. Landry, No. 42 Squadron; Captain H. W. G. Jones, No. 32 Squadron; Lieutenant R. B. Wainwright, No. 20 Squadron.

Missing.—Second Lieut. E. Hamilton and Captain C. L. M. Scott, No. 54 Squadron; Lieutenant C. H. March, No. 32 Squadron; Captain J. M. E. Shepherd, No. 1 Squadron.

Artillery Co-operation.

February 16th.

Twenty-eight targets were dealt with by aeroplane observations.

Artillery of the First Army obtained one direct hit on gun-pits, and eight on trench mortars.

Artillery of the Second Army successfully engaged three hostile batteries. Three gun-pits were hit, and an explosion of ammunition was caused.

Artillery of the Third Army obtained a direct hit on a hostile battery, and one on a trench mortar. Two hostile batteries, on which four direct hits were obtained, were silenced by artillery of the Fourth Army, and 29 O.K.'s were obtained on trench points.

Artillery of the Fifth Army successfully engaged a hostile battery.

Hostile Aircraft.

A German aeroplane, which was attacked by Second Lieut. D. McC. Kerr and Second Lieut. F. C. Elstob, No. 53 Squadron, fell out of control near Wytschaete.

Sergeant Smith and Lieutenant Aldred, No. 5 Squadron, brought down a German aeroplane, which crashed near Hebuterne.

A patrol of No. 32 Squadron encountered four hostile machines near Bapaume. The observer in one of the machines was hit, and seen to fall forward.

Photography.

Eighty-six photographs were taken during the day.

Casualties.

Wounded.—No. 23921, Sergeant H. G. Smith, No. 5 Squadron.

Missing.—Second Lieut. E. W. Lindley and Second Lieut. L. V. Munn, No. 16 Squadron.

February 17th.

Owing to adverse weather conditions, only one successful flight was carried out. This was a patrol by Second Lieut. T. Ure and Second Lieut. V. C. Manuel, No. 10 Squadron, during a raid by the XI. Corps. Flares lit by our men in the enemy's trenches were observed, and S.O.S. signals made by the enemy were also noted.

Two 20-lb. bombs were dropped, which were observed to burst on the hostile support trenches.

Headquarters, Royal Flying Corps,
   18th February 1917.

REPORT OF OPERATIONS No. 29.

HOME STATIONS.

The usual patrols and reconnaissances have been carried out whenever possible, and the instructional and practice flights from the various stations, and, with the exception of the incidents which follow, there is nothing of much importance to report from the Home Stations during the period under review.

March 1st.

A hostile machine dropped three bombs in the sea near Broadstairs, and afterwards nine bombs on the town. There appear to have been no casualties.

March 13th.

There is a report from Portland of this date to the effect that a seaplane, when on patrol, located wreckage of the ss. "Memnon," which had been sunk by a submarine, and, subsequently sighting the survivors in the ship's boat, directed a patrol boat to their assistance.

March 16th-17th.

Two hostile airships attempted a raid about 10.30 p.m. over the south-east counties. The movements of the airships seem to have been purposeless and indefinite, and apparently no attempt was made to attack any military objective, and though bombs were dropped in Kent, no damages or casualties have been reported.

Machines went up in pursuit from Eastchurch and Westgate.

March 12th.

A report (A. 0706) has been received from the R.N. Seaplane Station at Dundee, which gives particulars of an attack on a hostile submarine by Flight Sub-Lieut. McNicholl.

The submarine was reported to be approximately off Bell Rock at 3.24 in the afternoon, and at 3.40 Flight Sub-Lieut. McNicholl left in Short 827, No. 8645, with L.M. Jenkins acting as observer.

The submarine was sighted about two miles north-east of Bell Rock, a great part of the hull being visible above the water, but she submerged before the pilot could get the seaplane in a position to attack. Flight Sub-Lieut. McNicholl continued to patrol in the vicinity, and about five o'clock again sighted the submarine about six miles east-south-east of Bell Rock, and promptly manœuvred the seaplane into a position for attack. The observer released four 16-lb. bombs, which dropped in a direct line with the submarine at a distance of about 100 feet apart.

The first two appeared to drop short, but the third and fourth fell very close to the submarine, which was submerging at the time, and it was difficult to observe if she was actually hit.

A dark smoke was observed in the place where the submarine was located on both occasions when she submerged.

March 16th.

A report has been received from Westgate of the raid by a hostile seaplane on this date.

The raid was carried out at about 5.30 a.m., and altogether 13 bombs were dropped, but no material damage was done beyond the breaking of a few windows, and there were no casualties.

Squadron Commander Butler in Sopwith Triplane N. 5424, and Flight Sub-Lieut. Arnold in Bristol Scout 8951, got off at 5.35 and 5.37 a.m. respectively and searched the vicinity in the direction of the North Goodwin Lightship and the North Foreland without result. Flight Sub-Lieut. Bronson also patrolled in the vicinity of Elbow Buoy. Apparently the weather was very thick over 1,000 feet.

DUNKIRK.
March 1st to 15th.

No. 1 Wing.
March 1st.

During a photographic reconnaissance to Bruges, one of our machines was attacked by five hostile aircraft, one of which was destroyed and the others driven off.

On the same day another machine in a photographic flight to Wendingon was attacked by three enemy machines, but succeeded in driving them off.

Much useful information was collected in both these flights.

No. 8 Squadron.

On receiving news of the raid on Broadstairs a patrol was carried out along the coast, during which a large seaplane was engaged six miles off Ostende; she escaped, however, by diving directly into Ostende Harbour.

No. 4 Wing.

During a fighting patrol three enemy machines were encountered over Ghistelles, and one was thought to have been destroyed.

The weather at the beginning of March was very unfavourable for flying, and the usual fighting patrols had to be abandoned on most days. The patrols were carried out when possible, but nothing of importance transpired.

No. 3 WING, FRANCE.

A report (A. 0685) has been received with particulars of the raid carried out on Brebach on the 4th of March.

Squadrons Nos. 1 and 2 each supplied seven bombers and three fighters, and these machines started just after 10 o'clock in the morning. Nine bombers reached the objective. Flight Sub-Lieut. Page (Sopwith Bomber No. 5091) lost his way and dropped his bombs on the railway station at St. Avold.

There seems no doubt that the enemy appears to be collecting machines for the protection of the Saar Valley, one of the squadrons being met by 10 hostile machines on reaching the objective.

Flight Sub-Lieut. H. Edwards, with Gunlayer P. O. Walker (in Sopwith Fighter N. 5173) seem to have shot down one enemy machine, while another is claimed to have been accounted for by Flight Sub-Lieut. Patteson and Gunlayer P. O. Hinkler (in Sopwith Fighter 9410).

Altogether thirty-six 65-lb. bombs were dropped on the blast furnaces, and all the pilots returned safely.

The names of the pilots and passengers who took part in the raid—and who are not mentioned above—were as follows :—

Name	Machine
Squadron-Commander Draper / Gunlayer Pinchen	Sopwith Fighter N. 5174.
Flight Lieut. Wilson	Sopwith Bomber N. 5116.
Flight Sub-Lieut. Alexander	Sopwith Bomber N. 5091.
Flight Sub-Lieut. Sharman / Gunlayer Turner	Sopwith Bomber N. 5171.
Flight Sub-Lieut. Redpath	Sopwith Bomber N. 9742.
Flight Sub-Lieut. Wallace	Sopwith Bomber N. 5512.
Flight Sub-Lieut. Holyman	Sopwith Bomber N. 5098.
Flight Sub-Lieut. Shirriff	Sopwith Bomber 9669.
Flight Sub-Lieut. Masson	Sopwith Bomber N. 5107.
Flight Sub-Lieut. Macgregor / Gunlayer Lockyer	Sopwith Fighter 9722.
Flight Sub-Lieut. Kirkpatrick	Sopwith Bomber N. 5089.
Flight Sub-Lieut. Dissette	Sopwith Bomber N. 5115.

No. 8 Squadron.

The following letter was received by Captain Lambe from the French General commanding the Thirty-sixth Army Corps on the departure of No. 8 Squadron from France:—

"At the moment of your squadron leaving the district I wish to express my satisfaction and recognition of the services rendered during eight months in the sphere of operations of the Thirty-sixth Army Corps.

"Commander Haskins, seconded by the excellent pilots under his orders, has assured, with complete success, the difficult task of maintaining the mastery of the air, and of allowing the French Squadrons to fulfil their missions under the shelter afforded them by the English Squadrons from enemy attacks."

FORTNIGHTLY SUMMARY OF OPERATIONS CARRIED OUT BY THE ROYAL NAVAL AIR SERVICE, DUNKERQUE COMMAND.

From 15th to 28th February 1917.

Weather Conditions.

The weather conditions during the period under review have been unfavourable for flying except on four days, owing to the thick haze inland and heavy mist over the sea.

Fighter Patrols.

15th February.

Fighter patrols were carried out continually from dawn to dusk in the Dunkerque–Nieuport–Dixmude sector.
No hostile machines were encountered and there is nothing to report.

16th February.

Fighter patrols were carried out from dawn till dusk in the vicinity of Nieuport and Dixmude, escorting bombing machines attacking Ghistelles Aerodrome and the harbour of Bruges.

About 7 a.m. hostile machines dropped bombs on the outskirts of Dunkerque, but no damage of military importance was done. Three indecisive encounters took place with these machines.

February 26th.

Fighter patrols were carried out during the day along the coast and inland to Dixmude and Ypres and acted as escorts to a photographic reconnaissance. Several encounters took place during the day, but none appeared to be decisive.

Bombing Patrols.

February 28th.

Flight Sub-Lieut Cuckney on Short Bomber Seaplane No. 9050, accompanied by Flight Sub-Lieut. Fisher on Sopwith Seaplane No. N. 1017, carried out a bombing patrol between 3.8 p.m and 5.4 p.m. to verify report of German submarine on Breedt Bank.

No hostile submarine was observed and there was nothing to report.

Photographic Reconnaissances.

Some very successful photographs have been taken during this period.

February 26th.

Flight Lieut. Holden with Sub-Lieut. Betts on Sopwith No. 9419 carried out an excellent photographic reconnaissance to Zeebrugge between 11.50 a.m and 1.55 p.m.

Twenty-five plates were exposed over the Mole, Solway Works, Lock, and Darse, and the new emplacements on the east and west of the entrance to the Zeebrugge-Bruges Canal, and one plate over the Grossen Battery.

A large new battery was observed by the same reconnaissance to be under construction between Breedene and Clemskerke, and two new sheds, possibly the reported seaplane station, were observed on the east edge of the Nouveau Bassin Decchasse, Ostende, with a slipway running down to the water.

The reconnaissance machine was attacked off Wenduyne by three hostile machines. One and a half trays of ammunition were fired into the smallest of the enemy machines, upon which all three retired.

Very heavy and accurate anti-aircraft fire was experienced. Several hits were made and one longeron was broken right through.

Bombing Attacks.

February 16th.

During the early hours of the morning three machines carried out a bombing attack on Ghistelles Aerodrome.

Four 112-lb. and nineteen 65-lb. bombs were dropped and were observed to explode in the south and south-east corner of the aerodrome and very close to the railway siding. Others were observed to straddle the aerodrome from the north-east to south-west and over the searchlights and the headquarters buildings.

Flight Lieut. Brackley, who was the first pilot to arrive, observed the plan of the enemy's landing lights very clearly. After the first bomb had fallen all lights were extinguished.

The large searchlight on the aerodrome was again suddenly lit after the first bombs had dropped. Practically no anti-aircraft fire was experienced round the aerodrome and no searchlights were able to pick up the machines. About 12 searchlights were observed along the coast between Westende and Ostende.

The following pilots took part in this raid :—

    Short Bomber 9338. Flight Lieut. Brackley, Light Mechanic (Gunlayer) Woolley.

    Short Bomber 9336. Flight Sub-Lieut. Frame, Air Mechanic (Gunlayer) Young.

    Short Bomber 9776. Flight Lieut. Darley, Air Mechanic (Gunlayer) Kirby.

About the same time seven machines carried out a bombing attack on the hostile shipping and harbour of Bruges. Fifty-nine 22-lb. Le Pecq bombs were dropped, but it was impossible, owing to the bad visibility, to observe what shipping was in the harbour, although the bursts of all the bombs were clearly seen. Most of the bombs fell on the docks between the east and west bassins, several explosions being heard. One very large explosion was observed by all the pilots on the docks. The anti-aircraft batteries at Ostende and Bruges Harbour put up an intense and accurate fire ; no machine, however, was hit.

The following pilots took part :—

    Sopwith No. 9395. Flight Commander Wood.
    Sopwith No. 9397. Flight Sub-Lieut. Nelles.
    Sopwith No. 9394. Flight Lieut. Clarke.
    Sopwith No. N. 5221. Flight Lieut. Gardner.
    Sopwith No. 9376. Flight Lieut. Chadwick.
    Sopwith No. 9672. Flight Lieut. le Mesurier.
    Sopwith No. N. 5082. Flight Sub-Lieut. Bartlett.
    Sopwith No. N. 5093. Flight Sub-Lieut. Slade.

W/T Spotting.

February 16*th.*

    Flight Sub-Lieut. Wyatt with Lieutenant Greenwood on Sopwith No. 9897, attempted W/T spotting for the naval siege guns between 12.45 p.m. and 2.20 p.m., but owing to the thick mist the target was almost invisible.

Combats.

February 16*th.*

    About 7 a.m. hostile machines dropped bombs on the outskirts of Dunkerque, but no damage of military importance was caused.

    Flight Commander Wood on Sopwith No. 9395, and Flight Lieut. Le Mesurier on Sopwith No. 9672, both returning from the bombing attack on Bruges, encountered two of the hostile machines returning from Dunkerque. Both machines were brought to action, but, unfortunately, the first pilot had only a tray of ammunition left, which he fired at close range, and the gun of the second machine jammed, whereupon both pilots were forced to abandon the fight.

Flight Sub-Lieut. Powles, on Nieuport No. 3989, observed an L.V.G. three miles to seaward of Dunkerque, proceeding east at 10,000 feet. Pilot went in pursuit and opened fire on the enemy at a range of 150 yards when off Coxyde. He followed hostile machine, which immediately dived towards Westende, and opened fire again. When last seen the enemy machine had flattened out at about 2,000 feet over Westende.

At 5.10 p.m. Flight Sub-Lieut. Thorne, on Nieuport No. 8747, observed an Aviatik about five miles north-west of Dunkerque, which came suddenly through the clouds above him. Pilot fired about three-quarters of a tray, upon which the enemy machine climbed steeply and was lost in the clouds.

February 26th.

Considerable hostile aircraft activity was observed during the day, several encounters taking place, but none appeared to be decisive.

Flight Lieut. Holden with Sub-Lieut. Betts, whilst carrying out a photographic reconnaissance on Sopwith No. 9419, were attacked by three hostile machines, which joined formation at Wenduyne. About $1\frac{1}{2}$ trays of ammunition were fired by the reconnaissance machine in reply to the fire from enemy machines, upon which the latter retired when off Nieuport. One of the hostile machines was very much like a Sopwith Pup, whilst the other two were Aviatiks.

No. 11 Kite Balloon Section.

No ascents have been made by the kite balloon, but meteorological observations have been taken when the weather has been suitable.

Casualties.

February 26th.

Flight Sub-Lieut. Powles, on Nieuport Scout No. 3981, failed to return from escorting the photographic reconnaissance machine to Zeebrugge. It has since been learnt that he has been interned in Holland.

REPORT ON R.N.A.S. SQUADRONS. (A. 0682.)

Period 11th February to 24th February 1917 (inclusive).

Naval Squadron No. 3.

Several line patrols, practice and test flights carried out during the fortnight.

On 14th instant one hostile machine which was attacked near Walencourt went down in a nose-dive, but was not seen to crash. There was also one indecisive combat.

On the 15th instant two hostile machines were met in the neighbourhood of Bapaume; 40 rounds were fired at one of the machines at a range of 20 feet, which went down in a spin.

On the 16th instant two of our machines encountered 11 of the enemy's over Le Sars. Anti-aircraft report having seen a hostile machine diving vertically at the same time and place after a combat with Sopwith Scouts.

On 18th instant "B" Flight returned from Cormont, having done a week's course at the Aerial Musketry Range.

Naval Squadron No 1.

On the 15th instant the 18 machines of this squadron were flown from Furnes to Chipilly, where the squadron is attached to the Fifth Brigade, Royal Flying Corps.

No flying has been possible since this date owing to the weather.

Advanced Headquarters,
 Royal Flying Corps,
25th February 1917.

EASTERN MEDITERRANEAN STATION.

(Compiled from Weekly Operation Reports Nos. 48 and 49.)

Operations in Southern Bulgaria and on the Struma Front.

Thasos Air Station, "A" Squadron.

The offensive against the enemy lines of communication, and particularly against the Kanthi-Drama Railway, has been steadily maintained. As was briefly reported in W.O.R. No. 47, Yeni Keui Railway Bridge was attacked on 5th February.

The attack was made by three Henri Farmans escorted by two scouts, good practice being made by Flight Sub-Lieut. G. Gilmore with H. M. Green, Air Mechanic 1 (C), as observer in H.F. N. 3017, who came down to 3,000 feet over the bridge under considerable A.A. fire, and dropped two 100-lb. bombs, one of which hit the northern post buttress. A photograph of the bridge was taken after the attack by the same observer.

On returning from Yeni Keui, other objectives in the Nestos area were attacked by Flight Sub-Lieut. J. D. Haig with Sub-Lieut. A. W. C. Holcombe, R.N.V.R., as observer, in H.F. 9140.

One 16-lb. bomb was dropped in the centre of the fort to the west of Ingenez, and three 16-lb. bombs were dropped on a group of 20 transport wagons observed to the west of

Kich-Otmanli bridge. Two direct hits were made, and many of the wagons were totally destroyed.

On 10th February two further attacks were made on Yeni Keui bridge. During the first of these, carried out early in the morning, a train was observed proceeding over the bridge in the direction of Buk and travelling very slowly, possibly indicating that temporary repairs only had been made to the bridge damaged on 5th February.

The second attack was carried out at midday, good results being obtained by Lieutenant-Commander Moraitinis with Sub-Lieut. P. Psychas (both of the Greek Navy) in Henri Farman No. N. 3010, who dropped two 100-lb. bombs from 1,200 feet, one of which fell on the permanent way about 30 feet to the south of the bridge, and caused a considerable amount of the embankment to collapse.

Two 16-lb. bombs were dropped from another machine at the anti-aircraft gun in the village, silencing it for several minutes, while heavy bombs were dropped at the bridge.

During the nights of 10th–11th and 11th–12th February attacks were made on Buk Bridge by Flight Sub-Lieut. H. R. Aird with Sub-Lieut. J. E. Maxwell, R.N.V.R., observer, in H.F. No. 9137. In the second attack three 100-lb. bombs were dropped from 1,500 feet under heavy anti-aircraft fire, five runs being made over the bridge. Two of the bombs fell very close to the bridge, and a reconnaissance made on the following day showed that the northernmost pier of the bridge had been damaged close to the waterline, probably rendering the bridge unsafe for traffic.

During the afternoon of 12th February an attack was made on the railway line to the N. of Okjillar Station by five Henri Farmans and two escorts.

The following pilots and observers made good :—

(1) Flight Sub-Lieut. J. D. Haig, with Sub-Lieut. A. C. Holcombe, R.N.V.R. (H.F. No. 9140—C. U. No. 4023/27). Dropped three 100-lb. bombs at the railway line, two of which fell on the embankment close to the line, causing it to collapse.

(2) Flight Sub-Lieut. C. Gilmore with H. M. Green, Air Mechanic 1, in H.F. 3017. Dropped one 100-lb. bomb close to the embankment, and three 16-lb. bombs on permanent way at the entrance of one of the tunnels. The observer also took photographs of the tunnel and embankment from 4,000 feet.

(3) Sub-Lieut. Argyropolous with Sub-Lieut. N. Meletopoulos (both of the Greek Navy) in H.F. 3010 dropped two 100-lb. bombs from 3,500 feet, one of which fell on the permanent way, the other on the side of a cutting to the N. of the line, causing rocks and débris to be thrown on the track.

On 16th February a further attack was made on the railway line to the north of *Okjilar*. A small railway bridge to the north of the station was destroyed by a direct hit with a heavy bomb, and extensive damage was done to the embankment.

A reconnaissance of the *Sarishaban Ovasi*, Kavalla area and the *Pravi Orfano* valley was also carried out.

On the 17th February a photographic reconnaissance of the *Okjilar* area was made, and the destruction of the railway bridge at the north of the station caused by the bomb attack of the previous day was confirmed. The road bridge over the *Nestos* River, which had been damaged by the recent floods, was observed to have been repaired. A bomb attack on this target was accordingly made on the same day, a direct hit wrecking the bridge.

On 19th February another raid was made on the railway at *Okjilar*, the station being chosen for attack. Direct hits were made, and the station buildings were set on fire.

On the same day seaplanes were sent to assist one of H.M. ships, which was being attacked by aircraft (probably Gereviz seaplanes) off *Porto Lagos*. Enemy machines were at a great height and could not be engaged.

On 20th February a further attack was made on *Okjilar* Station, and a store dump observed in the vicinity of the station during the attack on the previous day. Heavy anti-aircraft fire, which at *Okjilar* since the summer of 1916 has been conspicuous by its absence, was experienced during the raid.

On 22nd February further reconnaissances of the *Sarishaban Ovasi* and the *Xanthi* area were made, and the road bridge over the *Nestos* at *Okjilar* was observed to be badly damaged and unfit for transport. Considerable anti-aircraft fire was again experienced in this area.

Stavros Air Station, "D" Squadron.

On 10th February reconnaissances were carried out over the Angista, Drama–Pravi–Orfano Valleys, a considerable amount of information being obtained. Two photographic reconnaissances were also made and 150 photographs were taken of the areas Semultos–Zdravik, Doksambos, Provista, and Dedeballi, Menteselli to Orfano, and the coast line.

During the latter reconnaissances proclamations were dropped on the enemy's lines in the vicinity of Provista and Orfano.

Troops quartered in the villages of Provista and Mustenga (Meshtian) were attacked with bombs.

On 11th February further reconnaissances of the Provista area and of the Angista and Orfano Valleys were made, and eight bombs were dropped at Karjani.

Early in the afternoon a hostile machine of Albatross type approached Stavros aerodrome. Pursuit was made by Flight

Lieut. C. E. Wood with Second Lieut. E. P. Hyde as observer in Nieuport Fighter No. N. 3175 (130 H.P. Clerget No. 1448). The hostile machine immediately turned back in the direction of Angista, but was overtaken over Semultos, the Nieuport being then 3,000 feet below him. Fire was opened and the chase continued, the range continually decreasing. Four trays of ammunition were fired and several hits were scored, although the Albatross endeavoured to avoid the fire by side-slipping. Eventually the hostile machine dived steeply, emitting dense volumes of black smoke, and was lost; the Nieuport's ammunition being finished, she returned home.

On 12th February two spotting flights were carried out for H.M. ships, one ship being spotted on to Razolivos, in which the Turkish Divisional Headquarters are situated, and another on to battery positions in the vicinity of Lungo ruins. Good shooting was made in both cases—a reconnaissance carried out on the following day reporting that Razolivos had suffered heavily from the bombardment.

Shore batteries were also spotted on to battery positions and dug-outs in the vicinity of Hovis Hill.

The *Angista* and *Orfano-Pravi* valleys were again reconnoitred, and photographs were taken of camps and store-dumps at Razolivos and Angista Station, where considerable activity was observed. Bombs were dropped on the ruins of Orfano village and on a transport park at Angista village, many of the carts and transport wagons being destroyed.

On 13th and 14th February flying was prevented by low clouds.

On 15th February the Angista was reconnoitred and bombs were again dropped at Angista village.

On 16th February a reconnaissances was carried out over the Angista and Orfano-Pravi valleys and over the whole front line area on the Neohori front.

On the following day the Angista and Pravi valleys were again reconnoitred and two reconnaissance flights were made over the region around Lakovikia. A photographic reconnaissance of the area immediately south-east of Neohori was also made.

During the afternoon of the same day six machines carried out a raid on the store dump at Mustenja (Meshtian), which had been previously located and kept under observation by Stavros aircraft. Twenty-four bombs were dropped, many of which were seen to explode on the dump and among farm buildings where transport wagons were packed. Stores were set on fire and secondary explosions were observed on the dump, possibly indicating that an ammunition store had been hit.

On 18th February the usual reconnaissances of the Angista valley and the front line area were carried out, a considerable amount of information being obtained—particularly in the vicinity of Angista station, where a large concentration of troops and transport were observed.

On 19th February two spotting flights were made for H.M. ships, and the duty monitor being spotted on to emplacements (N 1) in the *Dranli Nullah*. Reconnaissances of the Dedeballi-Provista-Semultos area and the Angista valley were also carried out.

On 20th February reconnaissances of the Lakovikia area were carried out at dawn and dusk, and two photographic reconnaissances of areas required by 80th Brigade were made. The daily reconnaissance of the Angista and Pravi valleys and one spotting flight were also carried out.

During one of the above flights Nieuport two-seater No. 3929 suffered engine failure when some distance behind the enemy's lines, but succeeded in landing behind our lines, the machine being slightly damaged, although pilot and observer were unhurt. On landing, the enemy instantly began shelling the machine, which had to be abandoned, but was recovered unhit at night.

On 22nd February three spotting flights were made and one reconnaissance of the enemy's lines was carried out.

(1) Thermi Air Station.—"B" Squadron.

Signalled reports of the following operations have been received:—

During the afternoon of 11th February a hostile biplane was observed 10 miles N. of Thermi steering east. Pursuit was made, but the machine retired in a northerly direction and no engagement took place.

Details have been received of an attack on the *Gedis Chai* railway bridge carried out on 13th February.

The attack was delivered by two bombers (Henri Farman Nos. 9141 and 3919) and Nieuport 2-Seater No. 3176 as escort.

After leaving the aerodrome H.F. 9141 had difficulty in attaining the height. The machines thus became separated and escorts had to be sent from *Thermi* on courses which would afford her protection (Bristol Scout N. 8999 and Nieuport 2-Seater No. N. 3173).

On arriving over the target (rather more than 60 miles from Thermi) H.F. 3919 came down to 3,000 feet and after a careful "sighter" with which drift was ascertained straddled with two salvos of light bombs. Two heavy bombs were then dropped in separate runs and a direct hit was scored on the northernmost pier of the bridge.

A photograph of the explosion of the bomb which made the direct hit was taken by the Observer of the Nieuport.

H.F. 3919 then proceeded along the line to *Mesilji* dropping hand grenades on the permanent way, which was also damaged. H.F. 9141 after easing her load by dropping two light bombs and using an hour's petrol; attained height and proceeded to the target. This machine also descended to 3,000 feet and made good practice in three runs over the target.

One heavy bomb damaged the S.W. end of the bridge, portions of masonry being seen to fall into the water.

All machines returned safely to the aerodrome except the two which were sent as escorts to H.F. 9141. One of these (Bristol Scout No. 8999) on returning to Thermi was drifted to the N.E. and passed over Aivalik. Petrol gave out when four miles north of the aerodrome and a landing had to be made on rough ground at Balgique, the machine being damaged but not wrecked.

The second escort (Nieuport N. 3173) burst its petrol tank when over Chandarli, but got back to Thermi, landing in the water near the aerodrome.

The occupants of both these machines were unhurt.

Pilots and Observers.

Flight Sub-Lieut. B. A. Trechman with Leading Mechanic William Edwin Jones, N. 14 R.F.R.—25 in H.F. 3919 (Canton Unne No. 3499, 150 h.p.).

Flight Sub-Lieut. J. L. Sinclair with Arthur Carder, leading mechanic, No. F. 2290, in H.F. 9141 (Canton Unne No. 4538, 155 h.p.).

Flight Sub-Lieut. T. R. Hackman with Sub-Lieut. G. E. Wright, R.N.V.R., in Nieuport two-seater No. N. 3176 (130-h.p. Clerget No. 1457).

Flight Lieut. H. E. Morgan with Sub-Lieut. A. E. H. Roberts, R.N.V.R., in Nieuport No. N. 3173 (Clerget No. 1046, Type 9Z, 110 h.p.).

Flight Sub-Lieut. J. S. Browne in Bristol Scout 8999 (100-h.p. Mono. No. 6334, B. 661).

H.M.S. "Ark Royal."

Test and practice flights in seaplanes were carried out on 11th, 12th, 16th, 17th, 18th, and 20th February, a W/T test for receiving and transmitting being made on the latter date.

On 17th February one of H.M. ships was escorted out to sea by seaplanes, and reconnaissance flights were made while target practice was carried out.

On 21st February, while proceeding from Salonica to Mudros, s.s. "Princess Alberta" was sunk by mine or torpedo off Strati Island. At 3.45 p.m. S.N.O. requested a seaplane might be sent out, and she accordingly left at 4 p.m. and sighted a ship's boat about 10 miles due west of Strati. The attention of a trawler was then attracted by the use of Very's Lights and the trawler followed the seaplane in the direction of the ship's boat, which was picked up containing eight survivors. The weather was bad with strong wind and rain squalls, and the seaplane was unable to land on the water to communicate, due to state of the sea.

Repair Base.

On 18th February, while carrying out a test flight over the East Coast of Lemnos, a British mine was observed apparently on the surface, half a mile South of Cape Voruskopo and about half a mile from the shore. S.N.O. was informed and the mine destroyed by trawlers.

Imbros Air Station.—" C " Squadron.

Reconnaissance of the Dardanelles shipping was carried out on 11th, 12th, 13th, and 15th February, low clouds preventing the reconnaissance from being made on the remaining days of the week.

At midday on 11th February a hostile aeroplane was reported over Tenedos. Flight Sub-Lieut. G. T. Bysshe, in Bristol Scout No. 8996 (100-h.p. Mono No. 5812), started in search, and when over Kum Kale observed an enemy seaplane below him, proceeding down Straits.

Descending to 1,000 feet off Helles he attacked, opening fire with both guns at 50 yards' range. Tracers were seen to enter the fuselage and top plane of the seaplane. After firing about 100 rounds both guns jammed, so the Bristol pilot continued out to sea and cleared the jams.

On turning he observed two seaplanes over Kum Kale, one diving steeply at about 2,000 feet. (This was probably the machine reported over Tenedos.) Both seaplanes proceeded up the straits flying very low, so the Bristol pilot came down to 500 feet off Eren Kbui, and opened fire on the first seaplane at 100 yards.

At least six tracers were seen to hit the machine in the vicinity of the pilot's and observer's seat, and it is believed that the observer was put out of action, as neither movement nor gun-fire was observed from the back seat during the second attack, although he had been active during the first engagement.

The hostile seaplanes, which were of the Gotha type, and almost as fast as the Bristol scout, were followed to Nagara, where they were seen to land and enter the seaplane sheds.

During the afternoon two anti-submarine patrols were carried out over the straits. During the first of these, carried out by a H.F. with two escorts, a Fokker was observed approaching from the direction of Kephez. The Fokker did not, however, come within firing distance, and sheered off, seeing the Nieuport fighters.

On 12th February a submarine patrol was carried out at dawn by two H.F.'s and two escorts. The Fokker was again encountered, and the H.F. and one escort were hit. The H.F. was forced to land in the vicinity of Kephez Point, and was burnt by the pilot and passenger (Flight Lieut. C. A. Maitland-Heriot and Sub-Lieut. W. C. Jameson, R.N.V.R.), who were apparently uninjured.

The Fokker was attacked by a second escort (Sopwith) while the H. Farman was still at 2,000 feet, driven off and chased, until she landed at the aerodrome N. of Chanak. The Sopwith (Flight Lieut. J. W. Alcock with Midshipman E. R. Snow as observer) returned to the position where the Henri Farman had landed, and observed the pilot and observer burning their machine. At the same time they encountered a second Fokker, and getting into a favourable position, directly over him at 50 yards distance gave him a whole tray from the Lewis gun and saw the Fokker nose-dive vertically towards thick scrub, but did not actually see the machine hit the ground.

Only signalled reports of this operation have been received; details will follow.

With reference to the above, the Constantinople Wireless Press (OSM) of 14th February states:—

"Dardanelles Front: An aeroplane piloted by the acting officer Meinecke attacked three enemy aeroplanes. One of the enemy planes was shot down, two English officers were taken prisoners. The shattered aeroplane, her machine gun, and three bombs were taken by us."

During the afternoon of 12th February a submarine was reported in Kusa Bay, Imbros. A machine was sent to search, but nothing was seen of her.

Owing to low clouds, the reconnaissance of the Dardanelles shipping was carried out on 16th, 17th, 18th, and 20th February only.. With the exception of a gunboat of 2,500 tons off Nagara on the morning of 17th, none but the usual shipping has been observed.

At midday on the 17th a Bristol Scout and Sopwith Bomber were sent to attack gunboat reported by the morning reconnaissance. Two 16-lb. bombs were dropped at the gunboat, one at the seaplane hangar at Kusa Burnu ($1\frac{1}{2}$ miles S. of Nagara Point), and 20 hand grenades were dropped in the camps to the S.W. of Kephez, previously located and bombed by Imbros aircraft. Many of the grenades were seen to explode close to the tents.

The Bristol Scout (pilot Flight Sub-Lieut. G. T. Bysshe) which was last seen by the Sopwith observer flying towards Maidos from Chanak, and apparently making for Imbros, failed to return from this flight. Search was made by aeroplanes and patrol boats, but no sign of the missing machine was seen, and no news of it has since been received from enemy sources.

During the afternoon of 19th February a submarine patrol was carried out over the entrance to the Straits, a report having been received that an enemy submarine was expected to leave the Dardanelles.

Anti-aircraft exercise was carried out with one of H.M. ships on 16th February.

CAPE STATION.

Zanzibar.

No. 8 Squadron, R.N.A.S.

A report (A. 0647) has been received of the work of this squadron for the month of December 1916, and contains a great number of interesting photographs taken by pilots during reconnaissances.

During the month under review 20 war flights were undertaken, and some very good flights have been made in seaplanes. This type of machine is now doing most of the work in this neighbourhood.

Flight Lieut. E. R. Moon with F. Wilmhurst as observer, in Seaplane 8254, made a flight over Tshidya on December 13th, which seems to have had a most demoralising effect on the enemy, who, according to native reports, retired northwards, after bombs had been dropped on the occupied trenches.

The Commanding Officer of the Portuguese Forces sent a signal to the S.N.O. expressing his thanks for the assistance which the seaplanes had given him in his operations.

Since August, Short seaplanes have been flying continuously, and have proved of great value—they stand the climate well, and also the strain of being continually hoisted in and out of ships. The type also behaves well in the "bumpy" conditions experienced in this atmosphere. 150-h.p. Sunbeam engines have flown for 150 hours without a breakdown—with one exception—a very creditable performance considering the climate.

The health of the squadron has been good.

ROYAL FLYING CORPS COMMUNIQUÉ No. 77. (A. 0686.)

From the 25th February to the 3rd March very little flying was possible owing to unsettled weather.

February 25th.

Several successful reconnaissances were carried out by Nos. 15, 23, and 24 Squadrons.

Four targets were dealt with by artillery with aeroplane observation.

Some successful photographic work was done, and bombs were dropped by aeroplanes of the First Brigade.

A Halberstadt Scout, which was attacked by Lieutenant H. Fowler and Lieutenant F. E. Brown, No. 2 Squadron, burst into flames and fell to earth near Lens.

Lieutenant Probyn and Lieutenant Wood, No. 34 Squadron, drove down a German aeroplane near Marrieres Wood. This machine is believed to have been destroyed.

Casualties.

Killed.—Lieutenant J. G. B. Baines, No. 23 Squadron (accident).

Wounded.—Lieutenant R. J. S. Lund, No. 29 Squadron (combat).

February 26th.

Bombs were dropped on places of military importance by aeroplanes of the First and Fifth Brigades.

One hundred and eighty-six photographs were taken during the day, and successful trench reconnaissances were carried out by the Fourth and Fifth Brigades.

Eleven targets were dealt with by artillery with aeroplane observation, and one explosion of ammunition was caused.

Lieutenant Pickthorne, No. 32 Squadron, dived at a hostile machine which was attacking a B.E. 2 E., and fired half a drum of ammunition at close range. The enemy went down in a vertical nose-dive, but was lost in the clouds.

Casualties.

Killed.—Lieutenant G. Vaughan Jones, No. 18 Squadron.

Wounded—Lieutenant J. F. Ferguson, No. 18 Squadron; Second Lieut. L. L. Carter, No. 29 Squadron; Lieutenant H. E. Bagot, No. 16 Squadron; Second Lieut. R. M. L. Jack (since died), No. 16 Squadron; Lieutenant H. Q. Nickalls, No. 52 Squadron; Captain E. Fletcher and Second Lieut. A. M. Morgan, No. 5 Squadron; No. P43412 Second Air Mechanic E. Campbell, No. 22 Squadron.

February 27th.

Twenty-eight targets were dealt with by artillery with aeroplane observation, and two explosions of ammunition were caused.

Some successful contact patrol work was done by aeroplanes of the Fifth Brigade, and bombs were dropped by machines of the First Brigade.

Three of our machines were brought down by hostile aircraft during the day.

Second Lieut. H. F. Mackain, pilot, and Second Lieut. J. A. E. R. Daly, observer, of No. 13 Squadron, whilst on artillery patrol at Arras, were surrounded by six hostile aircraft. One hostile aircraft dived on them from above. The observer opened fire, and the hostile machine dived straight towards its own lines. Noticing that the pilot had no control over the machine, Lieut. Daly concluded that he was either dead or wounded. He thereupon climbed from the observer's seat across the wing into the pilot's seat, and sitting on the pilot's lap with his left foot on the wing, rectified the machine and landed in the biggest field he could find.

Casualties.

Killed.—Captain J. McArthur, No. 12 Squadron; Second Lieut. E. A. Pope, Second Lieut. H. A. Johnson, No. 8 Squadron; Second Lieut. H. F. Mackain, No. 13 Squadron; No. 15814, Private J. Whiteford, No. 12 Squadren.

February 28th.

No work was possible.

Artillery Co-operation.

March 1st.

Thirty-two targets were dealt with by artillery with aeroplane observation. Twelve direct hits were obtained on miscellaneous targets by artillery of the First Army.

Artillery of the Fourth Army successfully engaged four hostile batteries, on which six direct hits were obtained. Five of these were obtained by the Ninth Siege Battery with observation by Lieutenant Davis, No. 9 Squadron. An explosion of ammunition was also caused,

Artillery of the Second, Third, and Fourth Armies secured a few direct hits on hostile batteries and trenches.

Hostile Aircraft.

A patrol of No. 25 Squadron was attacked by 11 Halberstadts near Mericourt. Second Lieut. Leith drove down a Halberstadt, which fell in a spinning nose-dive.

Captain A. G. Saxty and Second Air Mechanic McMillan, No. 70 Squadron, engaged and drove down an Albatross Scout near Vimy.

Photography.

Three hundred and twenty-four photographs were taken during the day.

Bombs were dropped on places of military importance by aeroplanes of the First and Second Brigades, and some successful reconnaissances were carried out.

No. 14 Section's balloon was attacked and destroyed by a hostile aeroplane during the day. The occupants made successful parachute descents.

Casualties.

Wounded.—Second Lieut. G. R. F. Waner, No. 25 Squadron; Lieutenant G. K. Simpson, No. 14 K.S.B.; First Air Mechanic W. Bond, No. 7653, No. 6 Squadron; Second Lieut. D. R. C. Gabell, No. 5 Squadron.

March 2nd.

A little work was carried out and some successful trench reconnaissances were accomplished by Third and Fifth Brigades.

Casualties.

Wounded.—Second Lieut. H. J. Q. Campbell, No. 8 Squadron, and Second Lieut. A. R. M. Scrase Dickens, No. 23 Squadron (accident).

Missing.—Second Lieut. D. S. Cravos, and No. 1054 Flight Sergeant A. G. Shepherd, No. 5 Squadron.

March 3rd.

Nothing to report.

Headquarters, Royal Flying Corps,
    4th March 1917.

No. 30.

CONFIDENTIAL.

ROYAL NAVAL AIR SERVICE.

OPERATIONS REPORT

(with Royal Flying Corps Reports attached).

17th to 31st **MARCH 1917.**

ROYAL NAVAL AIR SERVICE.

REPORT OF OPERATIONS

Completed from Reports during period
17th to 31st March 1917.

CONTENTS.

	PAGE
HOME STATIONS	2
DUNKIRK	3
No. 3 WING, FRANCE	4
ROYAL NAVAL AIR SERVICE SQUADRON WITH ROYAL FLYING CORPS	5
EASTERN MEDITERRANEAN	5
CAPE STATION	11
ROYAL FLYING CORPS COMMUNIQUÉS	13

HOME STATIONS.

WEATHER.

For the period under review the weather on the whole was unfavourable for aircraft work.

SUBMARINE PATROL WORK.

March 6th.

Newlyn.—A seaplane on patrol from Newlyn (Pilot, Flight Sub-Lieut. R. Deane) sighted a submarine, submerged, approximately 10 miles S.S.E. of Dodman Point. One 65-lb. bomb was dropped close to the boat, which then disappeared.

The seaplane remained in the vicinity for 20 minutes, but the submarine was not seen again.

Dover.—A seaplane on patrol from Dover on March 18th sighted an enemy machine N.E. of Ramsgate. The pilot gave chase but failed to overtake the enemy, who disappeared to seaward.

A seaplane on patrol from Dover on the 24th March encountered three enemy machines, seven miles north of Boulogne, and pursued them without success.

ENEMY RAIDS.

March 16th.

Seaplane Raid.—A hostile seaplane dropped 17 bombs in the vicinity of Westgate without causing any damage.

March 16th–17th.

Zeppelin Raid.—Hostile airships raided the south-eastern counties of England on the night of March 16th–17th.

In all, five Zeppelins were reported, two of which crossed the coast of Kent, one of the latter proceeding over land as far west as Polegate Air Station.

Bombs were dropped in the vicinity of Canterbury, Dymchurch, and the North Foreland without causing damage or casualties. No bombs were dropped near Polegate, and as far as can be judged no attempt was made to attack any special objective of military importance.

Naval aeroplanes went up from Eastchurch and Westgate but failed to sight the enemy.

The following morning one of the raiders was destroyed by A.A. fire at Compeigne to the north of Paris and proved to be the naval Zeppelin L 39.

DUNKIRK.

WEATHER CONDITIONS.

The weather conditions during the period under review have been unfavourable for flying owing to bad visibility, wind, and rain.

RECONNAISSANCES.

Only two observation flights were possible during this period.

March 23rd.

A reconnaissance was carried out to Ostend, the port appearing very quiet. Three torpedo boat destroyers were noted alongside the Quai des Paqueboats and a floating dry dock alongside the south end of the Bassin de la Marine. Only six other small vessels were observed in the harbour.

March 30th.

The second reconnaissance was made over Ostend and the surrounding country. Great lack of artillery activity was observed on the coast and across the flooded area.

Four T.B.D.'s were noticed steaming N.W. at high speed from a point about five miles north of Ostend.

The rearmost T.B.D. emitted a thick volume of grey smoke immediately after the commencement of anti-aircraft gunfire; it is thought that this was intended to form a smoke screen.

SPOTTING FLIGHTS.

Two spotting flights were carried out in conjunction with the naval siege guns on the 17th and 18th instant. That on the 18th instant had to be abandoned owing to low cloud banks.

FIGHTER PATROLS.

Fighter patrols were carried out each day of the period under review with the exception of the 20th instant. The enemy was engaged on the 24th and 25th without definite result.

No. 11 KITE BALLOON SECTION.

March 28th.

Two short ascents were made. There was nothing to report on either occasion, visibility being very bad.

ENEMY RAIDS.

Details of the enemy bomb raid on Dunkirk on Saturday, March 31st, have now been received. The first hostile machine dropped bombs at 21.40 B.S.T. and the raid ended at mid-night. The exact number of hostile machines which took part is not known. As far as can be ascertained between 60 and 70 bombs were dropped.

No military damage or casualties occurred, but a certain amount of civilian property was damaged.

Two civilians were killed and four or five wounded.

CASUALTIES.

News has been received that Flight Sub-Lieut. Branford, who escorted the photographic reconnaissance on March 1st, was forced to land in the following circumstances:—

> Two hostile aeroplanes attacked the reconnaissance machine. Flight Sub-Lieut. Branford outclimbed them and, diving down, opened fire, when one machine was observed to fall out of control.
>
> . Later Sub-Lieut. Branford's machine was hit by anti-aircraft fire and the engine damaged, forcing him to land in the sea. He managed to swim to the Dutch shore.
>
> His machine appears to have been destroyed.

No. 3 WING, FRANCE.

March 22nd.

A bombing raid was carried out against the ironworks and blast furnaces at Burbach. The flight, which consisted of six bombing and three fighting machines, left the advanced base of No. 3 Wing at 8 a.m. and was over the Saar Valley soon after nine.

Bombs of a total weight of 1,560 lbs. were dropped on the objective.

Only two German machines were seen; they were some distance away, and made no attempt to attack.

The cold was intense, and several cases of frostbite were reported. On the return journey the machines ran into heavy clouds.

We sustained no losses.

NAVAL SQUADRONS WITH THE ROYAL FLYING CORPS.

Period 25th—31st March.

Extracted from the Report of the Officer Commanding Royal Flying Corps in France.

WEATHER.

For the period under review, with the exception of March 4th and 6th, the weather was unfavourable for aircraft work.

FIGHTER PATROLS' ENGAGEMENTS WITH ENEMY.

March 4th.

Near Manancourt a hostile machine was driven down out of control by a Sopwith Scout.

One of our escorting aeroplanes accompanying a reconnaissance was attacked by three enemy machines. Fire was returned, and one of the attackers went down in a spin. Another of the escorting pilots dived at one of the enemy, firing 100 rounds at close range, when the enemy machine fell vertically.

On the same day three enemy machines attacked a pilot who was already engaging a Halberstadt Scout. He successfully disabled one of the former, who was seen to side-slip and fall rapidly.

Near Bapaume one of our pilots, sighting a German machine in the act of diving at a Sopwith, intercepted and engaged him and he was seen to fall out of control.

Two pilots failed to return, and another died of wounds.

EASTERN MEDITERRANEAN STATION.

Mudros, March 2nd, 1917.

Compiled from Weekly Reports Nos. 50, 51, 52, 53, and 54, dating from March 2nd, 1917, to March 30th, 1917.

Weather and Amount of Flying done.—The weather conditions on the whole seem to have been fair and favourable for flying. Occasional mists and cloudy weather have, however, made effective bomb-dropping difficult.

A heavy gale blew over the Marsh Aerodrome, Mudros, on March 7th and 8th, destroying a machine there.

THASOS AIR STATION.

("A" SQUADRON.)

February 27th.

Raid on Gereviz Aerodrome.—An attack was made at dawn upon Geveriz Seaplane Base by four Henri Farmans, two Sopwith Bombers, a Sopwith Fighter, and a Bristol Scout. Owing to unfavourable weather conditions bomb-dropping was difficult, and the full results obtained were not discernible, but two of the 65-lb. bombs appeared to have hit the south end of the hangar. There was a spirited fight between a large hostile seaplane (at the water's edge in the accompanying photograph, Fig. 1) and the Bristol Scout. The enemy machine was flying over the lake. The Bristol Scout dived down to within 1,000 feet four times and fired three trays, the Sopwith Fighter joining in from the rear and above. The enemy machine then descended to the lake and taxied for the shore, running up on the beach, where both pilot and observer deserted their machine.

The Sopwith then, from 260 feet up, fired three trays from his rear gun and 50 rounds from his forward gun, rendering the enemy machine useless.

Pilot—Flight Sub-Lieut. J. N. Ingham, Flight Sub-Lieut. N. H. Starbuck, R.N.V.R., as observer in Sopwith Fighter. Flight Sub-Lieut. P. K. Fowler in Bristol Scout.)

March 9th.

Photographic Reconnaissance. — A detailed photographic reconnaissance of the line from Xanthi to Drama was carried out. The photographs secured show that all damage to bridges and embankments inflicted in the February attacks have been repaired.

March 11th.

Bomb Raids.—Following the reconnaissance of March 9th five Henri Farmans bombed the permanent way south of Yeni-Keui and Okjilar Station, the following results being observed:—One 100-lb. bomb and one 65-lb. bomb dropped from 1,000 feet exploded amongst Okjilar Station buildings. One 65-lb. bomb scored a direct hit on the dump store. Six 16-lb. bombs were dropped on the line to the north of the station, all by the same machine. (Pilot—Flight Sub-Lieut. Haig. Observer, Flight Sub-Lieut. J. Maxwell, R.N.V.R.)

Two A.A. guns opened fire on the attacking machines, who retaliated with two 16-lb. bombs, which had the effect of silencing the guns for some minutes. The line was successfully bombed 1 mile north-west of Okjilar Station. Two

To face page 6.

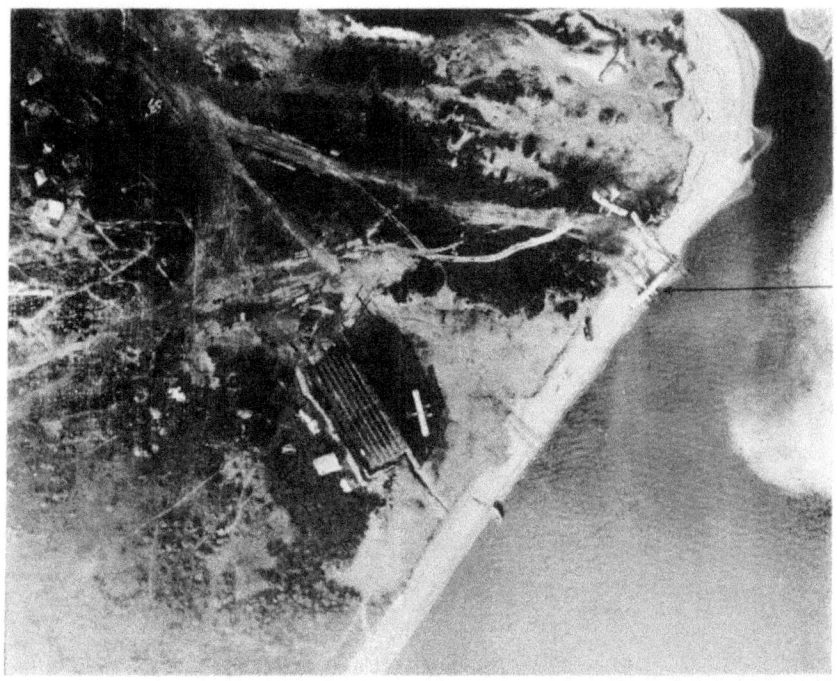

GEREVIZ SEAPLANE BASE WHICH WAS ATTACKED ON FEBRUARY 27TH.

The seaplane at water's edge was deserted by pilot and observer, and finally rendered useless by gunfire from one of the attacking machines.

FIG. 1.

100-lb. bombs were dropped on top of a tunnel, destroying it and blocking the line with débris. (Pilot—Flight Sub-Lieut H. D. Graham. Observer, Chief Petty Officer A. P. Marchant.)

March 17th.

Photographic Reconnaissance.—A photographic reconnaissance carried out over the railway north of Okjilar showed that the bombing of this line the previous day had been successful, the railway bridge and a considerable part of the track having been destroyed.

March 18th.

Enemy Raid.—An enemy aeroplane dropped bombs on the Thasos Aerodrome, all, however, failing to explode.

March 19th.

Bomb Attacks and Reconnaissances.—During a bomb raid on the line between Xanthi and Okjilar by four Henri Farmans one of the machines sighted a train with 10 or 12 coaches leaving Okjilar and proceeding in the direction of Yeni Keui. The train was pursued, but managed to reach the shelter of a tunnel, where it stopped, the two end coaches remaining outside the entrance to the tunnel. Two 65-lb. bombs were dropped from 4,000 feet, both falling directly on the line about 15 yards behind the coaches. Eight 16-lb. bombs were also dropped, one making a direct hit on the line, whilst others exploded on the embankment. (Pilot—Flight Sub-Lieut. C. Gilmour. Observer, H. M. Green, A.M. 1.)

A photographic reconnaissance of the Kavalla area resulted in securing 30 photographs of the Kavalla defences.

March 22nd.

Engagements with the Enemy. — A Halberstadt Scout attacked one of two Nieuport machines, and the Nieuport being hit in the engine was forced to descend. but the machine was burnt and completely destroyed before pilot and observer were taken prisoners. (Pilot—Flight Sub-Lieut. S. G. Beare. Observer, Second Lieutenant E. P. Hyde, M.G.C.)

(The Constantinople Wireless Press of March 23rd state that the pilot and observer of this machine, both lieutenants, were wounded and taken prisoners.)

March 23rd.

Engagements with the Enemy.—A Halberstadt machine engaged a Sopwith Bomber and a Sopwith Fighter. The enemy attacked the bomber, shooting away his aileron and elevator controls, riddling the machine and pilot's clothes with bullets. The enemy was then attacked by the Sopwith Fighter, who fired 200 rounds on him, causing him to make a hasty departure. Our machines returned safely to Thasos, the damaged bomber being skilfully landed. (Pilot—Squadron Commander J. R. W. Smythe-Pigott, D.S.O.)

Note on the Xanthi–Drama Railway.—From the statement of prisoners it would appear that the importance of the Xanthi–Drama Railway is enhanced by the fact that all food brought from Constantinople to the Front is transported along this line. As previously reported, the railway has been successfully attacked on frequent occasions, and the opinion has been expressed that it might be possible to entirely sever communication with the area west of Nestos by a large scale aircraft offensive.

STAVROS AIR STATION.
("D" SQUADRON.)

February 26th.

Spotting Flights.—In the afternoon H.M.S. "Raglan" was spotted on to a group of six waggons screened with bushes. A direct hit was made, and, judging from the large amount of smoke arising from the target, it is highly probable that the waggons were laden with ammunition.

February 27th.

Photographic Reconnaissances.—Photographic reconnaissances of Angista, the Pravi Valley, and the front line area were made, and 70 photographs were taken for the 80th Brigade of the region round Zdravik.

March 8th.

Engagements with the Enemy.—Whilst flying at 9,500 feet high 3 miles S.W. of Drama a fast hostile biplane was observed rapidly approaching our machine, a Nieuport two-seater. When over Angista Station the Nieuport observer was hit in the side, and, being short of ammunition, the pilot dived and flew along the ground, followed by the hostile machine. As the Nieuport machine gained ground and gradually drew away the enemy machine gave up the chase.

March 11th.

Bomb and Machine Gun Attack.—Two machines attacked and dispersed parties of sappers engaged in trench digging near Petelinos. Lewis gun was then used with good effect, about 12 casualties being observed.

IMBROS AIR STATION.
("C" SQUADRON.)

March 3rd.

Casualty.—After an evening reconnaissance Nieuport No. 8708 landed owing to engine failure in the Salt Lake at Kephalo. The pilot, Flight Sub-Lieut. Marlow was badly injured, and the observer, Midshipman Snow was killed.

THERMI AIR STATION.
"B" SQUADRON.

March 12th.

Reconnaissance.—A detailed reconnaissance of the Manisa district was made. The railway bridge was observed to have been repaired since the attack of the 13th February and the line is now in use.

March 13th.

Bomb Raid on Sanjak Kale.—The attack was carried out by one Henri Farman, escorted by a Nieuport two-seater. Two runs were made over the target, four 16-lb. bombs being dropped in the first and two 100-lb. bombs in the second. During the raid one hostile aeroplane approached the raiding machine but retired hastily refusing action.

March 19th.

Engagements with the Enemy.—Flight Sub-Lieut. H. T. Mellings in a Bristol Scout engaged an enemy machine near Thermi and pursued it as far as Symrna. He attacked vigorously, approaching to within 20 feet of the enemy machine. After a second attack the enemy observer ceased firing and was seen to be lying forward on his gun, apparently hit. Sub-Lieut. Mellings has carried out much valuable service, having frequently engaged the enemy single-handed.

ZEPPELIN RAID.

March 20th.

A Zeppelin raided Mudros at 11.30 p.m. and dropped 25 bombs. No damage was done, neither were there any casualties. After the attack, which lasted about seven minutes, the Zeppelin made off in a W.N.W. direction under heavy A.A. gun fire, apparently undamaged. She was pursued by a Schneider Cup Seaplane, which, however, was unable to sight the enemy owing to the darkness.

EAST INDIES AND EGYPT.

H.M.S. "ANNE," MEDITERRANEAN.

On the 22nd instant a reconnaissance of Shefr Amr, Nazareth, and Afule was made, a certain amount of idle rolling stock being observed in Afule Station. Anti-aircraft guns fired on the machine from Tubaun on the way inland. Very little road traffic was observed.

A further reconnaissance over Haifa, Nazareth, and the railway east and south-east of El Afule was carried out on the 22nd instant. The railways were found to be extremely quiet, and no movement of troops was observed on any of the roads. Both these reconnaisances were productive of very successful photographs.

Particulars have now been received of a reconnaissance carried out on the 28th February, across the saddle of Lebanon, over Rayak and Damascus, by Flight Commander Clemson, R.N.A.S., and Sub-Lieut. J. L. Kerry, R.N.V.R., as observer. The total length of the flight was 170 miles and involved the crossing of two mountain ranges whose lowest ridges are 4,000 feet above sea level.

Four examples of photographs (Figs. 2, 3, 4, and 5) taken on this noteworthy seaplane flight are attached.

H.M.S. "RAVEN II.," RED SEA.

During the period under review considerable reconnaissance work was accomplished and several lesser bombing operations were carried out.

March 17th.

A reconnaissance of the Turkish lines from Fiyush to Subar was made, the position of the enemy emplacements and trenches at Fiyush located, and two 16-lb. bombs dropped on a camp of some 30 tents about one mile south of Maht. One bomb scored a direct hit.

Later in the day a further reconnaissance of the same area was made, a small camp located at Bukai, and one 65-lb. bomb dropped on the camp at Subar village.

March 18th.

A reconnaissance of Fiyush was carried out and a satisfactory photograph of the area taken.

On the same day, at the request of the General Officer Commanding Lieut.-Colonel Alexander, General Staff Officer (1) was flown by Commander Samson over Fiyush, Waht and Darb, valuable information being obtained.

A mine search was made in Aden Waters on the 17th and 18th March in the belief that an enemy raider had laid mines in that area. None were seen, however.

March 18th.

Seaplanes from H.M.S. "Raven II." carried out a bombing attack on the enemy's positions before Aden and extended the operation to the camps in his rear. It is believed that this raid had considerable effect upon the moral of the Turkish troops.

On the morning of the 19th General Stewart, C.B., accompanied Commander Samson as observer on a reconnaissance over the enemy lines.

The General Officer Commanding Aden Field Forces has expressed his satisfaction, in a letter to Commander Samson, at the work carried out by H.M.S. "Raven II."

To face page 10.

A. 152. 6,700 ft.
ZAHLE
FIG. 2.

A. 167. 7,000 ft.
SADDLE OF LEBANON LOOKING N. FROM ZAHLE.
FIG. 3.

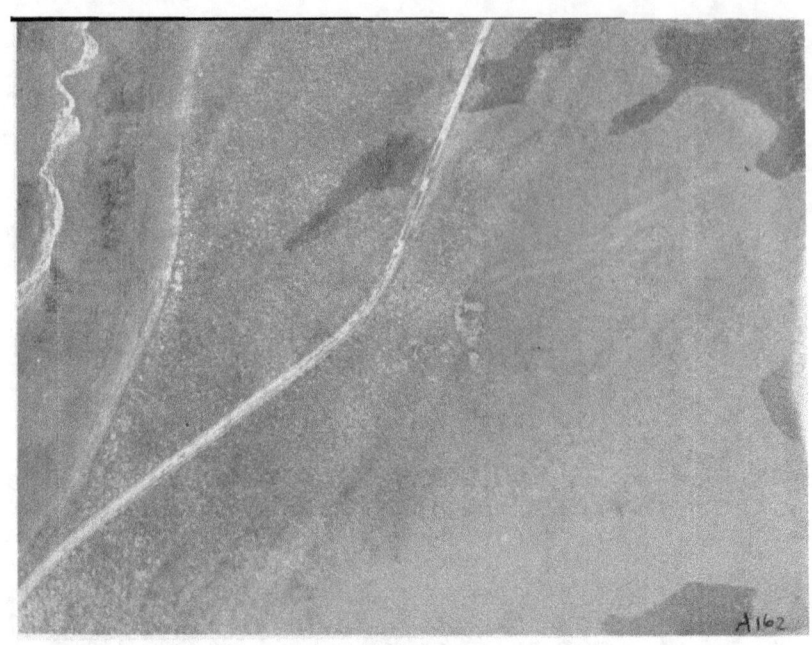

A. 162   7,000 ft.

BATTALION OF TROOPS PROCEEDING TO DAMASCUS
ON ROAD FROM N.W.

FIG. 4.

A. 165.   7,000 ft.

BODIES OF TROOPS BETWEEN DAMASCUS AND ZAHLE
S.E. OF AIN JEDEIDE.

FIG. 5

CAPE STATIONS.

ZANZIBAR—SQUADRON No. 8.

H.M.S. "MANICA."

On the morning of February 9th a seaplane carrying one incendiary and two 65-lb. bombs flew over Lindi Village and the district S.W. of Mrweka, with the object of locating an enemy gun reported to be stuck in the mud three miles from the latter place. The gun was not found.

Little was seén of the enemy, no movement being observed except in some trenches to the west of Mrweka; the bombs were dropped on these, and a small fire started, which was still burning when the machine returned to the ship.

ROYAL FLYING CORPS COMMUNIQUÉS.

ROYAL FLYING CORPS COMMUNIQUÉ, No. 79.

March 11th.

Reconnaissances.—Successful reconnaissances were carried out by all brigades, and much valuable information was obtained. Fires and explosions were reported behind the German lines.

Artillery Co-operation.—One hundred and two targets were dealt with by artillery with aeroplane observation.

Artillery of the First Army obtained 16 direct hits on nine gun-pits, and caused an explosion of ammunition.

Artillery of the Second and Third Armies each successfully engaged four hostile batteries.

Artillery of the Fourth and Fifth Armies successfully engaged 22 and 10 hostile batteries respectively, and artillery of the Fifth Army caused an explosion of ammunition.

Hostile Aircraft.—Hostile aircraft were extremely active, about 81 machines being observed on the First Army front.

Second Lieut. V. W. B. Castle, No. 1 Squadron, engaged an Albatross two-seater near Poezelhoek. This machine is reported to have fallen in flames.

A line patrol of six machines of No. 32 Squadron engaged nine hostile aircraft east of Bapaume. One of the hostile aeroplanes was destroyed by Lieutenent Pickthorne. Lieutenant Howe fired a double drum at another machine at a range of from 10 to 20 yards. The German pilot was seen to throw up his hands and to fall forward in his machine, which fell completely out of control.

A general engagement took place between hostile machines and aeroplanes of No. 18 Squadron. Lieutenant Boustead and Second Lieut. Smith destroyed one hostile machine and drove down a second out of control. At least three other hostile aircraft are believed to have been driven down during this fight.

Captain Oxspring, No. 54 Squadron, engaged and destroyed a hostile machine near Achiet-le-Grand.

A German machine was driven down out of control by two F.E.'s of No. 11 Squadron near Monchy-le-Preux.

Hostile machines were driven down out of control by Lieutenant Davies and 2/A.M. Taylor, No. 25 Squadron, Lieutenant Randall, No. 32 Squadron, and by Flight Commander Bell and Flight Lieut. Travers, Naval Squadron, No. 3.

A number of other hostile machines were driven off apparently damaged by aeroplanes of Naval Squadron No. 3 and Nos. 18 and 32 Squadrons.

No. 9 Section's balloon was attacked and brought down in flames by three hostile aircraft during the day. Both observers made successful parachute descents.

Five hundred and fifty-nine photographs were taken and 89 20-lb. bombs were dropped.

Lieutenant Dodson, No. 25 Squadron, took seven oblique photographs of the Vimy Ridge. He went well east of the position photographed and then took the photographs while facing west. They were taken from a height of about 2,000 feet and about 4 miles east of the lines.

March 12th.

Artillery Co-operation.—16 targets were dealt with by artillery with aeroplane observation.

Artillery of the Third and Fifth Armies each successively engaged two hostile batteries. During this week Lieutenant Summers and Second-Lieutenant Gellatly, No. 3 Squadron, carried out a very successful trench reconnaissance.

Much useful information was obtained by the Third, Fourth, and Fifth Brigades during reconnaissances.

March 13th.

Artillery Co-operation. — 15 targets were dealt with by artillery with aeroplane observation and an explosion of ammunition was caused.

Successful trench reconnaissances were carried out by the Second, Fourth, and Fifth Brigades, and many fires were again reported behind the German lines.

March 14th.

Very little work was possible owing to low clouds, mist and rain.

Two machines of No. 4 Squadron carried out successful trench reconnaissances and a successful contact patrol was done by Second-Lieutenant Barker and Lieutenant Goodfellow, No. 15 Squadron.

March 15th.

Reconnaissances.—Several successful trench reconnaissances were carried out by the Fifth Brigade. Several fires and explosions were seen in the enemy's lines during the afternoon. One especially large fire was seen in Achiet-le-Grand.

Artillery Co-operation. — 33 targets were dealt with by artillery with aeroplane observation.

Artillery of the Third Army successfully engaged four hostile batteries, one direct hit being obtained and one explosion seen.

Hostile Aircraft.—Captain Brand, No. 1 Squadron, destroyed an L.V.G., East of Zillebeke; Second-Lieutenant C. C. Clark, No. 1 Squadron, destroyed an Albatross Scout. A patrol of No. 1 Squadron engaged three Albatross Scouts. One of these fell out of control and the other two were driven down. A patrol of No. 11 Squadron destroyed a hostile machine near Hoppy and drove down a second machine out of control. A hostile aeroplane was destroyed by machines of No. 22 Squadron.

March 16th.

Reconnaissances.—Successful trench reconnaissances were carried out by Fourth and Fifth Brigades. A number of villages were seen on fire behind the enemy's lines.

Artillery Co-operation.—Artillery of the Fifth Army successfully engaged four hostile batteries with aeroplane observation; two-gun pits were demolished and one damaged.

Hostile Aircraft.—An offensive patrol of six F.E. 2 bs. of 25 Squadron; and two Sopwiths of No. 43 Squadron met eight hostile machines near Lens, which were immediately reinforced by eight more scouts. A combat lasting twenty minutes ensued, in which one hostile machine was brought down by Sergeant Mackie and Sergeant Brown, No. 25 Squadron; Lieutenant Munro, No. 43 Squadron; and Lieutenant Whitaker, No. 25 Squadron; each drove down a hostile machine out of control, and one other was driven down under control. All our machines returned.

A hostile aeroplane attacked No. 6 K.B. Section's balloon, but was driven off by Second Lieutenant Wills, No. 34 Squadron.

March 17th.

Reconnaissances.—Reconnaissances were carried out by all brigades and ninth wing. A large number of trench reconnaissances and contact patrols were carried out by the Third and Fourth Brigades. Several villages behind the enemy's lines were reported to be in flames.

Artillery Co-operation.—Eighty-three targets were engaged by artillery with aeroplane observation and 12 with kite balloon observation.

Artillery of the First Army obtained 10 direct hits on 10 gun-pits.

Artillery of the Second Army engaged 13 hostile batteries. Eight gun-pits were destroyed and two explosions caused amongst ammunition.

Artillery of the Third Army engaged eight hostile batteries, obtaining two direct hits.

Artillery of the Fourth Army engaged 11 hostile batteries, obtaining two O.K.'s.

Artillery of the Fifth Army engaged eight hostile batteries, damaging five gun-pits.

Hostile Aircraft.—Eighteen aeroplanes of the First Brigade taking photographs in the rear of the enemy's lines encountered 19 hostile machines. As the result of the fight three hostile machines were destroyed, three driven down damaged, and one driven down under control. The hostile formation was broken up, and the photographic machines completed their work.

A pilot of No. 1 Squadron and a pilot of No. 6 Squadron each brought down a hostile machine.

Eight other hostile aeroplanes were driven down completely out of control by pilots of the Second, Fourth, Fifth Brigades, and 9th Wing.

R. J. BARTON, Captain,
General Staff.

Headquarters, Royal Flying Corps.
18th March 1917.

ROYAL FLYING CORPS COMMUNIQUÉ, No. 80.

March 18th.

Reconnaissances.—Reconnaissances were carried out by all brigades and the 9th Wing.

Many successful patrols were carried out by the Third, Fourth, and Fifth Brigades, the advance of the cavalry and infantry being followed throughout the day.

Machines of the Third Brigade engaged a party of the enemy's cavalry from a height of 100 feet, three men being seen to fall. A working party with a balloon was also engaged and dispersed.

A machine of the Fourth Brigade engaged some snipers holding up our cavalry.

A machine of the Fifth Brigade engaged three small parties of the enemy with machine gun fire from a height of 1,200 feet.

Artillery Co-operation.—Thirty targets were engaged by artillery with aeroplane observation, and six with balloon observation.

Artillery of the First Army obtained two O.K.'s on two gun-pits.

Artillery of the Second Army engaged six hostile batteries, damaging one gun-pit.

Artillery of the Third Army obtained five direct hits on three hostile batteries, damaging one gun emplacement.

Bombing.—Machines of the 9th Wing dropped 28 20-lb. bombs on some sheds north-east of Valenciennes; large columns of smoke were seen to come from the sheds.

Hostile Aircraft.—A hostile machine was shot down by Lieutenant Belgrave and Second Lieutenant Truscott, No. 45 Squadron, and one driven down out of control by Flight Sub-Lieut. Casey, Naval Squadron No. 3.

March 19th.

Reconnaissances.—Reconnaissances were carried out by all brigades.

Machines of the 9th Wing carried out reconnaissances in the areas St. Quentin—Guise—Ribemont and St. Amand—Conde—Mons—Valenciennes.

A large number of contact patrols were carried out by machines of the Third, Fourth, and Fifth Brigades. In many cases pilots landed and reported to our cavalry and advanced infantry.

Bombs were dropped and machine-gun fire opened from the air on several parties of the enemy's cavalry and infantry.

Artillery Co-operation.—Only a small amount of artillery co-operation was possible, owing to low clouds.

An anti-aircraft battery was silenced by artillery of the Third Army after its location had been sent down by zone call.

Bombing.—Machines of the 9th Wing dropped 48 bombs on the ammunition depôt at Aulnoye from a height of 6,000 feet. Two direct hits were observed.

Hostile Aircraft.—Hostile aircraft were active well behind the enemy's lines.

Lieutenant Grevelink, No. 54 Squadron, drove down a hostile machine in flames.

Second Lieutenant Pennell, No. 27 Squadron, drove down a Halberstadt completely out of control.

A hostile machine was driven down out of control by Flight Sub-Lieut. Malone, Naval Squadron No. 3.

March 20th.

No flying possible owing to weather.

March 21st.

Reconnaissances were carried out by all brigades; villages reported burning west of Hindenberg line.

A number of useful contact patrols were carried out by the Third, Fourth, and Fifth Brigades, several machines landing and reporting to our advanced cavalry.

Artillery Co-operation.—19 targets were dealt with by artillery with aeroplane observation.

Hostile Aircraft.—Very few hostile machines seen.

Lieutenant Pickthorn, No. 32 Squadron, got on to the tail of an Albatross Scout, which he forced to land within our lines near Vaulx-Vraucourt, the pilot (Prince Frederick Charles of Prussia) being wounded.

March 22nd.

Reconnaissances.—Reconnaissances were carried out by all brigades.

A night reconnaissance was done by two machines of No. 11 Squadron.

Contact patrols were carried out by the Third, Fourth, and Fifth Brigades, in many cases machines landing and reporting to our infantry and cavalry. Several parties of the enemy were engaged by machine gun fire from a low altitude, a number of men being seen to fall.

Bombing.—Twenty 20-lb. bombs were dropped during the day.

Hostile Aircraft.—Little activity; there were two indecisive combats.

March 23rd.

Reconnaissances.—Machines of No. 18 Squadron carried out a very successful army reconnaissance. No defensive lines were seen behind the Hindenburg line within an area standing some 7 miles north, east, and south of Cambrai. Villages were seen to be burning or demolished west of the Hindenburg line, but none to the east.

Four new active aerodromes and the positions of several dumps were located.

Machines of No. 70 Squadron reconnoitred the Hindenburg line from Lens to La Fere, taking photographs of portions from Le Catelet to La Fere.

Contact patrols were carried out by machines of the Fourth and Fifth Brigades.

Artillery Co-operation.—Four targets were engaged with aeroplane, and ten with kite balloon observation.

Kite balloons of the Second Brigade successfully engaged three hostile batteries.

Seven active hostile batteries were located by balloons of the Third Brigade during the night.

Photography.—One hundred and twelve plates exposed.

Hostile Aircraft.—Activity below the normal.

March 24th.

Reconnaissances.—Second Brigade carried out three long reconnaissances, one of which was in the area Bruges–Ghent–Audenarde. The Hindenburg line was reconnoitred by machines of the Fourth and Fifth Brigades and 9th Wing. Villages were again seen burning to the west of this line.

A number of contact patrols were done by machines of the Fifth Brigade.

Second Lieutenant Coningham and Second Lieutenant Taylor, both of No. 32 Squadron, saw some German infantry attempting to clear away the wreck of a Halberstadt Scout.

They went down and scattered them with machine gun fire. Several casualties were left on the ground.

Artillery Co-operation.—Thirty-five targets were engaged by artillery with aeroplane, and two with kite balloon observation.

Artillery of the First Army engaged six hostile batteries, obtaining 11 O.K.'s on nine gun-pits, and causing an explosion. Twelve hostile batteries were successfully engaged by artillery of the Second Army, and 10 gun-pits were hit and five explosions caused amongst ammunition.

A siege battery of the Fifth Army obtained a direct hit on Queant Station.

Photography.—A total of 1,019 plates were exposed during the day, the Second Brigade taking a number in the neighbourhood of Ghent, the remainder being taken by the First, Third, Fourth and Fifth Brigades, chiefly in the neighbourhood of the Hindenburg and Drocourt lines.

Bombing.—Eighteen 112-lb. bombs were dropped by machines of No. 20 Squadron on Cambrai goods station. Four O.K's were obtained.

Machines of No. 27 Squadron dropped 12 112-lb. bombs on Busigny Station and sidings, several bombs bursting in the station and sidings.

Hostile Aircraft.—Hostile aircraft was active in the neighbourhood of Lens and Arras.

Flight Sergeant C. Ryder and Lieutenant J. E. S. Alexander, No. 2 Squadron, drove down a Halberstadt out of control.

During a reconnaissance by machines of No. 11 Squadron, two hostile machines were driven down completely out of control, one by Lieutenant E. T. Curling and Lieutenant H. E. Guy, the other by Second Lieutenant R. Savery and 2/A.M. Totterfield.

Flight Commander Bell, Naval Squadron No. 3, and Second Lieutenant Zink and 2/A.M. Walker, No. 18 Squadron, both drove hostile machines out of control.

A reconnaissance of No. 70 Squadron, consisting of six machines, were attacked by a hostile formation of 12 machines, two of which were driven down out of control. After 15 minutes' fighting only four hostile machines were seen, and they made no attempt to continue the combat.

Second Lieutenant Harker and Second Lieutenant Fernald, No. 57 Squadron, drove down a hostile machine out of control.

Most of the above machines were almost certainly destroyed, and in addition several others were driven down.

R. J. BARTON, Captain,
General Staff.

Headquarters, Royal Flying Corps,
    25th March 1917.

No. 31.

CONFIDENTIAL.

ROYAL NAVAL AIR SERVICE.

OPERATIONS REPORT

(with Royal Flying Corps Reports attached).

1st to 16th APRIL 1917.

ADMIRALTY WAR STAFF,
OPERATIONS DIVISION.
17th April 1917.

ROYAL NAVAL AIR SERVICE.

REPORT OF OPERATIONS

Completed from Reports during period
April 1st to 16th.

CONTENTS.

	PAGE
HOME STATIONS	2
DUNKIRK	2
ROYAL NAVAL AIR SERVICE SQUADRONS WITH ROYAL FLYING CORPS REPORTS ATTACHED	5
EASTERN MEDITERRANEAN	7
CAPE SQUADRON	15
ROYAL FLYING CORPS COMMUNIQUÉS	17

HOME STATIONS.

WEATHER.

Unfavourable weather conditions with occasional snow storms have made aircraft operations somewhat difficult during the period under review. Patrol work, instructional flying, bomb-dropping practice, have been carried out whenever possible.

DUNKIRK.

WEATHER.

The weather conditions governing the period under review have been unfavourable for offensive aircraft operations, notwithstanding which quite a number of bombing raids have been made on enemy stations. Rising ground mists made visibility bad during the night operations on April 6th, mentioned in a report from this station.

RECONNAISSANCES CARRIED OUT.

April 1st and 2nd.
Coastal reconnaissances were attempted, but had to be abandoned.

PHOTOGRAPHIC RECONNAISSANCE.

April 5th.
Photographs obtained of Seaplane Base, Zeebrugge, show that the bomb attack made by seaplanes the previous night had been successful.

Photographic machines and escort came under very heavy fire, but returned safely.

BOMB ATTACKS.

Carried out during the night and early morning intervening between the dates given.

Place	Date	Weight	Type
Zeebrugge	April 4th—5th	2,470 lbs.	Seaplanes.
,,	,, 5th—6th	4,030 lbs.	Seaplanes.
,,	,, 7th	1,572 lbs.	Aeroplanes.
,,	,, 7th—8th	3,289 lbs.	Seaplanes.
Bruges	,, 5th—6th	4,346 lbs.	Aeroplanes.
,,	,, 7th—8th	590 lbs.	Aeroplanes.
,,	,, 13th—14th	590 lbs.	Aeroplanes.
Arsenal south of Ghent.	,, 7th—8th	590 lbs.	Aeroplanes.
Ostend	,, 8th—9th	585 lbs.	Seaplanes.
,,	,, 13th—14th	2,664 lbs.	Aeroplanes.

April 4th–5th.

Seaplane Base.—Seaplanes carried out a night bombing attack at the seaplane base at Zeebrugge. Two 520-lb. bombs and twenty-two 65-lb. bombs were dropped. Photographs taken the next day showed the following results:—One direct hit on big main shed, probably by a 520-lb. bomb, and five direct hits on three smaller sheds.

April 5th–6th.

Seaplane Base.—Repeated air attacks were made on Bruges and Zeebrugge during the night with much success. Immense fires were observed at about 4 a.m.

A night attack was also made on the enemy torpedo boat destroyers lying alongside the Mole and Seaplane Base at Zeebrugge. All the torpedo boat destroyers put to sea upon the arrival of our aircraft.

Later in the night four of them returned and bombs were dropped in their vicinity. In the meantime the seaplane sheds were successfully bombed and much damage done. All our machines returned safely. Pilots, Flight Sub-Lieut. Potvin, Lieutenant R. Graham, D.S.C., Flight Sub-Lieut. E. J. Cuckney, Flight Sub-Lieut. P. S. Fisher, Flight Sub-Lieut. L. H. Slatter.

April 5th–6th.

No. 5 Wing (5th and 7th Squadrons).—An attack was carried out by the above squadrons on the junction and rolling stock at Bruges. The objective was clearly seen, and good shooting was made. Ten 100-lb. bombs, forty-two 65-lb. bombs, and twenty-eight Le Pecq bombs were dropped.

The machines came under heavy A.A. gun fire, aided by the enemy searchlights, but there were no hits, and all returned safely.

During the night raid of the 5th–6th on Zeebrugge Flight Sub-Lieut. Cuckney, Flight Sub-Lieut. Slatter, and Flight Sub-Lieut. P. S. Fisher carried out two attacks, leaving for the first about 9 p.m. and for the second soon after midnight.

Flight Lieutenant R. Graham, D.S.C., took part in the first attack and, descending to 400 feet, dropped his bombs during a glide to 300 feet. His machine was hit in several places by A.A. gun-fire, and was badly bumped by bombs exploding.

In connection with the night raids of the 4th–5th and 5th–6th mentioned above the following telegram has been sent to the Vice-Admiral, Dover:—

"Convey to Commodore, Dunkirk, their Lordships' appreciation of the successful attacks by R.N.A.S. on Seaplane Base, Zeebrugge, on the nights of the 4th and 5th April, which reflect great credit on officers and men concerned."

In recognition of their good work on this and other occasions His Majesty the King has been pleased to award to Flight

Lieutenant Ronald Graham, D.S.C., R.N.A.S., a bar to the Distinguished Service Cross, and to Flight Sub-Lieut. Ernest J. Cuckney, R.N.A.S., the Distinguished Service Cross.

April 7th.

No. 5 Wing (5th Squadron).—A bombing raid was carried out on Zeebrugge Mole by six Sopwith machines. Twelve 65-lb. bombs and 36 Le Pecq bombs were dropped, but accurate observation was difficult owing to heavy anti-aircraft gunfire. The escorting machines observed five explosions on or close to the objective. All machines returned safely.

April 7th–8th.

No. 5 Wing (7th Squadron).—Four Short bombers, each carrying two 100-lb. bombs and six 65-lb. bombs, left during the night to carry out a raid on the Arsenal south of Ghent. The weather at the time of starting was clear with a light north-easterly breeze, but shortly after their departure heavy cloud banks began to appear. Only one of the machines (Pilot—Flight Lieut. Brackley, and L. M. G./L. Woolley) succeeded in finding the objective, over which two runs were made. Two bombs exploded in west corner of Arsenal, two in the centre of buildings and the remainder well inside of the Arsenal grounds. This pilot put up a highly creditable performance having in the face of adverse weather conditions succeeded in reaching the objective and in making accurate shooting.

Flight Lieutenant Darley experienced engine trouble when close to Bruges, and finding it necessary to lighten his load dropped his bombs on the shipping in the docks. The other two machines lost their way owing to thick weather and returned.

Seaplane Base.—Attacks were carried out on Zeebrugge Mole by seaplanes of the R.N.A.S. on the night of the 7th and 8th, and many bombs were dropped.

April 8th–9th.

Short Bomber Seaplanes dropped nine 65-lb. bombs from 1,500 feet at the Submarine Repair Works at Ostend. Owing to the glare of searchlights the results could not be observed.

April 14th.

WING No. 5. (5th Squadron.)—A bomb raid was carried out on Seaplane Base at Ostend by eight machines. Sixty-three bombs, consisting of 16 65-lb. bombs and 47 Le Pecq 22-lb. bombs, were dropped on the objective from heights varying from 9,000 to 10,000 feet. Visibility was good, but the target was much obscured by banks of clouds, through holes in which, however, the pilots were able to view the objective only, but prevented actual results from being observed.

Five enemy destroyers were observed lying alongside Zeebrugge Mole, and one destroyer off the coast about five miles east of Ostend.

(**7th Squadron.**)—Four Short machines, each carrying six 65-lb. and two 100-lb. bombs, left for objectives East and West Basins, Bruges, with alternative Seaplane Base at Ostend, during the morning. The weather conditions delayed the departure of the machines, but the sky clearing somewhat and fairly good visibility obtaining from the moon, it was decided to despatch the machines. A high wind prevailed aloft. Two pilots failed to reach their objective owing to engine trouble. Flight Lieutenant Darley made apparently good shooting of objective Seaplane Base at Ostend, and Flight Lieutenant Brackley on objectives East and West Basins, Bruges, each machine dropping six 65-lb. bombs and two 100-lb. bombs. Both pilots experienced a very strong head wind on returning, a somewhat trying experience in this type of machine.

ENEMY RAIDS.

April 9th.

(**9th Squadron.**)—On the night of April 8th enemy aircraft were reported to be dropping bombs on Oudruick, and four machines were immediately sent to search.

In the vicinity of Ypres one enemy machine was sighted, but lost owing to the darkness.

NAVAL SQUADRONS WITH THE ROYAL FLYING CORPS.

25TH MARCH TO 16TH APRIL 1917.

Extracted from the Report of the Officer Commanding Royal Flying Corps in France.

Weather.—The weather conditions during the latter part of the period under review have been favourable for aircraft operations.

General Remarks.—Combats with enemy aircraft, many of a decisive character, resulting in a number of enemy machines being put out of action, is the prevailing feature of the operations during the period under review.

BOMB ATTACKS.

NAVAL SQUADRON No. 3.

April 6th.

While escorting a bombing raid one pilot engaged four hostile aircraft, which were preparing to attack the formation. The pilot followed one of the hostile machines down to 3,000 feet, and then saw it crash in a field. During the same patrol another machine was driven down and seen to crash near the Bois de Bourlon, whilst a third machine was driven down out of control.

April 8th.

Whilst escorting a bombing raid two hostile machines were driven down out of control.

From 8th April to 21st the squadron carried out offensive patrols, and acted as escort to bombing raids.

April 11th.

While acting as escort to a bomb raid three hostile machines were brought down, and three driven down out of control.

April 12th.

Two hostile machines were driven down out of control.

FIGHTER PATROLS—ENGAGEMENTS WITH ENEMY.

NAVAL SQUADRON No. 1.

Between April 6th and 11th a number of offensive patrols, well behind the enemy lines, were carried out.

Between April 6th and 19th, 11 hostile aircraft were engaged, seven of which were driven down out of control.

NAVAL SQUADRON No. 6.

April 5th.

Two hostile aircraft were engaged, one at 50 yards range and the other at 20 yards, both being brought down out of control. A third hostile machine was brought down in flames by a pilot of this squadron.

From April 6th to 10th the Squadron carried out offensive and line patrols, and during these dates had six combats with hostile aircraft, three of which were decisive.

NAVAL SQUADRON No. 7.

April 5th.

Flight Commander Dallas drove down a hostile machine out of control near St. Quentin.

NAVAL SQUADRON No. 8.

From the 5th to the 19th April this squadron carried out 24 offensive patrols, and engaged the enemy aircraft in 13 combats.

April 5th.

Flight-Lieut. Compston drove down a Halberstadt machine completely out of control. He says the Halberstadt was distinctly slower than the triplane.

CASUALTIES.

NAVAL SQUADRON No. 1.

April 6th.

Missing.—Flight Sub-Lieut. L. M. B. Weil, Flight Sub-Lieut. N. D. M. Hewitt (it is presumed they lost their way owing to bad weather).

NAVAL SQUADRON No. 6.

Missing.—Flight Sub-Lieut. R. K. Slater (believed to have been brought down in combat on 5th instant). Flight Sub-Lieut. Kingsford injured.

April 9th.

Flight Sub-Lieut. Thorne killed whilst on patrol. Squadron Commander J. J. Petre accidentally killed on 13th.

Flight Sub-Lieut. Paynter wounded while on patrol.

NOTE.—No further details have been received of the work of the units assisting the R.F.C.

EASTERN MEDITERRANEAN STATION.

Mudros, April 6th, 1917.

(Compiled from Weekly Reports Nos. 55 and 56, dating from March 30th to April 13th.)

Weather.—The weather conditions for the period under review have been generally good.

Reconnaissances, patrols, and practice flights have been carried out almost daily.

THASOS AIR STATION.

("A" SQUADRON.)

Remarks.—The salient feature of the work carried out from Thasos Air Station during the period under review has been a series of night bomb attacks on the enemy air station, and other objectives in the Drama-Kavalla and Xanthi areas.

March 30th.

Reconnaissances. — Reconnaissances were made of the Pravi-Kavalla area. A Sopwith Fighter, No. N. 5223, left to make a reconnaissance of the Phillipoppolis area, but failed to return. A seaplane searched the Gulf of Kavalla in the afternoon, but found no signs of the missing machine. The Sofia Wireless (F.F.) of the following day made this

statement:—" Lieutenant Esschwege (the pilot of the Drama
" Halberstadt Scout) shot down an enemy aeroplane in an air
" battle."

If this is true it is probable that the Sopwith was returning from the reconnaissance by way of Drama, having failed to pick up the Lower Nestos on account of low clouds on the hills. No mention is made as to whether pilot and observer were killed or taken prisoners. (Pilot, Flight Sub-Lieut. J. M. Ingham. Observer, Sub-Lieut. J. E. Maxwell, R.N.V.R.)

March 31st.

Bomb Attacks.—A successful night raid was carried out on Drama by a Henri Farman. One 16-lb. bomb made a direct hit on a hangar which was seen to collapse and one 100-lb. bomb was dropped from 500 feet on to the railway station, in which there were three trains, evidently carrying troops, as heavy rifle fire was experienced. It is felt certain that this bomb did considerable damage.

On the same evening bombs were dropped on Fort B, 3 miles from the east of Kavalla, and two were dropped on Fort A.

During the afternoon a wrecked German seaplane was picked up off Fenes Burnu and sent to Mudros for survey.

Anti-Submarine Patrols.—Anti-submarine patrols were carried out during the daytime in the vicinity of the base.

April 1st.

Bomb Attack.—Further attacks were made on Kavalla on this date, but the damage done could not be accurately estimated.

April 2nd.

Reconnaissance and Zeppelin Patrols.—A morning reconnaissance was made of the Sarishaban area, where new defence works have recently been located by aircraft. During the evening and early the following morning reports were received that a Zeppelin had been sighted. Reconnaissance machines set out on each occasion and thoroughly searched the coast area between Kavalla, Cape Balustra, Cape Makri, Nestos, Xanthi, and Gumuljina, but the enemy was not sighted. It is thought probable that the report was occasioned by a large flock of wild duck which were sighted by Trawler 43, and was reported by them to resemble an airship in the distance.

April 4th.

Bomb Attack.—Further attacks were made on Kavalla, but the damage done could not be accurately estimated.

April 5th.

Anti-Submarine Patrols.—Anti-submarine patrols were carried out by seaplanes in the Gulf of Kavalla and in the vicinity of Thasos.

April 5th and 6th.

Bomb Attacks.—During the night of 5th-6th one Henri Farman and one Short seaplane attacked the barracks at Pravi and at Leftera Bay. The Henri Farman dropped two incendiary bombs on the Pravi Barracks, both of which fell close to the target and started a large fire. Two 100-lb. bombs were then dropped from 4,000 feet, one making a direct hit practically in the centre of the barrack building.

The Short seaplane left the seaplane base at Thasos five minutes after the Henri Farman had proceeded to Pravi. Shortly after leaving the water bright flares were observed at intervals along the S.W. coast of Thasos. These were immediately fired on by machine-gun fire from the seaplane and extinguished at once, except one which was put out after a 16-lb. bomb had been dropped near it. The seaplane then proceeded to Leftera Bay and dropped two incendiary and three 16-lb. bombs on the barracks, one of which fell among the buildings.

For some weeks past signal fires have been observed on the hills in the Thasos area, particularly above Sutiros (a notorious Germanophil community) whenever a machine has left the aerodrome after dark. These have been increased recently in spite of warnings given to the inhabitants by the French Governor of the island.

April 8th.

A night raid was carried out by one Henri Farman on the seaplane base at Gereviz. In spite of intense A.A. fire, which was put up as a barrage over the target, five direct hits were made on the large wooden hangar from 1,100 feet. One 100-lb. bomb and four 16-lb. bombs were dropped. Owing to the darkness the damage could not be observed, but it is probable that the shed was totally wrecked.

STAVROS AIR STATION.
("D" SQUADRON.)

Result of Reconnaissances.—Tactical reconnaissances have been carried out daily during the period under review, and a routine reconnaissance of the enemy's front line area and the Angista Valley resulted in a considerable amount of information being obtained.

March 28th.

Enemy Raids.—Ten enemy twin-engined machines attempted to bomb Shnevece (12 miles north-east of Doiran Station), apparently unaccompanied by scouts. Four R.F.C. machines and two Sopwiths engaged the machines and succeeded in frustrating the attack of all enemy machines save one, the latter dropping a bomb on the objective.

Sub-Lieut. E. P. Hicks claims to have obtained a number of hits at close range, firing all his Lewis gun ammunition.

Kite Balloons, R.N.A.S. — One of our kite balloons was brought down by the enemy the previous day.

March 30th.

Spotting Flights.—During the morning H.M.S. "Raglan" was spotted on to camps to the south-east of Dranli. The second shell fired burst directly on a small camp and apparently completely destroyed the shelters, whilst five shells burst near another camp, destroying some sheds.

In the afternoon military batteries were spotted on to gun positions in and to the south-east of Tafel Kop, direct hits being made on the emplacements and communication trenches.

March 31st.

Photographic Reconnaissances.—A photographic reconnaissance of the Orfano-Karjani area and the region between Karjani and the sea resulted in 36 photographs being obtained of the enemy camps and defence works.

April 1st.

Photographs of Karacol, Provista, Razolivos, and Angista Station were obtained from a photographic reconnaissance.

April 4th.

Engagements with the Enemy.—Three Sopwith Fighters engaged four enemy scouts to the north of Lake Doiran. Two of the hostile machines, one of which was a Halberstadt, attacked the Sopwiths, but after a short action retired rapidly.

April 5th.

Four Sopwith Fighters co-operating with four R.F.C. machines engaged one enemy squadron of 12 twin-engined bombing machines with escorts which had just dropped bombs at Karasuli (on the Vardar River, S.W. of Doiran). The enemy squadron, which kept together throughout the raid, was pursued over his lines and was engaged for 45 minutes.

April 5th.

Spotting Flights.—H.M.S. "Edgar" was spotted on to emplacements at Karacol and to the east of Dranli Nullah. A direct hit was made on one of the Karacol emplacements and several rounds burst very close to the position, apparently causing considerable damage. Four direct hits were made on the target east of Dranli Nullah.

April 8th.

Enemy Raids.—An enemy squadron consisting of 14 machines appeared over Hadji Janas and dropped bombs on the aerodrome and dumps, without, however, causing any damage. The raiding machines were pursued and one twin-engined hostile aeroplane was shot down one mile south of Surlovo.

During the current week the enemy's bombing squadron has been brought into action six times, but details of these engagements are not yet available.

With reference to the engagement of April 8th, the Commander-in-Chief, British Salonika Army, sent the following telegram to Composite Flight at Hadji Janas:—

"Commander-in-Chief desires to record his appreciation of the work performed by the combined flight of R.N.A.S. and R.F.C. machines."

IMBROS AIR STATION.

("C" Squadron.)

Result of Reconnaissances.—A daily reconnaissance of the Dardanelles has been carried out and a considerable amount of enemy shipping activity observed, merchant ships and torpedo boat destroyers being sighted at Nagara, Ak Bachi, Liman, Chanak, and Sim Sighlar Bay.

April 2nd.

Bomb Attack.—A night raid was carried out on Nagara Seaplane Base by three machines. Bombs were dropped close to the sheds, but mists prevented results from being observed. An enemy camp to the north of Suvla was also bombed.

April 3rd.

Hostile Activity.—On the report that an enemy aeroplane was bombing a destroyer off Tenedos a machine was despatched to search, but failed to sight the enemy machine.

April 4th.

Spotting Flight.—At dawn H.M.S. "Grafton" was spotted on to emplacements on the Asiatic coast and succeeded in wrecking two and putting two others out of action.

April 5th and 6th.

Bomb Attack.—A night bombing attack was carried out by two B.E. 2 C's. One of these attacked a camp of large sheds, to the east of Suvla Salt Lake, dropping eight 16-lb. bombs, four of which appeared to fall directly in the centre of the camp. Shortly after the last bombs had been dropped flames were observed in the vicinity of the camp. The objective of the second machine was a large merchant ship which had been observed at Nagara during the previous day's reconnaissance, but on nearing the target the pilot observed two enemy seaplanes on the water off Nagara point. Two 65-lb. bombs were dropped at these, but no direct hits were observed.

April 10th.

Photographic Reconnaissance.—A photographic reconnaissance of Aivalik Harbour was carried out.

April 11th and 12th.

Bomb Attack.—A bomb attack was carried out by two machines on the night of 11th and 12th, the Gallipoli Flour Mills being the objective. A direct hit was probably made with one 100-lb. bomb. Four 16-lb. and four incendiary bombs were also aimed at the target, but the effect of these could not be observed owing to the flashes of A.A. gun fire.

THERMI AIR STATION.

("B" Squadron.)

March 30th.

Bomb Attack.—A bomb attack was carried out on the enemy aerodrome at Paradisos and Kassimir by two Henri Farmans, two Nieuport two-seaters, and a Bristol Scout. One Henri Farman and one Nieuport failed to return, and were probably brought down by a Fokker in the vicinity of Smyrna.

With reference to the above, the Constantinople Wireless Press (O.S.M.) of April 1st makes the following statement:—

"On March 30th at mid-day one of our aviators shot down two enemy planes in the vicinity of Smyrna. One was a Farman Biplane, the crew of which were taken prisoners. The other was a Nieuport aeroplane destroyer, which fell in the course of a battle in the air in the suburb of Budja. Both the crew were found dead."

The missing Henri Farman was last seen by the Bristol Scout engaged by a hostile machine believed to be a Fokker. The Henri Farman was closely followed, and in manœuvring lost about 4,000 feet in height. At 3,000 feet the Farman was seen to enter a cloud with the Fokker in close pursuit.

The Bristol dived to the assistance of the British machine, passing through the same cloud, but on emerging failed to see either machine. After searching the area flying at a low altitude the Bristol returned to Thermi.

Casualties.—

Missing.—Pilot — Flight Sub-Lieut. B. H. Trechman; Observer—L.M. W. A. Jones, No. 14, R.F.C., in Henri Farman

N. 3024 (quoted in enemy report as prisoners). Flight Lieutenant J. E. Morgan, Sub-Lieutenant A. Sandell, R.N.V.R., in Nieuport No. 9203 (quoted in enemy report as "found dead").

April 5th.

Reconnaissances carried out.—A reconnaissance of the Aivalik area was carried out.

April 6th.

A reconnaissance of the Smyrna Gulf and Harbour was carried out.

MUDROS.

H.M.S. "ARK ROYAL."

April 4th.

Schneider Cup No. N. 1018 proceeded by air to Thasos and came down in the water owing to engine trouble. A Schneider sent from Mudros eventually found the missing machine on the water 30 miles N.W. of Cape Murtzephalos (Lemnos), and a patrol launch subsequently towed her to Thasos Seaplane Base.

April 12th.

An experiment was carried out with box kites, supporting W/T aerial from seaplane drifting on the water. Results were satisfactory in a wind of from 15 to 20 miles per hour.

H.M.S. "RAVEN II."—RED SEA.

Supplementary Report to No. 1, March 19th.

March 17th.

A seaplane dropped two bombs on D'Abdullah, killing six Turks and wounding a number of others and destroying 10 tents. Turkish cavalry at Shajairat (3 miles west of Lahet) sighted a seaplane on Saturday morning and immediately sent messengers back to Lahet to give warning of its approach, and the Turkish ammunition depôt at Umackafaa (1 mile north-east of Lahet Palace) was immediately removed to Lahet.

According to intelligence reports there have been numerous casualties at D'Abdullah, Fiyush, and Subar, and a number of Turks retired from Fiyush Camp during the bombardment of Saturday.

March 18th.

A mountain gun was placed on Subar Hill and another south of D'Abdullah to fire at the seaplane.

EAST INDIES AND EGYPT SEAPLANE SQUADRON.

Extract from Summary of Operations (Section 2), March 19th—26th.

ADEN TO LACCIDIVES.

H.M.S. "Raven II.," in company with the French cruiser "Pothuau," left Aden on March 19th and proceeded to Laccadives Islands to search for an enemy raiding vessel reported in the Indian Ocean.

The following routine was carried out:—

For two hours before a flight "Raven II." steamed at 11 knots, stopped and hoisted out. As soon as the seaplane was clear of the ship "Raven II." proceeded at 11 knots, stopping again as required to hoist in the seaplane.

The weather conditions were perfectly suitable for seaplane flights, and at a height of 2,000 feet it was possible to see a vessel at a radius of 40 miles. Whenever smoke was seen on the horizon a seaplane was hoisted out and sent to investigate. Photographs were taken from the seaplanes of the ships encountered.

The general routine was for a seaplane to fly 20 miles on the port bow, then cross over to a position 20 miles away on the starboard bow, then return to the ship.

Date	No. of Flights.	Time in Air.
March 22nd	1	40 minutes.
March 23rd	2	1 hour 20 mins.
March 24th	2	1 hour 16 mins.

Laccadives (Section 3).

March 26th.

The ship arrived 10 miles west of Byramgore at 6 a.m. Two seaplanes were hoisted out and made the following reconnaissances.

Flight over Byramgore and 5 miles N.N.W. of north end.

Flight to Tree Island and Bitra.

The ship proceeded towards Tree Island, and as a sailing ship was sighted a seaplane was hoisted out to scout. The seaplane located the ship, which was found to be a dhow of about 25 tons anchored at the east side of the reef. The seaplane made a further reconnaissance 10 miles east and northeast of Byramgore. The ship arrived at Tree Island at 11.30 a.m. and two flights were made from this position. A seaplane

EAST INDIES AND EGYPT.

Photographs taken during Seaplane Reconnaissance in Search of Hostile Ships.

S. 29.
TARBURUDU, WATEDU, RAFURI, AND KANDUAU FROM N.W.

S. 30. NUMADA ISLAND FROM WEST. 1,000 ft.

o AS 3143

EAST INDIES AND EGYPT.

R. 280.   3,000 ft.
A BOMB DROPPING ON NORTH CAMP, SUBAR.

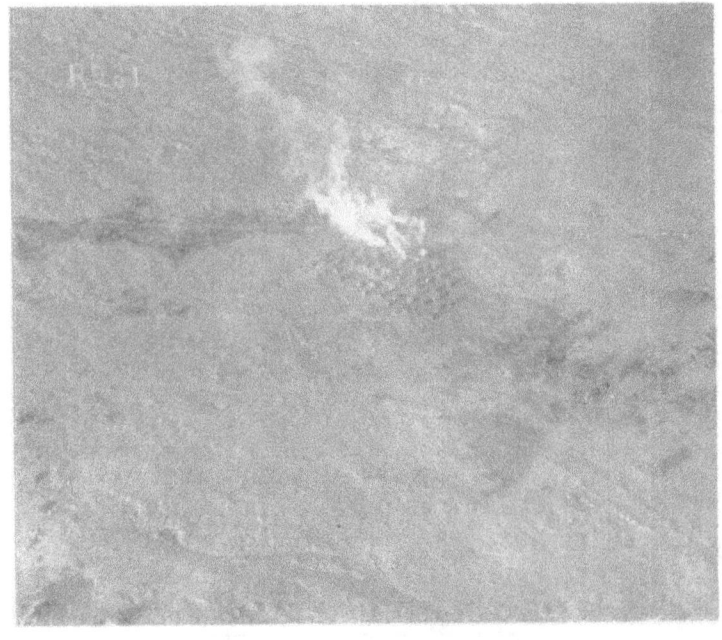

R. 281.   3,000 ft.
NORTH CAMP, SUBAR, ON FIRE AFTER BOMB EXPLOSION.

was sent with orders to fly to Chetlat and back. As at 2 p.m. the seaplane had not returned, both ships steamed 10 miles apart towards Chetlat. In addition, a seaplane was hoisted out to search. This seaplane located the missing machine at Chetlat. Communication was established and the seaplane was brought back to the ship. The trouble was found to be a broken piston necessitating changing the engine. The ships left Chetlat at 8 p.m. and proceeded towards Tinnagara.

No. of flights, 6.
Time in air, 5 hours 10 minutes.

March 28th.

From a position 10 miles south of Androth a seaplane made a flight over Androth and Kalpeni. This machine was severely damaged in alighting and ended up a complete wreck. The machine was hoisted in board and the engine and fittings salved.

No. of flights, 1.
Time in air, 1 hour 30 minutes.
During 26th, 27th, 28th March a heavy swell from southward was encountered, but this did not prevent the seaplanes getting off the water.

March 30th.

A reconnaissance off Umbali, Naguri, and Nilandu Islands was made from off Ihayandu Island. No hostile ships were observed.

CAPE STATION.

SQUADRON NO. 8, ROYAL NAVAL AIR SERVICE.

Chukwani, Zanzibar.

12th FEBRUARY 1917.

Extracts from Report of Squadron Commander F. W. Bowhill, R.N., of Work carried out by Squadron No. 8 during the month of January 1917.

January 6th.

Accident.—Seaplane No. 8254 was lost whilst flying over the Rufigi Delta. The accident was probably due to enemy gunfire, and it is not unlikely that the machine **caught** fire in the air.

Flight Sub-Lieut. Deans left from H.M.S. "Himalaya" at Nyrohoro in a seaplane to search for the missing machine. The pilot searched all creeks and channels in the area, and when returning by Ssimba Uranga Arm, observed seaplane in the water by left bank, 6 or 7 miles from mouth of Arm.

Flight Sub-Lieut. Deans landed his machine alongside, and found that the machine, which was lying in about 8 to 10 feet of water and 10 yards from the bank, was completely wrecked. The machine was upside down, and it seems probable from the position of the wreck that it had nose-dived into the water and turned over; also that it had been on fire, as the fabric under water was not burnt, whereas portions of the tail, rudder, and wings showing above water were burnt. There were no signs of pilot or observer, and after waiting for about 10 minutes and firing a Very's light, the machine returned to H.M.S. "Himalaya."

Casualties.—Commander the Hon. R. O. B. Bridgman, D.S.O., R.N., by drowning. Pilot, Flight Lieutenant E. R. Moon, taken prisoner of war.

January 8th.

Accident.—Seaplane 8642 was completely wrecked while flying from Zanzibar to Dar-es-Salaam.

At the latter part of the month (January) Squadron Commander F. W. Bowhill proceeded to Dar-es-Salaam to confer with Squadron Commander Nanson in reference to the stores he was taking over from No. 7.

General health of squadron good.

From Report dated March 6th. Work done during the month of February.

The military operations during the month have practically been at a standstill, therefore seaplane flights have not been required over the mainland.

February 10th.

Lindi.—A 65-lb. bomb dropped from a seaplane was successful in putting a 4·1-inch gun out of action. This gun has been a source of great trouble to the land forces.

The Senior Naval Officer, East Coast of Africa, states that from the reports of intelligence officers the seaplanes have killed a considerable number of the enemy during the last three months, causing great moral effect.

General health fairly good.

ROYAL FLYING CORPS COMMUNIQUÉS.

ROYAL FLYING CORPS COMMUNIQUÉ, No. 81.

March 25th.

Reconnaissances.—Successful reconnaissances were carried out by all brigades and 9th Wing, and much useful information was obtained.

Artillery Co-operation.—Fifty-five targets were dealt with by artillery with aeroplane, and 12 with kite balloon observation.

Artillery of the First Army obtained 11 direct hits on nine gun pits. Twenty-seven successful shots were also done on miscellaneous targets, and an explosion of ammunition was caused.

Artillery of the Second Army successfully engaged four hostile batteries, and caused an explosion of ammunition.

Eleven direct hits were obtained by artillery of the Third Army on hostile batteries, nine of which were obtained with observation by Second Lieutenant Morris and Second Lieutenant de Street, No. 8 Squadron, with the 213th Siege Battery. Four direct hits were obtained on trenches.

Hostile Aircraft.—Two hostile machines were brought down near Mercatel, on our side of the lines, by Lieutenants Binnie and Bower, of No. 60 Squadron.

A reconnaissance of No. 11 Squadron encountered seven hostile aircraft in the Scarpe Valley. Second Lieutenant Mackrell and Second Lieutenant Boddy, and Second Lieutenant Calvey and A. M. Hadlow drove down one machine, which is believed to have crashed. A second machine was driven down in a vertical nose dive. A hostile aeroplane attacked by a patrol of No. 54 Squadron was driven down and is believed to have crashed.

On the 24th instant, Sergeant Ridgway and Second Lieutenant Hare, No. 15 Squadron, whilst on a photographic flight, were attacked by hostile aircraft near Heninel. The hostile aircraft were driven off. The photographic machine was then hit by an anti-aircraft shell, which killed the observer, wounded the pilot, and considerably damaged the machine. Two hostile aircraft then attacked the machine, and the pilot was shot in the leg. He, however, succeeded in recrossing the line and landing his machine. The photographs of the Hindenburg line were of much value.

Photography.—202 photographs were taken.

Hostile Kite Balloons.—A hostile kite balloon was attacked by Captain Atkinson, of No. 1 Squadron, and brought down in flames near Wervicq.

March 26th.

Artillery Co-operation.—Four targets were dealt with by artillery aeroplane, and 16 with kite balloon observation.

Artillery of the First Army obtained a direct hit on a hostile battery. A number of small explosions were caused in houses, which were observed to burn for about 20 minutes. Two direct hits were obtained on trench points.

A direct hit was obtained on a trench target by artillery of the Third Army.

With observation by kite balloons of the First Army, artillery silenced three hostile batteries, and caused two explosions of ammunition.

With observation by kite balloons of the Second Army, artillery successfully engaged four hostile batteries.

March 27th.

Practically no work was possible owing to unfavourable weather.

Artillery Co-operation.—Kite balloons of the Third Army registered on six targets, and located 10 active hostile batteries.

March 28th.

Reconnaissances.—A reconnaissance of the First Brigade observed large fires in Billy Montigny and Henin Lietard, and just south of Lens. About a dozen fires were also seen in the Henin Lietard district.

Several fires were observed in Cambrai and in other places on the Fourth and Fifth Army fronts.

Large explosions were seen in Bois d'Havrincourt and in Hermies.

Artillery Co-operation.—37 targets were dealt with by artillery with aeroplane observation.

Artillery of the First Army obtained eight direct hits on five gun pits, and 13 direct hits on miscellaneous targets.

Artillery of the Third Army obtained five direct hits on hostile targets and two on trench targets.

Hostile Aircraft.—Second Lieutenant E. S. T. Cole, No. 1 Squadron, drove down an Albatross Scout out of control near Ronchin.

Second Lieutenant C. C. Clark, No. 1 Squadron, engaged an hostile machine near Lesquin, which he drove down completely out of control.

Photography.—204 photographs were taken during the day.

Bombing.—Bombs were dropped by machines of the First Brigade on Lens, and on dumps by machines of the Second Brigade.

March 29th.

Weather was unfavourable for air work.

Artillery Co-operation.—Eleven targets were dealt with by artillery with aeroplane observation, and 12 with observation by kite balloons.

Artillery of the First Army, with aeroplane observers, silenced four hostile batteries, and obtained 15 direct hits on trench points.

With kite balloon observation, two hostile batteries were engaged, in one of which a large explosion was caused.

Kite balloons of the Third Brigade reported the movement of 12 trains, registered on six targets, and located eight active hostile batteries.

March 30th.

Reconnaissances.—A reconnaissance of the First Army report that train movement proceeding north on the Pont-à-Vendin—Don—Haubourdin and Douai—Lille lines was above normal between 9.30 a.m. and 3.30 p.m.

Valuable information was obtained for the 7th Division by Second Lieutenant Barker, No. 15 Squadron.

Two explosions and three fires were observed in St. Emile.

An explosion occurred in Noreuil, and a house was seen to be destroyed.

A fire was also observed in Havrincourt.

Three parties of infantry in Hesbecourt were attacked by machine gun fire from the air by aeroplanes of the Fourth Brigade.

Artillery Co-operation.—Fourteen targets were dealt with by artillery with aeroplane observation.

Artillery of the Third Army obtained nine direct hits on a hostile battery with observation by Captain Thomas and Lieutenant Hutchison, No. 12 Squadron, who were observing for the 31st Siege Battery; 19 direct hits were obtained on trenches.

Hostile Aircraft.—Captain Gregory, No. 40 Squadron, observed and dived at two hostile machines near Bailleul, one of which he drove down apparently badly damaged.

March 31st.

A reconnaissance of the First Brigade observed fires in Liévin, Willerval, and one mile east of Roclincourt.

Considerable train movement was seen behind Queant and Baralle in the early morning. A large explosion was observed at Croisilles, and fires were seen burning in Pronville, Queant, and in other places.

Artillery Co-operation.— 28 targets were dealt with by artillery with aeroplane observation.

Artillery of the First Army obtained four direct hits on hostile batteries. Three gun pits were destroyed, and three explosions were caused, one of which was very large.

Artillery of the Third Army obtained 13 direct hits on hostile batteries, and damaged six emplacements. Seven direct hits were obtained on trenches.

Hostile Aircraft.—Major Scott, Squadron Commander, No. 60 Squadron, destroyed a hostile machine south-east of Arras. Captain Black, also of No. 60 Squadron, assisted Major Scott. A second hostile aeroplane was destroyed north-east of Arras by Lieutenant Bishop, of No. 60 Squadron.

A patrol of three Nieuports of No. 29 Squadron drove down a hostile machine out of control in the vicinity of Gavrelle.

Two other German machines were forced to land after having been engaged by Lieutenants Binnie and Molesworth, No. 60 Squadron.

R. J. BARTON, Captain,
General Staff.

Headquarters, Royal Flying Corps,
1st April 1917.

ROYAL FLYING CORPS COMMUNIQUÉ, No. 82.

April 1st.

Reconnaissances.—Two large explosions were observed in St. Quentin, and a large one in Quéant.

Artillery Co-operation.—Twenty-five targets were dealt with by artillery with aeroplane observation.

Artillery of the First Army obtained four O.K.'s on hostile batteries, and caused a large explosion.

Artillery of the Third Army obtained three direct hits on hostile batteries, and 13 on trench targets.

Artillery of the Fourth Army silenced a hostile battery.

Hostile Aircraft.—Second Lieutenant Gordon and Second Lieutenant Baker, No. 12 Squadron, engaged a hostile machine near Arras. The hostile aeroplane was seen to break in the air and to crash.

April 2nd.

Reconnaissances.—A successful reconnaissance was carried out by a machine of No. 43 Squadron, of the Izel—Drocourt line. A fire was observed in Givenchy.

The Drocourt—Quéant line was reconnoitred by an aeroplane of the Third Brigade.

Nos. 3 and 4 Squadrons carried out several successful contact patrols.

Captain Summers and Second Lieutenant Cleaver, No. 3 Squadron, observed two bodies of German troops, about 200 in each party, and reported them by zone call. Artillery fire was successfully brought to bear on them.

Much useful information was obtained for the Seventh Division by Second Lieutenant Barker and Second Lieutenant Goodfellow, No. 15 Squadron.

Artillery Co-operation.—Thirty-two targets were dealt with by artillery with aeroplane observation, and five with observation by kite balloon.

Artillery of the First Army obtained six O.K.'s on hostile batteries, and destroyed two gunpits. Five direct hits were obtained on trench points.

Artillery of the Second Army successfully engaged three hostile batteries, and caused an explosion of ammunition.

Artillery of the Third Army obtained seven direct hits on hostile batteries, and nine on trench targets. An emplacement was damaged and an explosion of ammunition took place.

Artillery of the Fifth Army obtained a direct hit on a gun position and damaged a gun-pit.

Hostile Aircraft.—On the 30th March, a patrol of No. 60 Squadron pursued six hostile aircraft to East of Douai in a very strong westerly wind. Second Lieutenant F. Bower was shot through the stomach, but flew west and landed his machine completely undamaged, except for enemy bullets, four miles south of Chipilly. Second Lieutenant Bower died from his wound the next day.

Second Lieutenant C. E. Berigny and Second Air Mechanic Bowen, No. 43 Squadron, engaged and drove down an Albatross Scout, which fell in flames east of Vimy.

Lieutenant O. M. Sutton, No. 54 Squadron, drove down a German aeroplane out of control east of Péronne.

A patrol of No. 24 Squadron engaged a number of hostile scouts near Bois D'Havrincourt, and destroyed two of them, one was destroyed by Lieutenant Crawford, and the other by Lieutenant Cockerell.

A line patrol of No. 57 Squadron engaged six single-seater Albatross S.E. of Arras. One of the hostile machines fell in flames, and a second went down apparently out of control.

Anti-aircraft of the First Army hit a hostile scout, which landed near Lens.

Anti-aircraft of Second Army brought down a hostile machine in flames near Pilckem.

A two-seater Albatross crossed the lines on the Fifth Army front, and was engaged and brought down by anti-aircraft fire. The machine was little damaged, and the passengers were taken prisoners.

April 3rd.

Reconnaissances.—Reconnaissances were carried out by the First, Second, Fourth, and Fifth Brigades.

Fires and explosions were reported by the Fourth Brigade.

Fifth Brigade observed an explosion in Riencourt-les-Cagnicourt, and fires in Boursies, Hermies, Metz-en-Couture, Bullecourt, Noyelles, and Marcoing.

Artillery Co-operation.—27 targets were dealt with by artillery with aeroplane observation.

Artillery of the First Army obtained two O.K.'s on hostile batteries, and a great many Y's and Z's. Many direct hits were obtained on trenches and on enemy's wire.

Artillery of the Second Army successfully engaged one hostile battery.

Artillery of the Third Army obtained a direct hit on a hostile battery, damaged an emplacement, and obtained 34 direct hits on trenches.

Hostile Aircraft.—Captain H. H. Balfour and Second Lieutenant A. Roberts, No. 43 Squadron, while on a photographic reconnaissance, were attacked by four hostile scouts, which they drove off. They were then attacked by two more, one of which they drove down in flames.

Bombing.—On the night of the 2nd-3rd instant, Second Lieutenant C. O. B. Beale, No. 42 Squadron, dropped two 112-lb. bombs on a blast furnace near Lille.

Photography.—630 photographs were taken.

Kite Balloons.—The balloons of Nos. 13 and 18 Kite Balloon Sections were brought down by hostile aircraft. The passengers in each made successful parachute descents.

April 4th.

Artillery Co-operation.—Fifty-four targets were dealt with by artillery with aeroplane observation, and 14 with observation by kite balloons.

Artillery of the First Army obtained seven direct hits on hostile batteries, and caused three explosions of ammunition. Eight direct hits were obtained on trench targets, and an explosion of ammunition took place.

Artillery of the Second Army successfully engaged one hostile battery.

Artillery of the Third Army engaged 36 hostile batteries, and obtained 15 direct hits. Ten explosions and a fire were caused. Seven emplacements were badly damaged, and seven direct hits were obtained on trenches.

One hostile battery was successfully engaged by artillery of the Fifth Army.

Three hostile batteries were silenced by artillery with observation by kite balloons of the First Brigade, and one hostile battery with observation by balloons of the Second Brigade.

Bombing.—On the night of the 3rd–4th two 112-lb. bombs were dropped near Perenchies by a machine of the Second Brigade.

Twenty-eight 20-lb. bombs were dropped on various targets by aeroplanes of the Third Brigade on the 4th instant.

April 5th.

Reconnaissances.—Reconnaissances were carried out by all Brigades and 9th Wing. Seven explosions were seen during the day between Lens and Arras. These were probably caused by our artillery fire.

Artillery Co-operation.—One hundred and nineteen targets were dealt with by artillery with aeroplane, and nine with kite balloon, observation.

Artillery of the First Army obtained four direct hits on hostile batteries, and caused an explosion of ammunition. A number of direct hits were obtained on trenches and on wire.

Artillery of the Third Army engaged 44 trench targets, and obtained two direct hits on a hostile battery.

Hostile Aircraft.—Our offensive patrols were successful in keeping hostile aircraft well over the lines, and our artillery machines were able to carry out their work without interference. There was much hard fighting during the day, and although the combats took place, mostly far over the enemy's lines, he suffered far more heavily than we.

Lieutenant C. R. O'Brien and Lieutenant Dickson, No. 43 Squadron, engaged three hostile machines east of La Bassée. One of these was driven down out of control, and the other two broke off the combat.

Flight Lieutenant Compston, Naval Squadron No. 8, on a Sopwith triplane, pursued three hostile aeroplanes and attacked the rear one, which went down out of control.

An Albatross Scout, which had been engaged by Sergeant Dempsey and Sergeant Nunn, No. 25 Squadron, fell out of control.

Second Lieutenant White and Private Allum, No. 20 Squadron, were attacked by two Albatross Scouts near St. Eloi. Two-thirds of a drum was fired at one of the hostile aircraft, which was forced down and landed near Neuve Eglise. The pilot, who was wounded, was taken prisoner.

Two Halberstadts were driven down out of control by a patrol of No. 20 Squadron. Captain Mahoney-Jones and Captain Knowles, who, with others, engaged these machines, believed that both were destroyed.

Many fights took place between machines of Third Brigade and the enemy, and the following is a short *résumé* of the day's fighting:—

A patrol of No. 48 Squadron, led by Captain Robinson, V.C., engaged 12 hostile aircraft near Douai. Captain Robinson engaged one hostile machine, which he drove down out of control. Another hostile machine, engaged by Lieutenant Pike and Lieutenant Griffiths, was brought down apparently out of control. These two officers lost the formation, and on returning home fought two rearguard actions, in one of which they drove down one hostile aeroplane.

A second patrol of No. 48 Squadron, led by Captain Wilkinson, saw three H.A. near Douai, and engaged and drove down two of them—one out of control. Later, they engaged another and drove it down.

Another patrol of No. 48 Squadron, led by Captain Tidmarch, engaged a two-seater H.A. east of Douai—the H.A. disappeared in the clouds. Lieutenant Berry engaged another H.A., S.E. of Douai, and drove it down in a steep spiral. Lieutenant Brockhurst then dived on a red single-seater, which was also driven down.

Flight Commander Norton, Naval Squadron No. 6, drove down one hostile machine in flames, and one out of control west of Douai. Flight Sub Lieut. Thorne, Naval Squadron No. 6, also drove down a hostile machine out of control.

An offensive patrol of five Nieuports of No. 29 Squadron fought six H.A. near Arras, and one of the H.A. was driven down out of control.

Lieutenant Langwill, with a patrol of No. 60 Squadron, engaged four H.A. One hostile machine dropped vertically and appeared to crash. During the patrol two other hostile machines were driven down out of control—one by Lieutenant Hall, and one by Lieutenant Elliott.

An Albatross Scout was driven down out of control by Lieutenant Rogers, No. 29 Squadron, near Vitry-en-Artois.

A patrol of No. 24 Squadron, Fourth Brigade, engaged three hostile machines near Honnecourt. Lieutenant Woolett drove down one of the hostile machines, which was seen to crash east of Honnecourt.

Flight Commander Dallas, Naval Squadron No. 1, drove down an Albatross Scout out of control S.E. of St. Quentin.

A patrol of No. 22 Squadron drove down a German aeroplane out of control near Honnecourt.

Lieutenant Huston and Second Lieutenant Blennerhassett, No. 18 Squadron, who were part of a formation which was on a photographic patrol, drove down two hostile machines out of control, and drove off several others, one of which is believed to have been hit.

Captain Platt and Second Lieutenant Margerison, No. 57 Squadron, drove down a single-seater biplane, which landed in a ploughed field.

Photography.—1,060 photographs were taken.

Hostile Balloons.—A hostile balloon was attacked by machines of No. 54 Squadron and brought down in flames. Captain Pixley, on his return flight, dived at a man on horseback and opened fire. Both horse and rider were seen to fall. Captain Hudson, when over Gouy, opened fire from a height of 200 feet on about 100 men unloading boxes from open trucks in the railway station. Some men were seen to fall, and the remainder scattered in all directions.

Bombing.—First Brigade.—Four 112-lb. bombs and two 20-lb. bombs were dropped on Don station at 11.45 a.m. One 112-lb. bomb was observed to burst on the railway line. The remainder were unobserved owing to mist.

In addition to the above, two 112-lb. bombs were dropped over the road and railway crossing behind Aubers; five 20-lb. bombs were dropped on Liévin; 12 on Bailleul, and four on the railway west of Avion.

Second Brigade.—On the night of the 4th–5th, two 112-lb. bombs were dropped on transport near Ghelewe. On the 5th, two 20-lb. bombs were dropped on Oosttaverne Wood.

Third Brigade.—Fourteen 20-lb. bombs were dropped on various targets.

Fourth Brigade.—Machines of the Fourth Brigade attacked railway sidings at St. Quentin. One bomb was seen to burst on the track and two in the station yard, and a fire was caused.

Fifth Brigade.—Twelve 112-lb. bombs were dropped on sidings and dumps at Marcoing. The bombs appeared to hit the objectives, but the results were difficult to observe owing to clouds and mist. Two bombs were also dropped on Quéant.

Ninth Wing.—A 230-lb. bomb was dropped on the railway at Pont-à-Vendin by a machine of No. 27 Squadron. A great quantity of earth was observed to have been thrown over the railway line, but the shell hole could not be observed.

Hirson bottle factory was attacked by machines of No. 27 Squadron from a height of 1,800 feet. A 230-lb. bomb destroyed two buildings in the factory enclosure. One bomb was observed to burst on the factory, and two on the engine depôt, and both places were set on fire.

Machines of No. 55 Squadron dropped a number of 20-lb. bombs on various objectives.

April 6th.

Reconnaissances.—Reconnaissances were carried out by all brigades and Ninth Wing, and fires were observed in Lens, Avion, Cavrelle, and Goulot Wood.

Artillery Co-operation.—123 targets were dealt with by artillery with aeroplane observation.

Artillery of the First Army obtained six O.K.'s on hostile batteries. Two pits were destroyed, one was set on fire, and two explosions of ammunition were caused. 27 direct hits were obtained on wire, and a number on the trenches.

Artillery of the Second Army successfully engaged two hostile batteries.

Artillery of the Third Army obtained 12 direct hits on hostile batteries, and damaged three emplacements. An explosion of ammunition was caused, and a large number of direct hits were obtained on trenches.

Hostile Aircraft.—There was considerable activity during the greater part of the day. As a result of our offensive patrols and bombing raids, hostile machines were again kept well to the east of the lines.

Second Lieutenant Pell, No. 40 Squadron, engaged and drove down a hostile machine south of Bailleul. This machine was observed by anti-aircraft to crash.

Second Lieutenant Roulstone and Second Lieutenant E. G. Green, No. 25 Squadron, saw a hostile scout attacking one of our artillery machines and immediately dived at it. The hostile machine was sent down in flames and crashed.

Second Lieutenant King and Corporal Emsden, No. 25 Squadron, attacked a Halberstadt Scout which was harassing a B.E. engaged on artillery work. The Halberstadt was destroyed.

Second Lieutenant Perry and Private Allum, No. 20 Squadron, engaged and destroyed a Halberstadt Scout near Ledghem.

Second Lieutenant Smart and Second Lieutenant Hampson, No. 20 Squadron, while on a bombing raid, attacked three hostile aircraft. The pilot of one of the hostile machines was shot, and the machine broke in the air and fell. The second machine was driven down in a spinning nose-dive, while the third, after having been attacked, dived vertically.

Second Lieutenant Cock and Second Lieutenant Murison, No. 45 Squadron, while on reconnaissance, destroyed a hostile machine near Lille, and a second was driven down out of control by this reconnaissance near Templeuve.

While on photographic work Lieutenant Laverack and Second Lieutenant Baker-Jones, No. 12 Squadron, were attacked by a hostile machine. As the result of the combat which ensued the hostile machine burst into flames and fell.

Lieutenant Smart, No. 60 Squadron, while on offensive patrol, engaged three hostile aircraft near Arras. One H.A. was driven down in a spin, and the other two were driven off. Later, this patrol of No. 60 Squadron engaged six hostile aircraft, and two of the hostile machines were driven down, and a third appeared to be hit.

Second Lieutenant Muir, No. 29 Squadron, engaged a two-seater biplane N.E. of Arras. The observer in the hostile machine was shot, whereupon the enemy pilot broke off the combat.

Lieutenant Holliday and Captain Wall, No. 48 Squadron, drove down a hostile machine out of control in the same locality, with the pilot apparently shot.

Second Lieutenant Price and Second Lieutenant Benjamin, of the same patrol, drove down a hostile machine out of control near Douai.

A formation of No. 54 Squadron, while acting as escort, was attacked by a fast hostile scout. The enemy pilot appeared to be very good and manœuvred with great skill. Finally, however, he was enticed to attack one of our machines from behind, whereupon Lieutenant Stewart dived at the hostile machine, and destroyed it.

A patrol of No. 22 Squadron also succeeded in destroying one hostile machine and driving a second down near Fontaine-Uterte.

Captain Hudson, No. 54 Squadron, and Lieutenant Arnot, No. 24 Squadron, each drove down a hostile aeroplane out of control.

Flight Commander Clayton, Naval Squadron No. 1, engaged a German machine which was painted partially red and drove it down out of control.

Flight Sub-Lieut. Culling, also of Naval Squadron No. 1, engaged a two-seater biplane N.E. of St. Quentin. The hostile machine was driven down completely out of control.

Captain McCallum, No. 23 Squadron, engaged four hostile aircraft. He drove down one machine apparently completely out of control, but, owing to the presence of the other hostile aircraft, he was unable to observe its ultimate fate.

Flight Lieutenant Breadner, Naval Squadron No. 3, while escorting B.E.'s on a bombing raid, engaged four hostile aircraft who were endeavouring to intercept the B.E.'s. He drove one down and followed, firing at it, until it was obviously out of control. This machine crashed near Bois de Bourlon. A second hostile machine was destroyed in the same locality by Flight Sub-Lieut. Fall, who was also one of the Naval escort.

Second Lieutenant Reid and Second Lieutenant Blennerhassett, No. 18 Squadron, drove down a hostile aeroplane which was interfering with a photographic reconnaissance. This machine fell completely out of control, and anti-aircraft report that it crashed. Second Lieutenant Parkinson and Second Lieutenant Power, of the same squadron, also fired on this machine.

Flight Sub-Lieutenant Carter, Naval Squadron No. 3, while acting as escort, drove down a German aeroplane out of control.

Second Lieutenant Vinson and Second Lieutenant Gwilt, No. 15 Squadron, were taking photographs over Bullecourt when they were attacked by six Albatross scouts. Unfortunately both machine guns fell out of the B.E., and it was forced to land near Lagnicourt, as one hostile machine pursued and continued firing at it. The pilot and observer jumped out and got into shell holes. The enemy artillery opened fire on our machine, but just before it was hit by an 8-inch shell Second Lieutenant Vinson managed to obtain the exposed plates, which produced good photographs of the Hindenburg line and of Bullecourt.

Second Lieutenant Collis, No. 23 Squadron, drove down a hostile machine near St. Quentin.

An offensive patrol of Sopwith Scouts of No. 66 Squadron shot the observer in a hostile machine, and he was seen to fall from the aeroplane. They drove off three hostile aircraft which were interfering with our artillery machines.

Photography.—700 photographs were taken during the day.

Bombing.—First Brigade.—On the night of the 5th-6th, eight 112-lb. bombs and 20-lb. bombs were dropped on Provin aerodrome. All the bombs dropped on the sheds and on the aerodrome.

On the 6th, 14 20-lb. bombs were dropped on Bailleul. Six of these burst on the railway and six on houses. Four 20-lb. bombs were dropped on Lens.

Second Brigade.—On the night of the 5th 6th, six 112-lb. bombs were dropped on various objectives. Two of these were dropped at a train on the Menin-Wervicq line from a height of 500 feet. One burst immediately in front of the train and destroyed the permanent way. The train stopped and was attacked with machine gun fire from the air by Captain Selby, No. 6 Squadron, who was slightly wounded by gun fire from the ground.

On the day of the 6th, 10 112-lb. bombs were dropped on Vyfwegen. Two of these were seen to burst on the railway line and two on a dump. 14 112-lb. bombs were dropped on Ledghem, and two 20-lb. bombs on hutments at Warneton.

Third Brigade.—On the night of the 5th-6th, Douai Aerodrome was attacked twice by machines of No. 100 Squadron. Four hangars were completely destroyed, and other damage was done. On the day of the 6th, 13 phosphorus and 97 20-lb. bombs were dropped on various targets.

Fourth Brigade.—On the night of the 5th–6th, six 112-lb. bombs were dropped on a railway junction south of St. Quentin.

On the day of the 6th, 30 20-lb. bombs were dropped on a railway dump at Essigny-le-Petit. Bombs were observed to explode on the railway line and on the dump.

Fifth Brigade.—Dumps and billets at Sauchy-Cauchy were bombed with 10 112-lb. bombs, which were observed to burst on and around the objectives. Several houses were completely demolished.

9th Wing.—Ath Railway Station was attacked by machines of No. 27 Squadron. Two 112-lb. bombs were observed to burst on the sidings, and one 230-lb. bomb was seen to burst on sheds north of the station, in which a fire started.

Aulnoye Railway Station was also attacked by the same squadron, and bombs were seen to burst on sheds and on the line.

Six de Havilland 4's of No. 55 Squadron attacked an ammunition dump at Valenciennes. The bombs were dropped from a height of 11,500 feet. Two bombs were seen to fall in the station, two near the engine depôt, and the remainder on and around the objective. On the return flight the de Havillands were pursued by hostile scouts, but owing to the superior speed of our machines the hostile aircraft was soon outdistanced.

Hostile Kite Balloons.—Five Nieuports of No. 40 Squadron proceeded to attack hostile kite balloons. The balloons were rapidly hauled down, but Second Lieutenant Todd succeeded in destroying one by firing three rockets into it at a range of about 10 yards. The balloon was then 500 feet from the ground.

Kite Balloons.—No. 24 balloon was up all night (5th–6th) and established communication with front line trenches. Situation reports were received by lamp signal and communicated to corps headquarters.

April 7th

Reconnaissances.—Reconnaissances of the First Brigade report fires at Corons, Gavrelle, Lens, Liévin, and Blache St. Vaast.

Second Lieutenant J. S. Black and Second Lieutenant S. Cooper, No. 16 Squadron, carried out a special reconnaissance at a height of 500 feet and made some useful observations. Their work was greatly facilitated by an effective shrapnel barrage by the Canadian Corps Artillery.

Artillery Co-operation.—Fifty-seven targets were dealt with by artillery with aeroplane observation.

Artillery of the First Army obtained 13 O.K.'s on hostile batteries. A gun-pit was completely destroyed, and an explosion was caused. Two direct hits were obtained on a dynamite store, and a large explosion took place. Many direct hits were obtained on wire and trenches.

Artillery of the Second Army successfully engaged one hostile battery.

Thirteen hostile batteries were successfully engaged by artillery of the Third Army, and several direct hits were obtained on trenches.

Hostile Aircraft.—A German aeroplane, said to resemble a Nieuport, attacked and destroyed one of our kite balloons. This machine had been observed by one of our artillery aeroplanes, but, until the attack on our kite balloon, the B.E. pilot had failed to realise that the machine was hostile.

Lieutenant Bishop, No. 60 Squadron, engaged and drove down a hostile machine, after which he attacked a hostile balloon on the ground and set it on fire.

Lieutenant Binnie, No. 60 Squadron, also attacked a hostile balloon on the ground, but, although hit, it did not burn.

Bombing.—Provin aerodrome was attacked twice during the day by the First Brigade. At 11 a.m., 14 20-lb. bombs were dropped, 10 of which fell on the aerodrome. One bomb dropped by Second Lieutenant D. Gordon, No. 10 Squadron, fell on the engine of a train going south-east on the Provin–Carvin railway. The boiler exploded, and the engine and trucks left the line. At 5.15 p.m., 26 20-lb. bombs were dropped. One bomb exploded amongst the rolling stock, seven on the aerodrome, and one destroyed a house on the edge of the railway.

The Second Brigade dropped 12 112-lb. bombs on Mouveaux aerodrome. The results were mostly unobserved, but two bombs were seen to explode on the aerodrome.

Photography.—Two hundred and twenty-one photographs were taken.

S. WOOD, Captain,
Headquarters, Royal Flying Corps, Staff Officer.
8th April 1917.

ROYAL FLYING CORPS COMMUNIQUÉ, No. 83.

April 8th.

Reconnaissances.—Reconnaissances were carried out by all Brigades. Considerable movement was reported on the Cambrai—Bapaume road.

Lieutenant Huston and Second-Lieutenant Smith, No. 18 Squadron, saw three small bodies of men in communication trenches in the Hindenburg Line near Bullecourt. They fired 400 rounds at these men from a height of 1,000 feet.

Artillery Co-operation. — 96 targets were dealt with by artillery with aeroplane, and 34 with kite balloon, observation.

Artillery of the First Army obtained 12 direct hits on hostile batteries and a number of trenches and wire.

Artillery of the Second Army successfully engaged 10 hostile batteries and five gunpits were damaged.

Artillery of the Third Army obtained eight O.K.'s, eight M.O.K.'s and 46 Z's on hostile batteries. Four emplacements were damaged and an explosion of ammunition was caused. A number of direct hits were obtained on trenches.

With observation by balloons of the First Brigade, a number of successful shoots were done on hostile batteries and trenches and four explosions were caused. Compass bearings were also taken during the night of hostile gun flashes and reports made to the corps concerned.

Three hostile batteries were successfully engaged by artillery with observation by balloons of the Second Brigade.

Balloons of the Third Brigade observed for a large number of successful shoots and reported a number of explosions and fires.

Hostile Aircraft. Flight Sub-Lieut. Little, Naval Squadron No. 8, engaged and destroyed a hostile machine near Lens.

Lieutenant Kitto and Second Air Mechanic Cant, No. 43 Squadron, while on line patrol, were attacked by five hostile aircraft. One of the hostile machines was driven down completely out of control.

Flight-Commander Arnold, Naval Squadron No. 8, drove down a hostile scout out of control near Beaumont.

Lieutenant Robertson and Second Lieutenant Fauvel, No. 20 Squadron, drove down a single-seater Albatross out of control near Tourcoing.

Lieutenant Bishop, No. 60 Squadron, drove down two hostile machines out of control, and forced three others to go down apparently damaged.

Major Scott, No. 60 Squadron, also drove down a hostile machine out of control.

A patrol of No. 48 Squadron drove down six hostile aircraft; two of them fell out of control.

No. 54 Squadron destroyed a hostile machine, and Naval Squadron No. 1 drove one down which is believed to have been destroyed.

Two H.A. were driven down out of control—one by Flight Sub-Lieut. Casey and one by Flight-Lieutenant Travers, both of Naval Squadron No. 3.

Captain McCallum, No. 23 Squadron, drove down a hostile machine and forced it to land in a field near the Canal du Nord.

An offensive patrol of No. 66 Squadron encountered six Halberstadt scouts, and three of them were driven down out of control by Captain Roberts and Lieutenants Montgomery and Lucas. Lieutenant Collier on the same patrol drove down a fourth machine in a damaged condition.

An offensive patrol of No. 57 Squadron engaged six hostile aircraft east of Arras; although none of the hostile machines were seen to fall, when the combat seized only three of them were seen.

On the evening of the 6th, a patrol of No. 57 Squadron engaged ten hostile aircraft south of Douai. The fighting was very severe and several of the hostile machines are believed to have been badly hit.

Hostile Kite Balloons.—Two hostile kite balloons were attacked and brought down in flames near Moorslede and Quesnoy respectively, by machines of No. 1 Squadron.

Bombing.—First Brigade.—On the night of the 7th–8th, five 112-lb. bombs and 22 20-lb. bombs were dropped on Provin aerodrome. The bombs were seen to fall on houses and on buildings round the aerodrome and on the aerodrome, and a house in Provin was set on fire. Two 112-lb. bombs were dropped on a battery which was firing flaming rockets; one was dropped on Hantay, and two on La Bassée.

Second Brigade.—On the night of the 7th–8th, nine 40-lb. bombs were dropped in conjunction with operations by the X Corps. All the bombs appeared to hit their objectives, and a fire was caused in Revinne Wood. Two 112-lb. bombs were dropped on a train on the Ledeghem—Roulers railway. The first bomb was released from a height of 500 feet and burst in front of the train. The second bomb was released from 300 feet and burst on the train. Four 112-lb. bombs were dropped on Wervicq aerodrome, and two on Perenchies railway station, which was damaged.

On the 8th instant, twelve 112-lb. bombs were dropped on Reckem; two of the bombs were observed to burst on the aerodrome.

Third Brigade.—Douai aerodrome was attacked twice during the night of the 7th–8th by machines of No. 100 Squadron. On the first raid, one phosphorus and 45 20-lb. bombs were dropped. Three hangars were destroyed and buildings near the aerodrome were hit. Eight bombs were dropped on Douai railway station. Three bombs were dropped on a motor transport convoy, and one direct hit was obtained. The convoy was then attacked by machine gun fire from the air. On the second raid, which took place about 2.40 a.m., a fourth hangar was destroyed. The bombs were dropped from an average height of 600 feet.

Fourth Brigade.—On the night of the 7th–8th, four 112-lb. bombs were dropped on Bohain station.

Fifth Brigade.—Two raids were carried out against a dump, and 13 112-lb. bombs were dropped. Two of the bombs were seen to burst on the dump and the remainder all round it.

Ninth Wing.—Aulnoye engine sheds were attacked by No. 27 Squadron and nine 112-lb. bombs were dropped from heights varying from 3,000 to 4,000 feet. The bombs were seen to burst on and around the sheds and considerable damage is believed to have been done. An ammunition dump at Valenciennes was attacked by machines of No. 55 Squadron with 10 112-lb. bombs, which were dropped from heights of 11,000 to 12,000 feet. The bombs were seen to burst on and around the dump.

April 9th.

Reconnaissances.—Successful reconnaissances and contact patrols were carried out during the day and much valuable information was obtained.

A machine of the First Brigade observed a hostile battery retiring and the pilot at once attacked with machine gun fire, and the guns were temporarily abandoned.

Artillery Co-operation.—61 targets were dealt with by artillery with aeroplane, and 55 with kite balloon, observation. Twenty-six hostile batteries were successfully engaged and four explosions of ammunition was caused.

Kite balloons of the Third Army carried out successful work by day and night, and observed 12 explosions and 11 fires.

Hostile Aircraft.—Flight Sub-Lieut. Little, Naval Squadron No. 8, drove down a hostile scout out of control.

Captain Wilkinson and Lieutenant Griffiths, No. 48 Squadron, destroyed a hostile two-seater near Lens and drove down an Albatross two-seater out of control.

Second Lieutenant Price and Second Lieutenant Benjamin, No. 48 Squadron, destroyed a hostile machine east of Arras.

Captain Wilkinson and Lieutenant Allen, Lieutenants Letts and Collins, in two machines of No. 48 Squadron, attacked five hostile aircraft near Arras. They destroyed one and drove down another out of control.

Flight-Commander Norton, Naval Squadron No. 6, drove down two hostile aircraft out of control near Cambrai.

No. 22 Squadron destroyed a hostile machine near Regny and drove down two in a damaged condition—one at Mont d'Origny and the other near Marcy.

Bombing. — First Brigade. — Six 112-lb. and four 20-lb. bombs were dropped on Pont-à-Vendin. Two 112-lb. bombs fell on the railway junction and one on the railway line, completely shattering the lines. Two 20-lb. bombs hit the station. Later in the day 22 20-lb. bombs were dropped on Pont-à-Vendin and all of them were seen to burst on the target. Thirty-seven 20-lb. bombs were dropped on Bois de l'Hirondelle and 18 of them were observed to burst on the wood and on the trenches near by.

Third Brigade.—On the night of the 8th–9th, eight 20-lb. bombs were dropped on Vitry by a machine of No. 100 Squadron. On the 9th, 28 20-lb. bombs were dropped on various targets.

April 10th.

Reconnaissances.—Reconnaissances were carried out by the First, Second, Third, and Fifth Brigades. Much useful information was obtained by machines on contact patrol duty.

Several machines of No. 43 Squadron came down as low as 400 feet, and attacked men marching and working on trains with machine gun fire.

Artillery Co-operation.—Eleven targets were dealt with by artillery with aeroplane observation, and 12 with kite balloon observation.

Hostile Aircraft.—Lieutenant T. N. Southorn and Second Lieutenant H. E. Freeman-Smith, No. 25 Squadron, were attacked by a formation of hostile scouts, and they drove one of them down out of control.

Bombing. — First Brigade. — Twelve 20-lb. bombs were dropped on Bois de l'Hirondelle, and 34 20-lb. bombs were dropped on various targets. Sixteen of these burst on houses at Arleux.

Second Brigade.—On the night of the 9th–10th, 44 20-lb. bombs were dropped on St. Savier Station, Lille, from a height of 10,000 to 12,000 feet. The bombs were seen to hit the station and a bridge crossing the canal. Six 20-lb. bombs were dropped on Roubaix Station.

Third Brigade.—On the night of the 9th–10th, No. 100 Squadron dropped 40 20-lb. bombs on Douai Railway Station and on moving trains. One train was wrecked, one was set on fire, and one was derailed.

April 11th.

Reconnaissances.—Reconnaissances were carried out by all brigades, and very successful contact patrol work was done by machines of the First, Third, and Fifth Brigades.

Second Lieutenant C. E. de Berigny and Second Air Mechanic E. Bowen, No. 43 Squadron, descended to a low altitude and opened fire on troops in Lens, and several soldiers were seen to fall.

Infantry were engaged on different occasions by machine gun fire by pilots of No. 60 Squadron.

Lieutenant Keller, No. 23 Squadron, attacked lorries from a height of 1,000 feet, and an explosion was caused in one of them, which blew up.

Artillery Co-operation.—Twenty-five targets were dealt with by artillery with aeroplane observation, and three explosions of ammunition were caused.

Artillery of the First Army obtained 17 direct hits on hostile batteries, and caused two explosions of ammunition. In addition to this, Captain Bird, No. 16 Squadron, observing for the Fifth Canadian Siege Battery, reported four pits of a five-gun battery completely destroyed. Infantry were also dispersed by artillery.

Hostile Aircraft.—An observer of the First Brigade reports having seen, as the result of combats, one machine crash, one fall in flames, and one fall out of control. He was, however, unable to say to whom they belonged.

Anti-aircraft report that they watched a fight between four Bristol Fighters (No. 48 Squadron) and four hostile aircraft. They saw two of the latter brought down and the other two break off the combat and fly east. Two Bristol Fighters were observed by No. 12 Squadron to land under control in hostile territory.

Second Lieutenants Riley and Hall, No. 48 Squadron, drove down a hostile machine out of control.

A German machine was also driven down out of control in the neighbourhood of Remy on the evening of the 10th.

Naval Squadron No. 3, when acting as escort to a bombing raid on Cambrai, were attacked by hostile machines. Flight Lieutenant Breadner engaged one machine, which fell completely out of control and in flames. Later, a formation of H.A. attempted to attack the bombing machines. Flight Lieutenant Breadner drove down an Albatross scout, and then attacked a second which went down in a spinning nose-dive and one wing was observed to break off.

Flight Sub-Lieut. Fall also drove down one of the attacking machines in flames. In the fighting he became detached from the rest of the formation and was attacked by three hostile machines. He drove down one of the hostile scouts out of control, but the remaining two continued to attack. After considerable fighting one of the H.A. broke off the combat. Flight Sub-Lieut. Fall, by skilful manœuvring obtained a favourable position from which to attack the remaining machine. He opened fire and the German aeroplane crashed. During certain periods the fighting took place at a height of only 50 feet from the ground. Flight Sub-Lieut. Fall landed at one of our aerodromes unhurt, but with his machine riddled with bullets from hostile gunfire from aircraft, infantry, and cavalry.

Flight Sub-Lieut. MacNeill, of the same escort, also drove down an enemy machine completely out of control, and there is practically no doubt that this machine was destroyed.

Lieutenant Brink and Second Lieutenant Smith, No. 4 Squadron, were both wounded while on reconnaissance, but the pilot returned and landed the machine on our side while followed by two hostile scouts, who continued firing at the machine on the ground. The observer got the pilot out of the machine, and then, with the assistance of a soldier who had come up to help, opened fire on the hostile scouts and drove them off.

Bombing.—Second Brigade.—On the night of 10th–11th two 112-lb. bombs were dropped on the Lille–Tourcoing Railway.

Fourth Brigade.—On the night of the 10th–11th and on the 11th, eight 112-lb. and 22 20-lb. bombs were dropped on Essigny-le-Petit Station. Bombs were seen to burst on the line amongst trains and on a dump at the station.

Fifth Brigade.—On the night of the 10th–11th and on the 11th, five 112-lb. and four 20-lb. bombs were dropped on Cambrai Station, and on the 11th, 30 20-lb. bombs were dropped on various objectives.

April 12th.

Reconnaissance.—Contact patrols were carried out by the First, Third, and Fifth Brigades, and valuable information was obtained.

Artillery Co-operation. — 10 targets were dealt with by artillery with aeroplane observation.

Hostile Aircraft.—Captain Wilkinson and Lieutenant Allen, Second Lieutenant Winkler and Second Lieutenant Moore, No. 48 Squadron, drove down out of control one of seven hostile machines which they engaged.

Second Lieutenant Hunt and Second Lieutenant Fearnside-Speed, No. 18 Squadron, and Flight Sub-Lieut. Armstrong, Naval Squadron No. 3, attacked and drove down a hostile machine completely out of control.

Flight Sub-Lieut. Armstrong and Flight Pierce, Naval Squadron No. 3, attacked and drove down a black single-seater H.A. completely out of control.

Flight Sub-Lieut. Whealey, of the same Squadron, also drove down a hostile machine out of control.

During the combat a German aeroplane was seen to fall with its wings completely broken. It is believed to have been brought down by Flight-Commander Mack, who is missing.

Bombing. — Bellicourt Canal Tunnel was attacked by machines of the Fourth Brigade. Six 112-lb. and 26 20-lb. bombs were dropped from a height of 800 feet, and some were seen to hit the objective.

April 13th.

Reconnaissances.—Many fires were observed in Lens and in other places in front of the First Army. Observation was made of trenches and in one case an empty trench was reported, and was at once occupied by our troops.

Second Lieutenant Howe, No. 32 Squadron, attacked a column of horse transport on the Arras–Cambrai Road. He fired two drums and great confusion was caused; some of the vehicles were seen to turn completely over and fall into a ditch.

Enemy troops and other objectives were attacked by pilots with machine gun fire from the air during the day.

Artillery Co-operation.—Twenty-six targets were dealt with by artillery with aeroplane observation.

Artillery of the First Army obtained 13 direct hits on hostile batteries. Nine pits were damaged and an explosion of ammunition was caused. Trenches were also hit.

Hostile Aircraft.—Lieutenant Ellis, No. 40 Squadron, engaged and destroyed an Albatross two-seater near Courrières.

Captain Oxspring, No. 66 Squadron, drove down a two-seater biplane near Douai.

Lieutenant Buck, No. 19 Squadron, assisted by another pilot, drove down an Albatross scout out of control.

Bombing.—First Brigade.—On the night of the 12th-13th, bombs were dropped on Henin Liétard, Billy Montigny, Dourges, Sallaumies, Mericourt and La Bassée. All the bombs were seen to burst, and considerable damage was done.

On the 13th, a number of 112-lb., 20-lb., and 40-lb. phosphorus bombs were dropped on various places of importance.

Second Brigade.—On the night of the 12th-13th, two 112-lb. bombs were dropped on Lambersart, and two 112-lb. bombs on Tournai, from a height of 2,000 feet. Two lorries were observed to be destroyed.

On the 13th, eight 112-lb. bombs were dropped on a dump at Werwicq from heights ranging from 7,000 to 9,000 feet. Some of the bombs were seen to explode on the dump, and a very large explosion was caused. A train near the dump was also damaged.

Mouveaux aerodrome was also attacked, and several bombs were observed to burst on the aerodrome.

Third Brigade.—Eighteen 20-lb. bombs were dropped on various objectives, including a railway bridge, which was hit.

Fourth Brigade.—Six 112-lb. bombs were dropped on the dump and station at Essigny-le-Petit. Thirty-two 20-lb. bombs were dropped on Busigny Station.

Fifth Brigade.—Eight bombs were dropped on railway stations, and much damage was done.

9th Wing.—Martinsydes, of No. 27 Squadron, dropped six 230-lb. and seven 112-lb. bombs on Henin Liétard Station.

April 14th.

Reconnaissances.—In front of the First Army considerable train movement was observed, and fires were seen in a number of places.

Successful contact patrols were carried out by machines of the First, Third, and Fourth Brigades.

Machines of No. 23 Squadron attacked enemy troops in Lens and other places with machine gun fire.

Artillery Co-operation. — 35 targets were dealt with by artillery with aeroplane observation and 32 with kite balloon observation.

Artillery of the First Army obtained eight O.K.'s on hostile batteries and caused an explosion of ammunition. Trench and other targets were successfully engaged.

Artillery of the Second Army successfully engaged two hostile batteries and caused an explosion of ammunition.

Second Lieutenant F. H. Holdsworth, No. 8 Squadron, observing for 149th Siege Battery, obtained eight O.K.'s, eight Y's and nine Z's on a hostile battery.

Artillery of the Fourth Army successfully engaged one hostile battery.

Nine hostile batteries were successfully engaged by artillery of the Fifth Army, and five gun-pits were damaged.

Hostile Aircraft.—F.E.'s of No. 25 Squadron engaged five hostile scouts of the Nieuport type, and one of them was destroyed by Sergeant Burtenshaw and Sergeant Brown. A second was destroyed by Second Lieutenant Malcolm and Corporal Emsden. The three other scouts were driven off.

Second Lieutenant Buckton and Second Lieutenant Barritt, No. 5 Squadron, were attacked by two Halberstadts. The B.E. was considerably shot about, and as the pilot was unable to flatten out, the machine flew into the ground and was completely wrecked. The occupants were uninjured. They took the guns from the wrecked machine and sought shelter in a sunken road. A patrol of eight Germans approached and our men opened fire on them with their guns. The Germans retreated and Second Lieutenants Buckton and Barritt shortly afterwards fell into the hands of a Canadian advance patrol and were able to give valuable information as to the position of the enemy and other points of importance. They found an R.E. 8 of No. 59 Squadron, which had been brought down a few days previously. The pilot and observer, Second Lieutenant R. W. M. Davies and Second Lieutenant J. C. D. Wordsworth, were both killed.

Flight Lieutenant Booker and Flight Sub-Lieut. Grundell, No. 8 Naval Squadron, each drove down an Albatross out of control.

Flight Sub. Lieut. Soar drove off three Albatross scouts.

On the evening of the 13th a patrol of No. 48 Squadron engaged about 20 hostile aircraft near Vitry-en-Artois. One of the hostile machines was destroyed by Captain Wilkinson and Lieutenant Allen, and a second was driven down completely out of control by Lieutenant Warren and Second Lieutenant H. B. Griffiths. One hostile machine was driven down by each of the following:—Second Lieutenant Jones-Williams, No. 29 Squadron; Second Lieutenant Savery and Corporal Tollerfield, No. 11 Squadron; Second Lieutenant Exley and Captain de Royer, No. 11 Squadron, and Flight-Commander Gerrard, Naval Squadron No. 1.

Second Lieutenant Aspinall and Lieutenant Parlee, No. 22 Squadron, destroyed an Albatross Scout, and Captain Strugnell, No. 54 Squadron, and Second Lieutenant Cole, also of No. 54 Squadron, each drove down a hostile machine out of control.

Five hostile aeroplanes were driven down by machines of No. 23 Squadron.

A hostile machine was driven down out of control by a Spad of No. 19 Squadron.

Photography.—Nearly 500 photographs were taken during the day.

Bombing.

First Brigade.—On the 13th, 42 20-lb. bombs were dropped on Henin Liétard, and 10 20-lb. bombs on Citié St. Anie

On the night of the 13th–14th, 56 20-lb. bombs were dropped on various targets, and a number of bombs were dropped on places of importance on the 14th.

Third Brigade.—On the night of the 13th–14th, No. 100 Squadron dropped 37 20-lb. bombs on railways and on Somain Station. One train was destroyed. During the day a number of bombs were dropped on various objectives.

Fourth Brigade.—On the night of the 13th–14th and on the 14th, 36 112-lb. and 20-lb. bombs were dropped on Bohain and Busigny Stations. Several of the bombs were seen to hit the stations.

S. WOOD, Captain,
Staff Officer.

Headquarters, Royal Flying Corps,
15th April 1917.

No. 32.

CONFIDENTIAL.

ROYAL NAVAL AIR SERVICE.

OPERATIONS REPORT

(with Royal Flying Corps Reports attached).

17th to 30th APRIL 1917.

NAVAL STAFF,
 OPERATIONS DIVISION.
 30th April 1917.

ROYAL NAVAL AIR SERVICE.

REPORT OF OPERATIONS

Completed from Reports during period
17th to 30th April 1917.

CONTENTS.

	PAGE
HOME STATIONS	2
DUNKIRK	4
No. 3 WING, FRANCE	8
ROYAL NAVAL AIR SERVICE SQUADRON WITH ROYAL FLYING CORPS	9
EASTERN MEDITERRANEAN	10
ROYAL FLYING CORPS COMMUNIQUÉS	17

HOME STATIONS.

SUBMARINE PATROL WORK.

April 20th.

   Felixstowe.—Whilst on patrol to the eastward of North Hinder a Large America seaplane sighted a hostile submarine on the surface about six miles N.E. of North Hinder. The machine increased to full speed, fired recognition signal and proceeded to attack. The seaplane got over the submarine as she submerged and dropped four 100-lb. bombs, taking as a target the foremost edge of the swirl. All the bombs exploded, but no results were observed.

April 23rd.

   Felixstowe.—Whilst on patrol a Large America seaplane sighted a hostile submarine about 20 miles E.S.E. of North Hinder in full buoyancy with three men on the conning tower. The machine at once proceeded to attack and met with gun-fire from high-angle guns. The submarine made no attempt to dive, and when in position the seaplane dropped four bombs. Immediately after the bombs had been dropped the submarine was observed to have a heavy list, and appeared to be turning over, and within a minute and a half had disappeared. The area was searched by two machines for five and a half hours, but nothing was observed, and it is thought probable that the submarine was destroyed.

   The pilots of this machine were Flight Commander F. C. Holmes and Flight Commander T. D. Hallam, D.S.C. On returning to Felixstowe Flight Commander Hallam transferred to another Large America, and proceeded to carry out a further search of the area in which the submarine was attacked. In all, he was in the air for over nine hours.

   In connection with the above engagement, the King has been pleased to approve the award of the following decorations to the Officers and C.P.O. named.

   To receive the Distinguished Service Cross :—
      Flight Commander F. C. Holmes.
   To receive a bar to the Distinguished Service Cross :—
      Flight Commander T. D. Hallam, D.S.C.
   To receive the Distinguished Service Medal :—
      C.P.O. Clements.

In addition, an expression of appreciation has been sent to the Officers and C.P.O. mentioned above by the Lords Commissioners of the Admiralty.

April 21st.

Newlyn.—One 65-lb. bomb was dropped on a submerged submarine. The pilot then circled round to make another attack, but after the disturbance caused by the explosion in the water had cleared, the submarine could not be sighted. The machine remained in the vicinity for twenty minutes and then zig-zagged over a large area for an hour and a half, but nothing was observed, and the result of the attack is not known.

April 24th.

Calshot.—In answer to an S.O.S. call heard by Portland Bill and other stations, seaplanes went to the assistance of the Italian steamship "Portofino," which was being attacked by an enemy submarine about 16 miles S.S.E. of Weymouth at about 07·40–07·50.

A Large America seaplane, No. 8655, sighted the submarine and proceeded to attack, dropping one 100-lb. bomb, which fell within 5 or 6 feet of the conning tower as submarine was submerging. A second bomb was dropped a few feet further ahead. The submarine went to the bottom in 30 fathoms of water and bubbles were seen to rise for the next half-hour, after which No. 8655 was compelled to return to her base. The state of the sea was calm.

Half an hour later the destroyer "Ambuscade" arrived on the spot, and saw the submarine break surface at a distance of about 3,000 yards.

The conning tower came out of water, and the boat then dived again very slowly. The "Ambuscade" proceeded to the spot at full speed and found the wake of the submarine clearly visible. The submarine was proceeding at about 3 knots, and it was obvious that she was only a short distance below the surface. The "Ambuscade" passed over her and dropped two depth charges, with the result that the submarine was destroyed. The submarine was sighted through the water immediately before the dropping of the charges.

It is very probable that the bombs dropped from the seaplane, although not damaging the submarine mechanically, had the effect of partially stunning the crew, which would account for her slow movements when she came to the surface and was attacked by H.M.S. "Ambuscade" about an hour later.

NOTE.—All the evidence seems to point to the necessity for aircraft to carry heavier bombs. In the case of this seaplane attack the shot seems to have been as near a hit as possible, yet the submarine was able to come up and dive again within an hour.

Type of machine and crew.—Large America seaplane, No. 8655 :—

    Flight Lieutenant C. L. Scott.
    Flight Sub-Lieut. L. T. Paine.
    L.M. Engineer D. S. Rennett.
    A.M.2 W/T W. R. Liddiard.

April 26th.

Calshot.—A Large America seaplane on patrol sighted an enemy submarine, which immediately submerged. The seaplane attacked, and one 100-lb. bomb was dropped as the submarine disappeared.

The seaplane continued the patrol, returning to the position in about two hours, when the submarine was again sighted and a further attack carried out. Two 100-lb. bombs were dropped and appeared to be aimed correctly. The seaplane was then compelled to return to the base owing to lack of petrol.

Type of machine and crew.—Large America seaplane, No. 8655 :—

    Flight Lieutenant C. L. Scott.
    Flight Sub-Lieut. F. E. Fraser.
    A.M.2 W/T Laycock.
    L.M. Engineer D. S. Rennett.

In connection with the above attacks the King has been pleased to make the following awards :—

    Flight Lieutenant C. L. Scott - D.S.C. and bar.
    Flight Sub-Lieut. L. T. Paine - D.S.C.
    Flight Sub-Lieut. F. E. Fraser - D.S.C.
    L.M. Engineer D. S. Rennett - D.S.M.
    A.M.2 W/T Laycock - - - D.S.M.

DUNKIRK.

WEATHER.

With the exception of a few days, the weather conditions during the period under review have been favourable for flying.

RESULT OF RECONNAISSANCES.

April 23rd.

A reconnaissance over Zeebrugge Mole observed a large number of enemy torpedo boat destroyers alongside the Mole and other shipping off Ostend. Four submarines and two torpedo boat destroyers were observed on the west side of Eastern Bassin.

Reconnaissance machines reported the presence of hostile destroyers in the vicinity of Blankenburgh and Zeebrugge during the afternoon. Naval machines were immediately despatched to attack them.

April 24th.

Three bombs were dropped by French reconnaissance machines on a submarine sixteen miles off Dunkirk. There were no hits, and the submarine then submerged.

KITE BALLOON OBSERVATION.

April 22nd.

No. 11 Kite Balloon Section.—Four ascents were made and heavy train movements were observed at Ostend and main lines.

PHOTOGRAPHIC RECONNAISSANCE.

April 23rd.

A photographic reconnaissance was made over Bruges.

BOMB ATTACKS ON TORPEDO BOAT DESTROYERS.

April 23rd.

No. 5 Wing (7th Squadron).—During the afternoon it was reported by reconnaissance machines that hostile destroyers had been seen off the coast, and three Handley-Page machines were despatched to attack them. They located five enemy destroyers between Blankenburgh and Zeebrugge steaming in a north-easterly direction five miles off the coast. The leading machine opened the attack, dropping sixteen 65-lb. bombs, one of which was observed to obtain a direct hit on the leading destroyer. The remaining four scattered and were attacked by the other two machines, which dropped 32 bombs close to the vessels. The destroyer which had been hit was then observed to take up a list to port and remained stationary. The other four destroyers went to the assistance of the disabled one. A hostile seaplane then attacked the Handley-Pages, but was easily driven off. It was reported later by reconnaissance machines that four enemy destroyers were seen entering Zeebrugge Harbour. It is, therefore, thought probable that one destroyer was sunk.

April 24th.

No. 5 Wing (5th Squadron).—A bombing patrol consisting of three machines, each carrying four 65-lb. bombs, was despatched at 10.40 a.m. with instructions to attack any destroyers lying at Zeebrugge Mole, and any other hostile ship they might observe on the way.

A destroyer was observed apparently anchored about one mile off the entrance piers at Ostend.

Two machines attacked, dropping eight 65-lb. bombs. The results were not observed, but it was noticed that two small vessels (probably patrol boats) afterwards closed alongside the destroyer. The third machine, having lost the formation, proceeded to Zeebrugge and attacked two destroyers which were seen lying alongside the Mole. Four 65-lb. bombs were dropped on the objective, but no results could be observed owing to A.A. gun-fire, which was very heavy and accurate. All the machines returned safely.

April 26th.

No. 5 Wing (7th Squadron).—On receipt of a signal reporting four enemy torpedo-boat destroyers off Ostend, four Handley-Page machines were despatched and observed the four destroyers about seven miles out to sea north of Ostend. Thirty-two 112-lb. bombs were dropped from 6,000 feet, all machines taking part in the attack. No direct hits were observed, but several bombs were seen to explode very close to the destroyers. A hostile seaplane appeared and several rounds were fired at it from one of our machines.

One Handley-Page, No. 3115, with pilot and three gun-layers, failed to return. Subsequent signals reported the machine in the sea and under heavy fire from the shore batteries.

The French came to the rescue and despatched two F.B.A. Flying Boats to assist the Handley-Page machine. Both Flying Boats came under heavy A.A. gun-fire from the shore. One succeeded in rescuing Gunlayer Kirby, who was wounded, and although the machine was hit in several places and badly damaged, it returned safely.

The other Flying Boat took off another of the crew from the wrecked machine, but, unfortunately, was unable to leave the water and coming under heavy A.A. gun-fire eventually fell into the enemy's hands. The fate of the remaining two of the Handley-Page crew is uncertain.

With reference to the above, Wing Captain C. L. Lambe makes the following statement :—

"I consider that the act of these two French pilots in attempting this rescue was one of exceptional gallantry, more especially since both machines had already their full crew on board, and it was a matter of considerable doubt whether they could have got off the water with an additional passenger."

French pilot—Quartier-Maitre Francois Cartigny. Observer—Matelot Paul Morvan.

(This machine rescued A.M. (Gunlayer) F. C. Kirby, wounded, and returned safely.)

Pilot—Enseigne de Vaisseau Morand du Jouffrey. Observer—Matelot Jules Bois.

(Machine and crew captured with one of the rescued crew of Handley-Page machine. News has been received by carrier pigeon that the occupants of this machine are not wounded.)

Missing.—Flight Sub-Lieut. Hood, Gunlayer L. M. Watson, A. C. M. Danzey.

The member of the crew rescued by French machine and afterwards captured by the enemy is one of the above three mentioned, but no name is given. The other two are not accounted for.

OFFENSIVE PATROLS—ENGAGEMENTS WITH ENEMY.

April 25th.

No. 4 Wing (4th Squadron).—Four Sopwith machines carried out an offensive patrol over the area Zeebrugge, Bruges, Ghistelles, Thourout, and Dixmude. When near Bruges six hostile machines were encountered, one of which was brought down by Flight Sub-Lieut. Chadwick, and at least one other driven down out of control.

April 26th.

No. 4 Wing (4th Squadron).—A Sopwith Scout, N. 6185, returning from an offensive patrol, observed a hostile machine low down over Dixmude travelling in a south-westerly direction. The Sopwith dived to within 100 yards of the enemy machine's tail and immediately opened fire. After about 25 rounds had been fired the hostile machine stalled and fell tail first, then crashed to earth. The Sopwith pilot is of the opinion that he killed the enemy machine's pilot during the action.

Pilot—Flight Sub-Lieut. C. J. Moir.

ENEMY ATTACK.

April 30th

No. 4 Wing (4th Squadron).—Whilst escorting a French photographic machine in the vicinity of Nieuport, a Sopwith Scout, N. 6168, was attacked by a hostile machine, which opened fire at close range, hitting the Sopwith in five places. The Sopwith dived, and from 15 yards beneath the enemy machine opened fire, raking his fuselage from one end to the other. The enemy machine toppled to one side, then dived completely out of control. The Sopwith followed down to 7,000 feet and observed the hostile machine still falling, but as A.A. gun-fire was very heavy and accurate did not venture any lower.

Pilot—Flight Sub-Lieut. L. F. W. Smith.

BOMB ATTACKS.

(Carried out during the period between the dates given.)

Zeebrugge Mole	April 30th—May 1st	2,940 lbs.	Seaplane.
Ostend	April 30th—May 1st	1,625 lbs.	Seaplanes.

April 30th–May 1st.

Seaplane Base.—Short seaplanes carried out a bomb attack during the night on Ostend and Zeebrugge Seaplane Bases. Twenty-five 65-lb. bombs were dropped at Ostend and two direct hits were observed, one on the corner of living quarters and one on the slip-way.

One 550-lb., twenty 100-lb., and six 65-lb. bombs were dropped on Zeebrugge Mole. Bombs were observed to explode on the target, but the results are not known.

All machines returned safely.

April 30th–May 1st.

No. 5 Wing (No. 7 Squadron).—Aeroplanes carried out a bomb attack on hostile shipping in Bruges Docks during the night. Visibility over the target was so poor that, except for the flash of the bombs, actual results could not be observed. It is thought, however, that one bomb must have hit one of the buildings in the vicinity of the Mine and Torpedo stores, as a dull explosion and a less vivid glow was observed. 2,592 lbs. of explosives were dropped, which were observed to straddle the target well.

No. 3 WING.

BOMB ATTACK ON FREIBURG.

Extract from Report of the 18th April from S.R. of Belfort.

On the 14th of April an aerial attack was made on Freiburg in Brisgau. Bombs were dropped on the Karlsruhe-Leopoldsoehe line, dislocating the permanent way and causing considerable damage to the station.

A subway under the line was hit by a bomb, completely destroying the roof, and about 20 soldiers who were sheltering beneath were killed or wounded. The Ophthalmic Institute was hit, but a statement made by the German newspapers that the

Women's Hospital was hit is false. On the day following the attack it was ascertained that there were 30 casualties, many of which were military.

NAVAL SQUADRONS WITH THE ROYAL FLYING CORPS.

Period April 22nd to May 5th.

Extracted from the Report of the Officer Commanding Royal Flying Corps in France.

Weather.—During the period under review the weather conditions have been favourable for flying.

SQUADRON No. 1.

The squadron has carried out 95 offensive patrols, and acted as escort to reconnaissances often as far as 10 to 20 miles behind the enemy front.

Large hostile machine formations have been encountered, and fighting has been severe. Of the 175 hostile machines engaged four have been observed to crash to the ground, one in flames, and 12 others have been driven down completely out of control.

During the fortnight a total of 713 hours' flying has been carried out.

Casualties.—Flight Sub-Lieut. A. P. Haywood, wounded in combat, April 27th.

SQUADRON No. 3.

This squadron has been employed for offensive patrols, also as escorts to bombing and photographic machines, and has on several occasions dispersed large formations of hostile machines intent on attacking the machines they were escorting.

During the period under review pilots of this squadron have brought down 14 hostile machines, and driven down 10 completely out of control.

Casualties.—Flight Sub-Lieut. Malone, D.S.O., missing April 30th.

(A message has been dropped by the German Flying Corps stating that this officer was killed on the above date.)

SQUADRON No. 6.

The squadron has carried out 13 offensive and 27 line patrols. Enemy machines have been engaged in four combats, resulting in one being sent down in flames and three others driven down completely out of control.

Casualties.—Flight Sub-Lieut. A. H. B. Fletcher, missing 29th April. Flight Sub-Lieut. R. W. Berridge, killed in flying, May 3rd.

SQUADRON No. 8.

This squadron has carried out 48 offensive patrols, four line patrols, nine escorts to photographic and bombing machines, in addition to flights after hostile aircraft reported in the vicinity. A total of 67 combats have taken place, resulting in seven hostile machines being brought down and seen to crash, and others being driven down completely out of control.

Casualties.—Flight Sub-Lieut. E. B. Walter, killed April 24th. Flight Sub-Lieut. Cuzner, missing April 29th. Flight Sub-Lieut. E. D. Roach, missing May 1st. Flight Sub-Lieut. D. Shields, wounded May 1st.

Fuller details of the work of the above units not available.

EASTERN MEDITERRANEAN STATION.

Mudros, April 20th, 1917.

*Compiled from Weekly Reports Nos. 57 and 58,
dated from April 13th to 28th.*

Weather.—The weather conditions during the latter part of the period under review have been unfavourable, heavy rain, low clouds and strong winds interfering with operations from all stations.

THASOS AIR STATION.

("A" SQUADRON.)

April 10th.

Bomb Attacks.—A bomb attack was carried out by a Henri Farman on Drama Aerodrome by moonlight. Three runs were made over the target, during which two 100-lb. bombs and four 16-lb. bombs were dropped. One 100-lb. bomb was observed to explode close to the large hangar in the centre of Aerodrome, causing a fire to break out which considerably damaged the hangar and spread to two petrol dumps close by. These fires were still observed burning when the machine was landing at Thasos. On the occasion of this night raid the signal fires on Thasos (mentioned in a previous report) were again repeated as soon as a bombing machine left for Drama, and there were continued fires lighted in succession from the Kavalla coast to Drama.

The French Military Governor of Thasos has issued a further order forbidding fires by night or day or any lights at night which can be seen from the enemy coast.

April 11th.

Result of Reconnaissances.—A reconnaissance carried out about two miles west of Kavalla resulted in a 3-gun howitzer battery position being located about 1,250 yards west of the western outskirts of the town and 500 yards inland.

Photographic Reconnaissance.—A photographic reconnaissance was carried out to definitely ascertain the extent of the damage caused by the bomb attack of the previous night. The observer states that one side of the centre hangar was completely blown away, and a photograph shows that the northeast corner of this and another hangar are damaged.

April 12th.

Spotting Flight.—A spotting flight was carried out for M. 20 on to an enemy howitzer battery position about 1,250 yards west of western outskirts of Kavalla and 500 yards inland. The position was bombarded.

April 14th.

Anti-Submarine and Coast Patrols.—Anti-submarine and coast patrol flights were carried out daily from April 14th to the 19th inclusive in the vicinity of the base.

April 22nd.

Local anti-submarine patrols were carried out on this and the following date.

April 25th.

Result of Reconnaissances.—A reconnaissance of the Xanthi-Port Lagos area was carried out, and a noticeable feature was the unusual absence of A.A. gun-fire, which may be taken as indicative that high-angle guns are being concentrated elsewhere to meet our offensive.

The accommodation at Gereviz Seaplane Base was observed to have been increased by the addition of another large hangar. When this station was reconnoitred on February 26th, four seaplanes, including one small fast scout, were observed outside the then existing sheds, and it is to be presumed from the creation of additional accommodation that a more intense offensive against the sea-borne patrols and Thasos Air Station may be expected.

April 28th.

Bomb Attack.—Seaplanes carried out a bomb attack on battery positions to the west of Kavalla, but results were not observed.

STAVROS AIR STATION.

("D" Squadron.)

April 13th.

Spotting Flights.—A machine from this station carried out a spotting flight for H.M.S. "Edgar" on to a camp at 49. Q. 6. and enemy billets at Dedeballi. Two direct hits were made on the first target, completely destroying at least two of the sheds in the camp. A direct hit was also scored on dug-outs just north of the sheds. Three direct hits were made on the second target.

A spotting flight was carried out for military batteries on to emplacements between Tafel Kop and Hovis Hill.

April 14th.

Reconnaissances.—Reconnaissances have been carried out almost daily from this station from the above date till April 26th, during which proclamations were dropped in enemy trenches, camps, and villages.

DETACHED SQUADRON WITH ROYAL FLYING CORPS.

"E" Squadron at Hadji Janos.

April 8th.

Engagements with Enemy.—As the result of an engagement with enemy machines in the region of Hadji Janos, a 200-h.p. Freidrichshafener machine carrying three guns was captured, and the crew, two officers and a N.C.O. mechanic, were taken prisoners.

April 13th.

Fighter Patrols.—Two Albatrosses were again pursued, and upon being attacked retreated rapidly.

April 22nd.

Enemy Raids.—After a period of inactivity the German bombing formation made its appearance in the region of Hadji Janos and was engaged by "E" Squadron. Five combats took place, during which two of our mechanics were wounded but not severely. Further details of the action are following later.

April 23rd.

Enemy machines bombed the British front line trenches at Hadji Janos, but were driven off by our machines and returned straight to Hudovo.

April 24th.

Enemy machines attacked the French area, but information was not received in time for these to be engaged.

April 25th.

Raids Carried Out.—Four naval machines escorted R.F.C. bombing machines on two raids, during the first of which four combats took place, the enemy being driven off on each occasion.

On returning from the second raid the enemy's bombing formation, consisting of 16 machines, was encountered. They were attacked by the four R.N.A.S. escorting machines. The enemy formation was broken and his squadron scattered.

We sustained no casualties or material damage.

IMBROS AIR STATION.

("C" SQUADRON.)

April 13th.

Result of Reconnaissances.—Owing to constant high winds reconnaissance of the Dardanelles was possible from the above date until the 15th (inclusive) only. During the latter two days large merchant ships were observed in the Straits.

April 15th.

A reconnaissance machine was sent to search for an enemy gun which was shelling Kephalo. No gun was found on the peninsula, but a gun emplacement with one gun was located on the next point north of Kum Burnu.

April 23rd.

Low clouds and high winds prevented any reconnaissance work being carried out from April 15th till the 23rd. On the latter date an evening reconnaissance observed a ship of about 3,000 tons at Nagara, another at Ak Bashi Liman, and a third at Kilia Liman.

During a reconnaissance our machine was pursued by an Halberstadt Scout.

This is the first time a Halberstadt Scout has been observed in the Dardanelles area, and its presence is an indication of the importance attached by the enemy to our constant surveillance of the Straits.

April 25th.

A reconnaissance was again made of the Dardanelles.

THERMI AIR STATION.

"B" Squadron.

Interesting details have now been received with regard to the bomb attack on the enemy aerodrome at Paradisos and Kassimir on March 30th (quoted in Operations Report No. 31).

It appears that Flight Sub-Lieut. B. H. Trechman, pilot, and Leading Mechanic W. A. Jones, No. 14 R.F.C., observer, in Henri Farman N. 3024, were engaged and brought down during this engagement by a bullet-proof Fokker, piloted by Budeke, and landed among a crowd of Turks. The pilot succeeded in keeping them off with his revolver until he had burnt his machine. He was then fêted by the enemy aviators and driven round the town in the Vali's carriage, being sent to Constantinople the following day. L.M. W. A. Jones, observer, being wounded in the foot, was taken to hospital in Smyrna.

Flight Lieutenant J. E. Morgan and Sub-Lieut. A. Sandell, R.N.V.R., in Nieuport No. 9203, brought down in the same action and quoted in an enemy report as "found dead," were accorded a military funeral.

April 14th.

Spotting Flight.—M. 22 was spotted on to the gun position B. to the north of Cape Bianco.

Reconnaissances.—A reconnaissance of the Chesme area was carried out.

April 18th.

Reconnaissances.—A reconnaissance of the Eleos Islands in the Mitylene Channel was carried out.

April 25th.

A reconnaissance of Aivali was carried out but nothing was observed.

MUDROS.

H.M.S. "ARK ROYAL."

Test and practice flights in seaplanes have been carried out whenever the weather conditions have permitted, but strong westerly winds have considerably curtailed all flying in the Northern Ægean during the latter part of the period under review.

EAST INDIES AND EGYPT.

H.M.S. "EMPRESS."

April 27th.

Since the last report H.M.S. "Empress" has joined the command of the Commander-in-Chief, East Indies and Egypt, and remains at Port Said.

Operations against Gaza.—On April 16th H.M.S. "Empress," escorted by the French destroyer "Courtelas," proceeded from Port Said at 9.45 p.m. to carry out a submarine patrol during the naval bombardment of Gaza.

During the following day seaplanes from H.M.S. "Empress" kept up a patrol searching for submarines, but owing to the weather conditions the chance of any being sighted was not great enough to counterbalance the risk incurred by the "Empress," the ship presenting a large and conspicuous target.

H.M.S. "Empress" therefore returned to the base in the evening.

Enemy submarines have recently been more active in Egyptian waters and have shown signs of operating nearer the ports of Alexandria and Port Said.

H.M.S. "RAVEN II."

The seaplane carrier H.M.S. "Raven II." and the French cruiser "Poltau" have returned from Ceylon from their reconnaissance of the Chagos and Maldive Groups.

As No. 14 Kite Balloon Section in Mesopotamia cannot be used until next August, owing to the heat, all the heavy gear is being stored, repaired, and put into good working order at Busra ready for further work, and the unit will proceed to Ceylon for the period they are not required at Mesopotamia.

ROYAL FLYING CORPS COMMUNIQUÉS.

ROYAL FLYING CORPS COMMUNIQUÉ, No. 84.

April 15th.

Reconnaissances.—Successful reconnaissances were carried out by the First, Second, Third, and Fifth Brigades.

Artillery Co-operation.—Fourteen targets were dealt with by artillery with aeroplane observation, and three with kite balloon observation.

Three hostile batteries were successfully engaged, and two gun-pits were hit by artillery of the Second Army.

Two hostile batteries were successfully engaged by artillery of the Third Army.

Artillery of the Fourth Army obtained two hits on trench points, and caused many casualties to infantry.

Second Lieutenant Buckingham and Second Lieutenant Cox, No. 15 Squadron, did an artillery patrol at a height of 500 feet. The zone call was sent down, and five parties of infantry, varying from 100 to 300 strong, were engaged by artillery. Two hostile batteries were silenced by artillery of the Fifth Army.

On the evening of the 14th Captain Coates and Second Lieutenant Cotton, No. 5 Squadron, while on artillery work, were attacked by five hostile aircraft. At the commencement of the fight Second Lieutenant Cotton was wounded in seven places, and Captain Coates was also wounded; but they succeeded in destroying one of the hostile aeroplanes and in landing safely, in spite of the fact that the machine was considerably damaged by machine-gun fire.

Second Lieutenant King and Corporal Taylor, No. 25 Squadron, attacked two hostile machines that were interfering with artillery patrols, and drove one of the hostile machines down in a badly-damaged condition.

Lieutenant de Burgh and Lieutenant Napier, No. 40 Squadron, dived on three hostile scouts, one of which landed in a field, and was seen to burst into flames.

Flight Sub.-Lieut. Grundell, Naval Squadron No. 8, drove down an Albatross two-seater out of control. This is in addition to the one already reported on the 14th instant.

On the evening of the 13th Lieutenant Beynon and Second Lieutenant Lutyens, No. 3 Squadron, engaged two hostile machines near Quéant. The observer had his collar-bone broken by machine-gun fire, but continued fighting, and one of the hostile machines was forced to land in a field. Some good photographs were taken during this flight.

Bombing.—Fourth Brigade.—Six 112-lb. bombs were dropped on Bohain Station on the night of the 14th/15th, and one of the bombs was seen to hit the station buildings, and others fell near the station.

April 16th.

Reconnaissances.—Successful reconnaissances were carried out by machines of the First, Second, Third, and Fifth Brigades, and some good contact patrol work was also done.

Artillery Co-operation.—Twenty targets were dealt with by artillery with aeroplane observation.

Artillery of the Third Army successfully engaged 10 hostile batteries, and caused an explosion of ammunition.

Artillery of the Fifth Army obtained 14 direct hits on two hostile batteries.

Hostile Aircraft.—Lieutenant Pidcock, No. 60 Squadron, engaged and drove down two hostile aircraft.

A photographic patrol of No. 18 Squadron engaged six hostile scouts over Cagnicourt. Second Lieutenant Young and Second Lieutenant Blennerhassett attacked one hostile aeroplane which was engaging one of our machines, and fired a whole drum into it. The hostile machine fell completely out of control. They then attacked and drove down a second machine. A third machine was driven down and fell out of control by Second Lieutenant Hunt and Second Lieutenant Partington.

Photography.—426 photographs were taken during the day.

April 17th.

Artillery Co-operation.—Three targets were dealt with by artillery with aeroplane observation, and 10 with kite balloon observation.

Lieutenant Wessel, No. 15 Squadron, successfully ranged the 152nd Siege Battery on to wire, and five direct hits were observed. This work was carried out under most unfavourable conditions, and at a height of 500 feet.

With observation by kite balloon, artillery of the Fourth Army successfully engaged a German balloon on the ground.

Bombing.—On the night of the 17th/18th No. 100 Squadron dropped 25 20-lb. bombs on a M.T. park near Cantin, and on two M.T. columns near Brebières. A train east of Douai was attacked with pom-pom fire from the air, and hits were observed on the engine. Two vehicles near Cantin were destroyed, and hits were also obtained on the second and third columns attacked.

Low clouds and rain prevented work on the 18th and 19th instant.

April 20th.

Reconnaissances.—Reconnaissances were carried out whenever possible, and a number of fires were observed in St. Quentin.

Second Lieutenant Hon. S. H. D'Arcy and Lieutenant A. E. Pickering, No 43 Squadron, descended to 200 feet and fired at small parties of men on the Gavrelle—Fresnes road. They also dived six times to within 200 feet of a trench near Plouvain which was filled with Germans, and fired over 200 rounds with the front gun and two drums with the Lewis gun.

Artillery Co-operation.—Seven targets were dealt with by artillery with aeroplane observation.

Hostile Aircraft.—Lieutenant Bishop, No. 60 Squadron, engaged and drove down in flames and out of control a German two-seater machine.

Photography.—314 photographs were taken during the day, 227 of which were by the 3rd Brigade.

Kite Balloons.—No. 29 Balloon, when in ballast at a height of 250 feet, was attacked from underneath by a hostile aeroplane. A large number of bullet holes were found in the balloon. At the time anti-aircraft were firing heavily at two other hostile machines which were evidently there for the purpose of drawing A.A. fire from the attacking machine.

April 21st.

Reconnaissances.—Successful reconnaissances were carried out, and fires were observed in a number of places on the First Army front.

Two drums of ammunition were fired into Lens at German infantry. Germans at Roeux and transport in several other places were attacked by machine-gun fire from the air.

Artillery Co-operation.—Thirty-two targets were dealt with by artillery with aeroplane observation.

Artillery of the Second Army successfully engaged two hostile batteries. Two gun-pits were hit and two explosions of ammunition were caused, one of which took place in a dump through the use of the zone call.

Artillery of the Third Army successfully engaged 11 hostile batteries.

Captain Mowcock and Lieutenant McCartney, No. 9 Squadron, observed a M.T. convoy on a road, and sent down a zone call. Artillery destroyed the road in front of the convoy, and then shelled and completely destroyed the convoy.

S. Wood, Captain,
Staff Officer.

Headquarters, Royal Flying Corps.
22nd April 1917.

ROYAL FLYING CORPS COMMUNIQUÉ, No. 85.

April 22nd.

Reconnaissances.—Successful reconnaissances were carried out by all brigades and 9th Wing.

Fires were observed in Lens and La Bassée, and in several other places on the fronts of the First, Fourth, and Fifth Armies. A very large explosion was seen in Neuvereuil.

Machines of No. 15 Squadron obtained valuable information concerning the Hindenburg Line and other trenches, and reported a number of explosions behind the Hindenburg Line.

Second Lieutenant Stocken, No. 23 Squadron, when returning from an attack on a hostile balloon, saw three groups of three limbers, drawn by four horses each, on the Arras-Cambrai road. He dived to within 100 feet of each group and fired at them. The horses bolted and some of the limbers overturned. He then attacked a party of troops in a courtyard, after which he recrossed the lines at about 200 feet.

Artillery Co-operation.—109 targets were dealt with by artillery with aeroplane observation, and 14 with observation by balloons.

Artillery of the First Army obtained 14 direct hits on hostile batteries and destroyed six gun-pits. Trenches and wire were also much damaged.

Artillery of the Second Army successfully engaged two hostile batteries.

Artillery of the Third Army successfully engaged 26 hostile batteries. Two emplacements were destroyed and an explosion of ammunition caused.

Three hostile batteries were successfully engaged by artillery of the Fourth Army. With observation by Captain Pirie, No. 34 Squadron, artillery obtained two direct hits, in addition to a large number of Y's and Z's, on a battery, damaged two gun-pits, and caused an explosion of ammunition.

Artillery of the Fifth Army successfully engaged four hostile batteries; two direct hits on gun positions were obtained, and two gun-pits were damaged.

Hostile Aircraft.—Evening of the 21st.—Flight Sub-Lieut. R. A. Little, Naval Squadron No. 8, observed five hostile machines attacking an F.E. of No. 25 Squadron. He at once dived at a scout that was attacking the F.E. from behind. The hostile machine fell completely out of control, and the other four broke off the combat. The F.E. was also firing at the hostile scout when it was attacked by Flight Sub-Lieut. Little.

Second Lieutenant R. G. Malcolm and Second Lieutenant J. B. Weir, No. 25 Squadron, dived at a formation of five hostile scouts. Flight Commander A. R. Arnold, Naval

Squadron No. 8, came to the assistance of the F.E. One of the hostile machines, after being badly hit, fell to pieces in the air, and crashed in our lines.

Second Lieutenant L. L. Morgan, No. 40 Squadron, engaged and drove down a hostile machine. Second Lieutenant Stocken, No. 23 Squadron, attacked a hostile machine (two-seater) near Sauchy Lestree. He followed it down to 800 feet and fired 200 rounds into it. The machine was seen to disappear into a small wood.

A German machine was driven down completely out of control near Cagnicourt by Lieutenant Keller, No. 23 Squadron.

Captain McCallum, also of No. 23 Squadron, drove down a hostile machine, in which the observer is believed to have been shot. Later, he and Lieutenant Keller forced another German machine down apparently damaged.

Flight Sub-Lieuts. Casey and Broad, Naval Squadron No. 3, attacked four Albatross Scouts. Flight Sub-Lieutenant Casey fired 80 rounds into one hostile machine, finishing at about 10 yards distance; the hostile machine was seen to fall out of control. He then attacked and drove down a second machine out of control. Flight Sub-Lieut. Broad also drove one down, which was afterwards seen crashed on the ground.

Flight Sub-Lieut. Malone, of the same squadron, drove down a German aeroplane out of control near Quéant.

Flight Lieutenant Travers, also of Naval Squadron No. 3, drove down a German machine completely out of control.

22nd April.

Flight Commander A. R. Arnold, Naval Squadron No. 8, in a Sopwith triplane, dived at one of several hostile aircraft, and fired about 60 rounds at close range. Unfortunately, his gun jammed, so he immediately out-climbed the hostile machines, cleared the jam, and re-engaged the hostile aircraft. A hostile machine was seen to fall in flames by other pilots, and is believed to have been brought down by Flight Commander A. R. Arnold.

Second Lieutenant J. S. Leslie and Lieutenant A. R. Sortwell, No. 16 Squadron, while on artillery duty were attacked by three hostile aircraft. One of the hostile machines was hit, and is believed to have been brought down, but owing to the presence of other hostile machines its fate was not ascertained.

Three Sopwith triplanes of Naval Squadron No. 8 attacked three hostile machines, and a running fight ensued, in which one of the hostile machines was driven down.

Second Lieutenant W. T. Walder, No. 40 Squadron, drove down a hostile machine out of control near Henin-Liétard. It was lost sight of in a cloud, but was shortly afterwards seen by another pilot completely wrecked on the ground.

When on offensive patrol, machines of No. 1 Squadron attacked eight H.A. south-east of Lille. Second Lieutenant

E. M. Wright drove one of the hostile machines down completely out of control. Captain E. D. Atkinson also drove down one out of control.

Major Scott, No. 60 Squadron, when on photographic duty, was attacked by five hostile aircraft. An offensive patrol of No. 60 Squadron dived to his assistance. One of the German machines was driven down out of control by Lieutenant Bishop. Later, Lieutenant Bishop engaged five hostile aircraft and drove them off east.

A hostile machine was destroyed by Second Lieutenant Patterson, and one was driven down out of control by Lieutenant Molesworth, both of the offensive patrol of No. 60 Squadron.

Lieutenants Pidcock and Henderson, of No. 60 Squadron, dived to the assistance of F.E.'s that were engaging a number of hostile machines, and drove two of the hostile aeroplanes down. The pilots state that there was considerable difficulty in fighting with the enemy, as they seemed unwilling to engage at close quarters and continually broke off the combats and flew east.

Flight Commander Dallas and Flight Lieutenant Culling, Naval Squadron No. 1, attacked about eight hostile aircraft over Douai. One of the hostile machines was destroyed and another driven down enveloped in flames by Flight Commander Dallas, while a third was driven down completely out of control by Flight Lieutenant Culling. The remaining hostile machines broke off the combat.

A patrol of No. 48 Squadron (Bristol Fighters) engaged a formation of 14 hostile aircraft. One of the hostile machines was driven down out of control by Captain Wilkinson and Lieutenant Allen, while two others were driven down by the patrol. The remaining hostile machines dived away east.

Captain Pickthorne, No. 32 Squadron, saw a German machine diving at a B.E. on artillery work. He at once flew at the hostile machine, which was driven off after being hit. Lieutenant W. E. Reed, No. 19 Squadron, while on offensive patrol observed a hostile machine approaching from the east. He secured a favourable position between the sun and the German machine, and then dived at it. About 200 rounds were fired at the hostile aeroplane, which fell completely out of control and in flames.

A hostile machine dived at a Sopwith Scout of No. 66 Squadron, but was itself attacked from behind by Lieutenant J. T. Collier. The pilot was hit and seen to fall forward, and the machine fell completely out of control. The German pilot appeared to manœuvre his machine with more than the average skill shown by the enemy.

Balloons.—Lieutenant D. de Burgh, No. 40 Squadron, attacked a hostile balloon with Le Prieur rockets. The balloon did not burst into flames, but was hauled down emitting a large amount of smoke.

Second Lieutenant E. S. T. Cole, No. 1 Squadron, attacked and destroyed a hostile balloon when about 20 feet from the ground. The engine of the Nieuport was hit, and the pilot crossed the lines considerably under 50 feet, while on more than one occasion the machine actually touched the ground on the enemy's side of the lines.

Captain Ellerton, No. 29 Squadron, attacked and brought down a balloon in flames. Lieutenants Essell and Jones-Williams, No. 29 Squadron, both attacked balloons, and although tracers were seen to enter the balloons, and smoke in each case rose from them, they were not seen to fall.

Second Lieutenant Ross, No. 60 Squadron, destroyed a balloon, and Lieutenant Molesworth and Second Lieutenants Penny and Lloyd, No. 60 Squadron, also attacked balloons, which were seen to be hit, and from which smoke issued.

The balloons of Nos. 3 and 14 sections were attacked and destroyed by hostile aircraft.

Bombing.—No. 18 Squadron dropped five 20-lb. bombs and 10 incendiary bombs on a drill ground at Cambrai. Some of the bombs were seen to hit the objective.

Photography.—700 photographs were taken during the day.

April 23rd.

Reconnaissances.—Reconnaissances were carried out by all brigades and 9th Wing.

1st Brigade report that areas near Salome and Marquillies appear to be flooded.

On a number of occasions, transport and German troops were attacked with machine-gun fire from the air from low altitudes.

Artillery Co-operation. — 88 targets were dealt with by artillery with aeroplane observation and 56 with observation by balloons.

Artillery of the First Army obtained eight direct hits on hostile batteries, and a number on wire and on trenches.

Artillery of the Second Army successfully engaged nine hostile batteries; 12 gun-pits were hit, and two explosions of ammunition caused.

Artillery of the Third Army successfully engaged 16 hostile batteries, and caused three explosions of ammunition.

Nine hostile batteries were successfully engaged by artillery of the Fourth Army. Three direct hits were obtained on gun-pits and one on an emplacement. With observation by Captain Pirie, No. 34 Squadron, all guns of one battery were destroyed, and one was blown into the air. Artillery of the Fifth Army successfully engaged four hostile batteries, and secured direct hits on trenches and on wire.

Hostile Aircraft.—Second Lieutenant C. E. de Berigny and Second Air Mechanic F. Bowen, No. 43 Squadron, drove down an Albatross, which landed in a ploughed field and turned over and crashed.

Lieutenant Mackenzie and Lieutenant Ellis, both of No. 40 Squadron, attacked a two-seater German machine, and drove it down out of control. Flight Sub-Lieutenant Little, Naval Squadron No. 8, drove down an Albatross two-seater in a damaged condition.

An indecisive combat took place between Flight Commander Arnold, Naval Squadron No. 8, and a single-seater Albatross Scout. The fight lasted about 20 minutes, and the German pilot showed great skill in manœuvring his machine, but was at a disadvantage, as the Triplane could out-manœuvre and out-climb the hostile machine.

Flight Commander Dallas and Flight Sub-Lieut. Culling, Naval Squadron No. 1, each engaged and drove down a German aeroplane out of control.

Four German aeroplanes were driven down out of control: one by Lieutenant Upson, two by Lieutenant Jones-Williams, and one by Lieutenant Rutherford, all of No. 29 Squadron.

Lieutenant Bishop, No. 60 Squadron, drove down a hostile machine, which landed. He continued attacking the machine, and believes that both the pilot and observer were killed or wounded. He then attacked and destroyed a hostile scout, which was attacking a Nieuport Scout from behind.

Captain Manning and Lieutenant Duncan, No. 11 Squadron, shot down a hostile machine out of control.

A patrol of No. 48 Squadron engaged 10 hostile aircraft over Vitry, and Lieutenant Holliday and Captain Wall, in one of the Bristol Fighters, destroyed a hostile machine, while a second German aeroplane was brought down out of control by the patrol, and a third was driven down severely damaged.

Lieutenant Parker, No. 11 Squadron, was attacked by 11 hostile aircraft and his machine was brought down in flames. The controls had been nearly all shot away and the observer—seriously wounded—had fallen partly out of the machine, but was held from falling out by Lieutenant Parker, who landed safely, and took his observer out of the burning machine and carried him to safety while under heavy shell fire.

On the evening of the 22nd, Flight Commander Dallas and Flight Sub-Lieut. Culling, Naval Squadron No. 1, met about 14 hostile aircraft, composed of scouts and two-seaters, flying from the east. The hostile machines were unable to keep formation owing to the Triplanes continually diving at the formation and firing short bursts as they passed. For about three-quarters of an hour, owing to the superior climbing powers and speed of the Triplanes, they were able to continue such tactics as suited their purpose. After two of the hostile machines had been destroyed by Flight Commander Dallas and one driven down out of control by Flight Sub-Lieut. Culling, the German formation was thoroughly disorganised, gave up its attempt to reach the lines, and retired eastwards.

Flight Lieutenant Breadner, Naval Squadron No. 3, engaged and brought down in our lines a double-engined pusher machine carrying a pilot and two observers. The officers were taken prisoners, but burnt the machine before being captured.

Flight Sub-Lieut. Malone, Naval Squadron No. 3, engaged a hostile machine and shot the pilot, and the machine crashed. He drove down a second hostile machine out of control and attacked a third. He then ran out of ammunition, and so returned to an aerodrome, obtained more ammunition, recrossed the line, and drove down another hostile machine out of control, while still another was forced down.

Captain Patrick, No. 23 Squadron, drove down two hostile machines and then attacked a third, which fell out of control.

Second Lieutenant Reid and Lieutenant Fearnside-Speed, No. 18 Squadron, drove down a hostile machine, which is believed to have fallen out of control.

A hostile machine was driven down by each of the following pilots of Naval Squadron No. 3 :—

Flight Sub-Lieuts. Pierce, Beamish, and Anderson.

Two hostile machines were driven down in a damaged condition by Flight Lieutenant Travers and Flight Sub-Lieut. Corby.

Captain A. Ball, No. 56 Squadron, attacked two Albatross two-seaters, one of which soon dived away east. After considerable manœuvring, Captain Hall obtained a favourable position underneath the second German machine, and fired about half a drum. The German aeroplane, which was painted with many colours, was destroyed. Later in the day, Captain Ball observed five Albatross Scouts over Cambrai. He dived at the nearest and fired about 150 rounds at close range, and the hostile machine fell in flames; while the remaining four hostile aircraft broke off the combat. Captain Ball had two other combats, and on each occasion the hostile machine dived away east.

Lieutenant Child, No. 19 Squadron, drove down an Albatross two-seater out of control.

A hostile machine was driven down out of control by Second Lieutenant Handley and Second Lieutenant Percival, No. 57 Squadron.

Second Lieutenant Pope and Lieutenant Nasmyth, No. 57 Squadron, drove down a hostile machine in a badly damaged condition.

Bombing machines of No. 55 Squadron, when returning to the aerodrome, were dived at by nine hostile aircraft. Second Lieutenant Pyott and Second Lieutenant Taylor, on a De Havilland four-machine, drove down one of the attacking machines out of control as it passed. The attacking machines were only able to fire at the De Havilland 4's owing to the fact that they were considerably higher and so gained speed in the diving. Having dived past, they were quite unable to attack a second time.

Machines of No. 66 Squadron, while acting as escort, engaged eight small hostile scouts of the Nieuport type. No hostile machines were seen to crash, but several were driven down after having been closely engaged, and there is little doubt that some were destroyed.

Major Harvey-Kelly, No. 19 Squadron, destroyed an Albatross Scout near Cambrai.

On the 22nd a hostile machine was brought down by gun-fire from the ground.

Photography.—573 photographs were taken during the day.

Bombing.—On the evening of the 22nd, No. 18 Squadron dropped 36 20-lb. bombs on the aerodrome at Champ-de-la-Manœuvre. A number of bombs were seen to drop on the aerodrome, but observation was difficult owing to constant interference by hostile aircraft.

No. 55 Squadron attacked huts and a dump at Boue. Twelve 112-lb bombs were dropped from an average height of 9,500 feet. Bombs were seen to fall on the dump and on the huts, and the latter were set on fire. This squadron also attacked Valenciennes railway station. Eight 112-lb. bombs were dropped from 9,500 feet, and several were seen to fall on the station and on the railway line.

No. 27 Squadron dropped forty-two 20 lb. bombs on Lecluse, Noyelle, and Brebières. A number of the bombs were seen to hit the objectives.

No. 27 Squadron also attacked a sugar factory at Lecelles. Ten 112-lb. bombs were dropped from 2,000 feet. The bombs were seen to burst on the factory and on railway trucks in the factory yard.

Balloons.—On the 22nd, the balloon of No. 33 Section was attacked and brought down by hostile aircraft.

The balloons of Nos. 5 and 16 Sections were attacked and considerably hit, but not destroyed.

April 24th.

Reconnaissances.—Successful reconnaissances were carried out by all brigades and 9th Wing, and a number of contact patrols were also successfully accomplished.

A number of fires and explosions were observed on the front of the First Army, and reports confirmed the flooding of certain areas reported yesterday.

A long reconnaissance was carried out by No. 45 Squadron, and information of much value was obtained.

Machine-gun fire was again used on enemy troops and transport.

Artillery Co-operation.—Ninety-three targets were dealt with by artillery with aeroplane observation, and 43 with observation by balloons.

Artillery of the First Army obtained 27 direct hits on hostile batteries and a number on trenches and wire.

Artillery of the Second Army succeesfully engaged 20 hostile batteries, when 34 gun-pits were hit, and five explosions of ammunition were caused.

Artillery of the Third Army successfully engaged 13 hostile batteries, on which a number of direct hits were obtained.

Ten hostile batteries were successfully engaged by artillery of the Fourth Army.

Artillery of the Fifth Army successfully engaged 13 hostile batteries. Nine direct hits were obtained, eight gun-pits were damaged, one demolished, and three explosions of ammunition were caused.

Hostile Aircraft.—A patrol of Naval Squadron No. 8 encountered a number of hostile machines and drove two of them down severely damaged. In one combat the observer was shot and seen to collapse.

Flight Lieutenant Booker, Naval Squadron No. 8, when leaving the aerodrome, observed A.A. firing at a hostile machine. He followed, steadily climbing, and eventually engaged it. The hostile machine flew east and was followed as far as Douai, when Flight Lieutenant Booker had to leave it owing to his having run out of ammunition. The hostile machine was very badly shot about.

Flight Sub-Lieut. Simpson, Naval Squadron No. 8, drove down a hostile machine out of control.

Second Lieutenant Hall, No. 40 Squadron, attacked a two-seater at very close range and shot the observer, and the hostile machine dived away.

Lieutenants Brewis and Napier, No. 40 Squadron, when returning from patrol encountered a two-seater Aviatik at 17,000 feet. They attacked and drove it downwards in a westerly direction. Flight Sub-Lieut. Little, Naval Squadron No. 8, also joined in the chase, and the hostile machine was forced to land in our lines in an undamaged condition and the occupants were taken prisoners.

Lieutenant Hazell, No. 1 Squadron, shot down a hostile machine in flames.

An escort of machines of No. 20 Squadron engaged 12 hostile aircraft near Roulers. One of the hostile machines was destroyed and one driven down out of control.

Flight Commanders Gerrard and Dallas, Naval Squadron No. 1, each drove down a hostile machine out of control.

Lieutenant Holliday and Captain Wall, No. 48 Squadron, destroyed a hostile machine near Cagnicourt, and drove another down out of control.

Three pilots of Naval Squadron No. 3 attacked a hostile machine over Quéant. The hostile machine endeavoured to fly east, but the wind was against it and the Naval pilots also intercepted it and drove it west. Two of the pilots' guns jammed, but the third, Flight Lieutenant Malone, continued to engage the hostile machine and drove it down in our lines. The observer was killed and the pilot wounded.

Sergeant Whiteman and Second Lieutenant Fearnside-Speed, No. 18 Squadron, brought down an Albatross Scout completely enveloped in flames.

Two Halberstadt Scouts were seen to collide in the air and break to pieces.

Flight Sub-Lieut. Carter, Naval Squadron No. 3, had several encounters during the day. In one with an Albatross Scout he eventually succeeded in hitting and driving the machine down and then followed behind, firing at it until it reached the ground where it crashed. On regaining his height he engaged another hostile machine and drove it down completely out of control.

Flight Sub-Lieuts. Whealy, Fall, Armstrong, Casey and Flight Lieut. Breadner, all of Naval Squadron No. 3, had decisive combats, and in every case the hostile machine was seen to fall completely out of control.

Captain Bryant and Second Lieutenant Couve, No. 18 Squadron, observing a hostile machine attacking an F.E., at once opened fire at it from behind and drove it down out of control.

Lieutenant Huston and Lieutenant Foord, No. 18 Squadron, drove down two hostile machines, one of which was seen crashed on the ground shortly after the fight.

A German machine was driven down out of control by Second Lieutenant Zink and Second Lieutenant Bate, No. 18 Squadron.

Second Lieutenant Traylen and Corporal Beebee, No. 18 Squadron, Second Lieutenant Hunt and Second Lieutenant Partington, No. 18 Squadron, drove down hostile machines in spinning nose-dives, after having been engaged at close quarters.

Two German machines were driven down damaged by a patrol of No. 23 Squadron.

Second Lieutenant Knaggs, No. 56 Squadron, on an S.E. 5, drove down an Albatross, painted red and green, out of control.

Three hostile machines were driven down apparently out of control by bombing machines of No. 55 Squadron.

A reconnaissance of No. 70 Squadron encountered six Halberstadt Scouts and drove three of them down, two falling out of control. One of these was shot down by Lieutenant Gotch and Lieutenant Kiburz, and the other by Sergeant Thomson and Second Air Mechanic Impey.

Lieutenant Barlow, No. 56 Squadron, engaged a hostile machine at about 10,000 feet. The fighting continued until the machines had gone down to within 1,000 feet of the ground, when the hostile machine fell and crashed.

A number of other hostile aircraft were driven down in a damaged condition by Nos. 66 and 56 Squadrons.

A very large number of other combats took place which were reported as "indecisive," but in nearly every case the hostile machine or machines dived away, and it is probable that in many cases they were badly damaged or even eventually fell out of control.

Photography.—1,368 photographs were taken during the day.

Bombing.—First Brigade.—On the evening of the 23rd, four 112-lb. and 35 20-lb. bombs were dropped on Quiry-la-Motte. Two of the heavy bombs were seen to hit a dump and the remaining bombs fell in the village, damaging and destroying several houses.

On the 24th, 41 20-lb. bombs were dropped on places of importance.

Third Brigade.—On the night of the 23rd/24th, machines of No. 100 Squadron went out in order to disorganise enemy traffic with bombs as far as possible. The machines went out in pairs, leaving the ground at about every two hours. Thirty-eight 20-lb. bombs were dropped in all. One bomb was dropped on Pont-á-Vendin from a height of 150 feet. A direct hit was obtained on an engine repair shop north-east of Lens from a height of 500 feet Lens, a motor transport column south of Lens, and the railway track east of Douai were successfully attacked. One pilot who had temporarily lost his bearings was fired at with a group of greenish-coloured rockets. These rockets clearly showed him a supply depôt beneath him, which he immediately bombed and hit. The first pilots observed fairly considerable movement east of Lens, but the presence of our machines caused most of the lights to be put out and trains to stop.

Fourth Brigade.—Busigny Station was attacked by machines of Nos. 9 and 22 Squadrons. Twenty-seven 20-lb. bombs and four 112-lb. bombs were dropped, and several of them were seen to burst in the station and on the railway line.

No. 9 Squadron bombed Bohain Station from an average height of 1,900 feet, and some of the bombs were observed to fall on the station and in the town.

9th Wing.—No. 55 Squadron dropped 49 20-lb. bombs on La Briquette aerodrome.

No. 27 Squadron dropped five 230-lb. bombs from a height of 2,000 feet on Ath. The bombs were seen to burst on sheds, on the railway line and on houses, and very considerable damage is believed to have been done. Later in the day No. 27 Squadron attacked Hirson Station with 230-lb. bombs. One bomb was seen to hit a train and derail an engine, and considerable damage was done.

Balloons.—A hostile balloon was brought down by Lieut. Molesworth, No. 60 Squadron, and Lieutenants Legallis and Essell, both of No. 29 Squadron, also destroyed one.

A hostile balloon was attacked by No. 54 Squadron but did not appear to catch fire. The balloon party on the ground was then attacked, and again, 20 minutes later, the pilots attacked the balloon party working on the balloon, which was now flat on the ground.

April 25th.

Reconnaissances.—Reconnaissances were carried out by the First, Second, Third, and Fifth Brigades.

The country north-west of Pont-a-Verdin is reported to be flooded.

Late in the evening of the 24th, two successful contact patrols were carried out by the First Brigade. In each case the call for flares was answered immediately.

A machine of No. 60 Squadron descended to a low altitude, and fired at infantry in a trench.

Artillery Co-operation.—Forty-eight targets were dealt with by artillery with aeroplane observation, and 66 with observation by balloon.

Artillery of the First Army obtained 10 direct hits on hostile batteries, and a number on trenches.

Artillery of the Second Army successfully engaged two hostile batteries, and three gun-pits were hit. Zone call was used with considerable success during an organised bombardment.

Artillery of the Third Army successfully engaged 14 hostile batteries.

Artillery of the Fourth Army successfully engaged two hostile batteries. Under zone call, two parties of infantry were dispersed, and a convoy was hit.

About 1,000 infantry in a trench were reported by zone call by Second Lieutenant Barker and Second Lieutenant Goodfellow, No. 15 Squadron, and were successfully engaged by artillery of the Fifth Army. They reported several other parties of infantry and two hostile batteries, and in most cases the shooting was successful. This pilot and observer also obtained valuable information and took valuable photographs. The work was all carried out at a very low altitude, under rifle and machine-gun fire. In addition to this, four other hostile batteries were successfully engaged by artillery of the Fifth Army, and two direct hits were obtained on gun positions, and two pits were damaged. A number of direct hits were also obtained on trenches.

Balloons of the 1st Balloon Wing successfully ranged Siege Artillery on to four hostile batteries, and on to trench and other targets, and one explosion of ammunition was caused.

Artillery, with observation by balloons of the 2nd Brigade, engaged nine hostile batteries, and caused an explosion of ammunition.

Artillery of the Fourth Army, with balloon observation, successfully engaged two hostile batteries, and obtained direct hits on houses at Bilhem. During the night of the 24th/25th, the balloon of No. 34 Section located eight hostile batteries.

Hostile Aircraft.—On the evening of the 24th, Second Lieutenant A. Roulstone and Second Lieutenant E. G. Green, No. 25 Squadron, were attacked while taking photographs by three Albatross Scouts. One of the hostile scouts was severely hit, the wing broke off, and the machine crashed.

On the 24th an escort composed of machines of No. 20 Squadron destroyed a hostile machine. This is in addition to those reported yesterday.

On the 25th Lieutenant C. R. O'Brien and Lieutenant J. L. Dickson, No. 43 Squadron, engaged four hostile scouts resembling Nieuports, which were painted red. One of the hostile scouts was driven down out of control, and was seen by A.A. observers to crash.

A patrol of No. 25 Squadron engaged 10 hostile scouts. Owing to the closeness of the fighting none of the hostile machines were observed by the patrol to fall, but A.A. observers report that one hostile machine fell in flames and one crashed.

Lieutenants Price and Benjamin, No. 48 Squadron, engaged and destroyed a German aeroplane.

A hostile aeroplane was brought down in our lines at H. 5.d. (Sheet 51B.).

Bombing.—On the night of the 24th/25th, machines of the Fourth Brigade dropped 19 20-lb. bombs on Estrees.

On the night of the 24th/25th, machines of No. 4 Squadron dropped six 20-lb. bombs on a convoy. After dropping the bombs the pilot attacked the convoy with machine-gun fire. In several other cases pilots engaged German infantry with machine-gun fire from the air.

Kite Balloons.—A German balloon broke loose and came down in our lines.

No. 7 Section's balloon was attacked by hostile aircraft on the 24th. Captain Sansom and Second Lieutenant W. M. Edwards made successful parachute descents, after which Captain Sansom repaired the balloon and at once reascended to the maximum height.

April 26th.

Reconnaissances.—A large number of fires and explosions were observed opposite the front of the First Army.

Some very successful contact patrols were carried out by machines of the Third Brigade.

Artillery Co-operation.—Eighty-nine targets were dealt with by artillery with aeroplane observation and 15 with observation by balloons.

Artillery of the First Army obtained 40 direct hits on hostile batteries. Two gun-pits were set on fire, and two explosions were caused; 141 active hostile batteries were reported by zone call. Direct hits were also obtained on wire and on trenches.

Artillery of the Second Army successfully engaged four hostile batteries. Nine gun-pits were hit and two explosions were caused.

Twenty-two hostile batteries were successfully engaged by artillery of the Third Army. Two direct hits were obtained on emplacements and two explosions of ammunition were caused.

The 202nd Siege Battery, with observation by Lieutenant Perimmer, No. 8 Squadron, obtained four direct hits on hostile batteries and two on emplacements.

Artillery of the Fourth Army successfully engaged five hostile batteries—three under zone call. A convoy of lorries was engaged under zone call and one lorry was destroyed.

Artillery of the Fifth Army successfully engaged six hostile batteries. Seven direct hits were obtained on gun positions and an explosion was caused. Two gun-pits were entirely demolished and two were damaged. The 94th Siege Battery, with observation by Lieutenant Poland, No. 15 Squadron, obtained six direct hits on a hostile battery, and two gun-pits were destroyed. This pilot then attacked a battery with his Lewis gun. Most of the work was done at a height of about 1,500 feet.

Hostile Aircraft.—A hostile scout made three determined attacks on No. 8 Section's balloon, and set it on fire when at a height of 500 feet.

A hostile machine was destroyed by a patrol of No. 41 Squadron, and a hostile balloon was brought down in flames by No. 1 Squadron.

Second Lieutenant Bartlett, No. 41 Squadron, engaged two hostile machines, one of which he drove down, and it is reported by artillery to have crashed.

Captain McCallum, No. 23 Squadron, with two other machines, attacked four hostile aircraft near Cambrai. Several other hostile machines joined in the fight, and two of the German machines were driven down in spinning nose-dives after having been engaged at close quarters by Captain McCallum.

Captain Ball, on an S.E. 5 of No. 56 Squadron, while on patrol at 13,000 feet, observed a number of hostile machines leaving an aerodrome at Cambrai, so he went and waited for them to get up. When the hostile machines were about 6,000 feet, he dived at the nearest one, firing at it with both his

Lewis and Vickers guns at a range of about 20 yards. The hostile machine crashed. He then found that five hostile machines had got between him and the lines. He endeavoured to get through this formation, but finding it difficult turned south-east, and was followed by the hostile machine, one of which was far in advance of the others. Captain Ball turned round and engaged this machine, which burst into flames and crashed. He then finished firing what ammunition he had left and crossed the lines at dusk, the speed of his machine enabling him to out-distance the pursuing aeroplanes.

Bombing.—1st Brigade.—Thirty 20-lb. bombs were dropped on places of military importance. Houses were set on fire in Avion, and in another place an explosion was caused.

5th Brigade.—Twenty-five 20-lb. and four incendiary bombs were dropped from an average height of 10,500 feet on Epinoy Aerodrome. A number of the bombs were seen to hit the aerodrome; one was seen to burst on a shed, while others fell in the village.

April 27th.

Reconnaissances.—A large number of fires and explosions were again reported on the front of the First Army.

Captain Neale, No. 16 Squadron, in spite of the fact that he had been wounded in the head, brought back valuable information.

Several pilots attacked German troops and transport with machine-gun fire.

Artillery Co-operation.—Fifty-nine targets were dealt with by artillery with aeroplane observation and 26 by balloons.

Artillery of the First Army obtained seven direct hits on hostile batteries; as well as hits on houses, trenches, and wire.

Artillery of the Second Army successfully engaged four hostile batteries; five gun-pits were hit and three explosions of ammunition were caused.

Ten hostile batteries were successfully engaged by artillery of the Third Army. With observation by Second Lieutenant F. H. Holdsworth, No. 8 Squadron, the 156th Siege Battery obtained four direct hits and a number of Y's and Z's on a hostile battery. With observation by Captain J. H. Norton, No. 13 Squadron, the 153rd Siege Battery obtained three direct hits on a hostile battery.

Artillery of the Fourth Army successfully engaged three hostile batteries and caused three explosions of ammunition. Motor transport was engaged successfully under zone call.

Artillery of the Fifth Army successfully engaged five hostile batteries, and obtained a number of direct hits on trenches and wire.

On the 26th, Lieutenant Trollope and Lieutenant Coury, V.C., No. 13 Squadron, observing for 20th Siege Battery, obtained three direct hits on a hostile battery and caused four explosions of ammunition.

Hostile Aircraft.— Anti-aircraft of the First Army brought down a hostile machine, which fell in flames near Willerval.

Six F.E.'s of No. 25 Squadron, while taking photographs, and escorted by six Sopwith triplanes of Naval Squadron No. 8, were heavily attacked by 12 hostile machines. As the result of the combat, one hostile machine was destroyed by Lieutenant C. Dunlop and Second Lieut. J. B. Weir, and two were driven down out of control—one by Sergt. J. H. R. Green and Second Lieutenant H. E. Freeman-Smith, and the other by Flight Lieut. C. D. Booker of the Naval Squadron.

Lieutenant H. E. O. Ellis, No. 40 Squadron, proceeded to attack a hostile balloon, but was attacked by four hostile aircraft. He succeeded in destroying one of these machines.

Flight Sub-Lieuts. Thornely and Simpson, Naval Squadron No. 8, each drove down a hostile machine, apparently out of control.

Machines of No. 6 Squadron drove down a German aeroplane out of control, and a patrol of No. 1 Squadron drove down a hostile machine in a badly-damaged condition.

Lieutenants Price and Benjamin, No. 48 Squadron, attacked and drove down a two-seater machine, which crashed in the River Scarpe, near Vitry.

Lieutenant Bishop, No. 60 Squadron, attacked a balloon, into which he fired 60 rounds. The balloon was seen to emit a great deal of smoke.

On the 26th, bombing machines of No. 20 Squadron destroyed one hostile machine, and a second was driven down out of control by Lieutenant Hay and A. M. T. Allum.

Captain Hudson and Second Lieutenant Charley, No. 54 Squadron, each drove down a hostile machine out of control, and Lieutenant Rome, of the same squadron, drove one down which is also believed to have fallen out of control.

A hostile machine was driven down out of control by each of the following pilots:—Captain Patrick, Second Lieutenant Keller, Second Lieutenant Stead, and Sergeant T. Evans, all of No. 23 Squadron.

Flight Sub-Lieut Casey, Naval Squadron No. 3, drove down a machine in a spinning nose-dive after being closely engaged.

Flight Sub-Lieut. Malone, Naval Squadron No. 3, attacked a hostile machine near Cambrai. Three other H.A. joined in the engagement, which took place at a height of 7,000 feet. Flight Sub-Lieut. Malone followed one machine down to 3,000 feet, firing at it, and was in turn followed by the three H.A. Eventually the first machine attacked was destroyed. When at a height of 1,000 feet, Flight Sub-Lieut. Malone turned west, but finding it impossible to evade the attacking machines, he pretended to land. As soon as his wheels touched the ground, he saw that the hostile machines were also just about to land, and at once put on his engine and flew off, and, although he was pursued by the three machines, they were unable to overtake him, and were driven east by heavy fire from our trenches.

Bombing.—First Brigade.—Twenty-nine 20-lb. bombs were dropped on places of importance. A fire was caused in Oppy, and houses were destroyed in Avion.

Second Brigade.—Twenty 112-lb. bombs were dropped on Rumbeke aerodrome, but no especial results were observed.

Third Brigade.—On the night of the 26th/27th, machines of No. 100 Squadron dropped 48 20-lb. bombs on trains and transport. Two trains were wrecked and derailed, and two M.T. convoys hit.

Fourth Brigade.—Twenty-four 20-lb. bombs were dropped on Estrees on the night of 26th/27th. Twenty-four 20-lb. and 10 112-lb. bombs were dropped on Bohain Station.

April 28th.

Reconnaissances.—Reconnaissances were carried out by the First, Second, Third, and Fourth Brigades.

Successful contact patrols were carried out by machines of the First and Third Brigades.

Captain Meintjes and Lieutenants Hoidge and Manville, No. 56 Squadron, went down to 500 feet and fired at German infantry between Vitry and Sailly.

Second Lieutenants Davies and Barny, both of No. 32 Squadron, and Captain Taylor, No. 23 Squadron, each went down to a very low altitude and attacked troops and other objectives with machine-gun fire.

Captain Crowe, Lieutenant Barlow, and Second Lieutenant Kay, of No. 56 Squadron, after escorting Sopwiths back to the line, returned to Douai and patrolled over the aerodrome at 3,500 feet.

Artillery Co-operation.—Thirty-three targets were dealt with by artillery with aeroplane observation, and eight with observation by balloons.

Artillery of the First Army successfully engaged two hostile batteries and destroyed two houses in the hostile battery positions.

Artillery of the Third Army successfully engaged six hostile batteries and caused an explosion of ammunition.

Enemy troops were engaged by artillery of the Fourth Army under zone call.

Artillery of the Fifth Army successfully engaged six hostile batteries and obtained five direct hits on gun-pits and caused an explosion of ammunition. Wire and trenches were also considerably damaged.

Hostile Aircraft.—Lieutenant Ellis, No. 40 Squadron, engaged a two-seater Aviatik from underneath. The hostile machine fell over and went down completely out of control.

Second Lieutenant Kennedy and Captain Le Royer, No. 11 Squadron, on the evening of the 27th, engaged and drove down a hostile machine in flames, while they destroyed a second south-west of Vitry, and drove down another apparently out of control.

Captain Ball, No. 56 Squadron, on an S.E. 5, drove down a hostile machine near Noyelles. He then attacked and destroyed an Albatross two-seater west of Cambrai. After this he waited above the clouds for any hostile machine or machines that might come up. Finally, he saw a two-seater Albatross, which he promptly pursued. The hostile machine put its nose down and fled. When at about 500 feet from the ground Captain Ball's machine was hit by anti-aircraft, and the controls, with the exception of a thread on the left elevator, were all shot away, and the fuselage was very severely damaged. The machine got into a spin, but the pilot cleverly pulled it out again and returned to the aerodrome, where he made a perfect landing.

Bombing.—1st Brigade.—Ten 20-lb. bombs were dropped on Henin-Liètard and two 112-lb. bombs on Lorgies. Houses in Lorgies were hit and badly damaged, and a large shed in Henin-Liètard was completely destroyed. Bombs were dropped on other places of military importance, and houses in Lens were hit.

5th Brigade.—Twelve 20-lb. bombs were dropped on Hendicourt and two on Quéant. A number of bombs were dropped on other places of military importance during the day.

No. 27 Squadron dropped five 230-lb. bombs from 6,500 feet on Busigny Station.

A dump at Bohain railway station was attacked by No. 55 Squadron. Eight 112-lb. bombs were dropped, but results were difficult to observe owing to a thick haze.

Information has been received that very serious damage was done at Ath on the 6th instant by the bombs dropped by machines of No. 27 Squadron.

S. WOOD, Captain,
Staff Officer.

Headquarters, Royal Flying Corps,
29th April 1917.

No. 33.

CONFIDENTIAL.

ROYAL NAVAL AIR SERVICE.

OPERATIONS REPORT

(with Royal Flying Corps Reports attached).

1st to 16th MAY 1917.

NAVAL STAFF,
  OPERATIONS DIVISION.
  16th May 1917.

ROYAL NAVAL AIR SERVICE.

REPORT OF OPERATIONS

(Completed from Reports during period
1st to 16th May 1917).

CONTENTS.

	PAGE
HOME STATIONS	2
DUNKIRK	4
ROYAL NAVAL AIR SERVICE SQUADRONS WITH ROYAL FLYING CORPS	11
EASTERN MEDITERRANEAN STATION	12
EAST INDIES AND EGYPT SEAPLANE STATION	19
ROYAL FLYING CORPS COMMUNIQUÉS	21

HOME STATIONS.

SUBMARINE PATROL AND ATTACKS.

May 1st.

Dover.—The French authorities at Boulogne report that Seaplanes B 3 and B 4 observed two enemy submarines about 25 miles west of Berck.

An attack was made on one of the submarines, four bombs being dropped, two of which fell about 10 yards from the superstructure of the submarine.

Results are uncertain, but some damage is thought to have been caused.

May 15th.

Calshot.—A special seaplane patrol was carried out over the Portland to Start Point area to search for an enemy submarine which had been reported in the vicinity.

The submarine was sighted, and getting into position the seaplane dropped one 65-lb. bomb over the spot where the submarine had submerged.

The seaplane circled over the area for some time, but no results were observed.

SEAPLANE ATTACK ON ZEPPELIN L 22.

May 14th.

Great Yarmouth.—Large America Type H 12, No. 8666, left Yarmouth at 3.30 a.m. G.M.T. to carry out a W/T reconnaissance patrol to Terschelling Light Vessel. She was armed with three Lewis guns with Brock, Pomeroy, and Buckingham ammunition and four 100-lb. bombs.

At 4.15 a.m., and when 80 miles from Yarmouth, W/T communication was suspended to avoid discovery. At 4.48 a.m. a Zeppelin was sighted dead ahead between 10 and 15 miles away and end on. The seaplane was then cruising at 60 knots at 5,000 feet, and two minutes later the Terschelling Light Vessel on the port hand was passed. Speed was increased to 65 knots and height to 6,000 feet. The Zeppelin appeared to be at about 3,000 feet. Three bombs were dropped to lighten ship at 5 a.m. and preparations were made to attack, Flight Sub-Lieut. Leckie taking the wheel.

Flight Lieutenant C. J. Galpin, R.N., went forward to the two Lewis guns mounted in parallel to the bow, whilst C.P.O. Whatling went aft to the rear gun. The Zeppelin turned north and then north-east exposing her broadside. The machine was then about 2 miles astern of the Zeppelin, so speed was increased to 75 knots, descending to 5,000 feet.

Owing to a background of dark fog and clouds the enemy seemed unaware of the presence of the seaplane until within half a mile of her, when she put her nose up and seemed to increase speed. The seaplane dived at her at 90 knots, coming up slightly astern at 3,800 feet, where it levelled out to 75 knots, overhauling the Zeppelin on her starboard quarter about 20 feet below the level of the gondolas. Fire was opened with both Lewis guns forward at 50 yards range, and incendiary bullets were observed entering her envelope on the starboard quarter slightly below the middle. After a few rounds the port gun jammed, but the starboard gun fired nearly a complete tray before jamming also. The Zeppelin was then 100 feet away, and the seaplane was turned to starboard whilst an effort was made to clear the starboard gun. As the machine turned, a light was observed glowing inside the Zeppelin envelope, and 15 seconds later when she came in sight on the other side of the seaplane she was hanging tail down at an angle of 45° with the lower half of her envelope thoroughly alight. Five or six seconds later the whole ship was a flaming mass, and she fell vertically by the tail.

C.P.O. Whatling, observing from the after hatch, saw the number L 22 painted under the nose before it was consumed. He also saw two of the crew jump out, but they had no parachutes.

When the airship had fallen to about 1,000 feet four large columns of water were seen to rise from the sea in quick succession either from bombs or engines becoming detached from the framework. After 45 seconds from first ignition the envelope was burnt off, and the bare skeleton plunged into the sea leaving a mass of black ash on the surface from which a column of brown smoke about 1,500 feet high sprang up.

The action took place at 5.15 a.m. in longitude 4° 35″ E., latitude 53° 25″ N., 18 miles N.N.W. of the north end of Texel Island.

It was evident that the seaplanes had 20 to 25 knots greater speed than the Zeppelin, though during the whole attack the seaplane engines were not opened right out. The Zeppelin's speed was certainly never more than 50 knots. The enemy appears to have attempted to return the fire, as a bullet hole was found in the left upper plane and another in hull amidship of the seaplane.

Flight Lieutenant C. J. Galpin, R.N., reported that the success of the attack was due to the good judgment and skill of Flight Sub-Lieut. Leckie, and that C.P.O. Whatling and A. M. Laycock both showed considerable coolness and promptitude in attending to their duties during this action.

Names of Crew.—Flight Lieut. Galpin, R.N.; Flight Sub-Lieut. Leckie; C.P.O. V. F. Whatling, W/T observer; A.M. J. R. Laycock.

ATTACK ON SHIPPING BY ENEMY TORPEDO-CARRYING SEAPLANES.

April 19th.

Ramsgate.—Six hostile seaplanes, three of them torpedo-carrying machines, and the others, apparently acting as escorts, carried out a raid in broad daylight on shipping in the vicinity of Ramsgate. As far as could be judged they were operating in pairs.

The North Goodwin Drifter Division was first attacked at 6.38 a.m. by six machines. One torpedo was dropped. The seaplanes went off in a westerly direction; one returned and renewed the attack but was driven off.

Four of the machines were seen by an armed trawler off the North Brake Buoy at 6.40 a.m. flying very low. One attacked the s.s. "Nyanza" at 6.45, dropping one torpedo. Two machines appeared off Ramsgate, circled round the Marshal Ney, and discharged one torpedo, which, entering Ramsgate Harbour, became embedded in the mud. No bombs were dropped.

May 1st.

Yarmouth.—An attack was made by two enemy seaplanes on the steamer "Gena" 7 miles east of Lowestoft at 5.45 a.m. G.M.T. The "Gena" was sunk by a torpedo dropped from one of the hostile machines. The ship's crew were all saved.

Estimates as to the height from which the machines released their torpedoes vary between 30 and 150 feet.

NOTE.—The method of attack was similar to that carried out by hostile aircraft on shipping off Ramsgate during the previous fortnight, the machines choosing their objectives, then circling round it at a very low altitude, and releasing a torpedo when the target appeared to them to be in the most favourable position.

DUNKIRK.

General Remarks. — Reconnaissance flights and fighter patrols have been carried out almost daily and many combats in the air have taken place in which a number of hostile machines have been destroyed and many driven down out of control.

Bomb attacks on enemy bases and shipping have been frequent and several tons of bombs have been dropped.

PHOTOGRAPHIC RECONNAISSANCES.

Photographic reconnaissances have been carried out almost daily and a number of excellent photographs obtained.

RESULT OF RECONNAISSANCE PATROL.

May 10th.

Seaplanes.—A special reconnaissance patrol to Zeebrugge and Thornton Ridge was carried out by two Short seaplanes, accompanied by two Sopwith Fighter seaplanes, and the following observations were made. Minelayers were sighted 3 miles north-west of Mole, one large ship was seen between Blankenburghe and Zeebrugge, 3 miles west of Zeebrugge, and five destroyers were observed off end of Mole.

OFFENSIVE PATROL—ENGAGEMENT WITH ENEMY.

May 1st.

Squadron No. 10 (Detached).—An offensive patrol by three Sopwith triplanes was carried out over Nieuport, Ostend, Thourout, and Dixmude. In the vicinity of Courtemarck Flight Sub-Lieut. Collishaw was attacked by an Albatross Scout at 10,000 feet. After manœuvring down to 9,000 feet the Sopwith got into a favourable position and opened fire. The enemy machine immediately went down out of control and commenced to spin. It was observed some thousand feet below to stall and again go into a spin, which continued until it struck the ground almost at the railway junction east of Courtemarck.

May 2nd.

No. 4 Wing (No. 4 Squadron).—Three Sopwith machines carried out an offensive patrol to Ostend, and on the return journey sighted an enemy machine which was attacked and brought down at Rosendaal. The observer was shot, and his body picked up 4 miles from where the machine crashed.

ESCORT TO PHOTOGRAPHIC RECONNAISSANCE.

May 3rd.

No. 1 Wing (No. 9 Squadron).—During a photographic reconnaissance escorted by three machines very heavy and accurate A.A. gunfire was experienced, the machines being hit in several places by splinters.

OFFENSIVE PATROL—ENGAGEMENT WITH ENEMY.

May 6th.

Squadron No. 10 (Detached).—During an offensive patrol, Flight Sub-Lieut. Epstein, in a Sopwith triplane, having lost the formation in the vicinity of Zarran, observed a hostile formation to the south, consisting of nine machines of the Halberstadt Scout type, flying at 19,000 feet. The Sopwith pilot manœuvred into a position between the enemy formation and the sun, then followed them for some distance south, when they dispersed formation, whereupon he attacked the rear machine of their right wing firing 75 to 100 rounds. Tracers were observed to enter the petrol tank, which exploded. The enemy machine turned over and commenced dropping erratically to the ground in flames. At this point the Sopwith was attacked by three other machines of the formation from above, and to avoid their fire the pilot side-looped for some minutes and eventually climbed away returning safely to the aerodrome.

May 9th.

No. 4 Wing (No. 4 Squadron).—Whilst patrolling in the vicinity of Ghistelles, Flight Lieutenant Shook, in a Sopwith Scout, observed a large two-seater Aviatik approaching, apparently spotting, The Sopwith dived on the enemy machine, opening fire, and was also joined by another Sopwith, which also opened fire, all three machines diving together. The enemy machine went into a spin and crashed in a field near Ghistelles. The crash was plainly visible owing to the floods.

A hostile kite balloon south of Ostend was also attacked and brought down.

May 11th.

No. 4 Wing (No. 4 Squadron).—An offensive patrol in formation was carried out by seven Sopwith machines between the fleet and the coast. The formation was attacked by an enemy formation of about 15 machines which were about 20,000 feet over Holland, apparently waiting for allied machines. This formation was in such a position with the sun behind it that it was very difficult to see them until they dived into our formation.

A number of combats took place in which three enemy machines were destroyed, many others driven down out of control, and probably another three destroyed. Our formation was split up during the fighting, and pilots were most of the time fighting against greater numbers. The Germans seem to be employing as fighters single-seater machines carrying two guns. They were faster than Sopwith Scouts and about the same climb. All machines returned safely, one being badly damaged by machine gun fire.

May 12th.

No. 4 Wing (No. 4 Squadron).—During an offensive patrol, in which a number of hostile aircraft were encountered, a Sopwith Scout sighted a single-seater enemy machine about 530 feet below and 5 miles to sea, east of Zeebrugge. The Sopwith dived on the enemy machine from behind, firing about 30 rounds, during which several tracers were observed to enter his fuselage. The enemy machine then side-slipped, going down completely out of control. This is confirmed by another pilot who saw the machine crash into the sea.

ENGAGEMENT WITH ENEMY.

May 12th.

No. 1 Wing (No. 9 Squadron).—An escort machine whilst accompanying W/T machines to Zeebrugge, was joined by three other machines (probably No. 4 Squadron), and off Zeebrugge they were attacked by four enemy machines, consisting of two two-seaters, one seaplane and one fighter. A general engagement took place lasting about 10 minutes, during which the enemy were driven down from 14,000 feet to 9,000 feet, when they made off inland. The same machine on the return journey encountered a two-seater seaplane, which was attacked. About 20 rounds were fired at close range, but the enemy did not reply, and when last seen was diving nearly vertically for Ostend. Flight Sub.-Lieut. Mott encountered a Halberstadt, and got in about 40 rounds at close range. The enemy machine descended in an almost vertical dive. A few minutes later the same pilot sighted and attacked a large two-seater aeroplane. He fired 50 rounds from very close range and saw tracers hitting it near the pilot's seat. The enemy machine fell completely out of control. Flight Sub-Lieut. Mott was unable to follow the machine down and make certain of its destruction as he was attacked by five other German aeroplanes. A running fight ensued, lasting 10 or 15 minutes, during which time the pilot got in about 50 shots, after which the enemy machines made off.

BOMB ATTACKS.

(Carried out during the Period between the two Dates given.)

Ostend (hostile shipping)	May 1st -	326 lbs.	Aeroplanes.
Ostend (hostile shipping)	May 2nd -	1,048 lbs.	Aeroplanes.
Ostend Seaplane Base	May 1st—2nd -	1,755 lbs.	Seaplanes.
Ostend Seaplane Base	May 3rd—4th -	3,632 lbs.	Aeroplanes.
Ostend Seaplane Base	May 9th—10th	2,240 lbs.	Seaplanes.
Bruges Docks (and shipping).	May 1st—2nd -	648 lbs.	Aeroplanes.
Bruges Docks -	May 6th—7th -	1,962 lbs.	Aeroplanes.
Bruges Docks -	May 9th—10th	6,322 lbs.	Aeroplanes.
Zeebrugge (hostile shipping).	May 1st -	305 lbs.	Aeroplanes.
Zeebrugge Mole	May 9th—10th	614 lbs.	Aeroplanes.

BOMB ATTACK ON HOSTILE SHIPP NG.

May 1st.

No. 5 Wing (No. 7 Squadron).—A bomb attack was carried out by aeroplanes during the afternoon on hostile shipping off Ostend and alongside Zeebrugge Mole. Four 65-lb. and three Le Pecq bombs were dropped at Ostend and three 65-lb. and five Le Pecq bombs at Zeebrugge Mole. Details of results are not given.

May 1st–2nd.

No. 5 Wing (No. 7 Squadron).—A night attack was carried out on the shipping and docks at Bruges. Four 112-lb. and two 100-lb. bombs were dropped. Good shooting was made and many explosions were observed on the Docks.

BOMB ATTACK ON SEAPLANE BASE.

May 1st–2nd.

Seaplanes.—A bomb attack on Ostend Seaplane Base was carried out by three Short Seaplanes during the night. Twenty-seven 65-lb. bombs were dropped. Visibility was not good, but the bombs were observed to fall over the objective. Considerable and accurate A.A. fire was experienced, which resulted in one machine being hit. All machines returned safely.

BOMB ATTACK ON HOSTILE SHIPPING.

May 2nd.

No. 5 Wing (No. 5 Squadron).—A bomb attack was carried out during the afternoon on hostile shipping entering Ostend. Eight 65-lb. and 24 Le Pecq bombs were dropped. No direct hits on vessels were observed, but one of the "overs" was seen to start a fire on the quay.

BOMB ATTACK ON SEAPLANE BASE.

May 3rd–4th.

No. 5 Wing (No. 5 Squadron).—A bomb attack was carried out during the night on the Seaplane Base at Ostend. Sixteen 112-lb., eight 100-lb., and 16—65-lb. bombs were dropped. All pilots found the objective easily, visibility being good. Shooting appears to have been extremely good, three direct hits being observed and two fires started in one of the sheds. A.A. fire was very active, but not accurate. All machines returned safely.

BOMB ATTACK ON BRUGES DOCKS.

May 6th–7th.

No. 5 Wing (No. 5 Squadron).—A bomb attack was carried out by nine Sopwith machines on Bruges Docks during the morning. Eighteen 65-lb. and 36 Le Pecq bombs were dropped in heights varying from 3,000 to 7,500 feet Visibility was fair, and a number of bombs were observed to explode on the targets. A large explosion was seen, followed by a series of blue flashes, similar to electrical short circuit; also a group of bombs were observed to burst on the submarine assembling shops. A.A. gunfire was heavy, and searchlights were active round the objective. Two machines stood off until the main attack had taken place in order to bomb any destroyers which might be observed in the canal. As none were seen they attacked the docks, and one group of bombs appeared to have made direct hits on the power-station close to submarine assembling shops.

Pilots report seeing a very bright light at about 8,000 feet near Zeebrugge, which burnt for several minutes, and another over east of Bruges at about 6,000 feet. The anti-aircraft defences at this place seem to have been considerably increased, and the hottest fire was reported by all pilots.

NOTE.—The A.A. gun-fire appears to have been the most intense yet experienced. The large flares observed in the sky near Zeebrugge and Bruges are of interest, and were presumably an attempt to illuminate the sky so as to render the machines visible to the gunners.

It is indicative of the difficulties of the defence that the time chosen for their use was so late that only one machine remained to be attacked.

BOMB ATTACKS.

May 9th–10th.

No. 5 Wing (Nos. 5 and 7 Squadrons).—Four Short Bombers and four Handley Page machines carried out a bomb attack during the night on Bruges Dock and Zeebrugge Mole. Eighteen 65-lb. and 46—112-lb. bombs were dropped on Bruges Docks, and two 112-lb. and six 65-lb. bombs were dropped on Zeebrugge Mole. Of the latter two exploded close to the Seaplane Shed, and the remainder in the vicinity of the Mole. The visibility was not good, and A.A. gun-fire and searchlights were extremely active which rendered observation difficult and the shooting appears to have been good. This is the first occasion on which Handley-Page machines have been used for night work at Dunkirk. All machines returned safely.

May 9th–10th.

Seaplanes.—A bombing raid on Ostend Seaplane Station was carried out by four Short Bomber Seaplanes during which 26—65-lb. bombs and one 550-lb. bomb were dropped. Results could not be ascertained owing to the extremely poor visibility.

ATTACK ON SUBMARINE.

May 7th.

No. 1 Wing (No. 9 Squadron).—During a search for hostile aircraft by six Sopwith Scouts between Dunkirk–Ostend and Gravelines–Deal, Flight Commander Hervey sighted a submarine about 15 miles off the coast in the vicinity of Ostend. He dived down to 400 feet and fired at it from both quarters, getting in about 50 rounds in each attack. Tracers were observed to hit the conning tower. The submarine then submerged.

KITE BALLOON OBSERVATION.

No. 11 Kite Balloon Section.—Ascents were made on five days, the total hours flown being 10 hours 31 minutes.

NAVAL SQUADRONS WITH THE ROYAL FLYING CORPS.

May 5th to the 19th, 1917.

Extracted from the Report of the Officer Commanding, Royal Flying Corps in France.

NAVAL SQUADRON No. 1.

This squadron has been attached to the 3rd Brigade R.F.C. during this period and has carried out 47 offensive patrols and escorts to reconnaissances.

During the fortnight 128 hostile machines were engaged, one of these was brought down and 10 driven down completely out of control, while several others were driven down apparently damaged.

Casualties.—Flight Sub-Lieut. O. B. Ellis. Flight Sub-Lieut. G. G. Bowman. Missing, 19th May.

NAVAL SQUADRON No. 3.

This squadron is attached to the 5th Brigade and has been used for offensive patrols and escorts to bombing and photographic machines.

Very little fighting has taken place, owing to the decrease in hostile aerial activity. Two hostile machines were driven down completely out of control, one of which went down in a spinning nose dive enveloped in black smoke. Several other combats took place, but were not decisive.

NAVAL SQUADRON No. 6.

This squadron has been attached to the 4th Brigade, R.F.C., and has been used for offensive and line patrols and escorts to photographic and bombing machines.

There have been four combats, in one of which a hostile machine was driven down out of control.

Casualties.—Flight Sub-Lieut. O. J. Gagnier, wounded on 11th May.

NAVAL SQUADRON No. 8.

This squadron has been attached to the 1st Brigade, R.F.C., and has been used for offensive patrols.

Thirty-five combats have taken place, in which one hostile machine was destroyed and five driven down completely out of control.

Casualties.—Flight Sub-Lieut L. E. B. Wimbush, wounded on the 9th May. Flight Sub-Lieut. E. D. Crundall, wounded on the 10th May.

(No further information available.)

EASTERN MEDITERRANEAN STATION.

MUDROS, MAY 4TH, 1917.

Compiled from Weekly Reports Nos. 59 and 60 dating from April 28th to May 11th.

Weather.—The weather conditions during the period under review have been generally good. The usual reconnaissances and patrols have been carried out.

The camp at Thasos is in process of being moved, and in order to get this done as quickly as possible no more operations than appear of immediate importance are being undertaken.

THASOS AIR STATION.

"A" SQUADRON.

April 28th.

A Reconnaissance was made of the Pravi-Kavalla area. A good deal of motor traffic was observed, but not sufficient to indicate any abnormal activity.

April 28th.

Bomb Attack.—A Henri Farman escorted by a Bristol Scout bombed an enemy battery to the west of Kavalla.

April 30th.

A Reconnaissance of the Gereviz seaplane base area was carried out, and the existence of another large shed and a further portable shed were observed.

Night Bomb Attack on Gereviz Seaplane Base.—Two Henri Farmans, Nos. N. 3017 and N. 3010, attacked the seaplane base at Gereviz from heights of 1,200 feet and 1,400 feet respectively. Ten A.A. guns with machine guns put up a barrage of fire over the sheds, hitting both machines. The radiator of

Flight Sub-Lieut. Aird's machine was hit, and his engine consequently failed over Thaso Poulo, in spite of which a successful landing was made.

May 1st.

Photographic Reconnaissance.—A coastal photographic reconnaissance was made as far as Lake Boru. A reconnaissance was also made of the Xanthi-Sarishaben and Kavalla area.

May 3rd–4th.

Reconnaissance.—During the night a number of coloured rockets were seen from Thasos aerodrome and Limena on the mainland coast between Kavalla and Leftera Bay. A Schneider seaplane with bombs was sent to reconnoitre. The rockets ceased before the seaplane was near the Greek coast, and by the time she was over Kavalla all lights in and around the town were extinguished. The coast was patrolled as far as Leftera Bay but nothing unusual could be seen, and so on the return journey the bombs were dropped on Kavalla forts.

About six months ago deserters gave the information that a system of coloured rocket signals had been devised for use in the event of an attempted landing by the Allies, and it is possible that the system was being tested.

May 4th.

Hostile Seaplane Bomb Attack on Monitor.—Information having been received that Monitor 20 was being bombed by two seaplanes off the coast of Thasos at 8.15 a.m. a Bristol Scout and a Schneider seaplane were sent to engage the enemy. By the time the machines reached M. 20 the enemy machines had disappeared and could not be picked up again. M. 20 was escorted until she was within 10 miles of Limenaria.

May 10th.

A Spotting Flight was undertaken for a monitor firing at a gun emplacement which has been erected at Karacol.

Patrols for mines and submarines in the vicinity of Thasos were also carried out.

STAVROS AIR STATION.

"D" Squadron.

Reconnaissance Flights have been made on the enemy Neohori and Lower Struma front almost daily. During these reconnaissances much detailed information relating to gun positions, new trench systems, camps, dumps, transport, and movement of troops were obtained, and photographs of positions where important changes were observed were taken.

April 29th.

A Reconnaissance was made to examine gun positions, and to report whether emplacements were occupied, and much useful information was gained.

May 1st.

A Reconnaissance of the Angista–Pravi area was made. It was observed, amongst other things, that there are now four large white hangars and four small ones on Drama Aerodrome, which, coupled with the information since received from French Intelligence that 17 German officer pilots had recently left Berlin for Drama, indicates that serious opposition in the air on this front is to be expected in the near future.

A reconnaissance of the enemy line on the Neohori front with photographs of battery positions was made later in the day.

May 6th.

A Spotting Flight was carried out for the military.

DETACHED SQUADRONS WITH R.F.C.

"E" SQUADRON AT HADJI JANOS.

April 22nd.

Enemy Raid.—An enemy bombing formation of 14 machines bombed the advance bivouacs on the front of the 12th Corps. The composite squadron of R.F.C. and "E" Squadron, R.N.A.S., attacked and dispersed the enemy formation. A number of engagements took place, the enemy machines being driven off in each case.

During this encounter, whilst attacking two enemy machines simultaneously, L.M. A. Carder was painfully wounded, but continued to serve his gun, firing two complete trays of ammunition into the enemy after being shot.

April 26th.

Bomb Attack.—Engagement with enemy. After successfully escorting an R.F.C. bombing squadron to bomb Cerniste dump in the morning, four R.N.A.S. and one R.F.C. machines again escorted an R.F.C. squadron in the afternoon to bomb Bogdanzi dump, When over the front line they encountered an enemy bombing formation of 16 machines, and a large number of combats took place. The enemy formation was broken up and dispersed, thus leaving the R.F.C. bombers to drop their bombs without interference.

One of the enemy twin-engined Friedrichshafener machines was driven down in flames near the edge of Doiran, the bulk of the machine falling in the enemy's lines, but the rudder fell in the British lines.

The fighting was of such a mixed character that it is not clear from the reports yet received as to who is entitled to the credit of having brought the machine down.

April 28th.

Enemy Raid.—A hostile formation of six twin-engined bombing machines, escorted by two Halberstadt Scouts appeared, and "E" Squadron left the aerodrome to engage them.

Flight Sub-Lieut. E. P. Hicks with Acting A.M. 1 Albert Edward King as gunner in Sopwith N. 5099, had a running fight with four twin-engined machines. He successively got into position 150 yards below the first two, and a drum of Lewis ammunition was fired into each. Then, climbing slowly, he got into position 30 yards below a third machine and gave it a complete drum. The fourth machine was attacked from a similar position, two drums of ammunition being fired into it. No detailed information has yet been received of operations undertaken by "E" Squadron after April 28th, but signalled reports indicate that on April 29th five flights were made, but no combats took place.

May 2nd.

Casualties.—When flying at 5,000 feet the wings of Sopwith No. 9748 folded up and the machine fell, killing both pilot and observer.

As the result of an investigation there appears no doubt that the machine was subjected to heavy A.A. fire and had been badly damaged. The pilot appeared to be aware of this, and was using the utmost care in coming down over the aerodrome, but as soon as he put the machine's nose down the wings folded up. So far as could be ascertained, there had been no defect in the construction nor in the condition of the machine; the accident was solely attributed to injury caused by gun fire.

Pilot—Flight Sub-Lieut. Holbroke L. Gaskell, killed.

Observer—2nd Lieutenant J. Watts, Royal Scots and R.F.C., killed.

May 6th–7th.

Bomb Attacks.—On the above dates "E" Squadron escorted "F" Squadron on their bombing expedition to Dedela and Paljorca respectively. On the first occasion no enemy aircraft were encountered, but on the second, one combat took place, of which, however, no details are yet available.

NOTE.—In spite of provocation, through "F" Squadron carrying out a number of effective bombing raids, and notwithstanding the greatly increased activity of all arms of the Allied forces on the Macedonian front, enemy aircraft have displayed singularly little activity during the latter part of the period, either in bombing or in defence, and what they have done has been at a considerable distance from the present sphere of "E" Squadron's work, that is, on the Serbian and French fronts around Monastir. "E" Squadron have, therefore, only been able to bring the enemy to action once during the week, and it seems as if the enemy had either suffered more severely in the actions of the preceding weeks than at first seemed likely, or they are waiting for reinforcements to enable them to accept action with a still greater superiority of numbers on their side.

"F" SQUADRON AT AMBERSKOJ.

Bomb Attacks.—This bombing squadron flew from Stavros, arriving at Amberkoj on April 29th, and on the 30th dropped 1,300 lbs. of bombs on an important dump store to the east of Bogdanci where A.A. fire was experienced. Eight bombs fell on stores and tents, while eight others fell in the dump enveloping it in flames. The five bombing machines were escorted by three fighters which formed part of the squadron.

May 1st.

Bomb Attack.—A raid was carried out in the early morning on Cestovo Dumps 1,210 lbs. of bombs being dropped. The majority fell among the sheds, stacks of stores and huts, doing considerable damage. In the afternoon a second expedition was made to Bogdanci Dumps, where 1,445 lbs. of bombs were dropped from 8,000 feet. Owing to the extremely hazy conditions at the time results could not be ascertained definitely, but a cloud of black smoke seen over the dumps indicated that the bombs had hit their targets.

May 3rd.

Bomb Attack.—A further attack was carried out on the Cestovo Dump, 1,445 lbs. of bombs being dropped, the majority of which burst in the south-east corner of the dump. One large shed was also seen to be damaged.

The composite fighting squadron escorted "F" squadron to the lines where they waited and formed a screen for the bombing flight on their return journey.

In the afternoon Cestovo was again visited, and a further 1,445 lbs. of bombs were dropped. Again haze prevented the estimation of results, but bombs were seen to explode in the dump.

May 6th.

Bomb Attack.—During the morning two raids were made on the enemy dumps near Dedeli, which is an important military depot eight miles north-west of Doiran on the main Doiran-Hudovo road. On each occasion 1,500 lbs. of bombs were dropped, direct hits being obtained on two large sheds, while two other sheds were badly damaged by heavy bombs dropping within twenty-five yards of them. Four bombs burst among the tents, and considerable damage was observed to have been inflicted on the stores and material.

May 7th.

Bomb Attack.—Two successful raids were carried out on bivouacs, transport, dug-outs, &c. near the enemy lines at Paljorca, four miles west of Doiran, 1,300 lbs. of bombs being dropped on each occasion.

May 8th–9th.

Bomb Attack.—Two further raids were made on similar targets close behind the enemy lines, and $1\frac{1}{2}$ tons of explosives were dropped.

May 10th.

Bomb Attacks.—A bomb attack was carried out on the main enemy aerodrome at Hudovo, 1,500 lbs. of bombs being dropped, several exploding close to the sheds. The special tents erected for the German bombing formation were found to have been removed, and their new position has not yet been located.

During their short visit to the Doiran front "F" Squadron has dropped nearly $7\frac{1}{2}$ tons of bombs on enemy camps, store and ammunition dumps, &c., five bombing machines taking part in each raid.

IMBROS AIR STATION.

"C" Squadron.

Result of Reconnaissances.—With the exception of the 27th of April the patrol of the Dardanelles has been carried out daily. Ships of between 2,000 and 3,000 tons were observed on several occasions in Kilia, Liman, Akbashi Liman, and off Chanak, but never more than three such ships in the Straits at the time.

April 29th.

Result of Reconnaissance.—A reconnaissance was made of the Gallipoli coast, and the position of the gun which shelled Kephalo on April 15th, and which was located on the 25th April, was verified.

May 5th.

Result of Reconnaissance.—Reconnaissance patrols of the Dardanelles on the above date, and the following day reported the usual small shipping. One T.B.D. was observed in the Narrows at anchor on both days.

May 7th.

Result of Reconnaissance.—During the morning reconnaissance machines again sighted a T.B D. in the Narrows. On the return journey three submarines were observed on the surface about one mile off Gully Beach steering S.S.W., and being escorted by two seaplanes. A Henri Farman escorted by a Nieuport was immediately sent to bomb the submarines, but on arrival over Gallipoli no trace of the submarines or seaplanes could be found. It is thought probable that the submarines were being escorted down the coast through the mine fields, preparatory to entering the Dardanelles.

May 8th.

Reconnaissance.—An aeroplane was sent to the Dardanelles on a reconnaissance flight, but nothing was observed owing to the Straits being enveloped in mist.

May 10th.

In order to carry out Vice-Admiral's orders of May 6th two Nieuport aeroplanes were prepared for the reconnaissance of the Dedeagatch coast to search for gun positions, and two seaplanes were flown from Mudros to Imbros on May 10th to carry out a reconnaissance of that area for mines. It was arranged that the two reconnaissances should take place together so that aeroplanes and seaplanes could afford protection to one another.

So far the weather has prove unsuitable for carrying out these reconnaissances, and the seaplanes remained temporarily at Imbros to seize the first opportunity.

THERMI AIR STATION.

"B" Squadron.

Very little flying has been undertaken during this period. On May 2nd a flight was made for the purpose of escorting a transport leaving Port Iero.

May 4th.

A patrol of two aeroplanes was carried out to the south of Mitylene, preparatory to two transports and their escorts putting to sea, and these were subsequently escorted until dusk.

A flight was also made in a Henri Farman for the purpose of tuning M. 22's W/T, but heavy rain began to fall and put and end to the flight before the operation had been completed.

The only other service flying which has been done during the week was on the 9th when two machines escorted a transport from Port Iero as far as Chios, one machine landing at Chios Aerodrome and remaining there for the time.

SUDA BAY SEAPLANE STATION.

The entrance to Suda Bay from Cape Drepano to Cape Tripiti has been patrolled daily during the week. On the 5th May seaplane No. 9759 was wrecked, the pilot being slightly injured. The engine was salved, but no further details as to the cause of the accident has yet been received.

EAST INDIES AND EGYPT SEAPLANE STATION.

(Extract of Report from Naval Commander-in-Chief, May 15th.)

H.M.S. "Empress."

On the report that an enemy submarine might be expected in Beirut Harbour between the 9th and 14th of May, seaplane carrier H.M.S. "Empress," escorted by two French destroyers, was despatched from Port Said with orders to attack the harbour at daylight on the 13th.

The attack took place at 5.30 a.m., and one 500 lb. and four 65 lb. bombs were dropped on the harbour. No submarine was observed, but it is thought that a store on the pier was demolished. Orders that no bombs were to be dropped on the town were adhered to.

INDIA AND CEYLON.

H.M.S. "Raven II."

May 9th.

Seaplane carrier H.M.S. "Raven II." escorted by a cruiser left for Maldive Islands to search for a missing seaplane which was reported to be practically intact at Nilandu Island in the Maldives. There are no particulars given as to whether the machine was recovered,

Lieutenant Meade, R.N.V.R., and Flight Sub-Lieut Smith, who were believed to have been drowned on April 21st, have arrived safely at Colombo. Further details of the adventures of these two officers have not yet been received.

"Raven II." with the Short seaplanes is returning to Egypt, and she will sail in the first available convoy from Bombay.

Two Sopwith seaplanes will be left at Colomba with the necessary personnel, so that they will be available for working from the cruisers.

ROYAL FLYING CORPS COMMUNIQUÉS.

ROYAL FLYING CORPS COMMUNIQUÉ.—No. 86.

April 29th.

Reconnaissances.—Reconnaissances were carried out by the 1st, 2nd, 3rd, and 5th Brigades, and 9th Wing, and successful contact patrols were accomplished, especially by No. 16 Squadron. Convoys and troops were engaged by our aeroplanes from low altitudes with machine gun fire.

Artillery Co-operation.—Eighty-one targets were dealt with by artillery with aeroplane observation and 27 with observation by balloons.

Artillery of the First Army obtained three direct hits on hostile batteries and caused two explosions of ammunition.

Artillery of the Third Army successfully engaged 24 hostile batteries and obtained 30 direct hits. Nine emplacements were damaged and 13 explosions of ammunition were caused. A large number of direct hits were also obtained on trenches.

With observation by Lieutenant J. P. V. Laverack, No. 12 Squadron, the 67th Siege Battery obtained four direct hits on a hostile battery and caused two explosions.

With observation by Captain J. H. Norton, No. 13 Squadron, the 153rd Siege Battery obtained nine direct hits on a hostile battery, damaging four emplacements and causing three explosions. The same pilot observed six direct hits on another hostile battery, and an explosion. On the 28th ult., the 153rd Siege Battery, with observation by Captain Norton, obtained eight direct hits on gun-pits and caused two explosions of ammunition.

Five hostile batteries were successfully engaged by artillery of the Fourth Army—eight direct hits were obtained, and one explosion was caused.

Artillery of the Fifth Army successfully engaged 22 hostile batteries and obtained 10 direct hits on gun positions. Four gun-pits were demolished, eight were damaged, and an explosion of ammunition was caused.

With observation by Second-Lieutenant Cooke and Second-Lieutenant Goodfellow, No. 15 Squadron, three active hostile batteries were silenced.

Hostile Aircraft.—Flight Sub-Lieut. Little, Naval Squadron No. 8, engaged and destroyed a two-seater Aviatik.

In the evening, Triplanes of Naval Squadron No. 8, drove off a scout that was attacking a B.E. When over Monchy-le-Preux, five more scouts were encountered, and a fight ensued which took the naval machines over Douai Aerodrome. Flight Sub-Lieut. Little, assisted by Flight Sub-Lieut. Minifie, of Naval Squadron No. 1, who joined in the fighting, destroyed one of the hostile machines, which crashed on Douai Aerodrome from a height of 2,000 feet. On his return flight, Flight Sub-Lieut.

Minifie engaged enemy infantry with machine gun fire from a height of 50 feet.

Captain Thayre and Captain Cubbon, No. 20 Squadron, shot down two H.A. in flames.

Hostile aircraft were driven down out of control by Lieutenant Knight and Flight Sergeant Cardno, No. 6 Squadron; Second Lieutenants Smart and Lewis, No. 20 Squadron; Second Lieutenants Conder and Neville, also of No. 20 Squadron, and Second Lieutenant Cole, No. 1 Squadron.

A patrol of Naval Squadron No. 1 engaged about 12 hostile aircraft over Epinoy Aerodrome. Flight Commander Gerrard and Flight Lieutenants Ridley and Rowley, drove down two of the hostile aircraft out of control, and Flight Sub-Lieut. Minifie destroyed one.

Captain Bishop, No. 60 Squadron, also destroyed a German aeroplane east of Epinoy.

Flight Commander Norton and Flight Sub-Lieut. Fletcher, Naval Squadron No. 6, drove down a German machine out of control.

An offensive patrol of No. 54 Squadron attacked two formations of hostile aircraft. The fighting was so close and severe that it was impossible to see what happened, but it is believed that one German machine was destroyed, and a number driven down, some of which probably fell out of control.

Flight Commander Norton, Naval Squadron No. 6, shot down an enemy machine, which fell in flames, and then hit the pilot in another machine, which fell apparently out of control.

Flight Sub-Lieut. Winter, of the same squadron, drove down a hostile aeroplane in a spin.

Flight Sub-Lieut. Casey, Naval Squadron No. 3, engaged and drove down a hostile machine, which burst into flames and fell, and Flight Sub-Lieut. Fall drove one down out of control.

Second Lieutenants Dinsmore and Bate, No. 18 Squadron, while on escort duty, attacked three hostile aircraft and drove one of them down in flames. They then attacked and crippled a second machine, which dropped out of the combat. The third machine, however, shot Lieutenant Bate and hit the F.E. badly. The pilot just succeeded in crossing the lines while followed closely by the German aviator, and landed. Second Lieutenant Dinsmore was then assisted by men of the Border Regiment, who observed the combat, and who saw one hostile machine wrecked on the ground and the other driven down.

Flight Lieutenant Breadner and Flight Sub-Lieuts. Carter and Broad, Naval Squadron No. 3, drove down a hostile machine in a severely damaged condition.

Lieutenants Huston and Foord, No. 18 Squadron, and Second Lieutenant Stocken, No. 23 Squadron, engaged and drove down several enemy machines.

A patrol of No. 57 Squadron observed several hostile aircraft engaging two S.E. 5's. The F.E.'s joined in the combat, and a pilot of one of the hostile machines, which was engaged by Captain McNaughton and Second Lieutenant Downing, was seen to fall from his machine, which crashed. Lieutenant Ryan and Second Lieutenant Soutten drove down another aeroplane completely out of control.

An encounter took place between six Albatross Scouts and three S.E.'s of No. 56 Squadron. One S.E. had both guns jammed, so outclimbed the H.A. in order to rectify the trouble, while the other two pilots continued the fight. One S.E. temporarily got into a spin and was followed by two scouts. Seeing this, Captain Meintjes immediately dived and drove them off, and one fell completely out of control and was undoubtedly destroyed. The other H.A. then broke off the combat.

A second patrol of No. 56 Squadron, led by Captain Ball, had two combats, and in each case the German aeroplanes were driven down.

Captain Crowe, Lieutenant Leach, and Second Lieutenant Kay, No. 56 Squadron, engaged seven hostile machines and drove two of them down out of control, while the remainder fled. These pilots then patrolled over Douau Aerodrome at a very low altitude, and although hostile machines were seen on the aerodrome, no endeavour was made to interfere with their patrol.

Photography.—1,080 photographs were taken during the day.

Bombing.—First Brigade.—On the evening of the 28th, four 112-lb. and 45—20-lb. bombs were dropped on the railway east of Drocourt and eight of the bombs were observed to burst on the railway. On the 29th, 24—20-lb. bombs were dropped on various targets. An explosion and a fire were caused in Avion, where bombs were dropped.

Second Brigade.—No. 20 Squadron dropped 23—20-lb. bombs on a dump at Bisseghem. Eight of the bombs were seen to burst on the dump, causing three fires and destroying a house near the dump.

Fifth Brigade.—Eleven 20-lb. bombs were dropped on Hendecourt.

9th Wing.—No. 27 Squadron dropped six 230-lb. bombs from a height of 7,000 feet on Bohain. Valenciennes Station was attacked by machines of No. 55 Squadron. 10—112-lb. bombs were dropped from a height of about 9,500 feet. Several of the bombs were seen to hit the station and railway, and one fell on a railway bridge. One of the bombs dropped by Captain Adams caused a large fire.

April 30th.

Reconnaissances.—Reconnaissances were carried out by all Brigades and 9th Wing, and successful contact patrols were carried out by the 3rd Brigade.

Transports, machine gun emplacements, and enemy troops were engaged with machine gun fire from the air.

Artillery Co-operation.—79 targets were dealt with by artillery with aeroplane observation and 30 with balloon observation.

Artillery of the First Army obtained four direct hits on hostile batteries and caused an explosion of ammunition. Many direct hits were also obtained on trenches.

Artillery of the Second Army successfully engaged seven hostile batteries.

Twelve hostile batteries were successfully engaged by artillery of the Third Army and four explosions were caused.

Artillery of the Fourth Army successfully engaged six hostile batteries. Six direct hits were obtained—two emplacements were damaged and a third was set on fire. The 9th Siege Battery obtained five O.K.'s, 12 Y.'s, and 10 Z.'s on a hostile battery, with observation by Lieutenant Rogers, No. 52 Squadron.

Seventeen hostile batteries were successfully engaged by artillery of the Fifth Army. Eight direct hits were obtained on gun pits, two of which were demolished, and two explosions of ammunition were caused. Wire and trenches were also much damaged.

Hostile Aircraft.—Flight Sub-Lieut. R. A. Little, Naval Squadron No. 8, drove down a German aeroplane out of control, and then attacked and drove down a second.

Flight Lieutenant Compston, Naval Squadron No. 8, drove down an Albatross Scout out of control, and then attacked and drove down another in a spinning nose dive.

Flight Lieutenant Booker and Flight Sub-Lieut. Knight, of the same squadron, drove down two hostile machines in a badly damaged condition.

Captain Brand, of No. 1 Squadron, engaged an Albatross two-seater, which he destroyed in our lines.

Second Lieutenant Cole, No. 1 Squadron, drove down a German aeroplane out of control, and then he and Captain Atkinson of the same squadron engaged and drove down two more out of control.

Flight Lieutenants Maynard, Haywood, and Rowley, Naval Squadron No. 1, each drove down a hostile aeroplane out of control, and Flight Commander Dallas, of the same squadron, who had about seven combats while on patrol, destroyed a two-seater Rumpler and drove down a German Nieuport completely out of control.

Captain Bishop, No. 60 Squadron, had eight combats during a patrol of two hours, and in six of these he engaged two or more enemy machines, and succeeded in bringing one down out of control and driving down two in a badly damaged condition.

A reconnaissance of No. 48 Squadron had many combats. Lieutenants Game and Malcomson drove down one of their opponents out of control, while Lieutenants Middleton and Clay, who had six different fights, also drove down an enemy machine out of control.

Anti-aircraft of the Third Army drove down one German machine out of control, and forced another to land after being hit.

Lieutenant Hyde, No. 54 Squadron, attacked a machine which appeared to fall out of control.

A photographic reconnaissance of No. 18 Squadron, led by Captain Bryant and Second Lieutenant Couve, engaged about 20 hostile machines. In the fight that ensued one enemy machine was driven down out of control, four were driven down damaged, and one was destroyed by Second Lieutenant Kaizer and Sergeant Russell. It is probable that one of the machines reported damaged was actually destroyed, for the pilot was seen to fall forward, but the machine was lost sight of. In spite of the hard fighting 24 photographs were taken.

Captain Patrick, No. 23 Squadron, engaged a German machine and shot the observer. He then engaged a two-seater Albatross, and, assisted by Second Lieutenant Stead of the same squadron, drove down the enemy machine, which landed in a field apparently much damaged. Captain Patrick and his patrol then engaged four H.A.'s, and one was hit by Captain Patrick, and fell completely out of control and on fire. Second Lieutenant O'Grady, of the same squadron, also drove down one of the hostile machines out of control.

Captain Summers and Lieutenant Cayley, No. 3 Squadron, dived at a German machine that was attacking a B.E., and drove it down.

Second Lieutenant Bell and Lieutenant McLeod, No. 18 Squadron, drove down a hostile aeroplane in a badly damaged condition. Later they engaged five more hostile machines and drove two of them down, spinning vertically, after being closely engaged.

Captain C. M. Crowe, Lieutenant J. O. Leach and Second Lieutenant Kay, No. 56 Squadron, saw a formation of eight hostile machines east of Douai, which were about to attack some F.E.'s. The S.E.'s immediately dived at and intercepted the German scouts, and a very hard fight took place. The German pilots appeared to be good, and manœuvred their machines skilfully. Finally, Captain Crowe succeeded in destroying one of the German aeroplanes. Lieutenant Leach observed Second Lieutenant Kay's machine going down in a spiral with a hostile machine at its tail, and he immediately dived and opened fire on the hostile scout, which crashed, and was seen to burst into flames.

Major L. A. Pattinson and Lieutenant A. H. Mearns, No. 57 Squadron, observed a formation of their F.E.'s fighting with

German machines, and immediately joined in the combat. They drove down one of the hostile machines in a damaged condition, while a second was driven down out of control by Lieutenant C. S Morice and Lieutenant F. Leathley; and several others were driven down damaged by the F.E.'s. The fighting was so intense that it was quite impossible to ascertain the fate of any machine that fell out of the combat.

Photography.—948 photographs were taken during the day.

Bombing.—First Brigade.—Eighteen 20-lb. bombs were dropped on places of military importance.

Second Brigade.—Thirteen 112-lb. bombs were dropped on a dump at Bisseghem by machines of No. 20 Squadron, and a large explosion was observed in the dump.

Third Brigade.—On the night of the 29th-30th machines of No. 100 Squadron dropped 32—20-lb. bombs on various objectives from heights ranging from 100 feet to 500 feet. Dorignies Station was hit, and three trains were attacked, and two were hit and derailed, one of which is believed to have been totally destroyed at Dorignies.

Fourth Brigade.—On the night of the 29th-30th six 20-lb. bombs were dropped on Estrees.

Fifth Brigade.—On the night of the 29th-30th four machines of No. 4 Squadron dropped 30—20-lb. bombs on troops and transport.

On the 30th No. 4 Squadron dropped four 112-lb. bombs, and 13—20-lb. bombs on Epinoy Aerodrome, and all the bombs were seen to burst on and around the aerodrome. Two machines of No. 18 Squadron also dropped seven 20-lb. bombs on this aerodrome.

In addition to this 26—20-lb. bombs were dropped on Hendecourt, six on Quéant, and four on Pronville, in which place a house was completely demolished.

9th Wing.—No 27 Squadron dropped 40—20-lb. bombs on Epinoy Aeradrome. One hangar was observed to be partially destroyed.

May 1st.

Reconnaissance.—Reconnaissances were carried out by all brigades and 9th Wing. Many fires and explosions were observed opposite the First Army Front. A special reconnaissance was carried out by Lieutenants O'Brien and Jones, No. 43 Squadron, at a very low altitude, and much useful information was obtained. An armoured B.E. of No. 53 Squadron flew at 500 feet, and successfully co-operated with an infantry raiding party.

Artillery Co-operation.—111 targets were dealt with by artillery with aeroplane observation, and 11 with observation by balloons.

Artillery of the First Army obtained nine hits on hostile batteries, causing two explosions, and two fires in gun-pits.

Artillery of the Second Army successfully engaged seven hostile batteries.

Artillery of the Third Army successfully engaged 14 hostile batteries, and caused four explosions of ammunition.

Two hostile batteries were successfully engaged by artillery of the Fourth Army, and two explosions were caused.

Artillery of the Fifth Army successfully engaged 29 hostile batteries. Nineteen direct hits were obtained on gun-pits, six gun-pits were destroyed and 16 damaged, and an explosion of ammunition took place.

The 93rd Siege Battery, with observation by Second Lieutenant Barker and Second Lieutenant Goodfellow, No. 15 Squadron, destroyed two machine gun emplacements with five direct hits.

Hostile Aircraft.—Six F.E.'s of No. 25 Squadron engaged about 15 hostile scouts near Douai. Second Lieutenant Malcom and Corporal Emsden destroyed one and drove down a second in a damaged condition.

Second Lieutenant King and Lieutenant Hobart-Hampden drove down another out of control, while several other scouts were driven down in a damaged condition during the fight.

Captain Brand, No. 1 Squadron, destroyed an Albatross two-seater near Warneton, and Captain Atkinson of the same squadron destroyed one near Zonnebeke.

Second Lieutenant Dalziel and Lance-Corporal Bradley, No. 20 Squadron, shot down an Albatross two-seater, which crashed near Messines.

An Albatross Scout, which was engaged by Second Lieutenant Cole, No. 1 Squadron, was brought down in our lines near Elverdinghe.

An Albatross two-seater was driven down out of control by Second Lieutenant Mansbridge, No. 1 Squadron, and another machine of the same type was driven down out of control by Captain Thayre and Captain Cubbon of No. 20 Squadron.

Anti-aircraft gunners of the Third Army brought down a German two-seater machine in our lines. Captain Strugnell, No. 54 Squadron, engaged and drove down a German machine in a spinning nose dive.

A photographic reconnaissance of No. 18 Squadron attacked 10 H.A.'s near Epinoy. Flight Sub-Lieut. Fall, Naval Squadron No. 3, one of the escort to the F.E.'s, assisted by Second Lieutenant Kaizer and Sergeant Russell, No. 18 Squadron, drove down one of the machines completely out of control. Lieutenants Parkinson and Anglin, on one machine, and Lieutenants Shaumer and Shackell, on another machine, drove down two of the hostile machines out of control. Second

Lieutenant Critchley and 2nd Air Mechanic Jones also drove down one out of control and a second in a badly damaged condition. A number of the German machines broke off the combat, and it is probable that most of them were hit. Captain Taylor and Lieutenant Eccles, both of No. 32 Squadron, attacked two Albatross two-seaters and drove them down. A green coloured machine was seen shortly afterwards destroyed on the ground, and is believed to be one which they drove down which was painted that colour.

A patrol of three machines of No. 56 Squadron saw six H.A.'s near Cambrai at 13,000 feet. The S.E.'s immediately attacked, and one of the German machines was destroyed by Captain Ball, while a second was driven down out of control by this pilot.

Second Lieutenant K. J. Knaggs, No. 56 Squadron, drove down an Albatross two-seater, which is believed to have fallen in the River Scarpe.

Lieutenant F. S. Wilkins, No. 19 Squadron, engaged and drove down an Albatross two-seater, which fell south-east of Arras. Second Lieutenant D. J. Bell, No. 27 Squadron, drove down a single-seater German machine in a spin.

Photography.—1,117 photographs were taken during the day.

Bombing. – First Brigade.—During the night of the 30th April–1st May, machines of No. 10 Squadron dropped six 112-lb. and 32—20-lb. bombs on Carvin Station from an average height of 2,500 feet. Direct hits were obtained on the railway and station and on houses. A searchlight was also bombed and extinguished. On the 1st inst., 22—20-lb. bombs were dropped on gun positions at Bauvin, 20—20-lb. bombs were dropped on Quiery-la-Motte, 24—20-lb. bombs on Izel, and a number of bombs were dropped on other objectives.

Second Brigade.—Fourteen 20-lb. bombs were dropped by No. 21 Squadron on Rumbeke Aerodrome, but no special results were observed.

Third Brigade.—On the night of the 30th April–1st May machines of No. 100 Squadron carried out two raids. In the first seven 112-lb. and three phosphorus bombs were dropped from on average height of 300 feet on St. Sauveur Station. A number of the bombs fell on large glass-roofed sheds at the station and caused several fires. The weather was unfavourable during the second raid, but a train on the Lille-Seclin line was bombed and wrecked, and two 112-lb. bombs were dropped on the railway track near Haubourdin.

Fourth Brigade.—Eighteen 20-lb. bombs were dropped on an ammunition depôt at le Catelet on the night of the 30th April–1st May.

Fifth Brigade.—On the night of the 30th April–1st May, Epinoy Aerodrome was attacked. Twenty-six incendiary bombs were dropped by No. 18 Squadron, and all the bombs fell on and around the aerodrome and near the hangars, and one bomb hit a house near the aerodrome, which burned furiously. The aeroplanes attacked several objectives with machine gun fire, and a machine gun, firing from the ground, was silenced. On the return of the F.E.'s, four B.E.'s of No. 4 Squadron left the ground and dropped three 112-lb. and 14—20-lb. bombs on the same aerodrome, and the majority of the bombs hit their objective. One 112-lb. bomb was dropped on a train north-west of Marquion, and the train was set on fire. These machines also attacked transport and other objectives with machine gun fire.

9th Wing.—Machines of No. 27 Squadron dropped 76—20-lb. bombs on Epinoy Aerodrome, but observation was difficult owing to interference by hostile aircraft.

May 2nd.

Reconnaissance.—Reconnaissances were carried out by 1st, 2nd, 4th, and 5th Brigades. Fires and explosions were again reported on the front of the First Army. A number of our machines when on artillery and other work went down to low altitudes and attacked enemy troops in trenches and on the roads, and also convoys, with machine gun fire.

Artillery Co-operation.—One hundred and forty-five targets were dealt with by artillery with aeroplane observation and 45 with balloon observation.

Artillery of the First Army obtained 18 direct hits on hostile batteries and a number on trenches and wire. Captain W. R. Snow, No. 10 Squadron, carried out a successful shoot on the night of the 1st/2nd with the 8th Canadian Siege Battery. Two direct hits were obtained on a gun-pit, and a battery was silenced. After this, Captain Snow dropped bombs on a sugar factory at Marquillies.

Artillery of the Second Army successfully engaged nine hostile batteries, and hit 11 gun-pits.

Artillery of the Third Army successfully engaged 28 hostile batteries, 13 direct hits and a large number of M.O.K.'s, Y.'s and Z.'s being obtained, and three gun-pits were damaged and two explosions seen. With observation by Captain J. H. Norton, No. 13 Squadron, artillery obtained three direct hits on station buildings at Corbehem, causing a fire in the station. With observation by the same pilot, the 251st Siege Battery obtained three direct hits and three M.O.K.'s on a hostile battery.

Eleven targets were successfully engaged by artillery of the Fourth Army. Four of these were active anti-aircraft batteries, and were silenced, six O.K.'s and five M.O.K.'s being obtained.

Artillery of the Fifth Army successfully engaged 22 hostile batteries. Twenty-four direct hits were obtained on gun positions and three explosions of ammunition were caused. Eight pits were destroyed and 10 damaged. Second Lieutenant Barker, No. 15 Squadron, ranged the 193rd Siege Battery on three machine gun emplacements, and five direct hits were obtained.

Hostile Aircraft.—On the evening of the 1st instant, Flight Sub-Lieut. Shields, Naval Squadron No. 8, attacked an Albatross Scout, which he drove down out of control. He was then attacked by seven more scouts and fought for a considerable time, but was forced down; his controls were shot away, and the machine crashed and was immediately shelled by the Germans. The pilot, who was injured, crept into a shell hole and remained there until rescued the next morning.

A formation of nine Albatross Scouts attacked six F.E.'s of No. 25 Squadron which were returning from a bomb raid. Captain Woollven and Sergeant J. H. Brown destroyed one of the scouts, and Second Lieutenant R. G. Malcolm and Sergeant Emsden destroyed a second.

Lieutenant K. Mackenzie, No. 40, Squadron, attacked five hostile aircraft, and destroyed one near Quiery-la-Motte.

Two German machines were driven down out of control—one by Flight Lieutenant Compston and the other by Flight Sub-Lieut. Simpson, Naval Squadron No. 8.

Lieutenant Cunnell and 2nd A.M. Sayers, No. 20 Squadron, drove down a German machine out of control near Comines.

Second Lieutenants Farnes and Davis, No. 48 Squadron, engaged and drove down a two-seater Albatross completely out of control.

A very keen engagement took place between 10 red Albatross Scouts and Bristol Fighters of No. 48 Squadron. One of the German machines was destroyed and one driven down out of control by Lieutenants Wrinkler and Moore, and another was driven down in flames by Lieutenant Scholte and Second Lieutenant Game. A fourth was driven down out of control by Second Lieutenants Harrison and Richards, while two others were driven down badly damaged.

Major Scott, No. 60 Squadron, was attacked by six hostile scouts, and in the fight which took place on his way back to the lines, one of the German machines was destroyed. A German machine was driven down in a damaged condition by Naval Squadron No. 1, and two balloons were forced down by the same squadron.

Captain Bishop, No. 60 Squadron, had nine combats during the day, and destroyed one of his opponents, while a second was driven down completely out of control, and a third was forced to land in a field. Lieutenant Fry of the same squadron also drove down a German machine damaged, and drove off several others.

Two hostile machines were driven down badly damaged by pilots of Naval Squadron No. 3.

Captain Ball, No. 56 Squadron, dived at a German scout, and was immediately attacked from behind by four other scouts, one of which shot past Captain Ball, who immediately fired a burst from his Vickers gun into the hostile machine, which went down, and was followed by Captain Ball, who continued to fire into it until it crashed. Then he climbed up in order to join a big fight which was taking place between hostile two-seaters and scouts, and, on our side, Sopwith Scouts, Bristol Fighters and F.E.'s. The fighting drifted to the east, and the hostile machines were generally out-manœuvred. After this combat, Captain Ball engaged a white two-seater Albatross, which he drove down out of control, but, owing to the dusk, he was unable to see what happened to it.

Captain Meintjes, No. 56 Squadron, dived at one of two Albatross two-seaters, and drove it down in a slow spiral; he throttled down and "sat on its tail" until both the occupants appeared to be shot, then turned to engage the second machine.

Second Lieutenant L. M. Barlow, also of No. 56 Squadron, engaged and drove down an Albatross two-seater completely out of control.

Captain Andrews, No. 66 Squadron, attacked a single-seater German machine, which was diving at some of our Martinsydes. The scout was driven down out of control, but was not watched, owing to the presence of a number of other H.A.

Balloons.—Lieutenant K. Mackenzie and Second Lieutenants Walder, Lemon, Thompson, Bond, and Morgan, No. 40 Squadron, crossed the lines at 50 feet and under in order to attack German balloons. Previous experience had shown the necessity of flying low in order to obtain satisfactory results in these attacks. These pilots had practised low flying, and had learnt how to use trees, houses, and the ground in screening them from infantry and machine gun fire. Artillery co-operated by putting a heavy barrage on the German trenches, leaving the pilots a certain area in which to cross. As a result of the attack, four German balloons were destroyed. One pilot, who went to within a few feet of the balloon, failed in his attack, owing to gun trouble.

A German aeroplane was brought down in our lines by machine gun fire from the trenches; the pilot was killed, and the observer taken prisoner.

Photography.—932 photographs were taken during the day.

Bombing.—1st Brigade.—On the night of the 1st–2nd, six 112-lb. and 30—20-lb. bombs were dropped on Carvin station and town. Many direct hits were observed on the railway and in the station, and two fires were caused in the town. Twelve 20-lb. bombs were also dropped on Marquillies Sugar Factory, and 10 of the bombs were observed to hit the objective, which caught fire.

On the 2nd inst. 24—20-lb. bombs were dropped on Fresnes, four of which burst on buildings. Bombs were also dropped on Neuvireuil and Lens, and 24—20-lb. bombs were dropped on Izel-les-Equerchin, and a large explosion was caused.

2nd Brigade.—No. 20 Squadron dropped 62—20-lb. bombs on a dump at Ledeghem station from a height of about 8,500 feet. Six of the bombs were observed to burst on the dump.

5th Brigade.—On the night of the 1st–2nd four F.E.'s, of No. 18 Squadron, and four B.E.'s, of No. 4 Squadron, dropped four 112-lb., 36—20-lb., and 12 incendiary bombs on Eswars Aerodrome. One shed was set on fire, and most of the bombs appeared to fall on the aerodrome. Three searchlights were attacked by machine gun fire and the lights were extinguished.

On the 2nd inst. 22—20-lb. bombs were dropped on Hendecourt, and 10—20-lb. bombs on Quéant.

9th Wing.—10—112-lb. bombs were dropped on Valenciennes Railway Station by machines of No. 55 Squadron, and three of the bombs were seen to explode on the railway track. No. 27 Squadron dropped 12—112-lb. bombs on Orchies Station.

May 3rd.

Reconnaissances.—Reconnaissances were carried out by the 1st, 2nd, 4th, and 5th Brigades. Fires were observed in a number of towns opposite the front of the First Army. Many flares were located and valuable reports made by contact patrol machines. Information was received that the Germans were massing for a counter-attack, and 13 machines of No. 43 Squadron went out in order to attack them with machine gun fire and to gather information. These aeroplanes flew at altitudes varying from 50 to 300 feet, and attacked the German troops, causing many casualties and breaking up formations. The pilots then flew over trenches which were seen to be packed with Germans and fired at them, and they also attacked transport and machine gun parties. All returned safely after having expended their ammunition.

In many other instances troops and transport were attacked from the air.

Artillery Co-operation.—Seventy-six targets were dealt with by artillery with aeroplane observation, and 48 with observation by balloons.

Artillery of the First Army obtained 14 direct hits on hostile batteries and a number on trenches and wire, and a house in a battery position was set on fire.

Artillery of the Second Army successfully engaged 14 hostile batteries. Fifteen gun-pits were hit and two explosions of ammunition caused.

Fourteen hostile batteries were successfully engaged by artillery of the Third Army, and four explosions were caused.

Artillery of the Fourth Army successfully engaged five hostile batteries under zone call. Ten direct hits were obtained, two emplacements were destroyed and two damaged.

Artillery of the Fifth Army engaged 21 hostile batteries successfully, and obtained 12 direct hits on gun positions. Four gun-pits were demolished, and an explosion was caused.

Captain Portal, No. 3 Squadron, ranged artillery on to cross roads and on to a battery position, and six direct hits were obtained on the latter, which destroyed two pits and damaged two others. He then ranged the 122nd Heavy Battery on to a hostile battery, which was silenced after having been hit. In addition to this, he ranged heavy batteries on to five hostile batteries, all of which were silenced.

Hostile Aircraft.—Flight Sub-Lieut. Little, Naval Squadron No. 8, engaged and drove down a German scout out of control.

On returning from a bomb raid, Captain F. H. Thayre and Captain F. R. Cubbon, No. 20 Squadron, attacked and drove down an Albatross two-seater. Our machines were then attacked by about 26 Albatross Scouts, led by a machine painted bright scarlet. As a result of the combat which ensued two of the German machines were destroyed by Captain Thayre and Captain Cubbon, and another was driven down out of control by Lieutenant Stevens and Second Lieutenant Wilkinson, No. 20 Squadron. Most of the hostile scouts were eventually driven off, and the remaining few were attacked and driven off with pistols, as our pilots had all run out of ammunition.

Lieutenant Porter and Second Lieutenant MacKay, No. 41 Squadron, each drove down a German machine out of control after very hard fighting between seven of our machines and 18 Albatross Scouts.

Second Lieutenant E. A. H. Ward and Lieutenant G. G. Bell, No. 22 Squadron, drove down a hostile aeroplane in a spinning nose dive.

Captain Patrick, Lieutenant Stead, and 2nd Lieutenant Doran, No. 23 Squadron, attacked a patrol of six enemy machines. Several of the German machines fell out of the combat after being closely engaged, but our pilots were unable to see what happened, but believe three of them fell out of control.

Captain Tolhurst and Lieutenant Blennerhassett, No. 18 Squadron, engaged four hostile machines and drove one down completely out of control.

An Albatross Scout landed in our lines in an undamaged condition.

Two German machines were destroyed by machine gun and rifle fire from the trenches.

Photography.—416 photographs were taken during the day.

Bombing.—First Brigade.—On the night of the 2nd–3rd, 18—20-lb. and two 112-lb. bombs were dropped on Carvin, from an average height of 2,000 feet, by machines of No. 10 Squadron. Many of the bombs were observed to burst on houses, and a fire was caused. Two 112-lb. and 10—20-lb. bombs were dropped on Harnes, and houses were hit. Four 20-lb. bombs were dropped on Provin at 11 p.m. with the same result; and eight 20-lb. and four incendiary bombs were dropped on Marquillies Sugar Factory, and the bombs were observed to burst on the factory. On the 3rd instant, 44—20-lb. bombs were dropped in Izel, and 11—20-lb. bombs on Avion, and were again seen to burst on houses in both places.

Second Brigade.—No. 20 Squadron dropped two 20-lb. bombs on a dump near Wigres, which caused two fires. This squadron also dropped 16—20-lb. bombs on Lichtervelde station from 8,000 feet, and 10 direct hits were observed, while houses were also damaged.

Third Brigade.—On the night of the 2nd–3rd, No. 100 Squadron dropped seven 112-lb. and 22—20-lb. bombs on stations and trains. One 112-lb. bomb was dropped on La Goulee Station, and one on the sheds east of Somain. Four 112-lb. bombs were dropped on Valenciennes stations and sheds. Four trains on lines radiating from Somain were bombed from 200 feet and derailed. Two 112-lb. bombs were dropped on the railway track between Valenciennes and Douai, and several trains were attacked with machine gun fire.

Fourth Brigade.—Three machines of the 3rd Wing dropped 18—20-lb. bombs on Estrees, and 13 of the bombs were seen to burst in the village.

Fifth Brigade.—On the night of the 2nd–3rd, one 112-lb., eight incendiary, 40 phosphorus, and three 20-lb. bombs were dropped on an ammunition dump at Iwny by No. 18 Squadron. Several bombs were observed to burst on and around the dump, and two explosions were caused, and a fire broke out. Pilots then attacked searchlights and other targets with machine gun fire.

No. 4 Squadron dropped 16—20-lb. bombs on various objectives, and one pilot fired 200 rounds at active batteries around Hendecourt. On the third instant, 20—20-lb. bombs were dropped on Hendecourt.

9th Wing.—Six Martinsydes of No. 27 Squadron dropped 48—20-lb. bombs on Brebières, and 12—230-lb. bombs on Don Station, which was attacked twice, and hit on each occasion. No. 55 Squadron dropped 11—112-lb. bombs on Brebières, and direct hits were obtained, and clouds of smoke were seen at the station after the attack. This squadron also dropped eight 112-lb. bombs from 1,200 feet on Busigny, and buildings at this junction were set on fire.

May 4th.

Reconnaissances.—Reconnaissances were by carried out by the First, Second, and Fifth Brigades and 9th Wing.

Successful contact patrols were carried out by machines of the First, Third, and Fifth Brigades, and while on this work infantry and convoys were attacked from low altitudes with machine gun fire.

Second Lieut. Barker and Second Lieutenant Goodfellow, No. 15 Squadron, fired 500 rounds at an enemy bombing party east of Bullecourt.

Artillery Co-operation.—Sixty-seven targets were dealt with by artillery with aeroplane observation, and 29 with observation by balloons.

Artillery of the First Army obtained 23 direct hits on hostile batteries. Two gun-pits were destroyed, one was set on fire, and eight explosions of ammunition took place. 22 active hostile batteries were reported by zone call.

Artillery of the Second Army successfully engaged 12 hostile batteries. 16 gun-pits were hit, and an explosion of ammunition was caused.

Artillery of the Third Army successfully engaged 17 hostile batteries. Three explosions were caused, and a fire was started. 115 hostile batteries were seen active, and on 21 of these there was observation of fire.

Eight hostile batteries were successfully engaged by artillery of the Fourth Army. Four O.K.'s and six M.O.K.'s were obtained on one battery. One emplacement was destroyed and four damaged.

Eight hostile batteries were successfully engaged by artillery of the Fifth Army. Six direct hits were obtained on gun positions. One gun pit was demolished, seven were damaged, and four explosions were caused.

With observation by balloons, five hostile batteries were engaged and 16 located.

On the 23rd ult., with observation by No. 33 Balloon Section, the 175th Siege Battery fired for effect on a quarry. After the infantry had advanced and taken the quarry, six Germans were captured, and it was found that a large number had been killed owing to the accurate shooting of the 175th Siege Battery. The presence of the enemy in large numbers in the quarry had been reported by aeroplane observation.

Hostile Aircraft.—On the evening of the 3rd instant an offensive patrol of Sopwith Triplanes of Naval Squadron No. 8 encountered five Albatross Scouts, and Flight Commander Arnold and Flight Lieutenant Johnston each drove one down out of control. Five other Albatross Scouts flew considerably higher, but did not take part in the combat.

On the 4th, while on artillery work, Second Lieutenant Ryder and Lieutenant Alexander, No. 2 Squadron, drove down an enemy aeroplane out of control.

A German aeroplane was attacked and driven down by Flight Lieutenant Booker, Naval Squadron No. 8.

Anti-aircraft gunners also drove down a German machine out of control.

Three machines of Naval Squadron No. 1 engaged a formation of eight hostile aircraft, which they drove East. These machines landed on Epinoy Aerodrome, and although the triplanes waited half an hour no attempt was made to attack them.

Flight Lieutenant Eyre, Naval Squadron No. 1, drove down a German machine, which is believed to have fallen out of control.

Captain Bishop and Lieutenant Fry, both of No. 60 Squadron, dived at one of two German aeroplanes and destroyed it.

Captain Letts and Lieutenant Smithers, No. 48 Squadron, destroyed a German machine, which crashed at Pelves.

Captain Davidson, No. 23 Squadron, engaged and drove down an enemy machine out of control east of Havrincourt.

An engagement took place between Spads of No. 19 Squadron and a hostile formation, and several of the enemy machines were driven down damaged after being closely engaged, while one, which was engaged by Lieutenant Hope, fell out of control.

A reconnaissance of No. 70 Squadron engaged about eight Albatross Scouts, and one was driven down out of control by Sergeant Skinner and Lieutenant Seth-Smith, while two others were driven down damaged.

While on photographic duty, de Haviland 4's, of No. 55 Squadron, encountered several hostile machines, and one was driven down out of control by Lieutenant Barnett and Second Lieutenant Durrant, and another by Second Lieutenants Stevens and Sandy, while two others were driven down damaged.

One of our balloons was destroyed and one damaged by hostile aircraft.

Photography.— 676 photographs were taken during the day.

Bombing.—First Brigade.—On the night of the 3rd-4th, 81—20-lb., six 112-lb., two incendiary, and two phosphorus bombs were dropped on Henin-Liétard, Harnes, Courrières, Annay, Pont-à-Vendin, Carvin, and Tourmignies Aerodrome. Two fires were caused in Henin-Liétard. The phosphorus bombs started a fire in Carvin, and direct hits were obtained on the railway line at Henin-Liétard and Harnes. Captain W. R. Snow, No. 16 Squadron, carried 16—20-lb. bombs and obtained six direct hits on hangars at Tourmignies Aerodrome. Searchlights were fired at with machine gun fire, and were immediately extinguished.

On the 4th, 65—20-lb. bombs were dropped on Noyelles, Avion, Billy Montigny, Sallaumines, and on trenches. Fifteen bombs were seen to hit houses in the towns of Noyelles and Sallaumines.

Second Brigade.—On the night of the 3rd–4th eight 20-lb. bombs were dropped by No. 20 Squadron on a dump at Wervicq, and eight direct hits were obtained.

On the 4th, 15—112-lb. bombs were dropped on Chateau-du-Sart Aerodrome from 8,000 feet. Four direct hits were obtained on hangars and four on sheds, which were seen to be on fire. In addition four 20-lb. bombs were dropped on a dump at Quesnoy, where an explosion was caused.

Third Brigade.—On the night of the 3rd–4th seven machines of No. 100 Squadron left the ground with bombs at intervals of half an hour in order to disorganise the enemy's communications. Forty 20-lb. bombs were dropped from altitudes varying from 50 to 1,000 feet on various objectives. Direct hits were obtained on sheds at Lens Station. A train was bombed from 50 feet and derailed, while two others south of Beaumont were attacked, and one is known to have been hit. Bombs were dropped in Mericourt Station, where two trains were seen, and on which two hits were obtained. Hangars in Carvin Aerodrome are believed to have been hit, while the results in several other cases were not observed.

No. 11 Squadron also went out and dropped bombs on various objectives, and attacked troops with machine gun fire.

Fourth Brigade.—On the night of the 3rd–4th 30—20-lb. and six 112-lb. bombs were dropped on an enemy rest-camp by machines of the 3rd Wing, and many direct hits were obtained.

Fifth Brigade.—On the night of the 3rd–4th an ammunition dump at Iwuy was attacked by machines of Nos. 4 and 18 Squadrons with 112-lb., 20-lb., phosphorus and incendiary bombs. One of the first machines obtained direct hits, and set the dump on fire. A number of other hits were obtained, and as the fire had spread and was burning the whole dump, and a number of explosions were observed to be taking place, the last machine proceeded to Eswars Aerodrome and dropped bombs there. During this raid a searchlight and active hostile batteries were attacked with machine gun fire.

9th Wing.—No. 27 Squadron dropped 47—20-lb. bombs on Eswars Aerodrome from 7,000 feet, and bombs were seen to burst between the sheds and close to 12 German aeroplanes on the aerodrome. No. 55 Squadron dropped 49—20-lb. bombs on La Brayelle Aerodrome.

S. WOOD, Captain,
Staff Officer.

Headquarters, Royal Flying Corps,
6th May 1917.

ROYAL FLYING CORPS COMMUNIQUÉ, No. 87.

May 5th.

Reconnaissances.—Reconnaissances were carried out by all brigades, and fires and explosions were reported opposite the front of the First Army.

Artillery Co-operation.—Eighty-nine targets were dealt with by artillery with aeroplane observation, and 16 with observation by balloons.

Artillery of the First Army obtained eight direct hits on hostile batteries and destroyed three gun-pits. Two houses in battery positions were set on fire, and five explosions were caused, while several direct hits were obtained on trenches.

Artillery of the Second Army successfully engaged six hostile batteries; five gun-pits were hit, and two explosions caused.

Artillery of the Third Army successfully engaged 27 hostile batteries; 13 direct hits were obtained, three pits were damaged, and four explosions were caused.

Eleven direct hits were obtained on various targets by artillery of the Fourth Army.

Artillery of the Fifth Army successfully engaged 26 hostile batteries; 15 direct hits were obtained on gun positions, four pits were demolished, 15 damaged, and five explosions were caused.

Hostile Aircraft..—Lieutenant Ellis, No. 40 Squadron, observed three Albatross scouts south of Douai and dived at them, but the three scouts immediately dived away, and at 500 feet one of them side-slipped and crashed; the second landed on its nose on Douai Aerodrome and turned completely over; while the third landed safely. Lieutenant Ellis was then attacked by a German Nieuport, and, after having gained position, his gun jambed, so he immediately dived, rectified the jamb, and returned to re-engage the German machine. He then ran out of ammunition, so got as close as possible and fired seven rounds from his Colt automatic pistol, and the German aeroplane went down, and was seen to break in the air and to crash.

Three hostile machines were driven down out of control—one by Second Lieutenant Walder, No. 40 Squadron; one by Second Lieutenants Richmond and Pritchard, No. 43 Squadron; and the third by Lieutenant Belgrave and Second Lieutenant Stewart, No. 45 Squadron.

Second Lieutenant Farquhar and Lieutenant Keller, No. 23 Squadron, each drove down a German machine out of control.

Captain Ball, No. 56 Squadron, when on patrol, saw two hostile aircraft coming towards Carvin from the direction of

Douai. As he had not gained much height, he flew away from the machines, climbing steadily. When the Germans had got quite near his tail, he did a sharp turn and got underneath one of the machines and opened fire. This machine fell out of control, and Captain Ball then manœuvred in order to get into a favourable position to attack the second. The German, however, simply flew straight at him, firing hard, so the S.E. returned fire, and the machines almost collided; then the hostile aeroplane went down. The S.E.'s engine was hit and the pilot was covered with oil. As there were no other enemy machines in sight, Captain Ball went down and saw both the hostile aeroplanes lying within 400 yards of each other completely wrecked on the ground. On his way home he met two more hostile aircraft, but as he had practically run out of ammunition, and as his sights were covered with oil, he put his nose down and returned to his aerodrome.

Lieutenant Lewis and Second Lieutenant Hoidge, No. 56 Squadron, each engaged and drove down a hostile machine out of control.

Anti-aircraft of the Third Army brought down a hostile machine, and anti-aircraft of the Fourth Army brought down two, one falling in on our lines.

Balloons.—On the 4th, No. 29 Balloon was brought down by a hostile aeroplane; it was repaired and went up again, and was brought down a second time. It was again repaired and went up a third time, and did some useful work during the night. The same observer, 24107 Flight Sergeant G. G. L. Blake, was in the balloon each time it was brought down and made successful parachute descents on each occasion.

Photographs.—Five hundred and one photographs were taken during the day.

Bombing.—First Brigade.—On the evening of the 4th, 30—20-lb. bombs were dropped on Izel-les-Equerchin, and 22 of them were seen to fall on houses. On the night of the 4th–5th, 34—20-lb. bombs were dropped on Brebières-Beaumont-Quiery-la-Motte, and Rouvroy and all the objectives were hit, and a fire was caused in Brebières. On the 5th, 30—20-lb. bombs were dropped on Neuvereuil, Rouvroy, and Avion. The railway and railway embankment at Rouvroy and the other objectives were all hit.

Second Brigade.—On the night of the 4th–5th, eight 20-lb. bombs were dropped on Reckem Aerodrome and eight on Coucou Aerodrome, where four direct hits were obtained on a shed. On the 5th, 54—20-lb. bombs were dropped on Poelcapelle Station and four on a château near Wicres.

Third Brigade.—No. 100 Squadron dropped eight 20-lb. bombs on various objectives. A train was derailed between

Brebières and Douai. Four machines of No. 11 Squadron left the ground between 11 p.m. and 12.40 a.m., and dropped bombs on Dury, Etaing, and on roads. All the objectives were hit, and machine gun fire was opened on villages.

Fourth Brigade.—Twenty-eight 20-lb. and 10—112-lb. bombs were dropped on H.V. gun position and railways.

Fifth Brigade.—On the night of the 4th–5th, an ammunition dump at Iwuy was attacked with 29—20-lb. bombs by machines of No. 18 Squadron. Two direct hits were obtained, and machine gun fire was opened on transport and other objectives. Four B.E.'s of No. 4 Squadron dropped four 112-lb. and 16—20-lb. bombs on convoys on the roads radiating from Cambrai. Direct hits were obtained on the convoys, and one explosion was caused, and the convoys were also fired at with machine guns.

On the 5th, 10—20-lb. bombs were dropped on Hendecourt.

May 6th.

Reconnaissances. — Fires and explosions were reported opposite the front of the First Army. Very successful contact patrols were carried out by machines of the Fifth Brigade. Lieutenant Keller, No. 23 Squadron, observed about 2,000 men drawn up in the square in Solesmes, and he engaged and dispersed them with machine gun fire.

Artillery Co-operation.—Eighty-three targets were dealt with by artillery with aeroplane observation, and 22 with observation by balloons.

Artillery of the First Army carried out 15 successful counter-battery shoots. One pit was completely blown up, a fire was caused in another, while many of the pits were badly damaged, and one explosion of ammunition was caused.

Artillery of the Second Army engaged 17 hostile batteries; 22 gun-pits were hit, and an explosion of ammunition was caused.

Artillery of the Third Army successfully engaged 22 hostile batteries; 10 direct hits were obtained, five emplacements were damaged, and two explosions caused.

Five hostile batteries were successfully engaged by artillery of the Fourth Army, and 14 by artillery of the Fifth Army, who obtained 12 direct hits on gun positions, destroying two, damaging seven, and causing an explosion of ammunition.

Captain Portal, No. 3 Squadron, ranged the 13th Siege Battery on a battery position, and four O.K.'s were obtained, badly damaging two pits, slightly damaging a third, and causing a large fire in a battery position; he also located and reported by zone call two active hostile batteries, one of which was seen to be engaged. He observed four parties of infantry, followed by six M.T. in Cagnicourt, and reported them by zone call. They were engaged by our artillery, and shells fell all round them and scattered the infantry.

Hostile Aircraft.—Second Lieutenant L. L. Morgan, No. 40 Squadron, engaged a hostile scout, which he drove down in flames; and Captain R. Gregory, of the same squadron, drove one down out of control.

Second Lieutenant Libby and Lieutenant Dickson, No. 43 Squadron, destroyed a German machine, which crashed near Petit Vimy.

Flight Lieutenant Booker, Naval Squadron No. 8, drove down an Albatross Scout out of control, and Second Lieutenant Leishman and Lance-Corporal Dillon, No. 25 Squadron, drove down one in a spinning nose-dive.

Flight Sub-Lieuts. Armstrong and Kerby, Naval Squadron No. 3, attacked an enemy machine, which they drove down out of control. Shortly after this, Flight Sub-Lieut. Kerby engaged an Albatross Scout, which also fell out of control.

While on offensive patrol, five F.E.'s of No. 20 Squadron, engaged two Albatross two-seaters. The Germans were soon reinforced by three formations of Albatross Scouts, composed of eight or nine machines each, coming from different directions. A general engagement commenced at about 5 p.m. at a height of 11,000 feet. The F.E. formation was broken up, but the machines kept well together. Captain Thayre and Captain Cubbon shot one German machine, from which the wings were seen to fall before it crashed. Second Lieutenant Conder and 2nd A.M. Cowell hit another machine, which fell out of control; and a third, which had been engaged at the same time, was driven down in a spinning nose-dive by Lieutenant Solly and 2nd A.M. Bemister. Second Lieutenant Conder's engine stopped, and he had to leave the formation, and was followed down by hostile aircraft. Lieutenant Solly immediately dived to his assistance, and one of the hostile machines was driven down in a vertical nose-dive. Lieutenant Condor's engine picked up, and he at once returned to the fighting. Just after this, Captain Thayre and Captain Cubbon set a German machine on fire, and then dived at and destroyed a hostile machine that was following closely one of ours going down temporarily out of control. At the same time, Second Lieutenant Heseltine and Second Lieutenant Kydd drove down a hostile scout out of control, and Lieutenant Solly, with 2nd A.M. Bemister as observer, hit another German machine, which fell in flames; while Second Lieutenant Babbage and 2nd A.M. Alfred shot down one of the German Scouts, which fell on our side of the lines. The F.E.'s all returned safely.

Fifteen hostile aircraft were encountered by five triplanes of Naval Squadron No. 1, and two of the hostile machines were driven down out of control—one by Flight Commander Dallas and the other by Flight Sub-Lieut. Culling.

While on photographic duty, a patrol of No. 60 Squadron was attacked by several hostile scouts. A patrol of Naval Squadron No. 1 dived to the assistance of the Nieuports, and during the fight Flight Sub-Lieut. Cockey drove one German machine down out of control, and Flight Commander Gerrard drove down another in a damaged condition.

Captain Ball, No. 56 Squadron, flying a Nieuport Scout at 11,000 feet, observed four red Albatross Scouts of a new type going towards Cambrai at 10,000 feet. He dived into the centre of the formation, which broke up, and then got underneath the nearest machine, into which he fired and which lost control and crashed. The remaining three German machines avoided combat, and Captain Ball states that they were easily out-manœuvred and appeared to climb and turn very slowly.

A hostile aeroplane was seen approaching No. 34 balloon, and was at once engaged by anti-aircraft gun fire and brought down.

Photography.—335 photographs were taken during the day.

Bombing.—First Brigade.—Forty-two 20-lb. bombs were dropped over Quiery-la-Motte, Izel-les-Equerchin and Sallumines. Houses in all three places were seen to be hit and destroyed.

Quiery-la-Motte was again attacked late in the evening, when 18—20-lb. bombs were dropped and nine were seen to explode on buildings.

May 7th.

Artillery Co-operation.—Ninety-three targets were dealt with by artillery with aeroplane observation, and 24 with observation by balloons.

Artillery of the First Army carried out 48 successful shoots on hostile batteries; 27 direct hits were obtained, eight explosions were caused, and five pits were destroyed. Ninety-one active hostile batteries were reported by zone call, and fire was quickly opened in response to these calls, and in most cases proved to be effective. Exceptionally good shoots were carried out by Captain Neale, No. 16 Squadron, and Lieutenant George, No. 2 Squadron.

Artillery of the Second Army successfully engaged 14 hostile batteries; 10 gun-pits were hit, and three explosions caused.

Artillery of the Third Army successfully engaged 29 hostile batteries; 17 direct hits were obtained, seven pits were damaged, and 13 explosions were caused. Thirty-five hostile batteries were seen active, on five of which there was observation of fire.

Seven hostile batteries were engaged successfully by artillery of the Fourth Army; four direct hits were obtained, and four explosions were caused. A balloon bed, machine-gun emplacement, and trenches were all hit.

Artillery of the Fifth Army successfully engaged 17 hostile batteries; 13 direct hits were obtained, three gun-pits were demolished, 11 damaged, and two explosions were caused.

Hostile Aircraft.—Captain Gregory, No. 40 Squadron, drove down an Albatross Scout in a damaged condition, and Flight Sub-Lieut. Simpson, Naval Squadron No. 8, drove down two Albatross Scouts much damaged.

Flight Sub-Lieut. Pailthorpe, Naval Squadron No. 8, was suddenly attacked by a hostile scout, which he turned and engaged and finally destroyed.

An offensive patrol of No. 45 Squadron engaged seven hostile aircraft near Lille. Lieutenant Belgrave and Second Lieutenant Stewart shot down one of the German machines in flames, and two of the hostile aircraft were driven down out of control—one by Second Lieutenant Cock and Lieutenant Murison and the other by Second Lieutenants Carleton and Vessey.

A bomb raid of No. 20 Squadron engaged about 10 hostile aircraft, and one was destroyed by Second Lieutenant Babbage and 2nd A.M. Aldred.

Captain Bishop, No. 60 Squadron, while escorting F.E.'s of No. 11 Squadron, drove down two German machines out of control, while a third was driven down out of control by Lieutenant Parker and 2nd A.M. Mee, No. 11 Squadron.

Flight Sub-Lieut. Millward, Naval Squadron No. 1, engaged two hostile aircraft and drove one of them down out of control.

Three German aeroplanes were forced to land after having been engaged by a patrol of No. 48 Squadron.

Second Lieutenant Stead, No. 23 Squadron, attacked an Albatross Scout and drove it down completely out of control.

A great deal of fighting took place during the day between S.E.'s of No. 56 Squadron and hostile formations, and during these combats Captain Meintjes and Lieutenant Hoidge each destroyed a German machine, while two others were driven down out of control—one by Lieutenant Lewis and the other by an S.E. formation.

Second Lieutenant Bell Irving, No. 66 Squadron, also drove down a hostile machine out of control, and Captain Andrews, of the same squadron, forced one to land in a field.

Balloons.—An attack on German balloons was carried out by seven machines of No. 40 Squadron. The pilots crossed the lines at about 20 feet, and, as on a previous occasion, artillery put a barrage on the trenches, but on this occasion 12 other aeroplanes crossed the lines at the same time at a considerable height in order to draw the attention of anti-aircraft gunners. As a result of the attack, seven German balloons were destroyed; three caught fire when high up, two burst into flames when near the ground, and two when on the ground.

The names of the pilots who took part in the attack are :—

Second Lieutenants Morgan, Hall, Cudemore, Redler, Mannock, Parry, and Captain Nixon, who failed to return.

Bombing.—First Brigade.—On the night of the 6th–7th, 42—20-lb. and six 112-lb. bombs were dropped on Pont-à-Vendin, Quiery-la-Motte, Brebières, and Izel. Considerable damage was done in all places, and fires were started in Quiery-la-Motte, while a train entering Pont-à-Vendin is believed to have been hit.

On the 7th, 38—20-lb. bombs were dropped on Izel-les-Equerchin. Twenty-three of the bombs were seen to fall on houses, many of which were destroyed, and two set on fire.

Second Brigade.—On the night of the 6th–7th, eight 20-lb. bombs were dropped on the railway workshops at Hellemmes by Lieutenant Satchell, No. 20 Squadron, from a height of 600 feet, and all the bombs hit the objective, and very considerable damage was done. Lieutenant Cunnell, of the same squadron, dropped eight 20-lb. and two incendiary bombs from 1,000 feet on La Madelaine Station (Lille). Six direct hits were obtained and one shed was seen to be in flames.

On the 7th, 56—20-lb. bombs were dropped on Bisseghem, where four hits were obtained on sheds; two 20-lb. bombs on Messines, and four 20-lb. bombs on a balloon winch near Sequedin.

Third Brigade.—On the night of the 6th–7th, No. 11 Squadron dropped 11—20-lb. bombs on villages. Machine gun fire was opened on transport and troops on the march from heights of 70 to 150 feet. Casualties were caused to men and horses, and convoys were much disorganised.

No. 100 Squadron dropped 12—20-lb. and four phosphorus bombs on trains. One train was derailed and totally destroyed near Carvin by bombs dropped from a height of 150 feet, and two trains in Beaumont Station were hit. Forty 20-lb. and two phosphorus bombs were dropped by this squadron on Dorignies Aerodrome. A fire was started in a factory alongside the aerodrome, and one shed was demolished.

Fifth Brigade.—On the night of the 6th–7th, four B.E.'s of No. 4 Squadron dropped 28—20-lb. bombs on various objectives. Houses in Bourlon village were hit, and machine gun fire was used on transport and other objects.

9th Wing.—On the night of the 6th–7th, 60—20-lb. bombs were dropped on various targets. On the 7th, 60—20-lb. bombs were dropped on Abseon by No. 55 Squadron.

May 8th.

Artillery Co-operation.—Forty-nine targets were dealt with by artillery with aeroplane observation, and 68 with observation by balloons.

Artillery of the First Army obtained 17 direct hits on hostile batteries. Nine pits were badly damaged, and an explosion caused.

Three hostile batteries were successfully engaged by artillery of the Second Army, and three gun-pits were hit.

Artillery of the Third Army successfully engaged 10 hostile batteries, causing one explosion and damaging one pit.

Four batteries were successfully engaged by artillery of the Fourth Army. Twelve direct hits were obtained and six emplacements damaged. With observation by Lieutenant Elliot, No. 52 Squadron, artillery obtained six O.K.'s, 10 Y.'s, and 20 Z.'s on a hostile battery, causing a fire and an explosion, and damaging all emplacements.

Artillery of the Fifth Army successfully engaged four hostile batteries, and a gun-pit was damaged, and an explosion caused. In addition to other work, Second Lieutenants Barker and Strudwick, No. 15 Squadron, reported by zone call seven parties of enemy infantry varying from 20 to 300 in number. They were all effectively engaged by our artillery, and in five instances observation of fire was sent down. They attacked two parties of men with machine gun fire. A barrage was also ranged on a trench which was reported to be strongly held, and many direct hits were obtained. Two active hostile batteries were also located and reported by zone call.

With observation by No. 20 Balloon Section, two active hostile batteries were silenced, and four explosions caused. This section also located 13 active hostile batteries. In addition to this, artillery of the First Army, with balloon observation, successfully engaged two hostile batteries, and caused three explosions of ammunition.

With observations by balloons of the Second Army, nine hostile batteries were successfully engaged.

With observations by balloons of the Fourth Army, three hostile batteries were successfully engaged, and four explosions and a fire were caused.

In addition to many trench shoots, artillery, with observations by balloons of the Fifth Army, silenced two hostile batteries and caused two explosions of ammunition.

Bombing.—Machines of the First Brigade dropped 24—20-lb. bombs on Quiery-la-Motte. Eighteen fell on houses, two of which were demolished, and the other six bombs fell on and damaged the road.

May 9th.

Artillery Co-operation.—Sixty-five targets were dealt with by artillery with aeroplane observation, and seven with observation by balloons.

Artillery of the First Army obtained 29 direct hits on hostile batteries. Four gun-pits were destroyed and 14 badly damaged; an explosion was caused, and one gun-pit was set on fire. Twenty-four area calls were sent down, and two batteries were silenced.

After having registered guns on to hostile batteries, aeroplanes handed over a number of shoots to balloons in order that they should continue the observation of fire.

Artillery of the Second Army successfully engaged six hostile batteries. Six pits were hit and three explosions were caused. Several direct hits were obtained on transport through zone call.

Nine hostile batteries were successfully engaged by artillery of the Third Army, and eight direct hits were obtained on trenches.

Artillery of the Fourth Army engaged one hostile battery.

Six hostile batteries were successfully engaged by artillery of the Fifth Army. Four direct hits on gun positions were obtained, and five gun-pits damaged.

Hostile Aircraft.—Three triplanes of Naval Squadron No. 8 attacked a large formation of hostile scouts. One of the naval pilots had to withdraw owing to his gun having jambed, and Flight Sub-Lieut. Wimbush, after having fought well, had to break off the engagement, as he was wounded, and his engine was hit. Flight Sub-Lieut. R. A. Little continued the fight and drove down one of the scouts after having been closely engaged, but was unable to see its fate owing to the presence of other German machines. After considerable fighting another triplane and some de Havillands came to his assistance, and the hostile machines withdrew. A little later a report was received that enemy machines were working west of Lens, and Flight Sub-Lieut. Little immediately went to look for them, and found L.V.G.'s working at 3,000 feet. He drove one of the German machines down out of control. He was then attacked by six more aeroplanes, one of which shot past him and was immediately attacked from behind and driven down damaged. He then ran out of ammunition, so put his machine into a spin, and thus evaded the attacking Germans and returned to his aerodrome.

Another patrol of five triplanes attacked a large formation of hostile aircraft, but the enemy refused to fight, and five of them went down and landed immediately.

Bombing machines of No. 20 Squadron engaged about 10 hostile aircraft near Courtroi, and Second Lieutenant Howe and Kydd drove one down out of control, while Lieutenant Hay and Sergeant Wait drove down a second out of control. Lieutenant Hazel, No. 1 Squadron, also drove down a German machine out of control.

An offensive patrol of No. 45 Squadron engaged about 15 hostile aircraft near Lille. Second Lieutenant G. H. Cock and Lieutenant J. T. G. Murison engaged two of the German machines at long range, and one fell out of control. The pilot then manœuvred in order to enable his observer to use his gun on three of the hostile aircraft which were diving at them. A burst of about 80 rounds hit one of the German machines in the centre section, and it immediately collapsed and fell, one of its wings being seen to fall off. Second Lieutenants W. A. Wright and E. T. Caulfield-Kelly also brought down one of the attacking machines, which broke in the air and crashed, and Second Lieutenant Johnston and 2nd A.M. Harriers drove down one out of control.

A patrol of No. 48 Squadron encountered eight hostile aircraft near Vitry, and Lieutenant F. P. Holliday and Captain Wall drove down two of them out of control.

Lieutenant Holliday and Captain Wall, on one machine, and Second Lieutenants Price and Moore, on another machine, of No. 48 Squadron, engaged two hostile aircraft near Vitry, and drove one of them down in a field, where they continued attacking it, and both the passengers are believed to have been killed.

Flight Commander Dallas, Naval Squadron No. 1, drove down a German machine in which the observer appeared to be killed, and Flight Sub-Lieutenant Bowman, of the same squadron, drove down a German machine badly damaged.

A photographic reconnaissance of No. 22 Squadron, with an escort of No. 54 Squadron, had a big fight with seven German machines. Captain C. M. Clement and Lieutenant M. K. Parlee, No. 22 Squadron, drove down one of the hostile machines out of control and then dived at three others that were following one of our Sopwith Scouts down. They were unable to get there in time, however, and the Sopwith Scout was forced to land in a field, but they eventually succeeded in engaging one of the German machines, which crashed quite near the Sopwith. Second Lieutenant M. B. Cole, No. 54 Squadron, opened fire at a large white two-seater which went down and was seen to crash by other pilots. Lieutenant E. J. Y. Grevelink, of the same squadron, drove down a black and white German scout which was also seen to crash. A third hostile aeroplane was destroyed by Lieutenant M. D. G. Scott, of the same squadron.

On the evening of the 7th, Captain H. Meintjes, No. 56 Squadron, with three other S.E.'s of the same squadron, dived at a German aeroplane, which they riddled with bullets and drove down. Then they saw four red Albatross Scouts, and Captain Meintjes engaged one at close range. Eventually the German machine got into a favourable position, and Captain Meintjes immediately put his machine into a spin. On shaking off the German machine, he at once regained height and dived at another scout with whom he fought for a considerable time and eventually out-manœuvred, and the hostile machine crashed. Shortly afterwards he engaged another machine of the same type, but he was shot through the wrist and the top of his central lever was carried away. Although suffering considerable pain and flying under great disadvantages, he succeeded in landing his machine undamaged on our side of the lines, and then fainted. Captain Albert Ball failed to return from this patrol, and no details as to what happened are available.

On the 9th, a reconnaissance of No. 70 Squadron was attacked by 15 hostile aircraft while taking photographs. Lieutenants Griffith and Allen fired at close range into one of the German machines, which immediately fell out of control. One of the Albatross Scouts dived on Lieutenant Crang's machine, but his observer, Lieutenant Sully, fired a burst at the attacking scout, which burst into flames and fell. Two other Albatross Scouts were driven down badly damaged.

Lieutenant McQuistan and Gunner Ellis of No. 55 Squadron drove down a German machine out of control.

Bombing.—1st Brigade. — Fifty-seven 20-lb. bombs were dropped on Izel-les-Equerchin and 30—20-lbs. on Quiery-la-Motte. Houses in both places were hit and destroyed. Late in the evening Izel-les-Equerchin was again attacked when 21—20-lb. bombs were dropped, and 15 of the bombs were observed to burst on buildings.

2nd Brigade.—No. 20 Squadron dropped 36—20-lb. bombs on Courtrai goods yard, and obtained three direct hits.

4th Brigade.—Nos. 22 and 52 Squadrons dropped 56—20-lb. bombs from about 8,500 feet on hutments in a wood east of Fontaine Uterte, and a number of direct hits were obtained, while a troop of horsemen were seen to gallop away from the wood.

5th Brigade.—Six 20 lb. bombs were dropped on Hendecourt.

9th Wing.—No. 27 Squadron dropped 10—112-lb. bombs from a height of 2,500 feet on Queue de Boue. Direct hits were obtained and a very large explosion took place, which temporarily upset one of our machines when at a height of 2,000 feet.

No. 55 Squadron dropped 60—20-lb. bombs on La Briquette Aerodrome.

10th May.

Artillery Co-operation. -- Seventy-nine targets were dealt with by artillery with aeroplane observation, and 54 with observation by balloons.

Artillery of the First Army obtained 13 direct hits on hostile batteries; two pits were destroyed, 10 were badly damaged, one was set on fire, and an explosion caused. Houses round battery positions were also badly damaged. Twenty-nine active batteries were reported by zone call.

Twenty-four hostile batteries were successfully engaged by artillery of the Third Army. Seventeen direct hits were obtained and a number af M.O.K.'s, Y.'s and Z.'s; one pit was destroyed, one damaged, and an explosion caused, and a number of direct hits were obtained on trenches.

Artillery of the Fourth Army successfully engaged three hostile batteries.

Sixteen hostile batteries were successfully engaged by artillery of the Fifth Army. Sixteen direct hits were obtained on gun positions, four gun-pits were demolished and 15 damaged, and four explosions of ammunition were caused.

With observation by Lieutenant Creagham, No. 15 Squadron, the 117th Battery destroyed two pits and caused two explosions and a fire, and damaged a third pit.

With observation by Captain Davidson and Second Lieutenant Toomer, No. 15 Squadron, the 152nd Siege Battery obtained four direct hits on a hostile battery, which was very considerably knocked about.

Artillery, co-operating with balloons of the 1st Wing, carried out a number of successful shoots on trench and other targets. Several batteries were silenced, and five explosions were caused, two of these being with observation by No. 24 Balloon, which, in addition, observed for 396 rounds, during which a large fire was caused, and very considerable damage done.

Hostile Aircraft.—Flight Sub.-Lieut. Little, Naval Squadron No. 8, went up to look for an enemy machine which was reported to be doing artillery work, and he encountered five Albatross Scouts, which he engaged. Finding himself outnumbered, he outclimbed them, but, on being joined by a pilot of Naval Squadron No. 1, dived at the German machines, and drove one down apparently much damaged, and probably out of control.

Lieutenant W. A. Bond, No. 40 Squadron, drove down a two-seater Aviatik in a spin.

Flight Sub-Lieut. Bennetts and Flight-Lieut. Compston, Naval Squadron No. 8, drove down a two-seater Albatross out of control; and Captain R. Gregory, No. 40 Squadron, also drove down out of control one of two German machines which he engaged.

Lieutenant Middleton and Second Lieutenant Malcolmson, No. 48 Squadron, engaged 10 hostile scouts, and after considerable fighting, one of the enemy machines was observed to crash.

A patrol of No. 24 Squadron engaged seven single-seater hostile scouts, and Captain Crawford, after having driven one of the German machines off the tail of a de Haviland, fired a whole drum into one of three machines, and it fell right over and went down out of control.

Flight Sub-Lieut. Gagnier, Naval Squadron No. 6, engaged and drove down an Albatross in a spinning nose-dive, after having been closely engaged.

A photographic reconnaissance of No. 55 Squadron had heavy fighting during the whole time they were over the lines. As a result of the fighting, one German machine was destroyed by Lieutenant Pitt and Second Lieutenant Holroyde, and two were driven down out of control—one by Captain Rice and Second Lieutenant Clarke, and the other by Second Lieutenant Webb and 1/A.M. Bond.

Photography.—662 photographs were taken during the day.

Bombing.—First Brigade.—On the night of the 9th–10th, 40—20-lb. and four phosphorus bombs were dropped on Meurchin, Pont-à-Vendin, Henin-Liètard and Annay. Three of the phosphorus bombs dropped in Pont-à-Vendin caused large fires, while considerable damage was done to buildings in Henin-Liètard, and a dump was set on fire. A battery was also attacked and silenced.

On the 10th, 54—20-lb. bombs were dropped on Izel-les-Equerchin, but observation was difficult owing to a thick mist. Four 20-lb. bombs were dropped on Bois du Biez, and a considerable amount of smoke was seen after the bombs had been dropped.

Second Brigade.—Sixty-three 20-lb. bombs were dropped on Reckem Aerodrome, and four direct hits were obtained on a shed.

Third Brigade.—On the night of the 9th–10th, No. 100 Squadron dropped 14—20-lb. and four 112-lb. bombs on Dorignies Aerodrome. Eight 20-lb. and two phosphorus bombs were dropped from 200 feet on a train on the Somain-Valenciennes line, and the train is believed to have been derailed and set on fire. Earlier in the evening, No. 11 Squadron went out and dropped 11—20-lb. bombs on various objectives, and also used their machine guns against enemy troops and transport.

Fifth Brigade.—On the night of the 9th–10th, two B.E.'s of No. 4 Squadron dropped eight 20-lb. bombs in Fontaine-Notre-Dame, and four 20-lb. bombs on Sauchy-Cauchy.

On the 10th, 10—20-lb. bombs were dropped on Hendecourt.

9th Wing.—Twelve 20-lb. bombs were dropped on various objectives.

May 11th.

Artillery Co-operation.—149 targets were dealt with by artillery with aeroplane observation, and 34 with observation by balloons.

Artillery of the First Army obtained 17 direct hits on hostile batteries; two gun-pits were destroyed, eight damaged, four set on fire, while four houses in a battery position were set on fire and seven explosions caused.

Thirty-three hostile batteries were successfully engaged by artillery of the Third Army; 19 direct hits were obtained, damaging four gun-pits, and 10 explosions were seen. Seventy-four hostile batteries were seen active, and on seven there was observation of fire. A number of direct hits were also obtained on trenches.

Artillery of the Fourth Army successfully engaged 12 hostile batteries, obtaining 18 O.K.'s and 30 M.O.K.'s; nine emplacements were damaged, and one explosion caused. Two active hostile batteries were silenced under zone call. The 9th Siege Battery, with observation by Captain Hall, No. 52 Squadron, obtained four O.K.'s and 28 M.O.K.'s on a hostile battery, and all four emplacements were damaged, and a fire and explosion caused. With observation by Lieutenant Rogers, No. 52 Squadron, five direct hits and 27 Y.'s were obtained on a hostile battery.

Twenty-nine hostile batteries were successfully engaged by artillery of the Fifth Army; nine direct hits were obtained on gun positions, four gun-pits were demolished, 15 damaged, and three explosions caused. The 152nd Siege Battery, with observation by Lieutenants Carter and MacDonald, No. 15 Squadron, obtained three direct hits on a hostile battery, demolishing four pits and causing an explosion.

Hostile Aircraft.—Flight Lieut. Booker, Naval Squadron No. 8, drove down three H.A. during the day.

A formation of No. 29 Squadron encountered eight Albatross Scouts, and after a sharp engagement Lieutenant Shepherd drove one down, which crashed, and two others were driven down out of control—one by Captain Chapman and the other by Lieutenant Wood.

A patrol of No. 60 Squadron, led by Major Scott, encountered five Albatross Scouts near Douai and drove them down. The patrol waited over Douai Aerodrome, but no hostile aircraft attacked them. During another combat this squadron drove down two German machines, and Lieutenant Jenkins drove down a third out of control.

No. 48 Squadron encountered a formation of 12 Albatross Scouts, and Lieutenant Holliday and Captain Wall destroyed one of the enemy machines and drove down a second out of control.

Second Lieutenant Smither and Lieutenant Rutherford on one machine, and Captain Letts and Lieutenant Jameson on another machine, also drove down a German machine out of control.

Second Lieutenant Messenger and Private A. Jee, No. 59 Squadron, attacked and destroyed a hostile machine.

While on patrol, Captain R. G. H. Pixley, No. 54 Squadron, encountered a two-seater hostile aeroplane, with which he fought for about 15 minutes and finally drove down, and the German machine was seen to crash into a house in a village.

He returned at a very low altitude, and ad his machine much damaged by gun fire from the ground, and by three German machines which dived at him.

Captain Patrick, No. 23 Squadron, encountered a German machine, which he hit, and from which the wings broke off as it fell in flames.

Three pilots of No. 32 Squadron drove down a German machine in a badly damaged condition.

Lieutenants C. A. Lewis and G. C. Maxwell, No. 56 Squadron, after considerable fighting, drove down one of their opponents out of control, and Major W. D. S. Sanday, No. 19 Squadron, drove down another German machine in a badly-damaged condition.

Photography.—548 photographs were taken during the day.

Bombing. Second Brigade.—No. 20 Squadron dropped 48—20-lb. bombs on a dump at Wervicq. Sixteen direct hits were obtained, which started two fires and caused a very big explosion. Two 20-lb. bombs were dropped on Don and one on Messines.

Fifth Brigade.— Eighteen 20-lb. bombs were dropped on Hendecourt, and a house was destroyed. In addition, 10—20-lb. bombs were dropped on a dump at Bourlon.

S. Wood, Captain,
Staff Officer.

Headquarters, Royal Flying Corps,
 13th May 1917.

ROYAL FLYING CORPS COMMUNIQUÉ.—No. 88.

May 12th.

On the evening of the 11th, patrols of Nos. 11 and 60 Squadrons co-operated effectively with infantry of the XVII. Corps by attacking enemy troops from a low altitude and by generally harassing the enemy.

In a number of other instances, our pilots and observers used their machine guns with good effect.

Artillery Co-operation.—123 targets were dealt with by artillery with aeroplane observation, and 125 with observation by balloons.

Artillery of the First Army obtained 15 direct hits on hostile batteries, five gun-pits were destroyed, 12 badly damaged, one set on fire, and two explosions of ammunition caused.

Artillery of the Second Army successfully engaged 10 hostile batteries; nine gun-pits were hit, and eight explosions were caused. Wire was also successfully cut by the 175 Brigade.

Twenty-one hostile batteries were successfully engaged by artillery of the Third Army; 16 direct hits were obtained, one pit was destroyed, four damaged, and seven explosions were caused. 102 hostile batteries were seen active, on 21 of which there was observation of fire.

Artillery of the Fourth Army successfully engaged nine hostile batteries, three under zone call; six direct hits were obtained, and an explosion caused. The 9th Siege Battery, with observation by Lieutenant Carbery, No. 52 Squadron, obtained three O.K.'s, and 10 M.O.K.'s on a hostile battery, destroying two pits and causing an explosion.

Twenty-six hostile batteries were successfully engaged by artillery of the Fifth Army; 37 direct hits were obtained, 16 gun-pits were demolished, 15 damaged, and five explosions were caused.

In addition to the number of targets registered by balloons, 110 active hostile batteries were located. In one wing, observations were given for over 1,150 rounds, and in another for over 600 rounds.

Two successful shoots, with cross observation from two balloons, were done, and a successful shoot, with combined observation by aeroplane and balloon, was carried out.

No. 21 Balloon ranged the 222nd Siege Battery on to a long column of horse-drawn transport in the Douai road, and the shooting was observed to be acurate and effective.

Hostile Aircraft.—Captain A. W. Keen, No. 40 Squadron, drove down out of control an Albatross two-seater, which was seen by anti-aircraft observers to crash, while a second two-seater hostile machine was driven down out of control by Second-Lieutenant Hon. S. H. D'Arcy and Lieutenant A. E. Pickering, No. 43 Squadron.

On the evening of the 11th, a formation of five Sopwith triplanes of Naval Squadron No. 8 encountered nine Albatross Scouts, which they immediately engaged. Flight-Lieut. Simpson drove one down out of control, and then dived on another scout, which burst into flames and fell. He then attacked two more and drove them down. Two other triplanes of the same squadron observed 15 Albatross Scouts over Douai, and Flight-Commander Booker dived into the formation, while the other triplane waited in order to guard him. The Albatross formation split up and dived away. Shortly afterwards, when reinforced by four de Havilland 4's, they again attacked a German formation, and Flight-Commander Booker drove one down out of control.

A bomb raid of No. 20 Squadron, escorted by Nieuports of No. 1 Squadron, engaged 12 hostile aircraft, and two of the German aeroplanes were driven down out of control—one by Lieutenant Street, and the other by Captain Honnet, both of No. 1 Squadron.

A patrol of No. 45 Squadron shot down a German machine in flames near Lille.

On the evening of the 9th, a combat took place, which was not previously reported owing to the fact that the pilot and observer who took part was wounded. This engagement took place between Lieutenants Price and Clay, No. 48 Squadron, and a hostile scout, which they drove down, and which crashed.

On the evening of the 11th, Flight Sub-Lieuts. Ellis and Millward, Naval Squadron No. 1, engaged six Albatross scouts, and drove one down out of control.

On the 12th, a patrol of No. 48 Squadron engaged six hostile aircraft, and drove one down out of control. In a later engagement this squadron drove down an Albatross Scout out of control. Second Lieutenant J. D. Atkinson, No. 29 Squadron, drove down an artillery machine in a damaged condition, and then attacked a balloon, which was hauled down, but he was unable to see if it were destroyed.

An offensive patrol of No. 54 Squadron, led by Captain Strugnell, dived at a large two-seater crossing the lines, and all the pilots opened fire at the German machine, which crashed in a field. Shortly afterwards, Captain Strugnell drove down another German machine, which crashed in a pond. Second-Lieutenant M. B. Cole, of the same squadron, while escorting F.E.'s, drove down a German machine out of control; his gun jambed, but he followed the German machine down until he saw it crash.

Offensive patrols of No. 23 and 32 Squadrons engaged several hostile formations, but the German machines soon scattered, and were unwilling to fight.

S.E.'s of No. 56 Squadron had several engagements, and one German machine was driven down out of control by Captain Brodbery and Lieutenants Maxwell and Lloyd.

Anti-aircraft of the First Army drove down a German machine out of control, and anti-aircraft of the Second Army brought one down, which fell in our lines.

Photography.—424 photographs were taken during the day.

Bombing—First Brigade.—On the evening of the 11th, 24—20-lb. bombs were dropped on Izel-les-Equerchin, and 18 were observed to hit houses. 92—20-lb. bombs were dropped on Quiéry-la-Motte during two raids; in the first, 10—20-lb. bombs were observed to fall on houses, and four fires were started, and in the second raid a number of bombs were seen to fall on houses. Eight 20-lb. bombs were dropped on Neuvereuil.

Second Brigade.—No. 20 Squadron dropped 72—20-lb. bombs on Ramegnies Chin Aerodrome, and six of the bombs burst on hangars, which were seen on fire when the machines left; sheds were also hit and seen on fire.

Third Brigade.—No. 100 Squadron dropped one 112-lb. and 16—20-lb. bombs between 9.30 p.m. and 3.30 a.m., and hits were obtained on a train near Evin from a height of 200 feet, while a train on the Lille–Tournai line is also believed to have been hit.

Fifth Brigade.—Fifty-four 20-lb. bombs were dropped on Hendecourt.

Information has been received that bombs dropped by the Second Brigade in April on Chateau Motte, on the Mouveaux road, fell on an officers' club. Eight or ten direct hits were obtained, and many officers were killed.

An ammunition train which was bombed near Hellemmes on the night of the 6th–7th May by Lieutenant Satchell, No. 20 Squadron, was hit.

Another report states that a good deal of damage was done in Bohain owing to a British aerial raid on (about) April 26th.

During a recent bombing raid, a troop train in Lille was hit, and 50 soldiers were killed.

Other reports state that the power station at Marais was successfully bombed, and the Hotel de l'Europe (town not known), which was also bombed, was an officers' billet, and much damage was done; one officer was killed and several wounded.

May 13th.

Reconnaissances.—A machine of No. 11 Squadron fired five drums into the trenches at Bullecourt in order to disperse a German attacking party.

Second Lieutenant Cook and Second Lieutenant Goodfellow, No. 15 Squadron, while doing contact patrol on the evening of the 12th, observed bombing between our troops and the enemy in progress, and repeatedly attacked the enemy with Lewis gun fire from a low altitude, and succeeded in driving them into their dug-outs. They also attacked enemy troops in the Hindenburg Line, and reported three active hostile batteries by zone call.

In a number of other instances machine-gun fire was used effectively.

Artillery Co-operation.—120 targets were dealt with by artillery with aeroplane observation, and 91 with observation by balloons.

Artillery of the First Army obtained 24 direct hits on hostile batteries; 19 pits were badly damaged, three were set on fire, and three explosions caused, while houses near battery positions were hit and set on fire.

Artillery of the Second Army successfully engaged 17 hostile batteries; 12 gun-pits were hit, and six explosions caused. A number of successful trench shoots were carried out, and one battery was silenced under zone call.

Twenty-nine hostile batteries were successfully engaged by artillery of the Third Army, which obtained 45 direct hits, damaged seven emplacements, and caused six explosions; 102

hostile batteries were seen active, on 16 of which there was observation of fire; two direct hits were obtained, and an explosion caused. Thirteen direct hits were also obtained on trench targets, where an explosion was observed. The 240th Siege Battery, with observation by Lieutenant A. P. D. Hill, No. 8 Squadron, obtained eight direct hits on a hostile battery, and caused an explosion. The 112th Siege Battery, with observation by Lieutenant W. B. Fryer, No. 12 Squadron, obtained five O.K.'s, 10 Y.'s, and 10 Z.'s on a hostile battery.

With observation by Second Lieutenant D. F. Stevenson, No. 12 Squadron, the 61st Siege Battery obtained four O.K.'s, 16 Y.'s, and three Z.'s on a hostile battery, where three emplacements were hit and an explosion caused.

Twenty direct hits were obtained on hostile batteries by artillery of the Fourth Army. Sixteen emplacements were damaged and four explosions caused. The 75th Siege Battery, with observation by Lieutenant Wills, No. 34 Squadron, obtained three direct hits which destroyed two emplacements, damaged another, and caused three explosions.

Twenty-nine hostile batteries were successfully engaged by artillery of the Fifth Army. Twenty-nine direct hits on gunpits were obtained, five pits were destroyed, 28 damaged, and four explosions caused. The 163rd Siege Battery, with observation by Lieutenants McGregor and Brown, No 3 Squadron, obtained five direct hits on a hostile battery, which destroyed two pits. They also reported by zone call four active hostile batteries, two of which were silenced, and, in addition, took 18 successful photographs.

In addition to a number of successful shoots with observation by balloon of the 1st Wing, artillery caused three explosions and a fire.

Seven batteries were successfully engaged and an explosion caused by artillery co-operating with balloons of the 5th Wing.

Hostile Aircraft.—During the evening, 15 flights were made from the advanced landing ground at St. Elroy on receipt of warnings from First Army wireless that hostile machines were at work, and nine of these machines were discovered and driven off.

When returning from a bomb raid on Reckem Aerodrome, F.E.'s of 20 Squadron were attacked by 12 Albatross Scouts, which were kept out of range by long-distance firing. Near Courtrai the German formation had increased to 30 machines, four of which dived on the tail of an F.E., piloted by Captain F. H. Thayre, who immediately turned and dived in the same direction, and his observer, Captain E. R. Cubbon, fired half a drum into one of the German machines which had dived past them. The enemy machine went straight down and burst into flames. Immediately afterwards three more hostile aircraft were attacked, and by stalling and firing both guns Captains Thayre and Cubbon shot down a second machine, which crashed.

Second-Lieutenant W. P. Scott and 2nd A.M. Cowell, of the same squadron, also shot down a German machine, which was seen to crash.

Lieutenant Drummond, No. 1 Squadron, engaged and drove down a German machine out of control.

A patrol of No. 29 Squadron encountered eight Albatross Scouts. Lieutenant Wray attacked one at close range and followed it down firing until it crashed. Lieutenant Sherwood, during the same encounter, drove down another completely out of control.

Lieutenant Fry, No. 60 Squadron, attacked an Albatross Scout which fell out of control.

Second-Lieutenants McGregor and O'Grady, No. 23 Squadron, drove down a German machine which was seen to fall in flames, and Captain Batrick and Second Lieutenant Stead, of the same squadron, also shot down a hostile machine, which fell in flames. In addition, patrols of this squadron drove down at least six more hostile aircraft badly damaged.

Lieutenants Huston and Foord, No. 18 Squadron, engaged and drove down a Halberstadt, which was seen to crash.

Captain J. O. Andrews, No. 66 Squadron, engaged an Albatross Scout, which he drove down out of control.

Balloons.—Lieutenant F. Sharpe and Lieutenant J. C. C. Piggott, No. 1 Squadron, went out to attack balloons. They crossed the lines at a very low altitude and had to "zoom" over hedges and other obstacles on the way. Armed Germans were seen, who made no attempt to fire, but simply stared at the machines, and in some cases endeavoured to hide. On his return trip Lieutenant Sharpe fired a drum at horses in a field, and then attacked a group of mounted officers and also transport and infantry.

Photography.—592 photographs were taken during the day.

Bombing.—1st Brigade.—Thirty-three 20-lb. bombs were dropped on Quiéry-la-Motte and many of the bombs were seen to burst on the road and on houses.

Thirty-six 20-lb. bombs were dropped on Harnes, and 33 of these were seen to hit houses and buildings. Eight 20-lb. bombs were dropped on Lens, and a barge in the canal on which four fell was destroyed.

2nd Brigade.—No. 20 Squadron dropped 61—20 lb. bombs on Reckem Aerodrome. Two direct hits were observed on hangars and a shed was set on fire.

5th Brigade.—Eight 20-lb. bombs were dropped on Hendecourt.

While on patrol the engine of a pilot of No. 60 Squadron "cut out" owing to the throttle end coming unscrewed. He overcame this difficulty by leaning right forward and holding the throttle open, but not before he found himself within 50 feet of the ground on the enemy's side of the lines.

May 14*th.*

Reconnaissances.—Several successful reconnaissances were carried out.

Captain Manning and Corporal Tollerfield, No. 11 Squadron, attacked German troops with machine-gun fire, and several of the enemy were seen to fall, and a hostile battery was also attacked and silenced.

Machines of the 5th Brigade engaged on contact patrol and artillery work used their machine guns with good effect on a number of occasions.

Artillery Co-operation.—121 targets were dealt with by artillery with aeroplane observation, and 90 with observation by balloons.

Artillery of the First Army obtained nine direct hits on hostile batteries; one pit was destroyed, one set on fire, 10 badly damaged, and five explosions were caused.

Artillery of the Second Army successfully engaged 10 hostile batteries; eight gun-pits were hit, and 10 explosions caused. A number of zone calls were sent down, and a direct hit was obtained on a battery. With observation by Lieutenant Wilson and Major Wright, No. 6 Squadron, artillery obtained five direct hits on a hostile battery and caused six explosions of ammunition, and the target was burning at the end of the shoot.

Twelve hostile batteries were engaged by artillery of the Third Army, and eight direct hits were obtained. Seventy-five hostile batteries were seen active, on 13 of which there was observation of fire. Four O.K.'s were obtained, and two explosions caused.

Eight hostile batteries were successfully engaged by artillery of the Fourth Army. Twenty-three direct hits were obtained, five emplacements damaged and one explosion caused. Two M.T. convoys were engaged and dispersed under zone call.

Twenty-nine hostile batteries were successfully engaged by artillery of the Fifth Army. Fourteen direct hits were obtained on gun-pits, four of which were destroyed, nine damaged, and an explosion caused.

Balloons of the 1st wing carried out seven successful shoots on hostile batteries, and five explosions were caused.

With observation by balloons of the Second Army, three hostile batteries were successfully engaged.

Thirty targets were successfully engaged by artillery co-operating with balloons of the Third Brigade.

With observation by balloons of the Fourth Brigade, four hostile batteries were successfully engaged, and five explosions were caused.

With observation by balloons of the Fifth Brigade, seven hostile batteries were silenced. Cross observation was given by two balloons for three shoots by the 5th R.M.A., all of which were successful.

Hostile Aircraft.—Second Lieutenant W. C. Campbell, No. 1 Squadron, while on special duty, shot down a Roland two-seater, which crashed near Zonnebeke.

Captain Curphey and Second Lieutenants Taylor and Wright, No. 32 Squadron, attacked German balloons. The observers in the balloons were seen to throw out their papers and descend by parachutes, and the balloons were hauled down. The De Havilands were then engaged by six Albatross Scouts, one of which was destroyed by Second Lieutenant Taylor. Captain Curphey was driven down, and his machine was seen to turn over on landing.

Second Lieutenants West-White and Garrett, No. 23 Squadron, engaged three hostile machines and drove all of them down, one of which was forced to land in a field.

Photography.—182 photographs were taken during the day.

Bombing.—5th Brigade.—Six 20-lb. bombs were dropped on Hendecourt.

May 15th.

Reconnaissances.—Successful reconnaissances were carried out by the Second and Third Brigades, and successful contact patrols by machines of the Fifth Brigade.

Artillery Co-operation.—Thirty targets were dealt with by artillery with aeroplane observation, and 66 with observation by balloons.

Artillery of the First Army obtained four direct hits on hostile batteries and damaged three gun-pits. Five hostile batteries were successfully engaged by artillery of the Second Army; five gun-pits were hit, and an explosion caused. Two active hostile batteries were silenced under zone call. With observation by Second-Lieutenants Dowdall and Protheroe, No. 53 Squadron, the 59th Siege Battery obtained four direct hits on a hostile battery, and one pit was set on fire.

Artillery of the Third Army successfully engaged one hostile battery. Forty-two hostile batteries were seen active, on six of which there was observation of fire.

Three hostile batteries were successfully engaged by artillery of the Fourth Army, and three by the Fifth Army.

With observations by balloons of the 2nd Brigade, artillery successfully engaged three hostile batteries and caused an explosion of ammunition, and three hostile batteries were successfully engaged by artillery with observation by balloons of both the 4th and 5th Brigades.

Hostile Aircraft.—While on line patrol, machines of No. 20 Squadron engaged seven hostile aircraft near Quesnoy, and Sub-Lieutenant Grout and 2nd A.M. Tyrrell destroyed one of the German machines, while a second was driven down out of control by Lieutenant A. N. Solly and 2nd A.M. Bemister.

Bombing.—2nd Brigade.—On the night of the 14–15th, No. 20 Squadron dropped 32—20 lb. bombs and three incendiary bombs on Gheluvelt Station. Five direct hits on the station and railway were obtained, and a large explosion was caused.

16th May.

Practically no work was possible owing to unfavourable weather.

No. 13 Squadron carried out four successful contact patrols.

Two hostile batteries were successfully engaged by artillery with observation by balloons of the 2nd Brigade, and a fire was started.

17th May.

The weather was very bad, and flying was practically impossible.

Captain Capel and Lieutenant Brooker, No. 13 Squadron, carried out a successful contact patrol under heavy gun fire and at a low altitude, and much useful information was obtained.

Later in the day, Lieutenant Robertson and Captain Tibbs, of the same squadron, did the same work at an altitude of about 500 feet, and also obtained valuable information, under heavy machine gun and rifle fire.

18th May.

Reconnaissances.—Successful reconnaissances and contact patrols were carried out.

Artillery Co-operation.—Fifty-nine targets were dealt with by artillery, with aeroplane observation.

Artillery of the First Army obtained eight direct hits on seven hostile batteries; four pits were destroyed and three damaged.

Artillery of the Second Army successfully engaged eight hostile batteries; nine gun-pits were hit and three explosions caused.

Fifteen hostile batteries were successfully engaged by artillery of the Third Army; 24 direct hits were obtained and two explosions caused. Thirteen hostile batteries were seen active, on three of which there was observation of fire, and an explosion was caused.

Artillery of the Fourth Army successfully engaged three hostile batteries; seven direct hits were obtained, two emplacements were destroyed, two damaged, and two explosions caused. With observation by Lieutenant Woodhouse, No. 52 Squadron, the 9th Siege Battery obtained four O.K.'s and a large number of Y.'s, Z.'s and M.O.K.'s on a hostile battery, where two pits were destroyed and one damaged. The 110th Siege Battery, with observation by Lieutenant Rogers, No. 52 Squadron, obtained three O.K.'s, 32 Y.'s and 28 Z.'s on a hostile battery, and two explosions were caused.

Five hostile batteries were successfully engaged by artillery of the Fifth Army, and one explosion was caused.

Hostile Aircraft.—Flight-Lieut. Little, Naval Squadron No. 8, observed a German two-seater from the aerodrome, and at once went up, and engaged it when at 10,000 feet N.E. of Lens. During the fighting the German observer was seen to fall. Finally the enemy machine went down, and was followed by Flight-Lieut. Little until he saw that it was out of control. This machine was seen to crash by artillery. Flight-Lieut. Little then engaged three Albatross Scouts, which he drove off.

A German aeroplane was brought down in our lines in the Third Army area by machine gun fire from the trenches.

Bombing.—First Brigade.—Twenty-two 20-lb. bombs were dropped on Sallumines by machines of No. 25 Squadron, and 18 of the bombs were seen to fall on buildings, which were damaged, and four fell on the railway.

Sallumines was again attacked by No. 25 Squadron in the evening, when 32—20-lb. bombs were dropped, and considerable damage was done.

May 19th.

Reconnaissances.—Reconnaissances were carried out by all Brigades, but observation was difficult owing to low clouds.

During successful work by machines of Nos. 4 and 15 Squadrons, many active hostile batteries and other targets were reported by zone call.

Artillery Co-operation.—Seventy-one targets were dealt with by artillery with aeroplane observation, and 12 with observation by balloons.

Artillery of the First Army obtained 19 direct hits on 12 hostile batteries; seven pits were damaged, and four explosions caused.

Artillery of the Second Army successfully engaged six hostile batteries, and two gun-pits were hit. A number of successful zone calls were sent down, and several hostile batteries were silenced.

Nine hostile batteries were successfully engaged by artillery of the Third Army; nine direct hits were obtained, and three explosions caused. Thirty-nine hostile batteries were seen active, on five of which there was observation of fire and two explosions were caused. A number of direct hits were obtained on trenches.

Artillery of the Fourth Army successfully engaged four hostile batteries—one under zone call; parties of infantry were also successfully engaged under zone call.

Seven hostile batteries were successfully engaged by artillery of the Fifth Army; four direct hits on gun positions were obtained, and six pits were damaged. A large number of hostile batteries were reported by zone call, and several were silenced.

Five hostile batteries were engaged by artillery with observation by balloons of the 1st Wing, and four explosions were caused.

Hostile Aircraft.— Second Lieutenant Hon. S. H. D'Arcy and Lieutenant A. E. Pickering, No. 43 Squadron, attacked a hostile scout, which went down out of control and is believed to have crashed.

At about 10 a.m. an Albatross Scout was seen over Le Hameau Aerodrome, and was immediately pursued by Lieutenant Fry, No. 60 Squadron, who engaged it and brought it down near St. Pol. The pilot was taken prisoner.

Flight Sub-Lieut. Culling, Naval Squadron No. 1, had eight engagements, and drove one of his opponents down out of control.

Flight Sub-Lieut Milward, of the same Squadron, also drove down a German machine out of control.

Captains Patrick and Keller and Second Lieutenant Stead, No. 23 Squadron, engaged a formation of 12 Albatross Scouts. A general engagement followed, and the German formation was driven east after one had been driven down badly damaged and several others driven down.

A patrol of No. 19 Squadron engaged a number of German machines, and one was destroyed by Captain W. J. Cairnes.

Balloons.—On the evening of the 18, six machines of No. 1 Squadron crossed the lines at about 20 feet and attacked German balloons, two of which were brought down in flames—one by Lieutenant H. J. Duncan and the other by Second Lieutenant T. H. Lines.

Second Lieutenant W. C. Campbell, No. 1 Squadron, while on patrol, attacked a German balloon and brought it down in flames.

When attacking a hostile balloon a pilot of No. 29 Squadron dived at a battery firing rockets and shot at the gunners with his machine gun.

Photography.—One hundred and eighty-six photographs were taken during the day.

Bombing.—First Brigade.—No. 25 Squadron dropped 20—20-lb. bombs on Sallumines, and 12 of the bombs were seen to fall on houses, which were destroyed.

Third Brigade.—Two 20-lb. bombs were dropped on Cherisy.

Fifth Brigade.—Three 20-lb. bombs were dropped on Hendecourt.

S. Wood, Captain,
Staff Officer.

Headquarters, Royal Flying Corps,
20th May 1917.

No. 34.

CONFIDENTIAL.

ROYAL NAVAL AIR SERVICE.

OPERATIONS REPORT

(with Royal Flying Corps Reports attached).

17th to 31st **MAY 1917.**

NAVAL STAFF,
OPERATIONS DIVISION.
31st May 1917.

ROYAL NAVAL AIR SERVICE.

REPORT OF OPERATIONS

Completed from Reports during period
17th to 31st May 1917.

CONTENTS.

	PAGE
HOME STATIONS - - - - - -	1
DUNKIRK - - - - - -	4
ROYAL NAVAL AIR SERVICE SQUADRONS WITH ROYAL FLYING CORPS REPORTS ATTACHED - - -	9
EASTERN MEDITERRANEAN - - -	11
ROYAL FLYING CORPS COMMUNIQUÉS - -	17

HOME STATIONS.

WEATHER.

High winds, mists, and unfavourable weather conditions generally have interfered with flying operations during the past fortnight.

The usual bomb-dropping practice, instructional flying and patrols, have been carried out whenever possible.

SUBMARINE PATROL WORK.

May 19th.

Felixstowe.—Seaplane No. 8663, whilst on a patrol, observed an enemy submarine 22 miles south of North Hinder. The seaplane got into position and bombs were dropped, but the results are not known.

May 20th.

Felixstowe.—Seaplane 8663 attacked an enemy submarine 10 miles N.E. of North Hinder. Bombs were dropped, and the submarine blew up with great violence and sank.

May 22nd.

Felixstowe.—A seaplane bomb attack was made on an enemy submarine 20 miles S.E. of North Hinder. The submarine dived about 10 seconds before bombs were dropped. Four were released over the spot where the submarine had submerged, and three exploded in the swirl, but results are not known.

May 24th.

Westgate.—During a seaplane patrol in the vicinity of the Kentish Knock, a submarine was sighted and bombed, but no effect was observed.

May 27th.

Scilly Isles.—On the report that an enemy submarine was in the vicinity, a search by seaplane was carried out. The submarine was sighted on the surface and opened fire with a machine gun, puncturing the seaplane's starboard radiator. Four 100-lb. bombs were dropped, two of which appeared to hit the mark.

May 29th.

Scilly Isles.—A seaplane patrol was carried out to search for an enemy submarine reported S.S.W. of Bishops Light. The seaplane attacked, dropping four 100-lb. bombs on the submarine as she submerged, after which black oil fuel and streaks of oil were observed on the surface.

SEAPLANE ATTACK ON ZEPPELIN.

May 24th.

Yarmouth.—During an early morning reconnaissance patrol to Terschelling, Curtiss Flying Boat No. 8666 sighted a super Zeppelin about 10 miles N.E. of Terschelling Island. The seaplane pursued, and at 3,000 feet got to within 300 yards astern, when the Zeppelin threw out a smoke screen, under cover of which he gained the clouds. Half a tray of ammunition was fired into him as he disappeared, but the effect could not be observed.

The same pilot and machine brought down L 22 on May 14th.

ENEMY TORPEDO-CARRYING SEAPLANES' ATTACK ON SHIPPING.

May 20th.

Lowestoft.—Two enemy seaplanes attacked S.S. Birchgrove, of Glasgow, near the Corton Channel Buoy in the Lowestoft area. Each Seaplane fired one torpedo and about 100 rounds from a machine-gun. The torpedoes were discharged from a thousand and two hundred yards respectively, one passing 10 feet astern, and the other under the ship's bottom. The Captain of the Birchgrove states that the torpedoes were dropped when the Seaplanes were about 12 feet above the water. The ship was hit by machine-gun fire and one bomb, but the damage done was not serious, neither were any of the crew hit. The enemy machines then made off in a south-easterly direction.

RAID BY HOSTILE AIRCRAFT.

May 25th.

An air raid was carried out over S.E. Essex and Kent during the afternoon by hostile machines thought to be about 16 in all. A large number of bombs were dropped in Kent, especially at Folkestone, resulting in heavy casualties amongst the civilian population, between 30 and 40 people being killed and 50 injured. Considerable damage was also done to shops and private houses.

Shorncliffe Camp was attacked, where an officer and 10 men were killed and 60 injured.

After leaving Shorncliffe and Folkestone, a number of machines passed over Dover town at a high altitude from west to east.

No bombs were dropped on Dover, and it is presumed that these machines had expended their supplies in the Folkestone-Shorncliffe attack. One of the enemy machines was engaged midway between Dover and Gravelines at 12,000 feet by Flight Lieutenant Leslie, in Sopwith Pup 3691 from Dover Station.

The Sopwith pilot fired about 150 rounds at ranges varying between 150 and 50 yards. Tracers appeared to be entering the enemy machine's fuselage, and large quantities of black smoke came from the engine. The Sopwith was then attacked from above and behind by two other machines, and was forced to abandon the attack on the first machine.

Whilst manœuvring to avoid these machines, the Sopwith fell in a spin which prevented the pilot observing what had happened to the machine he had attacked. Engine trouble then forced the Sopwith to return.

H.M.S. "Morris" reported seeing an aeroplane fall in the water north of the barrage. H.M.S. "Mentor" and several drifters searched the area thoroughly, but failed to find any signs of the enemy machine, which presumably sank.

The destruction of this machine is confirmed by information obtained from the crew of the aeroplane brought down in the Thames Estuary on June 5th.

Hostile aircraft were intercepted by R.N.A.S. machines from Dunkirk on their return journey, and a number of combats took place. (*See* Dunkirk.)

As far as can be ascertained from all reports, two enemy machines were completely destroyed and others driven down out of control.

DUNKIRK.

PHOTOGRAPHIC RECONNAISSANCE.

May 25th.

A photographic reconnaissance was carried out during the afternoon to Zeebrugge and five plates exposed in the vicinity of Lock Gates.

May 27th.

A photographic reconnaissance secured some very good photographs of Tirpitz Battery.

May 28th.

A photographic reconnaissance over Ghent resulted in some excellent photograhs being obtained.

RECONNAISSANCE.

Very little reconnaissance work has been carried out during this period owing to unsuitable weather conditions.

SPOTTING FLIGHTS.

May 27th.

Spotting was carried out during the afternoon. On the following day successful spotting was carried out for about 30 minutes, after which effective smoke screens obscured the objective.

(Nature of guns and objective not received.)

OFFENSIVE PATROL, ENGAGEMENTS WITH ENEMY.

May 24th.

No. 4 Wing (4th Squadron). — An offensive patrol was carried out by three Sopwith machines along the coast to Ostend, then inland over Ghistelles and Nieuport.

When off Ostend Bain a hostile aircraft was observed, going in a westerly direction, about 10 miles out to sea. Flight Sub-Lieut. Chadwick attacked and destroyed this machine north of Bray Dunes. This machine was observed by another pilot to fall to pieces in mid-air and drop into the sea.

During an offensive patrol Flight Sub-Lieut. Ellis attacked a single-seater Scout, 2 miles S.E. of Ghistelles, which he brought down, and observed to crash in a field.

May 25th.

No. 4 Wing (4th Squadron). — On a signal being received that hostile aircraft were over Dover, five Sopwiths left to intercept them on their return.

The formation sighted five hostile aircraft returning off Dunkirk about 30 miles out to sea and went in pursuit, bringing down a large twin-engine biplane north of Westende.

The enemy machine was seen to explode in mid-air, and wreckage was observed floating on the sea 15 miles from the shore.

No. 4 Wing (9th Squadron). — Four Sopwith machines also left to intercept hostile aircraft on their return from England. One pilot observed a large twin-engined enemy machine fall past him very close, in the vicinity of Nieuport. He followed it down and saw it break up.

It is presumed that this was the machine referred to under No. 4 Squadron.

Flight Sub-Lieut. Tanner met about 10 hostile machines some miles out to sea off Zeebrugge. He attacked a large

L.V.G. three times, which finally spun down towards the sea, but did not see it crash.

He engaged another machine, but owing to his engine failing, had to abandon the attack. This pilot observed a machine falling out of control off the coast between Ostend and Zeebrugge.

Flight Sub-Lieut. Le Boutillier engaged an enemy machine and got in nearly 100 rounds, and saw shots hitting. The enemy machine replied with about 10 rounds, then went down in a vertical nose-dive, obviously out of control.

May 26th.

No. 4 Wing (4th Squadron). — While returning from an offensive patrol, Flight Sub-Lieuts. Chadwick and Enstone observed an enemy machine over Furnes, which they attacked and brought down. This was confirmed later by Belgians who observed the hostile machine dive into the Forest d'Houthulst.

May 30th.

No. 4 Wing (9th Squadron).—During an offensive patrol over the Ostend-Bruges-Zeebrugge area by three Sopwiths, an enemy two-seater machine was sighted. One machine dived at it from its front while the other two pilots attacked from astern. The two latter had to abandon the fight owing to jammed guns, but the other pilot eventually got under the enemy machine's tail and finally caused it to nose-dive between Westende and Ostend.

He followed the machine down to 9,000 feet and observed it falling hopelessly out of control.

BOMB ATTACKS.

		Lbs.	
Hostile shipping	20th May	888	Aeroplanes.
St. Denis Westrem Aerodrome.	25th ,,	1,016	Aeroplanes.
St. Denis Westrem Aerodrome.	28th	953	
Zeebrugge Mole and hostile shipping.	27th	337	
Zeebrugge Mole and hostile shipping.	31st	1,209	
Zeebrugge Mole	31st	4,234	Aeroplanes and seaplanes.
Ostend Seaplane Base	27th	2,456	Aeroplanes.
,, ,, ,,	29th	1,842	,,
Ostend (Ateliers de la Marine).	31st	4,464	Aeroplanes and seaplanes.
Bruges Docks and shipping.	31st	2,362	Aeroplanes.

BOMB ATTACKS ON HOSTILE SHIPPING.

May 20th.

No. 5 Wing (5th Squadron).—A bomb attack was carried out by four machines on two destroyers, two miles north of Zeebrugge, during the afternoon. Four 112-lb. and 20 Le Pecq bombs were dropped, but the result could not be clearly observed. Four hostile machines were observed near Ostend, but these did not come sufficiently near to attack or be attacked.

BOMB ATTACK ON ENEMY AERODROME.

May 25th.

No. 5 Wing (5th Squadron).—A bomb attack was carried out by four machines on the aerodrome at St. Denis Westrem. Four 112-lb., eight 16-lb., and 20 Le Pecq bombs were dropped.

The aerodrome was considerably damaged, and several bombs exploded so close to eight large aeroplanes standing on the aerodrome, that damage to them is considered certain.

BOMB ATTACK ON ZEEBRUGGE MOLE AND HOSTILE SHIPPING.

May 27th.

No. 5 Wing (5th Squadron).—A bomb attack was carried out during the evening on Zeebrugge Mole and hostile shipping.

One 65-lb. and eleven 16-lb. bombs were dropped. Particulars of results are not given. When leaving the Mole a destroyer was observed eight miles north of Ostend. Six 16-lb. bombs were dropped from 4,000 feet, which fell in close proximity to the destroyer.

BOMB ATTACK ON SEAPLANE BASE.

May 27th.

No. 5 Wing (7th Squadron).—A bomb attack was carried out during the night on the Seaplane Base at Ostend by four Short bombers. All pilots found the objective, three of which dropped bombs on the target. Owing to the visibility being poor it was difficult to observe the results, but many explosions were seen in close proximity to the objective. In all twenty-four 65-lb. and eight 112-lb. bombs were dropped.

Pilots report that since last month many new powerful searchlights have been installed round the Bassin de Chasse.

BOMB ATTACK ON ENEMY AERODROME.

May 28th.

No. 5 Wing (5th Squadron).—Three machines carried out a bomb attack during the afternoon over the Aerodrome at

St. Denis Westrem. Two 112-lb., fourteen 16-lb., one 65-lb. and twenty Le Pecq bombs were dropped on the objective from 11,200 to 13,000 feet. Two direct hits were scored on one of the sheds, while several bombs were observed to explode in such proximity to eight large bombing machines standing on the Aerodrome that it is almost certain they were damaged.

A hostile seaplane was observed about two miles off Zeebrugge, flying at about 7,000 feet, going east. Anti-aircraft gun-fire was experienced but was inaccurate.

The visibility was good and all machines returned safely.

BOMB ATTACK ON SEAPLANE BASE.

May 29th.

No. 5 Wing (7th Squadron).—A bomb attack was carried out during the night on the Seaplane Base at Ostend, by four Short machines. Six 112-lb. and eighteen 65-lb. bombs were dropped on the target, and observed to explode in close proximity.

BOMB ATTACK ON ZEEBRUGGE MOLE AND SHIPPING.

May 31st.

No. 5 Wing (7th Squadron) and Seaplanes.—A bomb attack was carried out during the afternoon on Zeebrugge Mole and hostile shipping by four machines. Four 112-lb., one 65-lb., sixteen 16-lb., and twenty Le Pecq bombs were dropped on the Mole and two destroyers lying outside. Two direct hits were observed on east end of Mole, and a number of bombs seen to explode close to three destroyers getting under way outside the Mole.

A further attack was carried out in conjunction with seaplanes on Zeebrugge Mole at midnight. One 550-lb., six 65-lb., twelve 112-lb., and thirty 65-lb. bombs were dropped.

A fire was observed to have been started, which lasted for some minutes.

BOMB ATTACK ON BRUGES DOCKS AND SHIPPING.

May 31st.

No. 5 Wing (7th Squadron).—A bomb attack was carried out at midnight on Bruges Docks and shipping. Six 112-lb. and twenty-six 65-lb. bombs were dropped, but details of results are not stated.

BOMB ATTACK ON OSTEND.

May 31st.

No. 5 Wing (7th Squadron) and Seaplanes.—A bomb attack was carried out on Ateliers de la Marine, Ostend, by aeroplanes and seaplanes. Twelve 112-lb., forty 65-lb., and one 520-lb. bombs were dropped, but details of results are not stated.

ATTACKS ON ENEMY SUBMARINES.

May 24th.

Seaplanes.—A dawn submarine patrol was carried out by two seaplanes, during which a submarine was observed, stationary. The machines proceeded to attack and the submarine immediately started, full speed, steering a zigzag course, and submerging. Seaplane 9060 followed, and dropped two 100-lb. bombs from about 800 feet. The first bomb fell on the spot where submarine had disappeared and the second bomb dropped 20 yards over. The submarine appeared to turn to starboard, when nearly submerged.

Both bombs were seen to explode, delay action fuses being used.

A thin line of oil was observed on the surface later, but no further sign of the submarine was seen.

May 27th.

No. 5 Wing (5th Squadron).—During a bomb attack on hostile shipping off Ostend an enemy submarine was observed in the act of submerging. Six 16-lb. bombs were dropped and observed to explode on the spot where the submarine had dived.

KITE BALLOON OBSERVATION.

No. 11 Kite Balloon Section.—Ascents were made on two days, the total time flown being 51 minutes.

NAVAL SQUADRONS WITH THE ROYAL FLYING CORPS.

Period May 20th to June 2nd inclusive.

NAVAL SQUADRON No. 1.

This Squadron was attached to the Third Brigade R.F.C. until June 1st, when it was transferred to the 2nd Brigade R.F.C., 32 offensive patrols, in addition to escorts to reconnaissances, &c., having been carried out over the lines.

Hostile Aircraft.—Fifty-eight hostile machines were engaged during the fortnight, one of which was driven down completely out of control; several others were driven down apparently damaged.

NAVAL SQUADRON No. 3.

Enemy aircraft during this period were inactive, and consequently the number of combats fought have been less than usual.

On the 20th May one enemy machine was driven down out of control near Bullycourt, and a number of others were engaged, but the results were indecisive. On the 23rd May four enemy machines were driven down out of control after a considerable amount of fighting. On the 27th one pilot attacked a hostile machine that was attacking one of our aeroplanes, and after firing about 30 rounds the enemy machine crashed. The same pilot then attacked and drove down two more hostile machines in a spin.

There were no casualties during this period.

NAVAL SQUADRON No. 6.

This Squadron was attached to the 4th Brigade R.F.C., and carried out 23 offensive patrols and 6 escorting patrols. Eight combats have been fought, in which one hostile machine was driven down out of control and one driven down and forced to land in the enemy's lines. In one combat, Squadron-Commander Breese was slightly wounded.

Casualties.—Flight Lieutenant De Roeper, wounded 25th May 1917, Flight Sub-Lieut. Bailey, struck off strength, 23rd May 1917, Acting Flight Commander McLaren, struck off strength 26th May 1917.

NAVAL SQUADRON No. 8.

This Squadron, being attached to the First Brigade R.F.C., carried out 26 offensive patrols and 71 flights after hostile aircraft reported over our lines. One hostile machine has been brought down out of control.

Casualties.—Flight Lieutenant Pailthorpe, missing 23rd May 1917, Flight Sub-Lieut. Hall, wounded 23rd May 1917, Flight Sub-Lieut. Smith, missing 24th May 1917. *Ns+so*

Honours (Awarded by French through R.F.C.).—Legion d'Honneur (Croix de Chevalier), Squadron Commander Bromet, D.S.O.; Croix de Guerre, Flight Commander Booker.

NAVAL SQUADRON No. 10.

This Squadron, being attached to the Second Brigade R.F.C., has carried out 12 patrols, 16 flights after hostile aircraft, and two escorts. One hostile machine has been brought down and four driven down out of control.

Casualties.—Flight Sub-Lieut. Pattison, wounded; Flight Sub-Lieut. Disette, killed in accident.

EASTERN MEDITERRANEAN STATION.

Mudros, May 25th, 1917.

Compiled from Weekly Reports Nos. 61 and 62, dated from May 11th to 25th.

THASOS AIR STATION.

"A" SQUADRON.

May 12th.

Result of Reconnaissance.—On the statement of deserters that submarines were being assembled at Kavalla a reconnaissance of the enemy coast was carried out from north of Thasos to Leftura Bay. At the latter place rows of boats were observed drawn up on the beach near the pier. Bombs were dropped which damaged the pier.

No submarines were observed.

Note.—During the week ending May 25th the principal operation in which Naval Aircraft have been engaged has been in connection with the bombardment of Kavalla.

Recent information has disclosed a considerable degree of enemy activity at Kavalla. It was reported that a special party of Germans had been sent to erect craft which had arrived from Germany in sections.

From the description it was not clear whether these craft were submarine or surface vessels, but every indication pointed to some operation being afoot to which the enemy attached considerable importance. New minefields being located and the reported presence of additional heavy guns on the coast added emphasis to the point.

Accordingly orders were issued for Naval Aircraft to spot for the monitors detailed to carry out the bombardment, to provide the necessary escort to spotting machines, and to undertake a reconnaissance for submarines and mines during the bombardment.

Three machines were flown from Mudros to Thasos to assist in submarine and mine reconnaissances during the operations. All R.N.A.S. units on this front participated in the operations.

May 20th.

Spotting Operations and Bomb Attacks.—This squadron spotted for M. 33 and M. 29, bombarding the Custom House, Post Office, and any lighters found in Kavalla harbour.

F. Squadron of five bombers and three escorts, flying from Marian, timed their arrival within one minute of the first monitor opening fire, and dropped a few bombs in the Kavalla forts, of which one made a direct hit on an occupied emplacement. The squadron continued afterwards to circle over the forts, dropping an occasional bomb, and effectually preventing the enemy manning their guns.

The remaining machines of " E " squadron flew from Hadji Janos on the evening of the 19th to Marian to reinforce " F " Squadron's escort for the operations.

As the operations were expected to take four or five hours the duties were carried out in watches, the first machine leaving at 4.10 a.m.

One machine returned at 7 o'clock and reported that the small monitor had been spotted for one hour and three-quarters on to the Custom House (this building had been used for the erection of aircraft).

Sixteen O.K.'s were registered. Fires were started in the houses for 400 yards to the west of the Custom House, the Custom House itself, and the Post Office and warehouses used as barracks by the 19th Greek Regiment.

The other aeroplane, sent to spot for Raglan, piloted by Flight Sub-Lieut. J. D. Haig with Sub-Lieutenant Keightly, R.N.V.R., as observer, failed to return and there appears no doubt, from information supplied, that she was shot down by an enemy aeroplane, both pilot and observer being killed. The machine was subsequently seen from one of the escort machines of F. Squadron in the water with only the top plane showing above the surface and about six small boats around it.

The following piece of fiction, founded on fact, regarding the operations appeared in the Sofia Press Message of May 21st :—

"On May 20th from 5 to 9 o'clock 13 enemy ships of war bombarded the town of Kavalla, while twelve enemy aeroplanes dropped bombs on the town at the same time. Several houses have been destroyed. The military buildings have not been damaged and the military forces have received no harm. Lieut. Eschwege shot down an enemy aeroplane, which fell into the sea."

May 18th.

Bomb Attack on Gereviz.—A bomb attack on Gereviz Seaplane base was carried out at dawn by two Henri Farmans, escorted by a Bristol Scout, and 576-lbs. of bombs were dropped.

One bomb dropped close alongside one hangar and another between two hangars, probably causing some damage to them.

May 18th.

A Photographic Reconnaissance was carried out over the Kavalla area by two aeroplanes, and it was observed that one of the three guns in the battery 1,000 yards west of Kavalla, which had been bombarded on 24th April, had been removed.

May 21st.

A Photographic Reconnaissance was carried out over Kavalla to observe the results of the bombardment of the previous day.

A series of photographs were taken and the Custom House was seen to be damaged. Owing to a slight mist it was difficult to estimate other effects caused by the bombardment.

May 24th.

A Bomb Attack was made on the army bakeries at Pravi which supply the enemy forces on the lower Struma front. No report as to the damage has yet been received.

STAVROS AIR STATION.

"D" SQUADRON.

May 12th.

From the above date to the 16th inclusive, reconnaissance and spotting flights have been carried out daily.

May 18th.

Reconnaissance.—A careful reconnaissance was made by two machines of the enemy first and second trench line systems and the occupation of certain emplacements was confirmed.

May 21st.

Spotting Flights.—H.M.S. "Endymion" was spotted by a Henri Farman aeroplane on to an enemy battery while a Nieuport observed for M. 18 firing at another target in the vicinity. An enemy machine was obsered by the Nieuport pilot, who took up position to escort the Farman, and called up a second Nieuport to assist. H.M.S. "Endymion" thereupon ordered the machines to return to their aerodrome, they having already been spotting for over two hours.

May 24th.

Reconnaissances. — Two reconnaissances were carried out, during which proclamations were dropped.

DETACHED SQUADRON WITH ROYAL FLYING CORPS.

"E" Squadron at Hadji Janos.

May 12th.

Engagement with Enemy.—Two flights were made resulting in one combat. No decisive result was obtained.

Owing to the exigencies at other stations "E" Squadron has for the time been reduced to two pilots in addition to the Commanding Officer.

May 27th.

Accident.—Whilst the bombing squadron were preparing for their last operation on the Struma front prior to removing to Thasos, an accidental explosion destroyed 10 of their aeroplanes, killing four men and wounding five others. The loss of these machines was most unfortunate, as they were about to undertake important operations in Bulgaria which have now to be carried out by a smaller squadron destined originally for Mityleni.

"F" Squadron at Marian.

May 13th.

Bomb Attacks.—A bomb attack was carried out on Demirhissar Railway Station and dumps, 1,500 lbs. of bombs being dropped. Accurate shooting was hampered by bumpy weather, but two bombs were seen to fall among stores. Later in the dry Angista Station was attacked and 1,500 lbs. of bombs were dropped. Three large bombs burst on the railway line and several more on the edge of the station itself.

May 14th.

Poorna Railway Station, camp, and dumps were attacked and 1,500 lbs. of bombs dropped. A coalstack was hit and also a dump which was probably ammunition, as a large column of smoke was seen to rise to a great height.

May 15th.

Two successful raids were made on a large scattered camp half-way between Obaja and Spatovo, and 1,500 lbs. of bombs were dropped on each occasion, two direct hits being observed.

May 18th.

A bomb attack was made on Drama Air Station during the morning by five bombers with two escorts, during which 1,333 lbs. of bombs were dropped.

Four bombs made direct hits on buildings, and it is thought probable that some damage was caused to several hangars.

Over Angista, on the return journey, Flight Sub-Lieut. G. A. Magor was hit in the head by a piece of shell from enemy gunfire, but managed to bring his machine back safely to the base.

In the afternoon a camp lying W.N.W. of Razolivos was the object of attack.

Five bombing machines with one escort dropped 1,445 lbs. of bombs, scoring a number of direct hits.

The Major-General Commanding Twelfth Corps has expressed his satisfaction at the extremely efficient and effective work carried out by R.N.A.S. Squadrons, and his appreciation of the difficulties involved.

THERMI AIR STATION.

"B" Squadron.

May 17th.

The aeroplane which landed at Chios on May 9th returned to Thermi. No other flying has taken place during the period under review.

IMBROS AIR STATION.

"C" Squadron.

May 11th.

Reconnaissance.—The usual reconnaissance of the straits was made, one T.B.D. and one steamer of about 2,000 tons being observed.

May 12th.

Spotting Flight.—The Straits were reconnoitred at dawn, and M. 17 was spotted on to a gun position observed the previous day. The shooting was correct, but no direct hit on the gun was observed.

May 17th.

Spotting Flight.—Spotting was carried out for "Raglan" on to gun positions in 13.C.3 and 22.V.7 and 8, the nearest shot to the former being 100 yards, and the latter having the earthworks broken down by a shell which burst within 200 yards. Later in the afternoon "Raglan" was again spotted on to 13.C.3, making equally good shooting. M. 7 firing on the emplacement in 17.S. 8 and 9 was also spotted. Three small monitors fired altogether 120 rounds at 13.C.3, two direct hits being obtained and many other shells falling within 50 yards. The gun is reported to have been destroyed.

May 18th.

Spotting Flight.—During the morning two machines spotted for monitors firing at guns in squares 17.S.9, 13.C.3, and on

Hunter Weston Hill. A number of O.K.'s were registered, the vicinity of the guns being ploughed up, although no direct hits on the guns were made.

A large explosion was observed in square 17.S.5, resulting in a big column of black smoke. It is probable that this was from the destruction of an ammunition dump.

May 20th.

Enemy Attack on Air Station.—During the morning an 8·2-inch gun from the Peninsula opened fire on the air station. Six shells were fired, of which one fell in the lagoon, one on the edge of the aerodrome, one in the old air service headquarters, and three more over the Bessoneaux in the vicinity of the present quarters. No damage was done. The machines were removed from the aerodrome to a position of greater security behind the hill.

May 20th.

Spotting Flight.—Spotting was carried out for M.17, firing at the gun in square 13.J.3, but the gun replied, and having the superior range forced M.17 to move her position.

ROYAL FLYING CORPS COMMUNIQUÉS.

ROYAL FLYING CORPS COMMUNIQUÉ, No. 89.

May 20th.

Reconnaissance.—Successful reconnaissances and contact patrols were carried out, and during this work our aeroplanes frequently attacked enemy troops with machine gun fire.

A patrol of six Nieuports of No. 60 Squadron attacked hostile troops and other objectives with machine gun fire from 500 feet, while seven F.E.'s of No. 11 Squadron dropped bombs on trenches, and then attacked the occupants with gun fire.

Aeroplanes of No. 54 Squadron attacked a machine gun party from a height of 20 feet.

Artillery Co-operation.—128 targets were dealt with by artillery with aeroplane observation, and 87 with observation by balloons.

Artillery of the First Army engaged 14 hostile batteries; 14 direct hits were obtained, three pits were destroyed, six damaged, three explosions were caused, and two fires were started. Three direct hits were obtained on a house in Oppy, and it was destroyed.

Nine hostile batteries were successfully engaged by artillery of the Third Army, which obtained 14 O.K's. three M.O.K's, 35 Y.'s and 100 Z.'s; five gun-pits were damaged and eight explosions caused. Ninety-nine hostile batteries were seen active, on 20 of which there was observation of fire, and one pit was damaged. The 239th Siege Battery, with observation by Lieutenant Holdsworth and Sergeant Watson, No. 8 Squadron, obtained four O.K.'s on a hostile battery, and three emplacements were hit.

Artillery of the Fourth Army obtained 11 O.K.'s and eight M.O.K.'s on batteries; five emplacements were damaged, and a large explosion caused.

Nineteen batteries were successfully engaged by artillery of the Fifth Army, which obtained eight direct hits on gun positions; nine gun-pits were damaged, and two explosions caused.

With observation by balloons of the First Brigade, two hostile batteries were engaged and silenced, and other successful shoots were carried out on trenches and houses.

Artillery, with observation by balloons of the Second Brigade, carried out nine destructive shoots; two explosions were caused, and a fire was started in a hostile battery position, while four explosions were caused in a dump on to which artillery had been ranged.

648 rounds were observed by balloons of the Third Brigade.

On the 19th, balloons of the Fifth Brigade registered 17 trench points, and five batteries were successfully engaged, three of which were silenced, and one explosion was caused. 500 rounds were observed, and good observation work was done.

Hostile Aircraft.—An offensive patrol of No. 20 Squadron engaged 10 H.A. near Menin, and one was driven down out of control by Second Lieutenant Conder and Second Air Mechanic Cowell. Ten H.A. were also engaged by an offensive patrol of No. 45 Squadron, and two of the enemy machines were shot down in flames by Sergeant Cook and Lieutenant Blaiklock. A third was destroyed by Captain Jenkins and Lieutenant Eglington, while another was driven down out of control by Second Lieutenants Cock and Carey.

On the evening of the 19th, an engagement lasting three-quarters of an hour took place between 12 triplanes of Naval Squadron No. 1 and a large formation of H.A. Flight Sub-Lieut. Ellis shot down one of the German machines, from off which the wings were seen to break. Flight Commanders Dallas and Gerrard, Flight Lieut. Eyre and Flight Sub-Lieut. Minifie each shot down a German machine, which was seen to fall completely out of control.

On the 20th, Flight Lieut. Culling, Naval Squadron No. 1, attacked an Albatross, into which he fired 100 rounds at close range and it then fell out of control.

While on escort duty, Second Lieutenant A. M. Wray, No. 29 Squadron, attacked an Albatross, which was driven down and was seen to break up in the air. Second-Lieutenant Shepherd, of the same squadron, attacked a second hostile machine which burst into flames and fell. Second Lieutenant A. W. Gardner and Lieutenant P. D. McIntosh, No. 11 Squadron, drove down a German machine out of control and another in a damaged condition, while a third was driven down out of control, and the pilot is believed to have been killed by Captain Manning and Second Lieutenant A. M. West, also of No. 11 Squadron.

An escort composed of machines of No. 48 Squadron had several engagements, and Second Lieutenant Fraser and Private J. H. Muscott drove down one of their opponents out of control with the tail apparently broken. Second Lieutenant H. J. Pratt and Lieutenant H. Owen in one machine and Captain R. Barker and Lieutenant Jeff in another machine, drove down two of the German machines out of control after fighting superior numbers.

Flight Lieut. De Roeper, Naval Squadron No. 6, observed two H.A. at which he dived and opened fire. One of the hostile machines turned completely over and fell. Flight Sub-Lieut. Bailey, of the same squadron, also attacked a German machine, which is believed to have fallen out of control.

Captain Pitcher and Lieutenant Isles, No. 3 Squadron, engaged a German machine, which was last seen going down very steeply just over Havrincourt Wood. Information has now been received from the First Anzac Corps that this machine crashed in Havrincourt Wood and the pilot has been taken prisoner.

Flight Sub-Lieut. Rochford, Naval Squadron No. 3, attacked one of a formation of six H.A., which went down out of control.

Captain Patrick and Second Lieutenants Stead and O'Grady, No. 23 Squadron, saw three H.A. attacking an R.E., eight over Quéant, and immediately dived to the assistance of our machine. A long engagement took place between one of the German machines and Captain Patrick at heights varying from 1,000 to 200 feet, and the German machine was seen to fall temporarily out of control, but on flattening out crossed the trenches and was then observed by anti-aircraft to crash. In another instance, pilots of No. 32 Squadron observed several hostile scouts attacking an R.E. 8, and at once went to assist the R.E. 8, but the German machines flew away, and would not fight.

Much fighting took place between machines of No. 56 Squadron and hostile formations, and Lieutenant Hoidge and Captain Broadberry each drove down one of their opponents out of control.

Bombing.—First Brigade.—On the evening of the 19th, 24 20-lb. bombs were dropped on Wingles by machines of No. 25 Squadron.

On the 20th, 15 machines of No. 10 Squadron dropped 124 20-lb. bombs on an active anti-aircraft battery, which was silenced. Twenty-eight 20-lb. bombs were dropped on Sallaumines by No. 25 Squadron, and all the bombs were seen to burst on and around houses. Sallaumines was again attacked in the evening, when 28 20 lb. and four incendiary bombs were dropped, and damage was done to buildings nnd to the railway. Four 20-lb. bombs were dropped at a hostile battery, and were seen to burst near the objective.

Fifth Brigade.—Nine phosphorus bombs were dropped at hostile balloons, which were promptly hauled down, and 11 20-lb. bombs were dropped on Hendecourt.

Ninth Wing.—Six 230-lb. bombs were dropped on Carvin by machines of No. 27 Squadron. Two of the bombs were seen to burst on the railway line west of Carvin, and two on a depôt just south of the town. Sixty-four 20-lb. bombs were dropped on Cantin Aerodrome by machines of No. 55 Squadron, and the bombs fell on and near the aerodrome.

Photography.—880 photographs were taken during the day.

May 21st.

Reconnaissance.—Successful reconnaissances and contact patrols were carried out.

Second Lieutenants Barker and Strudwick, No. 15 Squadron, attacked a party of men with machine gun fire.

Artillery Co-operation.—Sixty-seven targets were dealt with by artillery with aeroplane observation, and 51 with observation by balloons.

Artillery of the First Army successfully engaged 11 hostile batteries and obtained six direct hits, destroying three pits, damaging ten and causing four explosions of ammunition, five direct hits were also obtained on a dump, and 20 active hostile batteries were reported by zone call.

Two hostile batteries were successfully engaged by artillery of the Second Army, and three gun-pits were hit.

Artillery of the Third Army successfully engaged 14 hostile batteries, obtaining 12 O.K.'s and causing an explosion. Seventy-nine hostile batteries were seen active, on eight of which there was observation of fire; a direct hit was obtained and an explosion caused.

Nine hostile batteries were successfully engaged by Artillery of the Fourth Army, and one was silenced under zone call; 25 O.K.'s and five M.O.K.'s were obtained, four emplacements were damaged and two explosions caused. The 240th Siege Battery with observation by Captain Murray, No. 52 Squadron, fired 100 rounds on a hostile battery and obtained eight direct hits. The 37th Siege Battery, with observation by Lieutenant Low, No. 9 Squadron, also fired 100 rounds on a hostile battery; four emplacements were damaged and a large explosion caused.

Four hostile batteries were successfully engaged by artillery of the Fifth Army; a direct hit was obtained on a gun position and two pits were damaged.

With observation by balloons of the Second Brigade, two hostile batteries were successfully engaged, and 17 batteries were located.

Six hostile batteries were engaged by artillery with observation by balloons of the Third Brigade, and an explosion was caused, while an active anti-aircraft gun was engaged and compelled to withdraw. Twenty-nine active hostile batteries were reported.

Hostile Aircraft.—In response to wireless calls 11 flights were made by machines of Naval Squadron No. 8 with the result that 15 hostile artillery machines were driven away.

Four machines of No. 25 Squadron while on photography were attacked by hostile scouts. Sergeant J. H. R. Green and Private H. Else fired three drums into one of the scouts, which side-slipped and then fell out of control, while a second machine was driven down out of control by Lieutenants A Roulstone and H. Cotton. One of the German machines is reported to have crashed by anti-aircraft observers.

Lieutenant W. C. Campbell, No. 1 Squadron, engaged and destroyed a German machine near Capinghem.

Flight Sub-Lieut. Nash, Naval Squadron No. 10, drove down a hostile machine out of control.

Anti-aircraft of the First Army brought down a hostile aeroplane which fell near Avion.

Bombing.—First Brigade.—Forty-four 20-lb. bombs were dropped on Rouvroy and Izel by No. 25 Squadron, and houses in both places and the railway in Rouvroy were hit.

Fifth Brigade.— Eleven 20-lb. bombs were dropped on Hendecourt.

May 22nd.

Reconnaissance.—Reconnaissances were carried out by the First, Second and Fourth Brigades, and a contact patrol by the Third Brigade.

Artillery Co-operation.—Forty-seven targets were dealt with by artillery with aeroplane observation and 71 with observation by balloons.

Artillery of the First Army successfully engaged 12 hostile batteries; 10 direct hits were obtained, seven pits were destroyed, four damaged, and eight explosions caused. Seventeen area calls were sent down.

Four hostile batteries were successfully engaged by artillery of the Second Army. Five pits were hit and an explosion caused, and some successful zone calls were sent down.

Artillery of the Third Army successfully engaged 10 hostile batteries, obtaining seven direct hits, damaging two gun-pits and causing an explosion.

Three hostile batteries were successfully engaged by artillery of the Fourth Army, which obtained seven O.K.'s and 10 M.O.K.'s and damaged two emplacements.

One hostile battery was successfully engaged by artillery of the Fifth Army and two direct hits were obtained; one pit was damaged and an explosion caused. Second-Lieut. Buckingham and Lieutenant Cox, No. 15 Squadron, observed 164 rounds fired by the 77th Siege Battery, which obtained 17 direct hits on a trench. This pilot and observer reported seven active hostile batteries by zone call, in addition to other work. Machines of the Fifth Brigade reported 41 active hostile batteries by zone call.

Balloons of the First Brigade, co-operating with artillery, carried out seven successful shoots on active hostile batteries, three of which were silenced and five explosions caused. After registration had been completed in one of the shoots the work was handed over to an aeroplane to carry out fire for effect.

Two hostile batteries were successfully engaged with observation by balloons of the Second Brigade.

No. 35 Balloon Section carried out a successful pre-arranged shoot in co-operation with No. 8 Squadron; the aeroplane observer left the battery with a satisfactory bracket and the balloon observer carried on the shoot. Balloons of the Third Brigade successfully ranged on 21 miscellaneous targets.

Artillery, with observation by the 5th Balloon Wing, engaged 16 hostile batteries, all of which were silenced, and an explosion was caused. Observations were given for over 460 rounds.

Hostile Aircraft.—Lieutenant G. F. Smith, No. 66 Squadron, drove down a German aeroplane out of control, and Second-Lieutenant Bell Irving, of the same squadron, drove one down in a badly damaged condition.

Bombing.—Six 20-lb. bombs were dropped on Hendecourt.

May 23rd.

Reconnaissances.—Second-Lieutenants Charles and Ward, No. 4 Squadron, obtained valuable information and also fired 250 rounds from their machine guns at enemy troops. In addition, four machines of No. 4 Squadron and one of No. 32 Squadron attacked battery positions and troops with machine gun fire.

Artillery Co-operation.—One hundred and twenty-two targets were dealt with by artillery with aeroplane observation and 53 with observation by balloons.

Artillery of the First Army obtained eight direct hits on hostile batteries, causing two fires in a battery, two explosions, and damaging two pits; 23 active hostile batteries were reported by zone call.

Eleven hostile batteries were successfully engaged by artillery of the Second Army; 15 gun-pits were hit and four explosions caused. Twenty-one direct hits were obtained on trenches and a number of successful zone calls were sent down.

Artillery of the Third Army successfully engaged 24 hostile batteries. Fifty-two hostile batteries were seen active, on three of which there was observation of fire.

The 103rd Siege Battery with observation by Lieutenants Hill and Lanos, No. 8 Squadron, obtained three O.K.'s on a hostile battery and caused explosions which lasted for 20 minutes.

Eight hostile batteries were successfully engaged by artillery of the Fourth Army; 10 direct hits were obtained, two emplacements were damaged, and one fire and a large explosion caused. With observation by Lieutenant Lines, No. 52 Squadron, the 110th Siege Battery obtained five direct hits and 23 Y.'s on a hostile battery.

Artillery of the Fifth Army successfully engaged 23 hostile batteries; 19 direct hits were obtained on gun positions, four pits were destroyed and 12 damaged, and an explosion caused. Lieutenants Wilmot and Morris, No. 3 Squadron, observed 100 rounds fired by the 23rd Siege Battery on an anti-aircraft battery, and six O.K.'s were obtained.

One hostile battery was engaged and silenced by artillery with observation by balloons of the First Brigade, while six hostile batteries were successfully engaged by artillery with Second Brigade balloon observation and one explosion was caused. A working party was also engaged and dispersed.

With observation by balloons of the Third Brigade 25 targets were successfully engaged and two explosions and a fire were caused.

Hostile Aircraft.—In response to wireless warnings from Compass Stations Flight Sub-Lieuts. Soar and Jenner-Parsons, Naval Squadron No. 8, went out and found a hostile two-seater, which they attacked and drove down out of control. Flight-Commander Booker and Flight-Lieutenant Little, also of Naval Squadron No. 8, observed a German machine from the aerodrome, which they promptly pursued and drove down out of control.

In the evening five Sopwith triplanes of Naval Squadron No. 8 and some Sopwith Scouts engaged 14 Albatross Scouts, and the fight lasted about half an hour. Two of the German scouts were driven down badly damaged—one by Flight-Lieutenant G. G Simpson and the other by Flight Sub-Lieut. Bennetts.

Flight Lieutenant R. A. Little, Naval Squadron No. 8, attacked three two-seater machines, but was then immediately attacked by four hostile scouts. He hit and drove down two of the enemy machines, when the Germans broke off the combat. On his way home he had several engagements with hostile formations.

While on patrol Second Lieutenant Mussared, No. 1 Squadron, shot down an Albatross two-seater near Poelcapelle, while a second was driven down out of control by Lieutenant Jenkin.

An offensive patrol of No. 20 Squadron engaged seven Albatross Scouts, and one was driven down out of control by Captain White and Second Lieutenant Lewis. A second offensive patrol of No. 20 Squadron, while over the enemy's lines, observed 10 Albatross Scouts, so turned and flew towards our lines. When near the lines the F.E.'s quickly turned and attacked the German machines, and one was destroyed by Captains Thayre and Cubbon, who then immediately attacked a second and drove it down out of control. After driving away the hostile formation our machines continued their patrol.

An escort of machines of No. 18 Squadron was attacked by seven Albatross Scouts, and one of the hostile machines, into which a drum was fired by Second Lieutenants Marshall and Blennerhassett, fell out of control and crashed.

Flight Lieutenant Breadner and Flight Sub-Lieuts. Fall and Glen, Naval Squadron No. 3, each engaged and drove down out of control a German machine, while a fourth was driven down badly damaged by Flight Sub-Lieutenant Orchard of the same squadron.

Five Spads of No. 19 Squadron engaged four Albatross Scouts, and Lieutenant Orlebar shot one down, which fell in flames.

Four German machines were driven down out of control by pilots of No. 56 Squadron, who had considerable fighting, and who manœuvred in order to use the sun to the best advantage before attacking hostile formations. Captain C. M. Crowe, Lieutenant C. A. Lewis, and Second Lieutenant A. P. F. Rhys-Davids each drove down one of their opponents out of control, while the fourth fell after being encountered by Captains P. B. Prothero and E. W. Broadberry.

Three other German machines were driven down badly damaged by machines of the Ninth Wing during the day, and one, after having been engaged by Captain Cairnes, No. 19 Squadron, landed in a field.

Photography.—522 photographs were taken during the day.

Bombing.—First Brigade.—Twenty-six 20-lb. bombs were dropped on Bois Bernard, and all the bombs were seen to fall on buildings in the village. Thirty 20-lb. bombs were dropped on Vendin-le-Vieil, but the results were mostly unobserved. Sixteen 20-lb. bombs were dropped on Wingles, and some were observed to hit houses in the village. In the evening machines of No. 25 Squadron dropped 71 20-lb. bombs and nine incendiary bombs on various objectives. Twenty-six of the bombs were dropped on Lens, 14 between Lens and Salkaumines, 36 on Wingles and four on La Bassée. Fires were started in Wingles and a direct hit was observed on a Metallurgique factory.

Fifth Brigade.—Ten 20-lb. bombs were dropped on Hendecourt.

9th Wing.—Six 230-lb. bombs were dropped by No. 27 Squadron on Orchies, but observation was difficult owing to mist and clouds.

May 24th.

Successful reconnaissances were carried out, and No. 45 Squadron reported train movements in the Lille area above normal.

Machine-gun fire was opened on German troops and a large explosion was observed at Hendecourt, which entirely destroyed a château in the wood.

Artillery Co-operation.—Sixty-seven targets were dealt with by artillery with aeroplane observation and 90 with observation by balloons.

Artillery of the First Army obtained 22 direct hits on hostile batteries; four pits were destroyed, 10 damaged, and an explosion was caused. Twenty-four O.K.'s were obtained on trenches, and 38 area calls were sent down.

Artillery of the Second Army successfully engaged 15 hostile batteries; nine gun-pits were hit, and three explosions caused.

Thirty zone calls were sent down, of which seven were seen to be answered, and in each case the hostile battery engaged was silenced.

Twenty hostile batteries were successfully engaged by artillery of the Third Army; 10 direct hits were obtained, two pits were damaged, and three explosions caused. Thirty-two hostile batteries were seen active, on two of which there was observation of fire.

Artillery of the Fourth Army successfully engaged nine hostile batteries, on which 33 O.K.'s and 10 M.O.K.'s were obtained. Ten pits were damaged and two explosions caused. The 9th Siege Battery, with observation by Lieutenant Glenny, No. 52 Squadron, fired 130 rounds at a hostile battery, and obtained 12 O.K.'s, destroying three emplacements and causing an explosion.

The same battery, with observation by Lieutenant Woodhouse, fired 140 rounds at another hostile battery, and obtained two O.K.'s and seven M.O.K.'s, and damaged all the pits.

Seventeen hostile batteries were successfully engaged by artillery of the Fifth Army, and 12 direct hits were obtained. One gun-pit was destroyed, 13 damaged, and five explosions were caused.

The 231st Siege Battery, with observation by Second Lieutenant Armstrong, No. 15 Squadron, obtained four direct hits on a hostile battery.

With observation by balloons of the First Brigade, artillery silenced four hostile batteries and carried out two successful shoots on trenches.

Artillery, with observation by balloons of the Second Brigade, successfully engaged seven hostile batteries and caused an explosion. Trench bombardments and wire-cutting shoots were also carried out.

Balloons of the Third Army received messages by heliograph and answered by Aldis lamp from seven miles distant. Nine targets were successfully ranged on by balloons of this army, and also by balloons of the Fourth Army.

Four hostile batteries were engaged and silenced by artillery with balloon observation of the Fifth Brigade.

Hostile Aircraft.— A patrol of six Sopwiths of No. 43 Squadron encountered nine hostile scouts and a general engagement took place. Captain K. L. Gopsill and Second Lieutenant E. H. Jones drove down one of the scouts, but were then attacked by two others, and Second Lieutenant Jones was wounded, but continued fighting, and, after 20 rounds had been fired, one of the attacking machines burst into flames and fell. Second Lieutenant C. H. Harriman and Second Air Mechanic O'Shea hit another scout, in which the pilot is believed to have been killed, and the machine fell out of control; while still another was driven down out of control by Second Lieutenant L. Gedge and C.S.M. L. M. Nava. Flight Commander Booker, of Naval Squadron No. 8, observed the combat from the aerodrome, and immediately left and joined in the fighting, and drove down a scout, which fell in flames and crashed. Shortly after this Flight Commander Booker and Flight Sub-Lieut. Macdonald engaged two H.A., and drove them both down out of control. A short time afterwards one was observed on the ground completely crashed.

Captain J. H. Letts and Lieutenant L. W. Allen, No. 48 Squadron, engaged four two-seater H.A. One of the German machines was driven down out of control and a second was badly damaged. The other two fled.

A patrol of No. 29 Squadron attacked a formation of nine H.A., which were fighting F.E.'s of No. 11 Squadron, and Second Lieutenant A. A. Shepherd drove one of the German machines down in flames and saw it crash. He then attacked and drove down a second in a badly damaged condition.

Lieutenant O. M. Sutton, No. 54 Squadron, engaged a German single-seater machine which flew straight at him, and it was only by a quick turn that Lieutenant Sutton avoided crashing into the hostile machine. As it was, his right-hand top plane hit the German machine, which broke to pieces in the air and fell. Although his top plane was badly broken, he succeeded in landing safely at his aerodrome. Lieutenant Steuart, of the same squadron, drove down an Albatross Scout in a spin, and followed it down. On two occasions the German flattened out but was immediately attacked and eventually fell out of control. This machine was seen to crash by anti-aircraft gunners.

Offensive patrols of No. 56 Squadron encountered several hostile formations. The German machines always broke off the combat, and in some cases refused to fight. Two were destroyed—one by Second Lieutenants Hoidge and Rhys-Davids, which fell in flames, and the second, which had a wing shot off, was destroyed by Second Lieutenant F. Williams. Two others were driven down out of control, one by the S.E. 5 formation and the other by Second Lieutenants Hoidge and Rhys-Davids, and this machine fell enveloped in smoke and the observer was seen to fall. The S.E. 5's saw De Havilland 4's, of No. 55 Squadron, drop bombs on Busigny Station, and observed a large column of smoke after the bombing machines had left.

Photography.—520 photographs were taken during the day.

Bombing.—First Brigade.—In the evening 28 20-lb. bombs were dropped on Wingles and La Bassée, and buildings in both places were hit.

Ninth Wing.—Twelve 112-lb. bombs were dropped on Busigny by machines of No. 55 Squadron. The results were mostly unobserved, but two were seen to burst on the railway.

May 25th.

Reconnaissances.—Successful reconnaissances were carried out by all brigades and Ninth Wing.

A successful long reconnaissance, including Le Cateau and Maubeuge, was carried out by Lieutenant Turner and Second Lieutenant R. Brett, No. 55 Squadron, and 18 photographs were taken.

Successful contact patrols were carried out by machines of the Third Brigade. Second Lieutenant C. Ryder and Lieutenant R. C. Rodger, No. 2 Squadron, descended to a low altitude and attacked and silenced a hostile battery. In several other instances machine-gun fire was used against enemy troops and transport.

Artillery Co-operation.— 114 targets were dealt with by artillery with aeroplane observation, and 111 with observation by balloons.

Artillery of the First Army obtained 16 direct hits on hostile batteries; three pits were destroyed, seven damaged, and six explosions caused. Three batteries were silenced under zone call and two explosions caused. Forty-eight active hostile batteries were reported by zone call, but in many cases the results of shoots were difficult to observe owing to a thick mist.

Artillery of the Second Army successfully engaged 35 hostile batteries, and 27 gun-pits were hit. Twenty-seven zone calls were sent down, including two reporting motor transport, which was engaged and dispersed.

Twenty-nine hostile batteries were successfully engaged by artillery of the Third Army; 27 direct hits were obtained, nine pits damaged, and five explosions caused. Thirty-six hostile batteries were seen active, on two of which there was observation of fire.

Artillery of the Fourth Army successfully engaged 14 hostile batteries; 15 O.K.'s and nine M.O.K.'s were obtained. 932 rounds were fired in a pre-arranged shoot, and 15 emplacements were damaged. The 37th Siege Battery, with observation by Lieutenant Lowe, No. 9 Squadron, obtained one O.K. and nine M.O.K.'s on a hostile battery, and all emplacements were damaged. The 52nd Siege Battery, with observation by Lieutenant Woodhouse, No. 52 Squadron, obtained two O.K.'s and 10 M.O.K.'s on a hostile battery. The 40th Siege Battery, with observation by Lieutenant Thornton, No. 9 Squadron, obtained two O.K.'s and five Y.'s on a hostile battery, and five direct hits on emplacements.

Twenty-five hostile batteries were successfully engaged by artillery of the Fifth Army; 27 direct hits on gun positions were obtained, 8 gun-pits were demolished, 16 damaged, and three explosions caused. Second Lieutenant Barker, No. 15 Squadron, ranged the 77th Siege Battery on two machine-gun emplacements, and observed 170 rounds. After this shoot he went down to 1,000 feet and examined the targets and saw that both were totally destroyed.

With observation by balloons of the First Brigade, artillery silenced four hostile batteries and caused an explosion of ammunition.

A successful wire-cutting shoot was carried out by balloons of the Second Brigade, over 300 rounds being fired, and two explosions were caused as the result of shoots on other targets.

Eleven hostile battery positions were successfully engaged by artillery with observation by balloons of the Third Brigade, and several explosions and fires were caused. 1,048 rounds were observed.

Balloons of the Fifth Brigade ranged artillery on three hostile batteries, all of which were silenced. One shoot, carried out with balloon observation, resulted in a fire and an explosion being caused.

Hostile Aircraft.—Second Lieutenant E. H. Stevens and Lieutenant V. Smith, No. 25 Squadron, were attacked by three hostile machines while taking photographs. Two of the H.A. were driven off, and the third was driven down out of control.

An offensive patrol of No. 20 Squadron engaged nine Albatross Scouts just after crossing the lines, and one of the scouts, attacked by Captains Thayre and Cubbin, was seen to break in the air and fall. Shortly afterwards this pilot and observer shot down a second machine in flames. During the engagement, Second Lieutenants Conder and Cowell drove down one of the hostile machines out of control.

An offensive patrol of No. 45 Squadron encountered nine hostile machines, and a general engagement took place. Second Lieutenant W. A. Wright and Lieutenant E. T. Caulfield-Kelly opened fire at one of the German machines which was diving at them from behind, and this machine immediately fell, then burst into flames, and was seen to crash. A second scout, which also attacked from behind, was driven down completely out of control, but its fate could not be ascertained owing to the presence of other hostile aircraft. Two other Albatross Scouts were driven down out of control during this encounter— one by Lieutenant Newling and Second Lieutenant Holland, and the other by Lieutenant Belgrave and Second Lieutenant Stewart.

In a later engagement between three machines of No. 45 Squadron and a large formation of Albatross Scouts Captain Mountford and Second-Lieutenant Vessey drove down two of their opponents out of control.

Second Lieutenant Mansbridge and Lieutenant L. F. Jenkin, No. 1 Squadron, each drove down a hostile machine out of control.

An offensive patrol of No. 24 Squadron encountered a formation of Albatross Scouts, and one attacked Lieutenant Woollett from behind, but Lieutenant Cockerell immediately drove it off and succeeded in destroying it.

A photographic reconnaissance of No. 18 Squadron engaged a formation of seven hostile aircraft, and drove one of the German aeroplanes down out of control.

Machines of Nos. 56, 66, and 19 Squadrons had considerable fighting. Second-Lieutenant A. P. F. Rhys-Davids, No. 56 Squadron, destroyed a two-seater Aviatik, while Captain C. M. Crowe, of the same squadron, drove a German machine down out of control. Lieutenant J. M. Child, No. 19 Squadron, and Second-Lieutenant F. A. Smith, No. 66 Squadron, each drove down a hostile machine out of control.

Bombing.—First Brigade.—Eighty-four 20-lb. bombs were dropped on Gloster Wood, Bois Bernard, and Beauchamps, and considerable damage was done to houses and trenches.

Second Brigade.—No. 20 Squadron dropped 18 20-lb. bombs on various targets. Two bombs were dropped on a balloon shed, which was totally destroyed.

Third Brigade.—No. 12 Squadron dropped eight 20-lb. bombs on a dump.

Fourth Brigade.—Fifty-one 20-lb. and three incendiary bombs were dropped by Nos. 22 and 9 Squadrons on sheds at Serain. Transport was observed to be hit, and cavalry were dispersed.

Fifth Brigade.—Twelve 20-lb. bombs were dropped on Hendecourt.

Ninth Wing.—Machines of No. 55 Squadron dropped 60 20-lb. bombs on Cantin Aerodrome, but the results were unobserved owing to the presence of a large number of hostile aircraft.

Six 230-lb. bombs were dropped on Busigny Station by machines of No. 27 Squadron from 8,000 feet, and five of the bombs were seen to fall on the railway line, and one is believed to have burst on a dump south of the station.

Photographs.—1,355 photographs were taken during the day.

S. WOOD, Captain,
Staff Officer.

Headquarters, Royal Flying Corps.
27th May 1917.

ROYAL FLYING CORPS COMMUNIQUÉ, No. 90.

May 26th.

Artillery Co-operation.—120 targets were dealt with by artillery with aeroplane observation, and 130 with observation by balloons.

Artillery of the First Army obtained 12 O.K.'s and 11 M.O.K.'s on hostile batteries, and five pits were destroyed, three damaged and four explosions caused.

Artillery of the Second Army successfully engaged 29 hostile batteries and 50 other targets. Eighteen gun-pits were damaged, five destroyed and four explosions and several fires caused.

Eighteen hostile batteries were successfully engaged by artillery of the Third Army, which obtained 11 O.K.'s, 11 M.O.K.'s, 80 Y.'s and 110 Z.'s, and caused three explosions. Thirty-three hostile batteries were seen active, on two of which there was observation of fire.

Ten batteries were successfully engaged by artillery of the Fourth Army, one of which was silenced under the zone call. Twenty-seven direct hits were obtained, 15 emplacements were damaged, and nine explosions caused. 1,149 rounds were fired in pre-arranged shoots on batteries. The 15th Siege Battery, with observation by Lieutenant Woodhouse, No. 52 Squadron, obtained three O.K.'s and seven M.O.K.'s on a hostile battery, destroying two emplacements and damaging two others. The 75th Siege Battery, with observation by Captain Williams, No. 9 Squadron, obtained four O.K.'s and eight Y.'s, which caused large explosions and a fire, the smoke of which was so dense that the shoot had to be abandoned.

Artillery of the Fifth Army successfully engaged 22 hostile batteries. Twenty-nine direct hits on gun positions were obtained, which destroyed six pits, damaged 21, and caused six explosions. Second Lieutenant Buckingham and Lieutenant Cox, No. 15 Squadron, registered batteries on to several trench points, and ranged the 117th Siege Battery on to a trench mortar emplacement, and two O.K.'s were obtained. They also located and reported by zone call five active hostile batteries, two H.T. and a few infantry, and opened machine-gun fire on the last two objectives.

With Balloon Observation.—Artillery of the First Army carried out successful trench shoots and caused an explosion, while wire was cut by artillery of the Second Army.

Artillery of the Third Army was successfully ranged on 46 targets, and engaged 16 hostile batteries, four of which had previously been ranged on by aeroplanes. Two of the shoots resulted in a number of explosions. Three N.F. targets were engaged, one was silenced and a fire broke out in a second. 1,000 rounds were observed, and 35 batteries were reported active.

Three hostile batteries were engaged by artillery of the Fourth Army, and one was silenced. Twenty-two successful shoots were carried out by artillery of the Fifth Army, and an explosion was caused, while 1,000 rounds were observed by balloon observers.

Hostile Aircraft.—A two-seater Aviatik was attacked and driven down out of control by Second Lieutenant R. W. Farquhar, No. 23 Squadron.

Flight Sub-Lieuts. McNeil and Parker, Naval Squadron No. 8, each drove down a hostile machine out of control.

An engagement took place between eight machines of No. 20 Squadron and 10 of No. 1 Squadron and 15 Albatross Scouts. One of the German machines, attacked by Lieutenants Satchell and Jenks, No. 20 Squadron, was seen to loop backwards; the pilot fell out and the machine was seen to crash. A second scout was driven down badly damaged by this pilot and observer. Lieutenants B. C. Cunnell and W. T. Gilson, of the same squadron, obtained a favourable position on one of the Albatross Scout's tails and followed it down firing until the German machine crashed. The German formation was eventually dispersed after seven others had been driven down out of control. The following pilots and observers succeeded in driving down one hostile aeroplane each out of control in this encounter: Captain White and Second-Lieutenant Lewis, Lieutenants Boucher and Birkett, Second-Lieutenants Conder and Second Air Mechanic Cowell, in three machines of No. 20 Squadron; and Captain Cronyn, Lieutenant Sharpe, Second-Lieutenant Fullard and Second-Lieutenant Mussared, in single-seater machines of No. 1 Squadron.

Two German machines were driven down out of control by pilots of the 9th Wing—one by Second-Lieutenant Rhys-Davids and one by Captain Broadway, of No. 56 Squadron.

Captain W. A. Bishop, No. 60 Squadron, engaged and drove down a German aeroplane near Izel-les-Equerchin.

Photography.—1,027 photographs were taken during the day.

Bombing.—First Brigade.—On the evening of the 25th, eighteen 20-lb. bombs were dropped on Izel, and all the bombs were seen to burst in the village.

On the 26th, eighty 20-lb. bombs were dropped on Drocourt, Bois Bernard, Vendin-le-Vieil, Pont-à-Vendin, Sallaumines, and considerable damage was done in all these places. Later in the day twenty-eight 20-lb. bombs were dropped on Pont-à-Vendin, and 22 of the bombs hit buildings, while six burst on the railway.

Second Brigade.—Twenty-four 20-lb. bombs were dropped on various targets, and two which fell on Houthem dump set two sheds on fire.

Fifth Brigade.—On the night of the 25th/26th four phosphorus and ten 20-lb. bombs were dropped by No. 18 Squadron on a dump, but the results were unobserved.

Ninth Wing.—No. 27 Squadron dropped forty-seven 20-lb. bombs on dumps at Iwuy from 10,000 feet, and a number of direct hits were obtained. One large explosion was caused in the Southern dump.

May 27th.

Reconnaissances.—Reconnaissances were carried out by all brigades and Ninth Wing.

Lieutenants Libby and Jones, No. 43 Squadron, carried out a specially long reconnaissance and made valuable observation of enemy movements.

Machine-gun fire was opened on enemy troops and transport in a number of cases during artillery and other work.

Artillery Co-operation.—110 targets were dealt with by artillery with aeroplane observation and 106 with observation by balloons.

Artillery of the First Army obtained 17 direct hits on hostile batteries. Seven pits were destroyed, nine damaged and five explosions caused Fifteen hostile batteries were reported by zone call.

Artillery of the Second Army successfully engaged 27 hostile batteries and 36 other targets. Twelve gun-pits were destroyed, nine damaged, and five explosions caused. Lieutenants Stock and Barr, No. 6 Squadron, obtained five O.K.'s and 10 M.O.K.'s on a hostile battery position with the 179th Siege Battery, and the target was completely obliterated.

Fourteen hostile batteries were successfully engaged by artillery of the Third Army. Five direct hits were obtained and an explosion caused. Thirty-five hostile batteries were seen active, on six of which there was observation of fire. One battery was silenced and one explosion took place. The 222nd Siege Battery, with observation by Lieutenants Devlin and Hare, No. 12 Squadron, obtained four O.K.'s and one M.O.K. on a hostile battery.

Ten batteries were successively engaged by artillery of the Fourth Army, of which three were anti-aircraft, and were silenced under zone call. Three direct hits were obtained on batteries and five emplacements damaged. The 75th Siege Battery, with observation by Lieutenant Glenny, No. 9 Squadron, obtained six direct hits on a hostile battery.

Artillery of the Fifth Army successfully engaged 20 hostile batteries and obtained 30 direct hits on gun positions. Seven gun-pits were demolished, 17 damaged, and six explosions caused. Lieutenants Carter and MacDonald, No. 15 Squadron, reported 15 active hostile batteries by zone call, and many of them were seen to be engaged, and observation of fire was given.

With Observation by Balloons.—Artillery of the First Army carried out three successful shoots on a hostile battery and caused an explosion.

Artillery of the Third Army was ranged on to transport entering Sailly-en-Ostrevent, which was engaged and hit. Twenty-nine targets were successfully ranged on and one N.F. target was engaged and silenced. Nine hostile battery positions were successfully engaged and an explosion caused.

Balloons co-operated successfully with aeroplanes and good shooting was done. A German balloon was hit and one hostile battery was successfully engaged by artillery of the Fourth Army.

Artillery of the Fifth Army silenced a hostile battery and carried out 17 successful shoots, causing one explosion.

Hostile Aircraft.—Captain R. Gregory, No. 40 Squadron, engaged a hostile scout at 19,000 feet, and the German machine was hit and fell out of control.

An offensive patrol of No. 20 Squadron engaged eight Albatross scouts near Ypres and one of the hostile machines was destroyed by Second Lieutenant R. E. Conder and Second Air Mechanic J. Cowell. Captains F. H. Thayre and F. R. Cubbon, No. 20 Squadron, observed an Albatross two-seater doing artillery work, and immediately attacked and destroyed it. They then attacked an Albatross Scout and drove it down.

An offensive patrol of No. 41 Squadron arranged to fly in two formations. One formation observed an Albatross two-seater being fired at by anti-aircraft and so dived in the direction of the shell bursts. The patrol leader fired a light in order to draw the attention of the other patrol. This light was seen by the German machine, which immediately dived away and found itself in the middle of the second patrol, which opened fire, and the German machine was driven down and seen to crash.

A patrol of No. 45 Squadron engaged 10 Albatross Scouts, and two were driven down out of control—one by Lieutenant Belgrave and Second Lieutenant Davies and the other by Second-Lieutenants Cock and Kelly.

A second offensive patrol of No. 45 Squadron engaged seven Albatross Scouts and one was destroyed by Second Lieutenants Fitchat and Hayes, while Captain Mountford and Second Lieutenant Vessey in one machine, and Second Lieutenant Cook and Second Air Mechanic Shaw in another machine, each drove down a scout out of control. Whilst on artillery work, Second Lieutenants Blofeld and Hunter, No. 45 Squadron, were attacked and both wounded by five Albatross Scouts, but they succeeded in destroying one of their opponents.

Second Lieutenants Middleton and Merchant, No. 48 Squadron, destroyed one of three Albatross Scouts which they engaged. Shortly afterwards they engaged a two-seater machine and drove it down out of control.

Captain Bishop, No. 60 Squadron, engaged and destroyed a German two-seater. Second Lieutenant Gunner of the same squadron engaged an enemy two-seater and shot the wings off before it crashed.

Second Lieutenant Phelan, also of No. 60 Squadron, destroyed a two-seater Albatross near Biache.

Flight Sub-Lieut. Ramsay, Naval Squadron No. 1, attacked a German machine near Bapaume and followed it down to 2,000 feet, when it was hit by anti-aircraft fire and fell in the German lines.

In the evening a patrol of No. 48 Squadron engaged a formation of hostile aircraft south of Douai, and one was destroyed by Captain Barker and Lieutenant Jeff. Four others were driven down out of control—one by Lieutenant Pike and First Air Mechanic Robertson, one by Lieutenants Warren and Benjamin, one by Lieutenants Fraser and Noss, and the fourth by Captain Letts and Lieutenant Malcolmson in one machine, and Second Lieutenants Smither and Jameson in another machine.

Flight Sub-Lieut. Glen, Naval Squadron No. 3, attacked a hostile machine which was about to attack an F.E., and followed it down until it crashed. Flight Sub-Lieut. Carter of the same Squadron drove down a German machine out of control.

Lieutenants Huston and Foord, No. 18 Squadron, while returning from a reconnaissance, engaged an Albatross Scout, which was hit and crashed. Flight Lieutenant Kerby, Naval Squadron No. 3, also fired at this machine as it was going down. Second Lieutenant West-White and Sergeant Cumberland, No. 18 Squadron, had their service tank shot through by hostile aircraft and the machine caught fire. The flames, however, were put out, and after finishing the patrol the pilot landed safely.

An offensive patrol of No. 56 Squadron engaged a formation of hostile two-seaters and scouts, and Second Lieutenant Barlow got to within close range of one machine and riddled it with bullets. This machine fell out of control, but soon flattened out when Second Lieutenant Barlow immediately dived at it again and drove it down out of control. The wings were seen to break off the German machine, which then went down like an arrow. After destroying this machine, Second Lieutenant Barlow turned quickly to engage another that was following him down, and after a short engagement the German machine fell out of control. Second Lieutenant Barlow then flew round and saw the first German machine in flames on the ground, and the second one crashed within half-a-mile of the first. Captain Crowe, No. 56 Squadron, observed a fight taking place between some of our machines and a hostile formation, and he took his patrol to join in the fighting. After several encounters he had a long engagement with a skilful opponent and eventually succeeded in driving him down and saw his machine crash.

A second patrol of No. 56 Squadron engaged a formation of hostile scouts, and Captain Prothero engaged one and drove it down out of control. Another hostile aircraft, however, secured a favourable position on his tail, and being unable to shake it off, he put his machine into a spin, but on flattening out he found the German machine still in a favourable position, so again put his machine into a spin. Second Lieutenant Hoidge observed the situation and dived at the German machine, which fell out of control. Lieutenant Lewis drove one of the hostile aeroplanes down in a spin, but was attacked himself from behind by another while changing drums. He put his machine into a spin, and was closely followed by the German, but on flattening out he secured a favourable position directly above the hostile machine and opened fire, driving it down out of control. The S.E.5's generally out-manœuvred the German formations, and in many cases easily scattered them. In a general engagement between our machines and two German formations, Captain Latta, of No. 66 Squadron, and an S.E. 5 drove down a hostile machine, and followed it down until, in order to escape without accident, it had to "zoom" over hedges and other obstacles as it was so near the ground. Fire was opened on our machines from a rocket battery, and Captain Latta immediately attacked and silenced the battery with machine gun fire.

Photography.—1,213 photographs were taken during the day.

Bombing.—1st Brigade.—On the night of the 26th/27th eight 112-lb. bombs were dropped on Don Railway Station by No. 100 Squadron. A thick ground mist made observation difficult, and it took the pilots three hours in some cases to locate the target.

On the 27th, 40 20-lb. bombs were dropped on Quiery-la-Motte. Considerable damage was done to the railway and to buildings. Thirty 20-lb. bombs were dropped on Pont-à-Vendin, and buildings, the railway and Metallurgique works were hit and damaged. Eight 20-lb. bombs were dropped on Harnes, 16 on Billy Montigny, and eight on Auchy by No. 25 Squadron, and buildings in all places were damaged.

Second Brigade.—Thirty-eight 20-lb. bombs were dropped on a dump at Houthem, and four direct hits were obtained.

Ninth Wing.—No. 55 Squadron dropped 11 112-lb. bombs on Bohain Station.

Miscellaneous.—Second Lieutanant L. L. Morgan, No. 40 Squadron, when returning from pursuing an artillery machine from the lines on the 24th inst. was hit when at 4,000 feet by one of our own shells. The shell exploded on the engine and carried away two cylinders, most of the engine bearers, the whole of the bottom R.H. longeron to behind the pilot's seat, and caused a compound fracture of the pilot's leg. Second Lieutenant Morgan, however, succeeded in bringing his machine back, and is progressing favourably.

May 28th.

Reconnaissances.—Reconnaissances were carried out by all brigades and Ninth Wing. Fires were observed in St. Quentin and a very large explosion was seen at Gouy. Machine gun fire was opened into German trenches and at German troops by several machines.

Artillery Co-operation.—127 targets were dealt with by artillery with aeroplane observation and 102 with observation by balloons.

Artillery of the First Army obtained 13 O.K.'s and 10 M.O.K.'s on hostile batteries; ten pits were damaged, one was destroyed and three explosions caused. Houses in battery positions were set on fire and a large number of hits were obtained on trenches.

Artillery of the Second Army successfully engaged 28 hostile batteries, seven gun-pits were destroyed, 13 damaged, and seven explosions and fires caused.

Thirty-three hostile batteries were successfully engaged by artillery of the Third Army, which obtained 25 O.K.'s, 14 M.O.K's, 84 Y.'s, and 95 Z.'s; one emplacement was destroyed, and six explosions took place. Thirty-four hostile batteries were seen active, on four of which there was observation of fire. The 102nd Siege Battery, with observation by Lieutenant Stevenson, No. 12 Squadron, obtained three O.K.'s and two M.O.K.'s on a hostile battery, causing one large and one small explosion.

Ten hostile batteries were successfully engaged by artillery of the Fourth Army; nine O.K.'s and 27 M.O.K.'s were obtained and 13 emplacements were damaged. The 40th Siege Battery, with observation by Lieutenant Phillips, No. 9 Squadon, obtained three O.K.'s and 12 Y.'s on a hostile battery, in which all the pits were badly damaged. Lieutenant Woodhouse, No. 52 Squadron, observing for the 9th and 15th Siege Batteries, obtained two O.K.'s and 22 M.O.K.'s, destroying four pits and damaging three.

Eighteen hostile batteries were successfully engaged by artillery of the Fifth Army. Seven direct hits were obtained on gun positions, one pit was destroyed and 13 damaged, while five explosions were caused.

With Balloon Observations.—Artillery of the First Army silenced one hostile battery, and as the result of many successful trench shoots four explosions took place.

Artillery of the Second Army fired over 2,000 rounds at 41 miscellaneous targets.

Twelve hostile batteries were successfully engaged by artillery of the Third Army, and 28 targets were successfully ranged on.

No. 16 Balloon Section ranged artillery on St. Rohart Factory, and a large explosion took place which destroyed the buildings.

Artillery of the Fourth Army successfully engaged one hostile battery.

Seventeen successful shoots were carried out by artillery of the Fifth Army, one hostile battery was silenced and an explosion caused.

Hostile Aircraft.—An Albatross Scout was attacked and driven down out of control by Flight Lieutenant P. Johnson, Naval Squadron No. 8.

Second Lieutenants C. S. Richmond and E. W. Pritchard, No. 43 Squadron, engaged three single-seater scouts and drove one down out of control. Their machine was then severely hit, but they returned safely owing to the arrival of Nieuport Scouts.

Lieutenant W. E. Bassett, No. 40. Squadron, drove down a two-seater hostile machine out of control.

An offensive patrol of No. 45 Squadron observed a large formation of Albatross Scouts which were being engaged by their own anti-aircraft guns—presumably as a ruse. The Sopwiths engaged the hostile aircraft and two were destroyed, one by Second Lieutenant W. A. Wright and Lieutenant Kelly, and the other by Second Lieutenants G. H. Cock and Corner. Both the German machines fell in flames.

In the evening, Second Lieutenant A. E. Godfrey and Lieutenant W. A. Bond, on Nieuports of No. 40 Squadron, encountered five hostile aircraft and drove one down completely out of control. Later in the evening Lieutenant Bond engaged and drove down a second machine out of control. Flight Sub-Lieut. Jenner-Parson, Naval Squadron No. 8, also drove down a hostile machine out of control. Two others were driven down badly damaged, and probably out of control, by Flight Commander Booker and Flight Sub-Lieut. Knight, Naval Squadron No. 8.

Major Scott, No. 6 Squadron, engaged eight hostile aircraft near Monchy and drove one down badly damaged.

Captain Prothero, Lieutenant Muspratt, and Second Lieutenant A. P. F. Rhys-Davids, No. 56 Squadron, each drove down a hostile machine out of control.

Second Lieutenant L. M. Barlow, No. 56 Squadron, drove down a German machine, which he followed to within 800 feet of the ground and forced it to land, after which he continued firing at it. Second Lieutenant C. C. Sharp, No. 66 Squadron, drove down an enemy machine out of control, while Second

Lieutenant T. C. Luke, of the same squadron, drove one down, which was last seen in a vertical nose-dive very near the ground.

Bombing.—On the night of the 27th–28th, No. 100 Squadron dropped one 230-lb. bomb on St. Sauveur Station, Lille. Captain McClaughry, who dropped this bomb, was at first baulked by searchlights, but flew round until he got immediately over his objective, and the bomb was seen to fall on the sheds.

Fifteen 112-lb., 10 20-lb., and two phosphorus bombs were dropped on Don Railway Station by the same squadron, and a large fire was caused. The bombs were dropped from an average height of 800 feet, and all were seen to hit and explode on the objective.

On the 28th, 14 20-lb. bombs were dropped on Marquillies and 16 20-lb bombs on La Bassée, and buildings in both places were hit.

Fifth Brigade.—Two 20-lb. bombs were dropped on a dump and six on Hendecourt.

Ninth Wing.—Martinsydes of No. 27 Squadron dropped six 230-lb. bombs on Busigny Station, where considerable damage is believed to have been done. No. 55 Squadron dropped 12 112-lb. bombs on Brebières Railway Station, but observation was difficult owing to clouds.

Photography.—702 photographs were taken during the day.

May 29th.

Artillery Co-operation.—Fifty-eight targets were dealt with by artillery with aeroplane observation and 145 with observation by balloons.

Artillery of the First Army obtained eight direct hits and nine M.O.K.'s on eight hostile batteries, destroying two pits, damaging three, and causing five explosions.

Artillery of the Second Army successfully engaged 11 hostile batteries; 13 gun-pits were damaged and six explosions caused. The 179th Siege Battery, with observation by Lieutenants Stocks and Barr, No. 6 Squadron, obtained one O.K. and seven M.O.K.'s on a hostile battery, which damaged three pits and caused three explosions.

Nine hostile batteries were successfully engaged by artillery of the Third Army and six O.K.'s were obtained.

Three hostile batteries were successfully engaged by artillery of the Fourth Army, which obtained eight O.K.'s and eight M.O.K.'s; six emplacements were damaged and three explosions caused.

Artillery of the Fifth Army successfully engaged four hostile batteries and obtained 10 direct hits on gun positions, all of which were damaged and one explosion caused. The 117th

Siege Battery with observation by Lieutenant McDonald, No. 15 Squadron, obtained five direct hits on a hostile battery, damaging all four pits and causing huge volumes of smoke.

With Balloon Observation.—Artillery of the First Army silenced six hostile batteries and caused an explosion, while artillery of the Second Army successfully engaged 40 miscellaneous targets and fired over 3,000 rounds.

Forty targets were also engaged by artillery of the Third Army, including 27 hostile batteries, which were successfully engaged, and two large explosions caused. Six targets were taken over from aeroplanes by balloons, and two shoots were carried out in conjunction with aeroplanes.

Seventeen targets, including a hostile battery, were successfully engaged by artillery of the Fourth Army.

Artillery of the Fifth Army silenced two active hostile batteries and successfully engaged 23 other targets.

May 30th.

Artillery Co-operation.—Eighty-two targets were dealt with by artillery with aeroplane observation and 65 with observation by balloons.

Artillery of the First Army obtained nine O.K.'s and 27 M.O.K.'s on hostile batteries, causing five explosions, one of which was very large.

Artillery of the Second Army successfully engaged eight hostile batteries; seven gun-pits were damaged and three explosions caused. Second Lieutenants F. James and Ireland, No. 53 Squadron, reported a hostile battery by zone call to the 171st Siege Battery, which obtained three O.K.'s, seven M.O.K.'s, and set two pits on fire.

Ten hostile batteries were successfully engaged by artillery of the Third Army, which obtained eight O.K.'s, 14 M.O.K.'s, 38 Y's, and 27 Z's, causing an explosion and two fires in gun-pits. Fifty hostile batteries were seen active, on three of which there was observation of fire.

Artillery of the Fourth Army successfully engaged four hostile batteries, one of which was silenced under zone call. Eight direct hits were obtained and five emplacements were damaged.

The 37th Siege Battery, with observation by Lieutenant Glenny, No. 9 Squadron, fired 120 rounds and obtained three O.K.'s and two M.O.K.'s, damaging three pits and causing a large explosion.

Seven hostile batteries were successfully engaged by artillery of the Fifth Army, which obtained 10 direct hits on gun positions, destroyed one gun-pit and damaged eight, while three explosions were caused. Lieutenant Harms, No. 3 Squadron, ranged the 232nd Siege Battery on a hostile battery, and three O.K.'s were obtained. Owing to heavy mist he discontinued the shoot, but in the morning carried on with the same battery, which obtained five more O.K.'s.

With Balloon Observation.—Artillery of the First Army silenced five hostile batteries.

Artillery of the Third Army successfully engaged 12 hostile batteries and one N.F. target, where a fire and several small explosions were caused in a dump near the battery. Six targets were taken over from aeroplane observation and successfully engaged, and a working party was also dispersed.

One hostile battery was silenced by artillery of the Fourth Army, and convoys were also engaged.

Artillery of the Fifth Army successfully engaged four hostile batteries.

Hostile Aircraft.—Major Sutcliffe and Lieutenant Grevelink, No. 54 Squadron, each engaged and drove down a German machine out of control.

Bombing.—First Brigade.—On the night of the 29th/30th, No. 100 Squadron dropped twelve 112-lb. bombs on various targets. A train bombed from 800 feet on the Lille—Tournai line at Tressins was hit. The pilot fired a Very's light from 400 feet and was then able to observe the effects of his bombs. Two other trains were hit, one at Wasquehal and the other on the Tournai line. Two bombs were seen to explode on Ascq from 1,000 feet, and a depôt between Lille and La Bassee was hit.

On the 30th, 22 20-lb. bombs were dropped on La Bassée.

Miscellaneous.—Second Lieutenants Shepherd and Leach and Lieutenant A. W. B. Miller, No. 29 Squadron, crossed the lines east of Bullecourt at about 20 feet and attacked German troops. Lieutenant Miller observed a party of Germans in two ranks and opened fire at 200 yards, and continued firing until he was just above them. A number of the men were seen to fall and the rest fled in all directions. Second Lieutenant Shepherd saw eight field guns, near which was a fire where about 20 gunners were seated. He fired into their midst and continued firing until the wheels of his undercarriage almost touched them, and several of the Germans were seen to fall into the fire; the remainder were dispersed.

May 31st.

Artillery Co-operation.—Sixty-nine targets were dealt with by artillery with aeroplane observation and 25 with observation by balloons.

Artillery of the First Army carried out successful shoots on six hostile batteries, obtaining four O.K.'s and two M.O.K.'s. Two pits were destroyed and one damaged.

Artillery of the Second Army successfully engaged 10 hostile batteries. Five gun-pits were destroyed, seven damaged, and three explosions caused. In four counter battery shoots, with observation by No. 53 Squadron, artillery obtained 22 direct hits in addition to a number of M.O.K's. Lieutenant Harvey and Second Lieutenant Paton, No. 53 Squadron, observing for Nos. 2 and 5 R.M.A. (15-in. Hows.) obtained 10 direct hits out of 23 rounds fired. Lieutenant Phillippo and Major Wright, No. 6 Squadron, observing for the 179th Siege Battery, obtained six direct hits on a hostile battery in which four pits were damaged.

Six hostile batteries were successfully engaged by artillery of the Third Army and seven by artillery of the Fourth Army, which obtained eight O.K.'s and 18 M.O.K.'s, damaging eight emplacements and causing an explosion. The 15th Siege Battery with observation by Lieutenant Woodhouse, No. 52 Squadron, obtained two O.K.'s and 13 M.O.K.'s, considerably damaging a hostile battery and causing an explosion.

Two hostile batteries were successfully engaged by artillery of the Fifth Army.

With Balloon Observation.—Artillery of the Second Army caused a number of explosions in a house near a battery position.

Two hostile batteries were engaged by artillery of the Fourth Army.

Hostile Aircraft.—Captain Bishop, No. 60 Squadron, engaged and destroyed a German machine.

Bombing.—First Brigade.—On the night of the 30th/31st, six 112-lb. bombs were dropped by No. 10 Squadron on Douvrin, Carvin, and Provin, and were seen to burst on buildings.

S. Wood, Captain,
Staff Officer.

Headquarters, Royal Flying Corps,
    3rd June 1917.

No. 35.

CONFIDENTIAL.

ROYAL NAVAL AIR SERVICE.

OPERATIONS REPORT

(with Royal Flying Corps Reports attached).

1st to 15th JUNE 1917.

NAVAL STAFF,
  OPERATIONS DIVISION.
  15th June 1917.

ROYAL NAVAL AIR SERVICE.

REPORT OF OPERATIONS

(Completed from Reports during period
1st to 15th June 1917).

CONTENTS.

	PAGE
HOME STATIONS	2
DUNKIRK	6
ROYAL NAVAL AIR SERVICE SQUADRONS WITH ROYAL FLYING CORPS	12
EASTERN MEDITERRANEAN STATION	13
CAPE STATION	19
ROYAL FLYING CORPS COMMUNIQUÉS	21

HOME STATIONS.

SUBMARINE PATROL WORK.

June 11th.

Felixstowe.—During a patrol Seaplane No. 8677 sighted an enemy submarine 10 miles N.W. of North Hinder, which dived about 40 seconds before seaplane could get into position to attack.

One 230-lb. bomb (which failed to explode) was dropped on the spot where submarine had submerged.

June 14th.

Felixstowe.—During a patrol Seaplane 8682 sighted an enemy submarine in the vicinity of Ymuiden Ridge, about 5 miles on the starboard bow. The seaplane proceeded to attack, but the submarine submerged 15 seconds before bombs were dropped. Four 100-lb. bombs were released, straddling the course of submarine about half a length ahead. All bombs exploded, and a large black patch on the water was observed. The seaplane circled over the spot for 5 or 6 minutes, but nothing further was observed.

SEAPLANE PATROL OBSERVATION.

June 11th.

Felixstowe.—Whilst on a patrol in the Felixstowe area, and in position, approximately 10 miles W. of North Hinder, Seaplane 8661 sighted six enemy seaplanes about 2 miles distant dead ahead at 11.20 a.m. The seaplane altered course and descending from 1,500 to 500 feet made a W/T signal, giving the position of enemy aircraft. As at 11.35 the enemy had disappeared from view, the seaplane resumed her original course and continued the patrol.

SEAPLANE ATTACKS ON ZEPPELINS.

June 5th.

Yarmouth.—Curtiss, Flying Boat 8666, left Yarmouth at 6.15 a.m. G.M.T. to carry out a Zeppelin patrol. There was a slight haze up to 6,000 feet which increased towards the Dutch coast. A direct course was made for Terschelling Lightship, climbing gradually to 6,000 feet. At 8 a.m. a Zeppelin was sighted at 53° 39″ N., 5° E., cruising at 2,000 feet about 6 miles to the N.E. of seaplane. The seaplane came down to 4,000 feet, but lost sight of the Zeppelin in the mist, and when next seen at 8.10 a.m., she was east by north and level with the seaplane at 4,000 feet. She fired one White light which was answered with one White Very's light from the seaplane.

The Zeppelin then commenced to climb, throwing out quantities of water ballast. The seaplane climbed to 9,500 feet, and, from immediately beneath her, opened fire at 600 yards range with the two guns forward and two amidships. The attack was carried on for twenty minutes, during which time ten trays of Brock, Pomeroy, and Buckingham ammunition were fired into the Zeppelin, the closest range obtained being about 1,000 feet. There is no doubt that some of the shots hit the airship but the tracer ammunition had burnt itself out before reaching the target.

At 8.45 a.m. the Zeppelin had reached 10,500 feet, and it was thought impossible to continue the fight with any prospect of success as anti-Zeppelin ammunition had run short, and with the westerly wind there was barely enough fuel to reach Yarmouth, so it was decided to return to the base.

At 9.17 a.m. seven enemy destroyers were observed steering east by north in 53° 34″ N., 5° 11″ E., their formation being two divisions in line abreast. They at once opened fire on the seaplane, but the shots fell short. The seaplane arrived at Yarmouth without further incident at 11.20 a.m.

June 14th.

Seaplane No. 8660 left Yarmouth shortly after 7 a.m. to search the area 25 miles east of Southwold for hostile aircraft indicated by enemy W/T signals. At 8.15 a Zeppelin was sighted about 15 miles eastward, steering west at 10,500 feet. Upon sighting the seaplane she threw out water ballast and went up to 15,000 feet, at the same time turning N.N.E. and making off. The seaplane went in pursuit and by 8.45 had reached a height of 12,500 feet, and could not be forced any higher. Four trays of Brock, Pomeroy, and Buckingham ammunition were fired into her from immediately beneath and bursts of tracer were observed going well on to the target, but it is thought the incendiary must have burnt out by the time it reached her. It is quite possible she was hit by explosive bullets, but no immediate results took place. Four tracers were seen to be fired at the seaplane.

After manœuvring for another hour and a half, to get up to the Zeppelin, with no effect, it was decided to break off the flight, and the seaplane returned to Yarmouth.

With regard to the accuracy of the number L 48, it was observed through binoculars from underneath, and on account of vibration it was very difficult to make certain whether the last number was 3, 6, 8, or 9.

June 14th.

Felixstowe. - During a hostile aircraft patrol Seaplane 8677, when off Vlieland, at 8.40 and flying at 500 feet, sighted a

Zeppelin L 43, 5 miles on the starboard bow, at about 1,500 feet steering due north.

The seaplane at once proceeded to attack at full speed, climbing to 2,000 feet. Flight Sub-Lieut. Hobbs, D.S.C., piloted the machine, Flight Sub-Lieut. Dickey manned the bow gun, while W/T operator H. M. Davis, A.M. 11., F. 20354, manned midship gun, and A.M.1. (E) A. W. Goody, F. 12237, manned the stern gun.

As the seaplane approached the Zeppelin it dived for her tail at about 100 knots. The midship gun opened fire with tracer ammunition, and when about 100 feet above, Sub-Lieut. Dickey opened fire with Brock and Pomeroy ammunition as the seaplane passed diagonally over the tail from starboard to port. After two bursts the Zeppelin was seen to be in flames. The seaplane turned sharply to starboard and passed over her again. She was by this time completely enveloped in flames and falling very fast. Three men were observed to fall out of her on her way down, and flames and smoke were observed for some time after the wreckage reached the water.

The seaplane then returned to Felixstowe.

ARMED YACHT ATTACK ON ENEMY SEAPLANES.

June 11th.

The armed yacht "Diana," based on Dover, shot down two of four Rumpler seaplanes in the early morning. One machine was destroyed, the pilot being rescued by another enemy machine. This machine was in turn attacked by the "Diana," and both pilots taken prisoner, the machine being so badly damaged that it sank while being towed into harbour. The remaining seaplanes flew away in a N.N.E. direction.

MERCHANT SHIPPING ATTACKED BY HOSTILE AIRCRAFT.

June 14th.

An attack was carried out on merchant shipping, during the afternoon, by five enemy torpedo-carrying seaplanes, approximately 15 miles S.E. of Harwich at 2.30 p.m.

The Greek steamer "Antonios," bound from Boulogne to the Tyne, was attacked about 5 miles off the Sunk Lightship; one of the seaplanes discharging a torpedo from about half a mile, which missed the ship by about 10 feet. The seaplane then flew over, and dropped two bombs, both of which missed by about 20 feet, at the same time opening fire with a machine gun which also missed.

S.s. "Canto" from Newcastle was also attacked, and three torpedoes discharged at her, as well as several rounds from a quick-firing gun, but no hits were made.

S.s. "Kankakee" was attacked and sunk 1 mile north of the Sunk Head Buoy. The hostile machine was observed approaching from a north-easterly direction on the port quarter. When about 2,000 yards off, the seaplane swooped to within a few feet of the water, and discharged a torpedo. The torpedo was not actually sighted until it was close to the ship, when the helm was immediately put over in order to avoid it, but was too late, the torpedo striking the vessel in No. 3 hold on the port side. Several of H.M. Patrol Boats came to her assistance and endeavoured to tow into port, but she sank about 1 mile north of Sunk Head Buoy

The Captain states that there was no time to clear ship's gun. Ships are being instructed that guns should be kept in instant readiness in these waters.

RAIDS BY HOSTILE AIRCRAFT.

June 5th.

Sheerness.—At about 6.25 p.m. a squadron of approximately 16 enemy machines was observed approaching Sheerness. They crossed the coast line in the vicinity of Maplin Sands, passed over Burnham, and proceeded south to Sheerness, where many bombs were dropped.

Near the village of Wakering ($4\frac{1}{2}$ miles N.E. of Southend) and round Shoeburyness 22 bombs were dropped. One man was killed and one seriously injured.

Five houses were demolished in Blue Town, Sheerness, and a bomb which fell in Sheerness Dockyard set fire to a store.

The machines left for seawards flying at approximately 17,000 feet pursued by naval machines. Heavy A.A. fire was opened by the shore batteries, and one machine was brought down in the sea near Nore Light Vessel and sank. Two of the crew of three were rescued in a badly injured condition; one of them has since died.

Two machines were attacked over the sea by Squadron Commander Butler in a Sopwith triplane and driven down, after which the Sopwith landed at Dunkirk. The total number of enemy machine losses are estimated to be two destroyed and four driven down out of control; it is considered that at least two of the latter must have been destroyed.

The enemy aircraft are reported to have been of a large type, some twin-engined and others single-engined, and in at least one case to have been armed with a gun firing bursting shell.

R.N.A.S. formations from Dunkirk engaged the returning raiders, and numerous encounters took place. (*See* Dunkirk.) Four of the R.N.A.S. machines from Dunkirk landed at Manstone.

The total casualties reported are: Killed 12, injured 36. Of these, 8 killed and 12 injured are military casualties.

June 13*th*.

London.—An air raid was carried out over London, Thames Estuary, Kent, and Essex by hostile aircraft, numbering approximately 15. Bombs were dropped on Margate at 9.45, presumably with the object of diverting attention from the principal objective, viz., London, which the raiders reached at about 10.35. Their course inland appears to have been by way of Burnham, Billericay, Romford, and East London. Bombs were dropped in the City of London, where considerable damage has been done to business premises. Two bombs fell in the Tower of London, but both failed to explode. The casualties in London are 158 killed and over 500 injured.

In Margate four bombs fell, but did very little damage; one man was slightly injured. Five bombs were dropped on Shoeburyness, but did no damage.

Flight Lieutenant Fox, R.N., in a Sopwith Pup 9940, whilst on a patrol over Kentish Flats, observed the enemy formation of 15 machines in the vicinity of Southend and Rochford at heights varying from 15,000 to 17,500 feet. At about 2 miles N.N.W. of West Shingles the Sopwith attacked one of the rear machines of the formation at close range at a height of about 15,000 feet.

One tray was fired and two or three tracers observed to enter the enemy machine's fuselage. The Sopwith was then attacked by three other machines, so descended about 500 feet, and proceeded east.

The pilot experienced some difficulty in changing trays, after which he observed three hostile machines some distance ahead and about 600 feet above, and went in pursuit. One of the machines was firing through its tail, to which the Sopwith replied until his gun jammed, owing to a tracer bullet becoming wedged in the barrel. Being unable to clear the jamb the Sopwith returned to Manstone.

DUNKIRK.

General Remarks.—Reconnaissance flights, photographic reconnaissances, and fighter patrols have been carried out almost daily. Many combats in the air have taken place, resulting in a number of hostile machines being destroyed and others driven down out of control.

Enemy bases and shipping have been frequently attacked and several tons of bombs have been dropped.

PHOTOGRAPHIC RECONNAISSANCES.

June 4th.

A photographic reconnaissance was carried out over Ostend, and photographs taken show that the Ateliers de la Marine suffered very extensive damage as a result of the bomb attack of May 31st, and the submarine shelter alongside was also hit.

SPOTTING FLIGHTS.

June 4th.

Spotting was successfully carried out during the morning for the fleet engaged in the bombardment of Ostend. It was only achieved with difficulty, as within a few minutes of the first few rounds being fired smoke screens were started which covered the entire harbour, and it is estimated that approximately 10 to 15 square miles were completely obscured. Before the target was hidden the spotting machine was able to range the guns on it.

OFFENSIVE PATROL—ENGAGEMENTS WITH ENEMY.

June 5th.

No. 4 Wing (No. 4 Squadron).—Three Sopwith machines left on an offensive patrol, and when off Ostend sighted about 16 hostile aircraft flying north. The Sopwiths started in pursuit, but only one machine (Flight Commander Newberry) managed to engage the enemy. Unfortunately he was compelled to break off the combat owing to continual gun jambs. The three Sopwiths landed at Manstone.

On report of hostile aircraft returning from England three Sopwith machines were sent up to intercept them. About 15 hostile aircraft were sighted between Nieuport and Ostende. Flight Commander Shook shot down two completely out of control, one of which, a single-seater, was seen to crash. Flight Sub.-Lieut. Enstone shot down one, which he saw break to pieces.

June 5th.

No. 4 Wing (No. 9 Squadron).—Seven Sopwith machines went up to intercept hostile aircraft on their return from England and encountered about 12 Albatross scouts off Ostende, which were apparently waiting to escort the bombing machines to their base.

A number of combats took place in which at least three hostile aircraft were driven down out of control. Flight Sub-Lieut. Shearer was forced to land at Manstone owing to his machine running out of petrol.

ATTACK ON ENEMY BALLOON.

June 4th.

No. 4 Wing (No. 4 Squadron).—While flying over Ostende at 18,000 feet, Flight Sub-Lieut. Smith, in a Sopwith scout, sighted a balloon in rear of Ostend moving along as though attached to a lorry. The pilot attacked and opened fire, and observed balloon to collapse and fall to the ground. A.A. and machine-gun fire was very heavy.

ENGAGEMENT WITH ENEMY.

June 6th.

No. 4 Wing (No. 4 Squadron).—Whilst acting as escort to a Belgian spotting machine, Flight Sub-Lieut. Smith, in a Sopwith machine, encountered five single-seater hostile aircraft near Handzaeme, and shot two of them down out of control, one of which was observed to crash in a field.

Flight Sub-Lieut. Hemming, in a Sopwith machine, was attacked by six hostile aircraft N.E. of Dixmude. He shot two of them down out of control and then got into a spin, but managed to return safely.

SEAPLANE OBSERVATION.

June 10th.

Seaplanes.—During a seaplane patrol a German seaplane was observed upside down in the sea 12 miles N.N.E. of Calais, being taken in tow by a patrol ship with two drifters assisting.

OFFENSIVE PATROL.

June 13th.

No. 4 Wing (No. 9 Squadron).—Seven Sopwith machines left to search for hostile aircraft on their return from England. The machines went out to sea, until level with the mouth of the Thames, then back to the Belgian coast, but saw nothing of the hostile aircraft.

Flight Sub-Lieut. Le Boutillier landed in England. Flight Sub-Lieut. Mellersh's engine failed in mid-channel; owing to haze he lost himself and was forced to land near Dominion Camp.

Whilst attempting an offensive patrol, Flight Sub-Lieut. Shearer, in Sopwith Triplane 5374, was seen to dive and spin about three miles from the Aerodrome. After flattening out once the machine started spinning again and finally crashed. The Pilot, Flight Sub-Lieut. Shearer, was killed.

ATTACK ON ENEMY SUBMARINE.

June 14th.

Seaplanes.—A special patrol was carried out, and observed an enemy submarine about 15 miles N.N.E. of Nieuport. This was attacked with two 100-lb. bombs, delay action. Submarine dived and bombs exploded close to the wake.

KITE BALLOON OBSERVATION.

No. 11 Kite Balloon Section.—Few ascents have been made during this period, owing to unsuitable weather conditions generally.

BOMB ATTACKS.

(Carried out during the Period between the two Dates given.)

St. Denis Westrem Aerodrome.	June 1st	769-lbs.	Aeroplanes.
St. Denis Westrem Aerodrome.	June 3rd—4th	10,856-lbs.	Aeroplanes.
St. Denis Westrem Aerodrome.	June 8th—9th	994-lbs.	Aeroplanes.
St. Denis Westrem Aerodrome.	June 14th—15th	1,219-lbs.	Aeroplanes.
Bruges Docks (Hostile Shipping).	June 2nd—3rd	994-lbs.	Aeroplanes.
Bruges Docks and Hostile Shipping.	June 3rd—4th	524-lbs.	Aeroplanes.
Bruges Docks and Hostile Shipping.	June 4th—5th	11,391-lbs.	Aeroplanes.
Zeebrugge Mole and Shipping.	June 2nd—3rd	1,842-lbs.	Seaplanes.
Zeebrugge Mole	June 3rd—4th	3,960-lbs.	Aeroplanes.
Houttave (Nieuwmunster) Aerodrome.	June 5th—6th	592-lbs.	Aeroplanes.

BOMB ATTACK ON AERODROME.

June 1st.

No. 5 Wing (No. 5 Squadron).—A raid was carried out on the St. Denis Westrem Aerodrome by three D.H. 4's and one Sopwith. Four 112-lb., one 65-lb., and sixteen 16-lb. bombs were released at heights of from 10,000 to 12,000 feet.

No direct hits were observed, but several bombs were seen to explode close to the sheds selected for attack.

BOMB ATTACK ON HOSTILE SHIPPING.

June 2nd–3rd.

No. 5 Wing (No. 5 Squadron).—About 4.30 a.m. a bomb raid was carried out on hostile shipping in Bruges Docks. Two 112-lb., two 65-lb., and forty 16-lb. bombs were dropped. One direct hit was observed on a large barge, and a bomb was seen to explode very close to a destroyer.

Bombing machines were attacked by hostile aircraft, but were successfully driven off, one being driven down completely out of control.

BOMB ATTACKS ON ZEEBRUGGE MOLE AND SHIPPING.

June 3rd.

Seaplanes.—During the evening one 550-lb., four 112-lb., twelve 65-lb., and four 16-lb. bombs were dropped on Zeebrugge Mole and two destroyers off the Mole, but no direct hits were observed.

BOMB ATTACK ON AERODROME.

June 3rd–4th.

No. 5. Wing (No. 7 Squadron).—During the night a bomb raid was carried out on the Aerodrome at St. Denis Westrem. Visibility was extremely good, and sixty-two 112-lb. and forty 65-lb. bombs were dropped over the objective, a number of direct hits being observed.

Searchlights over the Aerodrome and Ghent were very active, but A.A. gun-fire was inaccurate.

BOMB ATTACK ON ZEEBRUGGE MOLE.

June 3rd–4th.

No. 5 Wing (No. 7 Squadron).—Simultaneously with the above attack, the Mole at Zeebrugge was attacked, and twenty 112-lb., eighteen 65-lb., and one 550-lb. bombs were dropped over the target. The A.A. gun-fire was particularly heavy, one seaplane being hit in five places. The usual occulting lights on the coast were observed.

BOMB ATTACK ON AERODROME.

June 4th.

No. 5 Wing (No. 5 Squadron).—The night raid of June 3rd–4th on the St. Denis Westrem Aerodrome was followed up by another one at daybreak. Eight 65-lb. and thirty-six Le Pecq bombs were dropped. In the two raids just over 5 tons of explosives were dropped on the Aerodrome, and photographs taken later show several direct hits on sheds, which must have certainly caused internal damage.

BOMB ATTACK ON DOCKS AND HOSTILE SHIPPING.

June 3rd–4th.

No. 5 Wing (No. 5 Squadron).—Two Sopwiths carried out a bomb attack on Bruges Docks and hostile shipping, on which four 65-lb. and twelve Le Pecq bombs were dropped.

Two hits were observed on the North Bassin.

June 4th–5th.

No. 5 Wing (No. 7 Squadron).—During the evening a bomb attack was carried out on Bruges Docks and shipping. Twenty-eight 65-lb. and seventy 112-lb. bombs were dropped on the objective, and several were observed to explode on and in the vicinity of a group of buildings, reported to be submarine repair shops.

June 4th–5th.

No. 5 Wing (No. 5 Squadron).—A second attack on the same objective was made in the early hours of the morning, in which two 112-lb., eleven 65-lb. and thirty-six Le Pecq bombs were dropped.

During both raids intense anti-aircraft fire was experienced, but it was inaccurate.

BOMB ATTACK ON AERODROME.

June 5th–6th.

No. 5 Wing (No. 5 Squadron).—A bomb attack was carried out during the afternoon on the Aerodrome of Houttave (Nieuwmunster), and two 112-lb. and twenty-three 16-lb. bombs were dropped on the objective. A large explosion was observed on one of the hangars and four bombs were seen to explode close to machines standing on the Aerodrome.

June 8th–9th.

No. 5 Wing (No. 5 Squadron).—A bomb attack was carried out on the Aerodrome at St. Denis Westrem, and two 112-lb., two 65-lb., and forty 16-lb. bombs were dropped. The target was obscured by heavy banks of clouds, but, after waiting for a time, gaps appeared through which the objective could be seen. No direct hits were observed, but a number of bombs were seen to burst in the vicinity of a group of sheds.

June 14*th*-15*th*.

No. 5 Wing (No. 5 Squadron).—A bomb raid was carried out on the St. Denis Westrem Aerodrome, and two 112-lb., three 65-lb., and fifty 16-lb. bombs were dropped. Good shooting appears to have been made, and a number of direct hits were observed on sheds and huts, from which dense columns of smoke and flames were seen to rise. A.A. gun-fire was heavy and more accurate than usual.

REPORT ON R.N.A.S. SQUADRONS ATTACHED TO THE R.F.C.

Period 3rd June to 16th June inclusive.

NAVAL SQUADRON No. 1.

This squadron has been attached to the 2nd Brigade, R.F.C., and has carried out 35 offensive patrols over the enemy's lines, in addition to 16 special missions in the pursuit of enemy aircraft.

Enemy Aircraft.—Six decisive combats have taken place and numerous indecisive, with the result that two enemy aircraft were brought down and four driven down out of control. One of the machines destroyed was a two-seater, doing artillery work, which was brought down on our side of the lines.

Casualties.—
  Missing: Flight Lieutenant T. G. Culling, 8th June 1917. Flight Sub-Lieutenant T. R. Swinburne, 8th June 1917.
  Killed: Flight Sub-Lieutenant N. D. M. Wallace, 7th June 1917 (accidentally killed through his engine choking as he was taking off).
  Wounded: Flight Sub-Lieutenant L. H. Cockey, 4th June 1917 (wounded in foot during a fight with 20 enemy machines). Flight Sub-Lieutenant F. J. Nalder, 7th June 1917 (wounded in fight with two enemy machines).

NAVAL SQUADRON No. 6.

This squadron was attached to the Fourth Brigade, R.F.C., and carried out 12 offensive patrols and special missions in pursuit of enemy aircraft.

Enemy Aircraft.—During this period there were 10 combats, three of which were decisive; one enemy machine being brought down and two others driven down out of control.

Casualties.—Missing: Flight Sub-Lieut. Reeves, 6th June 1917.

NAVAL SQUADRON No. 8.

This squadron was attached to the First Brigade, R.F.C., and carried out 40 offensive patrols and 48 special missions in pursuit of enemy aircraft.

Enemy Aircraft.—There have been 34 combats, of which 11 were decisive; two machines being brought down and eight driven down out of control.

Honours.—Acting Flight Commander C. D. Booker, D.S.C., Flight Lieutenant G. G. Simpson, D.S.C.

NAVAL SQUADRON No. 10.

This squadron has been attached to the Second and Fifth Brigade, R.F.C.; many successful offensive patrols being carried out and special missions in pursuit of enemy aircraft.

Enemy Aircraft.—A large number of combats took place, in which 14 enemy machines were brought down and 18 driven down out of control.

Casualties.—

Missing: Flight Sub-Lieut. P. G. McNiel, 3rd June 1917.
Flight Sub-Lieut. L. H. Parker, 14th June 1917.
Wounded: Flight Sub-Lieut. J. H. Keens, 7th June 1917.

EASTERN MEDITERRANEAN STATION.

Mudros, June 1st, 1917.

(Compiled from Weekly Report No. 63, dating from May 25th to June 1st, 1917.)

THASOS AIR STATION.

"A" Squadron.

Reconnaissances have been carried out almost daily during the week of the Gulf of Kavalla and in the vicinity of Thasos for mines and submarines.

May 30th.

Bomb Attack.—A bomb attack was carried out at dawn on Gereviz Seaplane Base, but no report has yet been received which indicates the nature and extent of damage done.

This was made in retaliation to an attack by one enemy seaplane on Thasos Air Station on May 28th, when the enemy bombs did not even hit the Aerodrome and did no damage.

The crops in this area are almost ripe for burning, and measures are being taken to begin an offensive policy.

STAVROS AIR STATION.

"D" Squadron.

May 25th.

Results of Reconnaissance.—A reconnaissance of Angista Valley was carried out and a new dump located in the village of Tolos.

May 27th.

A Photographic Reconnaissance was made for the purpose of taking panoramic photographs of the coast line between Chai, Aghizi, and Orfano.

May 27th.

Result of Reconnaissance.—A reconnaissance was made of the area around Angista, where several new camps and some transport waggons were located among the trees. A further reconnaissance was made of the enemy lines on the Lower Struma front, and proclamations were dropped over enemy territory.

May 28th.

Result of Reconnaissance.—A reconnaissance was made of the enemy front line, where two guns on the S.E. bight of Tafel Kop were clearly seen.

May 29th.

Result of Reconnaissance.—The Angista Valley was again reconnoitred, the outstanding features observed being that the dump at Tolos had increased in size, and that the Angista Hospital had been enlarged to double its former size.

May 29th.

A Photographic Reconnaissance was made to take a line of photographs from Orfanos to Dedeballi.

May 30th.

A Bombing Flight was made, but no details have yet been received.

DETACHED SQUADRONS WITH R.F.C.

"F" Squadron at Marian.

Remarks.—The road and newly laid railway through the Kreshna Defile link up Sofia with the enemy front, along the Upper Struma, and westwards towards Dorian Lake, and along this route supplies for the enemy forces on that front require to be brought.

Interruption of traffic and damage to store and supply dumps had never been seriously dealt with on this route. Accordingly a large dump 3 miles N. of Livunovo, which lies at the southern edge of the Kreshna Defile, was selected as "F" Squadron's first objective.

May 25th.

Bomb Attack.—A bomb attack was carried out on the large dump (mentioned above) 3 miles N. of Livunovo, and 1,156 lbs. of bombs were dropped. Most of the bombs burst in the dump, one making a direct hit on a large shed. Three enemy aeroplanes were seen flying low over Livunovo, but they did not engage.

A further raid was carried out on the same day, in which 1,445 lbs. of bombs were dropped, which caused considerable damage. Three direct hits were observed on the main cluster of sheds; these caught fire. Three more bombs started a fire in a block of sheds on the southern side of the dump; one burst among 50 horses, which stampeded; two burst among some dark coloured stacks on the N.E. edge of the dump. The fire was observed to gradually envelop the dump, and flames from it were observed 20 miles away. On the following day it was seen that the main cluster of sheds was completely gutted and signs of two other large fires were apparent. The damage done must have been very considerable. Again two enemy aeroplanes, of a larger type than those seen in the morning, were observed flying low over Livunovo but did not engage.

May 26th.

Bomb Attack.—A bomb attack was carried out on a newly discovered enemy aerodrome 7 miles N. of Livunovo, consisting of 10 hangars hidden in a gully, and clustered close together, with the landing ground on the opposite side of the road. 1,445 lbs. of bombs were dropped, eight large bombs dropping right among the hangars and one obtaining a direct hit on a hangar.

The hangars are so close together that much damage must have been done to others, in addition to the one blotted out by the direct hit.

Two enemy machines were seen on the ground, but they did not attempt to come up and engage.

THERMI AIR STATION.
"B" SQUADRON.

May 26th.

Result of Reconnaissance.—A reconnaissance was made to observe the condition of the crops in the Menemem Plain. The bulk of the crops were still green, but some stretches were seen to be fit for burning.

May 27th.

Result of Reconnaissance.—A reconnaissance was made of shipping at Aivalik, but, apart from two large two-masted caiques and 10 small ones, nothing could be seen.

A useful reconnaissance of the coastal defences in this district was carried out at the same time, when a twin-gun emplacement was observed on the promontory east of Klavo Island, and two fresh emplacements were being dug on the west coast of Kara Tepe.

May 29th.

Destruction of Crops.—A first flight for the purpose of destroying crops was made in the vicinity of Illkili, when 24 incendiary bombs were dropped in the area where the crops appear to be farthest advanced.

May 30th.

Destruction of Crops.—Twenty incendiary bombs were dropped on wheat fields in the neighbourhood of Pergama. Considerable damage is reported to have been done on this and the previous day.

IMBROS AIR STATION.
"C" SQUADRON.

Remarks.—The R.N.A.S. from Imbros have been occupied principally in reconnaissance and spotting operations for monitors bombarding enemy gun positions.

May 25th.

Spotting Operations and Engagement with Enemy.—This was a day of considerable activity. In the early morning the enemy opened fire from the Peninsula on H.M.S. "Grafton." The triplane was immediately sent to cut off any enemy aeroplane spotting for the firing gun from its base. The triplane at 13,000 feet kept south of Helles and up the Asiatic side of the Straits in order to avoid notice, and then steered across towards Suvla and Anzac, but could not find any enemy machine. At the same time an escorted Nieuport was sent to locate the firing gun, which, however, ceased fire as soon as the Nieuport got into the air.

Later in the morning the enemy again opened fire on Kephalo Harbour, and a reconnaissance was made of the gun positions on the Peninsula, while the triplane patrolled the Straits for enemy aircraft. The gun again ceased fire and no hostile aircraft were seen. In the afternoon "Raglan" and M 17 were spotted on to enemy gun positions in the squares 13 J 3 and 5. During the spotting an enemy machine was sighted over Suvla and pursued, but was lost to sight when retreating low over the hills.

May 26th.

At dawn the triplane was sent out to attack any enemy aircraft attempting to spot for guns on the Peninsula. No aircraft were seen in the air, but a seaplane was sighted lying in Suvla Salt Lake. Afterwards a machine acted as a screen to prevent enemy aircraft observing H.M.S. "Grafton" moving her position. In the afternoon a photographic reconnaissance of Suvla Bay was made, and H.M.S. "Raglan" and M 17 were spotted on to enemy gun positions in square 13 J 3/5, while a gun in square 13 F 6 replied.

During the latter flight a. Halberstadt Scout, with two forward guns, attacked the spotting machine, a B.E., diving at her and firing about 50 rounds before the triplane (Pilot, Flight Sub-Lieut. H. T. Mellings, D.S.C.) which was escorting the B.E. could interfere. The triplane engaged the enemy and fired altogether about 200 rounds at him. Unfortunately, on several occasions, the belt of the Vickers gun stuck, ruining the triplane's attack and requiring both hands of the pilot to remedy it on each occasion. While the pilot was so engaged, the Halberstadt was able to manœuvre into favourable position for attacking. Twice during the action the two machines met, nose on, at short range. Eventually the Halberstadt broke off the action and retired. The triplane, whose gun belt had now stuck altogether, returned to the aerodrome. The Halberstadt was quite as fast as the triplane and was superior in climb. The following account of the action appeared in the Constantinople W/T Press:—

"One of our aviators, Lieutenant Kroneis, attacked an enemy airman on the 26th. The enemy machine fell into the sea east of the Island of Imbros. Shortly after this the same aviator compelled an enemy three-decker to land 100 metres north of the Bight of Kephalo and himself returned unharmed."

It is almost superfluous to state that the B.E. did not fall in the sea, but returned unharmed, and the triplane did not land north of Kephalo, but in the usual aerodrome to the south, after the enemy machine had gone home.

May 28th.

Two flights were made to spot "Raglan" on to guns in Square 13 F 6, which had been seen firing at her on 26th May.

"Raglan" fired six rounds at the enemy's 8·2-inch gun position. The fire was returned, the enemy making good shooting, their eighth and ninth rounds falling within 10 yards of the ship on either side.

On the second flight two direct hits were made on the emplacement, and the gun probably knocked out. During this flight an enemy scout came out, apparently with the object of attacking the spotting machine. The triplane, however, which was acting as escort engaged him at close range from under his tail and the enemy swung away to avoid action, coming within fairly close range of the spotting machine, which also gave him a burst of fire. The enemy thereupon headed away inland, and the triplane did not pursue as close escort was obviously desirable.

SUDA BAY SEAPLANE STATION.

May 27th.

A preliminary search was made by seaplanes for a supposed minefield off the Port of Candia, but without result.

Towards evening a second search was made under perfect observing conditions, but no mines were seen.

May 28th.

Two flights of about two hours' duration were made on this day, one in the early morning and again in the day watches, without any mines being seen. The same perfect conditions obtained, so that it was possible to see black rocks on the sea floor to a depth of 7, 8 and even 9 fathoms, and at low altitudes it was possible to observe the thin moorings of the Dan Buoys' 1-inch wire, leading away from the lower end of their staffs, 2 fathoms below the surface. The area is reported as being clear of mines, barring the possibility of mines having become embedded in the soft oozy bottom which exists in several places.

As well as demonstrating that the sweeping trawlers might well be diverted to more useful work, the presence of the seaplane put entirely new heart into the troops at Crete, and it is very evident that they at once felt assured that the British were doing everything in their power to help and protect the Greeks.

CAPE STATION.

Squadron No. 8, R.N.A.S.

ZANZIBAR.

March 11th.

A seaplane reconnaissance was carried out over the enemy positions outside Lindi. In the village of Mingoyo enemy entrenchments were observed, but no troops were visible. Proceeding towards Mrweka a gun position was observed, and the enemy fired at the seaplane without effect.

March 18th.

A Short seaplane carried out a photographic reconnaissance over Mingoyo, securing two photographs. No signs of the enemy were seen, but a few trenches were observed on the southern slopes.

March 28th.

A photographic reconnaissance was made by seaplane of Mingoyo, also a village two miles from Mingoyo, huts, trenches, and gun positions in the vicinity of Mrweka, and a general view of Mrweka itself.

April 1st.

One 65-lb. bomb was dropped on gun position at Mingoyo by seaplane. The bomb fell 50 feet short of the target, and results are not known.

April 12th.

One 65-lb. bomb was dropped on Mingoyo by seaplane, and the results are believed to be good. No enemy movements were observed.

April 25th.

A bomb attack was carried out by seaplane on Mingoyo, and two 65-lb. bombs were dropped on sheds, both making direct hits. Volumes of black smoke were observed after the bombs exploded, and it was evident that powder or ammunition must have been hit.

April 26th.

Two 65-lb. bombs were dropped by a seaplane on Mingoyo almost simultaneously, each hitting one of the sheds, on which a bomb was dropped the day before.

May 1st.

A bomb attack was carried out on Mayani, and two 65-lb. bombs were dropped almost simultaneously and fell on or near a trench. The seaplane was fired on continuously with rifle fire, one bullet striking the air speed indicator, and rendering it useless.

ROYAL FLYING CORPS COMMUNIQUÉS.

ROYAL FLYING CORPS COMMUNIQUÉ—No. 91.

June 1st.

Reconnaissances.—Reconnaissances were carried out by all brigades. Much valuable information with regard to enemy positions was obtained by Lieutenants Pember and Tymms, No. 5 Squadron, from a very low altitude. Machine gun fire was opened on parties of German infantry by our aeroplanes on a number of occasions.

Artillery Co-operation.—187 targets were dealt with by artillery with aeroplane observation, and 54 with observation by balloons.

Artillery of the First Army obtained 23 O.K.'s and 25 M.O.K.'s on hostile batteries. In many cases observation was difficult, but three pits were seen to be destroyed, six damaged, one set on fire, and one explosion caused. Fourteen active hostile batteries were reported by zone call and one was seen to be silenced.

Artillery of the Second Army successfully engaged 37 hostile batteries, eight gun-pits were destroyed, 18 damaged, and 12 explosions and fires caused. The 243rd Siege Battery, with observation by Lieutenants Home-Hay and Bradford, No. 53 Squadron, obtained 10 direct hits on a dump. Lieutenants Loutit and Holland, also of No. 53 Squadron, ranged the 120 Siege Battery on a hostile battery, with the result that one pit was set on fire by a direct hit, the second and third pits were completely destroyed, and three direct hits were obtained on the fourth.

Twenty-one hostile batteries were successfully engaged by artillery of the Third Army, which obtained 13 direct hits and caused two explosions. A number of O.K.'s were also obtained on trenches.

Artillery of the Fourth Army successfully engaged six hostile batteries, two of these being under zone call; nine direct hits were obtained and seven emplacements damaged.

Artillery of the Fifth Army successfully engaged 16 hostile batteries and obtained 11 direct hits, which destroyed two pits, damaged nine, and caused an explosion. Second-Lieutenant Penberthy and Lieutenant Ritter, No. 15 Squadron, ranged the 171st Siege Battery on to wire and observed for 235 shoots, out of which 50 O.K.'s and 50 M.O.K.'s were actually seen and the wire was destroyed. Balloon observation was also employed in this shoot. The 17th Siege Battery was ranged on wire by Second-Lieutenant Payne, No. 15 Squadron, and obtained 18 direct hits.

In the evening the 193rd Siege Battery, with observation by Second-Lieutenant Woollard and Lieutenant Firth, No. 15 Squadron, destroyed a gun-pit, severely damaged two others, and caused a large explosion and a fire.

With Balloon Observation.—Artillery of First Army engaged and silenced nine active hostile batteries and carried out a number of other successful shoots.

No. 24 Balloon was shelled by the Germans, and Lieutenant Higman, who was in the balloon, immediately threw out all ballast, which allowed the balloon to ascend to its maximum height. At the same time he located and reported the gun firing and our artillery silenced it.

Four hostile batteries were successfully engaged by Artillery of the Fifth Army.

Hostile Aircraft.—Two German two-seater machines were observed by Captain W. T. L. Allcocks, No. 40 Squadron, and he immediately engaged them and drove one down out of control and the second broke off the combat. Second-Lieutenant A. E. Godfrey, of the same Squadron, drove down a hostile aeroplane and followed it until it was lost in the mist falling out of control. Confirmation has now been received from infantry that this machine crashed.

On the evening of the 31st May, eight machines of No. 45 Squadron, while acting as escort to artillery machines, engaged two formations of Albatross Scouts. As the result of the fighting Captain Mountford and Second-Lieutenant Vessey drove down an opponent out of control, while a second was driven down out of control by Second-Lieutenants Findley and Blacklock.

A fiercely contested combat took place between eight machines of No. 20 Squadron and an Albatross formation of 17 Scouts. Lieutenant Cunnel and Second-Lieutenant Cambray shot down one of the scouts, which was seen to break to pieces in the air. A second was driven down out of control by Second-Lieutenants Taylor and Lingard.

On June 1st, Flight Sub-Lieuts. Disette and Page, Naval Squadron No. 10, drove down a two-seater Aviatik out of control, while an Albatross two-seater was driven down out of control by Flight Sub-Lieut. Reid of the same Squadron. Flight Sub-Lieut. Collishaw, also of Naval Squadron No. 10, shot down an Albatross Scout, which fell in flames before it crashed.

Sergeant Olley, No. 1 Squadron, engaged and drove down a two-seater machine out of control near Messines.

Second-Lieutenant A. S. Shepherd, No. 29 Squadron, engaged six H.A. near Brebières and drove two down, one out of control and a second badly damaged. Second-Lieutenant J. M. Leach and Lieutenant A. W. Miller, No. 29 Squadron, also drove down a hostile machine, each out of control, and damaged two others.

A patrol of No. 54 Squadron attacked an Albatross Scout, and after bursts of fire had been opened by Lieutenants O. M. Sutton and M. D. G. Scott, the Albatross fell out of control.

Squadron Commander Breese and Flight Sub-Lieut. Walton, Naval Squadron No. 6, also drove down an enemy machine out of control.

Photography.—542 photographs were taken during the day.

Bombing.—First Brigade.—On the evening of the 31st May, No. 25 Squadron dropped twenty-four 20-lb. bombs on Henin-Liètard and buildings were damaged.

On the night of the 31st May–1st June a very successful raid was carried out by No. 100 Squadron. One 230-lb. bomb was dropped on Orchies ammunition depôt, and the bomb was seen to explode with extreme violence and partly destroyed the depôt. Eight 112-lb. bombs were then dropped on the same objective and six direct hits were obtained from 800 feet, and all the bombs were seen to explode. Eleven 112-lb. bombs were dropped on the goods yard and sidings at Orchies, and six 20-lb. bombs were dropped on Templeuve goods siding.

On the 1st June No. 25 Squadron dropped twelve 20-lb. bombs on Bois Bernard and fourteen on La Bassée, and damage was done to buildings.

5th Brigade.—On the evening of the 31st May eight 20-lb. bombs were dropped by No. 18 Squadron on a dump north of Bois de Loison.

On the 1st June six 20-lb. bombs were dropped on Hendecourt.

June 2nd.

Artillery Co-operation. — 186 targets were dealt with by artillery with aeroplane observation, and 130 with observation by balloon.

Artillery of the First Army obtained 19 direct hits on hostile batteries; two pits were destroyed, 10 damaged, and three explosions and three fires were caused in battery positions.

Thirty-three hostile batteries were successfully engaged by artillery of the Second Army in addition to 65 other targets, seven gun-pits were destroyed, 11 damaged, and 13 fires and explosions caused. Fifty-six zone calls were sent down, and seven were seen to be answered.

Artillery of the Third Army successfully engaged 14 hostile batteries, and obtained 12 direct hits and caused three explosions.

Four hostile batteries were successfully engaged by artillery of the Fourth Army, seven direct hits and 12 M.O.K.'s were obtained on batteries, six emplacements were damaged, and four explosions caused. The 110th Siege Battery with observation by Lieutenant Lines, No. 52 Squadron, fired 220 rounds and obtained four O.K.'s on a hostile battery in addition to other good shoots. Lieutenant Phillips, No. 9 Squadron, reported about 60 infantry by zone call and artillery promptly opened fire.

Fifteen hostile batteries were successfully engaged by artillery of the Fifth Army, 18 direct hits on gun positions were obtained, one pit was destroyed, 13 damaged, and two explosions caused.

With Balloon Observation.—Artillery of the First Army silenced two hostile batteries and caused a fire.

Over 2,400 rounds were fired by artillery of the Second Army and four explosions and a fire were caused.

Artillery of the Third Army successfully ranged on 44 targets, including nine hostile battery positions.

Artillery of the Fourth Army engaged three hostile batteries and silenced one of them.

Hostile Aircraft.—An Albatross Scout which was engaged by Second-Lieutenant F. J. Gibbs, No. 23 Squadron, was driven down out of control.

An offensive patrol of No. 20 Squadron engaged eight Albatross Scouts, and Second-Lieutenant Trevethan and 2nd A.M. Cowell picked out the leader, whose machine burst into flames and crashed.

Second-Lieutenant Barager, No. 46 Squadron, engaged three Albatross Scouts and drove one down out of control.

A fight took place between an offensive patrol of No. 1 Squadron and eight Albatross Scouts, and Lieutenant Jenkins and Second-Lieutenant Mainsbridge each drove down one of their opponents out of control.

Captain Bishop, No. 60 Squadron, when 17 miles over the lines, saw seven machines, some of which had their engines running, on an aerodrome. He waited, and then engaged the first one that left the ground from a height of about 60 feet, and the hostile machine crashed on the aerodrome. Another left the ground, and Captain Bishop, who was hovering round, immediately dived at it, and, after 30 rounds had been fired, the German aeroplane crashed into a tree. Just after that two more left the ground at the same time, so Captain Bishop climbed to 1,000 feet and then engaged one of them, and it fell and crashed within 300 yards of the aerodrome. The fourth machine was driven down after a whole drum had been fired into it. After this exploit Captain Bishop returned safely, but with his aeroplane considerably shot about by machine gun fire from the ground.

Flight-Lieutenant G. G. MacLennan, Naval Squadron No. 6, while leading a patrol, engaged an Albatross Scout, which was driven down out of control, and is reported by anti-aircraft to have crashed.

No. 37 Balloon was attacked by a German machine, but owing to the accuracy of the machine gun and anti-aircraft fire the balloon was not destroyed.

Photography.—495 photographs were taken during the day.

Bombing.—1st Brigade.—On the night of the 1st–2nd, No. 10 Squadron dropped eight 112-lb. bombs on Provin Aerodrome, two on Salome, two on Pont-à-Vendin, which were seen to burst on the railway, and two on Marquilles, where a fire was caused in a dump.

On the 2nd, thirty-three 20-lb. bombs were dropped on Sallaumines by No. 25 Squadron.

5th Brigade.—Eight 20-lb. bombs were dropped on Hendecourt.

Miscellaneous.—Two aeroplanes of No. 60 Squadron and one of No. 32 Squadron fired into German trenches from about 150 feet.

June 3rd.

Reconnaissances.—In addition to successful reconnaissances by Brigades and 9th Wing, Captain Adams and Second-Lieutenant Durrant of No. 55 Squadron reconnoitred the Ypres–Menin–Courtrai–Thielt–Thourout area. The machine was followed by hostile aircraft, but they were unable to overtake it.

A very successful contact patrol was carried out by No. 16 Squadron.

Observation showed that Tourmignies, Phalempin, and Provin Aerodromes were in use on the night of the 2nd–3rd. Machines of the 4th Brigade attacked infantry, machine gun emplacement, and Germans in trenches from low altitudes.

Artillery Co-operation.—193 targets were dealt with by artillery with aeroplane observation and 107 with observation by balloons.

Artillery of the First Army obtained 28 direct hits on hostile batteries. Five pits were destroyed, seven damaged and seven explosions caused.

Forty-eight hostile batteries were successfully engaged by artillery of the Second Army. Nine gun-pits were destroyed, 17 damaged and 16 explosions and fires caused. Fifty-eight zone calls were sent down and 15 were seen to be answered. Two Siege Batteries with observation by Second-Lieutenants Hay and Bradford, No. 53 Squadron, destroyed all four gun-pits of a hostile battery. Observing for two other Siege Batteries, Second-Lieutenants James and Reade, No. 53 Squadron, reported three gun-pits of a hostile battery destroyed and two damaged. The 281st Siege Battery with observation by Second-Lieutenants Bowick and Debenham, No. 21 Squadron, destroyed two pits and damaged two others in a hostile battery.

Artillery of the Third Army successfully engaged 19 hostile batteries, 12 direct hits were obtained and three explosions caused. Thirty-three hostile batteries were seen active, on three of which there was observation of fire. A number of direct hits were obtained on trenches.

Ten hostile batteries were successfully engaged by artillery of the Fourth Army, which obtained 13 O.K.'s and 23 M.O.K.'s, 11 emplacements were damaged, and four explosions caused. 816 rounds were fired in pre-arranged shoots. The 37th Siege Battery with observation by Lieutenant Glenny, No. 52 Squadron, obtained six direct hits on a hostile battery, causing two explosions and damaging three pits. Lieutenant Woodhouse of the same squadron observed 175 rounds by the 9th Siege Battery and reported a direct hit, nine M.O.K.'s and an explosion. The 240th Siege Battery with observation by Lieutenant Elliott, No. 52 Squadron, fired 141 rounds, obtaining two O.K.'s, one M.O.K. and causing an explosion. During this shoot the battery was subjected to heavy hostile artillery fire.

Eight hostile batteries were successfully engaged by artillery of the Fifth Army, which obtained seven direct hits on gun positions which destroyed one pit, damaged six and caused four explosions.

Captain Portal and Lieutenant Aitken, No. 3 Squadron, successfully ranged the 34th Siege Battery on to a hostile battery and one pit was destroyed and an explosion caused. They also reported by zone call three active hostile batteries, one of which was an anti-aircraft battery, and sent down observations until all three were silenced.

With Balloon Observation.—Artillery of the First Army successfully engaged six hostile batteries, three of which were handed over by aeroplane observers.

Forty-nine targets were successfully engaged by artillery of the Second Army, and six hostile batteries were neutralised.

Transport was engaged by artillery of the Third Army, and 34 targets were successfully ranged on, including five N.F. targets and five hostile batteries.

Sixteen targets were dealt with by artillery of the Fourth Army and several hostile batteries were neutralised.

Hostile Aircraft.—Two two-seater fighting machines were engaged by Flight Commander Compston, Naval Squadron No. 8, and both were driven down damaged and probably out of control. A third machine was also engaged by this pilot and the engine was seen to be hit. In the evening Flight Commander Compston drove down a German Scout in a damaged condition, and Second-Lieutenant A. E. Godfrey, No. 40 Squadron, who attacked three H.A., drove one down out of control.

Lieutenant A. T. Rickards and C.S.M. Nava, No. 43 Squadron, engaged a German two-seater which burst into flames and fell.

Second-Lieutenant W. C. Campbell, No. 1 Squadron, observed an Aviatik two-seater flying towards our lines and immediately dived at it and opened fire at about 20 yards range, and the hostile machine went straight down and crashed.

Lieutenant Joske and Captain Pritt, No. 46 Squadron, each engaged and drove down an Albatross Scout out of control.

Corps machines of the Second Brigade were not interfered with at all by hostile aircraft. A pilot of No. 60 Squadron observed one of our machines being attacked by nine H.A., and he immediately dived at them, and the German machines were driven away. This pilot returned to his aerodrome, and, although slightly wounded, again went out in search of a hostile machine reported doing artillery work.

Flight Sub-Lieut. Collishaw, Naval Squadron No. 10, attacked an Albatross Scout, which fell out of control, and was seen to be on fire. Flight Sub-Lieut. Parker, of the same squadron, in an engagement with four H.A., shot one down, which was seen to crash. A third hostile aeroplane was destroyed by Flight Sub-Lieut. Reid, also of Naval Squadron No. 10.

Lieutenant A. W. Hogg, No. 41 Squadron, dived at a German machine, which immediately flew east. He, however, succeeded in getting in front of it, and forced it to fight, and, after a short encounter, the German machine crashed.

In a fight between an offensive patrol of No. 45 Squadron and about 25 H.A., one hostile machine was driven down and was seen to break in the air after having been engaged by Second-Lieutenant R. Watt and Corporal Harries. Another was driven down out of control by Second-Lieutenant Fitchat and Lieutenant Hates.

Lieutenant F. P. Holliday and Captain A. H. W. Hall, No. 48 Squadron, opened fire on an Albatross at about 20 yards range, and, after about 200 rounds, the tail of the German machine was seen to fall off.

Photography.—975 photographs were taken during the day.

Bombing.—First Brigade.—No. 25 Squadron dropped sixteen 20-lb. bombs on La Bassée and 22 on Marquillies Factory.

On the night of the 2nd–3rd, No. 10 Squadron dropped three 112-lb. bombs on Dourges Station, and all the bombs were seen to burst in the station and on the railway line. Two phosphorus and six 20-lb. bombs were dropped on Marquillies Sugar Factory, and a large fire was started. Two 112-lb. bombs were dropped on Phalempin Aerodrome, and twelve 20-lb. bombs were dropped on Provin Aerodrome, and both objectives were hit.

No. 100 Squadron dropped ten 112-lbs. and eight 20-lb. bombs on various targets between 10 p.m. and 1.15 a.m. Four trains were hit—one near Comines, one near La Madeline, one near Wasquehal, and a fourth, which was wrecked, was bombed from 900 feet near Wervicq. Menin Station was hit from 1,000 feet by two of the heavy bombs, and a fire was caused at Warneton by two more heavy bombs.

Second Brigade. Eight 30-lb. bombs were dropped on active batteries near Zandvoorde and Hollebeke on the night of the 2nd–3rd.

Third Brigade.—Fourteen 20-lb. bombs were dropped on various targets.

Fifth Brigade.—Six 20-lb. bombs on Hendecourt.

9th Wing.—No. 27 Squadron dropped 112-lb. bombs from an average height of about 6,000 feet on Vyfwegen dump, and a number of direct hits were obtained on the dump and on the railway, and a large volume of black smoke was seen, while one pilot felt the shock of an explosion.

June 4th.

Reconnaissances.—Successful reconnaissances were carried out by all brigades and 9th Wing. Lieutenant Stevens and Second-Lieutenant Sandy, No. 55 Squadron, reconnoitred the area around Bruges, Ghent, Audenarde, Courtrai, and took good photographs.

A number of valuable photographs were also taken by Lieutenants Bird and Russell, No. 55 Squadron, who reconnoitred the area Lille–Tournai–Roubaix and Tourcoing.

Artillery Co-operation.—214 targets were dealt with by artillery with aeroplane observation, and 164 with observation by balloons.

Artillery of the First Army successfully engaged 26 hostile batteries, 18 direct hits were obtained, five pits were destroyed, nine damaged and three explosions caused.

Artillery of the Second Army successfully engaged 55 hostile batteries, 10 gun-pits were destroyed, 33 damaged, and 10 explosion and fires caused. Seventy-six zone calls were sent down, and 16 were observed to be answered. The 243rd Siege Battery, with observation by Second-Lieutenant Turnbull and Lieutenant Prothero, No. 53 Squadron, completely destroyed a hostile battery position on which nine direct hits were obtained. The 89th Siege Battery, with observation by Captain Bowen and Lieutenant Bunt, No. 7 Squadron, destroyed one bridge and damaged another.

Twenty-four hostile batteries were successfully engaged by artillery of the Third Army; 11 direct hits were obtained, causing three explosions and a fire. Thirty-nine hostile batteries were seen active, on two of which there were observation of fire.

Ten hostile batteries were successfully engaged by artillery of the Fourth Army, which obtained 22 O.K.'s, 49 M.O.K.'s, and caused 17 explosions. Over 1,051 rounds were fired on batteries in pre-arranged shoots, and 21 emplacements were damaged. The 13th Siege Battery, with observation by Lieutenant Carbery, No. 52 Squadron, obtained four O.K.'s and 14 M.O.K.'s on a hostile battery; four pits were damaged and an explosion caused. Four O.K.'s and 20 M.O.K.'s were obtained by the 9th Siege Battery on a hostile battery with observation by Lieutenant Woodhouse, No. 52 Squadron. All pits were entirely destroyed, the whole battery position was damaged, and fires and explosions were seen.

Artillery of the Fifth Army successfully engaged 19 hostile batteries, eight direct hits on gun positions were obtained, one gun-pit was destroyed, eight pits were damaged, and three explosions caused.

With Balloon Observation.—Artillery of the First Army carried out 17 successful shoots on hostile batteries, six of which were silenced and an explosion caused. Four of these shoots were taken over from aeroplanes.

Artillery of the Second Army engaged 45 targets, of which 23 were hostile batteries. Seventeen batteries were neutralised, and a fire and three explosions were caused. Twenty-five active hostile batteries were reported during the Army demonstration.

Fifty-nine targets were engaged by artillery of the Third Army.

Five batteries, including an A.A. battery, were neutralised by artillery of the Fourth Army, and one battery position was set on fire.

Hostile Aircraft.—An offensive patrol of No. 1 Squadron engaged nine Albatross Scouts east of Hollebeke, and Lieutenant T. F. Hazel fired half a drum into one of them when the left wing was seen to break off the machine, after which it crashed. He then turned and fired the remainder of the drum into another hostile aeroplane at about 60 yards, and this machine went down in a spin and one wing was also seen to break off by other pilots of the patrol. Shortly afterwards, Lieutenant Hazel engaged four more H.A. and drove two down, one of which was forced to land. After this he joined in a fight between a number of our machines and 15 H.A., but the German machines avoided close fighting. Second-Lieutenant P. F. Fullard, of the same squadron, dived at one of four H.A., and this machine, which was painted with many colours, fell completely out of control. He then joined in the big fight between 15 H.A. and a number of our machines, but one of the German scouts obtained a favourable position on his tail so he put his machine into a spin. An S.E. 5 of No. 56 Squadron dived at the attacking scout and drove it down out of control. Second-Lieutenant Fullard then attacked a black and white Albatross Scout from underneath, and about 30 shots were seen to go into the German machine, which flew straight on, and then went into a spin, turned completely over and eventually crashed in a field.

Flight Commander Gerrard, who, with other machines of Naval Squadron No. 1 took part in the general engagement already referred to, fired 50 rounds at point blank range into a German machine which had driven a Nieuport Scout down in a spin, and the hostile machine fell completely out of control. Flight Commander Gerrard and a Nieuport Scout then attacked an Albatross Scout which had hit one of our machines. The Nieuport attacked from above and the triplane from below, and the hostile machine fell out of control and was seen to crash. Three of the German scouts were attacked by Flight Lieutenant Ramsey, but after a short engagement all three dived away.

In other engagements Second-Lieutenant Campbell, No. 1 Squadron, destroyed a two-seater L.V.G., and a patrol of Naval Squadron No. 10 drove down an Albatross Scout out of control.

In the evening an offensive patrol of No. 41 Squadron engaged four Albatross Scouts, and Lieutenant Baker drove one down out of control.

Second-Lieutenant Luxmoore, No. 46 Squadron, became separated from the rest of his patrol and was attacked by three Albatross Scouts. He secured a favourable position on the tail of one of the scouts, which he drove down and it crashed. The other two continued to attack, so he put his machine into a spin and thus evaded them.

Lieutenant F. Sharpe, No. 1 Squadron, dived at a Rumpler two-seater, and observed his tracers entering the pilot's and observer's seats, and the German machine fell out of control and crashed.

A Roland two-seater which had been engaged by Second Lieutenant Mussared, No. 1 Squadron, turned completely on its back and fell out of control with the engine full on. Anti-aircraft report that this machine eventually caught fire.

Captain Chapman, No. 29 Squadron, engaged a hostile machine and brought it down on our side of the lines, and the pilot was taken prisoner.

A bombing raid of No. 27 Squadron engaged nine Albatross Scouts, and had hard fighting during the whole of their time over the lines. In spite of this, the pilots dropped their bombs on the objective, and all the German machines were driven down, except one which broke off the combat. Captain D. J. Bell and Lieutenant D. V. D. Marshall attacked one of the Albatross Scouts which was diving at one of our machines, and one of the wings of the enemy machine was shot off. Captain Bell then engaged another machine, in which the pilot is believed to have been shot, and the German aeroplane fell completely out of control. Lieutenant Marshall also attacked and drove down another scout out of control. Second-Lieutenant M. Johnson also drove down one out of control, and Captain H. G. D. Wilkins hit one which turned over, but he was unable to watch it.

Machines of No. 56 Squadron on offensive patrol also had considerable fighting, and Second-Lieutenant A. P. F. Rhys-Davids drove down an enemy machine out of control, and, according to reports from other pilots, there is no doubt that this machine crashed.

Bombing machines of No. 55 Squadron when over Moorslede were attacked by about 10 H.A. One enemy machine dived at a De Havilland, in which were Lieutenants C. C. Knight and J. C. Trulock, and the latter fired two drums into the attacking machine, which fell out of control and crashed. After dropping the bombs this machine became detached from the rest of the formation and was cut off by six H.A., but the pilot succeeded in evading the German machines, and one was shot down in an attempt to attack the De Havilland from behind.

A reconnaissance of No. 70 Squadron was attacked the whole time by eight hostile scouts which dived and then immediately flew away, but all our machines returned safely, while two of the Germans were driven down badly damaged.

Spads of No. 19 Squadron and Sopwith Scouts of No. 66 Squadron also had heavy fighting, and Lieutenant A. B. Thorne, of the latter Squadron, drove down two German machines out of control, while Captain Latta and Lieutenant Robertson, also of No. 66 Squadron, drove one down badly damaged.

Photography. — 1,156 photographs were taken during the day.

Bombing. — **1st Brigade.** — On the night of the 3rd–4th, No. 100 Squadron dropped eighteen 112-lb. and twelve 20-lb. bombs on various targets. A train was bombed and wrecked between Quesnoy and Comines; another was hit with two 112-lb. bombs south of Quesnoy; two trains in Courtrai Station were hit from 500 feet with four 20-lb. bombs, and two 112-lb. bombs were dropped on Courtrai Station from 600 feet and burst on the rolling stock and caused an explosion. Ten 112-lb. and eight 20-lb. bombs were dropped on Menin Station and sidings, and all the bombs were seen to burst on the objective and caused a fire and a number of explosions followed by a volume of smoke. Two hours afterwards Menin Station was seen to be in flames.

On the 4th, No. 25 Squadron dropped fifty-six 20-lb. bombs on Sallaumines; eight of the bombs were seen to burst on the railway, eight on the road, and the remainder fell on buildings.

2nd Brigade. — Eight 20-lb. bombs were dropped on Warneton on the night of the 3rd–4th by machines of No. 20 Squadron.

3rd Brigade. — Twelve 20-lb. bombs were dropped on various targets.

5th Brigade. — On the night of the 3rd–4th, four F.E.'s of No. 18 Squadron dropped eight phosphorus and sixteen 20-lb. bombs on Proville Aerodrome, causing fires in hangars, houses, and sheds, all of which were hit. These pilots also attacked German infantry with machine gun fire.

9th Wing. — No. 27 Squadron dropped thirty-nine 20-lb. bombs on St. Denis Westrem Aerodrome, and direct hits were obtained on the Aerodrome and on a shed.

No. 55 Squadron dropped ten 112-lb. bombs on sidings at Ingelmunster, but owing to very heavy fighting the results were unobserved. This Squadron also dropped seventy-two 20 lb. bombs on Iseghem dump, and several fires were started in the dump.

June 5th.

Reconnaissances.—Reconnaissances were carried out by all brigades and 9th Wing, and a great deal of valuable information was obtained as to the enemy positions on the fronts of the First and Second Armies.

Lieutenant Barnett and Second-Lieutenant Durrant, on de Havillands of No. 55 Squadron, carried out two long reconnaissances embracing the area Leuze–Ath–Lessines–Grammont–Sotteghem–Audenard, and took 44 photographs.

Artillery Co-operation.—180 targets were dealt with by artillery with aeroplane observation and 208 with observation by balloons.

Artillery of the First Army successfully engaged 21 hostile batteries; 15 direct hits were obtained, five gun-pits were destroyed, 13 damaged, and five explosions took place.

Artillery of the Second Army successfully engaged 58 hostile batteries, destroying 19 gun-pits, damaging 27, and causing 21 explosions and fires. Seventy-seven zone calls were sent down, and 13 were seen to be answered. The 243rd Siege Battery, with observation by Lieutenants Hay and Bradford, No. 53 Squadron, engaged two hostile batteries and destroyed all four pits of one battery and three of the other. Second-Lieutenants James and Reade, No. 53 Squadron, ranged the 199th and 203rd Siege Batteries on to two hostile batteries, and one was completely destroyed and the other damaged. The 266th Siege Battery, with observation by Lieutenant Butler and Second-Lieutenant Ashwell, No. 53 Squadron, obtained direct hits on all four pits of a hostile battery and caused a large explosion, while the 184th Siege Battery destroyed gun-pits of a hostile battery with observation by Lieutenants Withers and Jenkins, No. 6 Squadron. Three pits were destroyed and two explosions caused in a hostile battery by the 83rd Siege Battery with observation by Lieutenant Wilson and Major Wright, also of No. 6 Squadron.

Twenty-four hostile batteries were successfully engaged by artillery of the Third Army; 10 direct hits were obtained. One pit was destroyed, four were damaged, and two explosions caused, while three other large explosions were seen which were probably caused by artillery fire. 43 hostile batteries were seen active, on five of which there was observation of fire.

Artillery of the Fourth Army successfully engaged eight hostile batteries, three under zone call; five direct hits were obtained and seven explosions were caused. The 15th Siege

Battery, with observation by Lieutenant Carbery, No. 52 Squadron, obtained three O.K.'s and 13 M.O.K.'s, destroying a pit, damaging three others, and causing several explosions in a hostile battery.

With Balloon Observation. — Artillery of the First Army successfully engaged 61 targets and silenced nine hostile batteries, causing an explosion and a fire in one of the battery positions.

Sixty-two targets were engaged by artillery of the Second Army, 20 of these being hostile batteries, and eight were neutralised.

Artillery of the Third Army engaged 66 targets, including 12 hostile batteries.

Artillery of the Fourth Army neutralised two hostile batteries. carried out two destructive shoots, and also successfully engaged a convoy of lorries.

Hostile Aircraft. — An offensive patrol of No. 20 Squadron attacked 4 H.A., and Lieutenant Cunnel and Sergeant Sayers shot one down in flames. A little later our formation again engaged a number of H.A. and Captains Thayre and Cubbon drove one down which crashed on Coucou Aerodrome.

Naval pilots of No. 10 Squadron had a general engagement with a number of Albatross two-seaters, and as a result of the fighting one of the German machines was shot down in flames, while a second was driven down out of control.

While over Menin a patrol of No. 45 Squadron was attacked by 18 H.A. Scouts, led by a red machine with black wheels. The leader of the German formation showed great pluck and skill and the fight lasted for 23 minutes. Lieutenants Frew and Dalton shot down one of the machines which fell in flames, and then dived on another which had secured a favourable position on the tail of one of ours, and after a burst of fire the German aeroplane fell completely out of control. Second-Lieutenants Macmillan and Webb also drove down one of their opponents which was seen falling out of control until very near the ground when it was lost sight of.

Lieutenant Hazel, No. 1 Squadron, and Second-Lieutenants Barager and Dimmock, No. 46 Squadron, each drove down a hostile machine out of control.

In a fight between 15 H.A led by a red machine and seven F.E.'s of No. 20 Squadron, one of our aeroplanes was driven down and followed by the red H.A. Lieutenant H. L. Satchell and Second-Lieutenant T. Lewis at once dived to the assistance of our machine, and a fight lasting about 15 minutes took place, in which the German pilot showed great skill and persistence. Eventually, however, after a burst of fire at very close range the enemy scout burst into flames and the wings were seen to fall off before it crashed.

Flight Sub-Lieut. Taylor, Naval Squadron No. 10, shot down a two-seater H.A. in flames, while two more were driven down out of control, one by Captain Barker and Sergeant Nicholson, and the other by Captain Letts and Lieutenant Jameson, No. 48 Squadron.

Continuous fighting took place between about 40 H.A. and machines of Nos. 22, 54, and Naval Squadron No. 6. As a result of the fighting at least three hostile machines were seen to fall out of control and one was afterwards seen completely wrecked on the ground.

No. 24 Squadron also had considerable fighting and drove down a German machine out of control, while the Cavalry Corps report having seen another crash.

Lieutenant Orlebar, No. 19 Squadron, drove down an enemy machine out of control, and Lieutenants Gotch and Kibury, No. 70 Squadron, hit one which was forced to land in a field.

In the evening Lieutenant W. A. Bond, No. 40 Squadron, while on offensive patrol, drove down a German machine out of control. He then attacked a second which was driven down and crashed. Second Lieutenant A. E. Godfrey of the same Squadron drove down a hostile scout out of control.

Major Scott, No. 60 Squadron, observed an Albatross Scout diving at a machine of No. 29 Squadron and he immediately dived at it, and after firing about five rounds the hostile aeroplane caught fire and crashed in our lines.

Photography.—677 photographs were taken during the day.

Bombing.—First Brigade.—On the night 4th–5th No. 10 Squadron dropped twenty-two 10-lb. and two 112-lb. bombs on Dourges, and all the bombs were observed to burst on buildings and on the railway. This squadron also dropped five 20-lb. bombs on both Tourmignies and Libercourt Aerodromes, six 20-lb. bombs on La Bassée, three phosphorus bombs on Violaines, two 112-lb. bombs on Provin Aerodrome, and ten 20-lb. bombs on Metallurgique, five of which burst on sheds, blowing in the roof and doing considerable damage. A phosphorous bomb was also dropped on Marquillies sugar factory and a very large explosion was caused. Two 20-lb. bombs were dropped on a searchlight at the factory.

No. 100 Squadron dropped one 230-lb. and fourteen 112-lb. bombs on various targets. The 230-lb. and six of the 112-lb. bombs were dropped on Roulers Station from 800 feet and direct hits were obtained. Two 112-lb. bombs were dropped on a station between Courtrai and Iseghem, and two on Wervicq Station, and both places were hit. Trucks in Comines Station were hit by two 112-lb. bombs which caused explosions and a fire, while two 112-lb. bombs were dropped on a train from 400 feet between Roulers and Menin.

On the 5th No. 25 Squadron dropped thirty-four 20-lb. bombs on Izel and twenty-eight 20-lb. bombs on La Bassée.

Direct hits were obtained on both places, and a fire was caused in the latter.

Second Brigade.—On the night of the 4th–5th six 30-lb. bombs were dropped on guns near Warneton.

Third Brigade.—On the evening of the 4th–5th No. 18 Squadron dropped four phosphorous and twenty-nine 20-lb. bombs on a dump at Sailly, and direct hits were obtained on the railway line and on the dump.

On the night of the 4th–5th No. 6 Squadron dropped eight phosphorous and sixteen 20-lb. bombs from 800 feet on Proville Aerodrome. A large fire was caused in sheds at the aerodrome, while a direct hit was obtained on an iron shed just south of the station.

9th Wing.—No. 27 Squadron dropped nine 112-lb. bombs from under 5,000 feet on Audenarde, and obtained direct hits on the station. No. 55 Squadron dropped sixty-four 20-lb. bombs on Bisseghem Aerodrome from 14,000 feet, and sixty-five 20-lb. bombs on Marcke Aerodrome from the same height.

June 6th.

All Brigades and 9th Wing reconnoitred large tracts of the enemy's territory, and during this and other work our aeroplanes went down to very low altitudes and attacked enemy infantry and other targets. In one case a motor cyclist was knocked off his bicycle, while in another a pilot attacked transport from 100 feet, killing six horses.

Artillery Co-operation.—161 targets were dealt with by artillery with aeroplane observation and 135 with observation by balloons.

Artillery of the First Army successfully engaged 17 hostile batteries; 16 direct hits were obtained, three pits were destroyed, five damaged, and eight explosions caused. Fifteen active hostile batteries were reported by zone call, and as a result an ammunition depôt was hit and a number of explosions took place.

Artillery of the Second Army successfully engaged 53 hostile batteries; 27 gun-pits were destroyed, 36 damaged, and 21 explosions caused. The 179th Siege Battery, with observation by Lieutenants Stock and Carson, No. 6 Squadron, obtained 13 O.K.'s and six M.O.K.'s on a hostile battery, completely destroying six gun-pits and causing two explosions. The 82nd Siege Battery, with observation by Second Lieutenants Kerr and Elstob, No. 53 Squadron, destroyed five gun-pits and caused a big fire and an explosion.

Twenty-nine hostile batteries were successfully engaged by artillery of the Third Army, which obtained 16 O.K.'s, eight M.O.K.'s, 88 Y.'s, and 119 Z.'s, and caused four explosions.

Six hostile batteries were successfully engaged by artillery of the Fourth Army, which obtained 14 O.K.'s and 33 M.O.K.'s.

Thirteen emplacements were damaged and nine explosions caused. Captain Carbery, No. 52 Squadron, ranged the 15th Siege Battery on to two hostile batteries, and nine direct hits and 26 M.O.K.'s were obtained. Two pits were destroyed, six damaged, and five explosions caused. The 110th Siege Battery obtained three O.K.'s and seven M.O.K.'s on a hostile battery with observation by Captain Murray, No. 52 Squadron, who observed for 170 rounds.

With Balloon Observation.—Artillery of the First Army silenced a hostile battery and carried out seven other successful shoots on hostile batteries and also on a number of trenches.

Artillery of the Second Army engaged 40 targets, of which 13 were hostile batteries; nine of these were engaged for destruction and four were neutralised.

Forty-one targets were successfully engaged by artillery of the Third Army. The Fifth Balloon Section took over two shoots on hostile battery positions from No. 12 Squadron, and in one case ammunition was set on fire, while in the other an explosion and three fires were caused.

Thirty-three targets were engaged by artillery of the Fourth Army.

Hostile Aircraft.—Six F.E.'s of No. 25 Squadron attacked three hostile scouts and drove one down out of control. Lieutenant Hazel, No. 1 Squadron, engaged a two-seater machine, which fell out of control near Houthem.

In an engagement between 13 of our machines and from 15 to 20 H.A., Flight Sub-Lieut. Collishaw, Naval Squadron No. 10, shot down two Albatross scouts in flames and drove down a third out of control, while Flight Sub-Lieut. Nash destroyed a two-seater Albatross and drove down an Albatross Scout out of control. During this encounter Flight Sub-Lieut. Reid destroyed a Halberstadt Scout and Flight Sub-Lieut. Page shot down an Albatross Scout, while three others were driven down out of control by Flight Sub-Lieuts. Keens, Sharman, and Alexander, who got one each. All our machines returned safely.

A general engagement took place between 30 of our machines and from 30 to 40 H.A., and after about 30 minutes' close fighting all the hostile machines were driven off. After the fight three of the German aeroplanes were seen crashed on the ground, and it is believed that at least five others were driven down out of control. Five pilots of No. 54 Squadron who took part claim a German machine each out of control, while several more are claimed by pilots of Naval Squadron No. 6, who also took part in the fighting.

Captain G. H. Bowman, No. 56 Squadron, drove down two H.A. out of control.

One H.A. was brought down by anti-aircraft of the Third Army.

Photography.—675 photographs were taken during the day.

Bombing.—First Brigade.—On the night of the 5th–6th No. 100 Squadron dropped one 230-lb. and twenty-four 112-lb. bombs on various targets between 10.15 p.m. and 3.20 a.m. Two 112-lb. bombs were dropped from 800 feet and on a train which was wrecked north of Roulers. Two 112-lb. bombs were dropped on Roulers Station, and five 112-lb. and one 230-lb. on Wervicq Station, where direct hits were obtained from 1,000 feet. The remaining bombs were dropped on trains and other objectives.

On the 6th No. 25 Squadron dropped twenty-eight 25-lb. bombs on La Poullerie Aerodrome.

Second Brigade.—Eight 30-lb. bombs were dropped on enemy front line trenches.

Third Brigade.—On the night of the 5th–6th No. 11 Squadron dropped eight 20-lb. bombs on Cantin Aerodrome from under 1,000 feet. During the day thirty-eight 20-lb. bombs were dropped on various targets.

9th Wing.—Reckem Aerodrome was attacked three times during the day by No. 55 Squadron, and one hundred and forty-four 20-lb. bombs were dropped from an average height of about 13,000 feet. Direct hits were obtained on the aerodrome, on sheds and on houses, which were set on fire. No. 27 Squadron dropped twenty-four 112-lb. bombs on railways and trains at Escanaffles. Several of the bombs were seen to fall on the track and one on the station from 5,000 feet.

June 7th.

Reconnaissances were carried out by all Brigades and 9th Wing, while contact patrols continued throughout the day, and all changes in positions were at once reported. One counter-attack was attempted but was immediately reported by our machines and did not develop owing to successful artillery fire.

Two special reconnaissances were carried out by aeroplanes of No. 43 Squadron, which came down as low as 500 feet and attacked German infantry and convoys. Troops massing in Warneton were attacked and scattered in all directions.

Second-Lieutenant MacGregor, No. 23 Squadron, left the ground before daybreak and flew over the Chateau du Sart Aerodrome. He descended to the level of the sheds and fired a large number of rounds into them. Machines of No. 41 Squadron also went out in order to attack and generally harass the enemy, and whenever troops were seen massing or marching on the road our machines would dive at them and continue firing until the enemy had completely scattered. Lieutenant Mussared, No. 1 Squadron, observed a body of men at Becelaere and fired several drums at them, and then emptied his revolver into their midst until they had all scattered.

Second-Lieutenant L. M. Barlow, No. 56 Squadron, crossed the lines at 1,500 feet, descended to 200 feet and then went to Bisseghem Aerodrome and flew up and down the sheds firing into them. After that he attacked a train by firing at it on one side and then turning round and firing on the other side as he passed. He then went to Wevelghem and opened fire on troops in the main street. From there he went to the station and fired into the trucks and then flew to Reckem Aerodrome and again fired many rounds into sheds from below the level of the sheds. A machine gun opened fire at him, so he immediately turned and attacked the gunners.

Captain P. B. Prothero, No. 56 Squadron, when driving away some hostile machines fired at several Germans sitting in a shell hole, and saw his tracers falling among the men.

Lieutenant Buck, No. 19 Squadron, left the ground shortly after 3 a.m. and attacked the sheds on Marcke Aerodrome.

Lieutenant C. S. Montgomery, No. 66 Squadron, crossed the trenches at 500 feet at dawn and then attacked a closed motor car and went so low that in the "zoom" to escape it his undercarriage just missed the car, which ran off the road and turned completely over. At Dadizeele he saw four gun teams being hitched to their guns, so he again attacked and caused great confusion. After that he dived at a party of infantry and dispersed them.

Second-Lieutenant Bell-Irving, also of No. 66 Squadron, attacked a party of about 100 infantry in a village and scattered them, but was wounded by machine gun fire and had to return.

Artillery Co-operation.—247 targets were dealt with by artillery with aeroplane observation and 27 with observation by balloons.

Artillery of the First Army carried out 13 successful shoots on hostile batteries; 12 pits were hit, four of which were destroyed, and two houses in battery positions were also destroyed. Several explosions were caused, one being very large which started a very big fire. Fifty area calls were sent down and many were seen to be answered.

Artillery of the Second Army successfully engaged 157 hostile batteries; two gun-pits were destroyed, one damaged and four explosions and fires caused. Three hundred and ninety-eight zone calls were sent down and 165 were seen to be answered. Seventy-two hostile batteries were silenced through zone call being sent down by No. 21 Squadron. Two batteries on the move were also reported in this way, and one was put out of action, and the other, after a few rounds, was silenced. Another battery on the move with caterpillar, five parties of infantry and four columns of motor transport were all hit through use of the zone call.

Artillery of the Third Army obtained 22 direct hits on hostile batteries. Three pits were destroyed, five damaged and an explosion caused.

Artillery of the Fourth Army successfully engaged 12 hostile batteries, one under zone call, and 30 O.K.'s and 94 M.O.K.'s were obtained. Nineteen emplacements were damaged, 15 explosions and five fires caused. One thousand five hundred and fourteen rounds were fired in pre-arranged shoots. The 37th Siege Battery obtained 11 O.K.'s and 10 M.O.K.'s on a hostile battery with observation by Lieutenant Glenny, No. 9 Squadron. Lieutenant Woodhouse, No. 52 Squadron, with the 9th Siege and 15th Siege Batteries, obtained six O.K.'s and 49 M.O.K.'s on hostile batteries, causing ten small explosions and three fires. Lieutenant Lewis, No. 52 Squadron, ranged the 15th Siege Battery on to a hostile battery and six O.K.'s and 19 M.O.K.'s were obtained.

Hostile Aircraft.—Six Spads of No. 23 Squadron encountered a formation of hostile machines and, in the combat which ensued, Captains Davidson and Wright engaged one machine which was driven down and Captain Wright fired into it as it fell from close range and the hostile machine crashed.

Second-Lieutenant A. E. Godfrey and Second-Lieutenant Mannock, No. 40 Squadron, each destroyed a hostile machine.

A patrol of Naval Squadron No. 8 encountered five hostile scouts and drove two of them down out of control, while a third went down in a spinning nose dive.

Lieutenant Lally and Second-Lieutenant Williams, No. 25 Squadron, drove down a German machine out of control and also assisted in the destruction of another.

Second-Lieutenant Redler, No. 40 Squadron, drove down a German machine out of control and Captain Patrick, No. 23 Squadron, forced one to land in a field.

Second-Lieutenant Anderson, No. 1 Squadron, drove down a hostile two-seater out of control and Lieutenants F. Sharpe and L. F. Jenkin, also of No. 1 Squadron, dived at an Albatross Scout, which they destroyed.

An offensive patrol of Naval Squadron No. 10 engaged 15 to 20 H.A., and as a result of the combat, two of the German machines were destroyed and three driven down out of control. Flight Sub-Lieut. Reid shot down one of these machines, while Flight Sub-Lieut. Sharman destroyed the second and drove another down out of control, while the other two were driven down out of control by Flight Sub-Lieuts. Collishaw and Nash.

An offensive patrol of No. 20 Squadron drove down a German machine which was seen to crash, and Lieutenant Joske, No. 46 Squadron, also destroyed a hostile aeroplane.

While on photography, Lieutenant Anderson and 1st A.M. Kirwan, No. 42 Squadron, were attacked by three H.A., but succeeded in destroying one of their opponents and driving the other two away.

Considerable fighting took place between machines of the 9th Wing and hostile formations, and, as a result of the combats, Captain Broadberry, No. 56 Squadron, Lieutenant Child, No. 19 Squadron, and Captain Andrews, No. 66 Squadron, each destroyed a German machine, while four others were driven down out of control: one by each of the following pilots— Second-Lieutenant Rhys-Davids and Rogerson, and Captain Broadberry, all of No. 56 Squadron, and Second-Lieutenant Taylor, No. 66 Squadron.

Lieutenant Sharpe, No. 1 Squadron, attacked and destroyed a hostile balloon.

Bombing.—First Brigade.—On the night 6th–7th No. 100 Squadron dropped three 230-lb. bombs and eight 112-lb. bombs on stations and railways. A 230-lb. bomb fell on Wervicq Station, while other bombs were dropped on a dump on the Warneton–Comines line, Quesnoy Station, and on hostile batteries.

On the 7th No. 25 Squadron dropped thirty-eight 20-lb. bombs on Chateau Du Sart Aerodrome, which was hit. This Squadron also dropped thirty 20-lb. bombs on Quesnoy, where considerable damage was observed to be done.

Second Brigade.—The Second Brigade dropped thirteen 20-lb. bombs on trenches on the night of the 6th–7th and thirty-one 20-lb. bombs on lorries on the 7th.

Third Brigade.—No. 11 Squadron dropped nineteen 20-lb. bombs on Douai Aerodrome, and two of the bombs were seen to burst on hangars.

9th Wing.—No. 27 Squadron dropped forty-four 20-lb. bombs on Bisseghem Aerodrome, and a number of direct hits were obtained. No. 6 Squadron attacked Rumbeke Aerodrome with ninety-one 20-lb. bombs, and direct hits were again obtained. No. 55 Squadron dropped forty-six 20-lb. bombs on Ramegnies Chin Aerodrome and one hundred and fifty-four 20-lb. bombs on Coucou Aerodrome.

Note.—In future the following abbreviation will be used for hostile aircraft in place of that (*i.e.*, H.A.) now in use :—

E.A.—Denoting Enemy Aircraft or Aeroplane.

S. WOOD, Captain,
Staff Officer.

Advanced Headquarters,
Royal Flying Corps,
    9th June 1917.

No. 36.

CONFIDENTIAL.

ROYAL NAVAL AIR SERVICE.

OPERATIONS REPORT

(with Royal Flying Corps Reports attached).

16th to 30th JUNE 1917.

NAVAL STAFF,
 OPERATIONS DIVISION.
 30th June 1917.

ROYAL NAVAL AIR SERVICE.

REPORT OF OPERATIONS

Completed from Reports during period
16th to 30th June 1917.

CONTENTS.

	PAGE
HOME STATIONS - - - - - -	2
DUNKIRK - - - - - -	5
ROYAL NAVAL AIR SERVICE SQUADRONS WITH ROYAL FLYING CORPS REPORTS ATTACHED - - -	8
EASTERN MEDITERRANEAN - - -	10
EAST INDIES AND EGYPT - - - - -	25
BRITISH ADRIATIC SQUADRON - - - -	26
ROYAL FLYING CORPS COMMUNIQUÉS - -	29

HOME STATIONS.

ANTI-SUBMARINE WORK CARRIED OUT BY AIRCRAFT, JUNE 1917.

NOTE.—During the month of June a distance of over 115,000 miles has been flown by aircraft carrying out anti-submarine patrols from stations round the coasts of the British Isles. Of this distance 65,846 miles have been covered by heavier-than-air machines and the remainder by airships. Submarines were sighted on 13 occasions, and seven attacked by the former, and possibly one has been sighted by the latter.

The traffic routes across the Channel and along the East and South Coasts have been regularly patrolled, and ships approaching the Scilly Isles have been met and escorted by seaplanes. Altogether 564 patrols have been carried out by aeroplanes and seaplanes. Airships have also done a large amount of work in escorting vessels on the East Coast and elsewhere.

WEATHER.

Strong wind and unfavourable weather conditions generally have interfered with flying operations during this period.

ANTI-AIRCRAFT PATROL—ENGAGEMENT WITH ENEMY.

June 17th.

Felixstowe.—A patrol in search of hostile aircraft was carried out during the morning by Large America Seaplane, No. 8677. The seaplane left Felixstowe at 5.5 a.m. B.S.T., steering 72° for two hours 20 minutes, and sighted the Dutch Coast at Vlieland at 7.25. Course was changed at 60°, which was held for 30 miles. At 7.55, and from a height of 3,000 feet two hostile destroyers, believed to be of the Krupp-Germania type, and one large submarine were sighted. The seaplane was about to investigate these when an enemy seaplane was observed approaching on the starboard bow about 3 miles away and at an approximate height of 1,000 feet, similar in appearance to British Short 225 h.p. type seaplane, but with a speed of approximately 70 knots.

The seaplane at once dived to a height of 1,000 feet and opened fire on the enemy machine at 200 yards range, with both forward Lewis Guns, as it passed across the port bow.

The hostile machine maintained a continuous machine-gun fire and circled round attempting to get under the tail of seaplane, which, however, successfully out-manœuvred the enemy machine, and opened fire with both forward and rear guns. Several bursts were observed to penetrate the fuselage and others to take effect on the nose and tail of machine. The enemy observer disappeared from view, presumably wounded, firing ceased, and the machine broke off the action pursuing an erratic course to the eastward, firing two red signal lights, and was lost to view close to the water. At 8.5 a.m. course was changed, and steered for Felixstowe at 1,000 feet. At 8.8 two hostile land machines were sighted about 2,000 feet above, and approximately 4 miles astern. The seaplane dived to 825 feet, and proceeded on its course at a speed of 75 knots. At 8.15 the hostile machines disappeared in a mist and the seaplane climbed to 1,000 feet, and continued its course, landing at Felixstowe at 10.20 a.m. B.S.T., having flown during this patrol a distance of 405 miles.

Names of Crew.—

Pilots: Flight Sub-Lieut. B. D. Hobbs, Flight Sub-Lieut. R. F. L. Dickey.
Engineer: A.-M. Anderson.
W/T Operator: A.-M. Caird.

SUBMARINE PATROL WORK.

June 25th.

Scilly Isles.—Whilst on a seaplane patrol in the Scilly Isles area, the conning tower of an enemy submarine was sighted on the port beam about 10 miles distant. At the same time a large steamer was observed (later recognised as a hospital ship) in the same direction. The seaplane altered course to attack the submarine, which was obviously getting into position to torpedo the hospital ship. Three 100-lb. bombs were dropped on the spot where submarine had submerged about two minutes previously, and five minutes later a large upheaval was observed where bombs had been dropped. This appeared in the form of a gigantic bubble, rising some distance above the sea level, and was distinctly visible for a minute or more. Warning was given to the hospital ship of the presence of submarine of which nothing further was seen.

ATTACK ON SUBMARINE.

June 27th.

Killingholme.—During a patrol between Spurn and Whitby Seaplane 8668, Flight Lieutenant Hards and Flight Lieutenant Robertson sighted and bombed an enemy submarine. A salvo of four 100 lb. bombs was dropped. A seaplane patrol of the following day reported seeing a large patch of oil on the water in approximate position where bombs had been dropped, but it is doubtful whether the submarine was damaged or sunk, in view of the further activity which occurred in the area soon afterwards.

June 28th.

Felixstowe.—During a patrol by seaplane 8662 (pilots Flight Lieutenant Mackenzie and Flight Sub-Lieut. Dickey), an enemy submarine was sighted and bombed about 10 miles west of North Hinder. It is believed to have been destroyed or severely damaged.

ZEPPELIN RAID.

June 16th–17th.

A night raid was carried out by four enemy airships over the area Isle of Thanet, Suffolk, and Norfolk. Bombs were dropped on Ramsgate by one of the Zeppelins, which was reported later over Foreness and Manstone, finally making off N.E. Another apparently crossed the Norfolk coast, and was reported at Framlingham, near Norwich, passing out to sea. She was reported at Lowestoft shortly after 2 a.m. and 60 miles N.E. of Lowestoft at 2.50 a.m. At 2 a.m. another Zeppelin, L. 48, appeared over Felixstowe and was reported later between Saxmundham and Aldeburgh, apparently disabled, and was seen to fall in flames shortly afterwards, 1 mile N.E. of Beston, near Westleton.

The fourth Zeppelin apparently did not cross the coast.

Six H.E. bombs were dropped on Ramsgate, causing considerable damage to houses, one bomb setting fire to a store in the naval base.

The Ramsgate casualties were three killed and 20 injured, one sailor and one soldier being included in the injured.

The other three Zeppelins were pursued by our aircraft, but Flight Sub-Lieut. Bittles, in Sopwith Seaplane, N. 1064, from Yarmouth, was the only pilot who succeeded in getting within range, attacking a Zeppelin at 11,000 feet, approximately 30 miles east of Lowestoft. One tray of ammunition was fired into the enemy airship from 100 feet below, all shots apparently taking effect, after which the Zeppelin climbed to 15,000 feet, and the Sopwith being unable to get within range returned to Yarmouth.

DUNKIRK.

WEATHER.

Unsuitable weather conditions generally, have affected flying operations during this period.

PHOTOGRAPHIC RECONNAISSANCE.

June 22nd.

Photographs were taken over Blankenberghe-Bruges Road-Zeebrugge-Bruges Canal, showing the ammunition sheds along the eastern side of the canal from Dudzeele to the entrance of Bruges Harbour, also of Zeebrugge Mole and Lock Gates. Steady work is being continued on the mole, and about 10 seaplanes could be seen outside the three Bessoneau tents north of the main seaplane shed. Great activity was shown around the lock gates, and new work is in progress. A submarine passing through the locks is clearly seen in one of the photographs.

Very little photographic work has been attempted during this period owing to unsuitable weather conditions.

SPOTTING FLIGHTS.

June 26th.

Spotting was attempted for the Dominion Battery, which was to fire on Ostende Harbour, but, owing to effective smoke screens over the whole of the harbour, observations were impossible. It was observed that as soon as the smoke screens over Ostende started, six vessels left steaming towards Zeebrugge.

OFFENSIVE PATROL, ENGAGEMENTS WITH ENEMY.

June 16th.

No. 4 Wing (No. 3 Squadron).—A patrol of six Sopwith Scouts, flying in formation over the area Thourout-Bruges-Ostende-Dixmude, encountered a formation of six 2-seater hostile aircraft north-east of Ypres. The patrol dived on these and broke up the formation, one of the enemy machines with the observer apparently killed or wounded going down in a spin, the others diving down to the east.

June 25th.

No. 4 Wing (No. 4 Squadron).—Whilst on patrol in the Ostende-Vassenaere-Thourout area, about nine two-seater hostile aircraft were engaged by three Sopwith machines. Sub-Lieut. Chadwick, in Sopwith N. 6345, shot down one of the enemy machines in flames. Other machines are believed to have been hit, but owing to clouds it was difficult to see actual results.

June 28th.

No. 4 Wing (No. 4 Squadron).—An offensive patrol of Sopwith Scouts observed a two-seater hostile aircraft, near Brayvdunes, proceeding in the direction of Dunkirk. The hostile aircraft was attacked at 16,000 feet and forced to return. Flight Sub-Lieut. Airey was slightly wounded in the neck, in spite of which he fired several shots at the hostile aircraft and was then compelled to break off the combat and return owing to petrol gauge being hit.

MINE PATROL—ENGAGEMENT WITH ENEMY.

June 19th.

Seaplanes.—At 4.20 a.m. a Short seaplane escorted by two Sopwith seaplanes started on a patrol in search of enemy mines and submarines.

Sopwith, Seaplane No. 1016, returned at 7 a.m. and reported that at 5.30 a.m. the patrol was attacked by three German fast single-seater seaplanes about 10 miles N.N.E. of Nieuport.

The Short machine 9057 (pilot, Flight Sub-Lieut. Paine, observer, Sub-Lieut. Rogers) and Sopwith 1015 (pilot, Flight Sub-Lieut. Potvin) were both shot down, the former making a good landing, but the latter appeared to fall sideways into the water.

Flight Lieutenant Graham in the third machine shot down one German machine, but during the engagement his pressure tank was damaged, so he landed beside a French T.B.D. and gave it instructions to proceed to the assistance of the other seaplanes. He was then taken in tow by a French trawler.

Seaplanes were sent to search for the damaged machines, and located the Short Seaplane (9057) on the water about 8 miles N.W. of Nieuport, and the German machine about 1 mile N.E. of this position. Four German T.B.D.'s were observed to come up and take off Flight Sub-Lieut. Paine from his machine. The damaged German seaplane was taken in tow.

From pigeon messages received it appears that the observer of 9057 is dead, and it is presumed he was killed instantly.

Nothing was seen of Sopwith N. 1015, and it is presumed that the pilot, Flight Sub-Lieut. Potvin, is dead.

CASUALTIES.

June 27th.

Seaplanes.—Owing to an explosion of some truckloads of ammunition, caused by a bomb or shell from hostile aircraft, three men were killed, ten wounded, and three slightly wounded. Station buildings were badly shaken, but seaplane sheds and seaplanes were only slightly damaged.

ATTACKS ON HOSTILE KITE BALLOONS.

June 27th.

A Sopwith machine carried out an attack on a kite balloon over the entrance to Ostend harbour. The Sopwith then took cover in the clouds to escape heavy A.A. gunfire, and upon descending was unable to locate kite balloon.

Another was attacked at 4,000 feet, south of Middlekerke, and a large number of shots were observed to enter the gas bag. The enemy observer descended by parachute, and kite balloon was at once hauled down.

Two kite balloons, one near Ghistelles and another near Middlekerke, were both hauled down upon the approach of our machines before they could be attacked.

Another kite balloon was attacked at 3,000 feet, east of Valdrloo, by a Sopwith. In spite of a large number of shots being fired the kite balloon was not hauled down, but the observer descended by parachute. The Sopwith gun was turned on him, and he was observed to become detached from the parachute, which remained floating. Later the same pilot attacked and sent down another kite balloon.

All pilots experienced heavy A.A. gunfire.

BOMB ATTACKS.

Bruges docks and hostile shipping.	June 16th–17th	931 lbs.	Aeroplanes.

BOMB ATTACKS ON DOCKS AND HOSTILE SHIPPING.

June 16th–17th.

No. 5 Wing (No. 5 Squadron).—A bomb raid was carried out on hostile shipping in Bruges docks during the morning in which two 112-lb., three 65-lb., and thirty-six 16-lb. bombs were dropped.

A large number of ships, some of which were thought to be destroyers, were observed in the West Bassin.

Bombs were dropped and observed to explode on the shipping. The west quay of the West Bassin was also attacked, where the wood store and junction of the railway sidings are situated. Bombs were observed to explode on these stores, and a cloud of brown smoke was seen to rise. Bombs were also observed to fall on the mine and ammunition stores, also the torpedo stores, situated on the east and west sides of the Eastern Bassin. A.A. fire in most cases was fairly accurate, and was particularly heavy over the objective.

KITE BALLOON OBSERVATION.

No. 11 Kite Balloon Section.—Ascents were made on four days, the total hours flown being about nine hours.

Owing to visibility being bad and weather conditions generally unsuitable, no observations were made.

NAVAL SQUADRONS WITH THE ROYAL FLYING CORPS.

PERIOD, 17TH TO 30TH JUNE, INCLUSIVE.

NAVAL SQUADRON No. 1.

This squadron has been attached to the 2nd Brigade, R.F.C., and has carried out 17 offensive patrols and 52 special missions in pursuit of enemy aircraft. A total of 293 hours flying has been done.

Numerous engagements with enemy machines have taken place, one of which was decisive. Flight Commander C. A. Eyre engaged an Albatross Scout, which was intent on attacking one of our balloons. The enemy machine rolled over, dived vertically, and went down out of control.

NAVAL SQUADRON No. 6.

This squadron has been attached to the 4th Brigade, R.F.C., and has carried out seven line patrols and one special mission in pursuit of enemy aircraft. The squadron has been in a quiet part of the front, and has had no combats.

NAVAL SQUADRON No. 3.

This squadron has been attached to the 3rd Brigade, R.F.C., and has carried out nine defensive and two offensive patrols, and three escorts to photography and bombing raids. Very few enemy aircraft have been seen, and no combats have taken place.

NAVAL SQUADRON No. 8.

This squadron has been attached to the 5th Brigade, R.F.C., and has carried out 23 offensive patrols and 47 special missions in pursuit of enemy aircraft. Many combats have taken place, two of which were decisive. On June 21st, Flight Lieutenant Little on an offensive patrol brought down an Albatross Scout after firing at it from below at very close range.

On June 26th, Flight Lieutenant Little attacked an Aviatik at 14,000 feet, firing a burst of about 20 rounds at close range. The H.A. caught fire and the pilot fell out. The observer crawled along the fuselage, and was seen to fall off a little later.

A large number of enemy machines doing artillery work were driven east by pilots of this squadron.

The following extract from First Army Wireless Telegraphy Summary is of interest:—

> "Our battle planes continue to hamper considerably hostile registration. At least 12 hostile machines have been driven away from the lines in sectors where warnings of hostile registration had been given. One hostile aeroplane sent the message "Air fight," and then ceased his calls abruptly. In the course of the week 10 observers ceased their calls abruptly without any closing signals."

Casualties. — *June 23rd.* — Flight Sub-Lieut. McAllister accidently killed.

NAVAL SQUADRON No. 10.

This squadron has been attached to the 5th Brigade, R.F.C., and has carried out 30 offensive patrols. Many engagements with enemy machines have taken place, five of which have been decisive.

On June 24th a patrol led by Flight Lieutenant Sharman, while escorting machines on photographic work, were attacked by 15 Albatross Scouts. One of these was brought down in flames, the tail plane and one right wing falling off.

On June 24th, Flight Lieutenant Collishaw fired 40 rounds into an enemy machine at a range of 25 yards; the machine was seen to crash. Three other combats took place, in which a hostile machine was driven down out of control.

Casualties.—*June 24th.*—Flight Sub-Lieut. A. B. Holcroft, missing. Flight Sub-Lieut. R. G. Saunders, missing.

June 25th.—Flight Sub-Lieut. G. E. Nash, missing.

EASTERN MEDITERRANEAN STATION.

MUDROS.

(Compiled from Weekly Reports, Nos. 64, 65, and 66, dating from May 31st to June 22nd, 1917.)

THASOS AIR STATION.

"A" SQUADRON.

May 31st–June 6th.

Bomb Attack on Gereviz.—A flight of three Henri Farmans escorted by two scouts left Thasos shortly after 3 a.m. on 31st May, arriving over Gereviz Seaplane Base soon after dawn, and dropped 15 bombs, weighing 864 lbs. One machine was detailed to drop small bombs at the anti-aircraft guns, while the other two bombers descended to 3,000 feet and attacked the seaplane base with heavy bombs, one of which fell 20 yards E.S.E. of the main shed, and must have damaged it.

A heavy barrage of fire was maintained over the seaplane base by the A.A. guns, two of the machines being hit.

It was noticed that repairs were in progress on the N.W. corner of the main shed, probably on account of damage done during the raid of the preceding day.

The look-out station at Limena reported enemy aircraft approaching Thasos soon after the return of the machines from Gereviz, and a Schneider Seaplane and a Sopwith Fighter were sent up to await their arrival. They did not, however, materialize.

June 1st.

A reconnaissance of the Sarishaban area was made to report on the condition of the crops. Those to the west of the town were seen to be ripe and ready for burning, while those nearer the sea were still green.

Enemy Raid.—In the evening at 9.30 p.m. a report was received from Mudros that a Zeppelin had been heard on the Drama-Kavalla line, and, as a matter of precaution, two $1\frac{1}{2}$ Strutter Sopwiths and a Schneider Cup Seaplane were sent up. Ten minutes after the machines had been got away the engine of an enemy machine, approaching from the direction of Drama, was heard, and the searchlight was switched on. The machine proved to be an aeroplane, not an airship, and it dropped three bombs at the new camp, one of which fell in the sea and the other two close to the searchlight, killing one rating, A. L. Shephard, A.C.M. 2., No. F. 17,635, and damaging a number of the tents.

The defending machines were unable to pick up the enemy machine in the dark.

Burning of Crops.—Local submarine patrols were carried out on 2nd and 3rd June, and on the latter day successful crop burning was undertaken in the Sarishaban area, which was continued with effect on the 4th and 5th, fires with large columns of smoke being observed from Thasos for many hours after bombs were dropped.

It is significant that the German W/T Press has mentioned the crop burning in the Sarishaban area in three successive issues, but has said nothing about the damage effected.

On the 4th June, Thasos Air Station was again attacked by enemy aircraft, which, however, did no damage. This was replied to by a night attack on Drama Air Station on 5th June. The amount of damage done could not be gauged in the dark.

Engagement with Enemy.—In returning from crop burning in the Sarishaban area on 5th June, a Henri Farman was attacked by an enemy aeroplane, and shot down, falling into the sea 3 miles S.W. of Kojun Nakla. The Greek pilot, Sub-Lieut. D. Argyropoulos, was drowned, and his body was recovered by a patrol launch. The observer, Sub-Lieut. Psychas, landed uninjured. The Sofia W/T Press states that Lieutenant von Eschwege shot down a " fighting machine," which fell in the sea.

The escorting Schnieder Seaplane overturned in landing near the Henri Farman on the water, the pilot, Flight Sub-Lieut. Brandon, being severely shaken. Only signalled reports of this occurrence and of operations since 2nd June have as yet been received.

On 6th June only local patrols were undertaken.

" F " Squadron, newly equipped, left Mudros for Thasos on 3rd June under command of Flight Lieutenant Bradley. Machines for the squadron had previously been sent to Thasos, and the Squadron was reported ready for action on 6th June.

" A," " F," and Greek Squadrons.

June 7th–14th.

During the week the usual establishment at Thasos has been strengthened by the presence of " F " Bombing Squadron, and a considerable amount of offensive work has been undertaken.

Bomb Attack on Gereviz.—On 7th June, " F " Squadron delivered an early morning attack on Gereviz Seaplane Base, dropping 1,300 lbs. of explosive bombs and nine large incendiary bombs. Six direct hits were observed on tents and sheds round the large hangar, while other bombs fell within 20 yards of the large hangar.

Burning of Crops.—Later in the morning, when the wind was strong, the squadron made a crop-burning expedition in the

Sarishaban Plain, and succeeded in starting 15 large fires, of which four were seen to be burning strongly four hours later. Two other incendiary expeditions were made in the afternoon, each by two fighting machines flying in company, both being successful. One fire was raised west of Irlati, which was still burning furiously when the last machine was over, and which had by that time consumed about 400 acres of standing crops.

Submarine patrols were also carried out during the day.

June 8th.

Burning of Crops.—" F " Squadron made one crop-burning flight, dropping 16 large and 12 small petrol bombs, and again raising several large fires which burnt fiercely for a long time. Incendiary candles, specially supplied from England, were also used in this and the previous day but seemed to have no effect. Submarine patrols were also made.

On 9th June " F " Squadron carried on the crop burning, on this occasion visiting the area east of the Nestos, and dropping 20 large and 12 small petrol bombs, which started nine large fires.

On 10th June the breeze was stronger and more favourable still for crop burning operations, so two expeditions were made by " F " Squadron, 30 petrol bombs being dropped each time. The breeze carried the fires along, and several were still seen to be burning on the following morning.

Enemy Raid.—At 7 p.m. an enemy aeroplane attempted a feeble retaliation, dropping bombs at Thasos Air Station Camp, none of which did any damage. Two Sopwith Fighters pursued him, one of which (pilot: Flight Lieutenant E. P. Hicks ; gun-layer : C. J. Goodwillie, L.M., O.N., F. 80) was able to get within 200 yards of his tail and gave him a tray of Lewis gun ammunition and about 20 rounds from the Vickers gun before the enemy dived into a cloud and was lost. The pursuing machines reported that the A.A. fire from the aerodrome was very good, three shells being observed to burst within an aeroplane's length of the enemy.

Reconnaissance and Bomb Attack on Gereviz.—The 11th of June was a day of some activity ; in the morning three Sopwith Fighters carried out an extended reconnaissance, Gereviz, Gumuljina, Xanthi, Narli, Okjilar, Buk, and Drama, all being visited and much useful information acquired.

In the afternoon " F " Squadron first of all attacked Gereviz Seaplane Base, 1,300 lbs. of explosive bombs being dropped, 14 bombs fell in a group round the large hangar, none being more than 24 yards from it. The eastern end of the hangar was blown in and much damage must have been done to its contents by splinters.

Afterwards the squadron proceeded with crop burning.

June 12*th.*

Crop Burning Flights, Engagements with Enemy.—Four Sopwith Fighters set out with orders to keep in formation as far as the Nestos River, where they were to split up, two going in company to make a photographic reconnaissance of Gereviz and drop petrol bombs there, while the other two, in company, dropped bombs on cornfields. The latter two machines lost touch momentarily, while picking up their targets, and the machine piloted by Flight Lieut. E. P. Hicks with A. E. King, A.M. 1, as gunlayer, was attacked by a Halberstadt. At first the gunlayer did not realise that an attack was imminent, thinking the machine was the other Sopwith. An engagement took place in which A. M. King was able to fire one tray, when a shot from the enemy pierced both tanks, and the Sopwith was obliged to glide to try and reach Thaso Poulo Island. The Halberstadt made repeated attacks under the Sopwith's tail, obliging the latter to loose height, and the glide which began three miles inland, finished in the water within 1,000 yards of the Bulgarian coast. Pilot and observer started to swim to Thaso Poulo, both being good swimmers. Machine guns from the shore continued to fire at them. It appears probable that A. E. King (A.M. 1, O.N. 4373) was struck by a bullet, as, after saying he was all right and talking about how they were brought down, he suddenly disappeared. Flight Lieutenant Hicks was picked up by a French motor boat, and the area was thoroughly searched for A. M. King, but only his lifebelt, inflated, could be found.

The second Sopwith could not find Flight Lieutenant Hicks' machine, and, assuming that he was gliding towards Thasos Aerodrome, after dropping his bombs, made a couple of circuits and not seeing anything of him, returned to Thasos. On discovering that Flight Lieutenant Hicks had not returned, he went over Sarishaban again in company with another Fighter, but failed to find either the Sopwith or the enemy.

Bomb Attacks on Gumuljina and Gereviz.—On 13th June attacks were made by " F " Squadron, first on store dump and railway station at Gumuljina, two 65-lb. bombs dropping in the station and 10 in the store dump, which had been located on the 11th June reconnaissance, and which must have been heavily damaged.

Afterwards Gereviz Seaplane Base was bombed, two 65-lb. bombs falling within 10 yards of the main shed. A third fell immediately over the door of the shed and hit a large seaplane which was lying there, completely destroying it.

On 14th June only local submarine patrols were made.

Only isolated patches of crop now remain. The crop-bearing area on both sides of the Nestos is reported as a whole to be practically destroyed. The earlier work was accomplished to a large extent by the Greek Squadron, and latterly by " F " Squadron assisted by scouts from " A " Squadron. In these operations 60 large and 220 small petrol bombs were used. Continued as it has been, with severe raids on Gumuljina and Gereviz, this work must have had a marked moral and material effect.

June 14th–22nd.

The week has been a quiet one at Thasos Air Station. No offensive operations of any magnitude have been attempted. During the previous week "F" Squadron had completed their work in crop burning and bombing various local objectives, and, their presence being required elsewhere, they were prepared for long-distance flight, and personnel of the squadron prepared to move by the 16th June.

On the 18th June, weather being favourable, the squadron left for Mudros by air, all machines arriving there safely.

Daily local anti-submarine patrols have been undertaken by "A" Squadron and the Thasos seaplanes.

On 20th June a photographic reconnaissance of the coast from Cale Deuthero to Cape Brassides was also effected.

STAVROS AIR STATION.

"D" Squadron.

June 1st–7th.

Reconnaisances.—On 1st June a reconnaissance was made of the lines of communication in the Angista Valley and an exhaustive reconnaissance of gun positions on the Lower Struma Front; reporting on the occupation and condition of the various emplacements was undertaken later in the day. A further reconnaissance of the enemy front line was made, and the opportunity was taken of dropping proclamations in the enemy trenches.

Since then several reconnaissance flights have been made daily, and a photographic flight was also undertaken on 4th June.

Only signalled reports have been received since 2nd June.

June 8th–13th.

Reconnaissance and Spotting Flights.—On 8th June a reconnaissance was made in the early morning, after which Monitor 28 was spotted on to gun position N. 1. Monitor 33 was spotted by another machine on to gun position N. 10. A photographic reconnaissance was made of the Lower Pravi Valley, and an extended reconnaissance of the Drama–Angista region for suitable bombing targets was attempted, but had to be abandoned in face of severe rain storms. In the evening field guns were spotted on to emplacement N. 7.

On 9th June two reconnaissances and one photographic flight were made. In returning from one of these flights a

130-h.p. Nieuport Fighter got into a nose spin near the ground, and both the pilot, Flight Sub-Lieut. J. W. Chuter, and observer, Sub-Lieutenant A. W. Henton, R.N.V.R., were killed.

On 11th June a reconnaissance of the front line and of Angista Valley was made, and shore batteries were spotted on to gun position N. 15. Three direct hits on the emplacement were recorded, but only one of the shells burst inside.

A flight was also made in a $1\frac{1}{2}$ Strutter Fighter to pursue an enemy machine which flew over Stavros, but the enemy out-distanced the $1\frac{1}{2}$ Strutter and could not be engaged.

Two spotting flights were made for ships guarding the British right on 12th June, and an attempt was again made to engage an enemy machine, which appeared over Stavros, again without success.

A front line reconnaissance was made on the 13th June.

June 16th–22nd.

Reconnaissance and Spotting Flights.—Low clouds and rain over the mountains on the Lower Struma front have hindered reconnaissances during the week.

On 16th June spotting flights were carried out for Monitor 32 firing on an enemy battery position. A spotting flight was also made for a field battery, but the number of low fleecy clouds made visibility bad, and after a few corrections had been given spotting was abandoned and a reconnaissance of new battery positions carried out. This was also interfered with by clouds, but valuable information was gained nevertheless.

Later in the day a reconnaissance of enemy lines of communication and of Angista and Pravi areas was made, but nothing more than the normal amount of transport was disclosed.

On 17th June a further attempt was made to spot shore batteries on to an enemy battery position, but heavy clouds being found at 3,000 feet the attempt had to be abandoned.

On 18th June spotting flights were made for Monitors 32 and 38, the former having to be curtailed on account of engine trouble with the aeroplane. A reconnaissance was also made to locate an enemy battery firing. The battery, however, ceased firing as soon as the aeroplane got into the air, and could not at the time be discovered.

On 19th June a reconnaissance was made of Pravi and Angista Valleys, a new battery position being located on the return journey.

On 20th June enemy aircraft reconnoitred the Struma front. Two Sopwith $1\frac{1}{2}$ Strutters were immediately sent in pursuit, but were unable to bring the enemy to action. Accordingly they carried out reconnaissances of the front line during their return journey. Two further reconnaissances were carried out later in the day. On both occasions the machines carried bombs, which they dropped on camps and bivouacs.

THERMI AIR STATION.
"B" Squadron.

June 1st–6th.

Crop Burning.—On 1st June a Henri Farman, Nieuport Fighter and Bristol Scout, all carrying incendiary bombs, and the latter two machines also acting as escorts, burnt crops in the Menimen Plain. The fields in this district are smaller than around Pergama, and there is not the same probability of large runaway fires: several good fires were, however, started in the most ripe of the fields.

Bomb Attack on Gun Positions.—In the afternoon a Henri Farman, escorted by a Nieuport Fighter, was sent to locate guns firing on Elios Island, and if found to bomb them. The guns were located in two fresh pits on Prygos Island. Two 112-lb. bombs and four 16-lb. bombs were dropped; the heavy bombs falling 30 yards and 10 yards respectively from the two emplacements.

On 2nd June a photographic reconnaissance was made of the gun positions on the Tuz Burnu, guns being identified in the emplacements.

Bomb Attack.—On 4th June Soma Coal Mines and Railway Station, where considerable activity has recently been reported, were chosen as objective for attack.

The Bristol Scout, (Pilot: Flight Sub-Lieut. Buckley) No. N 5393, 100-h.p. Mono. Gnome Engine, reached the objective first and dropped two 16-lb. bombs which fell just wide of the Station Buildings, and a third 16-lb. at a railway bridge 5 miles N. of the station, and then awaited the arrival of the other machines.

Henri Farman, No. N 3022, 155-h.p. Canton Unne, No. 4684, with Flight Sub-Lieut. C. Gilmour as pilot and L. H. Wright, A.M. 2, No. F 4315 as gunlayer, then arrived, but neither pilot or observer was able to locate the coal-pits, so the station, where a large number of loaded trucks were standing, was chosen for attack and extremely good shooting was made, three 112-lb. bombs being dropped from 5,000 feet, the first falling between the rails among the trucks at the southern end of the station, the second fell at the northern end of the station close to the locomotive shed and turntable, and the third fell among buildings in the middle of the station at the top of the Soma road. All three bombs must have caused considerable damage.

Nieuport Fighter, No. N 3183, 130-h.p. Clerget engine, with Flight Sub-Lieut. A. G. Woodward as Pilot, and T. C. Penna, P.O. No. J. 3286 as gunlayer, dived to 2,500 feet and dropped a line of three 16-lb. bombs, two of which scored direct hits on a large "T" shaped building which lies immediately on the southern side of the railway. The Nieuport was then obliged to leave the Henri Farman to be escorted by the Bristol as the Nieuport's petrol tank was seen to have split, and was leaking badly; she reached home practically dry of petrol, and the other two machines returned safely shortly afterwards.

In the afternoon crops were successfully burnt in Ayazmand Bay.

On 6th June corn fields were destroyed S. of Aivali.

June 8th–13th.

Crop Burning.—Early in the morning of 8th June, 20 incendiary bombs were dropped on cornfields in the Kara Ait district, but, although the bombs ignited, the fires did not spread much, probably because the wind blowing was much less on the surface there than at Thermi. A large field was seen to have been completely burnt out in the last raid.

In the evening a Henri Farman, escorted by a Bristol Scout, both carrying bombs, bombed the enemy troops who had established themselves on Gymno Island. A deserter stated that there were 200 irregulars who had been collected there for an attack on Thermi Air Station. The air station was prepared for attack, which, however, has not materialized.

On 10th June a reconnaissance of Aivali, and district, including Gymno Island, was made to verify military activity reported by a deserter, but no new works of any importance were seen. No guns were seen in the positions indicated, and only the usual number of small craft were in Aivali Harbour.

On 11th June 636 lbs of bombs were dropped at Grain Depôts near Aivali, but no direct hits were obtained.

Twenty-eight incendiary bombs were also dropped on the cornfields S. of Aivali.

On 13th June an attack was again made on Manissa Railway Bridge, when 636 lbs. of bombs were dropped. No direct hit was obtained, but one heavy bomb burst on the permanent way just north of the bridge.

June 16th–22nd.

Bomb Attack and Engagement with Enemy.—On 16th June a bomb attack was carried out on the granary N. of Aivali, 700 lbs. of bombs being dropped. One 112-lb. bomb dropped from Henri Farman, No. N 3022, by Flight Sub-Lieut. Gilmour with Air Mechanic E. M. Green as his observer, hit the outer wall of a building, seriously damaging it, while their two other 112-lb. bombs, dropped deliberately with a separate run for each, both fell very close to the building.

The Henri Farman was closely escorted by a Nieuport 2-seater which also dropped light bombs, and they had a roving escort of Bristol Scout and Sopwith Bomber. While bombing was in progress, the squadron was attacked by a Halberstadt Scout, but owing to the action of the Bristol Scout and Sopwith Bomber failed to approach within range of the Henri Farman and her immediate escort. When the Halberstadt was first observed, Flight Sub-Lieut. Hosking in the Bristol Scout immediately attacked, and during the engagement fired four trays of ammunition. During the progress of the fight, the enemy was driven well to the southward where he broke off the fight with his superior speed just when the Bristol's ammunition gave out. The Bristol immediately returned to the Aerodrome for fresh supplies, afterwards rejoining the squadron. The enemy meanwhile had returned to the attack, and was engaged by the Sopwith Bomber, piloted by Flight Sub-Lieut. L. H. Brake. The Sopwith not being so flexible in manœuvre as the Bristol only succeeded in firing some 60 rounds, observing tracers to pass through the enemy's fuselage. The fight was again broken off by the enemy, but not before considerable damage had been done to the Sopwith. The enemy used explosive bullets which, on striking anything hard, burst with sufficient violence to cause serious damage to steel fittings and main spars.

June 17th.

Fighter Patrols. Engagements with Enemy.—A fighter patrol of two Nieuports and two Bristol Scouts was sent to cruise over Aivali district, where the action of the previous evening had taken place. No enemy aircraft came up, but accurate A.A. fire was experienced from a position where the new enemy is probably situated. The opportunity was taken to drop a number of Thermit candles, one of which was seen to cause a fire in an olive grove.

On 18th June the triplane was flown from Mudros to Thermi in order to give "B" Squadron something with sufficient speed to attack Halberstadt Scouts on moderately even terms. A Fighter patrol was carried out over Aivali, but no signs of enemy could be seen, neither was the landing ground definitely located.

On 20th June, however, during the Fighter patrol, the enemy was seen to rise, and his landing place was located. Later in the day an action took place between the triplane and a Halberstadt Scout, of which only a signalled report as has yet been received. The triplane apparently out-manœuvred the Halberstadt, and drove him down in a large field immediately N. of the Illkeli-Pergama road, where a shed was observed. Later this shed was attacked with bombs, but no direct hit obtained.

On the 21st Wing Commander flew a seaplane from Mudros to Thermi Air Station in order to make arrangements regarding further operations.

IMBROS AIR STATION.

"C" SQUADRON.

June 1st–6th.

There has been less enemy activity in the Dardanelles area during the week, which may be attributable to the amount of mist which lies over the Straits in the morning and evening and the heavy winds blowing during the middle of the day.

On 1st June, in the morning, an enemy machine was reported to be approaching the island, and the triplane was sent up to locate it by the direction of A.A. fire and by ground signals. Visibility was very bad, and apparently the enemy sheered off without going over Imbros at all.

Owing to mist no morning reconnaissance was made of the Straits, and the evening reconnaissance reported only the usual small shipping.

On 2nd June an enemy machine was sighted from the ground about 6 miles off between Helles and Imbros. A Sopwith Fighter was sent in pursuit, but was unable to overtake the enemy.

Result of Reconnaissance.—At mid-day a reconnaissance was made of gun positions in Suvla Bay. Four were observed, but all were well screened, and although the machine came down to 4,000 feet it could not be seen whether they were occupied or not.

A reconnaissance was made of the shipping in the Straits in the evening. On 3rd June a fighting patrol was made in the morning, but no enemy machine ventured near Imbros. Subsequently a Sopwith was sent to climb high, so as not to be observed, and to wait for and locate any gun which opened fire from the Peninsula. No gun opened fire. The regular reconnaissance of shipping was made later.

On 4th June, at 10.45 p.m., an enemy machine bombed the shipping in Kephalo Harbour, but did no damage. Shortly after midnight a reprisal flight was made, and the new gun position on Suvla Point was bombed. A large explosion took place, and it is believed that an ammunition dump was hit.

The reconnaissance of shipping in the Straits was made on the 5th and 6th, and in the early morning of the latter date a submarine patrol was undertaken as a submarine had been reported during the night off Kephalo.

June 7th-13th.

Mist covered Gallipoli on the morning of the 7th June, so no shipping reconnaissance was carried out until the evening, when only the usual amount of shipping was seen.

Two flights were made by the triplane to try and discover an enemy machine heard making wireless signals, but no machine could be found.

In the morning firing was heard on the Peninsula and a machine was sent up to investigate, but only saw one large explosion S. of Gaba Tepe and what appeared to be the flash of a gun N. of Anzac. People on Imbros, however, assert that they saw about 30 rounds fired from S. of Gaba Tepe, and shrapnel burst towards the southern end of the Peninsula.

Bomb Attack on H.M.S. Edgar.—On 8th June an enemy aeroplane dropped bombs at H.M.S. "Edgar" at 8 a.m., and was pursued by the triplane, but had too much start and speed, so was lost in mist over Helles.

Two other reports were received during the day of enemy machines approaching the island, and on each occasion the triplane was sent up. Both proved false alarms.

Bomb Attack and Reconnaissance.—At 11.30 p.m. a B.E., piloted by Flight Sub-Lieut. Waistell, was sent to seek for a good target and make reprisals. The warehouses and engineering shop on the water front at Chanak were selected, and two 100-lb. bombs dropped. They must have done considerable damage, as a large column of smoke 200 feet high and lasting for 10 minutes was observed, while thick clouds of smoke poured from the water front. Heavy and fairly accurate A.A. fire, consisting of star shell and H.E., was experienced.

At mid-day, on 9th June, enemy aircraft were reported over Tenedos, and the triplane and a Strutter Fighter were sent to locate and attack them. A large biplane was seen over Helles at about 1,000 feet, and the triplane manœuvred to get the sun directly behind him, but the enemy had apparently observed the machine as it went low across the Straits and landed in a field N. of Kum Kale. A small machine, which had not been previously observed, landed beside it. The Sopwith Fighter did not arrive in time. In the evening the triplane, being out of truth, flew back to Mudros for adjustments, and a seaplane from Mudros arrived at Imbros.

On 10th June only one reconnaissance of the Straits was made owing to mist. An experimental flight was made during the heat of the day to ascertain the atmospheric conditions over a proposed new aerodrome which lies in a valley. In the evening a seaplane returning to Mudros was escorted until nearing Lemnos.

On 11th June a photographic flight over Ejelmer Bay and Suvla was made, and on the 12th a similar flight for the purpose of photographing the mainland coast opposite Tenedos.

On the 13th only an evening reconnaissance of the shipping was undertaken owing to mist in the morning. Nothing unusual was observed except a small launch alongside "River Clyde."

Enemy Activity.—In the afternoon firing was heard again on the Peninsula and to the southward. Shells were seen to fall three or four miles inland on the plain opposite Tenedos, and from 4 p.m. the hills to the N.E. of Anzac Beach were heavily shelled, both shrapnel and H.E., for about 40 minutes. A reconnaissance to see what the enemy was doing was made of the neighbourhood of Ari Burnu, but nothing was seen which indicated activity, except that three gun emplacements which had not previously been observed were seen in square 80 Q.

An enemy machine visited Imbros in the evening and a Sopwith Pup was sent in pursuit, but the enemy, which was a small seaplane, was much faster than the Pup.

June 16th–22nd.

Reconnaissances.—On 16th June no morning patrol of the Dardanelles was possible owing to mist. Evening reconnaissance reported only the usual shipping. During the afternoon a reconnaissance of squares 80 and 92 in the Anzac area, where firing had been observed, was carried out. No gun emplacements were seen, but several small camps were observed in that area.

In the evening of the 16th an enemy seaplane which reconnoitred Kephalo was pursued by a Sopwith Pup, which, however, was easily outdistanced by the seaplane, which had a superior speed, at 10,000 feet, to that of the Pup.

On the 17th June mist hung over the Straits practically all day, and although an evening reconnaissance was attempted, no part of the straits could be seen except Morto Bay, where a small lighter was working.

On June 18th a further attempt was made to carry out the reconnaissance of the Dedeagatch area, by order of Vice-Admiral Commanding. A seaplane from Mudros flew over Imbros Aerodrome, where she was picked up and escorted by two aeroplanes. On arriving near Dedeagatch, however, the machines ran into rainstorms and the reconnaissance had to be abandoned. In the evening a Fighter patrol was undertaken over the Island, on a report being received that an enemy aeroplane was approaching. The enemy, however, did not come over the harbour and could not be seen from the air.

On the 20th June a reconnaissance of the Dedeagatch area by one seaplane from Mudros, accompanied by two aeroplanes from Imbros, was carried out. Detailed reports of this reconnaissance have not yet been received, but signalled information states that, although under-water visibility was excellent, no mines were seen in the area. The coast from Enos to west of Dedeagatch was reconnoitred, but no gun position could be observed. About 30 caiques were lying in Dedeagatch inner harbour.

During the afternoon a machine was sent up to locate further firing which was heard, but observed nothing except a fire burning at Kum Kale.

On 21st June, besides the usual reconnaissances of the Dardanelles for shipping, a machine was sent up to locate a gun firing at Imbros. A gunflash was observed in square 17 P, while a dummy smoke puff was seen to rise in square 16 F 2. A flight was made to spot Monitor 17 on to two guns in square 116 N 5, no direct hit, however, being recorded. Another ineffectual chase of an enemy machine which visited the Island was also made.

MUDROS.

H.M.S. "ARK ROYAL."

June 1st–7th.

On 4th June a submarine patrol was carried out, a submarine having been reported 3 miles W.S.W. of Kombi.

During the remainder of the week test flights have been carried out when weather permitted, but strong winds have been prevalent during daylight hours. A Schneider Cup seaplane has stood by for defence of the port daily.

June 7th–14th.

Arrival of Handley-Page Aeroplane 3124.—On June 8th this machine arrived safely from England. She carried a crew of three officers, Flight Commander K. S. Savory, D.S.O., Flight Lieutenant H. McClelland, and Lieutenant P. T. Rawlings, R.N.V.R., with two E. ratings.

Thirty-two and a half hours were spent in the air on the journey, stops being made at Paris, Lyons, Frejus, Pisa, Rome, Naples, Otarnto, and near Salonika.

No untoward incident happened, but the reported aerodrome at Frejus proved to be very rough and soft and might easily have wrecked the machine. Bad weather was encountered between Pisa, and Naples which added to the flying time, and the first attempt to cross the Greek mountains had to be abandoned and many spares left at Otranto before the machine would get high enough to cross the mountains.

On the same day A.A. exercise was given to the fleet at Mudros. One machine delivered dummy bomb attacks from above, while another delivered a dummy torpedo attack on "Reliance," approaching from the sun.

From 10th to 14th June, patrols of the swept channel of Mudros Harbour have been undertaken each morning.

Test flights and a flight to drop a bomb with a modified fuse giving greater delay action, were also made.

June 14th–22nd.

On 16th and 17th June, extended patrols were carried out to the south and south-westward of the entrance to Mudros Harbour, the swept channel also being inspected.

On 18th June, in addition to making a similar patrol, a machine was sent to effect a mine reconnaissance in the Dedeagatch area, which, however, had to be abandoned before completion on account of rain storms.

On 20th June a patrol round Strati Island was carried out, and the reconnaissance for mines in Dedeagatch area was completed, the seaplane keeping in touch with the two aeroplanes detailed from Imbros to carry out reconnaissance in that area, in order to assist them should they be obliged to alight on the water.

On 21st June a reconnaissance to the westward of Strati for enemy submarines was made, and the usual inspection of the Mudros swept channel being effected on the return journey.

REPAIR BASE.

June 1st–7th.

The conversion of three Sopwith bombers into fighters, erection, testing, and packing for transport to outlying stations of two bombers and two fighters, and the repair of Sopwiths, Nieuports, and a B.E. and two Henri Farmans, has fully occupied the repair base.

June 7th–14th.

Repair base has done a large amount of work in rebuilding Sopwith's and Nieuport's and in erecting new machines. Two Sopwith Pups were erected within 24 hours of arrival in the port and one of them was tested within that time.

The first of the Curtiss bombers to arrive required a lot of work, as she had been damaged in transit, and was an old machine which required overhauling.

June 14th–22nd.

The usual tests of repaired machines and new machines erected on arrival have been made during the week, machines also being flown to Imbros and Mitylene after repair.

"F" Squadron arrived from Thasos on 18th June, and as the machines had done a considerable amount of hard work, a thorough overhaul of engines and machines has been undertaken preparatory to further operations by the Squadron.

MARSH AERODROME.

June 1st–7th.

Instructional flying and flights for training gunlayers have been carried out in the morning and evening when the weather is sufficiently good to permit of novices flying.

June 7th–14th.

Instructional flying, gunnery instruction, and practice on new type machines has continued daily.

June 14th–22nd.

Instructional flying and gunnery practice has been carried out daily. An accident took place on the 18th June, when a Greek pilot, under instruction, who had done some 12 hours' solo flying in a Henri Farman, attempted to turn with his engine throttled down and the machine over-banked. The machine side-slipped and then nose-dived from 600 feet, the pilot being killed and the machine destroyed by fire, which arose from the bursting of the petrol tank on the machine striking the ground.

AIRSHIP STATION.

June 1st–7th.

No flying has been done this week, the weather not having been sufficiently fine. Heavy bomb gears have been fitted to the airship during the week.

June 7th–14th.

The airship was deflated on 7th June in order to make use of the shed for the Handley-Page Aeroplane, which arrived the following day.

KASSANDRA AIRSHIP STATION.

June 1st–7th.

Twelve hours' patrolling were done on 1st June, after which the airship was laid up for adjustments and changing engines. Satisfactory trials were made on 5th June, since when no flights have been made on account of weather conditions.

June 7th–14th.

Except on the 10th June patrols of the entrance to the Gulf of Salonika were carried out daily during the week.

June 14th–22nd.

Patrols of the entrance to the Gulf of Salonika were carried out on 19th, 20th, and 21st June, over 11 hours flying being done on one of these days. On the remaining days of the week weather conditions prevented flying.

SUDA BAY SEAPLANE STATION.

June 1st–7th.

Patrols have been carried out both morning and evening off the entrance to Suda Bay during the week.

June 7th–14th.

Daily patrols, both morning and evening, have been carried out off the entrance to Suda Bay.

June 14th–22nd.

Daily patrols of the approaches to Suda Bay have been carried out both morning and evening, seaplanes remaining in W/T touch with the base during their patrols and reporting all shipping observed.

H.M.S. "PEONY."

June 1st.

On 1st June two reconnaissances were made of the Gulf of Kos, the first machine being hoisted out off Cape Phuka and examining the northern coast and the neighbourhood of Keramus and along to Budrum, both of which places had been reported as submarine supply bases at different times. Nothing of note was seen at either place, and Keramus seemed, from the nature of the country, very unlikely as a base.

Later in the morning a reconnaissance was made of the southern shore of the Gulf of Kos, but nothing to indicate the existence of a submarine base was discovered. The seaplane developed engine trouble, and was damaged in making a forced landing. In the evening the ship returned to Port Laki where repairs to seaplanes are being carried out.

Since 2nd June no reports have been received.

June 14th–22nd.

A report has been received from "Peony" for the week ending 16th June. During this period no service flying took place, owing to "Peony" boiler cleaning and coaling. The opportunity was, however, taken to exchange one of the Schneider seaplanes for a new seaplane which had been sent to Thermi Air Station in reserve for "Peony."

EAST INDIES AND EGYPT.

H.M.S. "EMPRESS."

H.M.S. "Empress" left Port Said at 11.45 a.m. on May 12th, arriving off Beirut at 4 a.m. on May 13th. Three seaplanes were hoisted out and left for the coast at 5.30 a.m. with orders to bomb submarines using Beirut Harbour as a base and petrol stores on eastern side of the harbour. No submarines were observed, but bombs were dropped in and just outside the harbour near the entrance. One 500-lb. and four 65-lb. bombs were dropped. No gun fire of any kind was experienced, and the guns reported in the town could not be located. It is considered probable that warning of the seaplanes approach was given and the smoke observed east of the town was a warning signal.

All machines return to the ship, and landed safely.

H.M.S. "Empress" was escorted by the French T.B.D.s "Courtelas" and "Pierrier." H.M.S. "Empress" returned to Port Said at 11 p.m. on 13th May.

Photographs of bomb explosions were taken.

BRITISH ADRIATIC SQUADRON.
No. 6 WING, R.N.A.S.
Otranto Air Station.

Enemy Activity.—On June 7th three hostile aeroplanes approached Brindisi at 3,400 metres. Two were driven off by anti-aircraft batteries, while the third attacked an airship which was on patrol. The airship sustained slight damage. Two Italian machines went up to attack. The first came down, killing the pilot. The other brought down an Austrian machine, killing the crew. An attempt to tow the Italian machine was made, but it sank.

Eight destroyers were sent out from Brindisi to attack a possible escort to the planes, and were twice attacked by enemy submarines.

Small craft and seaplanes were sent out to attack the submarines. The seaplanes dropped bombs on one of the submarines, which was thought to be damaged.

June 13th.

A British cruiser which passed through the Straits during the afternoon was escorted by seaplane from this station. A regular daily patrol is now being carried out.

June 14th.

Anti-Submarine Operations.—By arrangements with the Italian Authorities a submarine was sent to Otranto, and experiments were carried out with the motor launches and aircraft working in conjunction, the former fitted with hydrophones. The submarine, escorted by an Italian cruiser, arrived at a position 6 miles east of Otranto during the morning.

Two single-seater seaplanes and two 2-seater aeroplanes flew over the submarine at 2,000, 3,000 4,000 and 5,000 feet respectively. The seaplanes were able to follow the submarine as long as her periscope was showing, and guided by the wake of the periscope were able to distinguish the hull of the boat beneath the surface.

The aeroplane flying at 4,000 feet was able to locate the submarine as long as its periscope was showing, but lost sight of it when it dived, and owing to the many white waves breaking was unable to see or locate the submarine, though it afterwards broke surface with its periscope several times. The aeroplane flying at 5,000 feet arrived after the submarine had dived, and did not succeed in locating her at all.

June 17th.

Italian Flights.—Two Italian seaplanes flew over Pola from Venice and obtained photographs.

On return journey one machine attacked a large destroyer with her machine gun, but did no apparent damage. Both machines were fired on by anti-aircraft batteries, but only a few shots burst anywhere near them. The majority burst at 5,000 metres, while the planes were flying at 3,000 metres.

June 19th.

Anti-Submarine Patrol.—On the report that enemy submarines were operating in the vicinity of Gallipoli and Santa Maria de Leuca, all available aircraft at Otranto were sent at 5 a.m. the following morning on anti-submarine patrol work in this area. Two patches of oil were observed on surface, about 3 miles south of Molini Tower, but no submarines were sighted. While machines were away hostile aircraft attacked Otranto, but no damage was done.

S.S. "Antimous" with R.N.A.S. stores arrived at 2 a.m., June 23rd.

Four F.B.A. seaplanes have been accepted from the Italian Government, two of which will be sent to Malta in "Isonzo" on June 24th.

June 28th.

Enemy Activity.—Enemy aircraft attacked Valona, but no details regarding damage have yet been received.

ROYAL FLYING CORPS COMMUNIQUÉS.

ROYAL FLYING CORPS COMMUNIQUÉ.—No. 92.

The following details, in addition to those given in R.F.C. Communiqué No. 91, in connection with the aerial attack on German troops and transport on the 7th inst., are of interest :—

No, 43 Squadron. — Lieutenants Veitch and Bettinson attacked small bodies of troops in Dulemont from 500 feet.

Second Lieutenants Harriman and Dixon engaged small bodies of troops near Ploegsteert Wood.

Second Lieutenant D'Arcy and Lieutenant Pickering dived in order to fire on troops. The pilot was wounded in the leg and had to return.

Second Lieutenants Libby and Pritchard attacked a convoy of M.T. on the Wervicq–Comines Road. The leading wagon forced to pull across the road, and delayed the convoy. They then fired 250 rounds on troops massing at Warneton.

No. 1 Squadron.—Sergeant Olley fired on gunners of three anti-aircraft guns from 100 feet, and the men fled into the ditches. After this he engaged and scattered 300 men marching towards trenches.

Lieutenant Anderson fired 47 rounds at a machine gun emplacement and the gun ceased fire. Troops in small groups were then engaged and casualties caused. He also fired at troops in trenches from 500 feet, and the Germans rushed into dug-outs.

Lieutenant Campbell engaged and scattered troops on the east side of Polygon Wood, and fired on troops entraining at Houthem siding. After finishing all his ammunition he fired into the remaining troops with Very's lights.

Lieutenant Wilson fired on small bodies of troops, who scattered into ditches, and he also engaged troops in Houthem.

Lieutenant Rogers fired on a body of 250 troops and scattered them.

Lieutenant Buck, No. 19 Squadron, at dawn fired 70 shots into hangars on Marcke Aerodrome from 800 feet. He then forced a hostile machine which came up from Reckem Aerodrome to land in a field, after which he returned to Marcke and fired more shots into the hangars. When returning to the lines he fired on transport moving east.

Lieutenant Luke, No. 66 Squadron, attacked a G.S. wagon with six horses from below 500 feet; the horses swung across the road and the men took refuge in a ditch.

No. 56 Squadron.—Second Lieutenant Turnbull flew along and fired into the trenches from 1,500 feet.

Captain Bowman fired on 50 men marching in fours, and Lieutenant Lewis attacked a body of transport from 1,500 feet.

June 8th.

Reconnaissances.—Successful reconnaissances were carried out, and very valuable contact patrol work was done. The position of our troops, headquarters, and tanks was successfully located from low altitudes. The II. Anzac situation was obscure on the night of the 7th-8th, so Lieutenants MacDonald and Haultain, No. 42 Squadron, went out at dawn and cleared up the situation of our troops. On the night of the 7th-8th, No. 11 Squadron carried out a special patrol.

Artillery Co-operation.—One hundred and fifty-four targets were dealt with by artillery with aeroplane observation, and 53 with observation by balloons.

Artillery of the First Army successfully engaged 15 hostile batteries, 12 direct hits were obtained, one pit was destroyed, ten damaged, and four explosions caused, one of which was a quantity of ammunition.

Artillery of the Second Army successfully engaged 49 hostile batteries, four pits were destroyed, 11 damaged, and six fires and explosions caused. Eighty-four zone calls were sent down, and 24 were seen to be answered. Five hostile batteries were successfully dealt with by artillery, which had been ranged by Lieutenants Townsend and Prescot, No. 7 Squadron. A large number of zone calls were sent down reporting enemy infantry and motor transport, and in one case an excellent barrage on an enemy concentration in a new trench was produced. Four large bodies of infantry were reported by zone call by Lieutenants Fulljames and Reid, No. 53 Squadron, and in all cases the enemy were dispersed, and in one instance they corrected results of fire into the middle of the German troops.

Thirty hostile batteries were successfully engaged by artillery of the Third Army, 21 direct hits were obtained, five pits were damaged, and three explosions caused. Forty-three hostile batteries were seen active, on seven of which there was observation of fire, and two direct hits were obtained.

Six hostile batteries were successfully engaged by artillery of the Fourth Army—one under zone call—and 19 O.K.'s were obtained. The 9th Siege Battery, with observation by Lieutenant Lewis, No. 52 Squadron, obtained 13 O,K.'s and 14 Y.'s, with only one gun firing on a hostile battery.

On the night of the 6th-7th, Nos. 22 and 34 Balloon Sections moved up to within 3,000 yards of the line. Their balloons ascended before dawn and remained up all day until forced down by a thunderstorm in the evening, and although shelled they made very valuable reports on the movements of tanks and troops, and reported the actions of the enemy.

No. 34 Section's balloon was in direct telephonic communication with Second Army centre throughout the day. No. 2 Section's balloon was shelled, but rose to 5,000 feet and so got out of range.

Ten targets were successfully dealt with by artillery with observation by balloons of the Third Brigade, and seven by balloons of the Fourth Brigade. No. 29 balloon located and ranged artillery on a hostile battery which was shelling the headquarters of the 27th H.A.G., and the German battery was silenced. Transport was also reported and engaged.

Hostile Aircraft.—Captain K. C. Patrick, No. 23 Squadron, attacked four Albatross Scouts, and drove one down out of control. He was then attacked by 10 scouts, and escaped by spinning.

In the evening five Spads of No. 23 Squadron observed considerable transport, and so dived at and attacked it. While doing this two hostile scouts passed the Spads, three of which immediately turned to attack the German machines, while the other two continued firing at the transport. One of the scouts was driven down by Second-Lieutenants Collis and Langlands.

Major Dawe, No. 43 Squadron, attacked and drove down a German aeroplane which landed in a field.

Sergeant Mann and 2nd A.M. Harris, No. 25 Squadron, in an engagement between Albatross Scouts and a formation of F.E.'s drove down one of their opponents out of control.

Fight Sub-Lieut. Nalder, Naval Squadron No. 1, in an encounter with two E.A. was wounded, but succeeded in destroying one of the enemy machines.

An offensive patrol of No. 1 Squadron engaged six Albatross Scouts near Becelaere, and Second-Lieutenant Fullard shot down one of the German machines in flames, while a second was driven down out of control by Lieutenant Hazel. Another patrol of this squadron engaged eight Albatross Scouts in the same locality, and one was driven down out of control by Lieutenant Jenkin, while another was destroyed by Lieutenant Mussared.

An offensive patrol of No. 20 Squadron, encountered a large formation of E.A., and Second-Lieutenant Durrand and Sergeant Sayers drove down one of the German machines, which caught fire and fell to pieces before reaching the ground.

Captain W. A. Bishop, No. 60 Squadron, encountered a number of hostile scouts, and drove one down out of control. During this engagement he had fights with eight E.A.

Lieutenant R. T. C. Hoidge, No. 56 Squadron, took part in a number of engagements, drove down one of his opponents out of control and one in a damaged condition.

Photography.—Seven hundred and five photographs were taken during the day.

Bombing.—First Brigade.—On the night of the 7th–8th, No. 10 Squadron dropped twenty-four 20-lb. and seven phosphorous bombs on Haubourdin, and a very large fire was caused, which could be seen from our lines, and was still burning in the morning. This squadron also dropped twenty 20-lb. bombs on La Pouillerie Aerodrome, and direct hits were obtained.

No. 100 Squadron dropped five 230-lb., thirty-eight 112-lb., and eight 20-lb. bombs on various objectives between 10.5 p.m. and 3.45 a.m. Twelve of the 112-lb. bombs were dropped from a height of 900 feet on Menin Station and eight were seen to hit the target. Warneton and Courtrai Stations were both hit. Bombs were dropped on rolling stock at Roulers and on Wervicq Stations from a height of 700 feet, and six direct hits were obtained. A train leaving Menin Station was wrecked, and rolling stock between Warneton and Comines was hit, and a series of immense explosions took place and continued well into the day.

On the 8th, thirty-two 20-lb. bombs were dropped on Haubourdin by No. 25 Squadron.

Second Brigade.—No 20 Squadron dropped eighty-one 20-lb. bombs on various targets in the areas around Comines, Wervicq and Houthem.

Third Brigade.—On the night of the 7th–8th, No. 18 Squadron dropped eight phosphorous and six 20-lb. bombs on Proville Aerodrome, and a number of direct hits were obtained. The pilots then attacked various targets with machine guns and fired 1,500 rounds.

9th Wing.—No 27 Squadron dropped twelve 112-lb. bombs on Dadizele from 6,500 feet, and practically all the bombs fell on the objective.

No. 55 Squadron dropped sixty-four 20-lb. bombs on hutments on the road north of Becelaere.

June 9th.

Several contact patrols were carried out during the day, and parties of infantry were engaged with machine gun fire from low altitudes.

Two De Havilland 4's of No. 55 Squadron went out on very long reconnaissances, but were only able to do part owing to unsatisfactory weather.

Artillery Co-operation.—One hundred and twelve targets were dealt with by the artillery with aeroplane observation, and 13 with observation by balloons.

Artillery of the First Army successfully engaged 14 hostile batteries; six direct hits were obtained, two pits were destroyed, five damaged, and three explosions caused, which destroyed houses in battery positions. One hundred and thirty-six area calls were sent down and a number of hostile batteries were observed to be silenced.

Artillery of the Second Army successfully engaged 50 hostile batteries, two gun-pits were destroyed, 15 damaged, and three explosions caused. One hundred and sixty-four zone calls were sent down and 41 were observed to be answered, and a number of infantry targets were successfully engaged. The 323rd Siege Battery, with observation by Lieutenants Faulkner and Scar, No. 21 Squadron, obtained three O.K.'s and one M.O.K. on a hostile battery. A second hostile battery was then engaged by zone call, and two direct hits were obtained. Later in the day, the 104th and 114th Siege Batteries, with observation by the same pilot and observer, obtained six direct hits on two hostile batteries, damaging three gun-pits and causing two explosions, while a bridge near Warneton was destroyed.

Seven hostile batteries were successfully engaged by artillery of the Third Army, and eight direct hits were obtained, causing two explosions.

Artillery of the Fourth Army successfully engaged four hostile batteries, and obtained eight O.K.'s, and caused an explosion.

Five batteries were successfully engaged by artillery of the Fifth Army, which obtained four direct hits on gun positions and caused an explosion.

Nos. 9 and 38 balloons made ascents during the night in order to watch any preparations for a counter-attack by the enemy.

Hostile Aircraft.—Second Lieutenant J. L. Barlow, No. 40 Squadron, while proceeding to attack a German balloon, saw a two-seater Aviatik below him, so immediately dived at it, but was then attacked by eight Albatross Scouts from above and other Aviatiks from below. One of the Aviatiks dived past him, and, after being hit, fell out of control and crashed. Second-Lieutenant Barlow continued fighting, and saw another machine turn over and fall out of control, after which he broke off the combat, and recrossed the trenches at 80 feet. Lieutenant W. A. Bond, also of No. 40 Squadron, drove down a German machine out of control.

Second Lieutenants J. A. Loutit and V. J. Holland, No. 53 Squadron, while on artillery work, were attacked by six E.A., and in the engagement which followed the leader of the German machines fell out of control, and the rest broke off the fight.

An offensive patrol of seven machines of No. 1 Squadron encountered about 18 Albatross Scouts and very severe fighting took place. Second Lieutenant Campbell destroyed one of his opponents and drove down two others completely out of control; and Second Lieutenant Jenkin shot down a German machine, which crashed, and then attacked an Albatross Scout which fell in flames.

Another patrol of No. 1 Squadron engaged 15 Albatross Scouts near Zandvoorde, and Lieutenant Hazel and Second Lieutenant Stevens each drove one down out of control.

Second Lieutenants Trevethan and Dudbridge, No. 20 Squadron, shot down an Albatross Scout in flames during an encounter between machines of their squadron and 12 Albatross

Scouts. Later in the evening an offensive patrol of No. 20 Squadron engaged eight Albatross Scouts, and Second Lieutenants Strange and Tennant drove one down out of control.

Photography.—Three hundred and seventy-two photographs were taken during the day.

Bombing.—First Brigade.—On the night of the 8th-9th No. 100 Squadron dropped eight 112-lb bombs on Comines Station, four 112-lb. bombs on Warneton and one 230-lb. bomb on rolling stock between Comines and Warneton. A small fire and some explosions were caused by bombs dropped near Comines. Transport and men were attacked during this raid by machine gun fire.

No 25 Squadron dropped twenty-six 20-lb. bombs on Sallaumines. This squadron also dropped twenty-six 20-lb. bombs on Izel, and 16 of the bombs were seen to burst on buildings.

Second Brigade.—No. 20 Squadron dropped sixty-four 20-lb. bombs on a dump and on hutments at Houthem, and eight direct hits were obtained on the dump. Two wagons were hit by four 20-lb. bombs dropped on transport near Becelaere by the same squadron. Later in the evening this squadron dropped thirty-two 20-lb. bombs on Wervicq and Comines and on the dump at Houthem.

Third Brigade.—Twenty-three 20-lb. bombs were dropped on various targets.

June 10th.

Artillery Co-operation.—Thirty-one targets were dealt with by artillery with aeroplane observation and 15 with observation by balloons.

Artillery of the First Army obtained one O.K. and eight Y.'s on a hostile battery and exploded a quantity of ammunition. Three other explosions also took place during this shoot.

Artillery of the Second Army successfully engaged 13 hostile batteries; four gun-pits were destroyed, two damaged and four explosions caused. Twenty-four zone calls were sent down and seven were seen to be answered. The 179th Siege Battery, with observation by Captain McCall and Lieutenant Carson, No. 6 Squadron, obtained 30 O.K.'s on a hostile battery position which was completely destroyed.

With Balloon Observation.—Artillery of the Second Army engaged 15 targets and located 36 active hostile batteries.

Bombing.—Third Brigade.—Fourteen 20-lb. bombs were dropped on various targets during the day, and in the evening No. 18 Squadron dropped twenty-seven 20-lb. bombs on Cantin Aerodrome.

Photography.—One hundred and fifty-five photographs were taken during the day.

June 11*th.*

The fronts of the First and Second Armies were kept under observation whenever possible during the day, and reports were made concerning enemy movements.

Artillery Co-operation.—Thirty-five targets were dealt with by artillery with aeroplane observation and 13 with observation by balloons.

Artillery of the First Army successfully engaged a hostile battery and a trench mortar and obtained direct hits on trenches.

Artillery of the Second Army successfully engaged seven hostile batteries; 21 zone calls were sent down and five were seen to be answered.

Five hostile batteries were successfully engaged (prearranged shoots) by artillery of the Third Army.

June 12*th.*

Reconnaissances.—Reconnaissances were carried out whenever possible.

Lieutenant Matheson and Second Lieutenant H. Oliver, No. 55 Squadron, reconnoitred the area, Roulers-Deynze-Melle-Sotteghem-Ath-Audenarde-Courtrai and exposed 13 plates. During this reconnaissance the clouds prevented observation of certain points.

Artillery Co-operation.—One hundred and sixty-four targets were dealt with by artillery with aeroplane observation and 10 with observation by balloons.

Artillery of the First Army obtained 20 direct hits on hostile batteries; one gun-pit was destroyed, nine damaged, three explosions and three fires caused. Four hostile batteries were reported by zone call and one was silenced.

Artillery of the Second Army successfully engaged 22 hostile batteries; six gun-pits were destroyed, 11 damaged, and six explosions caused. The 180th Siege Battery, with observation by Captain Hodges and Lieutenant Elstob, No. 53 Squadron, obtained seven O.K.'s and five M.O.K.'s on a hostile battery, and two pits were completely destroyed. The 71st Heavy Battery, with the same observers, obtained five O.K.'s and one M.O.K. on another hostile battery. The 94th Siege Battery, with observation by Captain Grenfell and Lieutenant Flowers, No. 42 Squadron, destroyed two bridges and damaged a third at Frelinghein. The 83rd Siege Battery obtained 10 O.K.'s and 14 M.O.K.'s on a hostile battery position, where four pits were destroyed and two explosions caused, with observation by Lieutenants Withers and Barr, No. 6 Squadron.

Twenty-eight hostile batteries were successfully engaged by artillery of the Third Army; 21 direct hits were obtained, five pits were damaged, three explosions and two fires were caused.

Seven hostile batteries were successfully engaged by artillery of the Fourth Army, which obtained 13 O.K.'s and 11 M.O.K.'s.

Artillery of the Fifth Army successfully engaged 13 hostile batteries and obtained 32 direct hits on gun positions, destroying one pit, damaging 18, and causing an explosion. Lieutenant Quick, No. 21 Squadron, ranged the 237th Siege Battery on to a hostile battery and observed for 300 rounds.

With balloon observation of the First Brigade, artillery silenced two hostile batteries and obtained two direct hits on a house in which a trench mortar was active.

Hostile Aircraft. — An offensive patrol of four triplanes of Naval Squadron No. 8 encountered six Albatross Scouts; Flight Commander Compston shot down one which was seen to crash, and Flight Lieutenant Soar drove down an Albatross Scout out of control. Later two enemy two-seaters were attacked by the Naval pilots, and Flight Commander Booker and Flight Sub-Lieut. Jenner-Parsons drove one down in a spin. This machine (Aviatak) was then hit by anti-aircraft and landed in our lines near Arras, and the passengers, who were slightly wounded, were captured.

An Albatross Scout was driven down out of control by Sub-Lieut. Minifie, Naval Squadron No. 1, and a two-seater was destroyed by Sergeant Beadle, No. 1 Squadron.

As the result of an engagement between machines of No. 20 Squadron and eight Albatross Scouts, Lieutenant Solly and Second Lieutenant Kidd drove one of the German machines down out of control.

While on a photographic reconnaissance, Lieutenants Douglas and Houghton, No. 59 Squadron, were attacked by an Albatross Scout. After a short engagement the enemy machine burst into flames and broke up in the air before it crashed.

Bombing. — **First Brigade.** — No. 25 Squadron dropped twenty 20-lb. bombs on Izel-les-Equerchin, and 12 were seen to fall on buildings.

Second Brigade. — No. 20 Squadron dropped thirty-six 30-lb. bombs on Houthem dump, eight 30-lb. bombs on an anti-aircraft battery south of Comines, and twelve 30-lb. bombs on a balloon winch and shed near Comines.

Third Brigade. — Twenty-eight 20-lb. bombs were dropped on various targets.

June 13th.

Reconnaissances. — Some successful reconnaissances were carried out by Brigades and 9th Wing. Lieutenant Barnett and Second Lieutenant Miller, on a De Havilland, four of No. 55 Squadron, reconnoitred distant areas, including Ghistelles, Bruges and Ostend, and took some good photographs.

Artillery Co-operation.—Eighty-two targets were dealt with by artillery with aeroplane observation, and 46 with observation by balloons.

Artillery of the First Army successfully engaged three hostile batteries; two pits were damaged and two explosions caused.

Thirteen hostile batteries were successfully engaged by artillery of the Second Army, seven gun-pits were destroyed, one damaged and five explosions caused. The 321st Siege Battery, with observation by Lieutenant Stocks and Jenkins, No. 6 Squadron, obtained 24 O.K.'s on a six-gun battery position; all gun-pits were destroyed and the target was completely obliterated.

Fifteen hostile batteries were successfully engaged by artillery of the Third Army (prearranged shoots), 14 direct hits were obtained, one pit was destroyed, two damaged and three explosions and a fire caused.

Artillery of the Fourth Army successfully engaged five hostile batteries, and obtained seven O.K.'s and 16 M.O.K.'s, causing four fires.

Five hostile batteries were successfully engaged by artillery of the Fifth Army, which obtained eight direct hits on gun positions and damaged two pits.

With Balloon Observation.—Thirty-seven targets were dealt with by artillery of the Second Army, of which eight were hostile batteries engaged for destruction and three hostile batteries were neutralised. Two shoots were carried out in conjunction with aeroplanes, and a fire and four explosions were caused.

Hostile Aircraft.—In the evening an offensive patrol of Naval Squadron No. 8 attacked a formation of F.A. over Douai, and Flight Sub-Lieut. Knight and Flight Commander Arnold each drove down a hostile machine, both of which are believed to have fallen out of control.

Two Albatross two-seaters were engaged by a patrol of No. 41 Squadron, and one was destroyed by Lieutenant MacGowan. Lieutenant MacKay and Flight-Sergeant Barker, on one machine of No. 6 Squadron, and Lieutenants Poundall and Barton, on another machine, drove down two E.A. out of control.

An offensive patrol of No. 20 Squadron engaged 15 hostile scouts near Houthem, and Lieutenant Luchford and Second-Lieutenant Tennant drove one down out of control.

Photography.—Five hundred and seventy-five photographs were taken during the day.

Bombing.—First Brigade.—Thirty-six 20-lb. bombs were dropped on Vitry.

Second Brigade.—Eight 30-lb. bombs were dropped on Houthem hutments, eight 30-lb. bombs on Warneton Bridge, and four 30-lb. bombs on Wervicq Bridge.

Third Brigade.—Twenty-eight 20-lb. bombs were dropped on various targets.

June 14th.

Captain Turner and Lieutenant Brett, of No. 55 Squadron, carried out a long reconnaissance in the northern area right up to the coast and took 18 photographs. Other areas were reconnoitred by machines of all the Brigades.

Artillery Co-operation.—One hundred and three targets were dealt with by artillery with aeroplane observation and 11 with observation by balloons.

Artillery of the First Army successfully engaged 12 hostile batteries on which 10 direct hits were obtained. Three gun-pits were destroyed, 11 damaged, and six explosions caused, and houses in battery positions were set on fire.

Eight hostile batteries were successfully engaged by artillery of the Second Army; one pit was destroyed, three damaged, and two explosions were caused.

Artillery of the Third Army successfully engaged 21 hostile batteries, damaging three pits and causing three explosions. 142 direct hits were obtained on trenches.

One hostile battery was successfully engaged by artillery of the Fourth Army.

Artillery of the Fifth Army successfully engaged three hostile batteries; two gun-pits were damaged, and an explosion caused.

Hostile Aircraft.—Second-Lieutenants Richards and Wear, No. 20 Squadron, drove down an Albatross Scout out of control.

Lieutenant G. S. Buck, No. 19 Squadron, flying a 200 h.p. Spad on offensive patrol, observed a German Nieuport climbing above Spads and German machines which were fighting, apparently with the intention of "scalp hunting" (*i.e.*, taking no risks but diving at a disabled machine or one wholly unprepared for a sudden attack from above). Lieutenant Buck immediately flew up to him, and when the German found that he was unable to out-climb the Spad he put his nose down and fled. The Spad, however, easily followed him, and after 70 rounds had been fired from each gun the German machine fell out of control and crashed.

Captain G. H. Bowman, No. 56 Squadron, saw our anti-aircraft shells bursting over Armentières, so he immediately flew in that direction and observed two E.A. two-seaters going east and pursued them. The occupants of the German machines did not see him until he was very close, and he drove down one machine completely out of control. Later in the day he attacked and drove down another German machine out of control. Second Lieutenant Lewis, of the same squadron, forced one to land in a field.

In the evening Lieutenants Duff and Judd, No. 6 Squadron, destroyed a German machine which with others had attacked the R.E.S.

Six Albatross Scouts were engaged by an offensive patrol of No. 1 Squadron, and, as a result of the fighting Second-Lieutenant Fullard and Lieutenant Jenkin each drove one down out of control.

Flight Lieutenant Maynard, Naval Squadron No. 1, destroyed an Albatross Scout near Ypres.

Lieutenant Holliday and Captain Wall, No. 48 Squadron, destroyed a German machine and then engaged and drove down another out of control in the vicinity of Arleux.

Another German machine was driven down out of control by Captain K. L. Caldwell, No. 60 Squadron.

Flight Sub-Lieuts. Page and Sharman, Naval Squadron No. 10, each drove down an enemy machine out of control, and a third, after having been engaged by Second-Lieutenant Doran, No. 23 Squadron, also fell out of control.

Bombing.—First Brigade.—No. 25 Squadron dropped twenty-four 20-lb. bombs on Rouvroy.

Second Brigade.—Forty 30-lb. bombs were dropped on the area round Houthem, Quesnoy, and Comines by machines of No. 20 Squadron,

Third Brigade.—Thirty-six 20-lb. bombs were dropped on various targets.

June 15th.

Reconnaissances.—Reconnaissances were carried out by all Brigades and 9th Wing. Second-Lieutenants Stephens and Sandy on a De Havilland 4, of No. 55 Squadron, carried out a long reconnaissance and photographed Kain and Warcoing Aerodromes. Lieutenants Burd and Langmaid on another machine, of the same squadron, also carried out a long reconnaissance and took photographs at 21,000 feet.

Artillery Co-operation.—128 targets were dealt with by artillery with aeroplane observation and 130 with observation by balloons.

Artillery of the First Army successfully engaged 36 hostile batteries; 10 gun-pits were damaged and 11 explosions caused, two of which were very large and were presumably dumps. One battery position was completely destroyed and houses in a battery position were set on fire.

Artillery of the Second Army also successfully engaged 36 hostile batteries; two gun-pits were destroyed, three damaged, and an explosion caused.

Sixteen hostile batteries were successfully engaged by artillery of the Third Army; three pits were damaged and six explosions and two fires caused.

Artillery of the Fourth Army successfully engaged five hostile batteries and damaged seven emplacements.

Thirteen hostile batteries were successfully engaged by artillery of the Fifth Army; 10 gun-pits were destroyed, 17 damaged, and two explosions caused.

With Balloon Observation.—Artillery of the First Army carried out eight shoots on active hostile batteries, and seven were silenced. Eleven shoots on hostile battery positions were successful, and one explosion was caused. Twelve active hostile batteries were located and a number of direct hits were obtained on trenches.

Thirty-three targets were successfully engaged by artillery of the Second Army and trenches were severely damaged.

Artillery of the Third Army was successfully engaged on 81 targets.

A party of infantry and three hostile batteries were engaged by artillery of the Fourth Army, and very good shooting was done.

Artillery of the Fifth Army carried out five successful shoots on hostile batteries and registered a number of other targets.

Hostile Aircraft.—Flight Commander Booker, Naval Squadron No. 8, drove down one enemy machine out of control and another in a badly damaged condition.

Flight Lieutenant Eyre, Naval Squadron No. 1, pursued a hostile machine which, finding it could not escape, turned and fought. Eventually the German machine turned over, fell out of control, and crashed.

An offensive patrol of No. 1 Squadron engaged a formation of E.A., two of which were driven down out of control, one each by Second Lieutenants Campbell and Fullard.

Captain Taylor, Lieutenant Holman, and Second Lieutenant Barker, No. 41 Squadron, engaged an Aviatik which was being driven down by a Sopwith triplane, and the German machine crashed in our lines,

Flight Sub-Lieuts. Page and FitzGibbon, Naval Squadron No. 10, each drove down a German machine out of control, and another fell apparently out of control after having been engaged by Flight Sub-Lieuts. Collison and Sharman.

Captain Prothero and Lieutenant Maxwell, No. 56 Squadron, dived at a two-seater Albatross which they drove down and destroyed.

Second Lieutenant T. C. Luke, No. 66 Squadron, destroyed a German machine, and Captain Andrews, of the same Squadron, forced one to land.

Bombing.—First Brigade.—Thirty 20-lb. bombs were dropped on Courrières and eight 20-lb. bombs on Harnes.

Second Brigade.—Fifty 30-lb. bombs were dropped on the area round Houthem, Wervicq, and Comines.

Third Brigade.—Thirty-six 20-lb. bombs were dropped on various targets.

Fifth Brigade.—Sixteen 20-lb. bombs were dropped on Reckem Aerodrome.

S. WOOD, Captain,
Staff Officer.

Advanced Headquarters,
Royal Flying Corps,
17th June 1917.

ROYAL FLYING CORPS COMMUNIQUÉ.—No. 93.

June 16th.

Several reconnaissances were carried out; Lieutenants Matheson and Oliver, No. 55 Squadron, did a long reconnaissance of the northern area and took 10 photographs.

Ten contact patrols were done by machines of the Second Brigade.

In several instances machines on photographic and other work opened fire on German troops and transport with machine guns.

Artillery Co-operation.—One hundred and three targets were dealt with by artillery with aeroplane observation and 61 with observation by balloons.

Artillery of the First Army successfully engaged 13 hostile batteries on which they obtained 12 direct hits, destroying nine gun-pits, damaging 35, and causing four explosions and six fires.

Artillery of the Second Army successfully engaged 11 hostile batteries; one pit was destroyed, three damaged, and two explosions caused.

Twenty-nine hostile batteries were successfully engaged by artillery of the Third Army, which obtained 28 direct hits and 27 O.K.'s on trenches.

Seven hostile batteries were successfully engaged by artillery of the Fourth Army; 14 emplacements were damaged, and an explosion caused. Artillery, with observation by Captain Pirie, No. 34 Squadron, obtained nine M.O.K.'s on a battery, causing an explosion. With observation by Lieutenant Davis, No. 59 Squadron, six direct hits were obtained on a farm.

Artillery of the Fifth Army successfully engaged nine hostile batteries; six pits were destroyed, 10 damaged, and four explosions caused.

Fifty-eight targets were engaged by artillery with observation by balloons of the Third Brigade, and in addition to other good shoots transport and horsemen were dispersed.

Several targets were taken over from aeroplanes, and others were engaged in conjunction with aeroplane observation.

Hostile Aircraft.—On the evening of the 15th, Captain A. W. Keen, No. 40 Squadron, attacked an enemy machine, which he drove down in flames.

On the 16th, five Sopwiths of No. 43 Squadron attacked a two-seater Aviatik, all our machines opened fire, driving the German machine down, and it was seen to crash into a factory in Lens.

Flight Commander Compston and Flight Sub-Lieutenant Thorneley, Naval Squadron No. 8, attacked a German machine over Lens and drove it down. This machine fell on our side of the lines, and the observer, who was wounded, was captured, but the pilot killed.

Flight Lieutenants Little and Johnstone, of the same squadron, observed our A.A. shells bursting near St. Eloi, so proceeded in that direction, where they saw a German machine which they destroyed.

Second-Lieutenant W. C. Campbell, flying a Nieuport Scout of No. 1 Squadron, attacked a two-seater Albatross near Houthem at 9 a.m. and destroyed it. Ten minutes afterwards he attacked another two-seater Albatross in the same vicinity, and after firing a drum and a half the German machine fell and crashed. Immediately afterwards he attacked a third Albatross two-seater, but ran out of ammunition, so returned to the aerodrome and went off again. At 9.40 a.m. he encountered a large two-seater machine which had a tail similar to that of a Spad, and after emptying two drums into the German machine it fell out of control and crashed.

Captain Cock and Lieutenant Murison, on a Sopwith two-seater, of No. 45 Squadron, drove down a German machine out of control, and Second-Lieutenant Littler, No. 1 Squadron, drove down a two-seater Aviatik out of control.

On the evening of the 15th, Lieutenant F. P. Holliday and Captain A. H. Wall, No. 48 Squadron, while on a patrol alone encountered seven E.A. They decoyed the enemy machines up to a formation of Bristol Fighters of their squadron which they knew were coming from the north. A keenly-contested engagement took place, and Lieutenant Holliday and Captain Wall drove down one of the German machines out of control, and another was driven down out of control by Lieutenants Pratt and Owen and Lieutenants Fraser and Benjamin in two machines. Captain Baker and Lieutenant Munro in one machine and Lieutenant Binnie and 1st A.M. Reed in another drove down one of the German machines in flames, while the latter pilot and observer drove down another out of control, while still another was destroyed by Lieutenant R. B. Hay and Lieutenant Nutkins.

During the same evening, an offensive patrol, of No. 60 Squadron, engaged six enemy machines near Vitry and drove down two out of control.

On the 16th, an offensive patrol of No. 48 Squadron observed a two-seater Aviatik working east of Gavrelle, so our machines flew round in order to get a favourable position between the sun and the German, and then attacked at close range and the German machine crashed.

Later in the day, Lieutenant Pratt and Second-Lieutenant Owen, of the same squadron, drove down a German machine out of control near Estrée.

On the evening of the 15th, an offensive patrol of Naval Squadron No. 10 engaged a large number of E.A., and as the result of the fighting one German machine was destroyed, five others were driven down out of control, while the observer in a sixth machine was shot. All the naval pilots returned safely.

Flight Lieutenant Collishaw accounted for three of these machines, one he shot to pieces in the air and two others fell out of control, Flight Sub-Lieut. Reid was responsible for two and Flight Sub-Lieut. FitzGibbons for one.

Captain K. C. Patrick, No. 23 Squadron, observed nine Albatross Scouts attacking six F.E.'s and so dived to their assistance, and drove down one of the German machines out of control.

Captain C. M. Crowe, No. 56 Squadron, dived at one of two E.A., but after firing a few rounds his gun jammed, so he turned and changed drums. He then attacked two more E.A. and both opened fire on him, but one soon flew east, and the other was driven down and crashed. After this he met a large two-seater German machine with streamers and fired a drum into it, but it went down, obviously avoiding combat.

Bombing.—First Brigade.—Thirty-eight 20-lb. bombs were dropped on Drocourt.

Second Brigade.—Forty-nine 30-lb. bombs were dropped in the area Houthem–Comines–Wervicq.

Third Brigade.—Twenty-two 20-lb. bombs were dropped on various targets.

Photography.—Eight hundred and thirty-eight photographs were taken during the day.

June 17th.

Fifteen reconnaissances were carried out by the Brigades and 9th Wing.

Artillery Co-operation.—One hundred and thirty-seven targets were dealt with by artillery with aeroplane observation and 120 with observation by balloons.

Artillery of the First Army obtained 15 direct hits on hostile batteries, 18 gun-pits were damaged, 10 explosions and several fires caused. One battery position is believed to have been completely destroyed and a number of direct hits were obtained on trenches.

Artillery of the Second Army successfully engaged 22 hostile batteries and destroyed three gun-pits, damaged nine, and caused three explosions.

Thirty-four hostile batteries were successfully engaged by artillery of the Third Army; 37 direct hits were obtained, six explosions caused, and two pits were badly damaged. Ninety-three hostile batteries were seen active, on 10 of which there was observation of fire, and four of the batteries were silenced.

Six hostile batteries were successfully engaged by artillery of the Fourth Army, three emplacements were damaged, and an explosion and a fire caused.

Artillery of the Fifth Army successfully engaged 11 hostile batteries on which they secured 20 direct hits, destroying four pits, damaging three, and causing three explosions.

Artillery of the First Army silenced 10 hostile batteries with balloon observation and carried out 13 shoots on battery positions. Two fires were caused and a trench mortar was successfully engaged, while 19 other active hostile batteries were located.

Thirty-four targets were successfully engaged by artillery of the Second Army with balloon observation, of which 10 were hostile batteries.

Several shoots were taken over from aeroplanes by balloons.

Hostile Aircraft.—On the evening of the 16th, Second-Lieutenants D. M. MacKay and W. S. Cattell, No. 43 Squadron, were attacked by three E.A., two of which they drove away, and the third was driven down out of control.

On the 17th, an offensive patrol, No. 20 Squadron, engaged three two-seater Aviatiks near Zonnebecke; one was brought down by Second-Lieutenant Richards and Second-Lieutenant Wear. Lieutenant Jenkins, No. 1 Squadron, engaged and drove down an enemy machine out of control.

A machine of No. 11 Squadron drove down a German machine out of control, but haze prevented the final result being observed.

Lieutenants Douglas and Horton, No. 59 Squadron, attacked and drove an enemy machine which burst into flames before it crashed.

While on offensive patrol, Second-Lieutenant Gibbs and Captain Keller, No. 23 Squadron, saw three two-seater machines employed on artillery work, so manœuvred for position between the E.A. and the sun, and then dived on them. One went straight down and Second-Lieutenant Gibbs sat on its tail and followed it before it crashed. Captain Keller selected another machine on which he opened fire, and the German machine burst into flames and crashed.

Lieutenant W. B. Hutcheson and Sergeant Rose, No. 59 Squadron, engaged an Albatross Scout, which opened fire on them at close range. After considerable manœuvring the

German machine nose-dived, and then attempted to flatten out, but failed and crashed.

Lieutenants Dickenson and MacGowan, No. 41 Squadron, while on offensive patrol engaged a two-seater Albatross, and both pilots opened fire on the German machine, which fell out of control.

Another Scout which attacked Lieutenant W. E. Dawson and Sergeant Studholme, No. 4 Squadron, is believed to have fallen out of control.

Machines of the 9th Wing had a number of engagements. Second-Lieutenant R. T. C. Hoidge, No. 56 Squadron, attacked a number of two-seaters over La Bassée and drove one down, which was seen to crash. Captain Bowman and Lieutenant Lewis, of the same patrol, each drove down a German machine out of control.

The Spads of No. 19 Squadron took part in a number of engagements, and as the result two hostile machines were driven down out of control, one by Captain Leacroft and the other by the Spad formation, and two more were driven down obviously damaged.

Bombing.—First Brigade.—Six 20-lb., sixteen 20-lb., and eighteen 20-lb. bombs were dropped on Drocourt, La Bassée, and Metallurgique Factory, respectively.

Second Brigade.—Twenty-four 30-lb. bombs were dropped on the area round Houthem.

Third Brigade.—Twenty-nine 20-lb. bombs on various targets.

Fifth Brigade.—Sixteen 20-lb. bombs were dropped on Handzaeme Aerodrome.

9th Wing.—Thirty-eight 20-lb. bombs were dropped on Provin Aerodrome.

June 18th.

A number of reconnaissances were carried out by the brigades and 9th Wing, and valuable information was obtained from observation and from photographs.

During artillery and other work transport and enemy troops were frequently attacked from low altitudes with machine gun fire.

Artillery Co-operation.—Ninety-nine targets were dealt with by artillery with aeroplane observation and 132 with observation by balloons.

Artillery of the First Army successfully engaged 17 hostile batteries; one pit was destroyed, six damaged, and five explosions and three fires caused.

Fifteen hostile batteries were successfully engaged by artillery of the Second Army; one pit was destroyed, four damaged, and two explosions caused.

Third Army artillery successfully engaged 32 hostile batteries, on which 42 direct hits were obtained. Three pits were destroyed, 24 were damaged, and three explosions and one fire caused. The 18th Siege Battery, with observation by Lieutenants Brokensha and Iles, No. 3 Squadron, obtained four direct hits on gun-pits, and caused an explosion.

Two hostile batteries were successfully engaged by artillery of the Fourth Army, which obtained five O.K.'s, damaging two emplacements and causing an explosion.

Artillery of the Fifth Army successfully engaged nine hostile batteries, on which 14 direct hits were obtained. One gun-pit was destroyed, three damaged, and an explosion caused. The 323rd Siege Battery, with observation by Second-Lieutenant Bowick and Lieutenant Sear, No. 21 Squadron, obtained five O.K.'s on a hostile battery position.

With Balloon Observation. — Artillery of the First Army successfully engaged two hostile battery positions.

Thirty-eight targets were engaged, 16 of which were hostile battery positions, by artillery of the Second Army; eight of these batteries were engaged for effect, and four active batteries were silenced.

Artillery of the Third Army was successfully ranged on 59 targets, of which 13 were hostile battery positions. Many shoots were taken over from aeroplanes and successful results were obtained. Sixty hostile batteries were reported active.

Artillery of the Fourth Army successfully engaged three hostile batteries and one was silenced, while a number of men on a road were engaged and dispersed.

Artillery of the Fifth Army engaged and silenced two active hostile batteries.

Hostile Aircraft. — A patrol of four Sopwith Pups, of No. 46 Squadron, encountered 15 E.A., and although our machines were very much shot about none of the pilots were hit. Captain Pratt succeeded in driving down one of his opponents out of control.

On the evening of the 17th an offensive patrol of 20 Squadron engaged two formations of eight Albatross Scouts in each formation. Second-Lieutenant Alston and Lieutenant Chester shot down one of the German machines, while a second was destroyed by Lieutenant Strange and Second-Lieutenant Cambray.

On the 18th Lieutenant Ballard and Second-Lieutenant Lees, No. 6 Squadron, were attacked by nine Albatross Scouts over Zandvoorde; they shot down one of the Scouts, which fell to pieces in the air.

An offensive patrol of No. 20 Squadron engaged a number of Albatross Scouts, and, as the result of the fighting, Lieutenant Solly and Second-Lieutenant Cambray destroyed one of the German machines which crashed after the wings had broken off in the air, while several others were seen to go down, some of which were probably out of control.

Three machines of No. 1 Squadron, while searching for reported E.A., destroyed one of eight Albatross Scouts which they encountered.

Second-Lieutenants T. P. Middleton and Merchant, No. 48 Squadron, while on offensive patrol, lost formation, and were then attacked by seven E.A., but succeeded in destroying one of their opponents and returned safely.

Second-Lieutenants B. Wood and D. Bird, No. 29 Squadron, each shot down a hostile machine, which burst into flames and crashed.

During an offensive patrol of three machines of No. 41 Squadron and three R.E. 8's, of No. 6 Squadron, and a German formation of Albatross Scouts, Captain Taylor and Lieutenant MacGowan, No. 41 Squadron, each drove down an enemy machine, one of which was seen to break to pieces in the air.

Captain Harker and Lieutenant Barclay, No. 57 Squadron, when escorted by a De Havilland 4, were attacked by seven Albatross Scouts, one of which attempted to attack from behind, but was out-manœuvred and destroyed.

Flight Sub-Lieut. Reid and Flight Lieutenant Collishaw, Naval Squadron No. 10, each drove down a Halberstadt Scout out of control, and Lieutenant Orlebar, No. 19 Squadron, drove down a German machine in a badly damaged condition.

Photography.—Five hundred and thirty-three photographs were taken during the day.

Bombing.—Second Brigade.—Twenty-one 30-lb. bombs were dropped on Houthem ; an explosion was caused in the dump.

Third Brigade.—Twenty-two 20-lb. bombs were dropped on various targets.

Fourth Brigade.—Two 30-lb. bombs were dropped on Ribecourt Dump.

Fifth Brigade.—Sixteen 20-lb. bombs were dropped on Handzaeme Aerodrome.

June 19th.

Reconnaissances.—Early this morning Lieutenant Morice and Lieutenant Leathley, No. 57 Squadron, carried out a successful reconnaissance of the area Dixmude–Zarren–Cortemarck–Staden–Langemarck–Zonnebeke–Roulers–Ypres, gaining much useful information.

Second Lieutenant Evans and Lieutenant Willmott, No. 7 Squadron, carried out a successful reconnaissance early to-day, locating balloons and obtaining information. They also fired into hostile trenches, once from 800 feet and once from 1,500 feet.

Several pilots and observers fired into trenches while engaged on artillery work.

Artillery Co-operation.—Sixty-eight targets were dealt with by artillery with aeroplane observation and 68 with observation by balloon.

Artillery of the First Army successfully engaged 13 hostile batteries, on which 24 direct hits were obtained, destroying three pits, damaging seven, and causing six explosions and four fires.

Artillery of the Second Army successfully engaged 13 hostile batteries, damaging one and causing four explosions.

Seventeen hostile batteries were successfully engaged by artillery of the Third Army. Four pits were badly damaged, and a fire and an explosion were caused. A large number of direct hits were also obtained on trenches.

Fourteen direct hits were obtained on nine hostile batteries by artillery of the Fifth Army. Five pits were damaged and two explosions caused.

The 237th Siege Battery, with observation by Second Lieutenant Hermann, No. 21 Squadron, who observed for 100 rounds, obtained five O.K.'s on a hostile battery position, and caused an explosion.

Sergeant Edmunds and Lieutenant Torrance, No. 21 Squadron, observed for a successful shoot on a hostile battery on which five O.K.'s were obtained.

Bombing.—First Brigade.—Nineteen 20-lb. bombs were dropped on La Bassée and on a brewery near the town.

Third Brigade.—Twenty-two 20-lb. bombs were dropped on various targets.

Fifth Brigade.—Two 20-lb. bombs were dropped on a dump.

June 20th.

Reconnaissances.—An extensive reconnaissance was carried out by Captain Sutton and Lieutenant Leal, No. 9 Squadron, of the canal east of Boesinghe.

Artillery Co-operation.—Fifty-nine targets were dealt with by artillery with artillery observation and four with observation by balloons.

Artillery of the First Army successfully engaged 18 hostile batteries; two pits were destroyed, 12 damaged, and nine explosions and two fires caused. Twenty-nine hostile batteries were reported by zone call.

Artillery of the Second Army successfully engaged nine hostile batteries, destroying two pits and causing an explosion. Six zone calls were sent down. In one shoot Lieutenant Longton and Lieutenant Barr, observing for the 221st Siege Battery, obtained four O.K.'s on a hostile battery, destroying two pits and causing a fire.

In the Third Army twenty-four hostile batteries were successfully engaged, nine gun-pits damaged, and six explosions caused. A machine of No. 3 Squadron, co-operating with the 18th Siege Battery, obtained three O.K.'s on a hostile battery, damaging three pits and causing two explosions. A machine of No. 12 Squadron sent down a zone call on an active hostile battery; three of the pits were damaged, and two explosions caused.

Five gun-pits were damaged of eight hostile batteries engaged by artillery of the Fifth Army. No. 21 Squadron carried out four successful shoots on hostile batteries and reported five others by zone call. No. 4 Squadron carried out three successful shoots and reported 10 active hostile batteries by zone call.

Enemy Aircraft.—Slight activity on all Army fronts. Lieutenant A. W. Miller, No. 29 Squadron, brought down an Albatross Scout after firing 20 rounds at close range.

Lieutenants Blake and Roberts. No. 9 Squadron, while on photography, were attacked by eight Albatross Scouts, one of which was driven down out of control.

Bombing.—Third Brigade.—Thirty-four 20-lb. bombs were dropped on various targets.

Fifth Brigade.—Seven 20-lb. bombs were dropped on a dump.

Photography.—Seventy-one plates were exposed by machines of the First Brigade, and 57 by the Third Brigade.

Miscellaneous.—A machine of No. 12 Squadron descended to 1,000 feet and engaged the personnel of a hostile battery with machine gun fire.

Lieutenant Robbins and Second Lieutenant Ward, No. 4 Squadron, fired 140 rounds with their machine guns on the Ypres–Menin road.

June 21st.

Reconnaissances.—Much useful information was obtained from reconnaissances by machines of the Second, Third, and Fifth Brigades. Fires were reported all day in Quesnoy, Comines, and Warneton.

Artillery Co-operation.—One hundred and two targets were engaged by artillery with aeroplane observation and 27 with observation by balloons.

Artillery of the First Army carried out successful shoots on 19 hostile batteries, damaging 11 pits and causing eight explosions and three fires. Nine active hostile batteries were reported by zone call. Captain W. R. Snow, No. 10 Squadron, remained in the air for 4 hours 10 minutes through several rainstorms, and ranged three of our batteries on to three hostile batteries.

On the evening of the 21st, Captain J. C. Slessor and Second Lieutenant F. Tymms, No. 5 Squadron, carried out a successful shoot in continuous rain; the following morning these officers took some excellent photographs, 4,000 yards behind the enemy's lines at a height of 3,000 feet.

In the Second Army 12 hostile batteries were successfully engaged for destruction and 11 others neutralised; four gun-pits were damaged and one explosion caused. Thirty zone calls were sent down. The 161st Siege Battery, with observation by Second Lieutenant Kerr and Lieutenant Elstob, No. 53 Squadron, obtained seven O.K.'s on a hostile battery position, damaging all four gun-pits.

Twenty-four hostile batteries were successfully engaged by artillery of the Third Army, five pits being damaged and one fire and three explosions caused. The 213 Siege Battery, with observation by Major Ross and Lieutenant Spence, No. 8 Squadron, obtained two direct hits on a gun-pit, causing two explosions.

Artillery of the Fifth Army engaged nine hostile batteries, eleven gun-pits being damaged and two explosions caused. The 214th Siege battery, with observation by Captain Bolton and Lieutenant Torrance, No. 21 Squadron, demolished three gun-pits of a hostile battery. Thirty-one zone calls were sent down on active hostile batteries and a train.

Balloons.—First Army.—Four hostile batteries and eight other targets were successfully engaged with balloon observation.

Second Army.—Nine targets were engaged, five of which were hostile batteries. One of these shoots was carried out in conjunction with an aeroplane.

Third Army.—Five targets were successfully ranged on.

Fifth Army.—One hostile battery was successfully engaged.

No. 28 Section's balloon observed an enemy searchlight and picked up signals from it.

Nos. 9 and 32 Sections' balloons were brought down by enemy aircraft: all observers made successful descents. Two of the enemy machines were driven down out of control.

Enemy Aircraft.—Very little activity on all fronts, except Second and Fifth Brigades, where it was slightly above normal.

Flight Lieutenant Little, Naval Squadron No. 8, brought down an Albatross Scout near Courrières.

Four enemy machines were driven down out of control by Lieutenant Jenkins, No. 1 Squadron, Flight Commander Eyre, Naval Squadron No. 1, Second Lieutenants Campbell and McFerran, No. 1 Squadron, and Lieutenants Riddle and Laws, No. 42 Squadron.

Lieutenant Shepherd, No. 29 Squadron, engaged two enemy aircraft at close range. The pilot in one was seen to collapse, the machine going down completely out of control.

Five de Havilland 4's, of No. 57 Squadron, were attacked by 15 Albatross Scouts. The patrol leader turned towards our lines and succeeded in drawing the enemy machines after him, giving Lieutenant Morice an opportunity of diving on a machine 400 feet below him; he fired 30 rounds, whereupon the machine turned over on its back and went down completely out of control.

Captain McNaughton, No. 57 Squadron, drove down an Albatross Scout out of control.

Photography.— One hundred and ten plates were exposed.

Bombing.—First Brigade.—Twenty-four 20-lb. bombs were dropped on Sallaumines.

Second Brigade.—Seven phosphorous bombs were dropped on hostile balloons.

Third Brigade.—Twenty 20-lb. bombs were dropped on various targets.

Fifth Brigade.—Thirty-one 20-bombs were dropped on dumps.

Miscellaneous.—Machine gun fire was opened on troops in hostile trenches, on Railway Wood and roads round Zonnebeke by Lieutenants Glenny and Fogarty, No. 9 Squadron, Captain Bolton and Lieutenant Torrance, No. 21 Squadron, Second Lieutenants Davies and McNab, No. 4 Squadron, and Second Lieutenant Taylor and Lieutenant Thompson, No. 4 Squadron.

June 22nd.

Reconnaissances.—Successful reconnaissances were carried out by Nos. 8 and 57 Squadrons.

Artillery Co-operation.—Twenty-eight targets were dealt with by artillery with aeroplane observation and 42 with observation by balloons.

Artillery of the First Army carried out shoots on four hostile batteries, damaging four gun-pits and causing one explosion. Nineteen active hostile batteries were reported by zone call; several of these were silenced, and in two cases large explosions were caused.

In the Second Army four hostile batteries were engaged for destruction and five others neutralised; one gun-pit was damaged and three explosions caused. Fifteen active hostile batteries were reported by zone call.

Eight hostile batteries were successfully ranged on by artillery of the Third Army, two gun-pits being damaged and two explosions caused. Seven active hostile batteries were silenced as the result of zone call.

One target was successfully engaged after zone call by artillery of the Fourth Army.

In the Fifth Army three hostile batteries were successfully engaged, three gun-pits damaged, and an explosion caused. Second Lieutenants Gibson and Ivemay, No. 7 Squadron, reported by zone call seven active hostile batteries, all of which were seen to cease firing.

With Balloon Observation.—First Army.—Four hostile batteries were successfully engaged for destruction, and seven others neutralised and silenced; in one of these shoots, with co-operation by No. 37 Balloon, several explosions were caused and a fire started, which was still burning when the balloon descended.

Second Army.—One hostile battery was engaged for destruction and two others neutralised.

Third Army.—No. 28 Balloon Section successfully ranged on a hostile battery located by the Sound Ranging Section, which had been firing on No. 5 Section's balloon.

Fifth Army.—One hostile battery was engaged and silenced.

Enemy Aircraft.—Very slight enemy aircraft activity all day.

Photography.—Eighteen plates were exposed by machines of the Third Brigade.

Bombing.—Third Brigade.—Eighteen 20-lb. bombs were dropped on various targets.

R. J. BARTON, Captain,
General Staff.

Advanced Headquarters,
Royal Flying Corps,
24th June 1917.